WORKBO

Houghton
Mifflin
Harcourt

STECK-VAUGHN

MATHEMATICAL
REASONING

TEST PREPARATION FOR THE 2014 GED® TEST

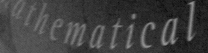

- Algebraic Problem Solving
- Quantitative Problem Solving
- Mathematical Practices

POWERED BY

PA✕EN

Houghton
Mifflin
Harcourt

POWERED BY

PA✕EN

Acknowledgments

For each of the selections and images listed below, grateful acknowledgement is made for permission to excerpt and/or reprint original or copyrighted material, as follows:

Images

Cover (bg) © Tetra Images/Corbis: **cover (inset)** © John Elk/Lonely Planet Images/Getty Images. **xii** Used with permission of Texas Instruments.

Mathematical Reasoning

Table of Contents

About the GED® Test

Welcome to the first day of the rest of your life. Now that you've committed to study for your GED® credential, an array of possibilities and options—academic, career, and otherwise—awaits you. Each year, hundreds of thousands of people just like you decide to pursue a GED® credential. Like you, they left traditional school for one reason or another. Now, just like them, you've decided to continue your education by studying for and taking the GED® Test.

Today's GED® Test is very different from previous versions of the exam. Today's GED® Test is new, improved, and more rigorous, with content aligned to the Common Core State Standards. For the first time, the GED® Test serves both as a high-school equivalency credential and as a predictor of college and career readiness. The new GED® Test features four subject areas: Reasoning Through Language Arts (RLA), Mathematical Reasoning, Science, and Social Studies. Each subject area is delivered via a computer-based format and includes an array of technology-enhanced item types.

The four subject-area exams together comprise a testing time of seven hours. Preparation can take considerably longer. The payoff, however, is significant: more and better career options, higher earnings, and the sense of achievement that comes with a GED® credential. Employers, colleges, and universities accept the GED® credential as they would a high school diploma. On average, GED® graduates earn at least $8,400 more per year than those with an incomplete high school education.

The GED® Testing Service has constructed the GED® Test to mirror a high school experience. As such, you must answer a variety of questions within and across the four subject areas. For example, you may encounter a Social Studies passage on the Reasoning Through Language Arts Test, and vice versa. Also, you will encounter questions requiring varying levels of cognitive effort, or Depth of Knowledge (DOK) levels. The following table details the content areas, number of items, score points, DOK levels, and total testing time for each subject area.

Subject-Area Test	Content Areas	Items	Raw Score Points	DOK Level	Time
Reasoning Through Language Arts	**Informational Texts—75%** **Literary Texts—25%**	*51	65	80% of items at Level 2 or 3	150 minutes
Mathematical Reasoning	**Algebraic Problem Solving—55%** **Quantitative Problem Solving—45%**	*46	49	50% of items at Level 2	115 minutes
Science	**Life Science—40%** **Physical Science—40%** **Earth and Space Science—20%**	*34	40	80% of items at Level 2 or 3	90 minutes
Social Studies	**Civics/Government—50%** **U.S. History—20%** **Economics—15%** **Geography and the World—15%**	*35	44	80% of items at Level 2 or 3	90 minutes

*Number of items may vary slightly by test.

Because the demands of today's high school education and its relationship to workforce needs differ from those of a decade ago, the GED® Testing Service has moved to a computer-based format. Although multiple-choice questions remain the dominant type of item, the new GED® Test series includes a variety of technology-enhanced item types: drop-down, fill-in-the-blank, drag-and-drop, hot spot, short answer, and extended response items.

The table to the right identifies the various item types and their distribution on the new subject-area exams. As you can see, all four tests include multiple-choice, drop-down, fill-in-the-blank, and drag-and-drop items. Some variation occurs with hot spot, short answer, and extended response items.

2014 ITEM TYPES

	RLA	Math	Science	Social Studies
Multiple-choice	✓	✓	✓	✓
Drop-down	✓	✓	✓	✓
Fill-in-the-blank	✓	✓	✓	✓
Drag-and-drop	✓	✓	✓	✓
Hot spot		✓	✓	✓
Short answer			✓	
Extended response	✓			✓

Moreover, the new GED® Test relates to today's more demanding educational standards with items that align to appropriate assessment targets and varying DOK levels.

- **Content Topics/Assessment Targets** These topics and targets describe and detail the content on the GED® Test. They tie to the Common Core State Standards, as well as state standards for Texas and Virginia.
- **Content Practices** These practices describe the types of reasoning and modes of thinking required to answer specific items on the GED® Test.
- **Depth of Knowledge** The DOK model details the level of cognitive complexity and steps required to arrive at a correct answer on the test. The new GED® Test addresses three levels of DOK complexity.
  - **Level 1** You must recall, observe, question, or represent facts or simple skills. Typically, you will need to exhibit only a surface understanding of text and graphics.
  - **Level 2** You must process information beyond simple recall and observation to include summarizing, ordering, classifying, identifying patterns and relationships, and connecting ideas. You will need to scrutinize text and graphics.
  - **Level 3** You must explain, generalize, and connect ideas by inferring, elaborating, and predicting. For example, you may need to summarize from multiple sources and use that information to develop compositions with multiple paragraphs. Those paragraphs should feature a critical analysis of sources, include supporting positions from your own experiences, and reflect editing to ensure coherent, correct writing.

Approximately 80 percent of items across most content areas will be written to DOK Levels 2 and 3, with the remainder at Level 1. Writing portions, such as the extended response item in Social Studies (25 minutes) and Reasoning Through Language Arts (45 minutes), are considered DOK Level 3 items.

Now that you understand the basic structure of the GED® Test and the benefits of earning a GED® credential, you must prepare for the GED® Test. In the pages that follow, you will find a recipe of sorts that, if followed, will guide you toward successful completion of your GED® credential.

GED® Test on Computer

Along with new item types, the 2014 GED® Test also unveils a new, computer-based testing experience. The GED® Test will be available on computer and only at approved Pearson VUE Testing Centers. You will need content knowledge and the ability to read, think, and write critically, and you must perform basic computer functions—clicking, scrolling, and typing—to succeed on the test. The screen below closely resembles a screen that you will experience on the GED® Test.

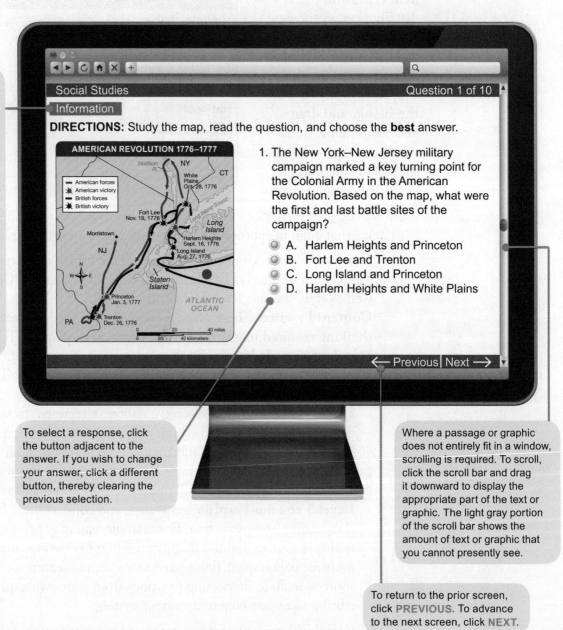

The **INFORMATION** button contains material vital to the successful completion of the item. Here, by clicking the Information button, you would display a map about the American Revolution. On the Mathematical Reasoning exam, similar buttons for **FORMULA SHEET** and **CALCULATOR REFERENCE** provide information that will help you answer items that require use of formulas or the TI-30XS calculator. You may move a passage or graphic by clicking it and dragging it to a different part of the test screen.

To select a response, click the button adjacent to the answer. If you wish to change your answer, click a different button, thereby clearing the previous selection.

Where a passage or graphic does not entirely fit in a window, scrolling is required. To scroll, click the scroll bar and drag it downward to display the appropriate part of the text or graphic. The light gray portion of the scroll bar shows the amount of text or graphic that you cannot presently see.

To return to the prior screen, click **PREVIOUS**. To advance to the next screen, click **NEXT**.

Contents of the computer screen:

Social Studies   Question 1 of 10

Information

DIRECTIONS: Study the map, read the question, and choose the **best** answer.

AMERICAN REVOLUTION 1776–1777

- American forces
- ★ American victory
- British forces
- ✦ British victory

Hudson R.
NY
White Plains Oct. 28, 1776
CT
Fort Lee Nov. 19, 1776
Long Island Sound
Long Island
Morristown
Harlem Heights Sept. 16, 1776
NJ
Long Island Aug. 27, 1776
N W E S
Staten Island
Princeton Jan. 3, 1777
ATLANTIC OCEAN
PA
Trenton Dec. 26, 1776
0   20   40 miles
0   20   40 kilometers

1. The New York–New Jersey military campaign marked a key turning point for the Colonial Army in the American Revolution. Based on the map, what were the first and last battle sites of the campaign?

- A. Harlem Heights and Princeton
- B. Fort Lee and Trenton
- C. Long Island and Princeton
- D. Harlem Heights and White Plains

← Previous | Next →

Some items on the new GED® Test, such as fill-in-the-blank, short answer, and extended response questions, will require you to type answers into an entry box. In some cases, the directions may specify the range of typing the system will accept. For example, a fill-in-the-blank item may allow you to type a number from 0 to 9, along with a decimal point or a slash, but nothing else. The system also will tell you keys to avoid pressing in certain situations. The annotated computer screen and keyboard below provide strategies for entering text and data for fill-in-the-blank, short answer, and extended response items.

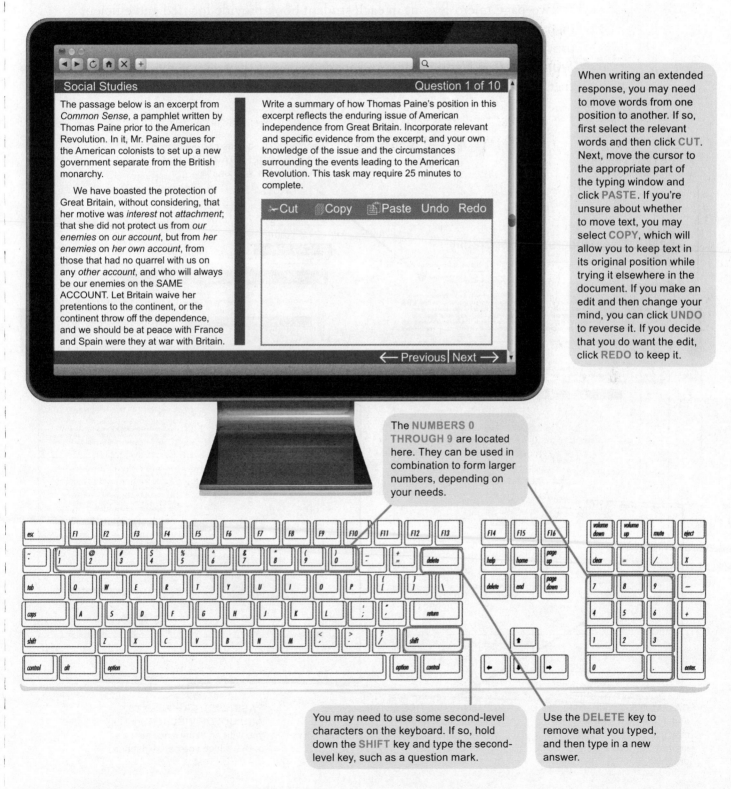

Social Studies   Question 1 of 10

The passage below is an excerpt from *Common Sense*, a pamphlet written by Thomas Paine prior to the American Revolution. In it, Mr. Paine argues for the American colonists to set up a new government separate from the British monarchy.

We have boasted the protection of Great Britain, without considering, that her motive was *interest* not *attachment*; that she did not protect us from *our enemies* on *our account*, but from *her enemies* on *her own account*, from those that had no quarrel with us on any *other account*, and who will always be our enemies on the SAME ACCOUNT. Let Britain waive her pretentions to the continent, or the continent throw off the dependence, and we should be at peace with France and Spain were they at war with Britain.

Write a summary of how Thomas Paine's position in this excerpt reflects the enduring issue of American independence from Great Britain. Incorporate relevant and specific evidence from the excerpt, and your own knowledge of the issue and the circumstances surrounding the events leading to the American Revolution. This task may require 25 minutes to complete.

⊷Cut   Copy   Paste Undo Redo

← Previous | Next →

When writing an extended response, you may need to move words from one position to another. If so, first select the relevant words and then click **CUT**. Next, move the cursor to the appropriate part of the typing window and click **PASTE**. If you're unsure about whether to move text, you may select **COPY**, which will allow you to keep text in its original position while trying it elsewhere in the document. If you make an edit and then change your mind, you can click **UNDO** to reverse it. If you decide that you do want the edit, click **REDO** to keep it.

The **NUMBERS 0 THROUGH 9** are located here. They can be used in combination to form larger numbers, depending on your needs.

You may need to use some second-level characters on the keyboard. If so, hold down the **SHIFT** key and type the second-level key, such as a question mark.

Use the **DELETE** key to remove what you typed, and then type in a new answer.

About *Steck-Vaughn*
Test Preparation for the 2014 GED® Test

Along with choosing to pursue your GED® credential, you've made another smart decision by selecting *Steck-Vaughn Test Preparation for the 2014 GED® Test* as your main study and preparation tool. Our emphasis on the acquisition of key reading and thinking concepts equips you with the skills and strategies to succeed on the GED® Test.

Two-page micro-lessons in each student book provide focused and efficient instruction. For those who require additional support, the companion workbooks, provide *twice* the support and practice exercises. Most lessons in the series include a *Spotlighted Item* feature that corresponds to one of the technology-enhanced item types that appear on the GED® Test.

The **REVIEW THE SKILL** section reteaches the skill.

Each lesson includes correlations to **ASSESSMENT TARGETS** that will help focus your studies.

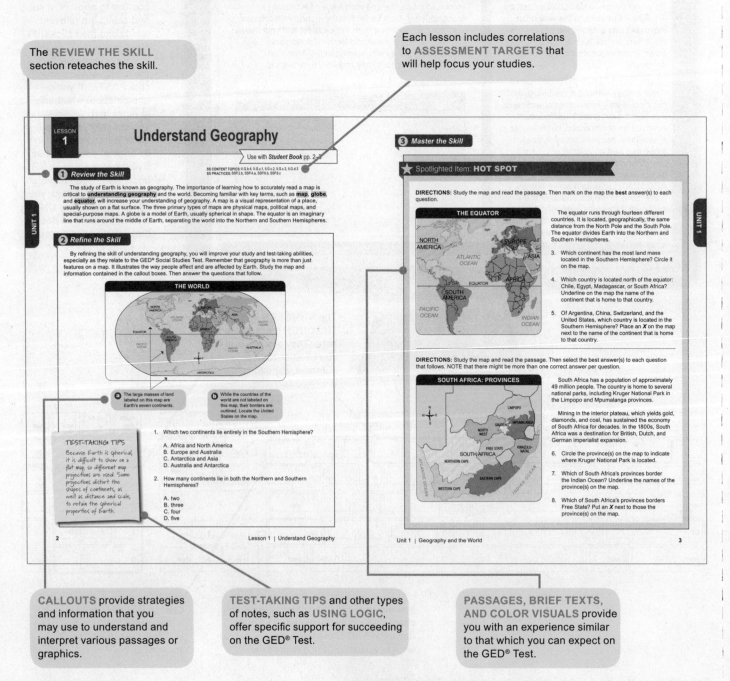

CALLOUTS provide strategies and information that you may use to understand and interpret various passages or graphics.

TEST-TAKING TIPS and other types of notes, such as USING LOGIC, offer specific support for succeeding on the GED® Test.

PASSAGES, BRIEF TEXTS, AND COLOR VISUALS provide you with an experience similar to that which you can expect on the GED® Test.

Student Book

Every unit in the student book opens with the feature *GED® Journeys*, a series of profiles of people who earned their GED® credential and used it as a springboard to success. From there, you receive intensive instruction and practice through a series of linked lessons, all of which tie to Content Topics/Assessment Targets, Content Practices (where applicable), and DOK levels.

Each unit closes with an eight-page review that includes a representative sampling of items, including technology-enhanced item types, from the lessons that comprise the unit. You may use each unit review as a posttest to gauge your mastery of content and skills and readiness for that aspect of the GED® Test.

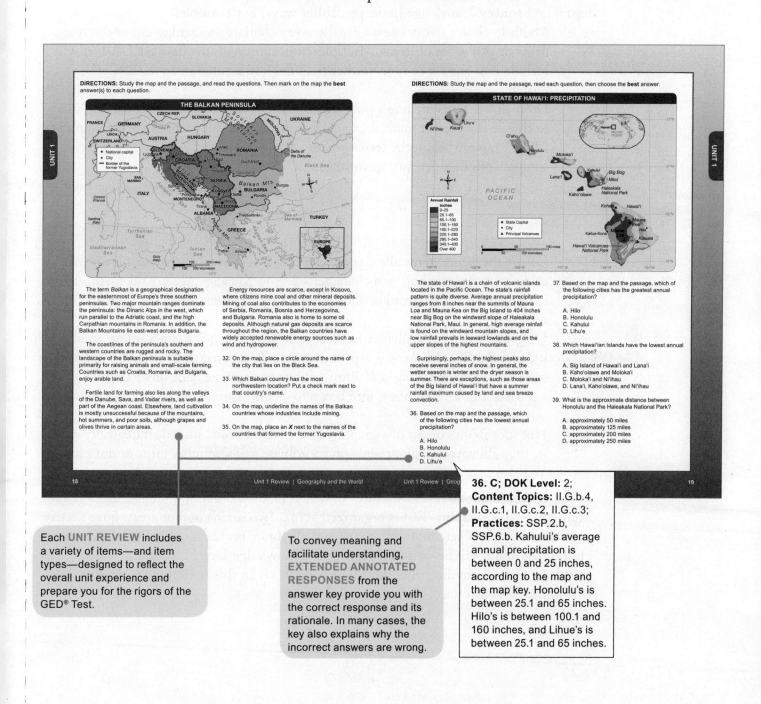

DIRECTIONS: Study the map and the passage, and read the questions. Then mark on the map the **best** answer(s) to each question.

THE BALKAN PENINSULA

The term *Balkan* is a geographical designation for the easternmost of Europe's three southern peninsulas. Two major mountain ranges dominate the peninsula: the Dinaric Alps in the west, which run parallel to the Adriatic coast, and the high Carpathian mountains in Romania. In addition, the Balkan Mountains lie east-west across Bulgaria.

The coastlines of the peninsula's southern and western countries are rugged and rocky. The landscape of the Balkan peninsula is suitable primarily for raising animals and small-scale farming. Countries such as Croatia, Romania, and Bulgaria, enjoy arable land.

Fertile land for farming also lies along the valleys of the Danube, Sava, and Vadar rivers, as well as part of the Aegean coast. Elsewhere, land cultivation is mostly unsuccessful because of the mountains, hot summers, and poor soils, although grapes and olives thrive in certain areas.

Energy resources are scarce, except in Kosovo, where citizens mine coal and other mineral deposits. Mining of coal also contributes to the economies of Serbia, Romania, Bosnia and Herzegovina, and Bulgaria. Romania also is home to some oil deposits. Although natural gas deposits are scarce throughout the region, the Balkan countries have widely accepted renewable energy sources such as wind and hydropower.

32. On the map, place a circle around the name of the city that lies on the Black Sea.

33. Which Balkan country has the most northwestern location? Put a check mark next to that country's name.

34. On the map, underline the names of the Balkan countries whose industries include mining.

35. On the map, place an *X* next to the names of the countries that formed the former Yugoslavia.

DIRECTIONS: Study the map and the passage, read each question, then choose the **best** answer.

STATE OF HAWAI'I: PRECIPITATION

The state of Hawai'i is a chain of volcanic islands located in the Pacific Ocean. The state's rainfall pattern is quite diverse. Average annual precipitation ranges from 8 inches near the summits of Mauna Loa and Mauna Kea on the Big Island to 404 inches near Big Bog on the windward slope of Haleakala National Park, Maui. In general, high average rainfall is found on the windward mountain slopes, and low rainfall prevails in leeward lowlands and on the upper slopes of the highest mountains.

Surprisingly, perhaps, the highest peaks also receive several inches of snow. In general, the wetter season is winter and the dryer season is summer. There are exceptions, such as those areas of the Big Island of Hawai'i that have a summer rainfall maximum caused by land and sea breeze convection.

36. Based on the map and the passage, which of the following cities has the lowest annual precipitation?

A. Hilo
B. Honolulu
C. Kahului
D. Lihu'e

37. Based on the map and the passage, which of the following cities has the greatest annual precipitation?

A. Hilo
B. Honolulu
C. Kahului
D. Lihu'e

38. Which Hawai'ian Islands have the lowest annual precipitation?

A. Big Island of Hawai'i and Lana'i
B. Kaho'olawe and Moloka'i
C. Moloka'i and Ni'ihau
D. Lana'i, Kaho'olawe, and Ni'ihau

39. What is the approximate distance between Honolulu and the Haleakala National Park?

A. approximately 50 miles
B. approximately 125 miles
C. approximately 200 miles
D. approximately 250 miles

18   Unit 1 Review | Geography and the World   Unit 1 Review | Geog   19

Each **UNIT REVIEW** includes a variety of items—and item types—designed to reflect the overall unit experience and prepare you for the rigors of the GED® Test.

To convey meaning and facilitate understanding, **EXTENDED ANNOTATED RESPONSES** from the answer key provide you with the correct response and its rationale. In many cases, the key also explains why the incorrect answers are wrong.

36. C; DOK Level: 2; **Content Topics:** II.G.b.4, II.G.c.1, II.G.c.2, II.G.c.3; **Practices:** SSP.2.b, SSP.6.b. Kahului's average annual precipitation is between 0 and 25 inches, according to the map and the map key. Honolulu's is between 25.1 and 65 inches. Hilo's is between 100.1 and 160 inches, and Lihue's is between 25.1 and 65 inches.

About the GED® Mathematical Reasoning Test

The new GED® Mathematical Reasoning Test is more than just a set of math items. In fact, it reflects an attempt to increase the rigor of the GED® Test to better meet the demands of a 21st-century economy. To that end, the GED® Mathematical Reasoning Test features an array of technology-enhanced item types. All of the items are delivered via computer-based testing. The items reflect the knowledge, skills, and abilities that a student would master in an equivalent high school experience.

Multiple-choice questions remain the majority of items on the GED® Mathematical Reasoning Test. However, a number of technology-enhanced items, including drop-down, fill-in-the-blank, drag-and-drop, and hot spot questions, will challenge you to master and convey knowledge in deeper, fuller ways. For example:

- Multiple-choice items assess virtually every content standard as either discrete items or as a series of items. Multiple-choice items on the new GED® Test will include four answer options (rather than five), structured in an A./B./C./D. format.
- Drop-down items include a pull-down menu of response choices, enabling you to choose the correct math vocabulary or numerical value to complete statements. In the example below, the terms *greater than*, *equal to,* and *less than* allow for comparisons between two quantities:

$$\sqrt{65} \qquad \begin{array}{l} \text{greater than} \\ \text{equal to} \\ \text{less than} \end{array} \qquad 7^2$$

- Fill-in-the-blank items allow you to type in a numerical answer to a problem using keyboard symbols or a character selector. You also may use fill-in-the-blank items to express one-word or short answers to questions about mathematical reasoning.
- Drag-and-drop items involve interactive tasks that require you to move small images, words, or numerical expressions into designated drop zones on a computer screen. You may use drag-and-drop options to organize data, order steps in a process, or move numbers into boxes to create expressions, equations, and inequalities.
- Hot spot items consist of a graphic with virtual sensors placed strategically within it. They allow you to plot points on coordinate grids, number lines, or dot plots. You also may create models that match certain criteria.

You will have a total of 115 minutes in which to answer about 46 items. The GED® Mathematical Reasoning Test is organized across two main content areas: quantitative problem solving (45 percent of all items) and algebraic problem solving (55 percent). Half of the items will be written at Depth of Knowledge Level 2. The TI-30XS calculator and a formulas page, such as that on p. xiv in this book, will be embedded within the test's interface.

About *Steck-Vaughn Test Preparation* for the 2014 GED® Test: Mathematical Reasoning

Steck-Vaughn's student book and workbook help unlock the learning and deconstruct the different elements of the test by helping you build and develop core mathematics skills. The content of our books aligns to the new GED® math content standards and item distribution to provide you with a superior test preparation experience.

Our *Spotlighted Item* feature provides a deeper, richer treatment for each technology-enhanced item type. On initial introduction, a unique item type—such as drag-and-drop—receives a full page of example items in the student book lesson and three pages in the companion workbook lesson. The length of subsequent features may be shorter depending on the skill, lesson, and requirements.

A combination of targeted strategies, informational callouts and sample questions, assorted tips and hints, and ample assessment help clearly focus study efforts in needed areas.

In addition to the book features, a highly detailed answer key provides the correct answer and the rationale for it so that you know exactly why an answer is correct. The *Mathematical Reasoning* student book and workbook are designed with an eye toward the end goal: success on the GED® Mathematical Reasoning Test.

Along with mastering key content and reading and thinking skills, you will build familiarity with alternate item types that mirror in print the nature and scope of the technology-enhanced items included on the GED® Test.

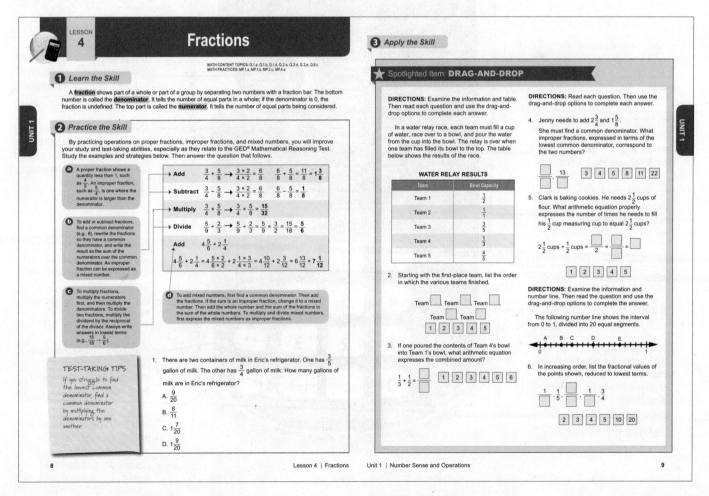

Calculator Directions

Certain items on the GED® Mathematical Reasoning Test allow for the use of a calculator to aid in answering questions. That calculator, the TI-30XS, is embedded within the testing interface. Students may also bring their own TI-30XS MultiView calculator to use on the test. The TI-30XS calculator will be available for most items on the GED® Mathematical Reasoning Test and for some items on the GED® Science Test and GED® Social Studies Test. The TI-30XS calculator is shown below, along with callouts of some of its most important keys. A button that enables the calculator reference sheet is located in the upper right corner of the testing screen.

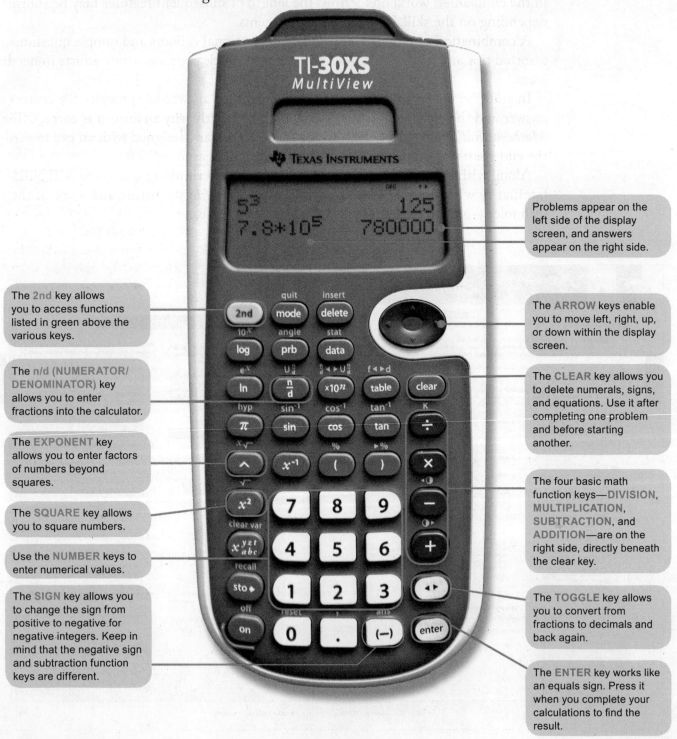

The **2nd** key allows you to access functions listed in green above the various keys.

The **n/d (NUMERATOR/ DENOMINATOR)** key allows you to enter fractions into the calculator.

The **EXPONENT** key allows you to enter factors of numbers beyond squares.

The **SQUARE** key allows you to square numbers.

Use the **NUMBER** keys to enter numerical values.

The **SIGN** key allows you to change the sign from positive to negative for negative integers. Keep in mind that the negative sign and subtraction function keys are different.

Problems appear on the left side of the display screen, and answers appear on the right side.

The **ARROW** keys enable you to move left, right, up, or down within the display screen.

The **CLEAR** key allows you to delete numerals, signs, and equations. Use it after completing one problem and before starting another.

The four basic math function keys—**DIVISION**, **MULTIPLICATION**, **SUBTRACTION**, and **ADDITION**—are on the right side, directly beneath the clear key.

The **TOGGLE** key allows you to convert from fractions to decimals and back again.

The **ENTER** key works like an equals sign. Press it when you complete your calculations to find the result.

Getting Started

To enable the calculator for a question that allows it, click the upper left portion of the testing screen. If the calculator displays over the top of a problem, you may move it by clicking it and dragging it to another part of the screen. Once enabled, the calculator will be ready for use (no need to push the **on** key). The directions below are for mathprint mode. Classic mode can be used by pressing the mode key and selecting classic.

- Use the **clear** key to clear all numbers and operations from the screen.
- Use the **enter** key to complete all calculations.

2nd Key

The green **2nd** key is located in the upper left corner of the TI-30XS. The **2nd** key enables a second series of functions, which are located above the keys and noted in green type. To use the 2nd-level function, click the **2nd** key, and then click the key with the 2nd-level function you need.

Fractions and Mixed Numbers

To enter fractions, such as $\frac{3}{4}$, click the **n/d (numerator/denominator)** key, followed by the numerator quantity [**3**]. Next, click the **down arrow** button (upper right corner of the calculator), followed by the denominator quantity [**4**]. To calculate with fractions, click the **right arrow** button and then the appropriate function key and other numerals in the equation.

To enter mixed numbers, such as $1\frac{3}{8}$, first enter the whole number quantity [**1**]. Next, click the **2nd** key and the **mixed number** key (1st level **n/d**). Then enter the fraction numerator [**3**], followed by the **down arrow** button and then the denominator [**8**]. If you click **enter**, the mixed number will convert to an improper fraction. To calculate with mixed numbers, click the **right arrow** button and then the appropriate function key and other numerals in the equation.

Negative Numbers

To enter a negative number, click the **negative sign** key (located directly below the number **3** on the calculator). Keep in mind that the **negative sign** key differs from the **subtraction** key, which is found in the far right column of keys, directly above the **addition (+)** key.

Squares, Square Roots, and Exponents

- **Squares:** The x^2 key squares numbers. The **exponent** key (^) raises numbers to powers higher than squares, such as cubes. For example, to find the answer to 5^3 on the calculator, first enter the base number [**5**], then click the exponent key (^), and follow by clicking the exponent number [**3**] and then the **enter** key.
- **Square Roots:** To find the square root of a number, such as 36, first click the **2nd** key, then click the **square root** key (1st-level x^2), then the number [**36**], and finally **enter**.
- **Cube Roots:** To find the cube root of a number, such as **125**, first enter the cube as a number [**3**], followed by the **2nd** key and ^ key. Finally, enter the number for which you want to find the cube [**125**], followed by **enter**.
- **Exponents:** To perform calculations with numbers expressed in scientific notation, such as 7.8×10^9, first enter the base number [**7.8**]. Next, click the **scientific notation** key (located directly beneath the **data** key), followed by the exponent level [**9**]. You then have 7.8×10^9.

Formulas for the GED® Mathematical Reasoning Test

Following are formulas that will be used on the new GED® Mathematical Reasoning Test. A button that will enable a formula reference sheet will appear in the upper left corner of the testing screen itself.

Area of a:

square	$A = s^2$
rectangle	$A = lw$
parallelogram	$A = bh$
triangle	$A = \frac{1}{2}bh$
trapezoid	$A = \frac{1}{2}h(b_1 + b_2)$
circle	$A = \pi r^2$

Perimeter of a:

square	$P = 4s$
rectangle	$P = 2l + 2w$
triangle	$P = s_1 + s_2 + s_3$
Circumference of a circle	$C = 2\pi r$ OR $C = \pi d$; $\pi \approx 3.14$

Surface area and volume of a:

rectangular/right prism	$SA = ph + 2B$	$V = Bh$
cylinder	$SA = 2\pi rh + 2\pi r^2$	$V = \pi r^2 h$
pyramid	$SA = \frac{1}{2}ps + B$	$V = \frac{1}{3}Bh$
cone	$SA = \pi rs + \pi r^2$	$V = \frac{1}{3}\pi r^2 h$
sphere	$SA = 4\pi r^2$	$V = \frac{4}{3}\pi r^3$

(p = perimeter of base with area B; $\pi \approx 3.14$)

Data

mean	mean is equal to the total of the values of a data set, divided by the number of elements in the data set
median	median is the middle value in an odd number of ordered values of a data set, or the mean of the two middle values in an even number of ordered values in a data set

Algebra

slope of a line	$m = \dfrac{y_2 - y_1}{x_2 - x_1}$
slope-intercept form of the equation of a line	$y = mx + b$
point-slope form of the equation of a line	$y - y_1 = m(x - x_1)$
standard form of a quadratic equation	$y = ax^2 + bx + c$
quadratic formula	$x = \dfrac{-b \pm \sqrt{b^2 - 4ac}}{2a}$
Pythagorean theorem	$a^2 + b^2 = c^2$
simple interest	$I = Prt$ (I = interest, P = principal, r = rate, t = time)
distance formula	$d = rt$
total cost	total cost = (number of units) × (price per unit)

Test-Taking Tips

The new GED® Test includes more than 160 items across the four subject-area exams of Reasoning Through Language Arts, Mathematical Reasoning, Science, and Social Studies. The four subject-area exams represent a total test time of seven hours. Most items are multiple-choice questions, but a number are technology-enhanced items. These include drop-down, fill-in-the-blank, drag-and-drop, hot spot, short answer, and extended response items.

Throughout this book and others in the series, we help you build, develop, and apply core reading and thinking skills critical to success on the GED® Test. As part of an overall strategy, we suggest that you use the test-taking tips presented here and throughout the book to improve your performance on the GED® Test.

> **Always read directions thoroughly so that you know exactly what to do.** As we've noted, the 2014 GED® Test has an entirely new computer-based format that includes a variety of technology-enhanced items. If you are unclear of what to do or how to proceed, ask the test provider whether directions can be explained.

> **Read each question carefully so that you fully understand what it is asking.** For example, some passages and graphics may present information beyond what is necessary to correctly answer a specific question. Other questions may use boldfaced words for emphasis (for example, "Which statement represents the **most** appropriate revision for this hypothesis?").

> **Manage your time with each question.** Because the GED® Test is a series of timed exams, you want to spend enough time with each question, but not *too* much time. For example, on the GED® Mathematical Reasoning Test, you have 115 minutes in which to answer approximately 46 questions, or an average of about two minutes per question. Obviously, some items will require more time and others will require less, but you should remain aware of the overall number of items and amount of testing time. The new GED® Test interface may help you manage your time. It includes an on-screen clock in the upper right corner that provides the remaining time in which to complete a test.

Also, you may monitor your progress by viewing the **Question** line, which will give you the current question number, followed by the total number of questions on that subject-area exam.

> **Answer all questions, regardless of whether you know the answer or are guessing.** There is no benefit in leaving questions unanswered on the GED® Test. Keep in mind the time that you have for each test, and manage it accordingly. If you wish to review a specific item at the end of a test, click **Flag for Review** to mark the question. When you do, the flag will display in yellow. At the end of a test, you may have time to review questions you've marked.

> **Skim and scan.** You may save time by first reading each question and its answer options before reading or studying an accompanying passage or graphic. Once you understand what the question is asking, review the passage or visual for the appropriate information.

> **Note any unfamiliar words in questions.** First attempt to re-read the question by omitting any unfamiliar word. Next, try to use other words around the unfamiliar word to determine its meaning.

> **Narrow answer options by re-reading each question and re-examining the text or graphic that goes with it.** Although four answers are *possible* on multiple-choice items, keep in mind that only one is *correct*. You may be able to eliminate one answer immediately; you may need to take more time or use logic or make assumptions to eliminate others. In some cases, you may need to make your best guess between two options.

> **Go with your instinct when answering questions.** If your first instinct is to choose **A** in response to a question, it's best to stick with that answer unless you determine that it is incorrect. Usually, the first answer someone chooses is the correct one.

Whole Numbers

Use with **Student Book** pp. 2–3

MATH CONTENT TOPICS: Q.1.d, Q.2.a, Q.2.e, Q.6.c
MATH PRACTICES: MP.1.a, MP.1.b, MP.1.c, MP.1.e, MP.2.c, MP.3.a

1 Review the Skill

Whole numbers are those numbers written with the digits 0 through 9. To determine the value of a digit in a whole number, first determine its place value. If one number (for example, *100*) has more digits than another number (*95*), it automatically has the higher value. However, if two numbers have the same number of digits, such as *200* and *195*, you must compare those digits from left to right.

In a table, you should read information and numbers from left to right and from top to bottom. In some cases, tables may include more information or data than you actually need to solve a problem. In such cases, you must know which information or data to use and which to ignore. Understanding place value will help you compare, order, and round whole numbers.

2 Refine the Skill

To understand more complex mathematical concepts and to solve problems successfully on the GED® Mathematical Reasoning Test, you first must master the concept of whole numbers. Examine the paragraph and table. Then answer the questions that follow.

An amusement park sells daily passes to visitors. The table below shows the number of daily passes sold each day of a week in July.

a When reading tables, start with the title. In this case, the title tells you that the table contains information about the number of passes sold over the course of one week in the summer. Additionally, tables contain rows and columns, which provide different, but related, types of information.

b When comparing numbers that contain the same number of digits, work from left to right to compare place values.

a NUMBER OF PASSES SOLD
(FOR THE WEEK OF JULY 19)

Sunday	4,586 **c**
Monday	3,989
Tuesday	4,209 **b**
Wednesday	4,001
Thursday	4,249
Friday	4,329
Saturday	5,683 **c**

c When you are asked to identify a trend, compare all of the information given. Look for ways that information changes over time or for numbers that are much smaller or larger than others to help in identifying trends.

TEST-TAKING TIPS

To maximize test-taking success, underline key words that could help you in solving the question. For example, the word *most* in question 1 indicates that you will compare to solve the problem.

1. On which day did the park sell the most daily passes?

A. Sunday
B. Monday
C. Thursday
D. Saturday

2. Based on the information, what trend can you identify?

A. Park attendance grew each day.
B. Park attendance fell each day.
C. The greatest daily attendance at the park was on the weekend.
D. Fewer total people visited the park during the week than on the weekend.

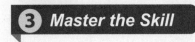
Master the Skill

DIRECTIONS: Study the information and table, read each question, and choose the **best** answer.

The seats in a large auditorium are identified by both numbers and letters. The range of numbers for each lettered row is shown in the chart.

SEAT NUMBERS

Letter of Row	Number Range
A	100–250
B	251–500
C	501–750
D	751–1000
E	1001–1250
F	1251–1500

3. In which row will you sit if your seat number is 1107?

   A. Row C
   B. Row D
   C. Row E
   D. Row F

4. A family of four has seat numbers 1000 through 1003. In which two rows in the auditorium will they sit?

   A. C and D
   B. D and E
   C. E and F
   D. D and F

5. Which row has the fewest number of seats?

   A. Row A
   B. Row B
   C. Row C
   D. Row E

6. How many rows have seat numbers in the thousands?

   A. 1
   B. 2
   C. 3
   D. 4

7. The auditorium plans to add two rows of seats continuing the pattern for rows B–F. With the addition, what will the last seat number be?

   A. 1600
   B. 1700
   C. 1900
   D. 2000

DIRECTIONS: Study the information, read each question, and choose the **best** answer.

In a dictionary, the following letters can be found on the associated pages:

P—pages 968–1096

Q—pages 1097–1105

R—pages 1105–1178

S—pages 1178–1360

8. With which letter does a word found on page 1100 begin?

   A. P
   B. Q
   C. R
   D. S

9. Which range of pages will include words that begin with the letter S?

   A. 998–1045
   B. 1046–1105
   C. 1117–1165
   D. 1234–1287

DIRECTIONS: Read each question, and choose the **best** answer.

10. Callie's job involves data entry. Which digits should she type in for the number twelve thousand, eight hundred two?

    A. 1, 2, 8, 0, 2
    B. 1, 2, 8, 2, 0
    C. 1, 2, 8, 0, 0, 2
    D. 1, 2, 0, 8, 0, 2

11. Romy's scores for her five social studies quizzes this semester are shown below.

    98, 75, 84, 92, 95

    What is the order of her social studies quiz scores from greatest to least?

    A. 75, 84, 92, 95, 98
    B. 75, 92, 95, 84, 98
    C. 95, 92, 98, 84, 75
    D. 98, 95, 92, 84, 75

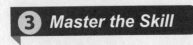

DIRECTIONS: Read the question, and choose the **best** answer.

12. Calvin is writing an essay. He wants to write the sentence "150,218 people lived in the city in 2013," but a good rule for writing is to avoid beginning a sentence with a numeral. What is a better way for Calvin to write his sentence?

   A. One hundred fifty thousand, two eighteen people lived in the city in 2013.
   B. One hundred fifty thousand, two hundred eighteen people lived in the city in 2013.
   C. One thousand fifty, two hundred eighteen people lived in the city in 2013.
   D. One hundred fifty thousand, twenty-one eight people lived in the city in 2013.

DIRECTIONS: Study the information and table, read each question, and choose the **best** answer.

The Northside Bowling Club recorded its nightly scores in the table below. The frequency is the number of scores falling within the corresponding range.

BOWLING SCORES

Score	Frequency
100–119	3
120–139	5
140–159	8
160–179	9
180–199	5

13. How many bowlers scored 100 to 139 points?

   A. 3
   B. 5
   C. 8
   D. 13

14. What score range had the highest frequency?

   A. 120–139
   B. 140–159
   C. 160–179
   D. 180–199

15. What score range had the lowest frequency?

   A. 100–119
   B. 120–139
   C. 140–159
   D. 180–199

DIRECTIONS: Study the information and table, read each question, and choose the **best** answer.

The table shows the number of people in different age groups who lived in San Francisco in 2010.

AGE GROUPS IN SAN FRANCISCO

Age Group	Population
< 5 years	31,633
5 to 9 years	31,564
10 to 14 years	30,813
15 to 19 years	33,334
20 to 24 years	56,054
25 to 34 years	180,418
35 to 44 years	133,804
45 to 54 years	107,718
55 to 59 years	35,026
60 to 64 years	30,258
65 to 74 years	53,955
75 to 84 years	37,929
> 84 years	14,227

16. Which age group had the fewest number of people?

   A. 10 to 14 years
   B. 15 to 19 years
   C. 60 to 64 years
   D. 85 years and over

17. Based on the table, the greatest number of people in San Francisco in 2010 were how old?

   A. 9 years or younger
   B. 10 to 24 years old
   C. 25 to 54 years old
   D. 75 years or older

DIRECTIONS: Read the question, and choose the **best** answer.

18. During jury selection, a clerk calls juror numbers. When a juror hears his or her number, he or she steps forward to speak with the judge. Bryan is juror number 807. When should he step forward to speak with the judge?

   A. when the clerk says "eighty and seven"
   B. when the clerk says "eight hundred seven"
   C. when the clerk says "eight hundred seventy"
   D. when the clerk says "eighty hundred and seven"

DIRECTIONS: Read the question, and choose the **best** answer.

19. A museum tracks its visitors each month. For its records, the museum rounds the number of monthly visitors to the nearest hundred. If 8,648 people visited the museum in July, what number will the museum record?

A. 8,500
B. 8,600
C. 8,700
D. 9,000

DIRECTIONS: Study the information and table, read each question, and choose the **best** answer.

Some people believe that, if you double the height of a child at age 2, the figure will equal the child's height as an adult. The table below shows the heights of six children at age 2.

HEIGHT OF 2-YEAR-OLDS

Child	Height (in.)
Ellie	32
Jake	34
George	33
Charlie	35
Kiera	34
Melanie	31

20. According to the above belief, which child will be the tallest adult?

A. Ellie
B. Jake
C. George
D. Charlie

21. If the belief holds true, which child will be the same height as Kiera in adulthood?

A. Ellie
B. Jake
C. George
D. Charlie

22. Who will be four inches taller than Melanie as an adult?

A. Charlie
B. Jake
C. Kiera
D. George

DIRECTIONS: Study the information and table, read the question, and choose the **best** answer.

The table shows sales of an automobile dealership over five weekends in the month of May.

SALES IN MAY

Weekend	Sales
Weekend 1	$168,000
Weekend 2	$102,000
Weekend 3	$121,000
Weekend 4	$119,000
Weekend 5	$305,000

23. On which weekend did the automobile dealership most likely run a promotion to sell more cars?

A. Weekend 1
B. Weekend 2
C. Weekend 3
D. Weekend 5

DIRECTIONS: Study the information and table, read each question, and choose the **best** answer.

Tom's Toy Store released its quarterly sales figures for the recent year. Sales are shown below.

QUARTERLY SALES

Quarter	Sales
Quarter 1 (January through March)	$79,000
Quarter 2 (April through June)	$131,000
Quarter 3 (July through September)	$119,000
Quarter 4 (October through December)	$151,000

24. In which quarter did the store make the most?

A. Quarter 1
B. Quarter 2
C. Quarter 3
D. Quarter 4

25. What is the store's order of quarterly toy sales from least to greatest?

A. Quarter 1, Quarter 2, Quarter 3, Quarter 4
B. Quarter 2, Quarter 3, Quarter 4, Quarter 1
C. Quarter 1, Quarter 3, Quarter 2, Quarter 4
D. Quarter 4, Quarter 2, Quarter 3, Quarter 1

Operations

MATH CONTENT TOPICS: Q.1.b, Q.2.a, Q.2.e, Q.3.a, Q.6.c
MATH PRACTICES: MP.1.a, MP.1.b, MP.1.c, MP.1.d, MP.1.e, MP.2.c, MP.3.a, MP.5.c

UNIT 1

1 Review the Skill

Addition, subtraction, multiplication, and division are the four basic math operations. Select an operation based on the information you need to find. For example, add to find a **sum**, or total. Subtract to find the difference between two numbers. Multiply to add the same number many times. Divide to separate a quantity into equal groups.

If adding, subtracting, or multiplying, work from right to left. If dividing, work from left (the divisor) to right (the dividend). In some cases, you may need to regroup numbers to complete the operation. If doing so, you'll want to align digits by their place value.

2 Refine the Skill

You will use one or more of the four basic operations to solve many problems on the GED® Mathematical Reasoning Test. You must understand when and why to use each operation to solve problems effectively. Examine the information and table. Then answer the questions that follow.

The table shows the number of boxes of cereal that a company produced each day in one week.

a To add, align place values. Then add the numbers in each column to find the sum. If the sum of a column exceeds 9, you must regroup.

b When using tables, ensure you read the title, column, and row headings for information. For example, all entries appearing in a column relate to the category heading at the top of the column. Sometimes tables may contain more information than you need to solve a problem. For that reason, you may need to evaluate the importance of information in a table as it relates to solving a problem.

COMPANY CEREAL PRODUCTION

Day of Week	Number of Boxes
Monday	4,596 **a**
Tuesday	4,025
Wednesday	3,548 **b**
Thursday	4,250
Friday	3,115 **c**

c Words in questions can provide clues about the needed operation. For example, question 2 states that cereal production increased 3 *times* from the previous Friday. The word *times* suggests that multiplication is the operation to use to solve the problem.

USING LOGIC

Addition and subtraction are opposites. Addition can, therefore, be used to check answers to subtraction problems, and vice versa. Multiplication and division are related in the same way.

1. What was the total number of boxes of cereal produced on Monday and Tuesday?

   A. 8,144
   B. 8,611
   C. 8,620
   D. 8,621

2. The following Friday, the factory increased production and produced 3 times as many boxes of cereal. How many boxes of cereal were produced the following Friday?

   A. 7,730
   B. 9,345
   C. 9,430
   D. 12,460

★ Spotlighted Item: **FILL-IN-THE-BLANK**

DIRECTIONS: Read each question. Then fill in your answer in the box below.

3. Alex saves $325 each month for college tuition. How much will he have saved after 6 months?

4. Angelo has paid $1,560 toward his car loan. If his loan is $2,750, how much does he still owe?

5. Tara pays the same amount for her electric bill each month. If she pays $72 per month, what is the total cost of her electricity for one year?

6. Four roommates equally share their monthly rent. Their monthly rent is $1,080. How much does each roommate pay per month?

7. Which whole number is the largest common factor of both the numbers 45 and 72?

8. A city budgets $567,800 for parks and recreation and $258,900 for facilities maintenance. How much is spent on these budget items together?

9. Mara gave 22 shirts, 14 pairs of pants, and 12 scarves to charity. How many clothing items did she give away altogether?

10. Eli is writing a 1,500-word essay for English class. He has written 892 words so far. How many words must he still write?

DIRECTIONS: Study the information and table below. Read each question. Then fill in your answer in the box below.

The table shows the cost for five people attending a professional football game.

COST OF ATTENDING GAME

Product/Service	Cost
Gasoline and parking	$50
Tickets	$335
Food	$80
Souvenirs	$75

11. If five friends decided to evenly share the costs, how much would each person expect to pay?

12. If two more friends decided to attend the game and all of the friends split the costs evenly as before, what would be the new total cost of attending the game?

★ Spotlighted Item: **FILL-IN-THE-BLANK**

DIRECTIONS: Study the information and table below. Read each question. Then fill in your answer in the box below.

The table shows Antonio's monthly budget.

MONTHLY BUDGET

Category	Amount Budgeted
Rent	$825
Utilities	$220
Food	$285
Recreation	$100
Auto Loan	$179
Auto Insurance	$62

13. What is the total amount included in Antonio's budget for rent, utilities, and food?

14. How much more money does Antonio allow in his budget for food than for his auto loan?

15. How much does Antonio pay toward his auto loan each year?

16. How much more per year does Antonio spend on rent than on utilities, food, and recreation combined?

17. To save $15 per month, Antonio decided to pay his auto insurance in one lump sum. What is the new amount he'll spend annually on auto insurance?

DIRECTIONS: Read each question. Then fill in your answer in the box below.

18. Annette works 5 days per week, 6 hours per day. She earns $13 per hour. How much does Annette earn, before taxes, in 4 weeks?

19. Andrew worked 54 hours one week and 39 hours the next week. He earns $11 per hour. How much did he earn, before taxes, in the 2 weeks?

20. In January, the Wilsons spent $458 on groceries. They spent $397 on groceries in February and $492 on groceries in March. What is the total amount the Wilsons spent on groceries for those three months?

21. A sports store ran a promotion on a specific tent. During the promotion, the store had tent sales of $23,870. If each tent cost $385, how many tents did the store sell?

22. What whole number greater than 1 is the smallest common factor of 45 and 75?

23. A pattern calls for 2 yards of material for a shirt and 5 yards of material for a dress. A seamstress makes five shirts and five dresses for a retail store. How many more yards of material does she use for the dresses than for the shirts?

DIRECTIONS: Read each question. Then fill in your answer in the box below.

24. Joanne drives 37 miles round-trip each day commuting to and from work. She works Monday through Friday. How many miles does Joanne drive in 4 weeks?

25. A charity wants to donate $12,500 to a food bank. It has already collected $4,020 in donations from local businesses and $3,902 in donations from individuals. How much more does the charity need to collect to meet its goal?

26. Mr. and Mrs. Dale paid $1,445 to have a new floor installed in their kitchen. The company installed 289 square feet of flooring. How much did the Dales pay for each square foot of flooring?

27. Maggie purchased a used car. She financed the car through the auto dealership. She will make equal monthly payments on the car for 3 years. If she owes a total of $13,392, what will be her monthly payment?

28. Maggie's friend Becky is thinking about buying a new car. If she pays $3,000 up front, she can finance the car over 5 years at a monthly payment of $265. What will Becky's cost for the car be over 5 years?

DIRECTIONS: Study the information and table below. Read each question. Then fill in your answer in the box below.

The table shows the prices of various stocks for purchase.

STOCK PRICE

Stock	Price Per Share
Computers4U	$30
Sun Cell Phones	$23
Online Airlines	$15
Virtual Reality, Inc.	$42

29. Mario wants to invest in an online travel service. How many shares of Online Airlines can he purchase for $270?

30. Karissa purchased 25 shares of Virtual Reality, Inc., and then sold all of them three months later for a profit of $7 per share. How much profit did Karissa make on her sale of Virtual Reality, Inc.?

DIRECTIONS: Read each question. Then fill in your answer in the box below.

31. What whole number is the largest common factor of both the numbers 30 and 42?

32. What is the smallest whole number that has both 12 and 15 as factors?

Integers

Use with **Student Book** pp. 6–7

MATH CONTENT TOPICS: Q.1.d, Q.2.a, Q.2.e, Q.6.c
MATH PRACTICES: MP.1.a, MP.1.b, MP.1.c, MP.1.d, MP.1.e, MP.3.a, MP.4.a

1 Review the Skill

Integers include positive and negative whole numbers as well as zero. Positive numbers may be written with or without a plus sign (+) before them. For example, +1 and 1 are both positive integers with the same value. However, negative numbers, such as −1, must feature a negative sign before them.

Use order of operations to add, subtract, multiply, and divide integers. There are specific rules to follow regarding the signs of integers when performing operations. If the difference between two integers (for example, −2 and 1) is negative, then the overall sign is negative. If the difference is positive (for example, 2 and −1), then the overall sign is positive.

2 Refine the Skill

To successfully solve problems with integers on the GED® Mathematical Reasoning Test, you must understand integer rules and the order of operations. Examine the information and table. Then answer the questions that follow.

The table shows the temperature at a weather station at various times during the day.

a Remember that, when you are asked to find change, subtract the original temperature from the new temperature. To answer question 1, subtract 68 from 65.

b To decide which operation to use, look for key words. In question 2, *dropped* tells you to subtract.

TEMPERATURE THROUGHOUT THE DAY

Time	Temperature (°F)
a 6:00 A.M.	68
9:00 A.M.	72
12:00 P.M.	75
3:00 P.M.	78
6:00 P.M.	76
9:00 P.M.	71
a 12:00 A.M.	65

CONTENT TOPICS

This lesson introduces number lines, absolute values, and differences in the context of integers. An integer's absolute value is its distance from 0; absolute values are always greater than or equal to zero, but never negative.

1. What is the change in temperature between 6:00 A.M. and 12:00 A.M.?

   A. −3°F
   B. +3°F
   C. −4°F
   D. +4°F

2. If the temperature dropped 4°F between 6:00 P.M. and 8 P.M., what would be the temperature at 8:00 P.M.?

   A. 69°F
   B. 70°F
   C. 71°F
   D. 72°F

DIRECTIONS: Read each question, and choose the **best** answer.

3. The Dow Jones Industrial Average opened trading one morning at 13,498. It closed that day at 13,416. Which integer describes the change?

    A. +82
    B. +18
    C. −18
    D. −82

4. In a card game, Deshon had −145 points. He then scored 80 points, and then 22 points. What is Deshon's score at this point?

    A. 247
    B. 87
    C. −43
    D. −87

5. A football team has possession of the ball. On their first play, they gain 8 yards. On their second play, they lose 10 yards. On their third play, they gain 43 yards. How far have they gone?

    A. 25 yards
    B. 33 yards
    C. 41 yards
    D. 51 yards

6. A mountain biker begins at the top of a mountain with an elevation of 8,453 feet. He rides 2,508 feet down the mountain before taking a break. He then rides another 584 feet up the mountain. At what elevation is he now?

    A. 11,545 feet
    B. 10,961 feet
    C. 9,037 feet
    D. 6,529 feet

7. Anna had $784 in her checking account on Friday. Over the weekend, she wrote checks for $23, $69, and $90. On Monday, she deposited $129. What was her balance after depositing the check?

    A. $913
    B. $731
    C. $692
    D. $655

DIRECTIONS: Read each question, and choose the **best** answer.

8. A diver begins at a height of 3 meters above the water on a diving board. In her dive, she reaches a height of 2 meters above the board. From this point, she drops 8 meters. Which integer describes her position at this point, with regard to the surface of the water?

    A. −3 meters
    B. −2 meters
    C. 2 meters
    D. 3 meters

9. If −7 is added to a number, the result is 12. What is the number?

    A. −5
    B. 5
    C. 12
    D. 19

DIRECTIONS: Study the information and table, read each question, and choose the **best** answer.

Four friends played a game. Each player kept track of the number of points she scored in each round.

POINTS SCORED EACH ROUND

Player	Round		
	1	2	3
Nikki	0	10	−15
Clara	−15	15	0
Donna	5	−10	−10
Dorothy	15	5	0

10. What was Donna's score after the end of Round 3?

    A. −25
    B. −15
    C. −10
    D. 0

11. How many more points did Dorothy score than Nikki?

    A. 5
    B. 10
    C. 15
    D. 25

DIRECTIONS: Read each question, and choose the **best** answer.

12. A submarine is at 3,290 feet below sea level. It rises 589 feet before dropping another 4,508 feet. Which integer describes its current position with regard to sea level?

    A. 7,209 feet
    B. 1,807 feet
    C. −1,807 feet
    D. −7,209 feet

13. Scott ran in a race. At one point in the race, he was in 10th position. He moved up 3 positions, fell back 4 positions, and then fell back 1 more position before the race ended. What position was he in when the race ended?

    A. 12th position
    B. 11th position
    C. 8th position
    D. 5th position

14. A cogwheel train transports skiers to the top of a mountain. There are two stations where skiers can get on and off the train. Station A is 5,993 feet above sea level. Station B is 10,549 feet above sea level. The peak of the mountain is 872 feet above Station B. How tall is the mountain at its highest point?

    A. −16,542 feet
    B. −11,421 feet
    C. 6,865 feet
    D. 11,421 feet

15. Jordan had $890 in her bank account. In one week, she withdrew $45 three separate times. What was the balance of her account at the end of the week?

    A. $755
    B. $800
    C. $845
    D. $935

DIRECTIONS: Examine the information and number line, read each question, and choose the **best** answer.

The number line shown below represents Erik's bicycle trip where he traveled from home (Point A), rode east to Point B, and then returned part way home to Point C; distances are in miles.

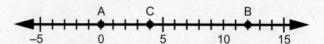

16. How far was Erik from home when he stopped at point C?

    A. 4 miles
    B. 8 miles
    C. 12 miles
    D. 16 miles

17. What was the total distance Erik traveled in going from home to Point C?

    A. 12 miles
    B. 16 miles
    C. 20 miles
    D. 24 miles

DIRECTIONS: Read each question, and choose the **best** answer.

18. Four team members each have −120 points. How many points do they have together as a team?

    A. −480
    B. −360
    C. 240
    D. 360

19. A group of rock climbers descended a rock face in three equal phases. If the rock face was 363 feet high, what number describes their change in height in each phase?

    A. −242 feet
    B. −121 feet
    C. 121 feet
    D. 242 feet

20. Brenda has her health insurance premium of $156 automatically withdrawn from her checking account each month. Which integer describes the change in her bank account due to her health insurance premium in one year?

    A. $1,872
    B. $936
    C. −$936
    D. −$1,872

21. Don played a game. He scored 3 points in the first round. After the second round, his total score was −10. How many points did Don score in the second round?

    A. −13
    B. −7
    C. 5
    D. 7

22. The number −7 is multiplied by −1. The product is then multiplied by −1. Finally, this product is multiplied by −1. What is the final product?

    A. −10
    B. −7
    C. −4
    D. 7

23. Karin owes her sister $1,554. She had budgeted an equal amount of money over the next 6 months to pay her sister back. How much money will Karin pay her sister each month?

    A. $257
    B. $258
    C. $259
    D. $260

24. If −10 is subtracted from a number, the result is 6. What is the number?

    A. −16
    B. −4
    C. 0
    D. 4

25. Jumana had $80 in her checking account. She deposited $25 on Monday. She wrote two checks for $75 each on Tuesday. She was charged with a $25 overdraft fee. What is Jumana's account balance?

    A. −$70
    B. −$60
    C. −$50
    D. −$40

26. In a year, Connor paid $3,228 for his car loan. He paid the same amount each month. Which integer describes the monthly change in his bank account after paying his monthly car payment?

    A. −$279
    B. −$269
    C. −$259
    D. −$249

27. Janet visited a skyscraper in Chicago. She entered the elevator on the ground floor and went up 54 floors. She then went back down 22 floors. She realized she should have gotten out of the elevator 5 floors above, so she rides the elevator up. On what floor is Janet now?

    A. 27
    B. 32
    C. 37
    D. 59

28. Cheryl receives $527 per month from her retirement fund. Which integer describes the amount she receives in 6 months?

    A. −$3,689
    B. −$3,162
    C. $2,635
    D. $3,162

29. Steve's fantasy baseball team led its league with 90 points. His team's point value did not change in five of the 10 statistical categories that make up the standings. In the other five categories, Steve's team was +2 in batting average, −1 in runs scored, +3 in stolen bases, −2 in wins, and −2 in strikeouts. What is his team's new point total?

    A. 89
    B. 90
    C. 91
    D. 92

Fractions

Use with *Student Book* pp. 8–9

MATH CONTENT TOPICS: Q.1.a, Q.1.b, Q.2.a, Q.2.d, Q.2.e, Q.3.a, Q.6.c
MATH PRACTICES: MP.1.a, MP.1.b, MP.1.d, MP.1.e, MP.2.c, MP.4.a

UNIT 1

1 Review the Skill

A **fraction** shows part of a whole or part of a group. A fraction bar separates two numbers, the **numerator** (above the fraction bar) and the **denominator** (below the fraction bar). An **improper fraction** has a numerator greater than the denominator. It shows an amount greater than one whole. A **mixed number** has a whole-number part and a fraction part. To compare and order fractions, you first must find a common denominator.

To add or subtract fractions, the fractions first must have **common denominators**. Next, you must add or subtract the numerators. To multiply fractions, multiply the numerators and then multiply the denominators. To divide fractions, multiply the dividend by the reciprocal of the divisor. To find the reciprocal, switch the numerator and the denominator in the fraction.

2 Refine the Skill

By refining the skills involved in operations with fractions, you will improve your study and test-taking abilities, especially as they relate to the GED® Mathematical Reasoning Test. Study the information and table below. Then answer the question that follows.

a Some problems will ask you to compare fractions with different denominators. These fractions are called *unlike fractions*. To solve problems with unlike fractions, rewrite the fractions using one common denominator. Then subtract the numerators to find the difference.

b When finding *how much more*, subtract the amounts. In question 1, it may be helpful to write the mixed numbers as improper fractions, since $\frac{1}{8} < \frac{1}{4}$.

The following chart shows the yards of fabric needed for each size of a dress pattern.

YARDS OF FABRIC NEEDED FOR DRESS PATTERNS

Size	45-in. Fabric (Yd)	60-in. Fabric (Yd)
XS	$3\frac{1}{4}$	$2\frac{3}{4}$
S	$3\frac{1}{2}$	$3\frac{1}{4}$
M	$3\frac{5}{8}$	$3\frac{3}{4}$
L	$3\frac{7}{8}$	$4\frac{1}{8}$
XL	$4\frac{1}{8}$	$4\frac{3}{8}$

TEST-TAKING TIPS

You can reduce some fractions before you multiply or divide to make your calculations simpler. To simplify, divide the numerator and denominator by the same number.

$$\frac{1}{2} \times \frac{4}{5} = \frac{1 \times \cancel{4}^{2}}{\cancel{2}_{1} \times 5} = \frac{2}{5}$$

1. Sharon is sewing an extra-small dress for her daughter and an extra-large dress for herself using 45-inch fabric. How much more fabric will she need for the extra-large dress than for the extra-small dress?

   A. $\frac{1}{8}$ yard

   B. $\frac{7}{8}$ yard

   C. $1\frac{1}{8}$ yards

   D. $2\frac{1}{4}$ yards

★ Spotlighted Item: **DRAG-AND-DROP**

DIRECTIONS: Read each question. Then use the drag-and-drop options to complete each answer.

2. Two out of every five students in a high school are male. What fraction of the high school students are male?

| 1 | 2 | 3 | 4 | 5 |

3. There are 64 students in the school band. There are 16 trumpet players. What fraction of the band are trumpet players?

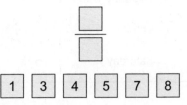

| 1 | 3 | 4 | 5 | 7 | 8 |

4. The school chess club celebrated its recent championship. The 15-member team went out for desert. Five members ordered pie, 4 ordered ice cream, 3 ordered cake, and 3 ordered milk shakes. What fraction of the chess club members ordered ice cream?

| 1 | 3 | 4 | 5 | 11 | 15 |

5. Anna withdrew $50 from her checking account. She spent $28 on a pair of shoes. What fraction of her money does Anna have left?

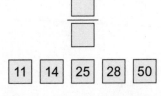

| 11 | 14 | 25 | 28 | 50 |

DIRECTIONS: Examine the information and table. Then read each question, and use the drag-and-drop options to complete each answer.

The table lists five students and the fraction of homework that each student completed.

VARIOUS STUDENTS' HOMEWORK COMPLETION

Student	Fraction Of Homework Completed
Dara	$\frac{2}{5}$
Natalia	$\frac{7}{10}$
Miguel	$\frac{1}{2}$
Ethan	$\frac{9}{10}$
Walt	$\frac{4}{5}$

6. List the students from the table above in order of the amount of homework they completed, beginning with the one that completed the most.

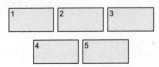

7. The fraction of homework completed by which two students in the table equals the fraction of homework completed by Ethan?

| | and | |

8. A restaurant served 72 customers for breakfast. Of those, 18 had omelets. What fraction of the customers had omelets?

| 1 | 2 | 3 | 4 | 6 | 18 | 36 |

UNIT 1

⭐ Spotlighted Item: **DRAG-AND-DROP**

DIRECTIONS: Read the question. Then use the drag-and-drop options to complete the answer.

9. Quentin is filling a glass that holds $1\frac{3}{4}$ cups of water. He is using a $\frac{1}{4}$-cup measuring cup.

   How many times will he have to fill the smaller measuring cup to equal $1\frac{3}{4}$ cups?

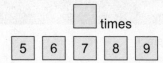

   ☐ times

   | 5 | 6 | 7 | 8 | 9 |

DIRECTIONS: Examine the information and number line. Then read each question, and use the drag-and-drop options to complete each answer.

   The number line below represents the speeds, in miles per hour, for five cars, labeled A through E. The time it takes the cars to travel 50 miles, in hours, is given by 50 divided by the speed.

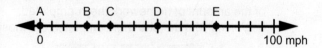

10. For which car is the time it takes to go 50 miles undefined?

   | A | B | C | D | E |

11. How many hours more does it take Car B to go the 50 miles than Car D?

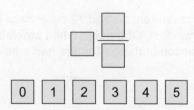

   | 0 | 1 | 2 | 3 | 4 | 5 |

DIRECTIONS: Examine the information and table. Then read each question, and use the drag-and-drop options to complete each answer.

   The table below shows the number of miles that Luke rode his bicycle over the course of one week.

LUKE'S WEEKLY BICYCLING MILEAGE

Day	Number of Miles
Sunday	$18\frac{2}{3}$
Monday	$25\frac{9}{10}$
Tuesday	$15\frac{1}{2}$
Wednesday	$12\frac{7}{8}$
Thursday	$32\frac{5}{6}$
Friday	$19\frac{7}{8}$
Saturday	$24\frac{5}{6}$

12. How many miles did Luke ride on the weekend?

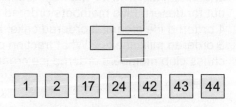

   | 1 | 2 | 17 | 24 | 42 | 43 | 44 |

13. How many fewer miles did Luke ride on Wednesday than he rode on Monday?

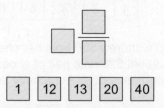

   | 1 | 12 | 13 | 20 | 40 |

DIRECTIONS: Read the question. Then use the drag-and-drop options to complete each answer.

14. Ginny has 26 tests to correct. It takes her $\frac{1}{9}$ of an hour to correct each test. How many hours will it take Ginny to correct all the tests?

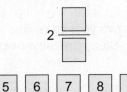

| 5 | 6 | 7 | 8 | 9 |

DIRECTIONS: Examine the information and number line. Then read each question, and use the drag-and-drop options to complete each answer.

The following number line shows the interval from 0 to 1, divided into 20 equal segments.

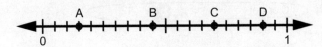

15. In decreasing order, list the fractional values of the points, reduced to lowest terms.

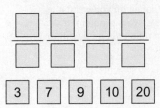

| 3 | 7 | 9 | 10 | 20 |

16. What is the distance between points B and D, expressed as a fraction reduced to lowest terms?

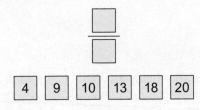

| 4 | 9 | 10 | 13 | 18 | 20 |

DIRECTIONS: Examine the information. Then read each question, and use the drag-and-drop options to complete each answer.

The distributive law of addition and subtraction is shown by: [(3)(5) + (3)(7)] = (3)(5 + 7).

17. Use the distributive law to simplify the following fraction.

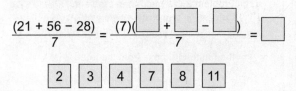

$$\frac{(105-40)}{5} = \frac{(5)(\square - \square)}{5} = \square$$

| 6 | 8 | 13 | 20 | 21 |

18. Use the distributive law to simplify the following fraction.

$$\frac{(21 + 56 - 28)}{7} = \frac{(7)(\square + \square - \square)}{7} = \square$$

| 2 | 3 | 4 | 7 | 8 | 11 |

DIRECTIONS: Read the question. Then use the drag-and-drop options to complete the answer.

19. Mario needs to work $32\frac{5}{6}$ hours this week. He has worked $19\frac{7}{8}$ hours so far. How many more hours must Mario work this week?

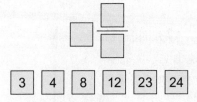

| 3 | 4 | 8 | 12 | 23 | 24 |

Ratios and Proportions

Use with **Student Book** pp. 10–11

MATH CONTENT TOPICS: Q.2.a, Q.2.e, Q.3.a, Q.3.b, Q.3.c, Q.6.c
MATH PRACTICES: MP.1.a, MP.1.b, MP.1.d, MP.1.e, MP.2.a, MP.2.c, MP.4.a

UNIT 1

1 Review the Skill

A **ratio** compares two numbers. The second or bottom number of a ratio does not necessarily represent a whole. A ratio with a denominator of 1 is known as a **unit rate**. When two ratios are written as equal, the equation is a **proportion**.

You may write a ratio as a fraction, using the word *to*, or with a colon (:). In all cases, remember to reduce a ratio to its simplest terms.

2 Refine the Skill

By refining the skill of solving ratios and proportions, you will improve your study and test-taking abilities, especially as they relate to the GED® Mathematical Reasoning Test. Study the table below. Then answer the questions that follow.

The number of students who play a given instrument in the school band is shown below.

a Write the proportion $\frac{3}{4} = \frac{x}{8}$ and then solve for *x* to solve the first problem.

b Problem 2 is a multi-step problem. Before you can write a ratio, you first need to find the number of girls who play clarinet. Next, subtract the number of boys from the total number of clarinet players.

c Remember that when you write a proportion to solve a problem, the terms in both ratios must be written in the same order.

BAND MEMBERS AND THEIR INSTRUMENTS

Instrument	Number of students
Flute	**a** 8
Percussion	5
Saxophone	4
Clarinet	**b** 12
Trumpet	5
Trombone	4
Tuba	2

TEST-TAKING TIPS

Include labels in your ratios to ensure you are writing numbers in the correct order. After you have written your ratio, read it in words. Check to ensure that it matches the stated problem.

1. The ratio of girls to total number of students in the band is 3 to 4. At that ratio, how many girls would you expect to play flute?

   A. 5
   B. 6
   C. 7
   D. 8

c 2. There are four male clarinet players. What is the ratio of male clarinet players to female clarinet players?

   A. 8:4
   B. 8:12
   C. 4:12
   D. 1:2

DIRECTIONS: Read each question, and choose the **best** answer.

3. On a swimming skills test, Olive performed 12 skills correctly. She performed 4 skills incorrectly. What is the ratio of incorrect skills to total skills?

    A. $\frac{1}{4}$

    B. $\frac{1}{2}$

    C. $\frac{2}{1}$

    D. $\frac{4}{1}$

4. Joe's basketball team won 38 games and lost 4 games this season. What is the ratio of games lost to games won?

    A. 38:4
    B. 4:38
    C. 19:2
    D. 2:19

5. A box of soup contains 8 cans. If the box costs $16, what is the unit rate?

    A. $0.50 per can
    B. $1 per can
    C. $2 per can
    D. $4 per can

6. A scale drawing of a living room has a scale of 1 inch:3 feet. If one wall is 4 inches long on the drawing, how long is the actual wall?

    A. 4 inches
    B. 7 feet
    C. 12 inches
    D. 12 feet

7. Annie drove 96 miles on Monday and 60 miles on Tuesday. What is the ratio of miles she drove on Monday to miles she drove on Tuesday?

    A. $\frac{2}{1}$

    B. $\frac{5}{8}$

    C. $\frac{8}{5}$

    D. $1\frac{3}{5}$

DIRECTIONS: Read each question, and choose the **best** answer.

8. A pancake recipe that serves 30 people calls for 12 eggs. Marti wants to make enough to serve only 10 people. What is the ratio of eggs to servings for the reduced recipe?

    A. 2 to 5
    B. 1 to 3
    C. 5 to 2
    D. 5 to 6

9. The ratio of wins to losses for the Wildcats rugby team was 8:3. If the team won 24 games, how many games did they lose?

    A. 8
    B. 9
    C. 19
    D. 64

10. There are 30 full-time and 12 part-time employees at the tire plant. What is the ratio of full-time to part-time workers?

    A. 2:1
    B. 4:1
    C. 5:2
    D. 7:2

11. A map scale states that 2 inches equal 150 miles. If two cities are 6 inches apart on a map, how many miles separate them?

    A. 300
    B. 450
    C. 600
    D. 900

12. There are 460 students in an elementary school. Of the students, $\frac{4}{5}$ ride the bus to school. How many students use a different method of transportation?

    A. 92
    B. 115
    C. 368
    D. 575

UNIT 1

★ Spotlighted Item: **DRAG-AND-DROP**

DIRECTIONS: Read each question. Then use the drag-and-drop options to complete each answer.

13. For each $5 given to a charity by an individual, the Bay Company will give $15 to that same charity. If individual contributions total $275, how many dollars will the Bay Company contribute?

$$\frac{\$5}{\$\boxed{}} = \frac{\$\boxed{}}{x}$$

$$x = \$ \boxed{}$$

| 15 | 91 | 125 | 275 | 825 |

14. In a school, the ratio of students to teachers is 14 to 1. If there are 406 students, how many teachers work at the school?

$$\frac{14}{\boxed{}} = \frac{\boxed{}}{x}$$

$$x = \boxed{}$$

| 1 | 28 | 29 | 203 | 406 |

DIRECTIONS: Read each question, and choose the **best** answer.

15. A person can burn about 110 calories by walking one mile. How many calories will a person burn by walking $4\frac{1}{2}$ miles?

   A. 440
   B. 495
   C. 550
   D. 615

16. Stuck in traffic, Trevor drove 48 miles in 3 hours. What was the unit rate of his speed?

   A. 16 miles per hour
   B. 45 miles per hour
   C. 48 miles per hour
   D. 144 miles per hour

17. In a 30-person office, 16 people drive to work and the rest walk or ride their bicycles. What is the ratio of people who drive to people who do not drive?

   A. 7:8
   B. 8:7
   C. 8:15
   D. 15:7

18. Thirty people were surveyed about their type of work. Two of every five people work in a field related to education. How many of the people surveyed work in education?

   A. 5
   B. 8
   C. 12
   D. 15

19. A recipe for a dessert sauce calls for 2 teaspoons of chocolate sauce and 3 teaspoons of caramel sauce. If Mary made 20 total teaspoons of dessert sauce, how many teaspoons of caramel did she use?

   A. 11
   B. 12
   C. 13
   D. 14

20. The ratio of cars to parking spots at a local business is 2:3. If there are 24 cars, how many parking spots are there?

   A. 16
   B. 32
   C. 36
   D. 48

DIRECTIONS: Read each question, and choose the **best** answer.

21. In a recent softball game, Allison threw 84 strikes out of 105 pitches. The remaining pitches were balls. What was Allison's ratio of strikes to balls?

   A. 4:1
   B. 5:1
   C. 5:2
   D. 6:1

22. The ratio of lifeguards to swimmers at a pool is 1:22. If there are 176 swimmers in the pool, how many lifeguards are there?

   A. 6
   B. 8
   C. 88
   D. 154

DIRECTIONS: Examine the information and table, read each question, and choose the **best** answer.

The table shows the number of miles Leila drove each week on a full tank of gas.

LEILA'S WEEKLY MILEAGE

Week 1	420 miles
Week 2	414 miles
Week 3	389 miles
Week 4	421 miles
Week 5	396 miles

23. If Leila's gas tank holds 18 gallons of gasoline, how many miles per gallon did her car get during Week 2?

   A. 22
   B. 23
   C. 46
   D. 28

24. What is the ratio of the number of miles Leila drove during Week 1 to the total number of miles she drove over the 5 weeks?

   A. 1:4
   B. 7:9
   C. 7:34
   D. 99:508

DIRECTIONS: Read each question, and choose the **best** answer.

25. The ratio of cats to people in a town is 3 to 8. How many people live in the town if there are 387 registered cats?

   A. 129
   B. 1,032
   C. 1,161
   D. 3,096

26. Ayla bought an 8-pound turkey for $24. How much would she spend for a 12-pound turkey?

   A. $3
   B. $16
   C. $28
   D. $36

DIRECTIONS: Examine the table, read each question, and choose the **best** answer.

BOOKSMART PUBLISHING

Position	Openings	Applicants
Graphic designer	5	25
Art researcher	3	27
Staff writer	4	48
Editor	2	12

27. Which position shows a ratio of 12 applicants to 1 opening?

   A. Graphic designer
   B. Art researcher
   C. Staff writer
   D. Editor

28. Due to an increase in workload, Booksmart recently announced plans to hire two project managers. The ratio of openings to applicants was 1:7. How many more applicants for the project manager position were there than applicants for the editor position?

   A. 2
   B. 14
   C. 15
   D. 26

Decimals

Use with **Student Book** pp. 12–13

MATH CONTENT TOPICS: Q.1.a, Q.2.a, Q.2.e, Q.6.c
MATH PRACTICES: MP.1.a, MP.1.b, MP.1.e, MP.2.c, MP.4.a

1 Review the Skill

A **decimal** shows a fraction of a number using the place value system. The value of decimal places decreases moving left to right. When you are solving problems involving money, you must know how to round decimals. Unless you are told otherwise, round answers involving money to the nearest penny, or hundredth.

To add or subtract decimals, align decimal points and perform the operation. To multiply decimals, multiply as you would whole numbers. Then count the decimal places in the factors to determine the number of decimal places in the product.

To divide decimals, set up the problem like you do with whole numbers. Adjust the problem so that there are no decimal places in the divisor. Then divide. Place the decimal in the quotient exactly above its place in the dividend.

2 Refine the Skill

By refining the skill of operations with decimals, you will improve your study and test-taking abilities, especially as they relate to the GED® Mathematical Reasoning Test. Study the information and table below. Then answer the questions that follow.

The Peterman family bowls once a week. Each member of the family has his or her own bowling ball. The mass of each bowling ball is shown in the table below.

a To compare a decimal to the tenths place with a decimal to the hundredths place, write a zero to fill the hundredths place. For example, 6.2 equals 6.20. You now can compare the hundredths digit.

b A whole number is understood to have a decimal point after the ones place. Write 6 kg as 6.0 kg to subtract. A decimal value with no whole number has a zero to the left of the decimal point. Write .2 kg as 0.2 kg.

MASS OF BOWLING BALLS (kg)

Julie	5.8 kg
Tay	5.2 kg
Christopher	**a** 6.2 kg
Mr. Peterman	7.2 kg
Mrs. Peterman	7.2 kg

USING LOGIC

When working with decimals, use estimation to check whether your answers are reasonable. Round numbers to the nearest whole.

a 1. How many of the Petermans' bowling balls have a mass greater than 6.25 kg?

A. 1
B. 2
C. 3
D. 4

b 2. Julie buys a new bowling ball that has a mass of 6 kg. How much greater is the mass of her new ball than the mass of her old ball?

A. 0.1 kg
B. 0.2 kg
C. 1.2 kg
D. 2 kg

⭐ Spotlighted Item: **FILL-IN-THE-BLANK**

DIRECTIONS: Study the table. Read each question. Then fill in your answer in the box below.

KATE'S DRIVING LOG

Day	Mileage
Monday	37.5 miles
Tuesday	38.1 miles
Wednesday	37.8 miles
Thursday	37.7 miles
Friday	38.3 miles

3. On which day did Kate drive the fewest number of miles?

4. What was Kate's total mileage during the week?

5. How many more miles did Kate drive on Friday than on Monday?

6. Kate's employer will reimburse her $0.45 per mile that she drives for work-related purposes. She drove 21.4 miles for personal reasons last week and the rest for work purposes. How much will she be reimbursed?

$

DIRECTIONS: Study the information and table, read the question, and choose the **best** answer.

7. Natalia completed her balance beam routine in a gymnastics meet with a score of 15.975. The table below shows the scores of three of Natalia's competitors. In what place did Natalia finish the competition?

BALANCE BEAM SCORES

Gymnast	Score
Johnson	15.995
Hen	15.98
Kalesh	15.97

A. first
B. second
C. third
D. fourth

DIRECTIONS: Read each question, and choose the **best** answer.

8. Bottled water at an amusement park costs $1.79. Dylan has $8. How many bottles of water could Dylan buy at the amusement park?

A. 4
B. 6
C. 7
D. 8

9. Isaiah works in quality-control at an ice cream factory. Each half-gallon container of ice cream must weigh more than 1.097 kg and less than 1.103 kg. Which of the following containers of ice cream would Isaiah reject?

A. Sample A – 1.099 kg
B. Sample B – 1.101 kg
C. Sample C – 1.121 kg
D. Sample D – 1.098 kg

DIRECTIONS: Study the information and table, read each question, and choose the **best** answer.

A library shelves its books using decimal numbers. The table shows the locations of the books in the library.

BOOK NUMBER LOCATIONS

Floor and Section	Book Number Range
Floor 1, Section A	14.598 – 17.654
Floor 1, Section B	17.655 – 21.584
Floor 2, Section A	31.858 – 35.784
Floor 2, Section B	35.785 – 42.955

10. Where would you find a book labeled with the number 17.653?

    A. Floor 1, Section A
    B. Floor 1, Section B
    C. Floor 2, Section A
    D. Floor 2, Section B

11. Mrs. Cafferty needs to shelve a book with the number 35.78. Where will she find the shelf for this book?

    A. Floor 1, Section A
    B. Floor 1, Section B
    C. Floor 2, Section A
    D. Floor 2, Section B

DIRECTIONS: Read each question, and choose the **best** answer.

12. Salami at a deli costs $3.95 per pound. What is the cost, without sales tax, of 2.3 pounds of salami?

    A. $9.08
    B. $9.09
    C. $9.90
    D. $10.08

13. At a home improvement store, Terese bought a new lamp for $14.89, a pack of light bulbs for $2.38, and a new light switch for $0.79. She paid with a $20 bill. How much change should be returned to her?

    A. $1.94
    B. $2.73
    C. $17.26
    D. $18.06

DIRECTIONS: Read each question, and choose the **best** answer.

14. Sylvia bought a computer on a finance plan. She will make 12 equal payments altogether to pay for the computer. If the cost of the computer was $675, what is the amount of each month's payment?

    A. $56.00
    B. $56.25
    C. $56.40
    D. $58.25

15. Tim scored 97.75 on his first mathematics exam, 92.5 on his second exam, and 98.25 on his third exam. What is the combined total of his scores on the three exams?

    A. 285.95
    B. 296.5
    C. 286.75
    D. 288.5

DIRECTIONS: Study the information and the table, read the question, and choose the **best** answer.

16. The batting averages of five baseball players are shown in the table.

BATTING AVERAGES

Player	Batting Average
A	0.279
B	0.350
C	0.305
D	0.298
E	0.289

The players with the top three batting averages are first in the batting lineup. They will bat in order from lowest batting average to highest batting average. Which lists the correct batting order?

    A. Player D, Player B, Player C
    B. Player B, Player C, Player D
    C. Player C, Player B, Player D
    D. Player D, Player C, Player B

DIRECTIONS: Read each question, and choose the **best** answer.

17. Shauna scored 9.25, 8.75, and 9.5 on three math quizzes. Which shows her scores listed in order from lowest to highest?

    A. 9.25, 8.75, 9.5
    B. 8.75, 9.25, 9.5
    C. 8.75, 9.5, 9.25
    D. 9.5, 9.25, 8.75

18. Angel hair pasta at Hometown Foods normally costs $2.29. This week, it is on sale for $2.05. Lorenzo bought 5 boxes on sale. How much money did he save?

    A. $0.24
    B. $1.20
    C. $1.24
    D. $7.96

19. A diver's score is calculated by adding the scores of three judges and then multiplying this sum by the degree of difficulty of the dive. Craig performed a dive with a degree of difficulty of 3.2. He received scores of 8, 8.5, and 7.5. What was his total score for the dive?

    A. 67.8
    B. 75.3
    C. 76.8
    D. 86.7

20. Walt took out a loan to buy his new car. He makes equal monthly payments. In a year, he pays $1,556.28. How much does he pay per month on his car loan?

    A. $128.29
    B. $129.69
    C. $130.99
    D. $131.09

21. A cyclist rode 115.02 miles in 5.4 hours. If he rode at a constant speed, how many miles per hour did he ride?

    A. 20.3
    B. 21.1
    C. 21.3
    D. 22.1

DIRECTIONS: Read the question, and choose the **best** answer.

22. In a dive meet, Morgan finished in second place. The first-place diver scored 218.65 points. The third-place diver scored 218.15 points. Which of the following could be Morgan's score?

    A. 218 points
    B. 218.05 points
    C. 218.105 points
    D. 218.5 points

DIRECTIONS: Study the table, read each question, and choose the **best** answer.

SHIPPING COSTS

Package Weight Range (Pounds)	Shipping Cost
0–4.65	$3.95
4.66–7.85	$5.55
7.86–10.95	$8.99
10.96–15.40	$12.30

23. Gary is shipping a package that weighs 6.8 pounds. How much will it cost?

    A. $3.95
    B. $5.55
    C. $8.99
    D. $12.30

24. Margaret placed 3 books in a box. Each book weighs 2.91 pounds. The box and packing materials weigh 1.6 pounds. How much will it cost to ship the package?

    A. $3.95
    B. $5.55
    C. $8.99
    D. $12.30

25. Tyler is shipping one package that weighs 4.51 pounds and another package that weighs 10.9 pounds. He pays with a $20 bill. What change will he receive?

    A. $4.59
    B. $7.06
    C. $12.94
    D. $15.41

Percent

Use with *Student Book* pp. 14–15

MATH CONTENT TOPICS: Q.2.a, Q.2.e, Q.3.c, Q.3.d, Q.6.c
MATH PRACTICES: MP.1.a, MP.1.d, MP.1.e, MP.2.c, MP.4.a

UNIT 1

1 Review the Skill

You can write fractions and decimals as percents. **Percents** are ratios that use the number 100 as the denominator. For example, 11 out of 100 is written as $\frac{11}{100}$. A percent is written with a percent sign, so $\frac{11}{100}$ equals 11%.

A percent problem includes a base, a part, and a rate. The **base** is the whole amount. The **part** is a portion of the base. The **rate** is a percent. You can also solve problems by using proportions or the percent formula **base × rate = part**.

2 Refine the Skill

By refining the skills of working with percents and solving percent problems, you will improve your study and test-taking abilities, especially as they relate to the GED® Mathematical Reasoning Test. Study the information below. Then answer the questions that follow.

The receipt from a restaurant is shown below.

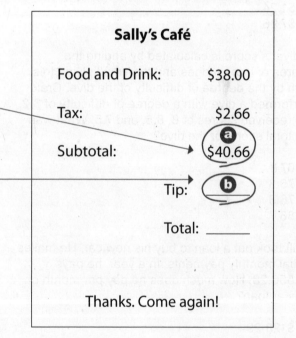

a To answer question 1, convert 15% to a fraction. Drop the percent sign, then write a fraction with the percent as the numerator and 100 as the denominator. Simplify.

b To answer question 2, first determine the 20% tip on the base of $40.66. Then add the tip to the subtotal to find the total.

Sally's Café

Food and Drink: $38.00

Tax: $2.66

Subtotal: **ⓐ** $40.66

Tip: **ⓑ**

Total: _____

Thanks. Come again!

TEST-TAKING TECH

Success on the new GED® Test requires the ability to use a mouse. For drop-down items, you must click an arrow to reveal the possible responses, and then click a second time to select the correct answer.

1. A waiter at Sally's received a 15% tip based on the subtotal of the check shown. What fraction of the subtotal was the tip?

   A. $\frac{1}{15}$

   B. $\frac{3}{20}$

   C. $\frac{1}{20}$

   D. $\frac{6}{15}$

2. A customer left a 20% tip on the subtotal shown. What is the total?

   A. $8.13
   B. $32.53
   C. $40.86
   D. $48.79

★ Spotlighted Item: **DROP-DOWN**

DIRECTIONS: Read each question, and choose the option that **best** completes each sentence.

3. Two-fifths of the children in first grade are dropped off at school by their parents.

   | Drop-down | % of first-graders are dropped off at school.

   A. 5
   B. 25
   C. 40
   D. 60

4. Of 140 sixteen-year olds, 85% have taken driver's education and earned their driver's licenses.

   | Drop down | students have taken driver's education and earned their licenses.

   A. 21
   B. 55
   C. 85
   D. 119

5. Each semester, about $\frac{3}{25}$ of students at a college study abroad.

   | Drop-down | of students study abroad.

   A. 9%
   B. 12%
   C. 22%
   D. 75%

6. A refrigerator costs $580. Sam bought the refrigerator for 30% off.

   Sam paid $ | Drop-down | for the refrigerator.

   A. 174
   B. 406
   C. 506
   D. 754

DIRECTIONS: Read each question, and choose the option that **best** completes each sentence.

7. Marie needs 500 fliers to be printed at a cost of $2 per flier. Because of the size of the order, the print shop is asking Marie to pay 30% up front.

   Marie must make a down payment of $ | Drop-down | .

   A. 60
   B. 150
   C. 300
   D. 530

8. As of January 1, Theo's monthly rent increased from $585 to $615.

   The approximate percent increase of Theo's rent was | Drop-down | %.

   A. 3
   B. 5
   C. 6.5
   D. 17

9. Ezra invested $3,000 for 18 months at a 3% annual interest rate.

   He will earn $ | Drop-down | interest on his investment.

   A. 90
   B. 135
   C. 900
   D. 1,350

10. Dan paid 20% down on a new car that cost $16,584.00. He will pay the balance in 24 equal monthly installments.

    He will pay $ | Drop-down | each month.

    A. 1,105.60
    B. 667.18
    C. 552.80
    D. 132.20

UNIT 1

⭐ Spotlighted Item: **DROP-DOWN**

UNIT 1

DIRECTIONS: Read each question, and choose the option that **best** completes each sentence.

11. Noelle works in sales and earns a salary of $2,500 per month, plus a commission of 8% of her total sales. Last month, Noelle's sales totaled $42,800.

    Noelle earned a total of $ | Drop-down | last month.

    A. 5,924.00
    B. 3,424.00
    C. 2,000.00
    D. 200.00

12. Remy took out a home-improvement loan to pay for new kitchen cabinets. The loan was for $10,000 at an annual interest rate of 5.6%. Remy paid off the loan in 36 months.

    She paid $ | Drop-down | in all.

    A. 10.680.00
    B. 11,680.00
    C. 12,016.00
    D. 12,760.00

13. Nina biked 45 miles in two days. She biked 36 miles the first day. Nina biked | Drop-down | of the miles the second day.

    A. 15%
    B. 20%
    C. 23%
    D. 25%

14. Eighty-two percent of the employees at a food processing plant belong to an employees union.

    82% = | Drop-down |

    A. 0.82
    B. 0.82%
    C. 8.2%
    D. 8.2

DIRECTIONS: Read each question, and choose the option that **best** completes each sentence.

15. The Wolves had 20 players on their soccer team, three of whom were freshmen.

    The percent of freshmen on the Wolves soccer team was | Drop-down | %.

    A. 5
    B. 10
    C. 15
    D. 20

16. The Panthers won 22 of their 34 games.

    The Panthers won about | Drop-down | % of their games.

    A. 67.4
    B. 64.7
    C. 61.7
    D. 58.8

17. Bryon recently purchased a new laptop computer. He put 20 percent down on the purchase. The computer cost $1,230.

    Bryon owes $ | Drop-down | after the down payment.

    A. 246
    B. 492
    C. 984
    D. 1,107

18. Jim makes and sells denim knapsacks for $10.50 apiece. The knapsacks cost $7 apiece to produce.

    Jim makes about | Drop-down | % profit on each knapsack.

    A. 33
    B. 50
    C. 75
    D. 125

DIRECTIONS: Study the information and table, read each question, and choose the option that **best** completes each sentence.

A parts factory records the number of each part sold in a monthly report. The report for May is shown below.

PARTS SOLD IN MAY

Part Number	Amount Sold
A056284	120,750
B057305	254,860
P183456	184,340
F284203	290,520
Q754362	308,205

19. About [Drop-down] % of the parts sold were part number Q754362.

    A. 22
    B. 25
    C. 26
    D. 27

20. If combined, the sales of part numbers B057305 and F284203 equal about [Drop-down] % of the parts sold in May.

    A. 22
    B. 25
    C. 46
    D. 47

DIRECTIONS: Read the question, and choose the option that **best** completes the sentence.

21. Jay took out a small-business loan for $210,000. The terms of the loan are 5% annual interest for four years.

Jay will pay back $ [Drop-down] by the end of four years.

    A. 420,000
    B. 252,000
    C. 168,000
    D. 42,000

DIRECTIONS: Read each question, and choose the option that **best** completes each sentence.

22. In March, the average number of passengers on a commuter train line was 5,478 per day. In April, this number dropped to 4,380 due to construction on the train line.

The ridership [Drop-down 22.1] by about

[Drop-down 22.2] from March to April.

Drop-Down Answer Options

22.1 A. increased B. decreased	22.2 A. 18% B. 20% C. 25%

23. There were 35 students signed up for an aerobics class. Then the class size increased by 20%.

There are now [Drop-down] students in class.

    A. 28
    B. 37
    C. 42
    D. 48

24. Delia earns $28,500 per year. She budgets $\frac{1}{5}$ of this for food and 0.35 of this for housing.

[Drop-down] % of her earnings is left to budget for other items.

    A. 15
    B. 45
    C. 55
    D. 85

25. The Kickers soccer team played 24 matches and won 75 percent of them.

The Kickers lost [Drop-down] of their matches.

    A. 6
    B. 8
    C. 14
    D. 16

Measurement and Units of Measure

Use with **Student Book** pp. 26–27

MATH CONTENT TOPICS: Q.2.a, Q.2.e, Q.3.a, Q.3.b, Q.3.c, Q.6.c
MATH PRACTICES: MP.1.a, MP.1.b, MP.1.d, MP.1.e, MP.2.c, MP.3.a, MP.4.a

1 Review the Skill

The most commonly used measurement systems are the U.S. customary system and the metric system. You probably use the **U.S. customary system** in your daily life to measure lengths and to cook. Basic units of measure in the U.S. system include the foot (length), pound (weight), and gallon (capacity). Basic units in the **metric system** include the meter (length), gram (weight), and liter (capacity).

You also measure **time** in standard units such as seconds, minutes, hours, days, weeks, months, and years. Units of time measurement are the same across the U.S. customary and metric systems. Many problems involving time use the formula **distance = rate × time**.

2 Refine the Skill

By refining the skill of measuring and converting between units, you will improve your study and test-taking abilities, especially as they relate to the GED® Mathematical Reasoning Test. Study the information below. Then answer the question that follows.

a When converting metric units from a larger unit of measure to a smaller unit, multiply by a power of 10. When converting a smaller unit to a larger one, divide by a power of 10.

b You can multiply by 1,000 by moving the decimal point three places to the right, by 100 by moving the decimal point two places to the right, and by 10 by moving the decimal point one place to the right. To divide, move the decimal point the corresponding number of places to the left.

Metric Units of Mass

1 kilogram (kg) = 1,000 grams (g)
1 gram (g) = 100 centigrams (cg)
1 centigram (cg) = 10 milligrams (mg)

CONVERTING METRIC UNITS OF MEASURE

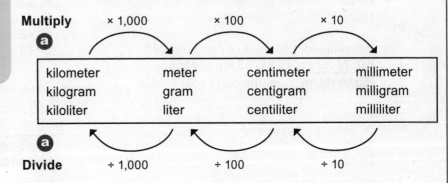

Multiply	× 1,000	× 100	× 10

kilometer	meter	centimeter	millimeter
kilogram	gram	centigram	milligram
kiloliter	liter	centiliter	milliliter

Divide	÷ 1,000	÷ 100	÷ 10

TEST-TAKING TIPS

First identify the unit of measure being called for in the answer. Then, convert each unit as needed before performing any other calculations, such as addition or subtraction.

1. A printmaker produces her own ink by mixing powdered pigments with water and alcohol. In the morning, she mixed 45 milligrams of red pigment. At noon, she mixed 2 grams of the same red pigment. Later in the afternoon, she mixed an additional 85 centigrams of red pigment. How many centigrams of red powdered pigment did the printmaker use?

   A. 33 cg
   B. 109.5 cg
   C. 289.5 cg
   D. 320 cg

DIRECTIONS: Study the information, read each question, and choose the **best** answer.

Cedric is making punch to take to a family reunion. He wants to triple the following recipe for Pineapple Punch.

Pineapple Punch
0.5 cup lemon juice
2 cups orange juice
1 cup sugar
5 pints ginger ale
4 pints carbonated water
8 slices canned pineapple

Liquid Capacity

1 cup (c) = 8 fluid ounces (fl oz)
1 pint (pt) = 2 cups
1 quart (qt) = 2 pints
1 gallon (gal) = 4 quarts

2. How many pints of orange juice will Cedric need?

A. 1 pt
B. 2 pt
C. 3 pt
D. 4 pt

3. How many quarts of carbonated water will Cedric need?

A. 2 qt
B. 3 qt
C. 4 qt
D. 6 qt

4. How many cups of ginger ale will Cedric need?

A. 7.5 c
B. 10 c
C. 13 c
D. 30 c

DIRECTIONS: Read the question, and choose the **best** answer.

5. For one print, an artist uses 50 milligrams of blue pigment, 55 centigrams of green pigment, and 3 grams of red pigment. How much greater is the mass of red pigment than the combined mass of the blue and green pigments?

A. 2.05 g
B. 2.4 g
C. 3.6 g
D. 12.5 g

DIRECTIONS: Study the information and table, read each question, and choose the **best** answer.

Sabrina is marking the route for an upcoming cross-country foot race. She keeps a record of the number of meters she marks each day.

Metric Units of Length

1 kilometer (km) = 1,000 meters (m)
1 meter (m) = 100 centimeters (cm)
1 centimeter (cm) = 10 millimeters (mm)

CROSS-COUNTRY RACE

Day	1	2	3	4
Meters Marked	700 m	600 m	800 m	1,000 m

6. How many kilometers of the cross-country route did Sabrina mark on Day 1?

A. 0.0007 km
B. 0.007 km
C. 0.07 km
D. 0.7 km

7. How many kilometers of the route had Sabrina marked by Day 4?

A. 0.31 km
B. 3.1 km
C. 31 km
D. 310 km

DIRECTIONS: Read each question, and choose the **best** answer.

8. If the fastest nerves in the human body can conduct impulses at 120 meters per second, determine how far an impulse can travel in 5 milliseconds?

A. 0.120 m
B. 60 cm
C. 600 m
D. 120 cm

9. Objects on the moon weigh generally one-fourth as much as they weigh on Earth. If a parcel weighs 3 kg on the moon, its weight on Earth would be what?

A. 12 mg
B. 120 cg
C. 3,000 mg
D. 12,000 g

UNIT 2

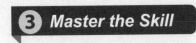

DIRECTIONS: Study the information and table, read each question, and choose the **best** answer.

SAPLINGS' GROWTH OVER 4 MONTHS

	May	June	July	August
Maple	55 cm	62 cm	83 cm	101 cm
Cherry	15 cm	18 cm	21 cm	23 cm
Oak	91 cm	98 cm	105 cm	121 cm
Ash	33 cm	38 cm	45 cm	57 cm

Metric Measures of Length

1 kilometer (km) = 1,000 meters (m)

1 meter (m) = 100 centimeters (cm)

1 centimeter (cm) = 10 millimeters (mm)

---

10. What was the height, in meters, of the tallest sapling in August?

    A. 1.01 m
    B. 1.21 m
    C. 2.3 m
    D. 12.1 m

11. What is the difference between the ash's height in May and its height in August?

    A. 0.24 m
    B. 2.4 m
    C. 24 m
    D. 240 m

DIRECTIONS: Study the information, read the question, and choose the **best** answer.

Metric Units of Length

1 kilometer (km) = 1,000 meters (m)
1 meter (m) = 100 centimeters (cm)
1 centimeter (cm) = 10 millimeters (mm)

---

12. A building shown in a magazine is 50 millimeters tall. Darlene is making a scale drawing of the building. She wants her drawing to be four times the size shown in the magazine. How tall will her drawing of the building be?

    A. 1 m
    B. 2 m
    C. 20 cm
    D. 150 cm

DIRECTIONS: Study the information, read each question, and choose the **best** answer.

Pure gold (24k) is golden yellow in color. However, alternate colors of gold may be formed by mixing pure yellow gold with metals of different colors in various proportions. Use the following recipe for making 10k use white gold for questions 13 and 14.

Recipe for making 10k white gold

37.5 grams pure gold
52 grams silver
4.9 grams copper
4.2 grams zinc
1.4 grams nickel

---

13. If a jeweler uses 112.5 grams of pure gold, determine the amount of silver that must be added to make 10k white gold.

    A. 0.156 kg
    B. 15.6 g
    C. 156 mg
    D. 52 g

14. A white gold necklace was analyzed and found to contain 0.007 kg of nickel. Determine the quantity of pure gold in the necklace.

    A. 18.75 g
    B. 45.9 g
    C. 187.5 g
    D. 262 g

15. Every 10 milliseconds, a mystery substance decreases its weight by half. Originally, the substance weighs 5 kilograms. Determine its weight after 3 centiseconds.

    A. 1,250 g
    B. 625 g
    C. 312.5 g
    D. 156.25 g

16. Every 20 seconds, a mystery substance doubles its weight. Originally, the substance weighs 40 mg. Determine how long it will take the substance to weigh 0.160 kg.

    A. 1,000 seconds
    B. 100 seconds
    C. 40 seconds
    D. 5 seconds

DIRECTIONS: Study the information, read each question, and choose the **best** answer.

Metric Measures of Capacity
1 kiloliter (kL) = 1,000 liters (L)
1 liter (L) = 100 centiliters (cL)
1 centiliter (cL) = 10 milliliters (mL)

17. Kyle is decorating his restaurant with tropical fish tanks. Three of the tanks each have a capacity of 448 L of water. Two of the tanks each have a capacity of 236 L of water. How many kiloliters of water will Kyle need to fill all of the tanks?

    A. 0.0186 kL
    B. 0.186 kL
    C. 1.816 kL
    D. 18.16 kL

18. Microbiologists gathered 15 vials of pond water. They filled 5 vials with 10 milliliters of pond water each, 5 vials with 1 milliliter of pond water each, and 5 vials with 0.1 milliliters of pond water each. How many centiliters of pond water did they gather in all?

    A. 0.555 cL
    B. 1.11 cL
    C. 11.1 cL
    D. 5.55 cL

19. The soccer team drank a combined 17 liters of water during the game. How many kiloliters did the team consume?

    A. .017 kL
    B. .17 kL
    C. 170 kL
    D. 1,700 kL

20. Ms. Lafayne has purchased 2 kL of paint to cover 4 walls in her new office. If each wall requires 450 L of paint, how much paint will she have left over?

    A. 0.2 kL
    B. 450 L
    C. 1.8 kL
    D. 2 kL

DIRECTIONS: Study the information, read each question, and choose the **best** answer.

Standard Measures of Length
1 foot (ft) = 12 inches (in.)
1 yard (yd) = 3 feet
1 mile (m) = 5,280 feet
1 mile = 1,760 yards

21. Hannah walks 875 yards on Monday, on Wednesday, and on Friday. She walks 2,625 yards on Tuesday and again on Thursday. About how many miles has she walked by the end of the day Friday?

    A. 1.5 mi
    B. 4 mi
    C. 4.5 mi
    D. 7.875 mi

22. Each place setting requires 18 inches of ribbon. If Mara makes 24 place settings, how many feet of ribbon will she need?

    A. 12 ft
    B. 36 ft
    C. 144 ft
    D. 432 ft

DIRECTIONS: Study the information, read each question, and choose the **best** answer.

A particular type of bamboo plant can grow 39 inches in 24 hours.

23. How far would such a plant grow in 60 seconds?

    A. 0.5 inch
    B. .00045 inch
    C. 1.63 inches
    D. 0.027 inch

24. At this rate, how many inches will the bamboo grow after 48 hours have elapsed?

    A. 0.027 inch
    B. 1.625 inches
    C. 48 inches
    D. 78 inches

Length, Area, and Volume

Use with *Student Book* pp. 28–29

MATH CONTENT TOPICS: Q.2.a, Q.2.e, Q.4.a, Q.4.c, Q.4.d, Q.5.a, Q.5.c, Q.5.f
MATH PRACTICES: MP.1.a, MP.1.b, MP.1.d, MP.1.e, MP.2.c, MP.3.a, MP.4.a

❶ Review the Skill

Perimeter is the distance around a polygon, such as a triangle or a rectangle. To find perimeter, measure and add the lengths of a polygon's sides. **Area** is the amount of space that covers a two-dimensional figure. The area of a rectangle may be determined by multiplying its width times its length. Area is expressed in square units, such as square feet, square centimeters, and so on.

Volume is the amount of space within a three-dimensional figure. A figure's volume, measured in cubic units, tells how many cubes of a given size would fill a given figure. One common three-dimensional figure is the rectangular prism. The surface area of a rectangular prism is the sum of the areas of its sides. A **cube** is a special rectangular prism with six congruent sides.

❷ Refine the Skill

By refining the skills of finding perimeter, area, and volume, you will improve your study and test-taking abilities, especially as they relate to the GED® Mathematical Reasoning Test. Study the information below. Then answer the questions that follow.

A farmer buys a plot of land. On a small part of the plot, he wants to build a house and fence off the yard. The following is a diagram of the farmer's plan.

VIEW OF FARMER'S LAND

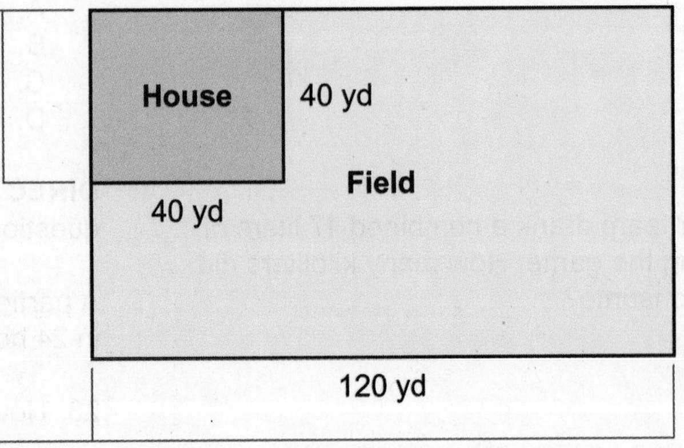

ⓐ The measurements of the smaller figure give you the information you need to determine that the figure is a square.

ⓑ The entire plot includes the house and the field. Recall that opposite sides of rectangles are equal in measure.

House   40 yd

Field

40 yd

80 yd

120 yd

TEST-TAKING TIPS

The text and figure in a test item may provide data about two or more figures. However, the question may only ask about one of the figures. Read the question carefully to understand exactly what you are being asked.

1. What is the perimeter of the small plot of land on which the farmer wants to build a house?

    A. 40 yd
    B. 80 yd
    C. 120 yd
    D. 160 yd

2. What is the perimeter of the entire plot of land?

    A. 160 yd
    B. 200 yd
    C. 240 yd
    D. 400 yd

Spotlighted Item: **DROP-DOWN**

DIRECTIONS: Study the information and figure, read each question, and choose the option that **best** completes each sentence.

The diagram below shows Erica's rectangular yard and square garden.

ERICA'S YARD

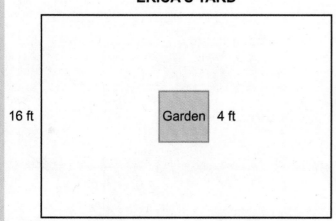

3. The perimeter of Erica's yard is 72 feet. The width is 16 feet. The measure of the length of Erica's yard is [Drop-down] ?

   A. 20 ft   B. 32 ft   C. 40 ft   D. 56 ft

4. The perimeter of the garden is [Drop-down] ?

   A. 8 ft   B. 12 ft   C. 16 ft   D. 20 ft

5. Erica wants to build a fence around her garden and another fence around her entire yard. To do so, she will need [Drop-down] of fencing.

   A. 16 ft   B. 56 ft   C. 72 ft   D. 88 ft

DIRECTIONS: Read each question, and choose the **best** answer.

6. A rectangle has a perimeter of 54 cm. The length is 16 cm. What is the width of the rectangle?

   A. 11 cm
   B. 19 cm
   C. 38 cm
   D. 864 cm

7. If a cube has a volume of 27 cubic ft, what is its surface area?

   A. 9 square ft
   B. 81 square ft
   C. 54 square ft
   D. 18 square ft

8. If the area of a figure is 64 square ft and its length is 16 ft, what is its width?

   A. 4 ft
   B. 4 cubic ft
   C. 16 cubic ft
   D. 256 ft

DIRECTIONS: Examine the figures, read the question, and choose the **best** answer.

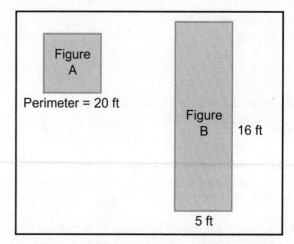

9. If Figure A is a square with a perimeter of 20 ft, determine the length of one side.

   A. 4 ft
   B. 5 ft
   C. 16 ft
   D. 20 ft

DIRECTIONS: Study the figures, read each question, and choose the **best** answer.

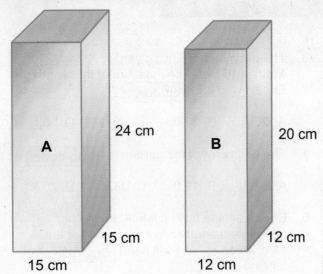

A 24 cm
15 cm
15 cm

B 20 cm
12 cm
12 cm

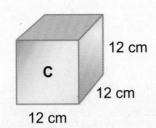

C 12 cm
12 cm
12 cm

DIRECTIONS: Study the information and figures, read each question, and choose the **best** answer.

TWO PACKING BOXES

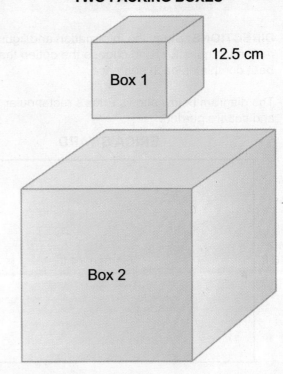

Box 1 12.5 cm

Box 2

Each box shown above is a cube. The length of Box 2 is three times the length of Box 1.

10. What is the volume of the smallest container?

    A. 36 cm³
    B. 156 cm³
    C. 1,560 cm³
    D. 1,728 cm³

11. What is the difference in volume between containers A and B?

    A. 576 cm³
    B. 1,440 cm³
    C. 2,520 cm³
    D. 3,672 cm³

12. An exporter needs to transport 8,000 cm³ of sand. Each container above costs $100 for shipping. Of the following choices, which is the most cost-effective way of transporting all of the sand?

    A. package sand in 7 units of container C
    B. package sand in 3 units of container B
    C. package sand in 1 unit of container A
    D. package sand in 2 units of container A

13. A painter is preparing work for an exhibit. He intends on painting the packaging boxes above. If one gallon of paint covers 1,000 cm² of the box, approximately how many gallons of paint will he need to paint both boxes?

    A. 15 gallons
    B. 10 gallons
    C. 9 gallons
    D. 1 gallon

14. Determine the volume of a cube if the surface area is 600 ft².

    A. 10 ft³
    B. 100 ft³
    C. 1,000 ft³
    D. 10,000 ft³

DIRECTIONS: Study the information and figures, read each question, and choose the **best** answer.

TWO SWIMMING POOLS

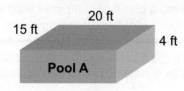

Pool A

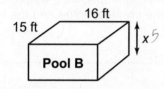

Pool B

Each pool model holds approximately the same amount of water. The height of Pool B is represented by x.

15. How much water can fit in Pool A?

  A. 80 ft³
  B. 300 ft³
  C. 1,000 ft³
  D. 1,200 ft³

16. What is the value of x?

  A. 4 ft
  B. 5 ft
  C. 6 ft
  D. 8 ft

17. What is the surface area of Pool A?

  A. 120 ft²
  B. 480 ft²
  C. 880 ft²
  D. 580 ft²

18. The surface area of Pool B is

  A. greater than the surface area of Pool A.
  B. less than the surface area of Pool A.
  C. equal to the surface of pool A.
  D. equal to twice the surface area of pool A.

DIRECTIONS: Study the information and figures, read each question, and choose the **best** answer.

Owen has a garage shaped like a rectangular prism. He built an addition in the shape of a cube.

OWEN'S GARAGE AND NEW ADDITION

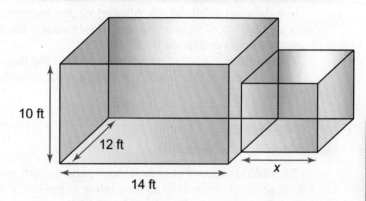

19. What is the volume of Owen's garage without the addition?

  A. 120 ft³
  B. 140 ft³
  C. 168 ft³
  D. 1,680 ft³

20. The volume of the addition is 512 ft³. What is the value of x?

  A. 6 ft
  B. 8 ft
  C. 11 ft
  D. 23 ft

21. What is the combined volume of Owen's garage with the new addition?

  A. 1,168 ft³
  B. 1,856 ft³
  C. 2,192 ft³
  D. 3,360 ft³

22. Owen wanted to add a drop ceiling to the garage that would reduce the ceiling height by 2 feet. What is the volume of the garage with the drop ceiling but without the addition?

  A. 1,344 ft³
  B. 1,400 ft³
  C. 1,440 ft³
  D. 1,536 ft³

UNIT 2

Mean, Median, and Mode

Use with *Student Book* pp. 30–31

MATH CONTENT TOPICS: Q.2.a, Q.2.e, Q.6.c, Q.7.a
MATH PRACTICES: MP.1.a, MP.1.b, MP.1.c, MP.1.d, MP.1.e, MP.2.c, MP.3.a, MP.4.a

UNIT 2

1 Review the Skill

The mean, median, mode, and range are different ways of describing a group of numbers called a data set. A **mean** describes the average of a set of numbers. For data sets without very high or low numbers, the mean can be useful. The **median** is the middle number in a set of data, where values are ordered from least to greatest.

In a data set of 30, 30, 43, 55, and 72, the median is 43 since it's the middle number in the data set. When a data set consists of an even number of data values, there are two middle numbers. To find the median, add those two middle numbers and divide the sum by 2.

The **mode** is the most common number in the data set, In the above example, 30—which appears twice in the data set—is the mode. The **range** is the difference between the greatest value and the least value in a data set.

2 Refine the Skill

By refining the skill of finding the mean, median, mode, and range, you will improve your study and test-taking abilities, especially as they relate to the GED® Mathematical Reasoning Test. Study the information below. Then answer the questions that follow.

Kyle wants to know how many runs his favorite baseball team scores per game. To do so, he sets up a table and records the number of runs the team scores each game.

a To find the range, identify the greatest number and the least number. Next, subtract the least from the greatest.

RUNS SCORED BY THE PATRIOTS

Game	Runs Scored
1	3
2	9 **a**
3	3
4	4
5	7
6	5
7	6
8	3
9	1 **a**
10	5

b To determine the mean, add all the data values and divide by the quantity of the data set. When a data set consists of an even number of data values, there are two middle numbers. In that case, add the two middle numbers, and divide by two to find the median.

1. What is the range of the data set that Kyle collected?

   A. 1
   B. 4
   C. 6
   D. 8

2. Kyle wants to determine the average number of runs scored by the Patriots. What is the mean of Kyle's data?

   A. 3
   B. 4.5
   C. 4.6
   D. 5.1

TEST-TAKING TIPS

Questions on the GED® Mathematical Reasoning Test may ask you to determine mean, median, and mode. Ensure that you closely read each question so that you provide the correct data description.

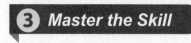

DIRECTIONS: Study the table, read each question, and choose the **best** answer.

FINAL EXAM SCORES

Student	Grades
David	87
Marla	72
Elena	75
Jeff	85
Tyrell	89
Jasmine	93
Kim	68
Chris	97
Jessica	85
Mel	70
Jean	91

3. What is the range of grades for the exam?

   A. 29
   B. 68
   C. 72
   D. 85

4. What is the mode for the set of exam grades?

   A. 29
   B. 82
   C. 85
   D. 93

5. What is the difference between Elena's grade and the median grade on the exam?

   A. 7
   B. 8
   C. 10
   D. 22

6. In this data set, what is the difference between the mode and the mean?

   A. 2.1
   B. 4.1
   C. 10.1
   D. 29

DIRECTIONS: Study the information and table, read each question, and choose the **best** answer.

Fred's bike shop tracked its sales for one year. Its monthly sales (rounded to the nearest ten dollars) are shown below.

BICYCLE SALES

Month	Sales
January	$8,320
February	$7,200
March	$11,820
April	$18,560
May	$23,630
June	$26,890
July	$24,450
August	$22,110
September	$23,450
October	$19,300
November	$15,340
December	$16,980

7. What is the median for January through June?

   A. $15,190
   B. $16,070
   C. $18,560
   D. $18,930

8. What is the mean sale for July through December? Round to the nearest dollar.

   A. $9,110
   B. $18,171
   C. $20,272
   D. $20,705

9. What is the range of sales throughout the year?

   A. $15,310
   B. $17,250
   C. $18,570
   D. $19,690

10. What is the difference between the mean and median for the year's sales?

   A. $389.17
   B. $759.17
   C. $1,129.17
   D. $3,939.17

UNIT 2

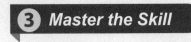

3 Master the Skill

DIRECTIONS: Study the information and table, read each question, and choose the **best** answer.

Jessica is conducting a random survey to find out how much time people spend on the Internet. The following table shows the results in hours per day.

HOURS PER DAY SPENT ON INTERNET

	Mon	Tues	Wed	Thurs	Fri	Sat	Sun
Jen	3	4.25	5	1	1.5	5.5	6
Mila	4	3.5	5.5	2.5	4	6	5.5
Trang	2	1.5	0.5	0.25	0.75	3	3
Ron	3.5	4.25	5	5.5	2.25	6.25	7
Yusef	2.5	1	1	1.5	0.5	5.25	7.5

11. What is the range for the data set showing the number of hours spent per day on the Internet?

    A. 0
    B. 3.4
    C. 5.5
    D. 7.25

12. What is the range for the number of hours per day that Ron spends on the Internet?

    A. 7
    B. 5
    C. 4.75
    D. 3.5

13. What is the median number of hours that Trang spends on the Internet in a day?

    A. 1.1
    B. 1.5
    C. 1.6
    D. 3

14. What is the difference between the mean of Wednesday's data and the mean of Sunday's data?

    A. 1. 25
    B. 1.5
    C. 2
    D. 2.4

15. What is the mode of the data set?

    A. 1
    B. 4.25
    C. 5.5
    D. 7.5

DIRECTIONS: Study the information and table, read each question, and choose the **best** answer.

The table below shows the number of points scored by the Pirates football team and their opponents for the first six games of the season.

FOOTBALL SCORES

Game	Points Scored By The Pirates	Points Scored By Opponents
1	24	0
2	7	14
3	13	21
4	12	6
5	0	12
6	36	30

16. What is the average number of points scored by the Pirates?

    A. 13.2
    B. 13.8
    C. 15.3
    D. 18.4

17. What is the median number of points scored by the Pirates' opponents?

    A. 12.5
    B. 13
    C. 14
    D. 16.5

DIRECTIONS: Read each question, and choose the **best** answer.

18. A group of four friends averaged 85% on a test. If the scores of 3 friends were 75%, 100%, and 70%, what was the score of the fourth person?

    A. 80%
    B. 85%
    C. 90%
    D. 95%

19. A group of 25 people took a pop quiz. Ten people had an average score of 80, while the remaining students had an average score of 65. What was the average score of the entire group?

    A. 68
    B. 70
    C. 71
    D. 80

DIRECTIONS: Study the table, and read each question. Then fill in the answer in the box.

AMOUNT OF MONEY TEENAGERS BROUGHT TO THE FAIR

Friends	Money ($)
Julie	100
Candy	50
Humza	200
Brian	?

20. If the mean amount of money the teenagers brought to the fair was $125, how much money did Brian have? Fill in the blanks to show your answer.

Brian brought _____ to the fair.

21. If the mean is $125, the range of the data set is _____ .

DIRECTIONS: Study the information and table, read each question, and choose the **best** answer.

PET OWNERSHIP

Number of Pets	Frequency
1	2
2	5
3	7
4	2
5	1

The results of a survey about pet ownership are displayed in the table above.

22. What is the mode for the data set?

   A. 2
   B. 3
   C. 4
   D. 5

23. What is the median for the data set?

   A. 1
   B. 2
   C. 3
   D. 4

24. What is the mean for the data set?

   A. 2.7
   B. 3
   C. 3.4
   D. 4

DIRECTIONS: Read the question, and choose the **best** answer.

25. Which data set below has a range of 6.5?

   A. 3, 0, 6.5, 4.5
   B. 6, 0.5, 3, 4.5
   C. 4, 6.5, 3, 0.5
   D. 3.5, 6.5, 6, 0.5

DIRECTIONS: Study the information and table, read the question, and choose the **best** answer.

The table shows the results of a cross-country team's times in a recent 3-mile race.

Name	Times (Minutes:Seconds)
Holly	25:21
Karen	21:07
Ana	20:58
Jessie	26:10
Sonya	23:27

26. What was the range of times run by members of the team?

   A. 4 minutes, 14 seconds
   B. 4 minutes, 23 seconds
   C. 5 minutes, 3 seconds
   D. 5 minutes, 12 seconds

UNIT 2

Probability

Use with *Student Book* pp. 32–33

MATH CONTENT TOPICS: Q.2.a, Q.2.e, Q.3.c, Q.3.d, Q.8.a, Q.8.b
MATH PRACTICES: MP.1.a, MP.1.b, MP.1.d, MP.1.e, MP.2.c, MP.3.c, MP.4.a, MP.5.a

1 Review the Skill

You likely check the weather forecast daily to learn about local temperatures, changing conditions, and the status of area roads and traffic. A weather forecast provides a **probability**, or chance, of certain weather events occurring. In math, probability compares the number of favorable outcomes to the number of total outcomes. Probability can be written as a fraction ($\frac{7}{10}$), ratio (7:10), or percent (70%).

One type of probability, called **theoretical probability**, describes the number of favored outcomes out of the number of total possible outcomes. For example, when you flip a coin, you have an equal chance of it landing on heads or tails. That can be expressed as 1 out of 2, $\frac{1}{2}$ (fraction), 1:2 (ratio), or as 50%.

Another type of probability, one based on the results of an experiment, is called **experimental probability**. As with theoretical probability, you can express experimental probability as a fraction, ratio, or percent. If you toss a quarter 10 times and get heads 4 times, the experimental probability is $\frac{4}{10}$, which simplifies to $\frac{2}{5}$.

2 Refine the Skill

If an event has a probability of 0%, it is considered to be *impossible*. If the probability is less than 50%, the event is considered to be *unlikely*. If the chances are greater than 50%, it is considered to be *likely*. If the probability of an event is 100%, it is considered to be *certain*. Read the text and examine the spinner. Then answer the questions that follow.

The spinner shown below has five equal sections.

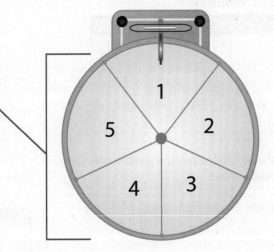

a Question 1 means that spinning 1, 4, and 5 are all favorable outcomes. Increasing the number of favorable outcomes generally increases the overall probability.

b Choice B is incorrect because it implies that there are four possible outcomes, when there are actually five possible outcomes.

c In addition, to find the probability of two consecutive events, you must multiply the probability of the first event by the probability of the second event.

TEST-TAKING TIPS

Compute and express probability in the way that is easiest for you. You may express probability as a fraction. If necessary, you can convert your answer to a ratio, percent, or decimal.

1. Which word best describes the chances of spinning a 1, 4, or 5?

   A. impossible
   B. unlikely
   C. likely
   D. certain

2. What is the probability of spinning a 3?

   A. 1:1
   B. 1:4
   C. 1:5
   D. 3:5

⭐ Spotlighted Item: **DROP-DOWN**

DIRECTIONS: Study the information and spinner, read each question, and choose the drop-down option that **best** answers each question.

Jay uses this spinner to conduct probability experiments.

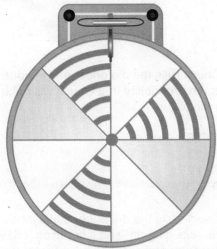

3. The probability that the spinner will land on a striped or white wedge is [Drop-down].

   A. 2:8   B. 3:4   C. 3:8   D. 6:6

4. The probability that the spinner will land on a yellow or striped wedge is [Drop-down].

   A. $\frac{1}{4}$ B. $\frac{3}{8}$ C. $\frac{1}{2}$ D. $\frac{5}{8}$

5. The probability is [Drop-down] that the spinner will land on a white or yellow wedge.

   A. $\frac{1}{4}$ B. $\frac{3}{8}$ C. $\frac{5}{8}$ D. $\frac{6}{8}$

6. The probability that, with two consecutive spins, the spinner will land on a yellow wedge and then a white wedge is [Drop-down].

   A. 0.09
   B. 0.38
   C. 0.58
   D. 0.63

DIRECTIONS: Study the information and figure, read each question, and choose the drop-down option that **best** answers each question.

Jenna has a bag of marbles that contains 7 striped marbles and 5 black marbles.

7. The probability that Jenna will pick a black marble is [Drop-down].

   A. 1:1   B. 5:12   C. 1:2   D. 7:12

8. Jenna picks a striped marble and does not replace it. Then Jenna picks a black marble and does not replace it. The probability that she will pick a striped marble on the third event is [Drop-down].

   A. 40%   B. 50%   C. 56%   D. 60%

9. In another experiment, using an unknown set of black and striped marbles, Jenna wants to find the probability of picking a striped marble. In the first event, she picks a black marble and places it back in the bag. In the second and third events, she picks a striped marble, replacing the marble after each pick. The experimental probability at this point of picking a striped marble is [Drop-down].

   A. $\frac{1}{3}$ B. $\frac{2}{3}$ C. $\frac{1}{2}$ D. $\frac{3}{4}$

UNIT 2

DIRECTIONS: Study the information and spinner, read each question, and choose the **best** answer.

Marta uses this spinner to conduct probability experiments.

10. What is the probability that Marta will land on either a yellow wedge or an odd number?

    A. 20%
    B. 40%
    C. 50%
    D. 100%

11. Marta spins and lands on 4. What is the probability that, on her second spin, she will land on 4?

    A. 1:2
    B. 1:4
    C. 1:6
    D. 2:5

12. What is the probability that Marta will land on 6, 2, or one of the white wedges?

    A. 1:2
    B. 2:3
    C. 5:6
    D. 6:6

DIRECTIONS: Study the information and figure, read each question, and choose the **best** answer.

Chuck is conducting probability experiments using a single die.

13. Chuck rolls the die once, and it lands on 2. What is the probability that Chuck will roll a 2 on his second turn?

    A. 1:6
    B. 1:3
    C. 1:2
    D. 2:3

14. Chuck rolls the die once, and it lands on 3. He rolls it again, and it lands on a 5. What is the experimental probability so far for landing on an odd number?

    A. 1:1
    B. 1:6
    C. 1:3
    D. 2:3

15. What is the probability that Chuck will roll an even number?

    A. 33.3%
    B. 50%
    C. 66.7%
    D. 83.3%

16. To win the game, Chuck must roll a total of 9 in two turns with the die. His first roll yielded a 5. What is the probability that his second roll will yield a 4?

    A. 1:36
    B. 1:6
    C. 1:3
    D. 2:3

UNIT 2

Ryan took a random survey of 100 cars. The following table displays the results.

SURVEY OF CARS

Color of Car	Amount
Black	32
Blue	15
Red	25
White	18
Other	10

17. Based on Ryan's survey, what is the probability that the next car he spots will be blue or red?

    A. 0.40
    B. 0.60
    C. 0.75
    D. 0.85

18. What is the probability that the next car Ryan sees will be a color other than black, blue, red, or white?

    A. 0%
    B. 10%
    C. 50%
    D. 100%

19. The probability is greatest for Ryan to see which color car next?

    A. blue
    B. red
    C. black
    D. white

20. What is the probability that the next car Ryan sees will be a color other than black or white?

    A. 20%
    B. 40%
    C. 50%
    D. 60%

DIRECTIONS: Study the paragraph, read the question, and choose the **best** answer.

Julian has a bag of marbles. He knows that the bag contains 10 marbles, some of them black and some of them red. He conducts experiments to predict how many of each color marble is in the bag.

21. In the first event, Julian picks a black marble. He replaces the marble. In the second and third events, he picks a red marble. He replaces the marble after each event. What is the experimental probability that he will pick a red marble next?

    A. $\frac{1}{5}$

    B. $\frac{3}{10}$

    C. $\frac{1}{3}$

    D. $\frac{2}{3}$

DIRECTIONS: Study the paragraph, read each question, and choose the the **best** answer.

Your bank PIN number must be 4 digits long. Each digit must be the number 0 through 9 and you may not use a number more than once.

22. How many possible combinations of PIN numbers do you have to choose from?

    A. 10
    B. 5,040
    C. 6,561
    D. 10,000

23. Your sister's PIN number is only 3 digits long. She must use the numbers 0 through 4 and also cannot use a number more than once. She believes she only has 15 different PIN options.

    Which of the following best describes your sister's calculations and the correct answer?

    A. She is incorrect because she added instead of multiplied. The correct answer is 5 × 5 × 5 = 125.
    B. She is incorrect because she cannot use a number more than once. The correct answer is 5 + 4 + 3 = 12.
    C. She is incorrect because she cannot use a number more than once and added instead of multiplied. The correct answer is 5 × 4 × 3 = 60.
    D. She is correct.

UNIT 2

Bar and Line Graphs

Use with *Student Book* pp. 34–35

MATH CONTENT TOPICS: Q.2.a, Q.2.e, Q.6.a, Q.6.c
MATH PRACTICES: MP.1.a, MP.2.c, MP.3.a, MP.4.a, MP.4.c

1 Review the Skill

People use graphs to organize and present data in a visual way. **Bar graphs** display and even compare data through horizontal and vertical bars. In both single-bar graphs and double-bar graphs, the bars show how pieces of data compare to one another. **Line graphs**, which can contain one or more lines, help you see how data increase or decrease over time.

A **scatter plot** is a type of line graph that shows how one data set can affect another. This relationship may be positive (extending upward from the origin to x- and y-points) or negative (extending downward from the y-axis to the x-axis), or it may not exist at all. Graphs and scatter plots often include scales and keys that give detail about the data.

2 Refine the Skill

By refining the skill of interpreting bar and line graphs, you will improve your study and test-taking abilities, especially as they relate to the GED® Mathematical Reasoning Test. Read the example and strategies below. Then answer the questions that follow.

The manager of the concession stands at a minor-league baseball stadium wants to know how sales of items compare. He also wants to see how the sales of individual items from the first to fifth innings of the game compare to sales from the sixth to ninth innings.

a Question 1 tells you the category to focus on for the answer. It also tells you what you are looking for: the amount and nature of the change.

b Carefully examine all the elements of the double-bar graph. The categories on the horizontal axis, the scale on the vertical axis, and the key all give essential information.

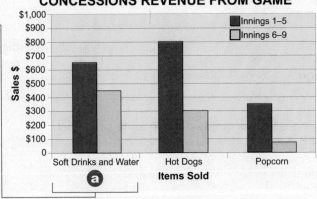

CONCESSIONS REVENUE FROM GAME

TEST-TAKING TIPS

Double-check your answer to ensure you used and correctly interpreted the proper bar on the double-bar graph.

1. What was the change in sales for soft drinks and water from the first part of the game to the latter part of the game?

    A. an increase of $100
    B. a decrease of $200
    C. an increase of $250
    D. a decrease of $300

2. Which statement about the double-bar graph is true?

    A. Soft drinks and water sold better in the latter part of the game.
    B. Hot dogs sold better throughout the game than soft drinks and water.
    C. Hot dogs show the greatest decrease in sales from the first part of the game to the latter part of the game.
    D. The sales of all products increased in the latter part of the game.

★ Spotlighted Item: **HOT SPOT**

DIRECTIONS: Study the information and graph, and read each question. Then mark on the graph the **best** answer to each question.

The bar graph shows the population of a city over a 60-year period.

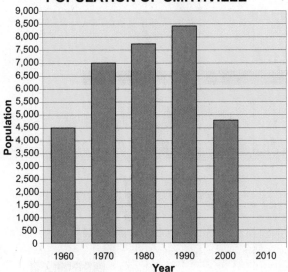

POPULATION OF SMITHVILLE

3. In which two years was the population roughly the same? Circle those dates on the graph.

4. In the year 2010, the population of Smithville was approximately half of its population in 1970. Draw a bar on the graph to show the population for 2010.

DIRECTIONS: Study the information and scatter plot. Then mark on the scatter plot the **best** answer to each question.

A local marketing company conducted a study that compared annual earnings of workers with their ages. Their findings are shown on the scatter plot below.

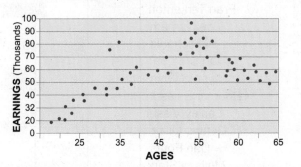

ANNUAL EARNINGS

5. Circle the age on the *x*-axis closest to the age that shows at which workers earn the highest average salary.

6. Circle the average earnings along the *y*-axis for someone who is 45 old.

7. The company hired a new vice president. She is 30 years old and makes an average of $80,000 per year. Place a dot on the graph that represents both her age and salary level.

The scatter plot at right shows real estate demand in various cities in the first two quarters of 2013.

8. Circle on the scatter plot those cities that are classified either as "booming" or "humming" housing markets.

9. Data were gathered for another city in which the asking price increased by 25% and the healthy market rank was 50. Place a dot on the graph that represents that city.

PRICE CHANGES AND HOUSING MARKET HEALTH

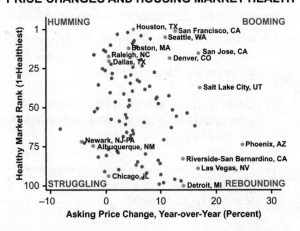

⭐ Spotlighted Item: HOT SPOT

DIRECTIONS: Study the bar graph about *Monday Night Football* announcers. Then mark on the bar graph the **best** answer to each question.

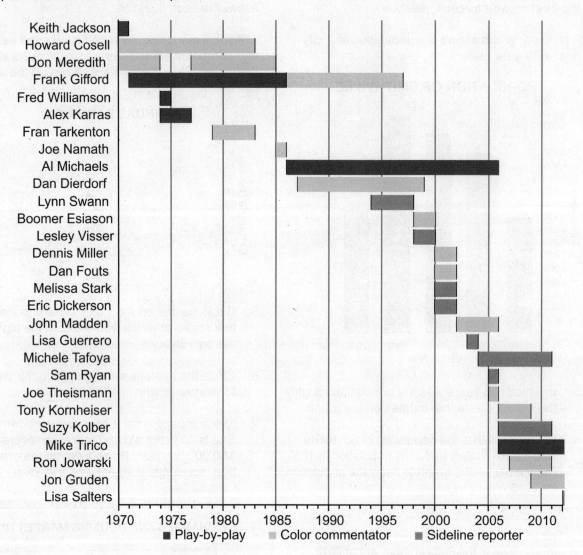

Keith Jackson
Howard Cosell
Don Meredith
Frank Gifford
Fred Williamson
Alex Karras
Fran Tarkenton
Joe Namath
Al Michaels
Dan Dierdorf
Lynn Swann
Boomer Esiason
Lesley Visser
Dennis Miller
Dan Fouts
Melissa Stark
Eric Dickerson
John Madden
Lisa Guerrero
Michele Tafoya
Sam Ryan
Joe Theismann
Tony Kornheiser
Suzy Kolber
Mike Tirico
Ron Jowarski
Jon Gruden
Lisa Salters

1970   1975   1980   1985   1990   1995   2000   2005   2010

■ Play-by-play   ■ Color commentator   ■ Sideline reporter

10. Place a check mark next to the name of the color commentator who had two separate stints on *Monday Night Football*.

11. Circle on the graph the names of the announcers who broadcast *Monday Night Football* in 2012.

12. Place an X next to the announcer(s) who appear to have had a one-season tenure on *Monday Night Football*.

13. Draw a box around the name of the announcer who handled both play-by-play and color commentator duties.

14. Place a star next to the name of the first announcer to serve as a sideline reporter on *Monday Night Football*.

15. Underline the name of the broadcaster who had the longest tenure as play-by-play announcer on *Monday Night Football*.

UNIT 2

DIRECTIONS: Study the information and bar graph, and read each question. Then mark on the graph the **best** answer to each question.

Every five years, ecologists record the type and number of mammals living in Pond Park. The bar graph below shows their counts for 2005 and 2010.

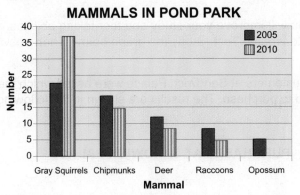

MAMMALS IN POND PARK

16. Circle the mammal that increased in numbers over the 5-year period.

17. Place an **X** next to the name of the mammal that was not seen at Pond Park in 2010.

DIRECTIONS: Study the information and bar graph, and read the question. Then mark on the graph the **best** answer to the question.

The following bar graph shows occupations of women in Centre City.

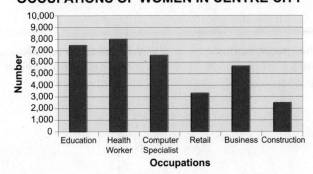

OCCUPATIONS OF WOMEN IN CENTRE CITY

18. Circle the occupation that is held by about twice the number of women who hold occupations in retail.

DIRECTIONS: Study the information and line graph, and read each question. Then mark on the graph the **best** answer to each question.

This line graph compares the average yearly rainfall for Anchorage, Alaska, to the average yearly rainfall in the United States.

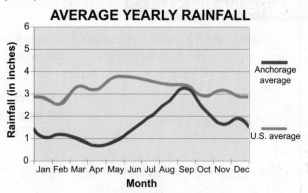

AVERAGE YEARLY RAINFALL

19. Circle on the graph the month in which the average rainfall for Anchorage and the United States is about the same.

20. Underline the month in which the average rainfall for the United States is the least.

DIRECTIONS: Study the information and line graph, and read the question. Then mark on the graph the **best** answer to the question.

The line graph shows the average amount of daylight throughout the year in Pine Town.

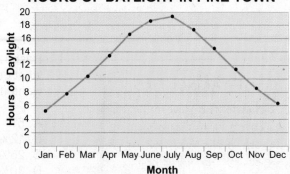

HOURS OF DAYLIGHT IN PINE TOWN

21. Circle on the graph the months that receive more than 17 hours of sunlight.

Circle Graphs

Use with *Student Book* pp. 36–37

MATH CONTENT TOPICS: Q.2.a, Q.2.e, Q.6.a
MATH PRACTICES: MP.1.a, MP.1.b, MP.1.d, MP.1.e, MP.2.c, MP.3.a, MP.4.c

UNIT 2

1 Review the Skill

Like other graphs, circle graphs present data visually. Unlike other graphs, which can compare data or show changes to data over time, a **circle graph** shows how different parts of a whole compare both to one another as well as to the whole.

Values in a circle graph may be shown as fractions, decimals, percents, or even as whole numbers. A circle itself represents one whole, or 100%. If a section is half of the whole, it represents $\frac{1}{2}$, 0.50, or 50%. If a section is a quarter of the circle, it represents $\frac{1}{4}$, 0.25, or 25%.

2 Refine the Skill

By refining the skill of interpreting circle graphs, you will improve your study and test-taking abilities, especially as they relate to the GED® Mathematical Reasoning Test. Study the graph below. Then answer the questions that follow.

The first 100 customers at Sandwich Palace were asked which menu item they planned to purchase. The results are shown in the following circle graph.

PURCHASES AT SANDWICH PALACE

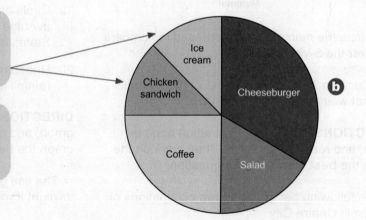

a Understanding that the ice cream and chicken sandwich categories combine to make up a quarter of the circle can help you determine the answer to question 1.

b The cheeseburger section of the graph covers more than 25%, or $\frac{1}{4}$. As a result, answer choices A and B are not reasonable.

TEST-TAKING TIPS

Estimate the value of a category in a circle graph in the way that is easiest for you. Then convert as necessary. For example, the value of the coffee category is about $\frac{1}{4}$, 0.25, 25%, or 25.

1. Based on the graph, about what percentage of people wanted to buy ice cream?

   A. 5%
   B. 12%
   C. 25%
   D. 30%

2. Which fraction shows the people who wanted cheeseburgers?

   A. $\frac{1}{5}$
   B. $\frac{1}{4}$
   C. $\frac{1}{3}$
   D. $\frac{2}{3}$

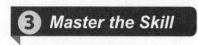

3 *Master the Skill*

DIRECTIONS: Study the information and graph, read each question, and choose the **best** answer.

As part of a civics project, Randall created a circle graph showing the most commonly used heating fuels in Smallsburg.

SOURCES OF HEATING FUEL IN SMALLSBURG

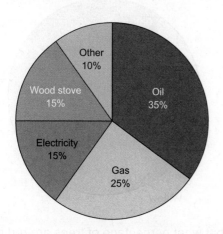

DIRECTIONS: Study the information and graph, read each question, and choose the **best** answer.

The following circle graph shows the voting habits of the residents of Middlesburg.

HOW MIDDLESBURG VOTES

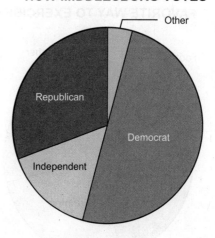

3. Which two sources of fuel together represent more than 50% of the total commonly used heating fuels?

   A. gas and wood stove
   B. oil and electricity
   C. wood stove and oil
   D. oil and gas

4. Which two sources of fuel are used by the same percentage of the population?

   A. wood stove and gas
   B. electricity and other
   C. oil and gas
   D. electricity and wood stove

5. What percentage of the population uses a source other than gas?

   A. 75%
   B. 50%
   C. 35%
   D. 25%

6. What percentage represents a heat source other than a wood stove?

   A. 10%
   B. 15%
   C. 85%
   D. 100%

7. For which party did half of the population vote?

   A. Republican
   B. Independent
   C. Democrat
   D. Other

8. About what percentage of the population voted for either Independent or Republican candidates?

   A. 15%
   B. 30%
   C. 45%
   D. 50%

9. Taken together, about what percentage of the population in Middlesburg voted for Independent or Other candidates?

   A. 10%
   B. 20%
   C. 30%
   D. 35%

10. If the town of Middlesburg consists of 200 people, about how many voted Independent?

   A. 25
   B. 30
   C. 40
   D. 50

UNIT 2

UNIT 2

DIRECTIONS: Study the information and graph, read each question, and choose the **best** answer.

Tom asked 100 of his friends and family members to name their favorite form of exercise. The circle graph below displays his findings.

FAVORITE WAY TO EXERCISE

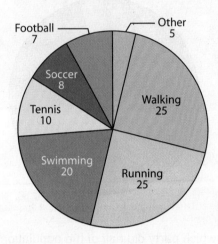

11. Which statement about the circle graph is accurate?

A. Less than 20% of people prefer walking.
B. The same number of people prefer soccer as prefer swimming.
C. Half of the people prefer either running or walking.
D. About 70 people prefer an exercise other than swimming.

12. About what fraction of people prefer an exercise other than running?

A. $\frac{1}{4}$
B. $\frac{1}{2}$
C. $\frac{3}{4}$
D. $\frac{9}{10}$

DIRECTIONS: Study the information and graph, read each question, and choose the **best** answer.

The circle graph shows the percentages of tree species in a state part.

TREE SPECIES

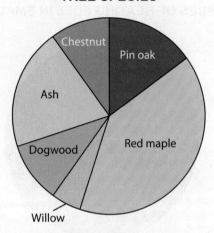

13. About what percentage of trees are red maples?

A. 10%
B. 20%
C. 30%
D. 40%

14. There are 400 trees in the park. About how many of them are ash trees?

A. 40
B. 80
C. 120
D. 150

15. Which tree species makes up about $\frac{1}{6}$ of the trees in the state park?

A. Pin oak
B. Chestnut
C. Dogwood
D. Ash

16. Which species accounts for more than one-quarter of the trees in the park?

A. Chestnut
B. Ash
C. Red maple
D. Willow

DIRECTIONS: Study the information and graph, read each question, and choose the **best** answer.

The circle graph shows the languages spoken by students at Marbletown International High School.

LANGUAGES SPOKEN BY STUDENTS

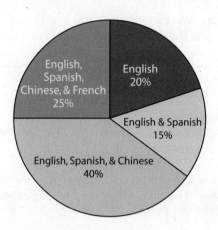

17. What percentage of students speak more than two languages?

    A. 15%
    B. 25%
    C. 40%
    D. 65%

18. What percentage of students do not speak Chinese?

    A. 20%
    B. 25%
    C. 35%
    D. 65%

19. Based on the circle graph, which statement is accurate?

    A. Half of the students speak French.
    B. One-fourth of the students speak Spanish.
    C. Less than half of the students speak two or more languages.
    D. All students speak English.

20. Based on the circle graph, which statement is accurate?

    A. More than 40% of students speak Spanish.
    B. Less than 50% of students speak Chinese.
    C. More than 30% of students speak French.
    D. No student speaks English and Spanish.

DIRECTIONS: Study the graph, read each question, and choose the **best** answer.

DIEGO'S MONTHLY BUDGET

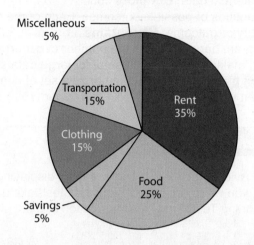

21. For every $100, about how much should Diego spend on food?

    A. $5
    B. $15
    C. $25
    D. $35

22. If Diego earns $2,200 this month, how much should he put into savings?

    A. $5
    B. $50
    C. $110
    D. $1,100

23. Based on the graph, which statement is accurate?

    A. Diego spends most of his monthly budget on food.
    B. Diego spends more on transportation and miscellaneous expenses than on food.
    C. Diego spends more on transportation than on clothing costs.
    D. Food and rent make up the largest percentage of Diego's monthly expenses.

Dot Plots, Histograms, and Box Plots

Use with **Student Book** pp. 38–39

MATH CONTENT TOPICS: Q.2.a, Q.2.e, Q.6.b, Q.7.a
MATH PRACTICES: MP.1.a, MP.1.b, MP.1.e, MP.2.c, MP.3.a, MP.4.a, MP.4.c

1 Review the Skill

Dot plots and histograms are useful ways of presenting the relative frequencies, or occurrences, of sets of numerical data. **Dot plots** consist of a number line and a series of dots. The number line represents a set of quantities of possible outcomes. Each of the dots, meanwhile, corresponds to an occurrence of specified quantity or outcome. **Histograms** are similar, but the number line is broken into intervals of equal width. Histogram bars represent the number of occurrences; bar lengths can be determined from an associated scale, making histograms useful for large data sets.

Box plots graphically summarize a set of numerical data using five characteristics of each data set: the median value, the lower (25%) and upper (75%) quartile values, and the maximum and minimum values.

2 Refine the Skill

By refining the skills of representing, displaying, and interpreting data using dot plots, histograms, and box plots, you will improve your study and test-taking abilities, especially as they relate to the GED® Mathematical Reasoning Test. Study the information and dot plot below. Then answer the questions that follow.

a A set of data may have more than one mode. Suppose, for example, that the number of students with two siblings were 5, rather than the 4 shown in the dot plot. Both the values 2 and 3 then would represent modes of the distribution, since both would have the maximum number of occurrences (5).

b Quantities, such as the median and the lower and upper quartiles, *summarize* the distribution.

A class of 16 students is asked to report on the number of brothers and sisters they each have. The number of siblings is plotted on the following dot plot.

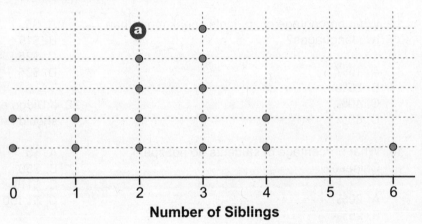

Number of Siblings

CONTENT TOPICS

The content standards that help make up the new GED® Mathematical Reasoning Test specifically mention the need to represent, display, and interpret data in dot plots, histograms, and box plots.

1. The mode of the distribution corresponds to what number of siblings?

   A. 2.5
   B. 3
   C. 5
   D. 6

2. What is the median number of siblings?

   A. 2.5
   B. 3
   C. 5
   D. 6

DIRECTIONS: Study the information and data display, read the question, and choose the **best** answer.

A swim club is open for 24 weeks from the middle of April through the middle of September. Monthly visitor totals are plotted below.

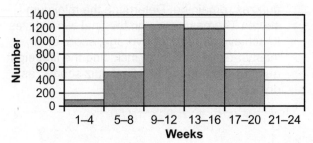

3. In which weeks did the greatest number of people visit the swim club?

   A. Weeks 1–4 and 5–8
   B. Weeks 9–12 and 13–16
   C. Weeks 13–16 and 17–20
   D. Weeks 17–20 and 21–24

DIRECTIONS: Study the information and data display, read each question, and choose the **best** answer.

Four chefs' dishes are judged by customers on a scale of 0 to 10. Box plots representing the scores each chef received are presented below.

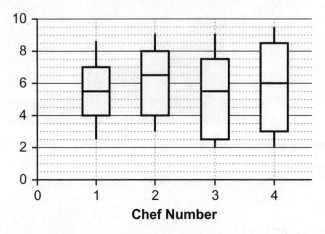

4. The chef with the highest median score is the winner. What is the number of the winning chef?

   A. 1
   B. 2
   C. 3
   D. 4

5. If the chefs were judged based on who had the highest upper quartile, which chef would have won?

   A. 1
   B. 2
   C. 3
   D. 4

DIRECTIONS: Study the information and dot plot, read each question, and choose the **best** answer.

Two 4-sided dice are tossed a total of 30 times. The dot plot below shows the sum of the two dice for each toss.

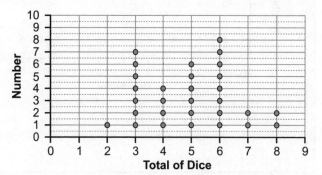

6. What is the median of the number of dice rolls?

   A. 4.5
   B. 5
   C. 5.5
   D. 6

7. What total of the dice represents the mode value?

   A. 6
   B. 5
   C. 4
   D. 3

8. What is the minimum value?

   A. 2
   B. 3
   C. 6
   D. 8

9. The 4-sided dice are tossed a very large number of times. Theoretically, what is the expected mode?

   A. 3
   B. 4
   C. 5
   D. 6

★ Spotlighted Item: **HOT SPOTS**

DIRECTIONS: Read each question, and place the dots on the graphs that follow.

10. Thomas has taken eight 10-point quizzes in his science class. His scores are as follows: 7, 8, 9, 6, 8, 7, 10, 6. Display the data on the dot plot.

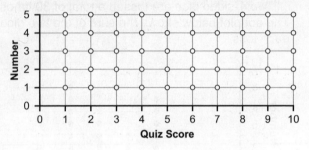

11. After taking the eight quizzes noted in the previous problem, Thomas has two 10-point quizzes remaining. Determine the minimum scores Thomas needs on the final two quizzes to achieve a mean, or average, score of at least 8. Graph the data, including the first eight quiz scores and the two final quiz scores, as a dot plot.

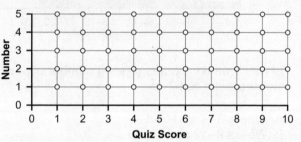

DIRECTIONS: Study the information and histogram, read the question, and choose the **best** answer.

A company that makes steel rods has one particular stock item that is supposed to be 60 cm long. The lengths of a random sample of 53 rods are measured, and the results are tabulated in the following histogram.

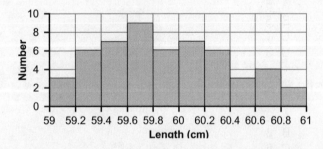

12. The company decides to reject rods with lengths that fall outside the range of 59.4 cm to 60.6 cm. Based on this sample, roughly what percentage of rods will be rejected?

A. 9.4%
B. 17%
C. 28.3%
D. 47.2%

DIRECTIONS: Study the information and histogram, read the question, and choose the **best** answer.

The following histogram lists the average number of viewers of a new movie, grouped by age.

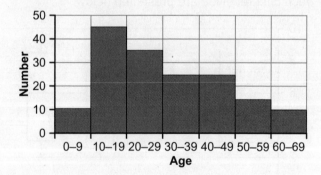

13. What is the mode age of viewers for the new movie?

A. 10 to 19
B. 20 to 29
C. 30 to 39
D. 40 to 49

UNIT 2

DIRECTIONS: Study the dot plot, read each question, and choose the **best** answer.

The 19 students in a keyboarding class are tested on the number of words they can type in a minute. Their results appear in the dot plot below.

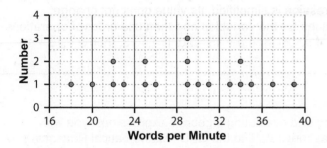

14. What is the median number of words per minute that students in the class can type?

   A. 25
   B. 26
   C. 29
   D. 34

15. What is the range of words typed per minute by students in the class?

   A. 15
   B. 17
   C. 19
   D. 21

DIRECTIONS: Study the histogram, read the question, and choose the **best** answer.

The teacher of the keyboarding class converted the data from a dot plot to a histogram.

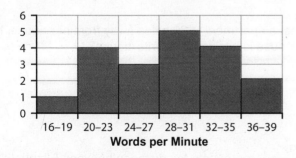

16. What is the mode of words typed per minute in the keyboarding class?

   A. 20 to 23
   B. 24 to 27
   C. 28 to 31
   D. 32 to 35

DIRECTIONS: Study the box plot and information, read each question, and choose the **best** answer.

Four thermostats placed in similar rooms are tested by setting the temperatures at 68°, letting the temperature settle for an hour, and then tabulating the temperature once every minute for an hour. The results are shown in the box plots below.

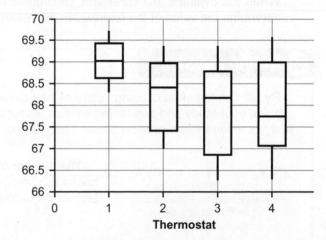

17. Which of the four thermostats does the best job minimizing the amount that the temperature varies?

   A. 1
   B. 2
   C. 3
   D. 4

18. Which thermostat maintains a median temperature closest to the set value?

   A. 1
   B. 2
   C. 3
   D. 4

19. Which thermostat exhibits the greatest range in temperature?

   A. 1
   B. 2
   C. 3
   D. 4

20. Which thermostat exhibits the smallest range in temperature?

   A. 1
   B. 2
   C. 3
   D. 4

Algebraic Expressions and Variables

Use with **Student Book** pp. 50–51

MATH CONTENT TOPICS: Q.1.b, Q.2.a, Q.2.e, Q.4.a, A.1.a, A.1.b, A.1.c, A.1.e, A.1.g, A.1.i, A.1.j
MATH PRACTICES: MP.1.a, MP.1.b, MP.1.e, MP.2.a, MP.2.c, MP.3.a, MP.4.a, MP.4.b

1 Review the Skill

Algebraic expressions translate words into number relationships by using numbers, operation signs, and variables. **Variables** are letters that represent numbers. A variable may change in value, which allows an expression to also have different values. When an expression is simplified, its value does not change.

When you evaluate an expression, you substitute values for the variables and then use order of operations to determine the value of the expression. For example, if $a = 5$, then $a + 15 = 20$. If $a = -5$, then $a + 15 = 10$.

2 Refine the Skill

By refining the skills of using variables and simplifying and evaluating algebraic expressions, you will improve your study and test-taking abilities, especially as they relate to the GED® Mathematical Reasoning Test. Examine the information below. Then answer the questions that follow.

a Look for key words. For example, *times* indicates multiplication. Phrases such as *increased by* indicate addition.

The number of miles between Elizabeth's house and her grandparents' house is 3 times the number of miles between her house and her older brother's apartment.

b You can evaluate an expression containing any number of variables as long as the variables are known. In this case, both x and y are given, so you can substitute those values for the variables to evaluate the expression.

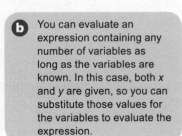

Elizabeth's house

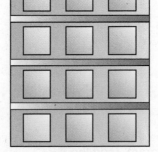

Brother's apartment

Grandparents' house

TEST-TAKING TECH

Subtraction and negative signs are entered differently in the calculator. Use the minus sign for subtraction. To enter a negative number, type the negative button: (-) followed by the number.

1. If Elizabeth's brother's apartment is 39 miles away from her house, how far away from her house is her grandparents' house?

   A. 13 miles
   B. 36 miles
   C. 42 miles
   D. 117 miles

2. If the expression $\dfrac{9x - y}{5}$ represents the distance between Elizabeth's house and her grandparents' house, and $x = 12$ and $y = 3$, what is the distance from Elizabeth's house to her grandparents' house?

   A. 16.2 miles
   B. 21 miles
   C. 22.2 miles
   D. 105 miles

UNIT 3

DIRECTIONS: Read each question, and choose the **best** answer.

3. The number of girls that registered to play basketball in a summer league is 15 fewer than twice the number of boys. If *b* is the number of boys, which expression describes the number of girls that registered?

   A. $\dfrac{2b}{15}$

   B. $\dfrac{1}{2}b + 15$

   C. $15 + 2b$

   D. $2b - 15$

4. There are *p* number of pencils in a pack. There are 50 packs in a box and 12 boxes in a case. Julia delivers 3 cases to a store. She opens a case to remove 1 pencil to use. Which expression represents the number of pencils that are left?

   A. $3 + 12 + 50 + p - 1$

   B. $3(12)(50)p - 1$

   C. $3(12)\left(\dfrac{50}{p}\right) - 1$

   D. $3(12)(50)p + 1$

5. Edward drove 4 times as many miles on Tuesday as he did on Wednesday and Thursday combined. Which expression describes the number of miles he drove on Tuesday in terms of the number of miles he drove on Wednesday (*x*) and Thursday (*y*)?

   A. $x + 4y$

   B. $\dfrac{4}{x + y}$

   C. $\dfrac{x + y}{4}$

   D. $4(x + y)$

6. The museum admission fee for a child is $4 more than one-half the admission fee for an adult. Which expression describes the amount paid for 12 children and 4 adults to visit the museum?

   A. $10a + 4$

   B. $10a + 24$

   C. $10a + 48$

   D. $14a + 16$

DIRECTIONS: Read each question, and choose the **best** answer.

7. Which expression represents the perimeter of the triangle shown below?

   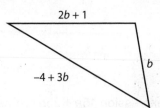

   A. $5b - 3$

   B. $6b + 3$

   C. $6b - 3$

   D. $-b + 4$

8. The age of Nick's grandfather is 5 years greater than twice the ages of his two grandchildren together. If *x* and *y* are the two grandchildren's ages, which expression describes Nick's grandfather's age?

   A. $2(x + y) + 5$

   B. $\dfrac{x + y}{2} + 5$

   C. $\dfrac{2(x + y)}{5}$

   D. $2x + 2y - 5$

9. A school sold adult tickets and children's tickets to a football game. The number of children's tickets sold was 56 more than one-third the number of adult tickets. Which expression describes the number of children's ticket sold?

   A. $\dfrac{1}{3}a - 56$

   B. $\dfrac{a}{3} + 56$

   C. $\dfrac{56a}{3}$

   D. $\dfrac{3}{a} + 56$

10. The number of students in an incoming freshman class is 3 times the number of students in the sophomore class divided by 4. Which expression describes the number of students in the incoming freshman class?

    A. $4y + 3$

    B. $\dfrac{3y}{4}$

    C. $\dfrac{4}{3y}$

    D. $3y - 4$

UNIT 3

DIRECTIONS: Read each question, and choose the **best** answer.

11. The expression 3(x + 2x) represents the distance between two cities. What is the distance if x = 4?

    A. 48
    B. 36
    C. 27
    D. 18

12. The expression 15a + 25b represents the amount of money a theater takes in per night if they sell a $15 seats and b $25 seats. How much money does the theater take in if a = 207 and b = 134?

    A. $5,115
    B. $5,175
    C. $6,455
    D. $7,185

13. The length of a rectangle is 3 less than 3 times its width. If w = the width of the rectangle, which expression represents the area of the rectangle?

    A. 3w − 3
    B. $\frac{1}{2}w(3w − 3)$
    C. w(3w − 3)
    D. $\frac{3w − 3}{2}$

14. The number of minutes that Erin spent on Project A is 45 less than one-half of her time spent on Project B. Which expression best represents her time spent on Project B, if t equals the number of minutes spent on Project A?

    A. 2t + 90
    B. 2t − 45
    C. $\frac{2t}{45}$
    D. $\frac{1}{2}t − 45$

DIRECTIONS: Read each question, and choose the **best** answer.

15. A number is half the value of the sum of a second number (x) and a third number (y). Which expression describes the first number?

    A. 2x + 2y
    B. $\frac{2}{x − y}$
    C. $\frac{x + y}{2}$
    D. 2(x + y)

16. On Monday, a cyclist rode 20 fewer than 3 times the number of miles he rode on Sunday. If he rode 30 miles on Sunday, how many miles did he ride on Monday?

    A. 40
    B. 50
    C. 60
    D. 70

17. Leo's age is 21 less than 2 times the age of his sister. If his sister is 23, how old is Leo?

    A. 21
    B. 23
    C. 25
    D. 46

18. A middle school has 374 male students. The number of female students is 56 more than one-half the number of male students. How many female students are in the middle school?

    A. 215
    B. 243
    C. 402
    D. 804

19. A store sells women's and men's shoes. In one day, the number of women's shoes sold was 12 more than 4 times the number of men's shoes sold. If 9 pairs of men's shoes were sold that day, how many pairs of women's shoes did the store sell?

    A. 24
    B. 48
    C. 60
    D. 108

20. Sean swam 8 fewer than twice as many laps as Antonio. If Antonio swam 15 laps, how many laps did Sean swim?

    A. 22
    B. 23
    C. 31
    D. 38

21. The number of students who scored above average on an exam was 34 fewer than twice the number of students who scored at an average level. If 45 students scored at an average level, how many scored above average on the exam?

    A. 34
    B. 56
    C. 66
    D. 90

22. The distance from Kristina's home to work is 15 miles less than 4 times the distance from her home to her parents' home. If the distance from her home to work is 33 miles, how far away is Kristina's home from her parents' home?

    A. 12 miles
    B. 18 miles
    C. 27 miles
    D. 60 miles

23. If -3 5 x, then what does $4y - 8(3 - 2x)$ equal?

    A. $-68y$
    B. $4y - 72$
    C. $4y - 24$
    D. $4y + 24$

24. Jada wrote a check to pay for gas. The amount of the check was $5 less than one-half the amount that she had deposited into her account that day. If she deposited $84, how much did she pay for gas?

    A. $37
    B. $42
    C. $74
    D. $79

25. A number is 3 times the value of the quotient of a second number (x) and a third number (y). Which expression describes the first number?

    A. $\dfrac{xy}{3}$

    B. $\dfrac{3}{x + y}$

    C. $\dfrac{3}{x} + y$

    D. $3\left(\dfrac{x}{y}\right)$

26. The length of a rectangle is 6 more than two-thirds the width, w. Which expression represents the perimeter of the rectangle?

    A. $\dfrac{10}{3}w + 12$

    B. $w\left(6 + \dfrac{2}{3}w\right)$

    C. $\dfrac{4}{3}w + 12$

    D. $\dfrac{10}{3}w + 6$

27. Rewrite the expression $\dfrac{y(x + 4)}{x(y + 4)}$ in terms of x, assuming $y = 2x$.

    A. 1

    B. $\dfrac{2(x + 4)}{6x}$

    C. $\dfrac{(x + 4)}{(x + 2)}$

    D. 2

28. Evaluate the expression $\dfrac{(x^2 - y^2)}{(x^2 + y^2)}$ when $x = 2$ and $y = -1$.

    A. $\dfrac{1}{3}$

    B. $\dfrac{3}{5}$

    C. 1

    D. $\dfrac{5}{3}$

Equations

Use with *Student Book* pp. 52–53

MATH CONTENT TOPICS: Q.2.a, Q.2.e, Q.3.a, Q.3.d, A.1.a, A.1.j, A.2.a, A.2.b, A.2.c
MATH PRACTICES: MP.1.a, MP.1.b, MP.1.e, MP.2.a, MP.2.c, MP.4.a

1 Review the Skill

An **equation** is a mathematical statement showing that two expressions are equal. You can solve equations by isolating the variable through inverse operations. If you have two equations with two variables, you can solve one equation for one of the variables, and then substitute that solution for the variable in the other equation. The formulas used to solve math problems all involve equations.

2 Refine the Skill

By refining the skill of solving equations, you will improve your study and test-taking abilities, especially as they relate to the GED® Mathematical Reasoning Test. Study the information below. Then answer the questions that follow.

The menu of a New England restaurant is shown below.

a There is usually more than one way to write an equation. In question 1, answer choices C and D are the same, because $\frac{4}{3}$ is the same as $4 \times \frac{1}{3}$.

b For question 2, use the equation $2(8) + 3t = 70$, where t represents the price of one lobster tail.

Seafood Heaven Menu	
ITEM	**PRICE**
Lobster Tail	Market Value
Clam Chowder	$8
Atlantic Salmon	$13
Crab Lettuce Wraps	$10
Cup of Lobster Bisque	$8

USING LOGIC

Note what the variable represents in your equation. The value of the variable may not necessarily be the answer. Question 2 asks for the cost of the lobster *tails*, not the cost of a single lobster *tail*.

a 1. If the price of lobster tails, *t*, on a given day was $4 more than one-third the price of the crab lettuce wraps, which equation could you use to find the price of lobster tails that day?

A. $3t + 4 = 10$

B. $t = \frac{1}{3}(10) + 4$

C. $\frac{4}{3}t = 10$

D. $(4)\frac{1}{3}t = 10$

b 2. Leon and his family ordered 2 cups of lobster bisque and 3 lobster tails. If their bill for these 5 items was $70, what was the total cost of the lobster tails?

A. $15
B. $18
C. $52
D. $54

DIRECTIONS: Read each question, and choose the **best** answer.

3. One number is 5 times the value of a second number. The sum of the numbers is 72. Which equation can be used to find the second number?

    A. $\dfrac{6}{x} = 72$

    B. $\dfrac{x}{6} = 72$

    C. $5x = 72$
    D. $6x = 72$

4. The amount John spent in restaurants one month is $55 more than twice the amount he spent on groceries. If he spent $y on groceries, which of the following equations could be solved to find the amount of money he spent in restaurants, r?

    A. $\dfrac{r}{2} + 55 = y$

    B. $r = 55 + 2y$
    C. $55 - 2r = y$

    D. $\dfrac{1}{2}r + 55 = y$

5. Patricia bought a printer. After she paid 6% sales tax, the total was $105.97. Which equation could be solved to find the price p of the printer before tax?

    A. $p + 0.06 = 105.97$
    B. $0.06p = 105.97$

    C. $\dfrac{105.97}{0.06} = p$

    D. $p + 0.06p = 105.97$

6. The admission to an amusement park for a child under 48 inches tall is $3 less than half the price of an adult ticket. If the admission for a child costs $26, which equation could be used to find the price of an adult's admission?

    A. $2a - 3 = 26$

    B. $\dfrac{1}{2}a - 3 = 26$

    C. $\dfrac{a}{2} + 3 = 26$

    D. $\dfrac{1}{2}a + 26 = 3$

DIRECTIONS: Read each question, and choose the **best** answer.

7. Rachel earns twice as much money as her husband. Together, they earn $1,050 each week. Which equation could be used to find Rachel's husband's weekly earnings?

    A. $3h = 1,050$
    B. $2h + 2 = 1,050$
    C. $2h = 1,050$

    D. $\dfrac{3}{2}h = 1,050$

8. Steven worked 2 more than one-third as many hours this week as he did last week. Last week, he worked 33 hours. How many hours did he work this week?

    A. 11
    B. 13
    C. 17
    D. 21

9. There are 36 inches in one yard. Which equation represents this situation, if i = number of inches and y = number of yards?

    A. $36i = y$
    B. $36 - i = y$
    C. $36y = i$

    D. $\dfrac{36}{i} = y$

10. In a recent survey, 419 people who listed soccer as their favorite sport were 13 less than 3 times the number of people who listed baseball as their favorite sport. How many people chose baseball as their favorite sport?

    A. 39
    B. 47
    C. 144
    D. 445

11. Ted recently sold half of his comic books and then bought 92 more. He now has 515 comic books. With how many comic books did he begin?

    A. 846
    B. 607
    C. 561
    D. 423

UNIT 3

★ Spotlighted Item: **DROP-DOWN**

DIRECTIONS: Read each question, and use the drop-down options to choose the **best** answer.

12. One number is two-thirds of another number. The sum of the numbers is 55.

    The greater number is [Drop-down].

    A. 22   B. 30   C. 32   D. 33

13. Karleen and her mother went on a vacation. Karleen paid for gas, and her mother paid for lodging. Karleen spent $65.25 more than one-fourth of what her mother spent. They spent a total of $659.

    Karleen spent $ [Drop-down].

    A. 475.00   B. 184.00   C. 164.75   D. 118.75

14. Emma purchased 3 bottles of ginger ale for $2.29 per bottle. She also purchased some boxes of crackers for $3.35 per box. Her total bill was $23.62.

    She bought [Drop-down] boxes of crackers.

    A. 4   B. 5   C. 6   D. 7

15. A store pays $53.80 for a carton of boxes of cereal. Each box of cereal costs $2.69.

    There are [Drop-down] boxes of cereal in a carton.

    A. 18   B. 19   C. 20   D. 21

DIRECTIONS: Read each question, and choose the **best** answer.

16. A barge travels downstream at an average speed of 15 miles per hour. It travels a distance of 60 miles. Which equation can be used to find how many hours the barge traveled?

    A. $15 = 60t$

    B. $\dfrac{t}{15} = 60$

    C. $\dfrac{60}{t} = 15 + t$

    D. $60 = 15t$

17. Ben and Brian both ride their bikes long distances on Saturday. Together, they rode 107 miles. If Ben biked 11 more miles than Brian, how many miles did Brian bike?

    A. 32
    B. 48
    C. 59
    D. 96

18. Mrs. Logan ordered 12 new desks and 20 new chairs for her classroom. The total cost of the desks and chairs was $1,260. If each chair cost $30, what was the cost of each desk?

    A. $50
    B. $55
    C. $58
    D. $60

19. If $y = \dfrac{1}{2}$, what does x equal when

    $4 - 2(3x - y) = 5x - 2\dfrac{1}{3}$?

    A. $-1\dfrac{2}{3}$

    B. $-\dfrac{2}{3}$

    C. $\dfrac{2}{3}$

    D. $1\dfrac{2}{3}$

UNIT 3

20. Kira has a total of 12 dimes and nickels in her pocket. The coins have a total value of $0.95. How many dimes are in Kira's pocket?

    A. 5
    B. 7
    C. 9
    D. 12

21. One number is 8 less than twice another number x. The sum of the numbers is 40. What is x?

    A. 16
    B. 12
    C. 10
    D. 8

22. Myra took her 5 children out for ice cream. Each child ordered a single scoop of ice cream on a cone. The clerk added $0.87 to Myra's bill for sales tax. Myra paid a total of $15.37. If each cone cost the same amount, what was the cost of one cone?

    A. $2.82
    B. $2.90
    C. $3.07
    D. $3.25

23. A cell phone at Store A costs $10 less than twice the cost of the same cell phone at Store B. If the phone costs $49.99 at Store B, how much does it cost at Store A?

    A. $89.98
    B. $99.98
    C. $109.98
    D. $119.99

24. Tickets to a baseball game are $9 for adults. A child's ticket is $2 more than half the price of an adult's ticket. Melanie buys 4 adult tickets and some children's tickets. If she paid $75 for the tickets, how many children's tickets did she buy?

    A. 3
    B. 4
    C. 5
    D. 6

25. Juan can either earn $200 per week plus 15% commission, or $300 per week plus 10% commission. What do Juan's sales need to be in order for the two earning options to pay the same amount?

    A. $10,000
    B. $2,000
    C. $400
    D. $20

26. A company held a fundraising event for a charity. Andrew contributed $25 less than twice as much as Michael. The sum of their contributions was $200. How much did Andrew contribute?

    A. $75
    B. $125
    C. $150
    D. $175

27. Xavier and Madeleine's ages add up to 28. Xavier is 4 years older than half of Madeleine's age. How old will Xavier be in 2 years?

    A. 12
    B. 14
    C. 16
    D. 18

28. Beth's rent is $74 less than 4 times her student loan payment. The total of these bills is $486. How much is Beth's student loan payment?

    A. $112
    B. $140
    C. $374
    D. $448

29. Ann's weekly salary is $543 less than twice Joe's weekly salary. If Joe earns $874 per week, what is Ann's weekly salary?

    A. $331
    B. $1,174
    C. $1,205
    D. $1,417

UNIT 3

Squaring, Cubing, and Taking Roots

Use with *Student Book* pp. 54–55

1 Review the Skill

MATH CONTENT TOPICS: Q.2.a, Q.2.b, Q.2.c, Q.2.d, Q.2.e, Q.4.a, Q.4.c, Q.4.d, Q.5.a

MATH PRACTICES: MP.1.a, MP.1.b, MP.1.e, MP.2.c, MP.3.a, MP.4.a, MP.4.b, MP.5.a, MP.5.b, MP.5.c

The **square** of a number is the result of multiplying the number times itself. Finding the **square root** of a number requires finding a second number that, when multiplied by itself, gives the first number. Since both positive and negative numbers, when squared, yield positive numbers, square roots of positive numbers have two mathematically possible values, while square roots of negative numbers are not defined for real numbers.

The **cube** of a number is the result of multiplying that number by itself three times; 3^3, for example, is $3 \times 3 \times 3 = 27$. Since the cube of a negative number is also negative, the **cube root** of a negative number exists and is also negative.

2 Refine the Skill

By refining the skills of squaring, cubing, and taking the corresponding roots of quantities, you will improve your study and test-taking abilities, especially as they relate to the GED® Mathematical Reasoning Test. Study the diagram and information below. Then answer the questions that follow.

a To answer question 1, remember that a square has four equal sides. To find the area of a square, multiply the length of one side by itself.

b For question 2, increasing all sides of a rectangle by the same scale factor has the effect of increasing the area by the factor squared. Similarly, increasing all sides of a rectangular prism by the same factor has the effect of increasing the volume by the factor cubed.

The diagram shows the area of Meredith's square garden.

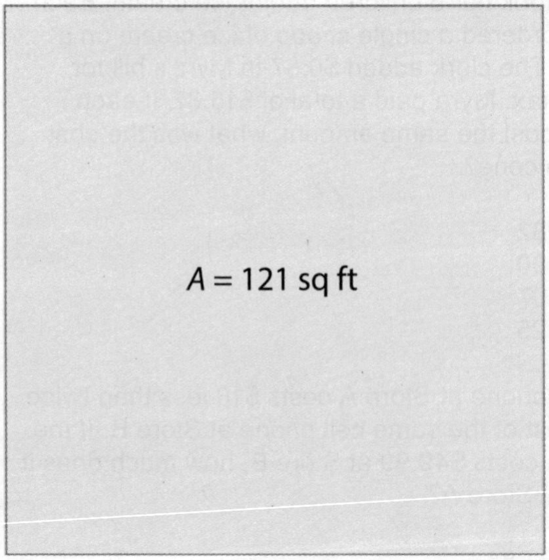

$A = 121$ sq ft

TEST-TAKING TECH

The on-screen calculator, the Texas Instruments TI-30XS MultiView™, features square and square-root functions, as well as more general abilities enabling cubes and cube roots.

1. Use the formula for the area of a square. What is the length of one side of Meredith's garden?

   A. 12 ft
   B. 11 ft
   C. 10 ft
   D. 9 ft

2. Meredith decides to double the length of each side of her garden. What will its new area be?

   A. 242 sq ft
   B. 363 sq ft
   C. 484 sq ft
   D. 605 sq ft

DIRECTIONS: Read each question, and choose the **best** answer.

3. A math website gives the number of questions in its daily quiz as a square root. Today, there are $\sqrt{144}$ questions. How many questions are there?

   A. 10
   B. 11
   C. 12
   D. 13

4. Amanda used her calculator to find $\sqrt{7,788}$. What is this number rounded to the nearest hundredth?

   A. 88.24
   B. 88.25
   C. 89.24
   D. 89.25

5. The length of a cube is 29 centimeters. What is the volume of the cube in cubic centimeters?

   A. 87
   B. 841
   C. 24,389
   D. 707,281

6. The area of a square is 6.7 square feet. What is the length of a side of the square to the nearest tenth of a foot?

   A. 2.5
   B. 2.6
   C. 2.9
   D. 3.4

7. The square root of 33 is between which two numbers?

   A. 4 and 5
   B. 5 and 6
   C. 6 and 7
   D. 7 and 8

8. The area of a square with sides of length x is x^2. What is the area of the square if $x = 7.8$ inches?

   A. 15.6 sq in.
   B. 49 sq in.
   C. 60.84 sq in.
   D. 62.41 sq in.

DIRECTIONS: Read each question, and choose the **best** answer.

9. Hannah is buying a carpet for her living room, which has an area of 216 square feet and is 50% longer than it is wide. What are the dimensions of the room?

   A. width = 12 feet; length = 18 feet
   B. width = 8 feet; length = 27 feet
   C. width = 27 feet; length = 8 feet
   D. width = 18 feet; length = 12 feet

10. Which set of integers solves the equation $x^2 = 16$?

    A. 4, −2
    B. 4, −4
    C. 2, 8
    D. −2, −8

11. A shipping container has a width equal to its height, a length 5 times its width, and a volume of 2,560 cubic feet. What are the dimensions of the container?

    A. width = 16 feet; height = 16 feet; length = 8 feet
    B. width = 8 feet; height = 40 feet; length = 8 feet
    C. width = 8 feet; height = 8 feet; length = 40 feet
    D. width = 40 feet; height = 8 feet; length = 8 feet

12. Jon's monthly car payment is the square of 19 minus the square root of 169. What is Jon's monthly car payment?

    A. $188
    B. $348
    C. $361
    D. $530

13. A soccer field for a youth league has an area of 4,000 square yards, and is 60% longer than it is wide. What is the length of the field?

    A. 50 yards
    B. 60 yards
    C. 70 yards
    D. 80 yards

14. A glass table is in the shape of a cube with a side length of 4 feet. The center of the table is a hollow cube with a side length of 1.5 feet. What volume of glass was used to make the table?

    A. 60.625 cubic feet
    B. 61.75 cubic feet
    C. 64 cubic feet
    D. 67.375 cubic feet

DIRECTIONS: Read each question, and choose the **best** answer.

15. The length of each side of a rectangular prism is increased by a factor of three. By what factor does the volume increase?

    A. 3
    B. 9
    C. 18
    D. 27

16. The length of each side of a rectangle increases by a factor of 2. By what factor does the area increase?

    A. 2
    B. 4
    C. 6
    D. 8

17. Justin's age in years is the solution, x, of the equation $\left(2 - \sqrt{x + 2}\right)^2 = 4$. How old is Justin?

    A. between 0 and 5 years old
    B. between 5 and 10 years old
    C. between 10 and 15 years old
    D. greater than 15 years old

18. The equation $x^2 = 25$ has two different solutions. What is the product of these two solutions?

    A. −25
    B. −5
    C. 5
    D. 25

19. The equation $(x - 1)^2 = 64$ has two different solutions. What is the product of these two solutions?

    A. 81
    B. 49
    C. −49
    D. −63

20. How many times greater is the cube of the positive square root of 64 than the square of the cube root of 64?

    A. 4
    B. 8
    C. 16
    D. 32

DIRECTIONS: Read each question, and choose the **best** answer.

21. The equation $(x - 6)^2 = 4$ has two different solutions. What is the product of these two solutions?

    A. −64
    B. −32
    C. 32
    D. 64

22. The area of one side of a cube is 30.25 square inches. What is the volume of the cube, rounded to the nearest cubic inch?

    A. 121
    B. 166
    C. 242
    D. 915

23. A square table has an area of 2,000 square inches. What is the length of each side, rounded to the nearest inch?

    A. 40 inches
    B. 44 inches
    C. 45 inches
    D. 50 inches

24. A small refrigerator is cubic in shape and has an outside width of 18 inches. What is the volume of the space the refrigerator takes up, expressed as cubic feet, to the nearest tenth of a cubic foot?

    A. 2.3
    B. 3.3
    C. 3.4
    D. 4.5

25. A child has a set of play blocks that are cubic in shape and measure 2 inches on each side. How many blocks does the child need to make a cubic stack with a volume of 1 cubic foot?

    A. 18
    B. 36
    C. 144
    D. 216

26. A relationship between the temperature measured in degrees Fahrenheit (F) and the temperature measured in degrees Celsius (C) is: $25(F - 32)^2 = 81C^2$. If the temperature measured in degrees Fahrenheit is 41, what is the temperature in degrees in degrees Celsius?

    A. 5
    B. 9
    C. 23
    D. 45

27. A model rocket accelerates from rest. While the fuel is still burning, the distance the rocket travels in feet, D, during a time t after launch expressed in seconds, is given by the equation $D = 400t^3$. The rocket is at a height of 1,350 feet when the fuel runs out. How long does the fuel burn?

    A. 1.4 seconds
    B. 1.5 seconds
    C. 1.8 seconds
    D. 3.4 seconds

28. Which number solves the equation $x^2 = -16$?

    A. 4
    B. −4
    C. −8
    D. No real solution.

29. Which number solves the equation $x^3 = -64$?

    A. 4
    B. −4
    C. −8
    D. No real solution.

30. Chris is laying floor tiles in his kitchen, which has a width of $\frac{3}{4}$ its length, and an area of 192 square feet. What are the dimensions of the room?

    A. 12 feet by 15 feet
    B. 12 feet by 16 feet
    C. 16 feet by 18 feet
    D. 8 feet by 24 feet

DIRECTIONS: Read each question, and choose the **best** answer.

31. Kelly is making a box that has a width equal to its depth, a length equal to three times the depth, and a volume of 192 cubic inches. What will the dimensions of the box be?

    A. depth = 4 inches; width = 4 inches; length = 12 inches
    B. depth = 2 inches; width = 4 inches; length = 8 inches
    C. depth = 4 inches; width = 4 inches; length = 8 inches
    D. depth = 12 inches; width = 4 inches; length = 4 inches

32. A ball is dropped out a window that is 9.8 meters above the ground. The height above the ground, h, at some time after it is dropped, t, is given by the equation $h = 9.8 - 4.9t^2$. How long does it take the ball to hit the ground, to the nearest tenth of a second?

    A. 0.7 seconds
    B. 1.4 seconds
    C. 1.5 seconds
    D. 2 seconds

33. For the numbers listed, select those for which the following expression is undefined: $\sqrt{(x^2 - 1.5)}$.

    A. 1.5, −1.5, −2
    B. 1.4, 1.6, −1.8
    C. 1.3, 2, −3
    D. −1, 0, 1

34. Rob recently refinanced his monthly student loan so that the payment equals the square of 14. In addition, Rob's monthly rent is the square of 21 minus the square root of 49. How much does Rob pay each month in student loans and rent?

    A. $396
    B. $445
    C. $630
    D. $686

35. For which expression is x not a real number?

    A. $x^3 = 8$
    B. $x^3 = -27$
    C. $x^2 = -49$
    D. $x^2 = 121$

UNIT 3

Exponents and Scientific Notation

Use with *Student Book* pp. 56–57

MATH CONTENT TOPICS: Q.1.c, Q.2.a, Q.2.b, Q.2.c, Q.2.d, Q.2.e, Q.6.c, A.1.a, A.1.d, A.1.e, A.1.f, A.1.i
MATH PRACTICES: MP.1.a, MP.1.b, MP.1.e, MP.2.c, MP.3.a, MP.4.a, MP.4.b, MP.5.a, MP.5.c

1 Review the Skill

Exponents show how many times a number is multiplied by itself. There are specific rules when performing mathematical operations on numbers with exponents. Sums and differences of quantities with exponents can be simplified if—and only if—they have the same base and exponents. For example, $2x^3 + 5x^3$ can be simplified to read $7x^3$. Multiplying or dividing two quantities written using exponents can be simplified if they have the same bases; the exponents add or subtract, respectively. For example, $(4x^4) \cdot (2x^7) = 8x^{11}$; $(4x^4) \div (2x^7) = 2x^{-3}$.

Scientific notation uses exponents and powers of 10 to write very small and very large numbers. Proper scientific notation requires that the decimal point be located just to the right of the first nonzero digit. The exponent is chosen so that the number has the correct magnitude.

2 Refine the Skill

By refining the skill of working with exponents and scientific notation, you will improve your study and test-taking abilities, especially as they relate to the GED® Mathematical Reasoning Test. Study the diagram below. Then answer the questions that follow.

The dimensions of the playing area of a football field are shown below.

a When dividing numbers involving scientific notation, the numbers can be divided first and then rewritten in proper notation, or they can be appropriately rewritten before division. For example, question 2 can be written as: $(150) \div (57.6 \times 10^3)$, which automatically will result in an answer expressed in proper notation.

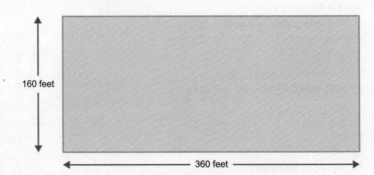

160 feet

360 feet

CONTENT PRACTICES

Solving algebraic expressions (MP.4.b) typically involve practices such as expanding terms, combining like terms, looking for common factors among terms, and canceling factors.

1. The area of the football field is the product of the length and the width—57,600 square feet. What is the area of the football field in square feet, expressed using scientific notation?

   A. 5.76×10^2
   B. 5.76×10^3
   C. 5.76×10^4
   D. 5.76×10^5

a 2. It takes 150 pounds of grass seed to reseed the field. If the seed is spread uniformly, how many pounds of seed go on each square foot?

   A. 2.6×10^{-2}
   B. 2.6×10^{-3}
   C. 2.6×10^{-4}
   D. 2.6×10^{-5}

DIRECTIONS: Read each question, and choose the **best** answer.

3. The North American feather-winged beetle is one of the world's smallest beetles. It is less than 0.0005 meters in length. What is this length written in scientific notation?

   A. 5×10^{-4}
   B. 5×10^{-3}
   C. 5×10^{-2}
   D. 5×10^{4}

4. The Smithsonian Institute has about 3^4 items in its Division of Old World Archeology Collection. About how many items are in this collection?

   A. 30
   B. 70
   C. 80
   D. 90

5. There are 3^4 students in one psychology class and 2^6 students in another psychology class. Which expression represents the total number of students in the two classes?

   A. 5^{10}
   B. 6^{10}
   C. $3^4 + 2^6$
   D. $3^4 \times 2^6$

6. Olivia was asked to write the number of siblings she has using exponents. She wrote 4^0. What is another way to write the number of siblings she has using exponents?

   A. 5^0
   B. 5^1
   C. 5^{-1}
   D. 4^1

7. The expression $4x(x^2 + 2y)$ is equal to which of the following expressions?

   A. $4x^3 + 2y$
   B. $4x^2 + 8xy$
   C. $4x^3 + 8y$
   D. $4x^3 + 8xy$

DIRECTIONS: Study the information and table, read each question, and choose the **best** answer.

The table shows the masses of the planets.

PLANET MASSES

Planet	Mass (kg)
Mercury	3.3×10^{23}
Venus	4.87×10^{24}
Earth	5.97×10^{24}
Mars	6.42×10^{23}
Jupiter	1.899×10^{27}
Saturn	5.68×10^{26}
Uranus	8.68×10^{25}
Neptune	1.02×10^{26}

8. Which planet has the greatest mass?

   A. Venus
   B. Earth
   C. Jupiter
   D. Uranus

9. Which planet has the least mass?

   A. Mercury
   B. Venus
   C. Earth
   D. Mars

10. About how many times greater is the mass of Jupiter than the mass of Mars?

    A. 3×10^2
    B. 3×10^3
    C. 3×10^4
    D. 3×10^5

11. About what is the sum of the masses of the planets?

    A. 2.7×10^{27}
    B. 2.7×10^{28}
    C. 3.8×10^{27}
    D. 3.8×10^{28}

⭐ Spotlighted Item: **DROP-DOWN**

DIRECTIONS: Read each question, and choose the drop-down option that **best** completes each equation.

12. $(5x^5 - 15x^4 + 10x^3) =$ Drop-down

    A. $5x^5(1 - 3x + 2x^2)$
    B. $5x^3(x^2 - 3x + 2)$
    C. $5x^{-3}(x^2 - 3x + 2)$
    D. $5x^{-5}(1 - 3x + 2x^2)$

13. $\dfrac{(x^4 + 5x^3) + x^2(x^2 - 2x)}{x^3} =$ Drop-down

    A. $\dfrac{(2x^3 + 5x^3 - 2)}{x^2}$
    B. $x^6(2x + 7)$
    C. $x^6(2x + 3)$
    D. $2x + 3$

14. $3(2x^2 - 1) - (5x^2 + x - 3) =$ Drop-down

    A. $(x^2 - 4x + 3)$
    B. $-x(2x + 1)$
    C. $x(x - 1)$
    D. $x(x + 1)$

DIRECTIONS: Read each question, and choose the drop-down option that **best** describes the given expression when it is evaluated at the specified value of x.

15. For $x = -1$: $\dfrac{(x^3)}{(x^3 - 1)}$ is Drop-down

    A. less than 0
    B. equal to 0
    C. greater than 0
    D. undefined

16. For $x = -1$: $\dfrac{(x^3)}{(x^3 + 1)}$ is Drop-down

    A. less than 0
    B. equal to 0
    C. greater than 0
    D. undefined

17. For $x = -1$: $\dfrac{(x - 1)^4}{(x^2 - 1)}$ is Drop-down

    A. less than 0
    B. equal to 0
    C. greater than 0
    D. undefined

DIRECTIONS: Study the information and table, read each question, and choose the **best** answer.

The table shows the distances of planets from the sun.

Planet	Distance from the Sun (km)
Mercury	5.79×10^7
Venus	1.082×10^8
Earth	1.496×10^8
Mars	2.279×10^8
Jupiter	7.786×10^8
Saturn	1.4335×10^9
Uranus	2.8725×10^9
Neptune	4.4951×10^9

18. Find the distance between Saturn and the sun. What is this number written in standard notation?

    A. 14,335,000 km
    B. 143,350,000 km
    C. 1,433,500,000 km
    D. 14,335,000,000 km

19. How many kilometers farther from the sun is Jupiter than Venus?

    A. 6.704×10^7
    B. 6.704×10^8
    C. 6.704×10^9
    D. 6.704×10^{16}

20. The approximate number of people who visited an amusement park in July can be written as 10^5. About how many people attended the park in July?

    A. 1,000
    B. 10,000
    C. 100,000
    D. 1,000,000

21. Which expression is equivalent to b^{-4}?

    A. b^4
    B. $\dfrac{1}{b^4}$
    C. $-b^4$
    D. $(-b)(-b)(-b)(-b)$

22. One of the largest genomes (sets of genetic material) is that of the marbled lungfish. Even so, this genome weighs only 1.3283×10^{-10} grams. What is this number expressed in standard notation?

    A. 0.0000013283
    B. 0.00000013283
    C. 0.000000013283
    D. 0.00000000013283

23. The perihelion of Pluto is 4,435,000,000 km. What is this distance written in scientific notation?

    A. 4.435×10^7
    B. 4.435×10^8
    C. 4.435×10^9
    D. 4.435×10^{10}

24. Which has the same value as 4.404×10^9?

    A. 0.4404×10^8
    B. 0.4404×10^9
    C. 0.4404×10^{10}
    D. 0.4404×10^{11}

25. If $3^x = 81$, what is the value of x?

    A. 1
    B. 2
    C. 3
    D. 4

26. The number of students who attend Shadyside High School can be written as 2^9. Sunnyside High School has 3 times the number of students as Shadyside. How many students attend Sunnyside High School?

    A. 171
    B. 512
    C. 1,536
    D. 4,096

27. Which statement is true about the following expression?

    $$(-5)^x$$

    A. If x equals an even number, the answer will be negative.
    B. If x equals an even number, the answer will be positive.
    C. If x equals an odd number, the answer will be positive.
    D. If x equals zero, the answer will be zero.

28. If $(3^x)(3^x) = 3$, what must the value of x be?

    A. -1
    B. 0
    C. $\dfrac{1}{2}$
    D. 1

29. What is the product of the values of x where the expression $(x^3 + 27)^{-1} (x^4 + 16)^{-1} (x^5 + 1)^{-1}$ is undefined?

    A. -3
    B. -2
    C. -1
    D. 3

30. A supercomputer can perform 5×10^{13} operations per second. How many operations can the computer perform in one hour?

    A. 1.8×10^{15}
    B. 1.8×10^{17}
    C. 3×10^{14}
    D. 3×10^{15}

UNIT 3

Patterns and Functions

Use with *Student Book* pp. 58–59

1 Review the Skill

MATH CONTENT TOPICS: Q.2.a, Q.2.b, Q.2.c, Q.2.e, Q.3.d, Q.6.c, A.1.b, A.1.e, A.2.c, A.7.a, A.7.b, A.7.c

MATH PRACTICES: MP.1.a, MP.1.b, MP.1.e, MP.2.a, MP.2.c, MP.3.a, MP.4.a, MP.4.b, MP.5.c

A **mathematical pattern** is an arrangement of numbers or terms in a particular order. The order of the arrangement follows a specific rule. You can identify the rule by describing what you would do to one term to get the next term. A **function**, which establishes relationships between *x*- and *y*-values, can be written as an algebraic rule. In a function, there is only one *y*-value for each *x*-value.

2 Refine the Skill

By refining the skill of identifying and extending patterns, you will improve your study and test-taking abilities, especially as they relate to the GED® Mathematical Reasoning Test. Examine the information and function table below. Then answer the questions that follow.

a Substitute 5 for *t* in the equation *distance = rate × time* + 20, or *d* = *r*(*t*) + 20, and solve to find the train's distance after 5 hours to answer question 1.

b The train is traveling 60 km each hour. However, after 1 hour, it is 80 km from Station A. This is because when it began its journey, it was already 20 km from Station A. This is shown as "+ 20" in the equation.

The distance of a train from Station A was measured at different times as the train traveled to Station B. A record of the train's position and time is shown in the table below.

DISTANCE OF TRAIN FROM STATION A

Time (*t*) in Hours	1	2	3	4	5
Distance from Station (*d*) in Km	80	140	200	260	

TEST-TAKING TIPS

You can use answer choices to help you solve a problem. Instead of determining the rule from the table, you can try each one to see whether it works.

1. How many kilometers from the station will the train be after 5 hours?

A. 290
B. 300
C. 310
D. 320

b 2. How many kilometers from the station was the train when it began its trip?

A. 20
B. 30
C. 50
D. 60

DIRECTIONS: Study the table, read each question, and choose the **best** answer.

x	−2	0	2	4	6
y	−8	−2	4	10	

3. Which equation expresses the relationship between *x* and *y*?

   A. $y = 3x − 2$
   B. $y = \frac{1}{4}x$
   C. $y = 2x + 3$
   D. $y = \frac{2}{3}x$

4. What number is missing from the table?

   A. 12
   B. 14
   C. 16
   D. 18

DIRECTIONS: Read each question, and choose the **best** answer.

5. What is the sixth term in the following sequence?

   $$1, 3, 9, 27, \ldots$$

   A. 729
   B. 243
   C. 81
   D. 9

6. Which value for *x* for the function $f(x) = \frac{1}{2}x$ results in $f(x) = 1$?

   A. −2
   B. $-\frac{1}{2}$
   C. $\frac{1}{2}$
   D. 2

DIRECTIONS: Read each question, and choose the **best** answer.

7. Solomon is following a pattern as he stacks the blocks shown below. How many blocks will he stack in the next figure in his sequence?

 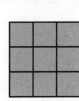 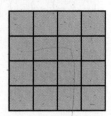

   A. 18
   B. 25
   C. 32
   D. 42

8. What is the next term in the sequence below?

   $$−5, −10, −20, −40, −80, \ldots$$

   A. −160
   B. −140
   C. −120
   D. −100

9. The function $f(x) = 50 − x^2$ was used to create the following function table. Which number is missing from the table?

x	−2	−1	0	1	2
f(x)	46	49	50		46

   A. 51
   B. 50
   C. 49
   D. 46

10. Which rule can be used to extend the following sequence?

    $$2, 4, 8, 16, 32, \ldots$$

    A. Add 4.
    B. Subtract 4.
    C. Multiply by 2.
    D. Divide by 2.

DIRECTIONS: Read each question, and choose the **best** answer.

11. What term in the sequence will have only one circle?

   A. fourth
   B. fifth
   C. sixth
   D. seventh

12. What is the seventh term in the following sequence?

$$-3, -6, -9, -12, -15, \ldots$$

   A. −18
   B. −21
   C. −24
   D. −27

13. For the function $f(x) = \dfrac{8}{x}$, which value for x results in a value of $f(x)$ that is less than 1?

   A. 6
   B. 7
   C. 8
   D. 9

14. How many triangles will the next term of the sequence have?

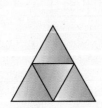

   A. 13
   B. 14
   C. 16
   D. 18

15. For the function $y = x^3$, which value for x results in a value for y that is equal to the value for x?

   A. 1
   B. 2
   C. 4
   D. 8

DIRECTIONS: Read each question, and choose the **best** answer.

16. The function $d = 55t$ describes the distance, d, a car will travel at a constant speed of 55 miles per hour in a certain amount of time, t. For which of the following values of t is the value of d equal to 220?

   A. 4
   B. 3.5
   C. 3
   D. 2.5

17. The increase in a population that grows annually at 1% can be described by the function $I = 0.01N$, where I is the increase and N is the initial population size. By what number does the population increase in a year if the initial population is 5,000?

   A. 5
   B. 10
   C. 25
   D. 50

18. $F = \dfrac{9}{5}C + 32$ describes the relationship between degrees Fahrenheit (F) and degrees Celsius (C). Which Celsius temperature is approximately 80° F?

   A. 26.7°C
   B. 44.4°C
   C. 62.2°C
   D. 176°C

19. The formula $I = (1{,}000)(r)(5)$ shows the amount of interest earned on a $1,000 investment over 5 years with a certain interest rate. What must the interest rate be to earn *at least* $250 interest on the investment in 5 years?

   A. 2%
   B. 3%
   C. 4%
   D. 5%

20. For the function $f(x) = \dfrac{1}{(x^2 + 1)}$, which value for x results in a value of $f(x)$ that is less than $\dfrac{1}{2}$?

   A. 1
   B. 0
   C. −1
   D. −2

DIRECTIONS: Study the information and table below, read each question, and choose the **best** answer.

An archer shot an arrow at an angle of 45 degrees. The distance and height of the arrow along its path were recorded at several points. The data is shown in the table below.

Distance (d) in Meters	1	2	3	4	5
Height (h) in Meters	0.8	1.2	1.2	0.8	

21. Which equation expresses the relationship between h and d?

    A. $h = d + 0.2d$
    B. $h = d - 0.2$
    C. $h = d - 0.2d^2$
    D. $h = d^2 - 0.2d^2$

22. What is the height of the arrow when it has traveled a distance of 5 meters?

    A. 0 meters
    B. 0.2 meters
    C. 0.4 meters
    D. 0.6 meters

DIRECTIONS: Read each question, and choose the **best** answer.

23. Kara substituted 1 for x into the function $f(x) = 3x^2 + 1$. Henry substituted a different value for x but found the same output. Which value of x would give the same output?

    A. 4
    B. 0
    C. −1
    D. −2

24. What is the eighth term in the following sequence?

$$2, -4, 8, -16, 32, \ldots$$

    A. −256
    B. −128
    C. 128
    D. 256

DIRECTIONS: Read each question, and choose the **best** answer.

25. The function $y = x^2$ was used to create the following function table. Which number is missing from the table?

x	−5	−1	0	$\frac{1}{2}$	
y	25	1	0	$\frac{1}{4}$	4

    A. −1
    B. 0
    C. 1
    D. 2

26. As you move below sea level, the pressure increases. Pressures at different depths are shown in the table.

Distance (d) in Meters Below Sea Level	0	10	20	30
Pressure (p) in Pounds Per Square Inch	14.7	29.4	44.1	58.8

Which equation expresses the relationship between d and p?

    A. $p = \dfrac{d}{10} + 14.7$

    B. $p = \dfrac{d}{10}(14.7) + 14.7$

    C. $p = 10d + 14.7$

    D. $p = \dfrac{d}{10}(14.7)$

27. In an experiment, a ball was dropped from a tall building at $t = 0$ seconds. The distance h the ball dropped at several different times is given in feet.

t	0.5	1	1.5	2	2.5
h	4	16	36	64	100

The relationship between distance and time is $h = \dfrac{1}{2}at^2$, where a is a constant determined from the data. What is the value for a?

    A. 28
    B. 32
    C. 36
    D. 40

UNIT 3

One-Variable Linear Equations

Use with *Student Book* pp. 60–61

MATH CONTENT TOPICS: Q.2.a, Q.2.e, Q.4.a, A.2.a, A.2.b
MATH PRACTICES: MP.1.a, MP.1.b, MP.1.e, MP.2.a, MP.3.a, MP.3.b, MP.4.a, MP.5.a, MP.5.c

① Review the Skill

A **one-variable linear equation** is an equation consisting of expressions involving only number values and products of constants and a variable. One such example is $3x + 3 = 9$. There may be variable terms on both sides of the equation. The solution of a one-variable linear equation is the value of the variable that makes the equation true.

To solve a one-variable linear equation, use **inverse operations** to isolate the variable. In the above example, subtract 3 from each side so that $3x = 6$. Next, divide each side by 3 so that $x = 6$.

② Refine the Skill

By refining the skill of solving one-variable linear equations, you will improve your study and test-taking abilities, especially as they relate to the GED® Mathematical Reasoning Test. Study the information below. Then answer the questions that follow.

a Multiply each quantity inside the parentheses by the quantity outside the parentheses.

b To solve question 1, remember to apply the negative sign. Use the distributive property to multiply each quantity inside the parentheses by −2.

c To solve question 2, apply the distributive property to both sides of the equation. Then use inverse operations to isolate and solve for *x*.

Solve the equation

$4(2x − 1) = 3x + 6$	
$4(2x) − 4(1) = 3x + 6$	← Distributive Property.
$8x − 4 = 3x + 6$	← Simplify.
$8x − 3x − 4 = 3x − 3x + 6$	← Subtract $3x$ from both sides.
$5x − 4 = 6$	← Simplify.
$5x − 4 + 4 = 6 + 4$	← Add 4 to both sides.
$5x = 10$	← Simplify.
$\dfrac{5x}{5} = \dfrac{10}{5}$	← Divide both sides by 5.
$x = 2$	← Simplify.

Check:

$4[2(2) − 1] \stackrel{?}{=} 3(2) + 6$

$4[4 − 1] \stackrel{?}{=} 6 + 6$

$4(3) \stackrel{?}{=} 12$

$12 = 12$

INSIDE THE ITEMS

Ensure that you check your solutions, especially with fill-in-the-blank questions. Substitute your solution into the original equation. If your solution makes the equation true, then it is correct.

b 1. What value of *x* makes the equation $8x = −2(3 − 2x)$ true?

A. −1.5
B. −0.6
C. −0.5
D. 0.5

c 2. Solve the equation for *m*.

$2(m + 3) = 5(6 − 2m)$

A. −3
B. 2
C. 6
D. 6.75

DIRECTIONS: Read each question, and choose the **best** answer.

3. Find the value of x that makes the equation true.

    $0.5(4x - 8) = 6$

    A. −1
    B. 1
    C. 5
    D. 7

4. Solve the equation for x.

    $3\left(\dfrac{2}{3}x + 4\right) = -5$

    A. −8.5
    B. −4.5
    C. −3.5
    D. −0.5

5. Drew's age is 3 more than one-half Tyler's age. The equation $d = \dfrac{1}{2}t + 3$ represents the relationship between their ages. If Drew is 17, how old is Tyler?

    A. 7
    B. 10
    C. 28
    D. 40

6. What is the value of x if $0.25(3x - 8) = 2(0.5x + 4)$?

    A. −64
    B. −40
    C. −24
    D. 24

7. Find the value of w that makes the equation true.

    $10w + 8 - 2(3w - 4) = -12$

    A. −7
    B. −1
    C. −3
    D. 1

DIRECTIONS: Read each question, and choose the **best** answer.

8. Solve the equation for b.

    $12b - 2(b - 1) = 6 - 4b$

    A. $\dfrac{2}{7}$
    B. $\dfrac{4}{7}$
    C. $\dfrac{2}{3}$
    D. $\dfrac{4}{3}$

9. If $(x - 4)$ is 5 more than $3(2x + 1)$, what is the value of x?

    A. −3
    B. −2.4
    C. −2
    D. −0.4

10. Amelia and Brandon solve the following equation.

    $-2(4x - 5) = 3x - (6 - x)$

    Amelia gets an answer of $\dfrac{4}{3}$. Brandon gets an answer of $\dfrac{8}{5}$. Who is correct?

    A. Amelia.
    B. Brandon.
    C. Both Amelia and Brandon.
    D. Neither Amelia nor Brandon.

11. If $0.1q - 0.2(3q + 4) = -0.3(5q + 3)$, what is q?

    A. 0.01
    B. 0.05
    C. 0.85
    D. −0.1

★ Spotlighted Item: **FILL-IN-THE-BLANK**

DIRECTIONS: Read each question. Then fill in your answer in the box below.

12. What value of *y* makes the equation true?

$$\frac{1}{2}(7y - 4) + y = 3y - \frac{1}{2}(6 - 5y)$$

y = [ ]

13. Solve the equation for *k*.

$$8k(4 - 6) - 2k = 16(3 - k)$$

k = [ ]

14. The congruent sides of an isosceles triangle are 4 feet less than 3 times as long as the third side. The equation $P = x + 2(3x - 4)$ gives the perimeter of the triangle. If the perimeter is 9.5 feet, what is the length of the third side?

[ ] feet

15. Solve the following equation for *a*.

$$4(2.25a + 0.75) = 12(2a + 3)$$

a = [ ]

16. What is the value of *z*?

$$-\frac{1}{5}(z + 12) = \frac{2}{5}(9 - 3z)$$

z = [ ]

17. A swimming pool with an initial volume of 9,250 gallons is emptying at a rate of 50 gallons per minute. The equation $w = 9{,}250 - 60(50t)$ represents the amount of water that remains in the pool after *t* hours. For how many hours has the pool been emptying if 5,500 gallons of water remain in the pool?

[ ] hours

DIRECTIONS: Study the diagram, read the question, and choose the **best** answer.

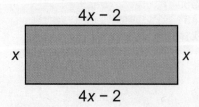

18. The perimeter *P* of the rectangle is equal to $2x + 2(4x - 2)$. If the rectangle has a perimeter of 35 inches, what is *x*?

A. 3.1
B. 3.9
C. 4
D. 4.2

DIRECTIONS: Read each question, and choose the **best** answer.

19. What is the value of *y*?

$$10y - 12 = 5(2y + 3) - y$$

A. −27
B. 27
C. −15
D. 15

20. Solve the following equation for *t*.

$$4\left(\frac{1}{8}t + 2\right) = 2(t - 8) - \frac{1}{2}t$$

A. 8
B. 12
C. 16
D. 24

UNIT 3

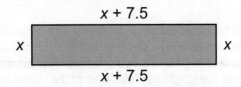

$x + 7.5$

x x

$x + 7.5$

21. The length of fencing around a garden with width x feet and length $x + 7.5$ feet is given by $f = 2x + 2(x + 7.5)$. If a total of 65 feet of fencing is used, what is the value of x?

   A. 12.5
   B. 14.375
   C. 18.125
   D. 20

DIRECTIONS: Read each question, and choose the **best** answer.

22. Keira is solving the equation $4(3x - 5) = -2(x + 7)$. She applies the distributive property and finds that $12x - 20 = -2x - 14$. Next, she groups together the variable terms and finds that $ax - 20 = -14$. What is the value of a?

   A. 6
   B. 10
   C. 14
   D. 26

23. Quentin solved the equation $0.5(7y - 6) = 2(2y + 1)$. His solution is shown in the table.

Step 1	$3.5y - 3 = 4y + 2$
Step 2	$-0.5y - 3 = 2$
Step 3	$-0.5y = -1$
Step 4	$y = 2$

In which step did Quentin make an error?

   A. Step 1
   B. Step 2
   C. Step 3
   D. Step 4

DIRECTIONS: Read each question, and choose the **best** answer.

24. Solve the following equation for b.

$10 - 3(2b + 4) = -4b - 2(5 - b)$

   A. −2
   B. 1
   C. 2
   D. 6

25. Lisa solved the equation $\frac{1}{4}(2x + 12) = 3(\frac{1}{4}x - 2)$. Her solution is shown in the table.

Step 1	$\frac{2}{4}x + 3 = \frac{3}{4}x - 2$
Step 2	$-\frac{1}{4}x + 3 = -2$
Step 3	$-\frac{1}{4}x = -5$
Step 4	$x = 20$

In which step did Lisa make an error?

   A. Step 1
   B. Step 2
   C. Step 3
   D. Step 4

26. What value of n makes the equation true?

$0.2(6n + 5) = 0.5(2n - 8) + 3$

   A. −10
   B. −6
   C. −4
   D. 0

27. If $3w - 2(0.5w + 1) = -4(2 + w)$, what is w?

   A. −6
   B. −1.5
   C. −1
   D. 3

28. Solve the following equation for x.

$2x + 3(5 - x) - 12 = 4(x + 2)$

   A. −2.4
   B. −1
   C. 0.2
   D. 1.4

Two-Variable Linear Equations

Use with *Student Book* pp. 62–63

MATH CONTENT TOPICS: Q.2.a, Q.2.e, Q.6.c, A.2.a, A.2.b, A.2.d
MATH PRACTICES: MP.1.a, MP.1.b, MP.1.e, MP.2.a, MP.2.c, MP.3.a, MP.4.a, MP.5.a, MP.5.c

1 Review the Skill

A system of **two-variable linear equations** may be solved by substitution or by linear combination. The solution is an ordered pair. To solve using **substitution**, solve one equation for one variable, substitute that value into the other equation, and solve for the second variable. To solve using **linear combination**, or elimination, multiply one or both equations by a factor so that the coefficients of one of the variables are opposites and cancel one another out.

If neither variable in the system has coefficients that are multiples of each other, find the **lowest common multiple** (LCM) of the coefficients of one variable. Then multiply each equation by a factor that results in a coefficient for that variable that is equal to the LCM.

2 Refine the Skill

By refining the skill of solving two-variable linear equations, you will improve your study and test-taking abilities, especially as they relate to the GED® Mathematical Reasoning Test. Study the information below. Then answer the questions that follow.

a The lowest common multiple (LCM) of 3 and 5 is 15. Multiply the first equation by 5 and the second equation by 3 to obtain y-coefficients that are opposites.

Solve the system of equations

$$\begin{cases} 2x + 3y = 7 \\ 3x - 5y = 1 \end{cases}$$

$$\begin{array}{l} 5(2x + 3y = 7) \longrightarrow 10x + 15y = 35 \\ 3(3x - 5y = 1) \longrightarrow \underline{9x - 15y = 3} \\ 19x + 0y = 38 \\ \dfrac{19x}{19} = \dfrac{38}{19} \\ x = 2 \end{array}$$

Substitute $x = 2$ and solve for y:
$$2x + 3y = 7$$
$$2(2) + 3y = 7$$
$$4 + 3y = 7$$
$$3y = 3$$
$$y = 1$$

b This system also could be solved by finding the LCM of the x-coefficients. The LCM of 2 and 3 is 6. Since both coefficients are positive, multiply one equation by a negative factor to result in coefficients that are opposites. Either multiply the first equation by 3 and the second equation by −2, or multiply the first equation by −3 and the second equation by 2.

c To solve the system in question 2, first write the equations in the form $Ax + By = C$. It is easier to work with the coefficients if the variables and constants are lined up in columns.

CONTENT TOPICS

Content Topic A.2.d includes solving a system of two linear equations by graphing, substitution, or linear combination. This lesson focuses on algebraic methods. You will learn about graphical methods in Lesson 9 of this unit.

1. What is the solution of the sytem of equations?

$$\begin{cases} 3x + 2y = -5 \\ 4x - 3y = -18 \end{cases}$$

A. (−3, 2)
B. (−2, 3)
C. (2, −3)
D. (3, −2)

c 2. What ordered pair is the solution of $\begin{cases} 3x - 2y = 7 \\ 7x + 3y - 1 = 0 \end{cases}$?

A. (−3, 1)
B. (−1, 2)
C. (1, −2)
D. (3, −1)

DIRECTIONS: Read each question, and choose the **best** answer.

3. Solve the system of linear equations.

$$\begin{cases} 2x + y = 13 \\ 4x - y = 17 \end{cases}$$

A. (2, 9)
B. (4, 5)
C. (4, −1)
D. (5, 3)

4. What is the solution of the system?

$$\begin{cases} 3x - 2y = 14 \\ x + 4y = -14 \end{cases}$$

A. (−2, −3)
B. (0, −7)
C. (2, −4)
D. (6, 2)

5. Solve the system.

$$\begin{cases} 6x - 2y = -10 \\ 4x + y + 2 = 0 \end{cases}$$

A. (−1, 2)
B. (0, −2)
C. (3, 14)
D. (2, 11)

DIRECTIONS: Study the system, read each question, and choose the **best** answer.

$$\begin{cases} 2x - 3y = 8 \\ 5x + 4y = -3 \end{cases}$$

6. By what factors could each equation be multiplied in order to solve the system by linear combination?

A. First equation by 2; second equation by 5
B. First equation by 3; second equation by 4
C. First equation by 3; second equation by 8
D. First equation by 4; second equation by 3

7. What is the solution of the system above?

A. (−2, −4)
B. (1, −2)
C. (4, 3)
D. (5, 1)

DIRECTIONS: Read each question, and choose the **best** answer.

8. Darnell solved the following system by linear combination.

$$\begin{cases} 4x - 5y = -7 \\ 7x - 3y = 5 \end{cases}$$

After multiplying each equation by a factor and adding the new equations together, Darnell has the equation −23x = −46. By what factors did Darnell multiply the two equations?

A. First equation by 3; second equation by −5
B. First equation by 3; second equation by 5
C. First equation by 7; second equation by −4
D. First equation by 7, second equation by 4

9. What is the solution of the following system?

$$\begin{cases} 4x - 5y = -6 \\ 3x + 2y = -16 \end{cases}$$

A. (2, −4)
B. (1, 2)
C. (−4, −2)
D. (4, 1)

DIRECTIONS: Study the table, read the question, and choose the **best** answer.

TICKET PRICES

	Adult	Child
Afternoon Show	$15	$8
Evening Show	$22	$16

10. A community group is planning a trip to the theater. There are *a* adults and *c* children in the group. An afternoon show will cost a total of $308. An evening show will cost a total of $520. The system of equations below represents the total cost for each show.

$$\begin{cases} 15a + 8c = 308 \\ 22a + 16c = 520 \end{cases}$$

How many adults will attend the show?

A. 12
B. 16
C. 24
D. 28

DIRECTIONS: Read each question, and choose the **best** answer.

11. Solve the system of linear equations.

$$\begin{cases} 2x - y = 3 \\ 3x - 2y = 2 \end{cases}$$

A. (5, 7)
B. (3, 2)
C. (−4, −5)
D. (4, 5)

12. Solve the following system.

$$\begin{cases} 4x + 2y = 2 \\ 2x - 2y = 10 \end{cases}$$

A. (2, 3)
B. (−2, 3)
C. (2, −3)
D. (−2, −3)

13. Solve the system of linear equations.

$$\begin{cases} 3x + 4y = 18 \\ 5x - 2y + 22 = 0 \end{cases}$$

A. (10, −3)
B. (−2, 6)
C. (−4, 1)
D. (2, −6)

14. What values of x and y make the following system true?

$$\begin{cases} 7x + 5y = -2 \\ 3x - 4y = -7 \end{cases}$$

A. (−1, 1)
B. (1, −1)
C. (4, −6)
D. (7, 7)

15. Solve the system of linear equations.

$$\begin{cases} 4x + 5y = 2 \\ 2x + 5y = -4 \end{cases}$$

A. (−2, 1)
B. (−2, 2)
C. (2, 6)
D. (3, −2)

DIRECTIONS: Read each question, and choose the **best** answer.

16. Liam solved the following system by linear combination.

$$\begin{cases} 9x - 4y = 2 \\ 5x - 3y = -2 \end{cases}$$

After multiplying each equation by a factor and adding the new equations together, Liam has the equation $7y = 28$. By what factors did Liam multiply the two equations?

A. First equation by −5; second equation by 9
B. First equation by −3; second equation by 4
C. First equation by 3, second equation by −4
D. First equation by 5; second equation by −9

17. Solve the system.

$$\begin{cases} 10x + 3y = 8 \\ 4x - 2y = 16 \end{cases}$$

A. (−5, −2)
B. (−2, 4)
C. (2, −4)
D. (5, 2)

18. Scott and Craig are solving the system below.

$$\begin{cases} 3x - 8y = 27 \\ 5x - 6y = 23 \end{cases}$$

Scott solves the system by multiplying the first equation by 5 and the second equation by −3. Craig solves the system by multiplying the first equation by 3 and the second equation by −4. Who is correct?

A. Craig
B. Scott
C. Both Craig and Scott
D. Neither Craig nor Scott

19. Solve the system.

$$\begin{cases} 2x - 3y = 7 \\ 4x + 6y = 26 \end{cases}$$

A. (5, 1)
B. (3, 2)
C. (2, 3)
D. (−1, 5)

Hannah used the steps below to solve the following system of equations:

$$\begin{cases} 5x + 4y = -2 \\ 2x + 3y = -5 \end{cases}$$

Step 1:	$3(5x + 4y = -2) \longrightarrow 15x + 12y = -6$ $-4(2x + 3y = -5) \longrightarrow -8x - 12y = 20$
Step 2:	$7x = -14$ $x = -2$
Step 3:	$5(-2) + 4y = -2$ $-10 + 4y = -2$
Step 4:	$4y = 8$ $y = 2$

20. In which step did Hannah make an error?

   A. Step 1
   B. Step 2
   C. Step 3
   D. Step 4

DIRECTIONS: Study the table, read the question, and choose the **best** answer.

OFFICE SUPPLY PRICES

	Paper (ream)	Pens (box of 12)
Regular Price	$7	$5
Sale Price	$4	$3

21. An office manager is ordering supplies. She needs r reams of paper and b boxes of pens. If she orders the supplies today, she will get the sale price and will spend a total of $205, before tax. If she misses the sale, she will spend a total of $355, before tax. The system of equations below represents the total cost during and after the sale.

$$\begin{cases} 4r + 3b = 205 \\ 7r + 5b = 355 \end{cases}$$

How many reams of paper will the office manager order?

   A. 15
   B. 20
   C. 30
   D. 40

DIRECTIONS: Read each question, and choose the **best** answer.

22. What is the solution of the system?

$$\begin{cases} 2x + 2y = 6 \\ 5y = 19 - 4x \end{cases}$$

   A. (-7, -4)
   B. (-4, 7)
   C. (4, -7)
   D. (7, -4)

23. Solve the system.

$$\begin{cases} 7x + 2y = -11 \\ 3x + 5y = 16 \end{cases}$$

   A. (-3, 5)
   B. (2, -2)
   C. (2, 2)
   D. (3, -5)

24. Yasmine is buying two types of flooring for her house. She needs a total of 1,200 square feet of flooring. Carpeting costs $3 per square foot. Hardwood costs $8 per square foot. The flooring will cost a total of $5,600. The system below represents the number of square feet of carpeting c and hardwood h Yasmine will buy. How many square feet of each type of flooring will Yasmine buy?

$$\begin{cases} c + h = 1,200 \\ 3c + 8h = 5,600 \end{cases}$$

   A. carpet = 400 sq ft; hardwood = 800 sq ft
   B. carpet = 500 sq ft; hardwood = 700 sq ft
   C. carpet = 600 sq ft; hardwood = 600 sq ft
   D. carpet = 800 sq ft; hardwood = 400 sq ft

25. In the system below, the variable a represents an integer.

$$\begin{cases} 9x + ay = 25 \\ 5x + 4y = 14 \end{cases}$$

If $x = 2$, what is the value of a?

   A. 1
   B. 2
   C. 5
   D. 7

Factoring

Use with *Student Book* pp. 64–65

MATH CONTENT TOPICS: Q.2.a, Q.2.e, Q.3.a, Q.4.a, Q.5.a, A.1.a, A.1.f, A.1.g, A.4.a, A.4.b
MATH PRACTICES: MP.1.a, MP.1.b. MP.1.e, MP.2.a, MP.2.c, MP.4.a, MP.4.b

1 Review the Skill

Factors are numbers or expressions that you multiply to form a product. Factors may have just one term (6 or 6x), two terms (for example, 6x + 4), or more than two terms. You can use the **FOIL method** to find the products of two factors with two terms apiece. With FOIL, multiply the *First*, *Outer*, *Inner*, and *Last* terms in that order.

Quadratic equations can be written in the form $ax^2 + bx + c = 0$, so that a, b, and c are integers and a does not equal zero. You can solve quadratic equations by factoring them into two, two-term factors and setting each factor to zero. Quadratic equations also can be solved by substituting a, b, and c into the quadratic formula that appears on the GED® Mathematical Reasoning Test.

2 Refine the Skill

By refining the skill of writing and solving equations by using factors, you will improve your study and test-taking abilities, especially as they relate to the GED® Mathematical Reasoning Test. Study the diagram and information below. Then answer the questions that follow.

a The equation for the area of the rug is a quadratic equation. Set it equal to zero to solve.

A rectangular area rug is shown in the diagram. The length of the rug is 2 feet less than the width. The area of the rug is 48 square feet.

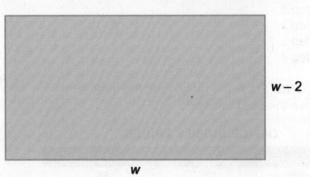

b The solutions for w are 8 and −6. The width of a rug cannot be negative, so w = 8 feet.

USING LOGIC

The FOIL method can be used to simplify (4 + x) (3 − x), but it is not needed to simplify (4x)(3x). The expression (4x)(3x) means 4x times 3x, which equals 12x^2.

a 1. Which equation represents the area of the rug?

    A. $w^2 = 48$
    B. $w^2 + 2w − 48 = 0$
    C. $w^2 − 2w − 48 = 0$
    D. $2w − 2 = 48$

2. What is the width, in feet, of the rug?

    A. −8
    B. −6
    C. 6
    D. 8

DIRECTIONS: Read each question, and choose the **best** answer.

3. Which of the following could be a value for z in the equation below?

   $(z - 3)^2 = 10$

   A. 3.3
   B. $\sqrt{10} + 3$
   C. 7
   D. 13

4. What is the product of $(x + 5)(x - 4)$?

   A. $x^2 + x + 20$
   B. $x^2 + 9x - 20$
   C. $x^2 + x - 20$
   D. $x^2 - x - 20$

5. The side of a square is represented by $x - 4$. What expression represents the area of the square?

   A. $x^2 + 16$
   B. $x^2 - 16$
   C. $x^2 - 8x - 16$
   D. $x^2 - 8x + 16$

6. The length of a rectangle is represented by $x + 2$ and the width of the rectangle is represented by $x - 5$. Which expression represents the area of the rectangle?

   A. $x^2 - 3x - 10$
   B. $x^2 - 10x - 3$
   C. $x^2 + 3x - 10$
   D. $x^2 + 3x + 10$

7. Which pair of solutions makes the quadratic equation $x^2 - 16 = 0$ true?

   A. −4 and 1
   B. −4 and 2
   C. −4 and 4
   D. 2 and −8

DIRECTIONS: Read each question, and choose the **best** answer.

8. The number of students in a classroom is 5 less than the number of pencils each student has. If x represents the number of students in the room, which expression represents the total number of pencils in the room?

   A. $x^2 - 5$
   B. $x^2 + 5x$
   C. $x^2 - 5x$
   D. $x^2 + 5$

9. Which expression is the same as $x^2 - 4x - 21$?

   A. $(x + 3)(x - 7)$
   B. $(x - 3)(x + 7)$
   C. $(x + 1)(x - 21)$
   D. $(x - 1)(x + 21)$

10. In the equation $x^2 + 8x - 20 = 0$, which of the following is a possible value of x?

    A. −10
    B. −8
    C. 8
    D. 10

11. If the area of a square is represented by $x^2 + 6x + 9$, which expression represents one side of the square?

    A. $x + 1$
    B. $x + 3$
    C. $x + 6$
    D. $x + 9$

12. The product of two consecutive integers is 42. Which quadratic equation could be solved to find the value of the first integer?

    A. $x^2 + 2x - 42 = 0$
    B. $x^2 + x - 42 = 0$
    C. $x^2 - 42x = 0$
    D. $x^2 - x + 42 = 0$

DIRECTIONS: Read each question, and choose the **best** answer.

13. The area of the square shown below is 49 square feet. What is the value of x?

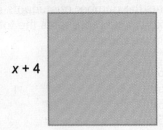

x + 4

A. −11
B. −3
C. 0
D. 3

14. The sum of the squares of two consecutive integers is 113. What are the two integers?

A. 4 and 5
B. 5 and 6
C. 6 and 7
D. 7 and 8

15. The product of two consecutive odd integers is 35. What is the second integer?

A. 7
B. 5
C. 3
D. 1

16. The product of two consecutive even positive integers is 48. Which quadratic equation could be solved to find the value of the first integer?

A. $x^2 + 4x − 48 = 0$
B. $x^2 + x − 48 = 0$
C. $x^2 − 48x = 0$
D. $x^2 + 2x − 48 = 0$

17. The length of a rectangle is 4 feet greater than its width. The area of a rectangle is 165 square feet. What is the length of the rectangle?

A. 11 feet
B. 13 feet
C. 15 feet
D. 19 feet

DIRECTIONS: Read each question, and choose the **best** answer.

18. A mini rocket is launched at 19.6 meters per second (m/s) from a 58.8-meter high launching pad for a class demonstration. The object's height h at time t seconds after launch can be represented by the equation $h = −4.9t^2 + 19.6t + 58.8$, where h is in meters. How much time will elapse before the projectile hits the ground?

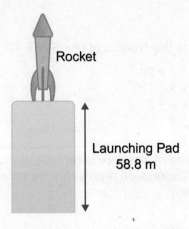

Rocket

Launching Pad
58.8 m

A. −2 s
B. 6 s
C. 5 s
D. 19.6 s

19. Hank is standing on a hotel balcony. He throws a ball to his friend on the street. The equation for the ball's height h at time t seconds after being thrown is $h = t^2 − 2t − 8$. How many seconds does it take the ball to reach the ground, or a height of 0?

A. 1
B. −2
C. 4
D. 8

20. Which of the following expressions result from the expansion of $(x + 6)^2$?

A. $x^2 + 12x + 12$
B. $x^2 + 36x + 12$
C. $x^2 + 12x + 6$
D. $x^2 + 12x + 36$

⭐ Spotlighted Item: **FILL-IN-THE-BLANK**

DIRECTIONS: Read the information and each question. Then fill in your answer in the box below.

A small agriculture-based company has created an equation to model its monthly revenues, where R represents the money made after all expenses, and x represents the kilograms of products sold.

$$R = x^2 + 20x - 300$$

21. If the company earned $809,600 last month, about how many kilograms of product were sold?

22. In a particularly bad month, when no products are sold, how much money does the company lose?

23. What is the revenue when 100 kg of product are sold ?

DIRECTIONS: Read each question, and choose the **best** answer.

24. While on vacation, Brian jumps off a 160-ft cliff into the sparkling blue waters below. At the same time, his friend tosses a ball over the cliff at 48 ft per second. The equation of the height (h) above water is represented by the equations below.

Brian: $h(t) = -16t^2 + 160$
Ball: $h(t) = -16t^2 - 48t + 160$

If both Brian and the ball leave the cliff at the same time, which of the following represents the difference in landing times?

A. 2 s
B. $(\sqrt{10} - 2)$ s
C. 10 s − 5 s
D. 5 s

25. Jimmy uses a ball of yarn to make an outline of a right angle triangle. The shorter leg is 6 units less than the longer leg. The hypotenuse is 6 units less than twice the shorter side. How long is the ball of yarn?

A. 24 units
B. 30 units
C. 144 units
D. 72 units

DIRECTIONS: Read each question, and choose the **best** answer.

26. Which of the following expressions results from the expansion of $(x - 8)^2$?

A. $x^2 - 16x - 64$
B. $x^2 - 16x + 64$
C. $x^2 - 8x$
D. 64

27. The area of the rectangle is 84 square feet. What is the longer side of the rectangle?

$w + 8$

A. 6 feet
B. 14 feet
C. 28 feet
D. 36 feet

Rational Expressions and Equations

Use with **Student Book** pp. 66–67

UNIT 3

1 Review the Skill

MATH CONTENT TOPICS: Q.2.a, Q.2.e, A.1.a, A.1.f, A.1.h
MATH PRACTICES: MP.1.a, MP.1.b, MP.1.d, MP.1.e, MP.2.a, MP.2.c, MP.3.a, MP.3.c, MP.4.a, MP.4.b, MP.5.a, MP.5.c

A **rational number** is a number written as $\frac{a}{b}$, where a and b are integers and $b \neq 0$. A **rational expression** is a fraction whose numerator, denominator, or both are nonzero polynomials. A rational expression is in its simplified form if its numerator and denominator have no common factors other than 1. A **rational equation** is an equation that contains rational expressions.

Completely factor each expression and divide out common terms from the numerator and denominator before adding, subtracting, multiplying, or dividing. Identify common terms in denominators to identify the lowest common denominator.

2 Refine the Skill

By refining the skills of performing operations with rational expressions and solving rational equations, you will improve your study and test-taking abilities, especially as they relate to the GED® Mathematical Reasoning Test. Study the information below. Then answer the questions that follow.

a To factor the quadratic trinomial $x^2 + bx + c$, find the numbers p and q so that $p + q = b$ and $pq = c$. Then, the factors are $(x + p)$ and $(x + q)$. In this example, $2 + 3 = 5$ and $(2)(3) = 6$, so the factors of $x^2 + 5x + 6$ are $(x + 2)$ and $(x + 3)$. Since the denominator of one expression is a factor of the denominator of the other expression, it is easier to see that the lowest common denominator is $(x + 2)(x + 3)$.

Factor to Find the Lowest Common Denominator (LCD)

$$\frac{4}{x + 2} - \frac{3x}{x^2 + 5x + 6} = \frac{4}{x + 2} - \frac{3x}{(x + 2)(x + 3)}$$

$$= \frac{4(x + 3)}{(x + 2)(x + 3)} - \frac{3x}{(x + 2)(x + 3)}$$

$$= \frac{4(x + 3) - 3x}{(x + 2)(x + 3)}$$

$$= \frac{4x + 12 - 3x}{(x + 2)(x + 3)}$$

$$= \frac{x + 12}{(x + 2)(x + 3)}$$

b Simplify a sum or difference by using the distributive property and then combining like terms. Simplify a product or quotient by factoring and dividing out common factors.

c To answer question 1, begin by factoring the numerator and denominator of each expression. Cancel out common terms to simplify each rational expression. Then, find the LCD of the simplified expressions.

MAKING ASSUMPTIONS

Recall that if $\frac{a}{b} = \frac{c}{d}$, then $ad = bc$. Similarly, if each side of a rational equation is a single fraction, then cross-multiplying can be used to solve the equation.

1. Simplify $\frac{3}{x + 1} + \frac{x - 2}{x^2 - 4}$.

A. $\frac{1}{(x + 2)}$

B. $\frac{1}{(x + 2)(x - 2)}$

C. $\frac{4x + 7}{(x + 1)(x + 2)}$

D. $\frac{4x^2 - x - 4}{(x + 1)(x^2 - 4)}$

2. Solve $\frac{5}{y - 1} = \frac{-10}{y^2 + 5y - 6}$.

A. −8

B. −7

C. −2

D. 1

DIRECTIONS: Study the information, read each question, and choose the **best** answer.

$$\frac{4x}{x^2 - 6x + 9} - \frac{3}{x - 3}$$

3. What is the lowest common denominator of the rational expressions?

   A. $(x - 3)$
   B. $(x - 3)(x + 3)$
   C. $(x - 3)(x - 3)$
   D. $(x - 3)(x^2 - 6x + 9)$

4. What is the numerator of the simplified difference of the rational expressions?

   A. $x + 9$
   B. $4x - 3$
   C. $7x - 9$
   D. $x^2 + 6x - 27$

DIRECTIONS: Read each question, and choose the **best** answer.

5. Simplify $\dfrac{x - 2}{x^2 + x - 6} + \dfrac{4x}{x + 3}$.

   A. $\dfrac{4x + 1}{x + 3}$
   B. $\dfrac{5x - 2}{x + 3}$
   C. $\dfrac{5x + 3}{x + 3}$
   D. $\dfrac{4x + 1}{(x + 3)(x - 2)}$

6. Simplify $\dfrac{x^2 - 16}{x} \div \dfrac{x^2 - x - 12}{x + 3}$.

   A. $\dfrac{x - 4}{x}$
   B. $\dfrac{x + 4}{x}$
   C. $\dfrac{x^2 - 16}{x(x - 4)}$
   D. $\dfrac{(x + 4)(x - 4)(x - 4)}{x}$

7. Solve $\dfrac{5}{x} + \dfrac{x + 1}{3x + 3} = \dfrac{2}{x}$.

   A. $x = -9$
   B. $x = -3$
   C. $x = 2$
   D. $x = 21$

DIRECTIONS: Read each question, and choose the **best** answer.

8. Evan simplified the expression $\dfrac{12 - 3x}{x^2 + 5x + 4}$.

   The steps of his solution are shown below.

Step 1	$\dfrac{12 - 3x}{x^2 + 5x + 4} = \dfrac{3(4 - x)}{(x + 1)(x + 4)}$
Step 2	$\dfrac{3(4 - x)}{(x + 1)(x + 4)} = \dfrac{-3(x + 4)}{(x + 1)(x + 4)}$
Step 3	$\dfrac{-3(x + 4)}{(x + 1)(x + 4)} = \dfrac{-3\cancel{(x + 4)}}{(x + 1)\cancel{(x + 4)}}$
Step 4	$\dfrac{12 - 3x}{x^2 + 5x + 4} = \dfrac{-3}{(x + 1)}$

   In which step did Evan make an error?

   A. Step 1
   B. Step 2
   C. Step 3
   D. Step 4

9. Solve $\dfrac{2}{x + 3} + \dfrac{2}{x - 3} = \dfrac{20}{x^2 - 9}$.

   A. $x = 2$
   B. $x = 3$
   C. $x = 5$
   D. $x = 10$

10. Simplify $\dfrac{8x}{x^2 + 10x + 16} \cdot (x + 2)$.

    A. $\dfrac{x}{x + 1}$
    B. $\dfrac{8x}{x + 8}$
    C. $\dfrac{8x^2 + 16x}{x + 8}$
    D. $\dfrac{8x(x + 2)}{x^2 + 10x + 16}$

11. Alicia has an average of 85% on her first four math tests. She wants to raise her average to 90% by scoring 100% on the next x math tests. The equation $0.90 = \dfrac{4(0.85) + 1.00x}{4 + x}$ represents the situation. On how many tests will Alicia need to score 100%?

    A. 2
    B. 3
    C. 4
    D. 5

DIRECTIONS: Study the information, read each question, and choose the **best** answer.

$$\frac{x}{5} + 1 = \frac{12}{2x + 8}$$

12. What is the lowest common denominator for the equation?

    A. $x + 4$
    B. $2x + 8$
    C. $5(x + 4)$
    D. $5(2x + 8)$

13. What is the value of x in the equation?

    A. $x = -1$ or $x = 10$
    B. $x = 1$ or $x = -10$
    C. $x = -3$ or $x = 5$
    D. $x = 3$ or $x = -5$

DIRECTIONS: Read each question, and choose the **best** answer.

14. Emma and Marco are finding the sum of the following rational expressions.

    $$\frac{x^2 - 25}{x^2 + 7x + 10} + \frac{4x + 8}{x^2 + 4x - 5}$$

    Emma says the lowest common denominator is $(x + 5)(x + 2)(x - 1)$. Marco says it is $(x - 1)$. Which explains who is correct?

    A. Emma is correct, because the common factor of $(x + 5)$ can be divided out of the numerator and denominator of the first addend.
    B. Marco is correct, because the constant term in the factor $(x - 1)$ is the least of the constant terms among the factors of the denominators.
    C. Emma is correct, because the common factor of $(x + 5)$ can be divided out of the numerator of the first addend and the denominator of the second addend.
    D. Marco is correct, because the common factors of $(x + 5)$ and $(x + 2)$ can be divided out of one of the numerators and at least one of the denominators.

15. Solve for x in $3 + \dfrac{4}{x - 6} = \dfrac{x + 6}{x^2 - 36}$.

    A. 10
    B. 6
    C. 5
    D. 4

DIRECTIONS: Read each question, and choose the **best** answer.

16. Simplify $\dfrac{x^2 + 2x - 15}{7x^2} \div (x - 3)$.

    A. $\dfrac{x + 5}{7x^2}$
    B. $\dfrac{(x + 5)(x - 3)}{7x^2}$
    C. $\dfrac{(x + 3)(x - 5)}{7x^2}$
    D. $\dfrac{x - 5}{7x^2}$

17. Simplify $\dfrac{x^2 - 25}{x^2 + 9x + 20} - \dfrac{2}{x + 4}$.

    A. $\dfrac{x - 7}{x + 4}$
    B. $\dfrac{x - 3}{x - 4}$
    C. $\dfrac{(x + 5)(x - 5)}{(x - 4)(x + 5)}$
    D. $\dfrac{x - 3}{x + 4}$

18. Solve $\dfrac{3}{x + 2} + \dfrac{2}{6x + 12} = \dfrac{5}{6}$.

    A. -6
    B. -2
    C. 2
    D. 6

19. Solve for x in $\dfrac{3}{x - 3} + 1 = \dfrac{4}{x^2 - 9}$.

    A. $1, -4$
    B. $3, -5$
    C. $-5, -3$
    D. $-1, 4$

20. Solve for x in $\dfrac{x + 2}{x - 6} = \dfrac{3x - 29}{x^2 - 13x + 42}$.

    A. $-3, -5$
    B. $3, -5$
    C. $-3, 5$
    D. $3, 5$

21. Simplify $\dfrac{(8x^2 - 18)}{(x^2 - 1)} \cdot \dfrac{(3x - 3)}{(4x + 6)}$.

    A. $\dfrac{3(2x - 3)}{(x + 1)}$
    B. $\dfrac{3(2x + 3)}{(x - 1)}$
    C. $\dfrac{6(2x - 3)}{(x + 1)}$
    D. $\dfrac{6(2x + 3)}{(x - 1)}$

22. Which of the following equations has a lowest common denominator of $(x + 4)(x - 3)$?

    A. $\dfrac{7}{2x + 8} + 1 = \dfrac{3}{3x - 9}$

    B. $\dfrac{2x - 4}{x^2 + 2x - 8} = \dfrac{3}{x + 4}$

    C. $\dfrac{x + 3}{x^2 - 9} = \dfrac{x + 5}{x^2 + 2x - 15}$

    D. $\dfrac{6}{3x + 12} + 2 = \dfrac{x^2 - 16}{x^2 + x - 12}$

23. In the simplified expressions below, a and b are integers and the lowest common denominator is $(x + a)(x + b)$.

    $$\dfrac{n}{(x + a)} + \dfrac{m}{(x + b)}$$

    Which expression, when added to the expressions above, would necessarily change the lowest common denominator?

    A. $\dfrac{2(x + b)}{(x - b)}$

    B. $\dfrac{(x - a)^2}{(x^2 - a)}$

    C. $\dfrac{(x + b)}{(x + b)^2}$

    D. $\dfrac{2(x - a)}{2x + 2a}$

24. A chemist has 100 mL of a 10% alcohol solution. She needs a 15% alcohol solution to perform an experiment. The equation below represents the number of milliliters, m, of a 25% alcohol solution that the chemist must add to the 10% alcohol solution in order to produce a 15% alcohol solution.

    $$0.15 = \dfrac{0.1(100) + 0.25m}{100 + m}$$

    How many milliliters of the 25% alcohol solution must the chemist add?

    A. 25
    B. 50
    C. 125
    D. 250

DIRECTIONS: Read each question, and choose the **best** answer.

25. Simplify $\dfrac{x^2 + 4x}{3x + 12} - \dfrac{4x}{x + 7}$.

    A. $\dfrac{-(x^2 + 3)}{x + 7}$

    B. $\dfrac{x^2 - 5x}{3x + 7}$

    C. $\dfrac{x^2 - 5x}{3x + 21}$

    D. $\dfrac{7 - 11x}{3x + 21}$

26. Simplify $\dfrac{x^2 + 6x - 16}{3x + 15} \cdot \dfrac{x^2 - 25}{x^2 - 4x + 4}$.

    A. $\dfrac{(x + 8)(x - 5)}{3}$

    B. $\dfrac{(x + 8)(x + 5)}{3(x - 2)}$

    C. $\dfrac{(x + 8)(x - 5)}{3(x - 2)}$

    D. $\dfrac{(x + 8)(x^2 - 25)}{(3x + 15)(x - 2)}$

27. What is the numerator of the simplified expression

    $$\dfrac{2}{5x - 10} + \dfrac{x + 1}{x^2 - 7x + 10} + \dfrac{1}{2 - x}?$$

    A. $x + 4$
    B. $-2(x - 8)$
    C. $2x + 20$
    D. $5(x - 2)(x - 5)$

28. Rebecca solved the equation $\dfrac{x}{x - 3} + \dfrac{1}{5} = \dfrac{3}{x - 3}$.

    The steps of her solution are shown in the table.

Step 1	$5(x - 3) \cdot \dfrac{x}{x - 3} + 5(x - 3) \cdot \dfrac{1}{5} = 5(x - 3) \cdot \dfrac{3}{x - 3}$
Step 2	$5x + (x - 15) = 5(3)$
Step 3	$6x = 30$
Step 4	$x = 5$

    In which step did Rebecca make an error?

    A. Step 1
    B. Step 2
    C. Step 3
    D. Step 4

Solving and Graphing Inequalities

Use with **Student Book** pp. 68–69

MATH CONTENT TOPICS: Q.2.a, Q.2.e, Q.4.a, Q.7.a, A.3.a, A.3.b, A.3.c, A.3.d
MATH PRACTICES: MP.1.a, MP.1.e, MP.2.a, MP.4.a, MP.4.b, MP.4.c

1 Review the Skill

An algebraic **inequality** states that two expressions are unequal. The expressions are separated by one of four symbols: greater than (>), less than (<), greater than or equal to (≥), or less than or equal to (≤). Inequalities are solved like equations. As you translate words into inequalities, remember that the inequality symbols always point to the lesser amount.

2 Refine the Skill

By refining the skills of solving and graphing inequalities, you will improve your study and test-taking abilities, especially as they relate to the GED® Mathematical Reasoning Test. Study the information below. Then answer the questions that follow.

a The formula for area is $A = l \times w$. Since the area must be at least 100 square feet, $l \times w$ can be greater than or equal to 100.

b In Question 2, the smallest width the plywood could have is the solution of the inequality.

Alex is using a rectangular piece of plywood to build a workbench. He wants the area of the workbench to be at least 100 square feet. The length of the plywood is 25 feet.

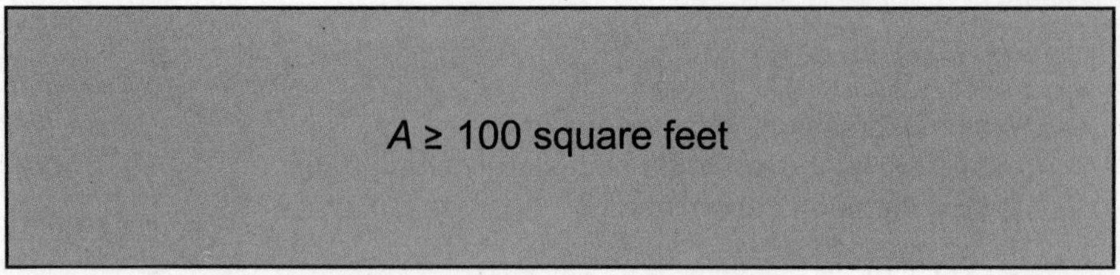

$A \geq 100$ square feet

25 feet

USING LOGIC

As you seek to graph inequalities on a number line, such as those on p. 95, you may wish to check your solution by substituting values for the variable. For example, if 3 is shaded on the number line, $x = 3$ should make the inequality true.

a 1. Which inequality could be solved to find the minimum width of the plywood?

A. $25 - w \leq 100$
B. $25 + w \geq 100$
C. $25w \leq 100$
D. $25w \geq 100$

b 2. What is the solution to the inequality?

A. $w \leq 4$
B. $w > 4$
C. $w \geq 4$
D. $w < 4$

DIRECTIONS: Read each question, and choose the **best** answer.

3. Which of the following inequalities is shown on the number line?

    A. $x \geq 3$
    B. $x \geq -3$
    C. $x \leq -3$
    D. $x > -3$

4. What is the solution to the inequality $x + 5 < 14$?

    A. $x < -9$
    B. $x \geq 19$
    C. $x \leq 19$
    D. $x < 9$

5. Which of the following inequalities is graphed on a number line using a closed circle?

    A. $x < 5$
    B. $x > -4$
    C. $x \geq -3$
    D. $x < -2$

6. Which shows the solution to the inequality $4(x - 1) \geq 8$?

    A.

    B. ![number line with open circle at 3, shaded left]

    C. ![number line with open circle at -1, shaded right]

    D. ![number line with closed circle at 3, shaded right]

7. What is the solution to the inequality $2x + 3 \geq 5x + 4$?

    A. $x < -\dfrac{1}{3}$
    B. $x \leq -\dfrac{1}{3}$
    C. $x \geq -3$
    D. $x < 3$

8. Which inequality is shown on the number line?

    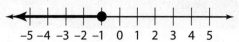

    A. $x > 1$
    B. $x \geq -1$
    C. $x < -1$
    D. $x \leq -1$

9. What is the solution to the inequality $2x - 7 \geq 15$?

    A. $x \geq 11$
    B. $x \geq 22$
    C. $x \leq 11$
    D. $x \leq 22$

10. When 4 times a number is added to 3, the result is greater than 2 less than 5 times that same number. Which of the following is the inequality?

    A. $4x + 3 > 5x - 2$
    B. $4x + 3 \geq 2 - 5x$
    C. $4x + 12 > 5x - 2$
    D. $4(x + 3) > 5(x - 2)$

11. Stacy pays $12 a month for basic cell phone service. Each minute she talks is an additional $0.10. If she budgets $25 a month for her cell phone bill, what is the maximum number of minutes she can talk each month?

    A. 12
    B. 120
    C. 130
    D. 1,300

12. Lydia purchased 3 gallons of milk. Her total was more than $9. What was the lowest possible price of 1 gallon of milk?

    A. $2.00
    B. $2.50
    C. $3.01
    D. $3.50

13. Dylan bowled two games and got scores of 122 and 118. He wants to bowl one more game and end up with an average of at least 124. Which inequality represents the score x that Dylan needs to get an average score of at least 124?

    A. $x \geq 132$
    B. $x \leq 132$
    C. $x \geq 240$
    D. $x \leq 240$

★ Spotlighted Item: **FILL-IN-THE-BLANK**

DIRECTIONS: Read each question. Then fill in your answer in the box below.

14. Complete the inequality that is shown on the number line.

x

15. Complete the inequality that is shown on the number line.

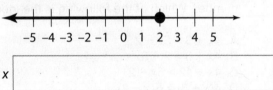

x

16. Solve the inequality $6x + 2 > 3x - 7$.

17. Solve the inequality $4y - 2 \leq 7y + 10$.

18. Kyle's pickup truck can carry a maximum load of 1,000 pounds. He wants to haul a load of cinderblocks that weigh 30 pounds each. Write an inequality that could be used to find how many cinderblocks Kyle can carry in his truck. Let c be the number of cinderblocks.

19. Matthew is training for a marathon. Today, he must jog and run a combined distance of more than 18 miles. He will run twice as far as he will jog. Write an inequality that could be used to find the minimum number of miles Matthew will jog. Let m be the number of miles.

20. Kiera is preparing a wall for a mural. She has enough white paint to cover an area of no more than 240 square feet. The mural will be 15 feet high. What is the maximum possible width of the mural?

feet

DIRECTIONS: Read each question, and choose the **best** answer.

21. Brit scored 45, 38, and 47 on her first three math quizzes. What is the minimum score she must earn on the fourth quiz to have an average quiz score of at least 44?

A. 43
B. 44
C. 45
D. 46

22. A store sold 156 football T-shirts. If the store has fewer than 34 of the T-shirts left, which expresses how many T-shirts the store had originally in terms of x?

A. $x \geq 190$
B. $x \leq 190$
C. $x > 190$
D. $x < 190$

23. Gabe makes a base salary of $1,500 per month. He also earns a 3% commission on all of his sales. What must the amount of his monthly sales be for him to earn at least $3,000 per month?

A. $50
B. $500
C. $5,000
D. $50,000

UNIT 3

24. In the second round of a card game, Allen scored less than 2 times the number of points that he scored in the first round. If he scored 10 points in the first round, which inequality shows the number of points that he could have scored in the second round?

    A. $y < 20$
    B. $y > 10$
    C. $y \leq 20$
    D. $y \geq 10$

25. A grocery store has spaghetti noodles on sale. The first box of noodles is $1.60. Each additional box is only $0.95. What is the maximum number of boxes of noodles Jax can buy with $4.50?

    A. 1
    B. 2
    C. 3
    D. 4

26. Alia wants to buy a new winter jacket and boots. The jacket costs $2\frac{1}{2}$ times more than the boots. If Alia cannot spend more than $157.50, what is the most she can spend on the boots?

    A. $37.50
    B. $45.00
    C. $63.00
    D. $112.50

27. The number of yards Michael swam on Tuesday was 400 less than 3 times the number of yards he swam on Monday. The number of yards he swam over the two days was less than 2,000. Which could be the number of yards Michael swam on Monday?

    A. 500
    B. 600
    C. 800
    D. 1,000

28. Jose's batting average last year was 0.266. Provided Jose has the same number of at-bats, what is the minimum batting average he can have this year to finish with a combined average of at least 0.300 over the two years?

    A. 0.283
    B. 0.334
    C. 0.366
    D. 0.444

29. Elena is taking a bus to visit a friend and is going to buy some reading material for the trip. She has $15 to spend and would like to buy one magazine and one book. The book costs $8.99. The sales tax is 6% of the purchase price. Which inequality represents the maximum price of a magazine that she could buy?

    A. $x \leq 15 - 1.06(8.99)$
    B. $x \leq 1.06(15 - 8.99)$
    C. $1.06x \leq 15 - 8.99$
    D. $1.06(8.99 + x) \leq 15$

30. The number of students who are enrolled in first-semester biology at a university is 30 fewer than twice as many as last year. If the enrollment for the class cannot exceed 100 students, what was the maximum number of students enrolled in the class last year?

    A. 35
    B. 65
    C. 70
    D. 100

31. A restaurant bill was less than $45. Three friends split the bill evenly. What is the greatest amount each friend could have paid?

    A. $11.99
    B. $12.99
    C. $13.99
    D. $14.99

32. In an English class, students must earn an average score of 80% or above on their written papers to earn at least a B in the class. Leah's scores on her first four papers are shown below.

    LEAH'S ENGLISH PAPER SCORES

Paper	Score (%)
1	78
2	85
3	82
4	74
5	?

    What is the minimum score Leah needs on her fifth and final paper to earn a B in the class?

    A. 79
    B. 80
    C. 81
    D. 82

The Coordinate Grid

Use with *Student Book* pp. 70–71

MATH CONTENT TOPICS: Q.2.a, A.5.a
MATH PRACTICES: MP.1.a, MP.1.d, MP.1.e, MP.3.a

1 Review the Skill

A **coordinate grid** provides a visual representation of points. These points, which include an *x*-value and a *y*-value, are known as **ordered pairs**. In an ordered pair, the *x*-value is always shown first. The grid itself is made by the intersection of a horizontal line (*x*-axis) and a vertical line (*y*-axis). The point where the number lines meet is called the **origin**, which is (0, 0).

Along with plotting points, coordinate grids help in drawing line segments and figures and performing **translations**, in which figures slide to a new position. The grid is divided into four **quadrants**, or sections. The upper-right section of a grid is the first quadrant. Move counterclockwise to name the remaining quadrants.

2 Refine the Skill

By refining the skills of locating and identifying points on the coordinate grid, you will improve your study and test-taking abilities, especially as they relate to the GED® Mathematical Reasoning Test. Study the grid below. Then answer the questions that follow.

Circle *G* is shown on the coordinate grid below.

a To find the coordinates of a point, start at the origin. Move along the *x*-axis to the *x*-coordinate and then along the *y*-axis to the *y*-coordinate.

b When you are asked to find a translation, pay close attention to the direction in which you are asked to translate the figure. This will determine which coordinate changes and whether it will increase or decrease.

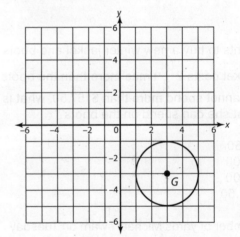

CONTENT TOPICS

Remember that the *x*-coordinate of an ordered pair is always written first. Also, remember that negative means *left* or *down*, and positive means *right* or *up*.

a 1. What are the coordinates of point *G*?

A. (3, −4)
B. (4, −3)
C. (−3, 3)
D. (3, −3)

b 2. If circle *G* and its center were translated up 1 unit and left 2 units, what would be the new location of point *G*?

A. (1, −2)
B. (−2, 1)
C. (4, −5)
D. (1, −4)

DIRECTIONS: Study the grid, read each question, and choose the **best** answer.

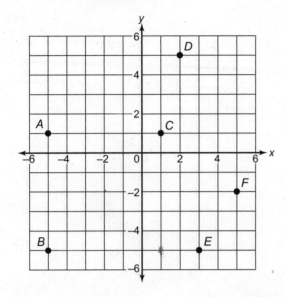

3. Which of the following ordered pairs identifies the location of point *D*?

   A. (2, 5)
   B. (5, 2)
   C. (−5, 2)
   D. (−2, −5)

4. Points *A*, *B*, and *C* mark three corners of a square. What is the location of the fourth corner needed to complete the square?

   A. (1, 5)
   B. (−5, −1)
   C. (−5, 1)
   D. (1, −5)

5. Points *C*, *F*, and *E* mark the corners of a rectangle. What is the location of the fourth corner needed to complete the rectangle?

   A. (−1, −3)
   B. (0, −2)
   C. (−2, −1)
   D. (−1, −2)

6. What is the new location of point *D* if it is translated 5 units down and 2 units to the right?

   A. (4, 0)
   B. (0, 4)
   C. (−3, 3)
   D. (0, 0)

7. If point *C* were the center of a circle and the circle were translated 2 units down, what would be the new location of point *C*?

   A. (−1, 1)
   B. (1, 3)
   C. (3, 1)
   D. (1, −1)

DIRECTIONS: Read each question, and choose the **best** answer.

8. Which of the following points is found in quadrant 2 of the coordinate grid?

   A. (2, 3)
   B. (−4, −3)
   C. (−2, 5)
   D. (1, −6)

9. Frank started at point (4, −3). He then moved down 1 and right 2. At which point did he land?

   A. (3, −1)
   B. (6, −4)
   C. (−4, 6)
   D. (−1, 3)

10. If point (*x*, −6) were translated 3 units down, what would be the new coordinates?

    A. (*x* − 3, −6)
    B. (*x* − 3, −9)
    C. (*x*, −9)
    D. (*x*, −3)

DIRECTIONS: Study the grid, read each question, and choose the **best** answer.

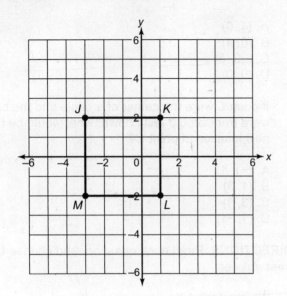

DIRECTIONS: Study the grid, read each question, and choose the **best** answer.

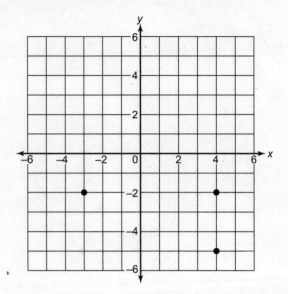

11. When square *JKLM* is translated 2 units up and 3 units to the right, the new location of point *J* is (0, 4). Which shows the new location of point *M*?

   A. (−1, −1)
   B. (0, 0)
   C. (0, −1)
   D. (0, −5)

12. Under a translation, the new point *M* is in the same location as the original point *K*. Which of the following describes the translation?

   A. 2 units up and 3 units to the right
   B. 3 units up and 3 units to the right
   C. 4 units up and 4 units to the right
   D. 5 units up and 4 units to the right

13. Point *N* is located in the center of square *JKLM*. When square *JKLM* is translated 1 unit up and 2 units to the left, what is the new location of point *N*?

   A. (−3, 1)
   B. (0, −2)
   C. (−1, 0)
   D. (1, 1)

14. Which of the following ordered pairs describes the location of a point that lies in the third quadrant?

   A. (2, 3)
   B. (−2, 3)
   C. (−3, −2)
   D. (3, −2)

15. The three points on the coordinate grid mark the corners of a rectangle. What is the location of the fourth corner needed to complete the figure?

   A. (4, −3)
   B. (−3, −4)
   C. (−3, −5)
   D. (−5, −3)

16. If you drew line segments to connect the three existing points on the coordinate grid, what figure would you draw?

   A. an equilateral triangle
   B. an obtuse triangle
   C. an isosceles triangle
   D. a right triangle

UNIT 3

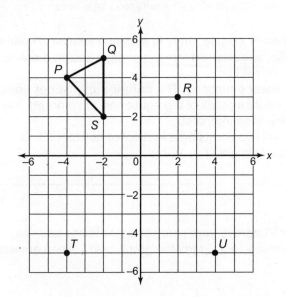

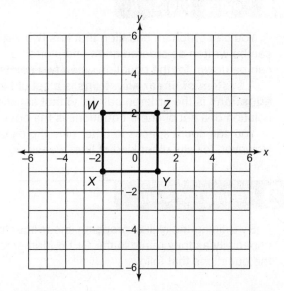

17. A point is translated down 2 units and ends at point *R*. How can you find the original location of the point?

    A. Add 2 units to the *x*-coordinate of point *R*.
    B. Add 2 units to the *y*-coordinate of point *R*.
    C. Subtract 2 units from the *x*-coordinate of point *R*.
    D. Subtract 2 units from the *y*-coordinate of point *R*.

18. Point *V* has the same *x*-coordinate as point *R* and the same *y*-coordinate as point *T*. What are the coordinates of point *V*?

    A. (−5, 2)
    B. (3, −4)
    C. (2, −5)
    D. (−4, 3)

19. The point (*x*, *y*) is translated to the location (*x* − 5, *y* + 3). If the same translation is performed on point *U*, what is its ending location?

    A. (−1, −2)
    B. (4, −5)
    C. (9, −8)
    D. (7, −10)

20. What is the point 6 units right and 3 units down from Point *X*?

    A. (4, −4)
    B. (4, −3)
    C. (−4, 4)
    D. (−5, 5)

21. Eva decides to increase the square *WZYX* by 2 units on all sides without moving the center. With the increase, what is the new location of point *W*?

    A. (2, 3)
    B. (−1, 1)
    C. (2, −2)
    D. (−3, 3)

22. Which point in the square *WZYX* lies in Quadrant 1?

    A. point *W*
    B. point *Z*
    C. point *Y*
    D. point *X*

23. Marco decided to translate the square 3 units to the right. What are the new coordinates for point *Z*?

    A. (4, 2)
    B. (1, 2)
    C. (4, −1)
    D. (1, −1)

UNIT 3

Graphing Linear Equations

Use with *Student Book* pp. 72–73

MATH CONTENT TOPICS: Q.2.a, Q.2.e, A.1.b, A.2.d, A.5.a, A.5.d
MATH PRACTICES: MP.1.a, MP.1.d, MP.1.e, MP.2.c, MP.3.a, MP.4.a

1 Review the Skill

You can graph an equation that has two variables. For each *x*-value, there is a unique *y*-value. These values can be written as ordered pairs and plotted on a grid. A **linear equation** forms a straight line on a graph. A line can be drawn for the equation when two points have been identified.

A **system of linear equations** is a set of two or more linear equations. The **solution of a set of linear equations** is the ordered pair (*x*, *y*) that satisfies, or is a solution of, all of the equations. On a graph, the solution of a set of linear equations is the point at which the lines intersect.

You can count spaces to determine the distance between two points on a vertical or horizontal line. However, for any other kind of line, please use the distance formula.

2 Refine the Skill

By refining the skill of graphing linear equations, you will improve your study and test-taking abilities, especially as they relate to the GED® Mathematical Reasoning Test. Study the graph below. Then answer the questions that follow.

a To answer Question 1, determine the equation of the line passing through the three points.

b To answer Question 2, use the following distance formula:
distance = $\sqrt{(x_2 - x_1)^2 + (y_2 - y_1)^2}$, where one point is ($x_1$, y_1) and the other is (x_2, y_2).

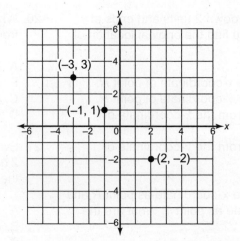

a 1. The points graphed on the grid above satisfy which of the following equations?

   A. $x - y = 0$
   B. $x + y = 0$
   C. $x - y = -1$
   D. $x + y = 1$

b 2. A line segment is drawn from point (−3, 3) to point (2, −2). What is the length of the line segment to the nearest tenth?

   A. 1.4
   B. 6
   C. 7.1
   D. 10

TEST-TAKING TIPS

Try to work backward from the answer choices. For Question 1, substitute the x- and y-values of one point into each equation. If the equation is not true, eliminate the answer choice.

UNIT 3

DIRECTIONS: Read each question, and choose the **best** answer.

3. Which ordered pair is a solution of $y = \frac{1}{2}x$?

   A. (4, 8)
   B. (1, 3)
   C. (4, 2)
   D. (1, 2)

4. What is the missing y-value if (2, y) is a solution of $-x = y + 1$?

   A. −3
   B. −2
   C. −1
   D. 1

5. What is the missing x-value if (x, −3) is a solution of $2x + 2y = -8$?

   A. −7
   B. −2
   C. −1
   D. 3

6. The graph of the equation $y = 4 - 3x$ would pass through which point on the coordinate grid?

   A. (1, −1)
   B. (4, 8)
   C. (3, 1)
   D. (2, −2)

7. What is the missing x-value if (x, 1) is a solution of $2x - y = 5$?

   A. −3
   B. 2
   C. 3
   D. 6

DIRECTIONS: Read the question, and choose the **best** answer.

8. Which of the following shows the graph of the equation $x + 2y = 2$?

   A.
   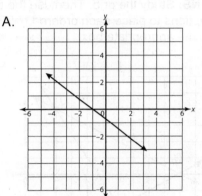

   B.
   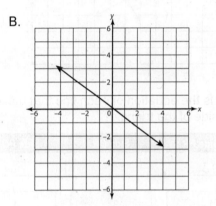

   C.
   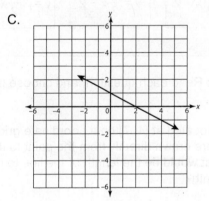

   D.
   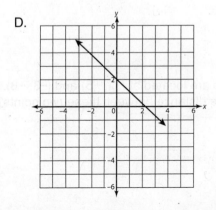

★ Spotlighted Item: DRAG-AND-DROP

DIRECTIONS: Study the grid. Then use the drag-and-drop options to place each ordered pair or equation in the appropriate box.

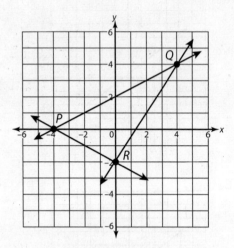

9. What is the equation of each line that makes up a side of the triangle?

Side *PR*	Side *QR*	Side *PQ*

$y = \frac{1}{2}x + 2$	$y = \frac{3}{2}x - 2$	$y = -\frac{1}{2}x - 2$

10. Which point is the solution of each pair of equations?

$y = \frac{1}{2}x + 2$ and $y = \frac{3}{2}x - 2$	$y = \frac{3}{2}x - 2$ and $y = -\frac{1}{2}x - 2$	$y = -\frac{1}{2}x - 2$ and $y = \frac{1}{2}x + 2$

(−4, 0)	(4, 4)	(0, −2)

11. Which points are located on each line?

$y = \frac{1}{2}x + 2$	$y = \frac{3}{2}x - 2$	$y = -\frac{1}{2}x - 2$

(2, −3)	(0, 2)	(2, 1)
(−6, −1)	(8, −6)	(6, 7)

DIRECTIONS: Read each question, and choose the **best** answer.

12. Point *B* is located at (4, 7) on a coordinate grid. If a line were drawn directly from the point to the origin, what would be the length of the line to the nearest tenth?

   A. 3
   B. 3.3
   C. 5.3
   D. 8.1

13. Two points are located at (−2, −5) and (−3, −8). What is the distance between these two points?

   A. 3.2
   B. 4.2
   C. 5.8
   D. 13.9

DIRECTIONS: Read each question, and choose the **best** answer.

14. The graph of the equation $y = -2x - 1$ passes through which point?

   A. (1, −3)
   B. (1, −2)
   C. (0, 1)
   D. (−1, 2)

15. Two points are located at (−3, −2) and (−4, 5). What is the distance between these two points?

   A. 3.2
   B. 7.1
   C. 8.2
   D. 9.1

DIRECTIONS: Read the question, and choose the **best** answer.

16. Which graph shows the solution of the equations $2x - y = 2$ and $y = -x + 1$?

A.

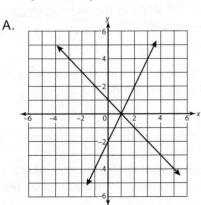

B.

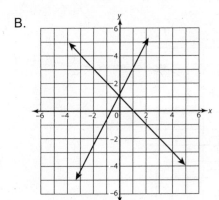

C.

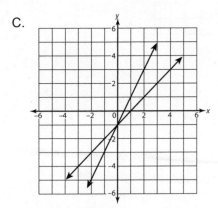

D.

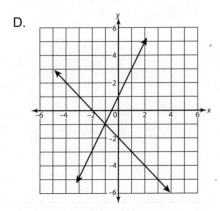

DIRECTIONS: Study the information and graph, read each question, and choose the **best** answer.

Rachel runs a small business. She produces and sells homemade fudge. The following graph shows Rachel's total revenue and total expenses based on the number of pounds of fudge sold.

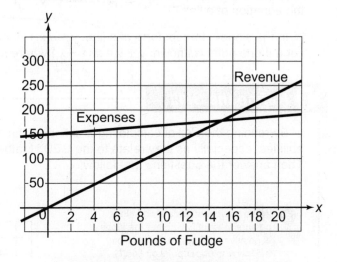

17. If the *Revenue* line passes through the point (4, 48), what is the equation of the *Revenue* line?

    A. $12x + y = 0$
    B. $4x - 5y = 0$
    C. $12x - y = 0$
    D. $4x + 5y = 0$

18. Rachel's start-up expenses total $150. What is the equation of the *Expenses* line?

    A. $x - 2y = 150$
    B. $x + 2y = 150$
    C. $2x - y = -150$
    D. $2x - y = 150$

19. The solution set of a revenue equation and an expense equation is called the break-even point. How many pounds of fudge must Rachel sell to reach the break-even point?

    A. 18
    B. 15
    C. 10
    D. 8

Slope

Use with **Student Book** pp. 74–75

MATH CONTENT TOPICS: Q.2.a, Q.2.e, Q.6.c, A.1.i, A.5.a, A.5.b, A.5.c, A.6.a, A.6.b
MATH PRACTICES: MP.1.a, MP.1.b, MP.1.e, MP.3.a, MP.4.a, MP.4.c

① Review the Skill

Slope is a number that describes the steepness of a line. Determine the slope between two points (x_1, y_1) and (x_2, y_2) by using the formula $m = \dfrac{y_2 - y_1}{x_2 - x_1}$. Use the slope-intercept form of a line ($y = mx + b$) to find the equation of a line.

In the slope-intercept form of a line, $y = mx + b$, m = slope and b = y-intercept. The slope-point form can be used if one point is known: $y - y_1 = m(x - x_1)$ where m is the slope and (x_1, y_1) is the point.

② Refine the Skill

By refining the skill of calculating and finding the slope, you will improve your study and test-taking abilities, especially as they relate to the GED® Mathematical Reasoning Test. Study the information below. Then answer the questions that follow.

a When you count grids to find slope, be sure to identify whether the slope is positive or negative. To get from the lower to upper point on line G, you must go up 3 and right 6. Write $\dfrac{3}{6}$ and simplify.

b Use the slope-intercept form of a line to find the equation of a line. Substitute the slope for m and the y-intercept for b. Ensure that you include the sign for each number.

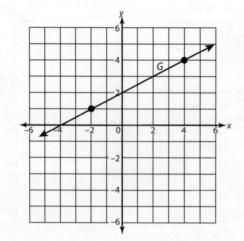

USING LOGIC

If you are given a point and a slope of a line, you can substitute the slope, x-value, and y-value into $y = mx + b$ to find the y-intercept. Then you can use the slope and y-intercept to write an equation for the line.

1. What is the slope of line G?

   A. -1

   B. $-\dfrac{1}{2}$

   C. 0

   D. $\dfrac{1}{2}$

b 2. What is the equation of line G?

   A. $y = -\dfrac{1}{2}x - 2$

   B. $y = -\dfrac{1}{2}x + 2$

   C. $y = \dfrac{1}{2}x + 2$

   D. $y = 2x + 1$

DIRECTIONS: Read each question, and choose the **best** answer.

3. The points (−4, 4) and (2, 3) lie on line *H*. What is the slope of line *H*?

   A. $-\dfrac{1}{6}$

   B. $-\dfrac{13}{2}$

   C. $-\dfrac{1}{2}$

   D. 2

4. What is the slope of a line that passes through points (−1, −2) and (−3, −4)?

   A. $-\dfrac{1}{2}$

   B. $\dfrac{1}{2}$

   C. 0
   D. 1

5. A linear equation is represented by $y = \dfrac{1}{2}x + 3$. The graph of which equation would be parallel to that of the equation above?

   A. $y = -\dfrac{1}{3}x + 2$

   B. $y = \dfrac{1}{2}x - 3$

   C. $y = 2x + 3$
   D. $y = x - 3$

DIRECTIONS: Read the information and question, and choose the **best** answer.

6. Line *B* has a slope of −1. It passes through point *K* at (4, −2), and it passes through point *L*, which has an *x*-coordinate of 2.

   What are the coordinates of point L?

   A. (2, −2)
   B. (0, 2)
   C. (2, 0)
   D. (−2, 2)

DIRECTIONS: Examine the grid, read the question, and choose the **best** answer.

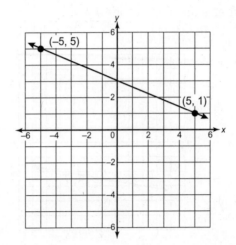

7. What is the equation of the line shown in the grid above?

   A. $y = -\dfrac{2}{5}x + 3$

   B. $y = -\dfrac{1}{3}x + 3$

   C. $y = \dfrac{2}{5}x + 3$

   D. $y = \dfrac{1}{3}x + 3$

DIRECTIONS: Study the information and grid, read the question, and choose the **best** answer.

8. Andrea paid an initial fee of $20 to set up her cell phone. Now she pays $30 per month for service. The amount she pays for cell phone service for a certain number of months can be graphed in the first quadrant of a coordinate grid. What is the equation of the line?

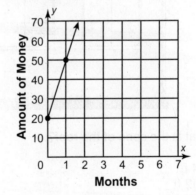

   A. $y = \dfrac{1}{3}x + 20$

   B. $y = 20x + 30$
   C. $y = 30x - 20$
   D. $y = 30x + 20$

DIRECTIONS: Examine the grid, read the question, and choose the **best** answer.

9. What is the slope of line *T*?

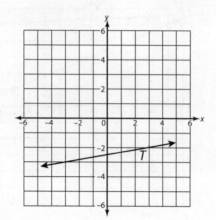

A. $-\dfrac{1}{3}$

B. $-\dfrac{1}{6}$

C. $\dfrac{1}{6}$

D. $\dfrac{1}{3}$

DIRECTIONS: Study the information and diagram, read the question, and choose the **best** answer.

The slope of the roof on the house below is $\dfrac{1}{3}$.

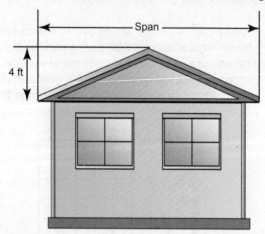

10. What is the span of the roof?

A. 4 ft
B. 12 ft
C. 18 ft
D. 24 ft

DIRECTIONS: Examine the grid, read the question, and choose the **best** answer.

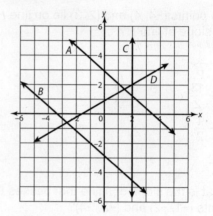

11. Which line shown on the grid above has a positive slope?

A. line *A*
B. line *B*
C. line *C*
D. line *D*

12. Which of the lines has an undefined slope?

A. line *A*
B. line *B*
C. line *C*
D. line *D*

DIRECTIONS: Read the information and each question, and choose the **best** answer.

Kaylia signs up for a cell-phone plan that costs $15 per month, plus 10 cents for every minute used.

13. If the monthly cost of Kaylia's cell phone bill was graphed, which numerical value would represent the slope of the graph?

A. 0.1
B. 0.15
C. 10
D. 15

14. What will be the amount of her bill if she uses 200 minutes in one month?

A. $15
B. $35
C. $50
D. $200

⭐ Spotlighted Item: **FILL-IN-THE-BLANK**

DIRECTIONS: Read each question. Then fill in your answer in the box below.

15. A ladder is leaning against a building and the top of the ladder touches the building 18 feet off the ground. The bottom of the ladder is anchored 4 feet away from the building. What is the slope of the ladder?

16. What is the slope of a line that passes through points (1, −3) and (4, 3)?

17. The points (−2, 0) and (3, 4) lie on line *D*. What is the slope of line *D*?

DIRECTIONS: Examine the table, read the question, and choose **best** answer.

Time (h)	Distance Traveled (km)
4	200
6	300
8	400

18. What is the rate of change in the table above?

A. 0.02 km/h
B. 50 km/h
C. 100 km/h
D. 200 km/h

DIRECTIONS: Read the question, and choose the **best** answer.

19. A helicopter takes off from the roof of a 200-foot high building. If it rises 90 ft/min, write an equation to model the height of the helicopter at time *t*.

A. $h = 90$
B. $h = 200$
C. $h = 90(t) + 200$
D. $h = 200(t) + 90$

DIRECTIONS: Read the information and each question, and choose the **best** answer.

When the sun sets at 6 P.M., the afternoon temperature of 90 degrees Fahrenheit begins to drop 4 degrees per hour and does not increase until the sun rises the next day. If the temperature drops below 60 degrees Fahrenheit for more than two hours, Maria's plant will die.

20. What is the temperature at midnight?

A. 4 degrees Fahrenheit
B. 24 degrees Fahrenheit
C. 64 degrees Fahrenheit
D. 66 degrees Fahrenheit

21. Which equation models the temperature change?

A. $y = 90 − 4x$
B. $y = 66 − 4x$
C. $y = 23 − 4x$
D. $y = 4 − 90x$

22. If the sun rose at 4:30 A.M., identify the correct statement from the choices below.

A. The temperature drops below 60 degrees Fahrenheit for 1 hour, so Maria's plant lives.
B. The temperature is above 60 degrees Fahrenheit so, Maria's plant lives.
C. The temperature drops below 60 degrees Fahrenheit for more than 2 hours, so Maria's plant dies.
D. The temperature is below 30 degrees Fahrenheit so, Maria's plant dies.

UNIT 3

Using Slope to Solve Geometric Problems

Use with *Student Book* pp. 76–77

MATH CONTENT TOPICS: Q.2.a, Q.2.d, Q.2.e, Q.6.c, A.5.a, A.5.b, A.6.a, A.6.b, A.6.c
MATH PRACTICES: MP.1.a, MP.1.b, MP.1.c, MP.1.d, MP.1.e, MP.2.c, MP.3.a, MP.4.a, MP.5.c

1 Review the Skill

If two lines have the same slope, they are **parallel** to one another. If two lines have slopes that are negative reciprocals of each other—for example, one being −3 and the other $\frac{1}{3}$—then the lines are **perpendicular** to each other.

Some geometric figures, such as squares and rectangles, are made up of line segments that are parallel or perpendicular to each other. Understanding slope can help you to analyze such figures.

2 Refine the Skill

By refining the skill of using slope to solve geometric problems, you will improve your study and test-taking abilities, especially as they relate to the GED® Mathematical Reasoning Test. Study the information and grid below. Then answer the questions that follow.

a The equations of the dashed lines can be deduced using the rules regarding slopes and the slope-point formula of a line: $(y - y_1) = m(x - x_1)$, where m is the slope and the point (x_1, y_1) is a point on the line.

b A good check to determine whether the slopes of perpendicular lines have been correctly determined: the product of the two slopes must equal −1. In this case, −3 multiplied by $\frac{1}{3}$ equals −1, which confirms that the lines are perpendicular.

The following graph shows a solid line with equation $y = -3x + 2$ and a point (−2, 2). The dashed lines pass through the point and are either parallel or perpendicular to the given line.

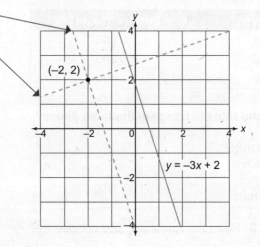

$(-2, 2)$

$y = -3x + 2$

INSIDE THE ITEMS

Finding the slope of a line perpendicular to another line with a given slope is a Level 1 DOK item. Simply invert and take the negative of the slope.

1. What is the equation for the line parallel to the given line?

   A. $(y - 2) = -3(x + 2)$

   B. $(y - 2) = -\frac{1}{3}(x + 2)$

   C. $(y + 2) = -3(x - 2)$

   D. $(y + 2) = -\frac{1}{3}(x - 2)$

2. What is the equation for the line perpendicular to the given line?

   A. $(y - 2) = \frac{1}{3}(x + 2)$

   B. $(y - 2) = 3(x + 2)$

   C. $(y + 2) = \frac{1}{3}(x + 2)$

   D. $(y + 2) = -3(x + 2)$

DIRECTIONS: Read each question, and choose the **best** answer.

3. A linear equation is represented by $y = \frac{1}{2}x + 3$.

   The graph of which equation would be parallel to that of the equation above?

   A. $y = \frac{1}{3}x + 2$

   B. $y = \frac{1}{2}x - 3$

   C. $y = -2x + 3$

   D. $y = x + 3$

4. A linear equation is represented by $y = -2x + \frac{3}{2}$.

   The graph of which equation would be perpendicular to that of the equation above?

   A. $y = -2x - 3$

   B. $y = -\frac{1}{2}x + 2$

   C. $y = \frac{1}{2}x - 3$

   D. $y = 2x + 3$

5. Which two lines in this graph are parallel to each other?

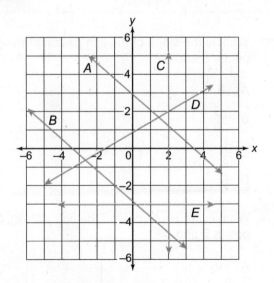

   A. line *A* and line *B*
   B. line *B* and line *C*
   C. line *C* and line *D*
   D. line *D* and line *E*

DIRECTIONS: Study the following grid, read each question, and choose the **best** answer.

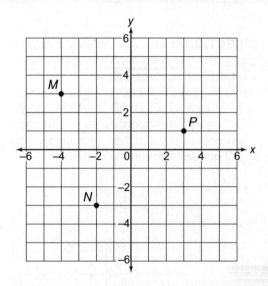

6. Which equation could reflect a line that is parallel to a line drawn through points *N* and *P*?

   A. $y = \frac{5}{4}x + 4$

   B. $y = -\frac{1}{5}x + 4$

   C. $y = 4x + 2$

   D. $y = \frac{4}{5}x - 4$

7. What would be the slope of a line that is parallel to a line drawn through points *M* and *P*?

   A. $-\frac{7}{2}$

   B. $-\frac{2}{7}$

   C. $\frac{2}{7}$

   D. $\frac{7}{2}$

8. What would be the slope of a line that is perpendicular to a line drawn through points *M* and *P*?

   A. $-\frac{7}{2}$

   B. $-\frac{2}{7}$

   C. $\frac{2}{7}$

   D. $\frac{7}{2}$

★ Spotlighted Item: **FILL-IN-THE-BLANK**

DIRECTIONS: Study the following information and grid. Then read each question, and fill in your answers in the boxes below.

Points A, B, C, and D form a rectangle. Points A and B have coordinates (−2, 0) and (0, 4), respectively, and the line joining points C and D passes through the origin.

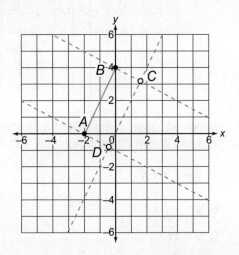

9. What is the equation of the line that passes through points C and D?

10. In decimal form, what is the slope of the line that passes through points B and C?

11. What are the x- and y-coordinates of point C in decimal form?

    x: _____ ; y: _____

12. What are the x- and y-coordinates of point D in decimal form?

    x: _____ ; y: _____

DIRECTIONS: Study the following information and figure, read each question, and choose the **best** answer.

Points A, B, and C form a right triangle, where side AB is perpendicular to side BC. Point A is at the origin, point B has coordinates (3, 1), and point C lies on the y-axis.

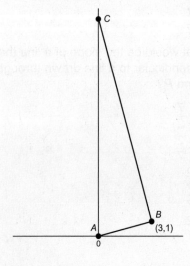

13. What is the slope of the line passing through points B and C?

    A. −3

    B. $-\dfrac{1}{3}$

    C. $\dfrac{1}{3}$

    D. 3

14. What is the y-intercept of the line passing through points B and C?

    A. −10
    B. 8
    C. 7
    D. 10

DIRECTIONS: Read each question, and choose the **best** answer.

15. A four-sided figure is formed by four points with the coordinates shown below. Roger argues that the figure is a rectangle because it looks like one, and the coordinates of the lower two points are the negatives of those of the upper two points. Which statement is true?

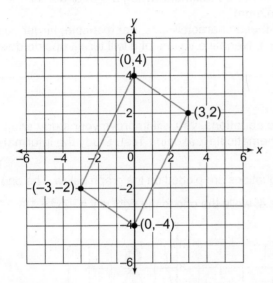

A. It is a rectangle; Roger is correct.
B. It is not a rectangle; the short sides are not parallel.
C. It is not a rectangle; the long sides are not parallel.
D. It is not a rectangle; the short sides are not perpendicular to the long sides.

16. A line is defined by points A and B, with coordinates (1, 3) and (2, 7), respectively. What is the equation of the line that is parallel to the line formed by A and B, but with the y-intercept increased by 2 units?

A. $y = \frac{1}{4}x + 1$

B. $y = \frac{1}{4}x + 2$

C. $y = 4x + 1$
D. $y = 4x + 2$

DIRECTIONS: Study the following information and figure, read each question, and choose the **best** answer.

A rectangular rug, shown below with points A, B, C, and D at its corners, is placed in a room and rotated, so that all four corner touch the walls. The size of the room in the y-direction is 14 ft, and points A and B are 12 ft and 6 ft from the lower left-hand corner, as shown.

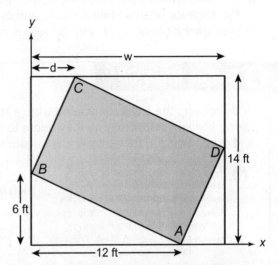

17. Treating the lower left-hand corner as the origin of a coordinate system, what is the equation of the line that passes through points A and B?

A. $y = -\frac{1}{2}x - 6$

B. $y = -\frac{1}{2}x + 6$

C. $y = -2x - 6$
D. $y = -2x + 6$

18. What is the slope of the line passing through points B and C?

A. 2
B. −2

C. $-\frac{1}{2}$

D. $\frac{1}{2}$

19. What is the distance, d, in feet?

A. 2
B. 4
C. 8
D. 14

Graphing Quadratic Equations

Use with **Student Book** pp. 78–79

1 Review the Skill

MATH CONTENT TOPICS: Q.2.a, Q.2.e, Q.6.c, A.1.e, A.1.f, A.1.g, A.4.a, A.4.b, A.5.a, A.5.e
MATH PRACTICES: MP.1.a, MP.1.b, MP.1.c, MP.1.d, MP.1.e, MP.2.a, MP.2.c, MP.3.a, MP.4.a, MP.4.b, MP.4.c, MP.5.a, MP.5.c

Quadratic equations are equations set in the form of $ax^2 + bx + c = 0$, where a is not zero. The word *quadratic* comes from the root *quad*, meaning "square." Therefore, a quadratic equation includes a squared variable, x^2. The x-value at the minimum or maximum may be found by using the formula of $x = \frac{-b}{2a}$.

Characteristics of quadratic equations include zero, one or two points where the plot of such an equation crosses the x-axis, one point where it crosses the y-axis, either a maximum (when $a < 0$) or a minimum (when $a > 0$), and symmetry with respect to that maximum or minimum.

Coefficients of an equation—a, b, and c—can quantify these characteristics. For example, larger values of a will contract a curve, while smaller values of a will expand it. Negative values of a will turn it upside down.

2 Refine the Skill

By refining the skills associated with graphing quadratic equations, you will improve your study and test-taking abilities, especially as they relate to the GED® Mathematical Reasoning Test. Study the information and graph below. Then answer the questions that follow.

a Symmetry can be used to identify additional points on the curve. For example, the left-hand curve goes through the point (0, 4). This is four units to the right of the minimum, which has an x-value of -4. Through symmetry, you can determine a point on the curve, with $y = 4$, four units to the left of the minimum, at $x = -4 - 4 = -8$, giving the point $(-8, 4)$.

b The larger the magnitude of a, the steeper the curve will be. The right-hand curve has a of magnitude 2, while the left-hand curve has a of magnitude $\frac{1}{2}$. The right-hand curve shows a more rapid change in y as one moves away from the maximum than is the case for changes in y as one moves away from the minimum of the left-hand curve.

Two quadratic equations are plotted on the graph below. The one to the left is $y = \frac{1}{2}x^2 + 4x + 4$, while the one to the right is $y = -2x^2 + 16x - 24$.

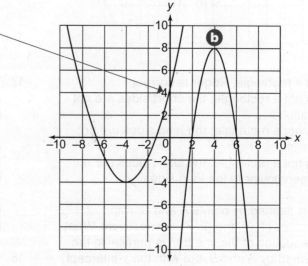

TEST-TAKING TECH

Hot spot questions appear as spotlighted items in this lesson. Because hot spot items allow students to actually plot points on a graph, they build a strong link between test preparation and the test-taking experience itself.

1. At what y-value does the right-hand curve cross the y-axis?

   A. -16
   B. -24
   C. -32
   D. -40

2. At what x-values does the left-hand curve cross the x-axis, expressed to the nearest tenth?

   A. $x = -6.8$, $x = -1.2$
   B. $x = -6.7$, $x = -1.2$
   C. $x = -6.8$, $x = -1.1$
   D. $x = -6.7$, $x = -1.1$

DIRECTIONS: Read each question, and choose the **best** answer.

3. Which value of y corresponds to the point where the curve defined by $y = 2x^2 - 5x + 3$ crosses the y-axis?

   A. $y = -5$
   B. $y = -3$
   C. $y = 3$
   D. $y = 5$

4. Indicate whether the curve defined by $y = -3x^2 + 12x - 5$ goes through a maximum or a minimum and the value of x at which it occurs.

   A. Minimum, $x = -2$
   B. Minimum, $x = +2$
   C. Maximum, $x = -2$
   D. Maximum, $x = +2$

DIRECTIONS: Study the diagram and information, read the question, and choose the **best** answer.

The following graph shows the path of a ball thrown horizontally from a height of 36 feet. The ball travels a horizontal distance of 6 feet by the time it lands.

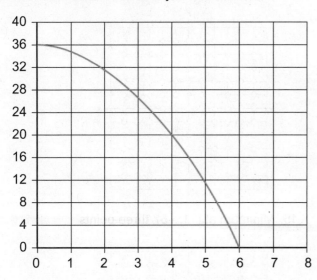

5. What is the quadratic equation corresponding to the path of the ball?

   A. $y = -x^2 - 36$
   B. $y = -x^2 + 36$
   C. $y = -x^2 + 6x - 36$
   D. $y = -x^2 + 6x + 36$

DIRECTIONS: Study the following diagram and information, read each question, and choose the **best** answer.

The following graph features plots of five different quadratic equations of the form $y = ax^2 + bx + c$, identified by letters A through E.

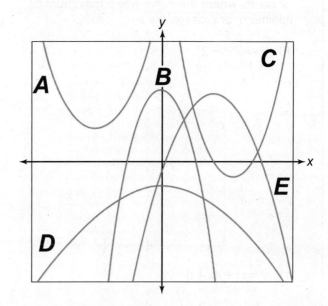

6. Which curves correspond to equations with $a < 0$?

   A. Curve A only
   B. Curve D only
   C. Curves A and C
   D. Curves B, D, and E

7. Which curves correspond to equations with $b = 0$?

   A. Curve D only
   B. Curves B and D
   C. Curve C only
   D. Curves A and C

8. Which curves correspond to equations with $\dfrac{b}{2a} > 0$?

   A. Curve A only
   B. Curve D only
   C. Curves C and D
   D. Curves C and E

9. Which curve corresponds to the equation with the most negative value of a?

   A. Curve B
   B. Curve C
   C. Curve D
   D. Curve E

⭐ Spotlighted Item: **HOT SPOT**

DIRECTIONS: Study the equation in each question and, on the graphs following each, mark all points where the curve has a maximum or minimum, or crosses the x- or y-axis.

10. $y = \frac{1}{2}x^2 - 2$

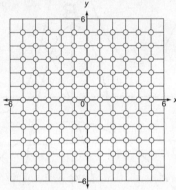

11. $y = x^2 + 4x + 3$

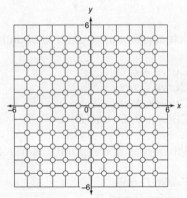

12. $y = -x^2 + 2x + 3$

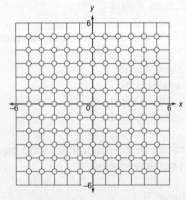

DIRECTIONS: The following questions feature plots of several points corresponding to a quadratic equation, the coordinates of the maximum or minimum, and the number of points that can be inferred from symmetry. Mark those symmetric points on the graph.

13. Minimum at (−1.5, −3.1); four points

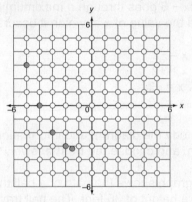

14. Maximum at (2, 5); three points

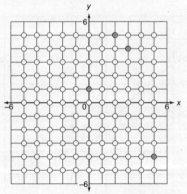

15. Minimum at (−1, −5); three points

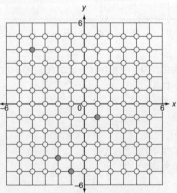

UNIT 3

DIRECTIONS: Study the following quadratic equation, read each question, and choose the **best** answer.

$$y = -2x^2 - 4x + 6$$

16. Which pair of x-values represent where the curve crosses the x-axis?

    A. $x = 3$, $x = 1$
    B. $x = 1$, $x = 3$
    C. $x = -1$, $x = 3$
    D. $x = -3$, $x = 1$

17. Which value of y represents where the curve crosses the y-axis?

    A. $y = -6$
    B. $y = -2$
    C. $y = 2$
    D. $y = 6$

18. Which value of x represents where the curve goes through a minimum?

    A. $x = 2$
    B. $x = 1$
    C. $x = -1$
    D. $x = -2$

DIRECTIONS: Study the graph, read the question, and choose the **best** answer.

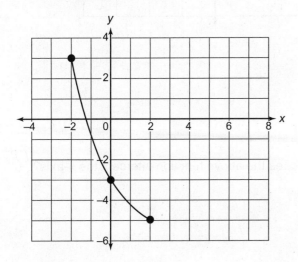

19. If the point at (2, −5) is the minimum, what positive value of x corresponds to a y-value of +3?

    A. 7
    B. 6
    C. 5
    D. 4

DIRECTIONS: Study the following information and diagram, read each question, and choose the **best** answer.

The diagram shows a ball player, standing at the origin, throwing a ball to another player. The ball's path, expressed in feet, obeys the equation $y = -\frac{1}{144}x^2 + x + 6$, which assumes the ball is 6 ft off the ground when it is thrown and caught.

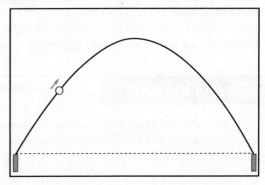

20. How far apart are the two ball players?

    A. 36 feet
    B. 72 feet
    C. 108 feet
    D. 144 feet

21. When the ball reaches its highest point, how far has it traveled horizontally?

    A. 36 feet
    B. 72 feet
    C. 108 feet
    D. 144 feet

22. How high off the ground is the ball at its highest point?

    A. 30 feet
    B. 36 feet
    C. 42 feet
    D. 72 feet

23. Suppose the ball were thrown harder, so that it reached its maximum height at a horizontal distance of 92 feet. How much greater would the *total* horizontal distance traveled be, assuming its path is still represented by a quadratic function?

    A. 0 feet
    B. 20 feet
    C. 40 feet
    D. 60 feet

Evaluation of Functions

Use with *Student Book* pp. 80–81

MATH CONTENT TOPICS: Q.2.a, Q.6.c, A.1.e, A.1.f, A.1.i, A.5.e, A.7.b
MATH PRACTICES: MP.1.a, MP.1.b, MP.1.e, MP.2.c, MP.3.a, MP.4.a, MP.4.b, MP.4.c, MP.5.b, MP.5.c

1 Review the Skill

A **function** includes three parts: the input, the relationship, and the output. For example, an input of *8* and a relationship of *x 7* produces an output of *56 (8 x 7 = 56)*. In the function $f(x) = x^2$, *f* is the function, *x* is the input, and x^2 is the output. The function $f(x) = x^2$ shows that the function *f* takes the *x* and squares it. So an input of *8* would result in an output of *64*: $f(8) = 8^2$.

Functions generally have one output (*y*-value) for each input (*x*-value). Functions and their properties or traits may be displayed in graphs, tables, and algebraic expressions. These include traits of quadratic functions: intercepts, maxima and minima, and symmetries. Calculation of isolated points located near intercepts and points where a function is undefined provide additional information about where a function is positive, negative, increasing, or decreasing, and estimates of where the function has relative maxima and minima.

2 Refine the Skill

By refining the skill of evaluating functions, you will improve your study and test-taking abilities, especially as they relate to the GED® Mathematical Reasoning Test. Study the information and graph below. Then answer the questions that follow.

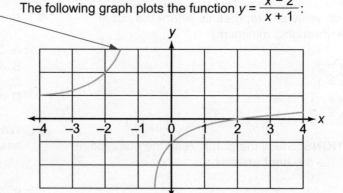

a Points where functions are undefined—such as *x*-values at which a denominator in a function becomes zero—are reflected in rapid changes in the function to *y*-values on either side of the graph.

The following graph plots the function $y = \dfrac{x - 2}{x + 1}$:

b Rational functions, which are ratios of polynomials, can feature both *x*-intercepts and points at which a function is undefined. These points are apparent in graphical representations of the functions, such as those in the graph to the right, and often can be determined from equations.

INSIDE THE ITEMS

When interpreting functions on graphs, ensure that you also review the same function in writing for clues. For example, the function above of $y = \dfrac{x - 2}{x + 1}$ provides clues that help you to answer Questions 1 and 2.

1. At what *x*-value does the above function intercept the *x*-axis?

   A. $x = -2$
   B. $x = -1$
   C. $x = 0$
   D. $x = 2$

2. For what *x*-value is the above function undefined?

   A. $x = -2$
   B. $x = -1$
   C. $x = 0$
   D. $x = 2$

3 Master the Skill

DIRECTIONS: Read each question, and choose the **best** answer.

3. Which equation corresponds to the graph below?

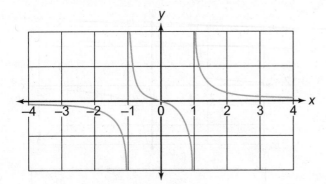

A. $y = \dfrac{-x}{(x + 2)(x - 2)}$

B. $y = \dfrac{-x}{(x + 1)(x - 1)}$

C. $y = \dfrac{x}{(x + 2)(x - 2)}$

D. $y = \dfrac{x}{(x + 1)(x - 1)}$

4. Which equation corresponds to the graph below?

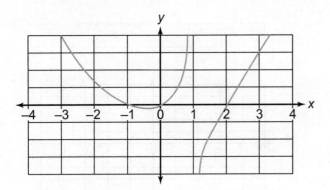

A. $y = \dfrac{x(x - 1)(x + 2)}{(x + 1)}$

B. $y = \dfrac{x(x + 1)(x - 2)}{(x - 1)}$

C. $y = \dfrac{-x(x - 1)(x + 2)}{(x + 1)}$

D. $y = \dfrac{-x(x + 1)(x - 2)}{(x - 1)}$

DIRECTIONS: Study the information and graph, read each question, and choose the **best** answer.

The following graph is a plot of the function $y = -x^3 - 2x^2$. Four x positions are labeled.

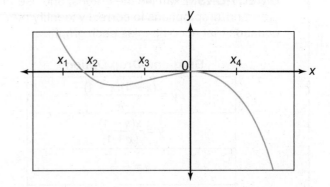

5. At which of the specified x-values is y positive?

A. x_1
B. x_2
C. x_3
D. x_4

6. At which of the specified x-values is the function increasing?

A. x_1 only
B. x_2 only
C. x_3 only
D. x_2, x_3, and x_4 only

7. In what x-interval does the curve go through a relative maximum?

A. to the left of x_1
B. between x_1 and x_2
C. between x_2 and x_3
D. between x_3 and x_4

8. At what y-value does the curve intercept the y-axis?

A. −2
B. −1
C. 0
D. 2

9. At what x-values does the curve intercept the x-axis?

A. −2 only
B. −2, 2
C. 0 only
D. 0, −2

UNIT 3

★ Spotlighted Item: **DRAG-AND-DROP**

DIRECTIONS: Examine the graphs, and use the drag-and-drop options to correctly identify the equation that accompanies each graph.

Drag-and-Drop Options

A	$y = \dfrac{(x + 1)(x - 1)}{x}$
B	$y = \dfrac{x(x - 1)}{(x + 1)}$
C	$y = -\dfrac{1}{x}$
D	$y = \dfrac{-(x + 1)(x - 1)}{x}$
E	$y = \dfrac{x(x + 1)}{(x - 1)}$
F	$y = \dfrac{-x(x - 1)}{(x + 1)}$

12.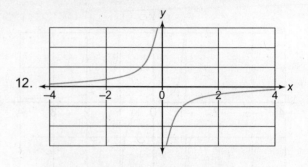

13.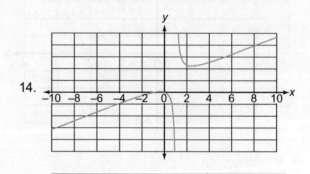

14.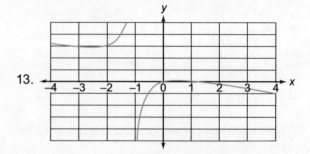

15.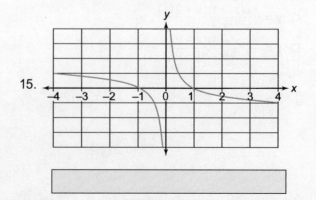

10.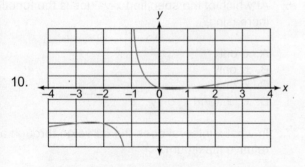

11.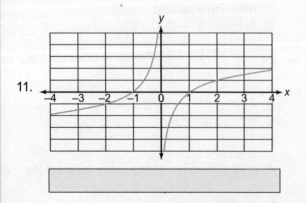

DIRECTIONS: Read each question, and choose the **best** answer.

16. Which equation corresponds to the graph below?

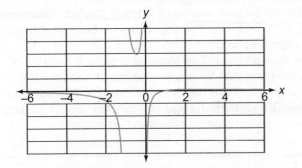

A. $y = \dfrac{-(x-1)}{x(x+1)}$

B. $y = \dfrac{-(x+1)}{x(x-1)}$

C. $y = \dfrac{(x-1)}{x(x+1)}$

D. $y = \dfrac{(x+1)}{x(x-1)}$

17. Of the following four graphs, which have exactly one output for each input?

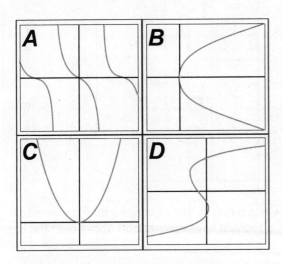

A. Graph *B* only
B. Graph *C* only
C. Graphs *A* and *C* only
D. Graphs *A*, *C*, and *D* only

DIRECTIONS: Read each question, and choose the **best** answer.

18. Which equation corresponds to the graph below?

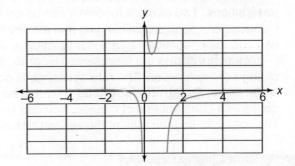

A. $y = \dfrac{-(x-1)}{x(x+1)}$

B. $y = \dfrac{-(x+1)}{x(x-1)}$

C. $y = \dfrac{(x-1)}{x(x+1)}$

D. $y = \dfrac{(x+1)}{x(x-1)}$

19. Which equation corresponds to the graph below?

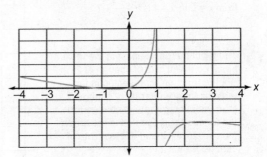

A. $y = \dfrac{x(x-1)}{(x+1)}$

B. $y = \dfrac{x(x+1)}{(x-1)}$

C. $y = \dfrac{-x(x-1)}{(x+1)}$

D. $y = \dfrac{-x(x+1)}{(x-1)}$

20. At the point at which the function $y = x^4 - 9x^3 + 6x^2 - 2x + 10$ crosses the *y*-axis, is the function positive or negative, and is it increasing or decreasing?

A. negative, decreasing
B. negative, increasing
C. positive, decreasing
D. positive, increasing

Comparison of Functions

Use with *Student Book* pp. 82–83

MATH CONTENT TOPICS: Q.2.a, Q.2.e, Q.6.a, Q.6.c, A.5.e, A.7.a, A.7.c, A.7.d
MATH PRACTICES: MP.1.a, MP.1.b, MP.1.d, MP.1.e, MP.2.a, MP.2.b, MP.2.c, MP.4.c, MP.5.a

1 Review the Skill

Functions can be represented by sets of ordered pairs, in tables, in graphs, algebraically, or by verbal descriptions. Two or more functions can be compared based on their slopes or rates of change, intercepts, the locations and values of minimums and maximums, and other features. You can compare two linear functions, two quadratic functions, or a linear function and a quadratic function.

Linear functions are represented by graphs that are straight lines. The slope of the line is the rate of change of the function. The rate of change is constant, meaning that for any two points on the line, the slope is the same. **Quadratic functions** are represented by graphs that are parabolas. Quadratic functions do not have a constant rate of change. You can find the **average rate of change** of a function over a particular interval by finding the ratio of the vertical change to the horizontal change between two points.

2 Refine the Skill

By refining the skill of comparing functions, you will improve your study and test-taking abilities, especially as they relate to the GED® Mathematical Reasoning Test. Study the information below. Then answer the questions that follow.

a The function represented in the graph is a quadratic function. The average rate of change from $x = 0$ to $x = 3$ is $\frac{2}{2} = 1$. The average rate of change from $x = 2$ to $x = 4$ is $\frac{7-1}{2} = 3$.

b The function represented in the table has a constant rate of change of 2. So, the function represented in the table has a greater rate of change than the average rate of change for the function represented in the graph for $x = 0$ to $x = 2$ and a lesser rate of change for $x = 2$ to $x = 4$.

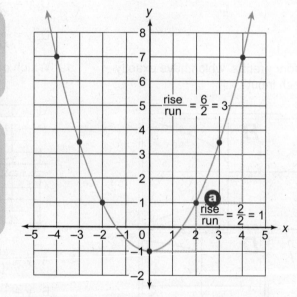

x	y
−4	−4
−3	−2
−2	0
−1	2
0	4
1	6
2	8
3	10
4	12

INSIDE THE ITEMS

On the GED® Mathematical Reasoning Test, you may see items in which two functions, presented in the same way or in a different ways, are separated by a dropdown menu populated by comparative terms.

1. Which function below has a lesser rate of change than the average rate of change of the quadratic function graphed above over the interval $x = 0$ to $x = 3$?

   A. $f(x) = 2x - 1$
   B. $f(x) = 0.5x + 3$
   C. $f(x) = 7x + 2$
   D. $f(x) = 1.5x - 4$

2. Over what interval is the rate of change of the quadratic function graphed above the same as the rate of change of the function $f(x) = -2x - 3$?

   A. $x = -4$ to $x = 0$
   B. $x = -4$ to $x = -2$
   C. $x = -3$ to $x = 2$
   D. $x = 0$ to $x = 4$

⭐ Spotlighted Item: **DROP-DOWN**

DIRECTIONS: Study the table, read each question, and choose the drop-down option that **best** answers each question.

x	y
−3	27
−2	12
−1	3
0	0
1	3
2	12
3	27

3. The *y*-intercept of the function represented by $f(x) = 6x + 4$ is [Drop-down] the *y*-intercept of the function represented in the table.

   A. less than   B. greater than   C. equal to

4. The rate of change of the function represented by $f(x) = 6x + 4$ is [Drop-down] the average rate of change of the function represented in the table, over the interval from $x = 0$ to $x = 1$.

   A. less than   B. greater than   C. equal to

5. The rate of change of the function represented by $f(x) = 6x + 4$ is [Drop-down] the average rate of change of the function represented in the table, over the interval from $x = 0$ to $x = 2$.

   A. less than   B. greater than   C. equal to

6. The rate of change of the function represented by $f(x) = 6x + 4$ is [Drop-down] the average rate of change of the function represented in the table, over the interval from $x = 1$ to $x = 3$.

   A. less than   B. greater than   C. equal to

7. The *y*-intercept of the function represented by $f(x) = -9x - 1$ is [Drop-down] the *y*-intercept of the function represented in the table.

   A. less than   B. greater than   C. equal to

8. The rate of change of the function represented by $f(x) = -9x - 1$ is [Drop-down] the average rate of change of the function represented in the table, over the interval from $x = -2$ to $x = -1$.

   A. less than   B. greater than   C. equal to

DIRECTIONS: Study the graph, read each question, and choose the **best** answer.

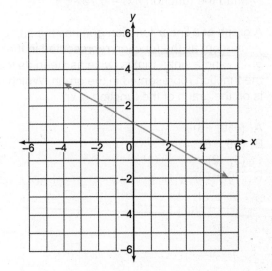

9. Which function has the same *y*-intercept as the function represented in the graph?

   A. $f(x) = x - 2$
   B. $f(x) = 2x^2 + 2$
   C. $f(x) = 3x - 1$
   D. $f(x) = 4x^2 + 1$

10. Which function has the same *x*-intercept as the function represented in the graph?

    A. $f(x) = x + 1$
    B. $f(x) = \frac{3}{2}x - 1$
    C. $f(x) = -x + 2$
    D. $f(x) = -\frac{3}{2}x - 2$

UNIT 3

DIRECTIONS: Study the graph, read the question, and choose the **best** answer.

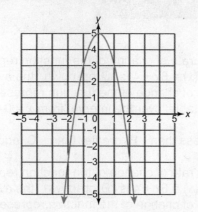

11. Which function has the same maximum value as the function represented in the graph?

    A. $f(x) = x^2 + 5$
    B. $f(x) = 2x^2 - 3$
    C. $f(x) = -2x^2 + 3$
    D. $f(x) = -3x^2 + 5$

DIRECTIONS: Study the graph, read the question, and choose the **best** answer.

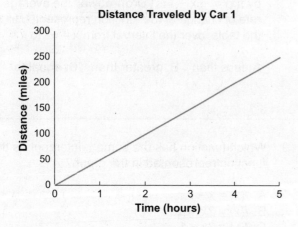

Distance Traveled by Car 1

12. The graph shows the distance traveled by Car 1, traveling at constant speed. The equation $d = 45t$ represents the distance, d, that Car 2 travels in t hours. Which statement explains which car is traveling at a greater speed?

    A. Car 1 is traveling at a greater speed, because the slope of the line in the graph is less than 45.
    B. Car 1 is traveling at a greater speed, because the slope of the line in the graph is greater than 45.
    C. Car 2 is traveling at a greater speed, because the slope of the line in the graph is less than 45.
    D. Car 2 is traveling at a greater speed, because the slope of the line in the graph is greater than 45.

DIRECTIONS: Study the graph, read each question, and choose the **best** answer.

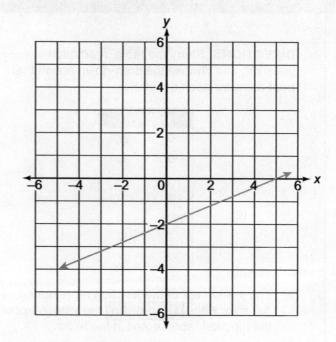

13. Which statement is true?

    A. The function represented in the graph has a greater rate of change and a greater y-intercept than the function $f(x) = 0.75x - 1$.
    B. The function represented in the graph has a greater rate of change and a lesser y-intercept than the function $f(x) = 0.75x - 1$.
    C. The function represented in the graph has a lesser rate of change and a greater y-intercept than the function $f(x) = 0.75x - 1$.
    D. The function represented in the graph has a lesser rate of change and a lesser y-intercept than the function $f(x) = 0.75x - 1$.

14. A graph of a linear function $g(x)$ has the same y-intercept as the function represented in the graph and a slope that is twice as steep as that of the function represented in the graph. Which point is on the graph of the function $g(x)$?

    A. $(-10, -6)$
    B. $(-5, -6)$
    C. $(5, -2)$
    D. $(10, -10)$

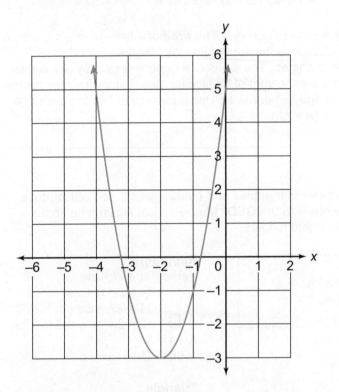

x	y
−4	6
−2	5
0	4
2	3
4	2

17. A linear function has a rate of change of −0.5 and a y-intercept of 5. Which statement is true?

A. The function has the same rate of change and y-intercept as the function represented in the table.
B. The function has a greater rate of change and y-intercept as the function represented in the table.
C. The function has a greater rate of change and the same y-intercept as the function represented in the table.
D. The function has the same rate of change and a greater y-intercept than the function represented in the table.

15. Alaina says the function $f(x) = x^2 − 2$ has the same minimum value as the function represented in the graph. Which explains Alaina's conclusion?

A. Alaina is correct, because both functions have a minimum value of −2.
B. Alaina is correct, because both functions have a minimum value of −3.
C. Alaina is incorrect, because the function represented in the graph has a minimum value of −3 and the function $f(x) = x^2 − 2$ has a minimum value of 2.
D. Alaina is incorrect, because the function represented in the graph has a minimum value of −3 and the function $f(x) = x^2 − 2$ has a minimum value of −2.

16. Which linear function has a rate of change that is equal to the average rate of change of the function represented in the graph over the interval from x = −3 to x = 0?

A. $f(x) = \frac{1}{4}x − 4$

B. $f(x) = \frac{1}{2}x + 1$

C. $f(x) = 2x − 6$
D. $f(x) = 4x + 7$

18. James says the function $f(x) = x + 8$ has the same x-intercept as the function represented in the table. Sam says that the function $f(x) = 0.25x − 2$ has the same x-intercept as the function represented in the table. Who is correct?

A. James
B. Sam
C. both James and Sam
D. neither James nor Sam

19. The ordered pairs below represent a linear function.

{(−6, −1), (−2, 1), (4, 4), (8, 6)}

Which is true of the function represented above?

A. The function is increasing at the same rate that the function represented in the table is increasing.
B. The function is increasing at the same rate that the function represented in the table is decreasing.
C. The function is decreasing at the same rate that the function represented in the table is increasing.
D. The function is decreasing at the same rate that the function represented in the table is decreasing.

UNIT 3

Triangles and Quadrilaterals

Use with *Student Book* pp. 94–95

MATH CONTENT TOPICS: Q.2.a, Q.2.e, Q.4.a, Q.4.c, Q.4.d, A.2.a, A.2.b, A.2.c
MATH PRACTICES: MP.1.a, MP.1.b, MP.1.d, MP.1.e, MP.2.a, MP.4.a, MP.4.b, MP.5.a

1 Review the Skill

A **triangle** is a closed three-sided figure with three angles or corners. The **area** of a triangle is $\frac{1}{2}bh$, where b is the base and h is the height. The **perimeter** of a triangle is the sum of its side lengths.

A **quadrilateral** is a closed four-sided figure with four angles. The sides of a quadrilateral may or may not be congruent or parallel. The perimeter of a quadrilateral is the sum of its side lengths. If the quadrilateral has two or more congruent sides, a formula can be used to find its perimeter. Use a formula to find the area of a rectangle ($A = lw$), a square ($A = s^2$), or a parallelogram ($A = bh$).

2 Refine the Skill

By refining the skill of computing the area and perimeter of triangles and quadrilaterals, you will improve your study and test-taking abilities, especially as they relate to the GED® Mathematical Reasoning Test. Study the information below. Then answer the questions that follow.

a To find the missing measure, use inverse operations to isolate the variable. Then perform the same operations on each side of the equals sign to keep the equation balanced.

w | $P = 34$ ft
$A = 66$ ft²
11 ft

Rectangle
Perimeter = $2l + 2w$
$34 = 2(11) + 2w$
$34 = 22 + 2w$
a $12 = 2w \rightarrow w = 6$ ft
Area = lw
$66 = 11w \rightarrow w = 6$

b The height of an acute or isosceles triangle, or of a parallelogram, may be shown as a line perpendicular to the base. The line can be shown inside or outside of the figure.

s ⟍ 8 ft
h | $P = 25$ ft
$A = 37.5$ ft²
10 ft

Triangle
Perimeter = side + side + side
$25 = 10 + 8 + s$
$25 = 18 + s \rightarrow s = 7$

Area = $\frac{1}{2}bh$

$37.5 = \frac{1}{2}(10)(h)$

$37.5 = 5h \rightarrow h = 7.5$

c An isosceles triangle has at least 2 congruent sides. Since the perimeter of a triangle is the sum of its side lengths, you can find the length of one congruent side by subtracting the length of the base from the perimeter and dividing the difference by 2.

TEST-TAKING TIPS

The information needed to solve geometry problems may be provided in the question, the diagram, or both. Ensure that you carefully study both the question and the diagram.

1. What is the side length of a square with the same perimeter as the rectangle above?

   A. 8.5 ft
   B. 16.5 ft
   C. 17 ft
   D. 34 ft

2. An isosceles triangle with a base of 8 cm has a perimeter of 28 cm. Which could be the length of each of the other two sides?

   A. 6 cm
   B. 10 cm
   C. 18 cm
   D. 20 cm

UNIT 4

★ Spotlighted Item: FILL-IN-THE-BLANK

DIRECTIONS: Study the figure and information and read each question. Then fill in your answer in the box below.

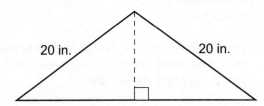

20 in.   20 in.

The perimeter of the triangle is 64 in.
The area of the triangle is 192 in².

3. What is the base of the triangle?

| |
| in. |

4. What is the height of the triangle?

| |
| in. |

DIRECTIONS: Read each question. Then fill in your answer in the box below.

5. A right triangle has an area of 30 cm². One of the sides that forms the right angle is 15 cm long. How long is the other side that forms the right angle?

| |
| cm |

6. The length of a rectangle is 2 times its width. The area of the rectangle is 32 in². What is the length of the rectangle?

| |
| in. |

7. A quilt is made up of squares, each with an area of $\frac{1}{4}$ ft². The squares are arranged in 12 rows of 10 squares each. The edge of the quilt is bordered with ribbon. What length of ribbon is required to border the quilt?

| |
| ft |

DIRECTIONS: Study the figures and information, read the question, and choose the **best** answer.

The square and the parallelogram below have the same perimeter.

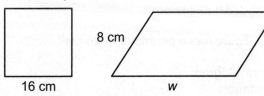

8 cm

16 cm   w

8. What is the perimeter of each figure?

A. 32 cm
B. 48 cm
C. 64 cm
D. 128 cm

DIRECTIONS: Study the figures and information, read the question, and choose the **best** answer.

The two figures below have the same area.

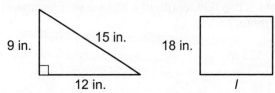

9 in.   15 in.   18 in.

12 in.   l

9. What is the area of each figure?

A. 54 in.²
B. 90 in.²
C. 108 in.²
D. 180 in.²

DIRECTIONS: Study the figure, read each question, and choose the **best** answer.

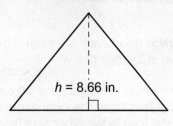

$h = 8.66$ in.

$A = 43.3$ in.^{2}

10. What is the base of the triangle above?

   A. 5 in.
   B. 10 in.
   C. 15 in.
   D. 20 in.

11. The triangle above is an equilateral triangle. What is the perimeter of the triangle?

   A. 15 in.
   B. 20 in.
   C. 30 in.
   D. 40 in.

DIRECTIONS: Read each question, and choose the **best** answer.

12. A parallelogram has an area of 58 square meters and a base of 5 meters. What is the height of the parallelogram?

   A. 5.8 m
   B. 11.6 m
   C. 24 m
   D. 26.5 m

13. What is the side length of a square with perimeter 0.5 meter?

   A. 0.125 m
   B. 0.25 m
   C. 1 m
   D. 2 m

14. Mary bought a cover for her rectangular swimming pool for $76.80. The material for the cover cost $0.15 per square foot. Her pool is 32 feet long. How wide is her swimming pool?

   A. 16 feet
   B. 24 feet
   C. 44.8 feet
   D. 51.6 feet

15. Kevin is buying a rectangular rug. He wants the rug to have an area between 30 and 40 square feet, and the length must be 7 feet. Which could be the width of the rug?

   A. 3.9 feet
   B. 4.4 feet
   C. 5.8 feet
   D. 6.2 feet

16. The perimeter of a rectangle is greater than its area. The rectangle has a perimeter of 24 feet. Which could be the length?

   A. 2 ft
   B. 3 ft
   C. 4 ft
   D. 5 ft

DIRECTIONS: Study the figures and information, read each question, and choose the **best** answer.

The four figures below have the same area.

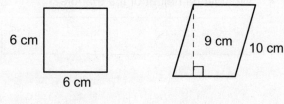

6 cm

6 cm

9 cm

10 cm

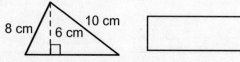

8 cm

6 cm

10 cm

4.5 cm

17. Which dimension has a value of 12 cm?

   A. base of triangle
   B. length of square
   C. length of rectangle
   D. width of parallelogram

18. Which figure has a perimeter of 25 cm?

   A. parallelogram
   B. rectangle
   C. square
   D. triangle

19. Which figure has the greatest difference between its area and perimeter?

   A. parallelogram
   B. rectangle
   C. square
   D. triangle

UNIT 4

20. Examine the parallelogram.

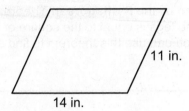

Which statement is correct?

A. The perimeter of the parallelogram is 25 in., because 11 + 14 = 25.
B. The area of the parallelogram is 154 in.², because 11 × 14 = 154.
C. The area of the parallelogram is 77 in.², because $\frac{1}{2}$(11)(14) = 77.
D. The perimeter of the parallelogram is 50 in., because 2(11) + 2(14) = 50 in.

DIRECTIONS: Examine the information and figure, read the question, and choose the **best** answer.

21. The isosceles triangle below is cut in half so that the height of each right triangle is the same as the isosceles triangle, and the base of each right triangle is one-half the base of the original triangle.

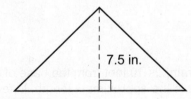

The area of the isosceles triangle is 75 square inches. What is the base of each right triangle?

A. 10 in.
B. 15 in.
C. 37.5 in.
D. 20 in.

DIRECTIONS: Study the figures and information, read each question, and choose the **best** answer.

Each triangle has an area of 30 cm².

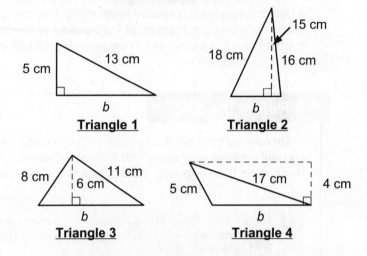

22. Which triangle has the longest base?

A. Triangle 1
B. Triangle 2
C. Triangle 3
D. Triangle 4

23. Which triangle has the greatest perimeter?

A. Triangle 1
B. Triangle 2
C. Triangle 3
D. Triangle 4

DIRECTIONS: Read each question, and choose the **best** answer.

24. Which of the following figures has the greatest width?

A. rectangle with area of 32 and length of 6
B. rectangle with area of 40 and length of 7
C. rectangle with area of 45 and length of 8
D. rectangle with area of 50 and length of 9

25. An isosceles triangle has a perimeter of 48 and one side length of 12. All of the following could be the length of one of the other two sides **except** which one?

A. 12
B. 18
C. 24
D. 30

UNIT 4

Pythagorean Theorem

Use with *Student Book* pp. 96–97

1 Review the Skill

MATH CONTENT TOPICS: Q.4.e, A.4.a
MATH PRACTICES: MP.1.a, MP.1.d, MP.1.e, M.P.2.b, MP.3.c, MP.4.b, MP.5.a

As you know, a **right triangle** has a right angle. The legs (shorter sides) and **hypotenuse** (longer side) of a right triangle have a special relationship that can be described by the **Pythagorean Theorem**. It states that, in any right triangle, the sum of the squares of the lengths of the legs is equal to the square of the length of the hypotenuse. It is expressed in equation form as $a^2 + b^2 = c^2$. You can use this theorem to find a missing length of a right triangle.

2 Refine the Skill

By refining the skill of using the Pythagorean Theorem to solve for the missing side of a right triangle, you will improve your study and test-taking abilities, especially as they relate to the GED® Mathematical Reasoning Test. Examine the diagram and strategies below. Then answer the questions that follow.

a The measurements of the legs of the right triangle are given. Solve for the hypotenuse to find the length of the ramp.

b To solve question 2, substitute 12 for 10 and solve for the hypotenuse. Remember that the hypotenuse is always the longest side of a right triangle.

A ramp was built to add wheelchair access to a public building. The ramp rises 2 feet, as shown in the diagram below.

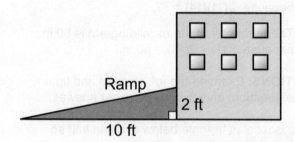

Ramp
2 ft
10 ft

UNIT 4

TEST-TAKING TIPS

Ensure that you're working with a right triangle before attempting to use the Pythagorean Theorem. It only applies to right triangles.

a 1. If the lower edge of the ramp is 10 feet from the base of the building along level ground, what is the approximate length, in feet, of the ramp?

A. 9.2
B. 9.6
C. 9.8
D. 10.2

b 2. The owners of the building are remodeling the front entrance. They would like to modify the ramp so that it begins 12 feet from the building. What will be the length of this new ramp?

A. 11.8 ft
B. 12.2 ft
C. 12.4 ft
D. 12.5 ft

⭐ Spotlighted Item: **FILL-IN-THE-BLANK**

DIRECTIONS: Study the coordinate plane, read each question, and fill in your answer in the box below.

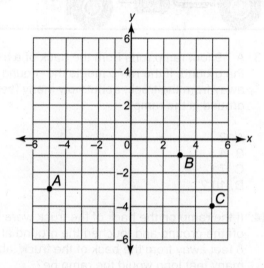

3. What is the distance between points *A* and *B*? Round your answer to the nearest hundredth.

4. What is the distance between points *A* and *C*? Round your answer to the nearest hundredth.

5. A new shape, Δ*JKL* is drawn on the given coordinates: *J* (−4, 4) *K* (−4, 0) *L* (2, 0). What is the distance between points *J* and *L*? Round your answer to the nearest hundredth.

6. What is the distance between points *K* and *L*?

7. What is the perimeter of Δ*JKL*? Round your answer to the nearest hundredth.

DIRECTIONS: Read the information and question, then choose the **best** answer.

Ella incorrectly determined the length of one of the legs of a right triangle. Her work is shown below.

$$4^2 + a^2 = 10^2$$
$$16 + a^2 = 100$$
$$a^2 = 116$$
$$a \approx 10.8$$

8. Which answer choice best describes why Ella's answer is incorrect?

A. She incorrectly found the square root of 116.
B. She incorrectly squared 10.
C. She incorrectly squared 4.
D. She added 16 when she should have subtracted.

DIRECTIONS: Read the figure and information below. Then read the question, and choose the **best** answer.

Dana designed the quilt square shown below.

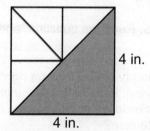

9. What is the length of the diagonal of the outside square? Round your answer to the nearest hundredth.

A. 5.66 in.
B. 4 in.
C. 2.83 in.
D. 2.01 in.

DIRECTIONS: Read the question, and choose the **best** answer.

10. A computer monitor is listed as measuring 21 inches This is the distance across the diagonal of the screen. If the screen is 16 inches wide, what is the height of the screen to the nearest tenth of an inch?

   A. 4.5
   B. 9.1
   C. 13.6
   D. 27.2

DIRECTIONS: Study the figure below, read the question, and choose the **best** answer.

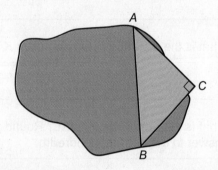

11. A surveyor wants to find the width of the pond. She placed stakes at points *A*, *B*, and *C*. She knows that Δ*ABC* is a right triangle. If the distance between *A* and *C* is 75 feet and the distance between *B* and *C* is 63 feet, what is the approximate width of the pond between points *A* and *B*?

   A. 12.2 feet
   B. 40.7 feet
   C. 54.5 feet
   D. 97.9 feet

DIRECTIONS: Read the question, and choose the **best** answer.

12. Caleb's empty binder forms a right triangle from the side view. If the binder is 3 inches tall and 11 inches wide, what is the approximate length of the hypotenuse?

   A. 8 in.
   B. 9.2 in.
   C. 11.4 in.
   D. 14 in.

DIRECTIONS: Study the diagram, read each question, and choose the **best** answer.

13. A 7.9 foot ramp runs from the back of a truck to the ground. If the ramp meets the ground 6.5 feet away from the truck, about how many feet off the ground is the ramp?

   A. 2
   B. 4.5
   C. 7.1
   D. 10.2

14. If the ramp on the back of the truck were 5 feet off the ground and touched the ground at a point 8 feet away from the back of the truck, about how many feet long would the ramp be?

   A. 3.6
   B. 5.3
   C. 9.1
   D. 9.4

DIRECTIONS: Read each question, and choose the **best** answer.

15. A right triangle has sides of 55 inches and 40 inches. What is the length of the hypotenuse to the nearest foot?

   A. 5
   B. 6
   C. 7
   D. 8

16. Laptop monitors are measured diagonally. Mona's laptop monitor measures 6 inches tall by 8.5 inches wide. What is her monitor's measurement?

   A. 10 inches
   B. 10.2 inches
   C. 10.4 inches
   D. 10.8 inches

UNIT 4

DIRECTIONS: Study the information and diagram, read each question, and choose the **best** answer.

Henry is building a walkway through a rectangular garden as shown in the diagram below.

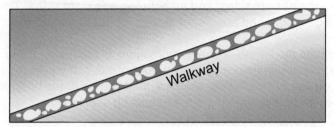

17. If the length of the garden is 30 yards and the width of the garden is 17 yards, what is the approximate length of the walkway in yards?

    A. 34.5
    B. 24.7
    C. 21.4
    D. 13.3

18. If the length of the walkway is 40 yards and the width of the garden is 12 yards, what is the approximate length of the garden in yards?

    A. 28.4
    B. 38.2
    C. 41.8
    D. 52.3

DIRECTIONS: Read each question, and choose the **best** answer.

19. A 15-foot ladder is placed against the side of a building so that it reaches 12 feet up the side of the building. How far away from the building is its base?

    A. 8 feet
    B. 9 feet
    C. 10 feet
    D. 11 feet

20. The ladder is extended to 18 feet. It now reaches 16 feet up the side of the building. About how far away from the building is its base now?

    A. 8.2 feet
    B. 9 feet
    C. 9.2 feet
    D. 10 feet

21. The 18-foot ladder is placed 6 feet from the side of the building. About how far up the building does it reach now?

    A. 13 feet
    B. 15.2 feet
    C. 17 feet
    D. 17.1 feet

DIRECTIONS: Study the figure and information below, read each question, and choose the **best** answer.

The front view of a dollhouse is shown below.

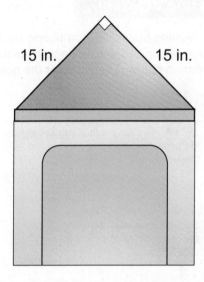

15 in.   15 in.

22. What is the approximate width of the dollhouse in inches?

    A. 17.5
    B. 18.6
    C. 19.2
    D. 21.2

23. What is the perimeter of the triangular section of the roof?

    A. 45 inches
    B. 51.2 inches
    C. 112.5 inches
    D. 225 inches

24. If the height of the rectangular section is 18 inches, what is the perimeter of the front view?

    A. 69.2 inches
    B. 87.2 inches
    C. 90.4 inches
    D. 108.4 inches

Polygons

Use with *Student Book* pp. 98–99

1 Review the Skill

MATH CONTENT TOPICS: Q.2.a, Q.2.e, Q.4.c
MATH PRACTICES: MP.1.a, MP.1.b, MP.1.d, MP.1.e, MP.2.c, MP.3.a, MP.3.b, MP.4.a, MP.5.b

A **polygon** is any closed figure with three or more sides. A polygon is named according to its number of sides. For example, a pentagon has five sides, a hexagon has six sides, and an octagon has eight sides. The perimeter of a **regular polygon** is the product of its side length and number of sides. The perimeter of an **irregular polygon** is the sum of its side lengths.

If you know the perimeter, you may be able to determine the length of one or more sides of the figure. If you know the perimeter and side length of a regular polygon, you can determine the number of sides. If you know the perimeter and number of sides of a regular polygon, you can determine the side length. If you know the perimeter and some side lengths of an irregular polygon, you may be able to determine the remaining side lengths.

2 Refine the Skill

By refining the skill of computing side length and perimeter of polygons, you will improve your study and test-taking abilities, especially as they relate to the GED® Mathematical Reasoning Test. Study the information below. Then answer the questions that follow.

a The perimeter of a regular polygon is *ns*, where *n* is the number of sides and *s* is the side length. If you know the perimeter, work backward to find the side length: $s = p \div n$.

b The perimeter of an irregular polygon is the sum of its side lengths. Subtract the known side lengths from the perimeter to find the remaining side length.

c To answer question 2, multiply the number of feet by 12 to find the answer in inches.

Each figure has a perimeter of 27 feet.

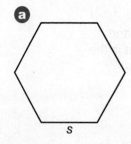

a

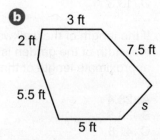

b

3 ft

2 ft

7.5 ft

5.5 ft

s

5 ft

s

UNIT 4

TEST-TAKING TIPS

Carefully read and analyze each figure, question, and answer option to ensure understanding. In question 2, for example, the calculated side length requires a conversion from feet to inches.

1. What is the length of each side of the regular hexagon?

   A. 3.375 feet
   B. 4.5 feet
   C. 5.4 feet
   D. 21 feet

2. What is the difference, in inches, between the side length of the regular hexagon and the unknown side length of the irregular hexagon?

   A. 5 in.
   B. 6 in.
   C. 12 in.
   D. 48 in.

DIRECTIONS: Study the information and figure, read each question, and choose the **best** answer.

The figure below has a perimeter of 32 meters.

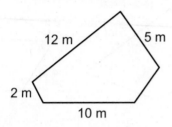

12 m 5 m

2 m

10 m

3. What is the missing side length in the figure?

   A. 3 m
   B. 5 m
   C. 5.8 m
   D. 6.4 m

4. What is the side length of a regular pentagon with the same perimeter?

   A. 5.8 m
   B. 6.2 m
   C. 6.4 m
   D. 15.4 m

DIRECTIONS: Read the question, and choose the **best** answer.

5. The park map shows a walking path that connects the entrance, the snack bar, the fountain, and the playground. The total distance along the walking path is 135 yd.

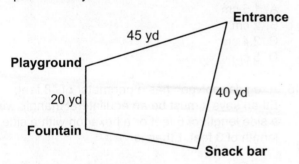

Entrance

45 yd

Playground

20 yd 40 yd

Fountain

Snack bar

What is the length of the path between the fountain and the snack bar?

   A. 30 yd
   B. 45 yd
   C. 70 yd
   D. 105 yd

DIRECTIONS: Read each question, and choose the **best** answer.

6. Which regular polygon has the greatest side length?

   A. square with perimeter 36 feet
   B. octagon with perimeter 32 feet
   C. hexagon with perimeter 30 feet
   D. pentagon with perimeter 35 feet

7. The figure below has a perimeter of 70 cm. What is the missing side length in the figure?

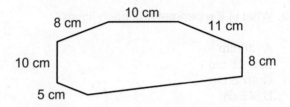

10 cm

8 cm 11 cm

10 cm 8 cm

5 cm

   A. 10 cm
   B. 18 cm
   C. 21 cm
   D. 52 cm

8. A regular polygon has a perimeter of 21 inches and a side length of 3.5 inches. How many sides does the polygon have?

   A. 4
   B. 5
   C. 6
   D. 7

9. Eli bends a piece of wire into a regular octagon with a side length of 2.5 in. Then he bends the same piece of wire into a regular pentagon. What is the side length of the pentagon?

   A. 3 in.
   B. 4 in.
   C. 5.5 in.
   D. 7.5 in.

UNIT 4

DIRECTIONS: Study the information and figures, read each question, and choose the **best** answer.

The figures below have the same perimeter and the figure on the left is a regular pentagon.

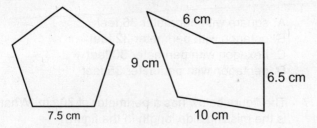

10. What is the perimeter of each figure?

    A. 30 cm
    B. 31.5 cm
    C. 37.5 cm
    D. 45 cm

11. What is the missing side length in the irregular polygon?

    A. 6 cm
    B. 6.3 cm
    C. 7 cm
    D. 7.5 cm

DIRECTIONS: Study the information and figure, read the question, and choose the **best** answer.

12. The figure below has a perimeter of 33.5 inches.

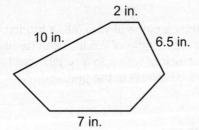

The two missing side lengths are equal. What is each unknown side length?

    A. 4 in.
    B. 5 in.
    C. 8 in.
    D. 16 in.

DIRECTIONS: Study the information and figures, read the question, and choose the **best** answer.

13. Examine the irregular polygons below.

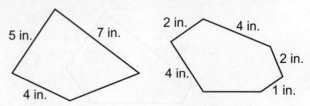

Which statement provides enough information to find the missing side length of the irregular hexagon?

    A. The two figures have the same perimeter.
    B. The quadrilateral has a perimeter of 22 in.
    C. The two figures have the same perimeter of 22 in.
    D. The missing side length of the quadrilateral is 6 in.

DIRECTIONS: Read each question, and choose the **best** answer.

14. A box has a cross-section that is a regular octagon with a side length of 3.5 centimeters. Ella wraps a 40-centimeter ribbon around the box and cuts off the extra ribbon. The extra ribbon fits perfectly around a box whose cross-section is a regular hexagon. What is the side length of the regular hexagon?

    A. 1.5 cm
    B. 2 cm
    C. 2.4 cm
    D. 5 cm

15. A regular polygon has a perimeter of 18 feet. Ethan says it must be an equilateral triangle with a side length of 6 feet or a hexagon with a side length of 3 feet. Ethan is

    A. correct, because 3 × 6 = 18 and 6 × 3 = 18.
    B. correct, because the side length must be a whole number.
    C. incorrect, because it could have a side length of 9 feet or 18 feet.
    D. incorrect, because the polygon could have 8 sides with a side length of 2.25 feet.

DIRECTIONS: Read each question. Then use the drag-and-drop options to complete each answer.

16. A regular octagon with a perimeter of ☐ inches has a side length of ☐ inches.

| 4.5 | 5 | 40 | 45 |

18. A regular ☐ with a perimeter of 12 inches has a side length of ☐ inches.

| pentagon | octagon | 1.5 | 2 |

17. A regular ☐ with a perimeter of ☐ cm has a side length of 9 cm.

| hexagon | pentagon | 50 | 54 |

19. A regular ☐-sided figure with a perimeter of 31.5 cm has a side length of ☐ cm.

| 7 | 8 | 3.5 | 4.5 |

DIRECTIONS: Study the information and figure. Read the question. Then choose the **best** answer.

20. Daniel installed a swimming pool in the shape of a regular hexagon. He surrounded the swimming pool with a deck and built a hexagonal fence around the deck. The outside edge of the deck is 6 feet wider than the side of the pool. The fence has a perimeter of 108 feet.

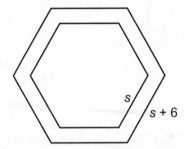

How long is each side of the swimming pool?

A. 12 ft
B. 18 ft
C. 24 ft
D. 17 ft

DIRECTIONS: Read each question, and choose the **best** answer.

21. The shortest side of an irregular pentagon is 3 inches long. The longest side is 9 inches long. Which could be the perimeter of the pentagon?

A. 15 in.
B. 24 in.
C. 57 in.
D. 76 in.

22. The figure on the left is a regular polygon.

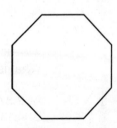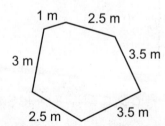

If the perimeter of the regular polygon is 1.5 times the perimeter of the irregular polygon, what is the side length of the regular polygon?

A. 2 m
B. 3 m
C. 4 m
D. 5 m

Circles

Use with **Student Book** pp. 100–101

MATH CONTENT TOPICS: Q.2.a, Q.2.e, Q.4.b, A.2.a, A.2.b, A.2.c
MATH PRACTICES: MP.1.a, MP.1.b, MP.1.d, MP.1.e, MP.2.c, MP.4.a, MP.4.b

1 Review the Skill

A **circle** is a closed figure with no sides or corners. All points on a circle are equidistant from the center. The distance from the center of a circle to any point on the circle is called the **radius**. The **diameter** is the distance across a circle through its center. The diameter is always twice the radius. The distance around a circle is known as its **circumference**.

To find a circle's circumference, use the formula $C = \pi d$. To find a circle's area, use the formula $A = \pi r^2$. You may find a circle's circumference or area if you know either its radius or its diameter. If you know the radius of a circle, you may double it to find the diameter. If you know the diameter of a circle, you may divide it by 2 to find the radius.

2 Refine the Skill

By refining the skills of finding the circumference and area of a circle, you will improve your study and test-taking abilities, especially as they relate to the GED® Mathematical Reasoning Test. Study the information below. Then answer the questions that follow.

a For both questions, you know the circumference and want to find the diameter. Use the formula for circumference and then work backward.

b Note that the information provided is in *inches*. For question 2, multiply the number of stones by the diameter of a stone. Then divide by 12 (inches in a foot) to find the number of *feet*.

Elizabeth created a path through her garden with identical round paving stones like those shown below. The circumference of each stone is 25.9 inches.

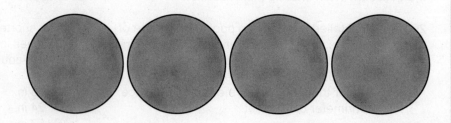

CONTENT TOPICS

Content Topic Q.4.a states that students must "compute the area and circumference of circles." In so doing, they should determine the radius or diameter when given the area or circumference.

1. What is the approximate diameter of each stone in inches?

   A. 2.87
   B. 4.13
   C. 6.48
   D. 8.25

b 2. If Elizabeth uses 35 stones, about how many feet long will her garden path be?

   A. 24
   B. 76
   C. 92
   D. 289

⭐ Spotlighted Item: **FILL-IN-THE-BLANK**

DIRECTIONS: Study the information and diagram below, read each question, and write your answer in the box below.

The circles below have the same center. The radius of the smaller circle is 3 inches. The radius of the larger circle is 7 inches.

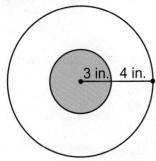

3. What is the approximate circumference of the smaller circle?

	inches

4. What is the approximate circumference of the larger circle?

	inches

DIRECTIONS: Read each question, and write your answer in the box below.

5. A birdbath has a diameter of 30 inches. What is the approximate circumference of the birdbath in inches?

6. Linda is cutting circle shapes for a bulletin board. If she wants to cut a circle that has a circumference of 25.12 inches, what should the radius of the circle be in inches?

7. Jenna's sports bottle has an approximate circumference of 19 inches. What is the diameter of the sports bottle to the nearest inch?

	inches

DIRECTIONS: Read each question, and choose the **best** answer.

8. Lydia is using a tire to build a sandbox. She is cutting plywood to use as a cover for the tire.

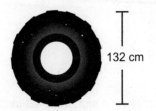

132 cm

About how many square centimeters of plywood does Lydia need to cover the tire?

A. 414
B. 828
C. 13,678
D. 54,711

9. Mr. Dunn is painting a large circle in the middle of a gymnasium. The diameter of the circle is 12 feet. What is the approximate area of the circle?

A. 18.84 ft²
B. 37.68 ft²
C. 75.36 ft²
D. 113.04 ft²

10. What is the radius of a circle that has a circumference of 50.24 inches?

A. 8 inches
B. 16 inches
C. 20 inches
D. 32 inches

UNIT 4

DIRECTIONS: Study the information and diagram, read each question, and choose the **best** answer.

The circular mirror below has a frame that is 2 inches wide. The diameter of the mirror and frame together is 11 inches.

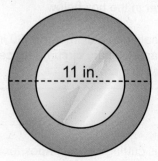

11 in.

11. What is the radius of the mirror without the frame?

A. 3.5 in.
B. 4.5 in.
C. 7 in.
D. 9 in.

12. What is the area of the mirror only in square inches?

A. 34.5
B. 38.5
C. 40.8
D. 95

13. What is the area of the frame only to the nearest tenth of square inch?

A. 151.5
B. 95
C. 56.5
D. 12.6

14. What is the approximate circumference of the mirror with the frame?

A. 34.54 inches
B. 35.64 inches
C. 47.10 inches
D. 94.99 inches

15. The area of a second mirror is 1.5 times the area of the mirror alone described above. About what is the diameter of the second mirror?

A. 4.3 inches
B. 8.6 inches
C. 12 inches
D. 17.5 inches

DIRECTIONS: Study the information and diagram below, read each question, and choose the **best** answer.

A circular tablecloth is shown in the diagram below.

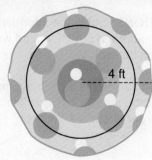

4 ft

16. About how many square feet is the tablecloth?

A. 200.96
B. 100.48
C. 50.24
D. 25.12

17. Tomas places the tablecloth on a circular table that has a diameter of 6 feet. About how many square feet of the tablecloth will hang over the edge of the table?

A. 12.56
B. 21.98
C. 50.24
D. 78.50

DIRECTIONS: Read each question, and choose the **best** answer.

18. Jonna is sewing a front cover for a circular pillow. The pillow has a diameter of 15 inches. To sew the front cover, she must cut the fabric two inches wider than the pillow all the way around. What is the minimum area, in square inches, of the piece of fabric she will use?

A. 706.5
B. 283.4
C. 226.9
D. 95

19. Carol is making a sign from felt circles that she will tie together in a row. One circle has a circumference of 37.68 inches. How many circles will she need to tie together to have a banner that is 60 inches long?

A. 2
B. 3
C. 4
D. 5

DIRECTIONS: Study the information and diagram, read each question, and choose the **best** answer.

A hotel swimming pool is in the shape of a sideways number eight.

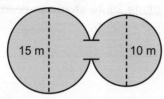

20. What is the approximate area of the swimming pool in square meters?

    A. 78
    B. 255
    C. 471
    D. 1,019

21. If the diameter of the smaller section is increased by 45 cm, what will be the approximate area of the entire enlarged pool?

    A. 79.9 square meters
    B. 255.57 square meters
    C. 262.35 square meters
    D. 269.89 square meters

DIRECTIONS: Read each question, and choose the **best** answer.

22. A large circle has a radius of 6 meters. A smaller circle has a radius of 2 meters. Which statement is correct?

    A. The circumference of the larger circle is 3 times the circumference of the smaller circle, and the area of the larger circle is 3 times the area of the smaller circle.
    B. The circumference of the larger circle is 3 times the circumference of the smaller circle, and the area of the larger circle is 9 times the area of the smaller circle.
    C. The circumference of the larger circle is 9 times the circumference of the smaller circle, and the area of the larger circle is 3 times the area of the smaller circle.
    D. The circumference of the larger circle is 9 times the circumference of the smaller circle, and the area of the larger circle is 9 times the area of the smaller circle.

23. What is the approximate difference in square inches between the areas of the two circles?

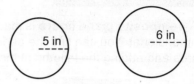

    A. 1
    B. 3.14
    C. 6.28
    D. 34.54

24. Dillon is building a model airplane. The front tires each have a diameter of 3.5 inches. What is the total circumference of the two tires to the nearest whole number?

    A. 7 in.
    B. 11 in.
    C. 20 in.
    D. 22 in.

DIRECTIONS: Study the information and diagram, read each question, and choose the **best** answer.

Ava hung a circular sunshield in a window in her living room to block the afternoon sun.

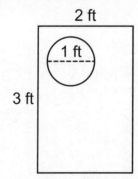

25. What is the approximate area of the sunshield in square feet?

    A. 3.14
    B. 1.57
    C. 1
    D. 0.79

26. About what percent of the area of her window is covered by the sunshield?

    A. 13%
    B. 16%
    C. 17%
    D. 50%

Composite Plane Figures

Use with *Student Book* pp. 102–103

MATH CONTENT TOPICS: Q.4.a, Q.4.b, Q.4.d
MATH PRACTICES: MP.1.a, MP.1.b, MP.1.c, MP.1.d, MP.3.a

① Review the Skill

A **composite plane figure** is made up of several shapes or parts of shapes. Composite plane figures are 2-dimensional. You can find the perimeter or area of a composite plane figure shape by dividing it into simpler figures and adding the lengths of the sides or the areas of each simple figure.

② Refine the Skill

By refining the skills of recognizing composite plane figures and calculating their area and perimeter, you will improve your study and test-taking abilities, especially as they relate to the GED® Mathematical Reasoning Test. Study the information below. Then answer the question that follows.

a Question 1 asks you to find the area of the actual tablecloth. Calculate numerical values for the actual product by first multiplying by 2. Next, calculate the area of each component shape to find the total area of this irregular figure. For example:

Total area = Area of semicircle + rectangle + semicircle

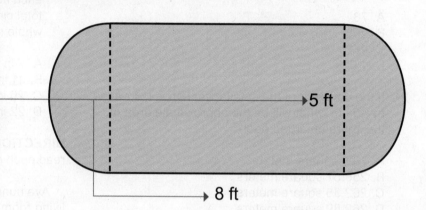

USING LOGIC

You can sometimes arrive at an answer by closely analyzing the figure. For example, calculating the area of one circle gives the same value as calculating 2 semicircles and then adding them together.

1. The image above represents a sketch of the top view of a sample tablecloth. If the actual tablecloth has dimensions twice as large as the sample, determine the approximate area of the actual tablecloth.

   A. 40 ft²
   B. 78.5 ft²
   C. 179.63 ft²
   D. 238.5 ft²

2. What is the approximate area of the two semicircular regions in the sample tablecloth?

   A. 19.63 ft²
   B. 47.9 ft²
   C. 55.7 ft²
   D. 59.63 ft²

3 Master the Skill

DIRECTIONS: Study the information and figure, read each question, and choose the **best** answer.

The diagram below shows Laura's living room space.

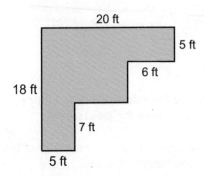

3. Laura is carpeting her living room. How many square feet of carpet will she need?

   A. 76
   B. 189
   C. 219
   D. 317

4. Laura needs tacking strips to go on the floor around the outer edge beneath the carpet. How many feet of tacking strips will she need?

   A. 72
   B. 76
   C. 78
   D. 85

DIRECTIONS: Study the information and figure, read the question, and choose the **best** answer.

The following image was painted on the floor of a second grade classroom.

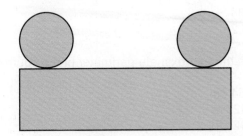

5. The radius of each circle is 3 cm. The area of the rectangle is 226.1 cm. What is the area of the entire figure to the nearest square centimeter?

   A. 36
   B. 226.1
   C. 254.4
   D. 282.62

DIRECTIONS: Read the question, and choose the **best** answer.

6. Corinne ordered a pizza with a diameter of 16 in. The pizza was cut into 8 equal slices. She ate 3 slices. What is the approximate area of the remaining pizza?

   A. 75.36 sq in.
   B. 100.48 sq in.
   C. 125.6 sq in.
   D. 200.96 sq in.

DIRECTIONS: Study the information and figure, read the question, and choose the **best** answer.

Adam is tiling the bathroom floor shown below.

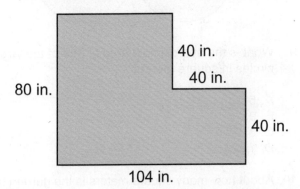

7. If each tile is 8 inches by 8 inches, how many tiles does he need to cover the floor?

   A. 64
   B. 105
   C. 116
   D. 124

DIRECTIONS: Study the figure, read the question, and choose the **best** answer.

8. A theater company builds a backdrop above the stage for a play. If the height of the triangle is 3 m, what is the area of the backdrop?

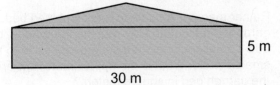

   A. 30 m²
   B. 150 m²
   C. 195 m²
   D. 360 m²

A. 30 m²

UNIT 4

DIRECTIONS: Study the information and figure, read each question, and choose the **best** answer.

The diagram shows the setup of the main garden bed in a rose garden. The two larger circles are congruent.

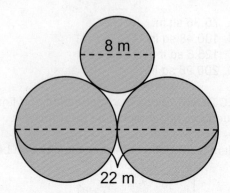

8 m

22 m

9. What is the approximate area of one of the larger circles in square meters?

   A. 50
   B. 95
   C. 379
   D. 1,520

10. About how many square meters is the garden bed?

    A. 145
    B. 190
    C. 240
    D. 290

11. The gardener considered merging the three garden beds into one even larger circle that has the same area as the three circles. What would the diameter of the new, larger circle-shaped bed be?

    A. 17 m
    B. 17.2 m
    C. 17.5 m
    D. 17.8 m

12. Rather than consolidate to one combined bed, the gardener decided to stay with the three beds, but add 1 smaller circled bed congruent in size to the smaller circle. What is the approximate new area of the garden bed in square meters?

    A. 190 m²
    B. 240 m²
    C. 290 m²
    D. 580 m²

13. The gardener decided to extend a 10-meter rectangular bed from the diameter of one of the smaller beds. What is the approximate area of the extension?

    A. 12.56 m²
    B. 25.12 m²
    C. 54.88 m²
    D. 100.48 m²

DIRECTIONS: Study the information and figure, read each question, and choose the **best** answer.

Stew drew the figure below. The diameter of the semicircle is also the height of the rectangle.

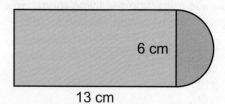

6 cm

13 cm

14. The semicircle at the end of the rectangle is exactly one half of a complete circle. What is the approximate area of the semicircle in squared centimeters?

    A. 9.42
    B. 14.13
    C. 28.26
    D. 78.39

15. What is the approximate area of the figure in square centimeters?

    A. 87.42
    B. 92.13
    C. 96.84
    D. 106.26

16. What is the approximate perimeter of the figure?

    A. 50.84 cm
    B. 47.42 cm
    C. 41.42 cm
    D. 38.84 cm

17. If the figure were twice as tall, what would be the approximate area?

    A. 156.37
    B. 174.84
    C. 184.26
    D. 212.52

UNIT 4

The figure shows an isosceles triangle set on top of a rectangle.

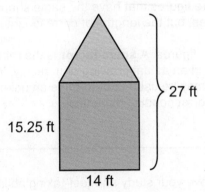

18. What is the height of the triangle?

    A. 11.75 ft
    B. 13.5 ft
    C. 14 ft
    D. 15.25 ft

19. What is the area of the figure?

    A. 56.3 ft²
    B. 75 ft²
    C. 295.75 ft²
    D. 378 ft²

20. What is the perimeter of the figure?

    A. 56.7 ft
    B. 68 ft
    C. 71.9 ft
    D. 75 ft

21. Suppose that the two shapes were pulled apart, and that the triangle has all sides equal to its base. Fencing is needed to enclose each shape. How much fencing is needed?

    A. 100.5 ft
    B. 93.75 ft
    C. 58.5 ft
    D. 42 ft

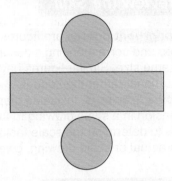

A few Grade 3 students create a huge division sign from paper, as outlined above. The rectangular portion measures 24 inches by 18 inches, and the diameter of each circle is also 18 inches.

22. What is the approximate area of the entire shape measured in square inches?

    A. 432
    B. 508
    C. 941
    D. 1,200

23. The students wish to paint all parts of the sign, except one of the circles. What is the approximate area will they paint?

    A. 470
    B. 686
    C. 941
    D. 1,200

24. If each container of paint covers 100 square inches, what is the minimum amount of paint containers required to paint the entire figure?

    A. 6
    B. 7
    C. 10
    D. 12

25. If the length of the rectangle is doubled, what would be the new area of the entire figure?

    A. 50.24 sq in.
    B. 654.17 sq in.
    C. 1,372.7 sq in.
    D. 5,000 sq in.

Scale Drawings

Use with *Student Book* pp. 104–105

MATH CONTENT TOPICS: Q.3.b, Q.3.c
MATH PRACTICES: MP.1.a, MP.1.b, MP.1.d

1 Review the Skill

Congruent figures are figures that are exactly the same shape and size because their corresponding angles and corresponding sides are equal. **Similar figures** are figures that have the same shape, but not the same size. Similar figures have equal corresponding angles, but the lengths of corresponding sides are proportional rather than equal.

Scale drawings, including maps and blueprints, are similar figures. A **scale factor** is the ratio of a dimension in a scale drawing to the corresponding dimension in an actual drawing or in reality. You can use ratios to determine the scale factor of a drawing. Proportions may be used to determine an unknown dimension in an actual or scale drawing, given the scale factor and the corresponding dimension.

2 Refine the Skill

By refining the skill of proportional reasoning, you will improve your study and test-taking abilities, especially as they relate to the GED® Mathematical Reasoning Test. Study the diagram and information below. Then answer the questions that follow.

a Read question 1 carefully to understand the part of the proportion that is unknown. Here, you know the length of the actual object and need to find its length in the floor plan.

b Question 2 is seeking the length of the larger living room. Ensure that you read each question carefully to understand its meaning.

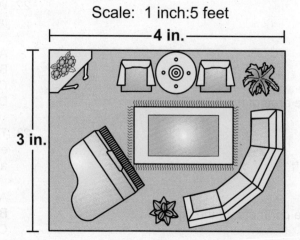

Scale: 1 inch:5 feet

4 in.

3 in.

USING LOGIC

Use common knowledge to determine whether your answer makes sense. For example, it would be reasonable for a room to be 12 feet wide and 8 feet long, not 12 inches wide or 12 inches long.

1. The length of the area rug in the actual living room is 8 feet. How many inches long is the area rug in the floor plan?

   A. 0.625 in.
   B. 0.975 in.
   C. 1.6 in.
   D. 5.8 in.

2. A similar floor plan will be used to build a smaller living room in the basement. If the smaller floor plan has a length of 3 inches, what is the length of the smaller living room?

   A. 3 feet
   B. 15 feet
   C. 20 feet
   D. 24 feet

UNIT 4

DIRECTIONS: Study the figures and information, read the question, and choose the **best** answer.

A 4-inch by 6-inch photograph is enlarged proportionally, as shown in the diagram.

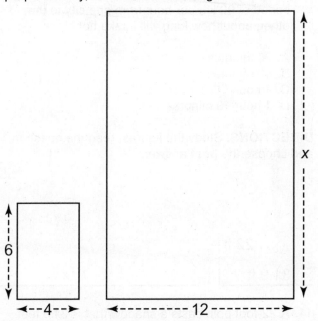

3. What is the measure, in inches, of the longer side in the enlargement?

   A. 9
   B. 12
   C. 15
   D. 18

DIRECTIONS: Read each question, and choose the **best** answer.

4. Two towns on a map are 3.5 inches apart. The map scale is 1 inch:5.5 miles. What is the actual distance, in miles, between the two towns?

   A. 2.25
   B. 9.25
   C. 11.25
   D. 19.25

5. Lake Superior is 350 miles in length. If the map scale is 1 inch:25 miles, how many inches long is Lake Superior on the map?

   A. 14
   B. 16
   C. 325
   D. 8,750

6. Peri biked 19.2 miles. She drew a map of her route for a friend using a scale of 2 inches = 3.2 miles. How many inches long is Peri's route on the map she drew?

   A. 8
   B. 10
   C. 12
   D. 31

DIRECTIONS: Study the figure, read each question, and choose the **best** answer.

On the map below, 2 centimeters represent 6.5 kilometers in actuality.

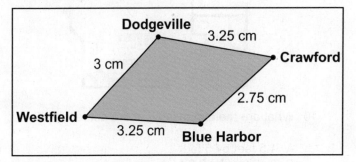

7. To the nearest tenth of a kilometer, what is the actual distance in kilometers between Dodgeville and Crawford?

   A. 4
   B. 9.8
   C. 10
   D. 10.6

8. About how many more kilometers would you drive from Blue Harbor to Dodgeville through Westfield than from Blue Harbor to Dodgeville through Crawford?

   A. 0.1
   B. 0.4
   C. 0.6
   D. 0.8

DIRECTIONS: Read the question, and choose the **best** answer.

9. Bloomington is 48 km from Orchard Point. On a map, these towns are 4 cm apart. What is the scale of this map?

   A. 1 cm = 16 km
   B. 1 cm = 12 km
   C. 1 cm = 8 km
   D. 1 cm = 0.5 km

DIRECTIONS: Study the diagram, read each question, and choose the **best** answer.

In this floor plan, the scale is 0.5 inch = 5 feet.

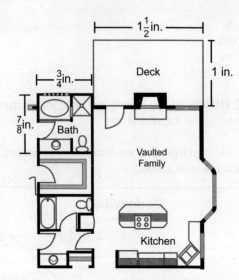

10. What are the dimensions of the actual deck?

    A. 1.5 feet by 5 feet
    B. 0.15 feet by 0.8 feet
    C. 5 feet by 7.5 feet
    D. 10 feet by 15 feet

11. What is the actual length of the longer side of the bathroom?

    A. $8\frac{3}{4}$ ft

    B. $8\frac{1}{2}$ ft

    C. 8 ft

    D. $4\frac{3}{8}$ ft

12. What are the dimensions of the actual bath?

    A. $7\frac{1}{2}$ feet by $8\frac{3}{4}$ feet

    B. $5\frac{1}{2}$ feet by $8\frac{1}{2}$ feet

    C. 5 feet by 8 feet

    D. $4\frac{3}{8}$ feet by $7\frac{1}{2}$ feet

DIRECTIONS: Read the question, and choose the **best** answer.

13. A map scale is 3 cm:18 km. Two cities are 10 cm apart on the map. If Stacey drives at an average speed of 90 km per hour from one city to the other, about how long will it take her?

    A. 20 minutes
    B. 40 minutes
    C. 1 hour
    D. 1 hour 10 minutes

DIRECTIONS: Study the figures, read the question, and choose the **best** answer.

	55 ft
22 ft	
31.9 ft	x

14. A 22-foot pole casts a shadow that is 31.9 feet long. At the same time of day, about how many feet long would a 55-foot building's shadow be?

    A. 31.9
    B. 37.9
    C. 64.9
    D. 79.8

DIRECTIONS: Read each question, and choose the **best** answer.

15. An animal that is 4.2 feet tall casts a shadow that is 3.8 feet long. At the same time of day, a second animal casts a shadow that is 6.8 feet long. About how tall is the second animal?

    A. 7.5 ft
    B. 7.2 ft
    C. 6.4 ft
    D. 6.2 ft

16. A model car has a scale of 1 inch:32 inches. If the length of the bumper of the actual car is 108.8 inches, about how many inches long is the bumper on the model car?

    A. 3.1 in.
    B. 3.3 in.
    C. 3.4 in.
    D. 3.6 in.

UNIT 4

17. A scale drawing of a square lot has a perimeter of 22 cm. The scale of the drawing is 2 cm:5 yd. How long is one side of the square in actuality?

    A. 2.2 yd
    B. 5.5 yd
    C. 13.75 yd
    D. 55 yd

DIRECTIONS: Study the information and diagram, read each question, and choose the **best** answer.

Michael had to submit the scale drawing below with his application for a permit to build a new deck.

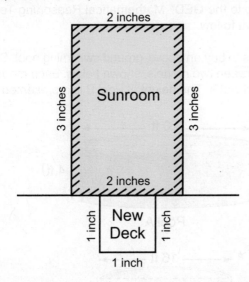

18. If the longer side of the actual sunroom is 30 feet long, what is the scale of the map?

    A. 1 in.:7 ft
    B. 1 in.:10 ft
    C. 1 in.:15 ft
    D. 1 in.:20 ft

19. If the map has a scale of 0.5 in.:6.5 ft, what are the actual dimensions of the new deck?

    A. 3.25 feet by 3.25 feet
    B. 7 feet by 7 feet
    C. 10 feet by 10 feet
    D. 13 feet by 13 feet

DIRECTIONS: Study the information and figures, read the question, and choose the **best** answer.

The following right triangles are similar. Line segment CB corresponds to the segment GF.

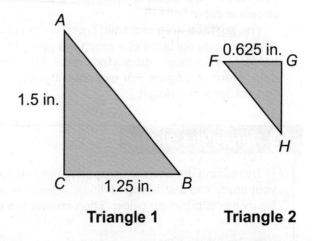

Triangle 1   **Triangle 2**

20. What is the scale factor between Triangles 1 and 2?

    A. 0.78
    B. 1.5
    C. 2
    D. 2.4

DIRECTIONS: Read the question, study the figure, and choose the **best** answer.

21. A carpet company makes two sizes of a popular carpet. The carpets are similar, and the length (longer side) of the smaller carpet is 10 ft. What is the width of the smaller carpet?

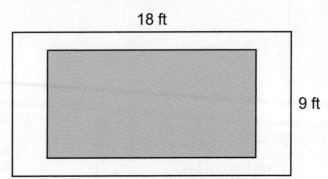

    A. 1.8 ft
    B. 5 ft
    C. 16.2 ft
    D. 162 ft

UNIT 4

Prisms and Cylinders

Use with *Student Book* pp. 106–107

MATH CONTENT TOPICS: Q.2.a, Q.2.e, Q.5.a, Q.5.b, Q.5.c, A.2.a, A.2.b, A.2.c
MATH PRACTICES: MP.1.a, MP.1.b, MP.1.d, MP.1.e, MP.2.a, MP.2.c, MP.4.a, MP.4.b, MP.5.b

1 Review the Skill

A **solid figure** is a 3-dimensional figure. The **volume** of a solid figure is the amount of space it occupies. The volume of a prism or cylinder is the product of the area of its base and its height. Volume is measured and shown in cubic units (^{3}).

The **surface area** of a solid figure is the sum of the areas of its two bases *and* the area of its lateral surfaces. The surfaces of a prism are polygons. Use formulas for the areas of triangles, rectangles, and other polygons to compute the surface area of a prism. Such formulas will help you to determine the complete dimensions of a figure. For example, if you know the area of the base of a cylinder and it's surface area, you can calculate the height.

2 Refine the Skill

By refining the skills of computing the surface area and volume of prisms and cylinders, you will improve your study and test-taking abilities, especially as they relate to the GED® Mathematical Reasoning Test. Study the information below. Then answer the questions that follow.

a The volume of the two pools is the same. For question 1, since the diameter and height are both given for Pool A, find the volume of this pool.

b Remember that the formula for volume of a cylinder uses the radius, not the diameter. For both questions, divide the diameter by 2 to find the radius.

Genevieve wants to buy an above-ground swimming pool. She is trying to decide between two models, shown below. Each model holds the same amount of water. The height of Pool B is represented by *x*.

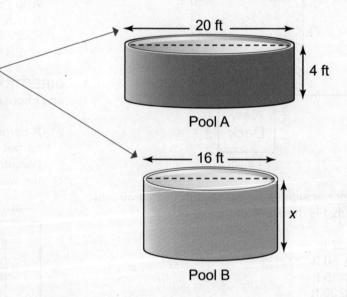

Pool A — 20 ft, 4 ft

Pool B — 16 ft, *x*

TEST-TAKING TIPS

Questions relating to solid figures and volume may ask you to solve for diameter, radius, or area of a base, or the length, width, or height of a figure. Read each problem carefully to decide what to solve.

1. What is the volume, to the nearest cubic foot, of each pool?

   A. 400
   B. 1,005
   C. 1,256
   D. 5,024

2. What is the height, in feet, of Pool B?

   A. 4.25 ft
   B. 6.25 ft
   C. 8 ft
   D. 10 ft

DIRECTIONS: Read each question, and choose the **best** answer.

3. A grocery store sells Italian sausage in the cylindrical tube-shaped package shown below.

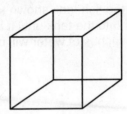

10 in.

If the radius of the package is about 1.5 inches, how many cubic inches is the package?

A. 70.65
B. 93.40
C. 104.67
D. 141.30

4. A cylinder has a diameter of 10 meters and a height of 7 meters. What is the volume of the cylinder?

A. 109.9 m³
B. 549.5 m³
C. 1725.4 m³
D. 2198 m³

DIRECTIONS: Study the information and figure, read each question, and choose the **best** answer.

The cube-shaped box below has a length, width, and height of 18 inches.

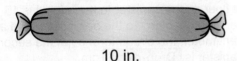

5. What is the volume of the box to the nearest cubic foot?

A. 3
B. 36
C. 324
D. 5,832

6. What is the surface area of the box to the nearest square foot?

A. 14
B. 19
C. 324
D. 1944

DIRECTIONS: Read each question, and choose the **best** answer.

7. Anaya's perfume bottle is a rectangular prism. The bottle is 2.5 centimeters wide and 13 centimeters tall. If the volume of the bottle is 97.5 cubic centimeters, what is the length of the perfume bottle to the nearest whole centimeter?

A. 2.5 cm
B. 3 cm
C. 3.3 cm
D. 7.5 cm

8. A shipping package has the shape of the triangular prism shown below.

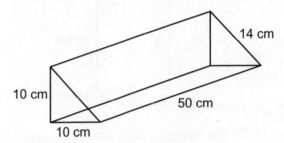

14 cm

10 cm

50 cm

10 cm

Assuming the package has no gaps or overlaps, how much cardboard is needed to produce the shipping package?

A. 1,300 cm²
B. 1,750 cm²
C. 1,800 cm²
D. 2,500 cm²

9. Calvin says that the surface area of a cube is always greater than its volume. Which side length of a cube shows that Calvin is incorrect?

A. 0.5 ft
B. 2 ft
C. 5 ft
D. 8 ft

10. What is the diameter of a cylinder with a volume of 235.5 cubic inches and a height of 3 inches?

A. 2.5 in.
B. 5 in.
C. 10 in.
D. 25 in.

Spotlighted Item: **DROP-DOWN**

DIRECTIONS: Study the information and figure, read each question, and choose the **best** answer from the drop-down list.

An open-top flour canister has a circumference of 31.4 centimeters and a height of 20 centimeters. The bottom and outside are made of cardboard and the lid is made of plastic.

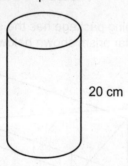

20 cm

11. To the nearest square centimeter and assuming there is no overlap, the area of cardboard needed to make the canister is ⬚ Drop-down ⬚ cm².

    A. 157   B. 314   C. 628   D. 707

12. A second canister holds the same volume of flour as the canister to the left but is 15 centimeters high. To the nearest tenth of a centimeter, the circumference of the second canister is ⬚ Drop-down ⬚ cm.

    A. 33.3   B. 36.2   C. 72.5   D. 133.3

DIRECTIONS: Study the information and figures, read the question, and choose the **best** answer from the drop-down list.

The two prisms have the same volume.

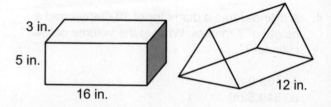

3 in.

5 in.

16 in.

12 in.

13. The area of the base of the triangular prism is ⬚ Drop-down ⬚ in².

    A. 10   B. 11   C. 15   D. 20

DIRECTIONS: Study the figure, read the question, and choose the **best** answer.

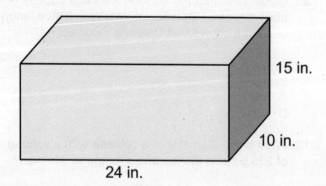

15 in.

10 in.

24 in.

14. Alyssa has the fish tank shown to the left. If she pours water into the tank until it is half full, how many cubic inches of water will be in the tank?

    A. 7,200
    B. 3,600
    C. 1,800
    D. 450

DIRECTIONS: Study the information, read the question, and choose the **best** answer.

A can of soda is 3 inches in diameter and holds 28.26 cubic inches

15. What is the height of the can?

    A. 1 inch
    B. 3 inches
    C. 4 inches
    D. 6 inches

UNIT 4

DIRECTIONS: Study the information and figure, read each question, and choose the **best** answer.

A company makes paper cups by rolling rectangular pieces of paper stock, like the one shown below, into cylinders. Each cup has a height of 10 cm.

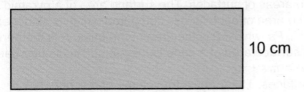

10 cm

16. If a cup has a radius of 3.5 centimeters, what is the volume of the cup in cubic centimeters?

   A. 384.7
   B. 219.8
   C. 192.3
   D. 109.9

17. If a cup has a radius of 3.5 centimeters, what is the lateral area of the cup in square centimeters?

   A. 35
   B. 70
   C. 110
   D. 220

DIRECTIONS: Read the question, and choose the **best** answer.

18. A food service company ships boxes that contain 40 cans of shortening. Each can has a radius of 2 inches and a height of 5 inches. The cans are placed in a box like the one shown below. After the cans are placed in the box, how much empty space is in the box?

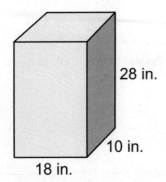

28 in.

10 in.

18 in.

   A. 2,512 cubic inches
   B. 2,528 cubic inches
   C. 3,784 cubic inches
   D. 4,973 cubic inches

DIRECTIONS: Read the question, and choose the **best** answer.

19. Kaya is planting flowers in the cylindrical-shaped flowerpot shown below.

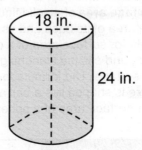

18 in.

24 in.

She begins by filling the bottom 3 inches of the flowerpot with rocks. Then she fills the rest of the pot with potting soil. About how many cubic inches of potting soil does she use?

   A. 760
   B. 5,340
   C. 6,100
   D. 21,360

DIRECTIONS: Study the information and figure, read each question, and choose the **best** answer.

A rectangular prism with volume 4,050 cubic inches has a base that is twice as long as it is wide. Its height is 25 inches.

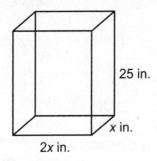

25 in.

x in.

2x in.

20. What is the length of the prism?

   A. 4.5 in.
   B. 9 in.
   C. 18 in.
   D. 27 in.

21. What is the surface area of the prism?

   A. 1,674 in.²
   B. 1,198 in.²
   C. 837 in.²
   D. 599 in.²

UNIT 4

Pyramids, Cones, and Spheres

MATH CONTENT TOPICS: Q.2.a, Q.2.e, Q.5.d, Q.5.e, A.2.a, A.2.b, A.2.c
MATH PRACTICES: MP.1.a, MP.1.b, MP.1.d, MP.1.e, MP.2.a, MP.2.c, MP.3.a, MP.4.a, MP.4.b

① Review the Skill

A **pyramid** is a 3-dimensional figure with one polygon base and triangular faces. The volume, or amount of space a pyramid takes up, is $V = \frac{1}{3}Bh$. A **cone** has one circular base. The volume of a cone is $V = \frac{1}{3}\pi r^2 h$.

The **surface area** of a solid figure is the sum of the areas of surfaces. The surface area of a pyramid is the sum of the area of its base and its triangular faces. The area of each face is computed using its slant height. The formula for surface area of a pyramid is $SA = B + \frac{1}{2}Ps$, where B is the area of the base, P is the perimeter of the base, and s is the slant height. Meanwhile, the surface area of a cone is the sum of its circular base and its curved surface. The formula for surface area is $SA = \pi rs + \pi r^2$.

A **sphere** is shaped like a ball and has no bases or faces. The formula for volume of a sphere is $\frac{4}{3}\pi r^3$. The formula for surface area of a sphere is $4\pi r^2$.

② Refine the Skill

By refining the skills of computing the surface area and volume of pyramids, cones, and spheres, you will improve your study and test-taking abilities, especially as they relate to the GED® Mathematical Reasoning Test. Study the information below. Then answer the questions that follow.

a The volume of the two buildings is the same. For question 1, since the diameter and height are both given for Shed A, you can find the volume of this shed.

b Remember that the formula for volume of a cone uses the radius, not the diameter. Divide the diameter by 2 to find the radius. Then multiply the calculated radius by 2 to find the diameter of Shed B.

A farmer is planning to build a conical grain storage shed on his property. To save on construction costs, he is choosing between two standard sizes, shown below. Each model holds the same amount of grain. The diameter of Shed B is represented by x.

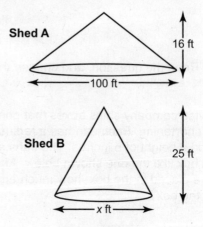

UNIT 4

CONTENT TOPICS

Standards Q.5.d and Q.5.e require you to compute volume and surface area of pyramids, cones, and spheres. You also may need to solve for diameter, radius, or area of a base, or the length, width, or height of a figure.

a 1. What is the volume, to the nearest cubic foot, of each shed?

A. 41,867
B. 65,417
C. 125,600
D. 167,467

b 2. What is the diameter, in feet, of Shed B?

A. 20
B. 40
C. 80
D. 160

DIRECTIONS: Read each question, and choose the **best** answer.

3. Walt inflates a beach ball with a diameter of 15 inches. About how many cubic inches of air does he blow into the ball?

   A. 710
   B. 1,770
   C. 2,820
   D. 10,600

4. A square pyramid has a height of 9 cm and a base with an area of 36 cm². What is the volume of the square pyramid to the nearest cubic centimeter?

   A. 108
   B. 162
   C. 324
   D. 432

5. A sphere has a surface area of about 28.26 cubic inches. What is the radius of the sphere?

   A. 1.5 cm
   B. 2.1 cm
   C. 3 cm
   D. 6 cm

DIRECTIONS: Study the information and figure, read each question, and choose the **best** answer.

The square pyramid below has a volume of 64 cubic feet and a surface area of 144 square feet.

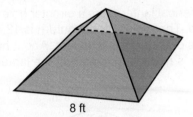

8 ft

6. What is the height of the pyramid?

   A. 2.25 ft
   B. 3 ft
   C. 5 ft
   D. 12 ft

7. What is the slant height of the pyramid?

   A. 2.25 ft
   B. 4 ft
   C. 5 ft
   D. 13 ft

DIRECTIONS: Study the information and figures, read each question, and choose the **best** answer.

The Snow Cone Hut sells snow cones in three sizes. Diagrams of the three sizes are shown below.

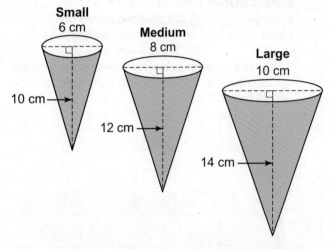

Small
6 cm
10 cm

Medium
8 cm
12 cm

Large
10 cm
14 cm

8. What is the volume of the smallest cone to the nearest cubic centimeter?

   A. 94
   B. 141
   C. 283
   D. 376

9. The smallest container has a slant height of 10.4 centimeters. To the nearest square centimeter, what area of paper is needed to make the smallest container? Assume no overlap.

   A. 94 cm²
   B. 98 cm²
   C. 188 cm²
   D. 196 cm²

10. About how many more cubic centimeters does the large size hold compared to the medium?

    A. 44
    B. 117
    C. 165
    D. 274

11. The owner replaced the smallest cone with a cone that has a 5-centimeter diameter and a 9-centimeter height. About how many cubic centimeters larger was the old snow cone size?

    A. 35 cm³
    B. 59 cm³
    C. 131 cm³
    D. 141 cm³

★ Spotlighted Item: **DRAG-AND-DROP**

DIRECTIONS: Read each question, and build the equation by using the drag-and-drop options to place quantities in the appropriate boxes.

12. To the nearest cubic inch, what is the volume of a cone 8 inches tall with a diameter of 10 inches?

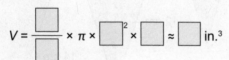

$$V = \frac{\square}{\square} \times \pi \times \square^2 \times \square \approx \square \text{ in.}^3$$

| 1 | 3 | 4 | 5 | 8 | 10 | 41.8 | 209 |

13. What is the volume of the pyramid shown below?

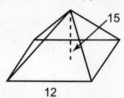

$$V = \frac{\square}{\square} \times \square \times \square = \square \text{ ft}^3$$

| 1 | 3 | 6 | 12 | 15 | 24 | 125 | 144 | 720 |

DIRECTIONS: Study the information and figures, read each question, and choose the **best** answer.

An ice sculpture company is experimenting with freezing blocks in the shapes of square pyramids as shown in the diagram below.

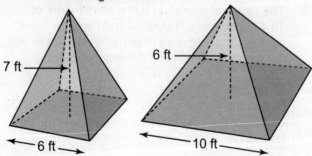

Pyramid A   Pyramid B

14. What is the volume of Pyramid A?

A. 28 cubic feet
B. 42 cubic feet
C. 84 cubic feet
D. 98 cubic feet

15. What is the volume of Pyramid B?

A. 20 cubic feet
B. 60 cubic feet
C. 120 cubic feet
D. 200 cubic feet

16. Pyramid C has the same volume as Pyramid A and the same base edge length as Pyramid B. About how tall is Pyramid C?

A. 2.5 ft
B. 5 ft
C. 6.5 ft
D. 16.7 ft

DIRECTIONS: Read the question, and choose the **best** answer.

17. A spherical lantern has a circular hole cut out of its top. The radius of the lantern is 12 inches. The radius of the hole is 3 inches. About how much paper is needed to construct the lantern?

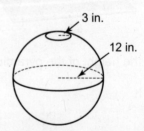

A. 1,780 square inches
B. 1,810 square inches
C. 7,200 square inches
D. 7,230 square inches

18. A team of sand sculptors is building a dinosaur with spikes on its back. The shape they have chosen for the spikes is a cone. If they build spikes that contain about 550 cubic inches of sand with diameter 10 inches, how many inches high are the cones?

    A. 5
    B. 7
    C. 10
    D. 21

19. What is the volume, to the nearest cubic foot, of a square pyramid with a side length of 2 feet 6 inches and a height of 3 feet 3 inches?

    A. 6
    B. 7
    C. 9
    D. 21

DIRECTIONS: Study the information and figure, read each question, and choose the **best** answer.

The space inside the teepee shown below measures 803.84 cubic feet.

16 ft

20. What is the height of the teepee to the nearest foot?

    A. 3
    B. 4
    C. 12
    D. 24

21. If 563 square feet of material is used to make the teepee and its floor, what is the slant height of the teepee to the nearest inch?

    A. 7 feet 2 inches
    B. 14 feet 5 inches
    C. 40 feet 10 inches
    D. 42 feet 3 inches

DIRECTIONS: Study the information and figures, read each question, and choose the **best** answer.

An architect is designing a glass greenhouse in the shape of a square pyramid. The triangular faces will be constructed from glass and the square base will be constructed from wood. The two designs below have the same volume.

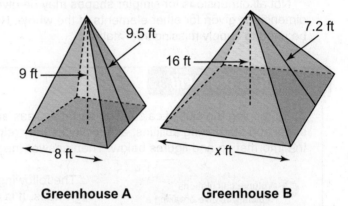

9 ft   9.5 ft   16 ft   7.2 ft

8 ft   x ft

Greenhouse A   **Greenhouse B**

22. What is the volume of each greenhouse?

    A. 48 cubic feet
    B. 72 cubic feet
    C. 192 cubic feet
    D. 576 cubic feet

23. What area of wood will be needed for Greenhouse B?

    A. 6 square feet
    B. 12 square feet
    C. 16 square feet
    D. 36 square feet

24. The architect wants to minimize the amount of glass that will be used to build the structure. Which explains the design she should choose?

    A. She should choose Greenhouse A, because the surface area of Greenhouse A is less than the surface area of Greenhouse B.
    B. She should choose Greenhouse A, because the total area of the triangular faces of Greenhouse A is less than the total area of the triangular faces of Greenhouse B.
    C. She should choose Greenhouse B, because the surface area of Greenhouse B is less than the surface area of Greenhouse A.
    D. She should choose Greenhouse B, because the total area of the triangular faces of Greenhouse B is less than the total area of the triangular faces of Greenhouse A.

Composite Solids

Use with *Student Book* pp. 110–111

MATH CONTENT TOPICS: Q.2.a, Q.2.e, Q.5.a, Q.5.b, Q.5.c, Q.5.d, Q.5.e, Q.5.f, A.1.a, A.1.c, A.1.g, A.2.c, A.4.b
MATH PRACTICES: MP.1.a, MP.1.b, MP.1.c, MP.1.d, MP.1.e, MP.2.a, MP.2.c, MP.3.a, MP.4.a, MP.4.b, MP.5.c

1 Review the Skill

Calculations involving the surface areas and volumes of **composite solids** often can be made easier by breaking a composite solid into simpler shapes. In doing so, one must be careful to ensure the pieces recombine into the original shape.

Not all dimensions for simpler shapes may be given explicitly. Some may be inferred from the geometry and dimensions given for other elements of the whole. Relationships such as the Pythagorean Theorem also can be used to supply missing information.

2 Refine the Skill

By refining the skill of calculating surface areas and volumes of composite solids, you will improve your study and test-taking abilities, especially as they relate to the GED® Mathematical Reasoning Test. Study the information and figures below. Then answer the questions that follow.

a Volume calculations typically involve breaking a solid into simple shapes that have well-defined volume formulas. In this case, the solid is a combination of a rectangular prism and a square pyramid.

b Problems involving the surface area of a composite solid must be read carefully to identify exactly the surfaces that are of interest. In this case, one might be interested in the walls of the building, but not the floor or the ceiling.

The following represents a storage shed, 20 ft by 20 ft, with 12-ft high walls. It is capped with a square pyramid, 30 ft by 30 ft, that adds an additional 12 ft to its height.

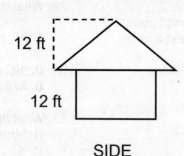

SIDE

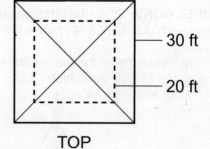

TOP

CONTENT TOPICS

Problems that use composite solids may be stated numerically or through variables. In the latter case, algebraic manipulation may result in simplified expressions that make calculations easier.

1. What is the volume occupied by the lower, square part of the shed?

   A. 400 cubic feet
   B. 900 cubic feet
   C. 4,800 cubic feet
   D. 10,800 cubic feet

2. What is the total volume occupied by the shed?

   A. 6,400 cubic feet
   B. 8,400 cubic feet
   C. 10,200 cubic feet
   D. 15,600 cubic feet

UNIT 4

DIRECTIONS: Read each question, and choose the **best** answer.

3. For the back-to-school season, a store is selling a container of paper clips in the shape of a pencil as shown below. The radius of the pencil container is 3 cm. What is the volume of the container to the nearest cubic centimeter?

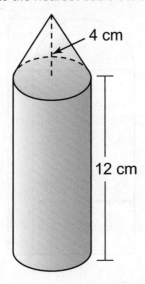

A. 226
B. 301
C. 377
D. 452

4. A theater company built the stage shown below. What is the volume of the figure?

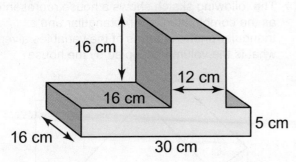

A. 1,632 cm³
B. 2,316 cm³
C. 5,312 cm³
D. 5,472 cm³

DIRECTIONS: Study the information and diagram, read each question, and choose the **best** answer.

The revolving restaurant on top of a downtown skyscraper is in the shape of a cylinder with a vaulted ceiling shaped like a cone, as shown in the diagram below.

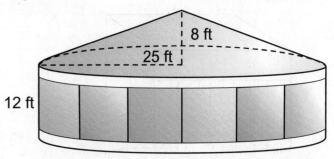

5. What is the volume of the cone-shaped section of the restaurant in cubic feet?

A. 209.3
B. 5,233.3
C. 7,850
D. 15,700

6. What is the approximate volume, in cubic feet, of the inside of the restaurant?

A. 5,233
B. 18,317
C. 23,550
D. 28,783

7. The owners of the restaurant decide to add insulation to the interior of the restaurant. As a result, the radius of the entire restaurant is reduced by 1 foot and the height of the cone-shaped section is reduced by 1 foot. By approximately how many cubic feet does the volume of the inside of the restaurant decrease?

A. 2,256
B. 2,859
C. 4,220
D. 4,668

8. If r is the radius of the restaurant, h is the height of the wall of the cylindrical portion, and s is the slant height of the conical ceiling, which equation represents the combined surface area of the wall and ceiling?

A. $A = \pi r (2h + s)$
B. $A = \pi r (2h - s)$
C. $A = \pi r (h + s)$
D. $A = \pi r (h - s)$

UNIT 4

DIRECTIONS: Study the information and diagram, read each question, and choose the **best** answer.

The following is a sketch of a sturdy work table composed of a rectangular top, 4 ft wide × 8 ft long × 0.5 ft thick, and four cylindrical legs, each 4 ft long with a diameter of 0.5 ft.

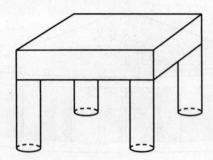

9. What is the total volume of the table, including the legs, to the nearest tenth of a cubic foot?

    A. 16 cubic feet
    B. 17.6 cubic feet
    C. 19.1 cubic feet
    D. 20 cubic feet

10. If the material used to make the table top weighs 50 lb per ft^3, and the material used to make the legs weighs 120 lb per ft^3, how much does the table weigh?

    A. 377 pounds
    B. 423 pounds
    C. 800 pounds
    D. 1,177 pounds

11. What is the combined surface area of the table top and vertical portion of the legs, expressed to the nearest square foot?

    A. 101 square feet
    B. 76 square feet
    C. 63 square feet
    D. 51 square feet

12. A varnish is applied to the top of the table, the four sides of the table, and the lateral surfaces of the legs. To the nearest square foot, what is the total area of the table that is varnished?

    A. 50 square feet
    B. 57 square feet
    C. 69 square feet
    D. 101 square feet

DIRECTIONS: Read each question, and choose the **best** answer.

13. The following shows a sketch of a grain silo that is composed of a cylinder forming the bottom and a hemisphere forming the top. What is the volume contained within the silo, expressed in terms of height H and radius R?

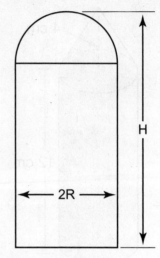

    A. $V = \pi R^2 \left(H + \frac{1}{3}R \right)$

    B. $V = \pi R^2 \left(H - \frac{1}{3}R \right)$

    C. $V = \pi R^2 \left(H + \frac{2}{3}R \right)$

    D. $V = \pi R^2 \left(H - \frac{2}{3}R \right)$

14. The following sketch shows a house represented as the combination of a rectangular and a triangular prism. In terms of the variables given, what is the volume occupied by the house?

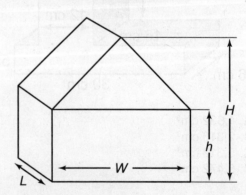

    A. $V = LW(H + h)$
    B. $V = LW(H - h)$
    C. $V = \frac{1}{2}LW(H + h)$
    D. $V = \frac{1}{2}LW(H - h)$

The following sketch represents a monument. The bottom portion is a square prism with a width of 50 feet and a height of 400 feet. The top is a square pyramid with a height of 60 feet.

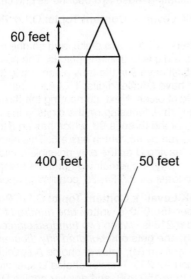

15. What is the volume of the bottom portion of the monument?

    A. 80,000 cubic feet
    B. 500,000 cubic feet
    C. 785,000 cubic feet
    D. 1,000,000 cubic feet

16. What is the total volume of the monument?

    A. 130,000 cubic feet
    B. 383,000 cubic feet
    C. 1,050,000 cubic feet
    D. 1,150,000 cubic feet

17. To the nearest 100 square feet, what is the combined surface area of the walls and the top of the monument?

    A. 21,600 square feet
    B. 64,900 square feet
    C. 86,000 square feet
    D. 86,500 square feet

The following sketch represents a water tower with a hemispherical top of diameter 48 feet, a cylindrical bottom of height 40 feet and diameter 8 feet, and a 20-foot high section joining the two. The total volume is 45,350 cubic feet.

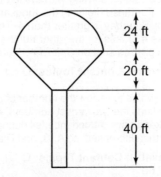

18. What is the combined volume of the spherical and cylindrical sections rounded to the nearest ten?

    A. 5,630 cubic feet
    B. 28,940 cubic feet
    C. 30,950 cubic feet
    D. 59,890 cubic feet

19. Suppose the water tower contains 36,280 cubic feet of water. About what percent of its maximum capacity does the water tower hold?

    A. 80%
    B. 60%
    C. 53%
    D. 30%

20. What is the combined surface area of the wall of the cylindrical section and the hemispherical section rounded to the nearest 10?

    A. 8,240 square feet
    B. 5,630 square feet
    C. 4,620 square feet
    D. 3,620 square feet

21. If one gallon of paint covers 400 square feet, how many gallons would be needed to paint the hemispherical top?

    A. 9
    B. 10
    C. 11
    D. 12

UNIT 4

Answer Key

UNIT 1 NUMBER SENSE AND OPERATIONS

LESSON 1, *pp. 2–5*

1. D; **DOK Level:** 1; **Content Topics:** Q.1.d, Q.6.c; **Practice:** MP.1.e
All the numbers contain the same number of digits, so individual place values, starting with the left-most digit, must be compared. For these digits, in the thousands place, only the number for *Saturday* is greater than 4. The thousands-place digits are 4 or less for the other numbers. This means the number of passes sold on *Saturday, 5,683*, was greatest.

2. C; **DOK Level:** 1; **Content Topics:** Q.1.d, Q.6.c; **Practice:** MP.1.e
By using place value to review the number of passes sold each day, one finds the two largest numbers, *4,586* and *5,683*, occur on weekend days. Attendance fell during the first part of the week and then increased, so A, B, and D are all incorrect.

3. C; **DOK Level:** 1; **Content Topics:** Q.1.d, Q.6.c; **Practice:** MP.1.e
The number 1107 is larger than *1001* and smaller than *1250*, so seat *1107* is located in *Row E*.

4. B; **DOK Level:** 2; **Content Topics:** Q.1.d, Q.6.c; **Practice:** MP.1.e
Seat 1000 is located in row *D*. Seats 1001 through 1003 are located in *Row E*. So the family will be seated in both *Rows D and E* (choice B).

5. A; **DOK Level:** 2; **Content Topics:** Q.1.d, Q.2.a, Q.6.c; **Practices:** MP.1.a, MP1.b, MP.1.e
The difference between the highest and lowest seat numbers in *Row A* is less than 200. The differences between highest and lowest seat numbers for the other rows are all greater than 200, eliminating those as possibilities. So *Row A* has the fewest number of seats.

6. C; **DOK Level:** 1; **Content Topics:** Q.1.d, Q.2.a, Q.6.c; **Practice:** MP.1.a, MP.1.e
Review of the seat numbers show that seat *1000* is in *Row D*, and that *Rows E* and *F* both have seat numbers in the thousands. So there are 3 rows with seat numbers in the thousands.

7. D; **DOK Level:** 2; **Content Topics:** Q.1.d, Q.2.a, Q.6.c; **Practices:** MP.1.a, MP.1.b, MP.1.e
The number of the final seat of each row after *Row A* is 250 greater than that of the preceding row. That indicates that the final seat number of the row following *Row F* likely will be 250 greater than 1500, or 1750. Similarly, the final seat number of the next row after that—the last seat number of the two added rows—likely will be 2000 (choice D).

8. B; **DOK Level:** 1; **Content Topic:** Q.1.d; **Practice:** MP.1.e
The number *1100* is larger than *1097* and smaller than *1105*, so the word is found among the pages covering the letter *Q*. The number *1100* does not fall within the range of pages for any other letter.

9. D; **DOK Level:** 1; **Content Topic:** Q.1.d; **Practice:** MP.1.e
Words beginning with S can be found on pages *1178–1360*. Pages *1234–1287* (option D) can be found within this range. The page range listed for A, *998–1045*, falls entirely within the page range for the letter *P*, so A can be eliminated as a choice. Choices B and C may be similarly eliminated.

10. A; **DOK Level:** 1; **Content Topic:** Q.1.d; **Practice:** MP.1.e
Twelve thousand is written as *12,000. Eight hundred two* is written as *802*. Combining the two gives *12,802* (option A). Option B places the 2 in the tens place, and so would read as a number concluding with *twenty*. Options C and D have six digits, meaning the first digit is in the hundred-thousands place, eliminating those two options as choices.

11. D; **DOK Level:** 2; **Content Topic:** Q.1.d; **Practice:** MP.1.e
The numbers all have two digits, and so one must first compare the digits in the tens places. The numbers *98, 92*, and *95* all have *9* in the tens place, while the numbers *75* and *84* have smaller digits. This eliminates A and B as possible choices. Next, comparing the three numbers beginning with *9*, focusing on the digits in the ones places, the largest of the three is *98*, which has an *8* in the ones place, followed by *95*, which has a *5*. This eliminates C as an option, leaving D as the only possible choice. Proceeding in the same way, the remaining numbers are ordered from greatest to least as *92, 84, 75*, confirming choice D.

12. B; **DOK Level:** 1; **Content Topic:** Q.1.d; **Practice:** MP.1.e
The number 150,000 is written *one hundred fifty thousand*. The number 218 is written *two hundred eighteen*. Combining, one gets *one hundred fifty thousand, two hundred eighteen* (B). Answer choice A specifies a 2, rather than the correct 200. Answer choice C specifies 1,000 and 50, rather than 150,000, and answer choice D uses a 21 and an 8 in place of 218.

13. C; **DOK Level:** 1; **Content Topics:** Q.1.d, Q.2.a, Q.6.c; **Practices:** MP.1.a, MP.1.b, MP.1.e, MP.2.c
There were 3 bowlers that scored between 100 and 119. Another 5 scored between 120 and 139. Adding the two together—3 bowlers and 5 bowlers—gives 8 bowlers scoring between 100 and 139.

14. C; **DOK Level:** 2; **Content Topics:** Q.1.d, Q.6.c; **Practices:** MP.1.a, MP.1.e
Comparing the various numbers in the frequency column, one finds the largest value is 9, occurring for the score range 160–179.

15. A; **DOK Level:** 2; **Content Topics:** Q.1.d, Q.6.c; **Practices:** MP.1.a, MP.1.e
Comparing the various numbers in the frequency column, one finds the smallest value is 3, occurring for the score range 100–119, choice A.

16. D; **DOK Level:** 2; **Content Topics:** Q.1.d, Q.6.c; **Practices:** MP.1.a, MP.1.e, MP.2.c
All the numbers are greater than 30,000 except for 14,227, corresponding to those 85 years and over (D). Of the four population choices, all are five-digit numbers, and as such can first be compared using digits in the ten-thousands places. Choices A, B, and C all have 3 in the ten-thousands places, while D has a 1, giving it the fewest number of people.

17. C; **DOK Level:** 3; **Content Topics:** Q.1.d, Q.2.a, Q.6.c; **Practices:** MP.1.a, MP.1.b, MP.1.c, MP.1.e, MP.2.c, MP.3.a
The total population of the age group 25 to 54 years old can be found by adding three age group numbers, each greater than 100,000. The results for the other age groups all involve adding two or three numbers, each less than 100,000. That ensures that C is the correct answer. One also could do the actual sums.

18. B; DOK Level: 1; **Content Topic:** Q.1.d; **Practice:** MP.1.e
The 8 is in the hundreds place and the 7 is in the ones place, so 807 is written as *eight hundred seven* (B). Answer choice A indicates an 80, rather than 800. Answer choice C uses a 70 rather than the specified 7. Answer choice D's use of the phrase *eighty hundred* incorrectly indicates a number of 8,000.

19. B; DOK Level: 1; **Content Topic:** Q.1.d; **Practice:** MP.1.e
The number in the hundreds place is 6. Since the number in the tens place (4) is less than 5, the number 6 is unchanged when rounding; the answer is 8,600. Answer choice A involves rounding to the nearest 500. Answer choice C involves round up to the hundreds place, not rounding down to the nearest hundred. Answer choice D involves rounding to the nearest 1,000.

20. D; DOK Level: 3; **Content Topics:** Q.1.d, Q.2.a, Q.2.e, Q.6.c; **Practices:** MP.1.a, MP.1.c, MP.1.e, MP.3.a
One can reason that if adult height is two times a child's height at age 2, then the tallest child at age 2 will also be the tallest adult. In that case, the tallest adult will be Charlie, who is the tallest child at age 2. All other children have heights less than Charlie's. One also could actually perform the multiplications and compare.

21. B; DOK Level: 3; **Content Topics:** Q.1.d, Q.2.a, Q.2.e, Q.6.c; **Practices:** MP.1.a, MP.1.c, MP.1.e, MP.3.a
One can reason that if adult height is two times a child's height at age 2, then two children of the same height at age 2 will have the same height as adults. In that case, the child with the same height as Kiera (Jake) also will have the same height as an adult. None of the other children have the same height as Jake, and so are eliminated as possibilities. One also could perform the multiplications and compare.

22. D; DOK Level: 2; **Content Topics:** Q.1.d, Q.2.a, Q.2.e, Q.6.c; **Practices:** MP.1.a, MP.1.c, MP.1.e, MP.3.a
Melanie's height as an adult is expected to be twice her height at age 2, or 2 × 31 = 62 inches. The person who is four inches taller than that as an adult—66 inches—would be half that height, or 33 inches, at age 2. That person is George (choice D). Alternately, one can reason that a four-inch difference as an adult will correspond to a two-inch difference at age 2. The person who is two inches taller than Melanie at age 2 is, again, George.

23. D; DOK Level: 2; **Content Topics:** Q.1.d, Q.6.c; **Practices:** MP.1.a, MP.1.e
This problem can most easily be solved by focusing on the digits in the hundred-thousands place. Weekend 5 is the only weekend with sales above $300,000, so it is *most likely* the weekend in which the dealership ran a promotion.

24. D; DOK Level: 2; **Content Topics:** Q.1.d, Q.6.c; **Practices:** MP.1.a, MP.1.e
Reviewing the numbers in the *Sales* column, one can immediately eliminate the first quarter, since it is the only one with sales less than $100,000. The remaining quarters all have sales numbers with the digit 1 in the hundred-thousands place, so one must compare the digits in the ten-thousands place. The largest is the digit 5 for quarter 4, making that quarter the one with the best sales (choice D).

25. C; DOK Level: 2; **Content Topics:** Q.1.d, Q.6.c; **Practice:** MP.1.e
Quarter 1 is the only quarter with sales less than $100,000, and as such is listed first. That eliminates choices B and D. Sales for the remaining three quarters can be sorted by comparing digits in the ten-thousands place. Quarter 3 comes next, eliminating answer choice A and leaving C as the answer. Finally, ordering the last two quarters, Quarter 2 and Quarter 4, confirms that choice.

LESSON 2, *pp. 6–9*
1. D; DOK Level: 1; **Content Topics:** Q.2.a, Q.2.e, Q.6.c; **Practices:** MP.1.a, MP.2.c
The solution requires adding the number of boxes produced on Monday (4,596) and Tuesday (4,025). Start in the ones digit, (6 + 5), or 11; the 1 in the ones place is also the ones digit in the sum, while the 1 in the tens place carries over. As a result, in the tens digit, you have (1 + 9 + 2), or 12. The 2 is the tens digit of the sum, and the 1 carries over. Continuing this way, one gets a final result of 8,621.

2. B; DOK Level: 1; **Content Topics:** Q.2.a, Q.2.e, Q.6.c; **Practices:** MP.1.a, MP.2.c
The request for *3 times* indicates that you need to multiply the number of boxes produced on Friday (3,115) by 3. The result is 9,345.

3. $1,950; DOK Level: 1; **Content Topics:** Q.2.a, Q.2.e; **Practice:** MP.1.a
To get the correct answer, multiply the cost per month (*$325*) by the number of months (*6*). Begin by multiplying *6* by *5* in the ones place to get *30*. Keep the *0* in the ones place and carry the *3* to the tens place. Next, multiply *6* by *2* in the tens place, for *12*, and add the *3* tens carried from the ones place for *15*. Keep the *5* in the tens place and carry the *1* to the hundreds place. Finally, multiply *6* by *3* in the hundreds place, for *18* hundreds. Add the *1* carried from the tens to the hundreds place for *19 hundreds*. Adding *19 hundreds + 5 tens + 0 ones* results in $1,950.

4. $1,190; DOK Level: 1; **Content Topics:** Q.2.a, Q.2.e; **Practice:** MP.1.a
The amount still owed is the amount already paid (*$1,560*) subtracted from the original loan (*$2,750*). The result is *$1,190*.

5. $864; DOK Level: 1; **Content Topics:** Q.2.a, Q.2.e; **Practices:** MP.1.a, MP.1.b, MP.1.d
First, recognizing that there are *12 months* in *one year*, the total cost is the amount of the monthly bill (*$72*) multiplied by the number of months (*12*). To multiply *72* by *12*, start with multiplying *72* by the *2* in the ones column of 12, giving a partial product of *144*. Multiplying *72* by *1* in the tens column of 12 and adding a zero placeholder gives a partial product of *720*. Adding the partial products (*720 + 144*) gives $864.

Answer Key

6. $270; DOK Level: 1; **Content Topics:** Q.2.a, Q.2.e; **Practice:** MP.1.a
Noting that the four roommates share the rent *equally*, each roommate pays the total monthly rent (*$1,080*) divided by *4*. Divide the first two digits of the dividend (*10*) by the divisor (*4*), giving *2* as the hundreds digit of the quotient. Multiplying *4* by *2*, writing the product (*8*) under the *10* in the dividend, and subtracting gives a *2*. Next, after you carry down the ones digit in the dividend (*8*), divide *28* by the divisor (*4*), getting *7* as the tens digit in the quotient. Finally, because *4* cannot divide into the remaining *0*, you add *0* as the ones digit in the quotient. There is no remainder, so the answer is $270.

7. 9; DOK Level: 3; **Content Topics:** Q.1.b, Q.2.a, Q.2.e; **Practices:** MP.1.a, MP.1.b, MP.2.c, MP.3.a, MP.5.c
The first step involves listing all whole numbers that divide into *45* with no remainder: 1, 3, 5, 9, 15, and 45. The list of numbers that divide into *72* with no remainder includes: 1, 2, 3, 4, 6, 8, 9, 12, 18, 24, 36, and 72. There are two numbers in common between the two lists (3 and 9) with 9 being the largest common factor.

8. $826,700; DOK Level: 1; **Content Topics:** Q.2.a, Q.2.e; **Practice:** MP.1.a
Finding the amount spent *together* requires adding *$567,800* and *$258,900*. Adding both the ones and tens columns gives a *0*. In the hundreds column, adding 9 + 8 gives 17. Regroup by moving the 1 to the thousands column so that you have 7 + 8 + 1, giving 16, Again regroup by moving the 1 to the ten-thousands column so that you have 6 + 5 + 1, giving 12. Regroup one final time to the hundred-thousands column, so that you have 5 + 2 + 1, giving 8 hundred thousands. The result is $826,700.

9. 48; DOK Level: 1; **Content Topics:** Q.2.a, Q.2.e; **Practice:** MP.1.a
Finding the number of items given away *altogether* requires the addition of *22*, *14*, and *12*. The answer is 48.

10. 608; DOK Level: 1; **Content Topics:** Q.2.a, Q.2.e; **Practice:** MP.1.a
The number of words he must still write is the number written so far (*892*) subtracted from the total required (*1,500*). The answer is 608 words.

11. $108; DOK Level: 2; **Content Topics:** Q.2.a, Q.2.e, Q.6.c; **Practices:** MP.1.a, MP.1.b, MP.3.a
Noting that the five friends are sharing the costs *evenly*, one needs to find the total cost of the game and divide it by 5. The total cost is the sum of the individual costs of the four products and services listed: $540. Dividing that sum by *5* gives the result of $108.

12. $756; DOK Level: 2. **Content Topics:** Q.2.a, Q.2.e, Q.6.c; **Practices:** MP.1.a, MP.2.c
The average cost of a friend to attend the game is $108. Adding two friends, with the costs and cost-sharing remaining the same, would increase the price to $756 (*$108 × 2 = $216; $216 + $540 = $756*).

13. $1,330; DOK Level: 1; **Content Topics:** Q.2.a, Q.2.e, Q.6.c; **Practices:** MP.1.a, MP.1.b, MP.2.c
Identifying the top three rows of the table as containing the relevant information and adding the three budgeted amounts in those rows (*$825*, *$220*, and *$285*), one gets $1,330. The other categories in the table (*Recreation / Auto Loan / Auto Insurance*) are unnecessary to answer this question.

14. $106; DOK Level: 1; **Content Topics:** Q.2.a, Q.2.e, Q.6.c; **Practice:** MP.1.a
Focusing on the two rows for *Food* and *Auto Loan*, and noting that *how much more* suggests finding a difference, subtract *$179* from *$285*. The result is $106.

15. $2,148; DOK Level: 1; **Content Topics:** Q.2.a, Q.2.e, Q.6.c; **Practices:** MP.1.a, MP.1.d
Recognizing that there are 12 months in a year, and focusing on the *Auto Loan* row, multiply *$179* by *12*, giving a yearly amount of $2,148.

16. $2,640; DOK Level: 2; **Content Topics:** Q.2.a, Q.2.e; **Practices:** MP.1.a, MP.1.b
First, find the amount per year that Antonio spends on rent. That row of the table shows that Antonio spends $825 per month on rent. With 12 months in a year, Antonio spends $9,900 annually ($825 × 12) on rent. Next, add the monthly costs for utilities ($220), food ($285), and recreation ($100), which sum to $605 per month. Multiply $605 × 12 months to arrive at a combined cost of $7,260 annually. Finally, subtract $7,260 from $9,900 to find that Antonio spends $2,640 more on rent per year than on the combined categories of utilities, food, and recreation.

17. $564; DOK Level: 2; **Content Topics:** Q.2.a, Q.2.e; **Practices:** MP.1.a, MP.1.b
First, find the amount per month that Antonio spends on auto insurance ($62). Next, subtract $15 from $62 to find the new monthly total ($47). From there, multiply $47 times 12 months to find the lump-sum total he'll spend on auto insurance ($564).

18. $1,560; DOK Level: 2; **Content Topics:** Q.2.a, Q.2.e; **Practices:** MP.1.a, MP.1.b
From the information given, the total number of hours Annette works is found by multiplying *6 hours per day* by *5 days per week* (*30 hours per week*), and then multiplying the result by *4 weeks*. The resulting 120 hours is then multiplied by the amount she makes each hour (*$13*), giving a total of $1,560.

19. $1,023; DOK Level: 2; **Content Topics:** Q.2.a, Q.2.e; **Practices:** MP.1.a, MP.1.b
The total number of hours Andrew worked during the two weeks is the sum of *54 hours* and *39 hours*: 93 hours. Multiplying that result by the amount he earns each hour (*$11*), gives a total of $1,023.

20. $1,347; DOK Level: 1; **Content Topics:** Q.2.a, Q.2.e; **Practice:** MP.1.a
The total amount spent on groceries is found by adding the amount spent each of the three months (*$458, $397, and $492*), giving a result of $1,347.

ANSWER KEY

21. 62; DOK Level: 1; **Content Topics:** Q.2.a, Q.2.e; **Practice:** MP.1.a, MP.1.b

If total tent sales were *$23,870*, and the cost of each tent was *$385*, divide *$23,870* by *$385* to get the number of tents sold: 62.

22. 3; DOK Level: 3; **Content Topics:** Q.1.b, Q.2.a, Q.2.e; **Practices:** MP.1.a, MP.1.b, MP.2.c, MP.3.a, MP.5.c

The first step involves listing all whole numbers that divide into *45* with no remainder: 1, 3, 5, 9, 15, and 45. The list of numbers that divide into *75* with no remainder includes 1, 3, 5, 15, 25, and 75. The numbers in common between the two lists include *1, 3, 5,* and *15,* with *3* being the smallest common factor that is greater than one.

23. 15; DOK Level: 2; **Content Topics:** Q.1.b, Q.2.a, Q.2.e; **Practices:** MP.1.a, MP.1.b, MP.1.c, MP.3.a

The quickest way to find the solution is to recognize that it takes 3 more yards of material to make a dress than it does to make a shirt. The difference in making five of each, then, is found by multiplying *5* by *3,* to give 15 yards. Alternately, one can find, using multiplication for each case separately, the amount of material needed for five shirts (*10 yards*), and subtracting it from the amount needed for five dresses (*25 yards*).

24. 740; DOK Level: 2; **Content Topics:** Q.2.a, Q.2.e; **Practices:** MP.1.a, MP.1.b

Recognizing that Joanne works *five days each week,* traveling *37 miles each day,* find by multiplication that she drives a total of 185 miles each week. Multiplication of that result by *4 weeks* gives the result of 740 miles.

25. $4,578; DOK Level: 1; **Content Topics:** Q.2.a, Q.2.e; **Practices:** MP.1.a, MP.1.b

The sum total of the donations given so far is: ($4,020) + ($3,902) = $7,922. The additional donations needed to meet the goal is the difference between that amount and the goal of $12,500: ($12,500) − ($7,922) = $4,578.

26. $5; DOK Level: 1; **Content Topics:** Q.2.a, Q.2.e, Q.3.a; **Practices:** MP.1.a, MP.1.b

Finding the cost per square foot requires dividing the total cost of *$1,445* by the number of square feet (*289*), giving a result of $5 for each square foot.

27. $372; DOK Level: 2; **Content Topics:** Q.2.a, Q.2.e, Q.3.a; **Practices:** MP.1.a, MP.1.b, MP.1.d, MP.1.e

First recognizing that there are 12 months in a year, find by multiplication that Maggie will be making equal payments for a total of *36* months. The amount she will pay each month will be the total of *$13,392* divided by *36* months, or $372.

28. $18,900; DOK Level: 2; **Content Topics:** Q.2.a, Q.2.e; **Practices:** MP.1.a, MP.1.b

First determine that 5 years = 60 months. Next, multiply the monthly payment of $265 by 60 months to find a total payment of $15,900. Finally, add the $3,000 up-front payment to the financed payment of $15,900 to arrive at an overall cost of $18,900 for the car.

29. 18; DOK Level: 1; **Content Topics:** Q.2.a, Q.2.e, Q.6.c; **Practices:** MP.1.a, MP.1.b, MP.2.c

Focusing on the Online Airlines row of information, note that each share costs *$15*. Finding the number of shares that can be purchased for *$270* requires dividing that amount by *$15*, giving 18 shares.

30. $175; DOK Level: 1; **Content Topics:** Q.2.a, Q.2.e, Q.6.c; **Practices:** MP.1.a, MP.1.e, MP.2.c

The total profit made is found by multiplying the profit for each share ($7) by the total number of shares (25), giving $175.

31. 6; DOK Level: 3; **Content Topics:** Q.1.b, Q.2.a, Q.2.e; **Practices:** MP.1.a, MP.1.b, MP.2.c, MP.3.a, MP.5.c

The list of whole numbers that are factors of 30 are: 1, 2, 3, 5, 6, 10, 15, and 30. The whole numbers that are factors of 42 include: 1, 2, 3, 6, 7, 14, 21, and 42. The largest factor the two lists have in common is 6.

32. 60; DOK Level: 3; **Content Topics:** Q.1.b, Q.2.a, Q.2.d; **Practices:** MP.1.a, MP.1.b, MP.2.c, MP.3.a, MP.5.c

Start listing the multiples of 12 and 15 to find the least common multiple. For 12: 12, 24, 36, 48, 60, 72, 84, ... For 15: 15, 30, 45, 60, 75, 90, ... The least common multiple is 60.

LESSON 3, pp. 10–13

1. A; DOK Level: 1; **Content Topics:** Q.1.d, Q.2.a, Q.2.e, Q.6.c; **Practices:** MP.1.a, MP.4.a

To find the change, subtract the temperature at 6:00 A.M. (65°F) from the temperature at 12:00 A.M. (68°F). Recall that this is the same as adding the first number with the negative of the second: (65°F) + (−68°F). One gets a result of −3°F.

2. D; DOK Level: 1; **Content Topics:** Q.1.d, Q.2.a, Q.2.e, Q.6.c; **Practices:** MP.1.a, MP.4.a

Since the temperature *dropped,* subtraction of 4°F from the temperature at 6:00 P.M. (76°F) is indicated. Again, the problem can be written as follows: (76°F) + (−4°F). The result is 72°F.

3. D; DOK Level: 1; **Content Topics:** Q.2.a, Q.2.e; **Practices:** MP.1.a, MP.4.a

Finding the change requires subtracting the opening value from the closing value: 13,416 − 13,498. This is the same as +13,416 + (−13,498), which gives −82.

4. C; −43; DOK Level: 2; **Content Topics:** Q.2.a, Q.2.e; **Practices:** MP.1.a, MP.4.a

Finding the score requires addition. First add −145 points and +80 points, to get −65 points. Then add that result to +22 points to get −43 points. Note also that the order doesn't matter. One could start by adding +80 points and +22 points to get +102 points, and then add that to −145 points. When adding more than two numbers, regrouping them can sometimes make the process easier.

5. C; DOK Level: 2; **Content Topics:** Q.2.a, Q.2.e; **Practices:** MP.1.a, MP.4.a

Finding how far they have gone requires addition. First add +8 yards and −10 yards to get −2 yards. Then add +43 yards to that result to get +41 or 41 yards.

6. D; DOK Level: 2; **Content Topics:** Q.2.a, Q.2.e; **Practices:** MP.1.a, MP.4.a

First subtract the 2,508-foot drop from the starting 8,453-foot altitude, giving 5,945 feet. Adding the subsequent 584-foot increase gives a final result of 6,529 feet. Other answer choices reflect incorrect computations.

Answer Key

7. B; DOK Level: 2; **Content Topics:** Q.2.a, Q.2.e;
Practices: MP.1.a, MP.1.b, MP.1.c, MP.1.e, MP.4.a
Note that writing checks subtracts money from Anna's
checking account, while depositing money adds to it.
One could solve a subtraction problem for each of the
three checks, followed by an addition problem to handle
the deposit. Again, since order doesn't matter, one can
make the problem a bit easier by first adding the original
balance to the deposit: $784 + $129 = $913. Then one can
add the amounts for the checks: $23 + $69 + $90 = $182.
Subtracting the two results: $913 − $182 = $731. Some
students may find ordering the problem this way makes
arriving at the solution easier.

8. A; DOK Level: 2; **Content Topics:** Q.2.a, Q.2.e;
Practices: MP.1.a, MP.4.a
This problem requires first adding 3 meters and 2 meters
to get a maximum height of 5 meters above the water.
Subtracting the 8-meter drop from that value gives: +5
meters + (−8 meters) = −3 meters.

9. D; DOK Level: 2; **Content Topic:** Q.2.a; **Practices:**
MP.1.a, MP.1.b, MP.3.a, MP.4.a
One way of solving this problem is to take 12 and reverse
the function of −7 to +7, so that 12 + 7 = x. Then solve for x,
so that $x = 19$.

10. B; DOK Level: 2; **Content Topics:** Q.2.a, Q.2.e, Q.6.c;
Practices: MP.1.a, MP.4.a
One can subtract the 10 points lost in the second round from
the 5 points gained in the first round to get −5 points after
two rounds. Subtracting another 10 points gives a total of
−15 points after three rounds. Alternately, one can sum the
negative results from the second and third rounds to get −20
points, and then add that to the +5 points of the first round.

11. D; DOK Level: 2; **Content Topics:** Q.2.a, Q.2.e, Q.6.c;
Practices: MP.1.a, MP.4.a
Adding Dorothy's three scores (15, 5, 0) gives a total of 20.
Adding Nikki's scores (0, 10, −15) gives a total of −5. The
difference between the two scores is (20) − (−5), which can
be written as (20) + (5) = 25.

12. D; DOK Level: 2; **Content Topics:** Q.2.a, Q.2.e;
Practices: MP.1.a, MP.4.a
First, add the 589-foot rise to the starting position of −3,290
feet, giving −2,701 feet. Then subtract the subsequent
4,508-foot drop to get a final result of −7,209 feet.

13. A; DOK Level: 2; **Content Topics:** Q.2.a, Q.2.e;
Practices: MP.1.a, MP.4.a
Add the changes in position (+3, −4, and −1) to get a total
change of −2, meaning he fell back 2 positions. Moving back
2 positions from 10th position would put Scott in 12th position
when the race ended.

14. D; DOK Level: 2; **Content Topics:** Q.2.a, Q.2.e;
Practices: MP.1.a, MP.2.c, MP.4.a
The location of the peak of the mountain, relative to Station
B, is given. The height of Station B, relative to sea level, is
also given. The height of the mountain, relative to sea level,
is given then by the sum of those two numbers: (10,549
feet) + (872 feet) = 11,421 feet. Note that the height of
Station A, while given, is unnecessary to solve the problem.

15. A; DOK Level: 2; **Content Topics:** Q.2.a, Q.2.e;
Practices: MP.1.a, MP.1.b, MP.1.c, MP.1.e, MP.3.a, MP.4.a
One could perform three subtraction problems, subtracting
$45 from the bank balance each time, to get the final result.
It is probably easier to note, however, that the total amount
removed from the account is (3)($45) = $135, and then
subtract that amount from the initial bank balance:
($890) − ($135) = $755.

16. A; DOK Level: 3; **Content Topics:** Q.1.d, Q.2.a, Q.2.e;
Practices: MP.1.a, MP.1.b, MP.1.c, MP.1.e, MP.4.a
The distance between Erik's home and Point C can be
found by simply counting the number of spaces on the
number line. Alternately, one can find the distance from
Erik's home by noting that the distance increased by 12
miles during the first part of his ride, and then decreased 8
miles after he turned around. The final distance from home,
then, is (12 miles) − (8 miles) = 4 miles.

17. C; 20 miles; DOK Level: 3; **Content Topics:** Q.1.d, Q.2.a,
Q.2.e; **Practices:** MP.1.a, MP.1.b, MP.1.c, MP.1.e, MP.4.a
Erik travels a distance of 12 miles in going from home to
Point B, found by counting spaces on the number line. He
then travels an additional distance of 8 miles in going from
Point B to Point C. The total distance he traveled is the sum
of the two: (12 miles) + (8 miles) = 20 miles.

18. A; DOK Level: 1; **Content Topics:** Q.2.a, Q.2.e;
Practices: MP.1.a, MP.4.a
Each of the four players has the same number of points
(−120), so multiply to get the total: (4) × (−120). Note that the
signs are different so the answer will be negative: −480.

19. B; DOK Level: 1; **Content Topics:** Q.2.a, Q.2.e;
Practices: MP.1.a, MP.4.a
The 363-foot descent was divided into three equal phases.
To find the change in height in each phase, noting that
descent means a negative change in height, divide −363
feet by 3 to get −121 feet.

20. D; DOK Level: 1; **Content Topics:** Q.2.a, Q.2.e;
Practices: MP.1.a, MP.1.d, MP.4.a
Recognizing that there are 12 months in year, and that
a withdrawal represents a negative change in Brenda's
checking account balance, multiply (12)(−$156) = −$1,872.

21. A; DOK Level: 2; **Content Topics:** Q.2.a, Q.2.e;
Practices: MP.1.a, MP.4.a
The number of points Don scored in the second round is the
difference between his total score and his score at the end
of the first round: (−10) − (+3) = −13.

22. D; DOK Level: 2; **Content Topic:** Q.2.a; **Practices:**
MP.1.a, MP.4.a
One way of solving this problem is to simply perform the
three multiplications requested, starting with (−7)(−1) = 7.
Alternately, you can arrive at the conclusion that multiplying
by −1 an odd number of times will result in a change in sign.

23. C; DOK Level: 1; **Content Topics:** Q.2.a, Q.2.e;
Practices: MP.1.a, MP.4.a
Karin is paying back the $1,554 loan in 6 equal steps. The
amount of each payment is $1,554 ÷ 6 = $259.

24. B; **DOK Level:** 2; **Content Topic:** Q.2.a; **Practices:** MP.1.a, MP.4.a, MP.1.b, MP.3.a, MP.4.a
Note that subtracting −10 is the same as adding +10. So the problem could be rewritten as, "If 10 is added to a number, the result is 6." Since the result of 6 is less than 10, the number being sought must be negative. Reasoning from there, the number must be −4.

25. A; **DOK Level:** 2; **Content Topics:** Q.2.a, Q.2.e; **Practices:** MP.1.a, MP.1.b, MP.1.c, MP.1.e, MP.4.a
Again, recognizing that deposits represent positive increases in Jumana's balance, and checks and fees represent negative changes, the positive and negative changes can be grouped. The $25 dollar deposit added to the $80 initial balance equals +$105. The two checks and overdraft fee sum to (−$75) + (−$75) + (−$25) = −$175. The net result (+$105) + (−$175) = −$70.

26. B; **DOK Level:** 2; **Content Topics:** Q.2.a, Q.2.e; **Practices:** MP.1.a, MP.1.d, MP.4.a
Recognizing that there are 12 months in a year and that the loan payments represent a negative change in Connor's bank account, the change each month is (−$3,228 ÷ 12) = −$269.

27. C; **DOK Level:** 2; **Content Topics:** Q.2.a, Q.2.e; **Practices:** MP.1.a, MP.4.a
The answer to this problem requires the sum of three numbers: (+54) + (−22) + (+5) = 37.

28. D; **DOK Level:** 1; **Content Topics:** Q.2.a, Q.2.e; **Practices:** MP.1.a, MP.4.a
During the 6 months, Cheryl receives 6 × $527 = $3,162.

29. B; **DOK Level:** 2; **Content Topics:** Q.2.a, Q.2.e; **Practices:** MP.1.a, MP.4.a
To find the fantasy baseball team's new total, add the positive increases (+2 + +3 = +5) and the negative decreases (−1 + −2 + −2 = −5). Next, add them together: 5 + −5 = 0. There was no change to the team's score, so it remains at 90 points.

LESSON 4, pp. 14–17
1. B; **DOK Level:** 1; **Content Topics:** Q.1.b, Q.2.a, Q.2.e, Q.6.c; **Practices:** MP.1.a, MP.2.c, MP.4.a
The phrase *How much more* indicates a subtraction problem. Identifying the relevant information, one gets $4\frac{1}{8} - 3\frac{1}{4}$, which can be rewritten as improper fractions: $\frac{33}{8} - \frac{13}{4}$. Rewriting in terms of the common denominator of 8, one gets $\frac{33}{8} - \frac{26}{8} = \frac{7}{8}$ yards.

2. $\frac{2}{5}$; **DOK Level:** 1; **Content Topics:** Q.2.a, Q.2.e; **Practices:** MP.1.a, MP.4.a
The whole is represented by the number 5; the portion being considered is the 2 male students out of every 5. So the fraction is: $\frac{2}{5}$.

3. $\frac{1}{4}$; **DOK Level:** 1; **Content Topics:** Q.2.a, Q.2.e; **Practices:** MP.1.a, MP.4.a
The total is 64 students, and the number being considered is 16 trumpet players, so the fraction is $\frac{16}{64}$. Both the numerator and denominator can be divided by 16, so the reduced fraction is $\frac{1}{4}$.

4. $\frac{4}{15}$; **DOK Level:** 1; **Content Topics:** Q.2.a, Q.2.e; **Practices:** MP.1.a, MP.2.c, MP.4.a
The total number given is 15 members, and the number being considered is the 4 members that chose ice cream. So the fraction is $\frac{4}{15}$; no reduction of the fraction is possible.

5. $\frac{11}{25}$; **DOK Level:** 1; **Content Topics:** Q.2.a, Q.2.e; **Practices:** MP.1.a, MP.1.d, MP.4.a
The total is $50, while the amount being considered is the ($50 − $28) = $22 Anna has left. So the fraction is $\frac{22}{50}$, which can be reduced to $\frac{11}{25}$.

6. Ethan, Walt, Natalia, Miguel, and Dara. DOK Level: 2; **Content Topics:** Q.1.a, Q.2.a, Q.2.e, Q.6.c; **Practices:** MP.1.a, MP.1.b, MP.1.d, MP.4.a
The most direct way of ordering the students is to recognize that all the fractions given have 10 as a common denominator. So the list, in order given, can be expressed as: $\frac{4}{10}, \frac{7}{10}, \frac{5}{10}, \frac{9}{10}, \frac{8}{10}$. From there, sequence the numerators from largest to smallest.

7. Miguel and Dara; **DOK Level:** 2; **Content Topics:** Q.1.b, Q.2.a, Q.2.e, Q.6.c; **Practices:** MP.1.a, MP.1.b, MP.1.d, MP.1.e, MP.4.a
The easiest way to determine the answer to this question is to refer to the list of fractions, expressed in terms of the common denominator of 10, written out in the previous problem. The numerator for Ethan is 9, and the two students being sought would have numerators that sum to that same value of 9. It is quickly evident by looking at the numerators in the list that the only two students with numerators that sum to 9 are Miguel (5) and Dara (4). Hence, they are the two students being sought.

8. $\frac{1}{4}$; **DOK Level:** 1; **Content Topics:** Q.2.a, Q.2.e; **Practices:** MP.1.a, MP.4.a
The total number is 72, while the number being considered is the 18 that had omelets. So the fraction is $\frac{18}{72}$. Both the numerator and denominator can be divided by 18, so the fraction can be reduced to $\frac{1}{4}$. Note also that if it is not immediately obvious that a fraction can be reduced to that extent, one can proceed in steps. For example, for some students it may be more obvious that the numerator and denominator can be divided by 9, giving a fraction $\frac{2}{8}$; the reduction to the final result then becomes more obvious.

9. 7; **DOK Level:** 1; **Content Topics:** Q.2.a; Q.2.e; **Practices:** MP.1.a, MP.4.a
The phrase *How many times* indicates division. To divide $1\frac{3}{4}$ cup ÷ $\frac{1}{4}$ cup, express the first number as an improper fraction and multiply by the reciprocal of the second number: $\left(\frac{7}{4}\right)\left(\frac{4}{1}\right) = 7$.

UNIT 1 *(continued)*

10. A; **DOK Level:** 3; **Content Topics:** Q.2.a, Q.2.d, Q.2.e, Q.3.a; **Practices:** MP.1.a, MP.1.b, MP.4.a
As noted in the information provided, the time it takes for a car to travel the 50 miles is the number 50 divided by the speed of the car. For the time to be *undefined*, the speed of the car must be zero. The car with zero speed is Car A. Note that, in this question, the lower a car's speed, the longer the time it takes to travel the 50 miles; in the case of Car A, the time is undefined because, since the car is not moving, it never travels the specified distance.

11. $1\frac{1}{2}$ hours; **DOK Level:** 1; **Content Topics:** Q.1.b, Q.2.a, Q.2.e, Q.3.a; **Practices:** MP.1.a, MP.2.c, MP.4.a
The time for Car B to travel the distance is 50 miles divided by 20 mph, while the time for Car D to travel the distance is 50 miles divided by 50 mph. Expressed as fractions the difference in time is $\left(\frac{50}{20} - \frac{50}{50}\right)$ hours = $\left(2\frac{1}{2} - 1\right)$ hours = $1\frac{1}{2}$ hours

12. $43\frac{1}{2}$ miles; **DOK Level:** 1; **Content Topics:** Q.1.b, Q.2.a, Q.2.e, Q.6.c; **Practices:** MP.1.a, MP.4.a
Identifying the number of miles Luke rode on those two days and adding, one gets: $24\frac{5}{6} + 18\frac{2}{3}$. Expressing the two fractions in terms of the common denominator of 6, one gets $24\frac{5}{6} + 18\frac{4}{6}$, giving a total of $42\frac{9}{6}$. Expressing the improper fraction as a mixed number and reducing gives $42 + 1\frac{3}{6} = 43\frac{1}{2}$.

13. $13\frac{1}{40}$; **DOK Level:** 1; **Content Topics:** Q.1.b, Q.2.a, Q2.e, Q.6.c; **Practices:** MP.1.a, MP.2.c, MP.4.a
The phrase *How many fewer* indicates a subtraction problem. Identifying the relevant numbers for the two days specified gives: $25\frac{9}{10} - 12\frac{7}{8}$. Expressing the two fractions in terms of their lowest common denominator of 40 gives: $25\frac{36}{40} - 12\frac{35}{40} = 13\frac{1}{40}$. No further reduction of the fraction is possible.

14. $2\frac{8}{9}$ hours; **DOK Level:** 1; **Content Topics:** Q.2.a, Q.2.e; **Practices:** MP.1.a, MP.4.a
When a rate and a total are given, multiplication is usually indicated. Multiplying the 26 tests by the hours per test gives the fraction $\frac{26}{9}$ hours. Expressed as a mixed fraction, it gives $2\frac{8}{9}$ hours.

15. $\frac{9}{10}, \frac{7}{10}, \frac{9}{20}, \frac{3}{20}$; **DOK Level:** 2; **Content Topics:** Q.1.a, Q.2.a; **Practices:** MP.1.a, MP.1.b, MP.4.a
Solving this problem requires reading values for each point from the number line, and reducing them to lowest terms as needed. Beginning with the largest number (Point D), the fraction is $\frac{18}{20}$; since both the numerator and denominator can be divided by 2, this fraction reduces to $\frac{9}{10}$. The next point (Point C), has a fractional value of $\frac{14}{20}$, which can be reduced to $\frac{7}{10}$. Point B corresponds to $\frac{9}{20}$, which cannot be reduced. Finally, Point A has a fractional value of $\frac{3}{20}$, which also cannot be reduced.

16. $\frac{9}{20}$; **DOK Level:** 1; **Content Topics:** Q.1.b, Q.2.a; **Practices:** MP.1.a, MP.2.c, MP.4.a
The distance between points B and D are found by subtraction: $\frac{18}{20} - \frac{9}{20} = \frac{9}{20}$.

17. $\frac{(5)(21 - 8)}{5} = 13$; **DOK Level:** 3; **Content Topics:** Q.1.b, Q.2.a; **Practices:** MP.1.a, MP.1.b, MP.1.d, MP.1.e, MP.4.a
In this case, the information provided shows that 5 is a factor of 105 and 40 that is being factored out of the sum in the numerator. The resulting difference in the numerator is $(21 - 8)$. Noting that the 5 in the numerator and the 5 in the denominator cancel, all that remains is the difference $(21 - 8)$, which equals 13.

18. $\frac{(7)(3 + 8 - 4)}{7} = 7$; **DOK Level:** 3; **Content Topics:** Q.1.b, Q.2.a; **Practices:** MP.1.a, MP.1.b, MP.1.d, MP.1.e, MP.4.a
In this case, the information provided shows that 7 is the factor of 21, 56, and 28 that is being factored out of the parenthesized expression in the numerator. The resulting expression is $(3 + 8 - 4)$, which equals 7. Since the other 7 in the numerator cancels with the 7 in the denominator, 7 is the correct resulting answer.

19. $12\frac{23}{24}$; **DOK Level:** 1; **Content Topics:** Q.1.b, Q.2.a, Q.2.e; **Practices:** MP.1.a, MP.4.a
When finding *How many more*, subtract the number of hours Mario already has worked from the number he needs to work: $32\frac{5}{6} - 19\frac{7}{8}$. Converting the fractions using the common denominator of 24, $32\frac{20}{24} - 19\frac{21}{24} = 31\frac{44}{24} - 19\frac{21}{24}$, where the first number has been rewritten by "borrowing" a 1 from the integer to make the subtraction of the fractions easier. The result is $12\frac{23}{24}$.

LESSON 5, pp. 18–21

1. B; **DOK Level:** 2; **Content Topics:** Q.2.a, Q.2.e, Q.3.c, Q.6.c; **Practices:** MP.1.a, MP.1.d, MP.1.e, MP.2.a, MP.4.a
The proportion $\frac{3}{4} = \frac{x}{8}$ represents the situation. The top number in the ratio is the girls and the bottom number is the total number of band members. The cross product is 24. Dividing the cross product by 4 gives a quotient of 6.

2. D; DOK Level: 2; **Content Topics:** Q.2.a, Q.2.e, Q.3.c, Q.6.c; **Practices:** MP.1.a, MP.1.d, MP.1.e, MP.2.a, MP.4.a
The total number of clarinet players is 12. There are 4 male clarinet players, so there are $12 - 4 = 8$ female clarinet players. The ratio of male clarinet players to female clarinet players is 4:8, or 1:2. It is important to write the numbers in the ratio in the same order in which they are described.

3. A; DOK Level: 2; **Content Topics:** Q.2.a, Q.2.e, Q.3.c; **Practices:** MP.1.a, MP.1.d, MP.1.e, MP.2.a, MP.4.a
The total number of skills is the sum of the number of correct skills and the number of incorrect skills: $12 + 4 = 16$. The ratio of incorrect skills to total skills is 4:16, or 1:4. It is important to write the numbers in the ratio in the same order in which they are described.

4. D; DOK Level: 2; **Content Topics:** Q.2.a, Q.3.c; **Practices:** MP.1.a, MP.1.e
The ratio of games lost to games won is 4:38, which can be simplified to 2:19. It is important to write the numbers in the ratio in the same order in which they are described.

5. C; DOK Level: 1; **Content Topics:** Q.2.a, Q.2.e, Q.3.a, Q.3.c; **Practices:** MP.1.a, MP.1.e, MP.2.a, MP.4.a
A unit rate is a ratio with a denominator of 1. To find the unit rate per can, divide the total cost by the number of cans: $16 \div 8 = 2$. The unit rate is $2.

6. D; DOK Level: 2; **Content Topics:** Q.2.a, Q.2.e, Q.3.b, Q.3.c; **Practices:** MP.1.a, MP.1.e, MP.2.a, MP.4.a
The proportion $\frac{1}{3} = \frac{4}{x}$ represents the situation. The top number in each ratio is the number of inches and the bottom number is the number of feet. The cross product is 12, so the missing number is 12. The scale is a ratio of inches to feet, so the correct answer is 12 feet. It is important to read the units carefully.

7. C; DOK Level: 1; **Content Topics:** Q.2.a, Q.3.c; **Practices:** MP.1.a, MP.1.e
The ratio of miles on Monday to miles on Tuesday is 96:60, which simplifies to 8:5. It is important to write the numbers in the ratio in the same order in which they are described.

8. A; DOK Level: 2; **Content Topics:** Q.2.a, Q.3.c; **Practices:** MP.1.a, MP.1.d, MP.2.c
The ratio of eggs to servings in the reduced recipe will be the same as the ratio of eggs to servings for the original recipe. The ratio of eggs to servings is 12 to 30, which simplifies to 2 to 5.

9. B; DOK Level: 2; **Content Topics:** Q.2.a, Q.2.e, Q.3.c; **Practices:** MP.1.a, MP.1.e, MP.2.a, MP.4.a
The proportion $\frac{8}{3} = \frac{24}{x}$ represents the situation. The top number in each ratio is the number of wins and the bottom number is the number of losses. The cross product is 72. Dividing the cross product by 8 gives a quotient of 9.

10. C; DOK Level: 2; **Content Topics:** Q.2.a, Q.3.c; **Practices:** MP.1.a, MP.1.e
The ratio of full-time to part-time employees is 30:12, which simplifies to 5:2. It is important to compare the correct quantities, full-time employees to part-time employees.

11. B; DOK Level: 2; **Content Topics:** Q.2.a, Q.2.e, Q.3.b, Q.3.c; **Practices:** MP.1.a, MP.1.e, MP.2.a, MP.4.a
The proportion $\frac{2}{150} = \frac{6}{x}$ represents the situation. The top number in each ratio is the number of inches and the bottom number is the number of miles. The cross product is 900. Dividing by 2 gives a quotient of 450.

12. A; DOK Level: 2; **Content Topics:** Q.2.a, Q.2.e, Q.3.c; **Practices:** MP.1.a, MP.1.d, MP.1.e, MP.1.a, MP.4.a
The proportion $\frac{4}{5} = \frac{x}{460}$ represents the situation. The top number in each ratio represents the number of students who ride the bus and the bottom number represents the total number of students. The cross product is 1,840. Dividing the cross product by 5 gives a quotient of 368. Subtract the number of students who ride the bus from the total number of students: $460 - 368 = 92$. So, 92 students use a different method transportation to school.

13. $\frac{5}{15} = \frac{275}{x} = \$825$; **DOK Level:** 2; **Content Topic:** Q.3.c; **Practices:** MP.1.a, MP.1.d, MP.2.a
The ratio of individual contributions to Bay Company contributions is $\frac{5}{15}$. The top number in each ratio is the amount of individual contributions and the bottom number in each ratio is the amount that the Bay Company will contribute. The total amount of Bay Company contributions is x, or unknown. Multiply 15 by 275 to get a cross product of 4,125, and divide that figure by 5 to find a quotient of $825 contributed by the Bay Company.

14. $\frac{14}{1} = \frac{406}{x} = 29$; **DOK Level:** 2; **Content Topics:** Q.3.c; **Practices:** MP.1.a, MP.1.d, MP.2.a
The ratio of students to teachers is 14:1. The top number in each ratio is the number of teachers. The bottom number in each ratio is the number of students. The total number of teachers is x, or unknown. The cross product is 406. Dividing by the third number, 14, gives a quotient of 29.

15. B; DOK Level: 2; **Content Topics:** Q.2.a, Q.2.e, Q.3.a, Q.3.c; **Practices:** MP.1.a, MP.1.e, MP.2.a, MP.4.a
The unit rate is 110 calories per hour. Multiply the unit rate by the number of hours, or set up and solve as a proportion: $4\frac{1}{2} \times 110 = 495$.

16. A; DOK Level: 1; **Content Topics:** Q.2.a, Q.2.e, Q.3.a, Q.3.c; **Practices:** MP.1.a, MP.1.e, MP.2.a, MP.4.a
A unit rate is a ratio with a denominator of 1. To find the unit rate, divide the number of miles by the number of hours: $48 \div 3 = 16$.

17. B; DOK Level: 2; **Content Topics:** Q.2.a, Q.2.e, Q.3.c; **Practices:** MP.1.a, MP.1.d, MP.1.e, MP.2.a, MP.4.a
The number of people who walk or ride their bicycles is the difference between the total number of people and the number of people who drive: $30 - 16 = 14$. The ratio of people who drive to people who walk or ride is 16:14, which simplifies to 8:7.

Answer Key

UNIT 1 (continued)

18. C; **DOK Level:** 2; **Content Topic:** Q.3.c; **Practices:** MP.1.a, MP.1.d, MP.2.a
The ratio of people who work in education to total people is 2:5. The top number in each ratio is the number of people who work in education. The bottom number is the number of people. The total number of people who work in education is x, or unknown. Multiply to find a cross product of 60. Then divide the cross product of 60 by the third number, 5, to find a quotient of 12 people in the field of education.

19. B; **DOK Level:** 2; **Content Topic:** Q.3.c; **Practices:** MP.1.a, MP.1.d, MP.2.a
The ratio of teaspoons of caramel sauce to teaspoons of dessert sauce is 3:5, because 2 + 3 = 5. The top number in each ratio is the number of teaspoons of caramel sauce. The bottom number in each ratio is the number of teaspoons of dessert sauce. The total number of teaspoons of caramel sauce is x, or unknown. Multiply to find a cross product of 60. Next, divide that figure by the third number, 5, to find a quotient of 12 teaspoons of caramel sauce.

20. C; **DOK Level:** 2; **Content Topics:** Q.2.a, Q.2.e, Q.3.c; **Practices:** MP.1.a, MP.1.e, MP.2.a, MP.4.a
The proportion $\frac{2}{3} = \frac{24}{x}$ represents the situation, whereby the top number in each ratio is the number of cars and the bottom number is the number of parking spots. The cross product is 72. Dividing the cross product by 2 gives a quotient of 36 parking spots.

21. A; **DOK Level:** 2; **Content Topics:** Q.2.a, Q.2.e, Q.3.c; **Practices:** MP.1.a, MP.1.e, MP.2.a, MP.4.a
Before you can establish a ratio, you first must find the number of balls to go along with the number of strikes. To that end, subtract 84 from 105 = 21 balls. From there, you can establish your ratio of 84:21, which simplifies to 4:1.

22. B; **DOK Level:** 2; **Content Topics:** Q.2.a, Q.2.e, Q.3.c; **Practices:** MP.1.a, MP.1.e, MP.2.a, MP.4.a
The proportion $\frac{1}{22} = \frac{x}{176}$ represents the situation. The top number in each ratio is the number of lifeguards and the bottom number is the number of swimmers. The cross product is 176. Dividing by the third number, 22, gives a quotient of 8 lifeguards.

23. B; **DOK Level:** 2; **Content Topics:** Q.2.a, Q.2.e, Q.3.a, Q.3.c, Q.6.c; **Practices:** MP.1.a, MP.1.b, MP.1.d, MP.2.a, MP.4.a
Leila traveled 414 miles in Week 2 on 18 gallons of gasoline, so her unit rate was 414 ÷ 18 = 23 miles per gallon.

24. C; **DOK Level:** 2; **Content Topics:** Q.2.a, Q.2.e, Q.3.c; **Practices:** MP.1.a, MP.1.d, MP.1.e, MP.2.a, MP.4.a
The total number of miles is 2,040. The ratio of miles driven in Week 1 to total number of miles is 420:2040, which simplifies to 7:34.

25. B; **DOK Level:** 2; **Content Topics:** Q.2.a, Q.2.e, Q.3.c; **Practices:** MP.1.a, MP.1.e, MP.2.a, MP.4.a
The proportion $\frac{3}{8} = \frac{387}{x}$ represents the situation. The top number in each ratio is the number of cats and the bottom number is the number of people. The cross product is 3,096. Dividing by 3 gives a quotient of 1,032 people.

26. D; **DOK Level:** 2; **Content Topics:** Q.2.a, Q.2.e, Q.3.c; **Practices:** MP.1.a, MP.1.e, MP.2.a, MP.4.a
The proportion $\frac{8}{24} = \frac{12}{x}$ represents the situation. The top number in each ratio is the number of pounds and the bottom number is the cost. The cross product is 288. Dividing by 8 gives a quotient of $36.

27. C; **DOK Level:** 2; **Content Topics:** Q.2.a, Q.2.e, Q.3.c, Q.6.c; **Practices:** MP.1.a, MP.1.e, MP.2.a, M.2.c, MP.4.a
The ratio of openings to applicants for the staff writer position is 4:48, which simplifies to 1:12.

28. A; **DOK Level:** 2; **Content Topics:** Q.2.a, Q.2.e, Q.3.c, Q.6.c; **Practices:** MP.1.a, MP.1.e, MP.2.a, M.2.c, MP.4.a
The proportion $\frac{1}{7} = \frac{2}{x}$ represents the situation. The top number in each ratio is the number of positions and the bottom number is the number of applicants. The cross product is 14. There were 14 applicants for the project manager position. There were 12 applicants for the editor position: 14 − 12 = 2.

LESSON 6, pp. 22–25

1. B; **DOK Level:** 2; **Content Topics:** Q.1.a, Q.6.c; **Practice:** MP.1.a
Compare each number in the table to 6.25. First compare the digits in the ones place. Since 7 is greater than 6, 7.2 is greater than 6.25 and both Mr. Peterman's and Mrs. Peterman's bowling balls have masses greater than 6 kg. Similarly, since 6 is greater than 5, 5.2 and 5.8 are less than 6.25 Tay's and Julie's balls have a mass less than 6.25 kg. The mass of Christopher's ball, 6.2 kg, has the same digits in the ones and tenths places as 6.25. Write 6.2 as 6.20 to compare the hundredths digits. Since 0 is less than 5, 6.20 is less than 6.25 and Christopher's ball has a mass less than 6.25 kg. Therefore, 2 of the bowling balls have a mass greater than 6.25 kg.

2. C; **DOK Level:** 2; **Content Topics:** Q.2.a, Q.2.e, Q.6.c; **Practices:** MP.1.a, MP.1.b, MP.1.e, MP.2.c, MP.4.a
To find the difference in masses, subtract 5.8 from 6. A whole number is understood to have a decimal point after the ones place, so write 6 kg as 6.0 kg, then subtract, remembering to regroup. 6.0 − 5.8 = 0.2.

3. Monday; **DOK Level:** 2; **Content Topics:** Q.1.a, Q.6.c; **Practice:** MP.1.a
All of the mileages have the same digit in the tens place, so look at the ones place. Since 8 is greater than 7, eliminate Tuesday and Friday. Next, look at the tenths place. Since 5 is less than both 8 and 7, the least mileage is 37.5, which Kate drove on Monday.

4. 189.4 miles; **DOK Level:** 2; **Content Topics:** Q.2.a, Q.2.e, Q.6.c; **Practices:** MP.1.a, MP.1.b, MP.1.e, MP.2.c, MP.4.a
The total mileage is the sum of five daily mileages. Align the decimal point and add place by place, being careful to regroup as needed. 37.5 + 38.1 + 37.8 + 37.7 + 38.3 = 189.4 miles.

5. 0.8 mile; **DOK Level:** 2; **Content Topics:** Q.2.a, Q.2.e, Q.6.c; **Practices:** MP.1.a, MP.1.b, MP.1.e, MP.2.c, MP.4.a
Subtract Kate's mileage on Monday from her mileage on Friday, being careful to regroup. 38.3 − 37.5 = 0.8 mile.

6. **$75.60; DOK Level:** 3; **Content Topics:** Q.2.a, Q.2.e, Q.6.c; **Practices:** MP.1.a, MP.1.b, MP.1.e, MP.2.c, MP.4.a
Kate's total mileage is the sum of the mileages in the table: 37.5 + 38.1 + 37.8 + 37.7 + 38.3 = 189.4 miles. Subtract the number of miles she drove for personal use: 189.4 − 21.4 = 168 miles. Multiply that mileage by $0.45: 0.45 × 168 = $75.60.

7. **C; DOK Level:** 2; **Content Topics:** Q.1.a, Q.6.c; **Practice:** MP.1.a
Order the balance beam scores from greatest to least. All of the scores have the same digits in the tens, ones, and tenths places, so compare the hundredths and thousandths places. Since 9 is greater than 8 and 7, the highest score was 15.995, so Natalia did not finish in first place. Since 8 is greater than 7, the next highest score was 15.98, so Natalia did not finish in second place. Compare 15.975 and 15.970. Since 5 is greater than 0, Natalia finished in third place.

8. **A; DOK Level:** 2; **Content Topics:** Q.2.a, Q.2.e; **Practices:** MP.1.a, MP.1.b, MP.1.e, MP.2.c, MP.4.a
To estimate an answer, round decimals to the nearest whole number. $1.79 is about $2, so divide $8 by $2, which is 4.

9. **C; DOK Level:** 2; **Content Topics:** Q.1.a, Q.6.c; **Practice:** MP.1.a
Compare the weight of each sample to the minimum and maximum weights allowed. The weights of Samples A and D have the same ones, tenths, and hundredths digits as 1.097. The thousandths digits are greater than 7, so Samples A and D are above the minimum weight. Samples A and D are also below the maximum weight because the tenths digit in the maximum weight, 1, is greater than the tenths digits in the samples' weights, 0. The weights of Samples B and C have the same ones digits as 1.097. The tenths digit is greater than 0, so Samples B and C are above the minimum weight. The tenths digits in these samples' weights are the same as the tenths digit in the maximum weight, so look at the hundredths digits. Since 2 is greater than 1, Sample C is heavier than allowed, so Isaiah would reject it.

10. **A; DOK Level:** 2; **Content Topics:** Q.1.a, Q.6.c; **Practice:** MP.1.a
Compare the number of the book to the range for each floor and section. The book's number has the same tens, ones, tenths, and hundredths digits as the highest number in Floor 1, Section A, and the lowest number in Floor 1, Section B. Look at the thousandths digits. Since 3 is less than 4, the book will be in Floor 1, Section A.

11. **C; DOK Level:** 2; **Content Topics:** Q.1.a, Q.6.c; **Practice:** MP.1.a
To compare a decimal to the hundredths place with a decimal to the thousandths place, rewrite the decimal with a 0 in the thousandths place. Compare 35.780 to the numbers in the table. The book's number has the same tens, ones, tenths, and hundredths digits as the highest number in Floor 2, Section A, and as the lowest number in Floor 2, Section B. Look at the thousandths digit. Since 0 is less than 4, the book will be in Floor 2, Section A.

12. **B; DOK Level:** 2; **Content Topics:** Q.2.a, Q.2.e; **Practices:** MP.1.a, MP.1.b, MP.1.e, MP.2.c, MP.4.a
The cost of the salami is the product of the price per pound and the number of pounds. Multiply: 2.3 × 3.95 = 9.085. Round the answer to the nearest penny, or hundredth: $9.09.

13. **A; DOK Level:** 2; **Content Topics:** Q.2.a, Q.2.e; **Practices:** MP.1.a, MP.1.b, MP.1.e, MP.2.c, MP.4.a
To find Terese's change, subtract the total cost from $20. Add the costs of the items, regrouping as necessary: $14.98 + $2.39 + $0.79 = $18.06. Subtract the total from $20.00. $20.00 − $18.06 = $1.94.

14. **B; DOK Level:** 2; **Content Topics:** Q.2.a, Q.2.e; **Practices:** MP.1.a, MP.1.b, MP.1.e, MP.2.c, MP.4.a
The amount of each equal payment is the quotient of the total cost and the number of months. Divide: $675.00 ÷ 12 = $56.25.

15. **D; DOK Level:** 2; **Content Topics:** Q.2.a, Q.2.e; **Practices:** MP.1.a, MP.1.b, MP.1.e, MP.2.c, MP.4.a
The combined total of Tim's three scores is the sum of the three numbers. Add the numbers, being sure to align decimal points, and regrouping as necessary. 97.75 + 92.5 + 98.25 = 288.5.

16. **D; DOK Level:** 2; **Content Topics:** Q.2.a, Q.2.e, Q.6.c; **Practices:** MP.1.a, MP.1.b, MP.1.e, MP.2.c, MP.4.a
The top three batting averages are the three greatest numbers in the table. All of the numbers have a 0 in the ones place, so compare the digits in the tenths place. Players B and C both have a 3 in the tenths place. Compare the hundredths places for these numbers. Since 5 is greater than 0, Player B has the highest batting average and Player C has the second-highest batting average. Next, compare the batting averages of the remaining players. All have a 2 in the tenths place, so compare the digits in the hundredths place. Since 9 is greater than 8 and 7, Player D has the third-highest batting average. Players B, C, and D have the highest batting averages, so they will bat in the order of Player D, Player C, and Player B.

17. **B; DOK Level:** 2; **Content Topics:** Q.1.a, Q.6.c; **Practice:** MP.1.a
Compare the digits in the ones place. Since 8 is less than 9, the lowest score was 8.75. Next, compare the tenths places of the two remaining scores. Since 5 is greater than 2, 9.5 was the greatest score. In order from lowest to highest, the scores are 8.75, 9.25, 9.5.

18. **B; DOK Level:** 2; **Content Topics:** Q.2.a, Q.2.e; **Practices:** MP.1.a, MP.1.b, MP.1.e, MP.2.c, MP.4.a
The normal price of 5 boxes of pasta is 5 × $2.29 = $11.45. The sale price of 5 boxes of pasta is 5 × $2.05 = $10.25. Subtract to find the savings: $11.45 − $10.25 = $1.20. Alternately, the savings on each box of pasta is $2.29 − $2.05 = $0.24, so the savings on 5 boxes of pasta is 5 × $0.24 = $1.20.

19. **C; DOK Level:** 2; **Content Topics:** Q.2.a, Q.2.e; **Practices:** MP.1.a, MP.1.b, MP.1.e, MP.2.c, MP.4.a
Add to find the total of the judges' scores, being careful to align decimal points and regroup as needed: 8 + 8.5 + 7.5 = 24. Multiply the judges' score by the degree of difficulty: 3.2 × 24 = 76.8.

20. **B; DOK Level:** 2; **Content Topics:** Q.2.a, Q.2.e; **Practices:** MP.1.a, MP.1.b, MP.1.e, MP.2.c, MP.4.a
There are 12 months in a year, so divide the amount of the loan by 12, regrouping as needed. $1,556.28 ÷ 12 = $129.69.

Answer Key

UNIT 1 (continued)

21. **C; DOK Level:** 2; **Content Topics:** Q.2.a, Q.2.e; **Practices:** MP.1.a, MP.1.b, MP.1.e, MP.2.c, MP.4.a
The number of miles per hour, or rate, is equal to the quotient of the total distance and the number of hours. Divide 115.02 by 5.4, being careful to place the decimal point correctly. 115.02 ÷ 5.4 = 21.3 miles per hour.

22. **D; DOK Level:** 2; **Content Topic:** Q.1.a; **Practice:** MP.1.a
All of the answer choices have the same digits in the hundreds, tens, and ones places, so compare the tenths places. Write 218 as 218.0. Since 0 is less than 1, 218 and 218.05 are too low. Compare the hundredths places. Since 0 is < 5, 218.105 is too low. Since 5 is between 1 and 6 in tenths place, Morgan's score could be 218.5.

23. **B; DOK Level:** 2; **Content Topics:** Q.1.a, Q.6.c; **Practice:** MP.1.a
Compare the weight of Gary's package to the weights in the table. Compare the digits in the ones place. Since 6 is less than 7, Gary's package falls in the weight range of 4.66–7.85. So, it will cost $5.55 to ship the package.

24. **C; DOK Level:** 3; **Content Topics:** Q.1.a, Q.2.a, Q.2.e, Q.6.c; **Practices:** MP.1.a, MP.1.b, MP.1.e, MP.2.c, MP.4.a
The total weight of the package is the weight of the books and the weight of the packaging materials. The books weigh 3 × 2.91 = 8.73 pounds. Add the weight of the packaging materials: 8.73 + 1.6 = 10.33. Compare the weight to the weights in the table. Since the tens and ones digits of the weight of the package are the same as the tens and ones digits in 10.95 and 10.96, compare the tenths digit. Since 3 is less than 9, the package falls in the weight range of 7.86–10.95 and the shipping cost is $8.99.

25. **B; DOK Level:** 3; **Content Topics:** Q.1.a, Q.2.a, Q.2.e, Q.6.c; **Practices:** MP.1.a, MP.1.b, MP.1.e, MP.2.c, MP.4.a
First, find the cost to ship the package that weighs 4.51 pounds. Since the ones digit is the same as the ones digits in 4.65 and 4.66, compare the tenths digit. Since 5 is less than 6, the package falls in the weight range of 0–4.65 and will cost $3.95 to ship. For the second package, which weighs 10.9 pounds, the tens, ones, and tenths digits are the same as in 10.95 and 10.96, so compare the hundredths digits. 10.9 is equal to 10.90, and 0 is less than 5, so the package falls in the weight range of 7.86–10.95 and will cost $8.99 to ship. Add the two shipping costs, aligning the decimal points and regrouping as needed: $3.95 + $8.99 = $12.94. Subtract from the amount paid: $20.00 − $12.94 = $7.06.

LESSON 7, pp. 26–29

1. **B; DOK Level:** 1; **Content Topics:** Q.2.a, Q.2.e, Q.3.d; **Practices:** MP.1.a, MP.1.e
To write a percent as a fraction, drop the percent sign and write the percent as a fraction with denominator 100.
Simplify. $\frac{15 \div 5}{100 \div 5} = \frac{3}{20}$.

2. **D; DOK Level:** 2; **Content Topics:** Q.2.a, Q.2.e, Q.3.c, Q.3.d; **Practices:** MP.1.a, MP.1.e, MP.2.c, MP.4.a
To find the amount of the tip, use the equation **base × rate = part**, where the base is $40.66, the rate is 20% or 0.2, and the part is unknown. Multiply: 0.20 × $40.66 = $8.13.
Alternately, set up and solve the proportion $\frac{part}{40.66} = \frac{20}{100}$.
Add the amount of the tip to the subtotal to find the total: $40.66 + $8.13 = $48.79.

3. **C; DOK Level:** 1; **Content Topics:** Q.2.a, Q.2.e, Q.3.d; **Practices:** MP.1.a, MP.1.e
To write a fraction as a percent, divide the numerator by the denominator. Then multiply the decimal by 100 and add the percent sign. 2 ÷ 5 = 0.4, 0.4 × 100 = 40. So, 40% of first graders are dropped off at school.

4. **D; DOK Level:** 2; **Content Topics:** Q.2.a, Q.2.e, Q.3.c, Q.3.d; **Practices:** MP.1.a, MP.1.e, MP.2.c, MP.4.a
Use the equation **base × rate = part**, where the base is 140, the rate is 85% or 0.85, and the part is unknown. Multiply: 0.85 × 140 = 119. Alternately, set up and solve the proportion $\frac{part}{140} = \frac{85}{100}$.

5. **B; DOK Level:** 1; **Content Topics:** Q.2.a, Q.2.e, Q.3.d; **Practices:** MP.1.a, MP.1.e
To write a fraction as a percentage, divide the numerator 3 by the denominator 25.
This gives you 0.12 or 12 hundredths. $\frac{12}{100}$ is 12%.

6. **B; DOK Level:** 2; **Content Topics:** Q.2.a, Q.2.e, Q.3.c, Q.3.d; **Practices:** MP.1.a, MP.1.d, MP.1.e, MP.2.c, MP.4.a
First, find the amount of the discount. Use the equation **base × rate = part**, where the base is $580, the rate is 30% or 0.3, and the part is unknown. Multiply: 580 × 0.3 = 174. Subtract the discount from the original price to find the price that Sam paid: $580 − $174 = $406.

7. **C; DOK Level:** 2; **Content Topics:** Q.2.a, Q.2.e, Q.3.c, Q.3.d; **Practices:** MP.1.a, MP.1.d, MP.1.e, MP.2.c, MP.4.a
Marie needs to pay 30% of the cost of the fliers as a down payment. The total cost of the fliers is $2 × 500 = $1,000. Use the equation **base × rate = part**, where the base is $1,000, the rate is 30% or 0.3, and the part is the amount of the down payment. Multiply: 1,000 × 0.3 = $300.

8. **B; DOK Level:** 2; **Content Topics:** Q.2.a, Q.2.e, Q.3.d; **Practices:** MP.1.a, MP.1.e, MP.2.c, MP.4.a
To find the percent increase, first find the amount of the increase by subtracting the original rent from the new rent: $615 − $585 = $30. Divide the amount of change by the original salary and write the decimal as a percent. $30 ÷ $585 = 0.051 ≈ 5%.

9. **B; DOK Level:** 2; **Content Topics:** Q.2.a, Q.2.e, Q.3.d; **Practices:** MP.1.a, MP.1.e, MP.2.c, MP.4.a
Use the equation $I = prt$, where I is the amount of interest earned. In this case, p is the amount of the investment, $3,000; r is the interest rate, 3% or 0.03; and t the time, 18 months, or 1.5 years. $I = 3,000 × 0.03 × 1.5 = 135$.

10. **C**; **DOK Level:** 3; **Content Topics:** Q.2.a, Q.2.e, Q.3.c, Q.3.d; **Practices:** MP.1.a, MP.1.d, MP.1.e, MP.2.c, MP.4.a
Find the amount that Dan paid down by using the equation **base × rate = part**, where the base is $16,584, the rate is 20% or 0.2, and the part is unknown. $16,584 × 0.2 = $3,316.80. Alternately, set up and solve the proportion $\frac{part}{16,584} = \frac{20}{100}$. Subtract the down payment (part) from the cost of the car: $16,584 − $3,316.80 = $13,267.20. Finally, divide the balance by the number of months, 24, to find the monthly payment: $13,267.20 ÷ 24 = $552.80.

11. **A**; **DOK Level:** 2; **Content Topics:** Q.2.a, Q.2.e, Q.3.c, Q.3.d; **Practices:** MP.1.a, MP.1.d, MP.1.e, MP.2.c, MP.4.a
First, find the amount that Noelle earned in commission. Use the equation **base × rate = part**, where the base is $42,800, the rate is 8% or 0.08, and the part is unknown. Multiply: $42,800 × 0.08 = $3,424.00. Add Noelle's salary to her commission to find her total earnings: $2,500.00 + $3,424.00 = $5,924.00.

12. **B**; **DOK Level:** 2; **Content Topics:** Q.2.a, Q.2.e, Q.3.d; **Practices:** MP.1.a, MP.1.e, MP.2.c, MP.4.a
Use the equation $I = prt$, where I is the amount of interest paid. In this case, p is the amount of the investment, $10,000; r is the interest rate, 5.6% or 0.056; and t the time, 36 months, or 3 years. $I = 10,000 × 0.056 × 3 = 1,680$. Add the amount of the loan, $10,000, to the amount of interest paid, $1,680, to find the total amount Remy paid: $10,000 + $1,680 = $11,680.00.

13. **B**; **DOK Level:** 2; **Content Topics:** Q.2.a, Q.2.e, Q.3.d; **Practices:** MP.1.a, MP.1.d, MP.1.e, MP.2.c
To determine the percentage of miles that Nina biked on the second day, first determine the percentage of miles that she biked on the first day. On the first day, she biked 36 out of a possible 45 miles. Set $\frac{36}{45}$ as a fraction and reduce by the greatest common multiple. In this case, both 36 and 45 are divisible by 9, so $\frac{36}{45}$ reduces to $\frac{4}{5}$. To find the percentage equivalent to $\frac{4}{5}$, divide the denominator into the numerator to get 0.8, which converts to 80%. Nina biked 80% of her miles (36 of them) on the first day, meaning she biked 20% of her miles on the second day.

14. **A**; **DOK Level:** 2; **Content Topics:** Q.2.a, Q.2.e, Q.3.d; **Practices:** MP.1.a, MP.1.e
To write a percent as a decimal, drop the percent sign and divide by 100. 82% = 0.82. It is important to drop the percent sign, as 0.82% is not equal to 82%.

15. **C**; **DOK Level:** 2; **Content Topics:** Q.2.a, Q.2.e, Q.3.d; **Practices:** MP.1.a, MP.1.d, MP.1.e, MP.2.c
To determine the percentage of freshmen players on the Wolves soccer team, divide 3 by 20 to find 0.15. To check your response, multiply 0.15 times 20 to get 3, which confirms the answer. Next, convert 0.15 to 15% to arrive at the correct response.

16. **B**; **DOK Level:** 2; **Content Topics:** Q.2.a, Q.2.e, Q.3.d; **Practices:** MP.1.a, MP.1.e
The Panthers won $\frac{22}{34}$ of their games. To write a fraction as a percent, divide the numerator by the denominator. Then multiply by 100 and write the percent sign. 22 ÷ 34 ≈ 0.647, which is 64.7%.

17. **C**; **DOK Level:** 2; **Content Topics:** Q.2.a, Q.2.e, Q.3.c, Q.3.d; **Practices:** MP.1.a, MP.1.d, MP.1.e, MP.2.c
To find the amount that Bryon put down, use the equation **base × rate = part**, where the base is $1,230, the rate is 20% or 0.2, and the part is unknown. 1,230 × 0.2 = 246. Subtract the down payment of $246 from the cost of $1,230 to find the amount Bryon owes: $1,230 − $246 = $984.

18. **B**; **DOK Level:** 2; **Content Topics:** Q.2.a, Q.2.e, Q.3.d; **Practices:** MP.1.a, MP.1.d, MP.1.e, MP.2.c
The percent profit is the percent increase from the production cost to the selling price. Jim's profit on each knapsack is the difference between the selling price and the production cost: $10.50 − $7 = $3.50. To find the percent profit, divide the profit by the production cost. Then multiply by 100 and write the percent sign: $3.50 ÷ $7.00 = 0.5 = 50%.

19. **D**; **DOK Level:** 2; **Content Topics:** Q.2.a, Q.2.e, Q.3.d, Q.6.c; **Practices:** MP.1.a, MP.1.e
To find the percent of parts that were part number Q754362, divide the number of parts that were Q754362 by the total number of parts. The total number of parts is 1,158,675. 308,205 ÷ 1,158,675 = 0.266, which is about 27%.

20. **D**; **DOK Level:** 2; **Content Topics:** Q.2.a, Q.2.e, Q.3.d, Q.6.c; **Practices:** MP.1.a, MP.1.e
The combined sales of part numbers B057305 and F284203 was 545,380. Divide the number of parts that were B057305 or F284203 by the total number of parts. The total number of parts is 1,158,675. 545,380 ÷ 1,158,675 = 0.4706, which can be rounded to 47%.

21. **B**; **DOK Level:** 2; **Content Topics:** Q.2.a, Q.2.e, Q.3.d; **Practices:** MP.1.a, MP.1.e, MP.2.c, MP.4.a
Use the equation $I = prt$, where I is the amount of interest paid. In this case, p is the amount of the loan, $210,000; r is the interest rate, 5% or 0.05; and t the time, 4 years. $I = 210,000 × 0.05 × 4 = 42,000$. Add the amount of the loan, $210,000, to the amount of interest paid, $42,000, to find the total amount Jay will pay back: $210,000 + $42,000 = $252,000.

22.1 **B**; 22.2. **B**; **DOK Level:** 2; **Content Topics:** Q.2.a, Q.2.e, Q.3.d; **Practices:** MP.1.a, MP.1.e, MP.2.c, MP.4.a
The number of riders dropped, so the ridership decreased. To find the percent of the decrease, first find the amount of the decrease by subtracting the number of riders in April from the number of riders in March: 5,478 − 4,380 = 1,098. Then, divide the amount of change by the original number of riders and write the decimal as a percent. 1,098 ÷ 5,478 ≈ 0.20 = 20%.

23. **C**; **DOK Level:** 2; **Content Topics:** Q.2.a, Q.2.e, Q.3.c, Q.3.d; **Practices:** MP.1.a, MP.1.e, MP.2.c, MP.4.a
The number of students increased by 20%. To find the number of new students, use the equation **base × rate = part**, where the base is 35, the rate is 20% or 0.2, and the part is unknown. Multiply: 35 × 0.2 = 7. Add the number of new students, 7, to the original number of students, 35: 35 + 7 = 42.

Answer Key

UNIT 1 *(continued)*

24. B; DOK Level: 2; Content Topics: Q.2.a, Q.2.e, Q.3.d;
Practices: MP.1.a, MP.1.d, MP.1.e, MP.2.c
Delia's total budget is 100% of her earnings. To find the percent of her earnings left to budget for other items, convert each number in the problem to a percent.
Convert $\frac{1}{5}$ to a decimal by dividing the numerator by the denominator, then convert the decimal to a percent by multiplying by 100: $1 \div 5 = 0.20 = 20\%$. Convert 0.35 to a percent by multiplying by 100: $0.35 = 35\%$. Subtract from 100% to find the percent of earnings left: 100% − 20% − 35% = 45%.

25. A; DOK Level: 2; Content Topics: Q.2.a, Q.2.e, Q.3.c, Q.3.d; **Practices:** MP.1.a, MP.1.d, MP.1.e
If they won 75% of the matches, they lost 25%. Find 25% of 24: $\frac{25}{100} \cdot \frac{24}{1} = \frac{600}{100} = 6$.

UNIT 2 MEASUREMENT/DATA ANALYSIS

LESSON 1, *pp. 30–33*
1. C; DOK Level: 2; Content Topics: Q.2.a, Q.2.e;
Practices: MP.1.a, MP.1.b, MP.1.d, MP.1.e, MP.2.c, MP.3.a
First, convert all units to centigrams:
45 mg ÷ 10 = 4.5 cg
2 g × 100 = 200 cg
Total red pigment used = 4.5 cg + 200 cg + 85 cg = 289.5 cg.

2. C; DOK Level: 2; Content Topics: Q.2.a, Q.2.e, Q.3.c;
Practices: MP.1.a, MP.1.b, MP.1.d, MP.1.e, MP.2.c, MP.3.a, MP.4.a
The original recipe requires 2 cups of orange juice. Since the recipe is to be tripled, Cedric needs to multiply each ingredient by 3. He will need 2 × 3 = 6 cups of orange juice. Next, set up an equation to help with conversion of units:
$$\frac{1\ pint}{2\ cups} = \frac{x}{6\ cups}$$
2x = 6
x = 3 pints
Answer choice A does not account for the tripling of the recipe. Answer choices B and D result from improper conversion of units.

3. D; DOK Level: 2; Content Topics: Q.2.a, Q.2.e, Q.3.c;
Practices: MP.1.a, MP.1.b, MP.1.d, MP.1.e, MP.2.c, MP.3.a
The original recipe required 4 pints of carbonated water. Since the recipe is to be tripled, Cedric will need 12 pints.
Set up an equation to help with conversion of units:
$$\frac{2\ pints}{1\ quart} = \frac{12\ pints}{x}$$
2x = 12
x = 6 quarts
Answer choice A does not account for the tripling of the recipe. Answer choices B and C result from improper conversion of units.

4. D; DOK Level: 2; Content Topics: Q.2.a, Q.2.e, Q.3.c;
Practices: MP.1.a, MP.1.b, MP.1.d, MP.1.e, MP.2.c, MP.3.a, MP.4.a
The original recipe required 5 pints of ginger ale. Since the recipe is to be tripled, 15 pints will be required.
Set up an equation to help with conversion of units:
$$\frac{1\ pint}{2\ cups} = \frac{15\ pints}{x}$$
1x = 30 cups
Answer choice B does not account for the tripling of the recipe. Answer choices A and C result from improper conversion of units.

5. B; DOK Level: 2; Content Topics: Q.2.a, Q.2.e;
Practices: MP.1.a, MP.1.b, MP.1.d, MP.1.e, MP.2.c, MP.3.a
First, convert all units to grams:
50 mg ÷ 1,000 = 0.05 g of blue pigment
55 cg ÷ 100 = 0.55 g of green pigment
Next, add the blue pigment and green pigment so that 0.05 g + 0.55 g = 0.6 g. Then, subtract the combined mass of the blue and green pigment from the mass of the red pigment: 3 g − .6 g = 2.4 g.

6. D; DOK Level: 2; Content Topics: Q.2.a, Q.2.e;
Practices: MP.1.a, MP.1.b, MP.1.d, MP.1.e, MP.2.c, MP.3.a
Set up an equation to help with conversion of units:
$$\frac{1\ km}{1,000\ m} = \frac{x}{700\ m}$$
1,000 x = 700
x = 700 ÷ 1,000
x = 0.7 km
This eliminates answers A through C, which all result from improper conversion of units.

7. B; DOK Level: 2; Content Topics: Q.2.a, Q.2.e, Q.3.c;
Practices: MP.1.a, MP.1.b, MP.1.d, MP.1.e, MP.2.c, MP.3.a, MP.4.a
By Day 4, she marked: 700m + 600m + 800m + 1,000m = 3,100 m.
Set up an equation to help with conversion of units:
$$\frac{1\ km}{1,000\ m} = \frac{x}{3,100\ m}$$
1,000 x = 3,100
x = 3,100 ÷ 1,000
x = 3.1 km
This eliminates answers A, C, and D, which all result from improper conversion of units.

8. B; DOK Level: 3; Content Topics: Q.2.a, Q.2.e, Q.3.c;
Practices: MP.1.a, MP.1.b, MP.1.d, MP.1.e, MP.2.c, MP.3.a, MP.4.a
Convert milliseconds (ms) to seconds.
5 ms = 0.005 s
distance = rate x time
distance = 120 m/s × 0.005s
distance = 0.6 m
Convert 0.6 m to cm by multiplying by 100m, so that 0.6m × 100 = 60 cm.

9. **D**; **DOK Level:** 2; **Content Topics:** Q.2.a, Q.2.e, Q.3.c; **Practices:** MP.1.a, MP.1.b, MP.1.d, MP.1.e, MP.2.c, MP.3.a, MP.4.a

Weight on the Earth: $\dfrac{1\ Moon}{4\ Earth} = \dfrac{3\ kg\ Moon}{x\ kg\ Earth}$; $x = 4 \times 3\ kg = 12\ kg$

$12\ kg \times 1{,}000 = 12{,}000\ g$

Answers A through C are eliminated because of improper conversion of units. Answer choice C is also eliminated because it does not reflect the increase in weight that objects have on Earth.

10. **B**; **DOK Level:** 2; **Content Topics:** Q.2.a, Q.2.e, Q.6.c; **Practices:** MP.1.a, MP.1.b, MP.1.d, MP.1.e, MP.2.c, MP.3.a

Answer choices A and C result from reading the chart inaccurately (for example, the tallest sapling is 121 cm, not 101 cm or 23 cm). Answer choice D results from incorrect conversion of units.

11. **A**; **DOK Level:** 2; **Content Topics:** Q.2.a, Q.2.e, Q.3.c, Q.6.c; **Practices:** MP.1.a, MP.1.e

The difference in height is 57 cm − 33 cm = 24 cm.
24 cm ÷ 100 = 0.24 m.

12. **C**; **DOK Level:** 2; **Content Topics:** Q.2.a, Q.2.e, Q.3.b, Q.3.c, Q.6.c; **Practices:** MP.1.a, MP.1.e

Her drawing will be 4 × 50 mm = 200 mm tall. Next, convert 200 mm to cm by dividing by 10 to give 20 cm.

13. **A**; **DOK Level:** 2; **Content Topics:** Q.2.a, Q.2.e, Q.3.c, Q.6.c; **Practices:** MP.1.a, MP.1.b, MP.1.d, MP.1.e, MP.2.c, MP.3.a, MP.4.a

Set up a ratio to help find the unknown quantity:

$\dfrac{Gold}{Silver} = \dfrac{37.5\ g}{52\ g} = \dfrac{112.5\ g}{x}$

$37.5x = 5{,}850$

$1x = 156\ g$

$156\ g \div 1{,}000 = 0.156\ kg$

Answer D can be eliminated because it does not contain the digits *156*. Answer choices B and C result from improper conversion of units.

14. **C**; **DOK Level:** 2; **Content Topics:** Q.2.a, Q.2.e, Q.3.c, Q.6.c; **Practices:** MP.2.c, MP.3.a, MP.4.a

Set up a ratio to help find the unknown quantity. Note that, when setting up an equation, numbers must always be in the same units. In this case, .007 kg first must be converted to grams.

$0.007\ kg \times 1{,}000 = 7g$

$\dfrac{Gold}{Nickel} = \dfrac{37.5\ g}{1.4\ g} = \dfrac{x}{7\ g}$

$1.4x = 262.5\ g$

$1x = 187.5\ g$

15. **B**; **DOK Level:** 3; **Content Topics:** Q.2.a, Q.2.e, Q.3.a, Q.3.c, Q.6.c; **Practices:** MP.1.a, MP.1.b, MP.1.d, MP.1.e, MP.2.c, MP.3.a, MP.4.a

Convert 3 cs to ms: (3 cs × 10 = 30 ms)

Time	Weight
0	5 kg
10 ms	2.5 kg
20 ms	1.25 kg
30 ms	0.625 kg

Converting 0.625 kg gives 625 g. Answer choice A represents the quantity of mystery substance left at $t = 20$ ms. Answer choice C represents the quantity of mystery substance left at $t = 40$ ms. Answer choice D represents what is left at $t = 50$ ms.

16. **C**; **DOK Level:** 2; **Content Topics:** Q.2.a, Q.2.e, Q.3.a, Q.3.c, Q.6.c; **Practices:** MP.1.a, MP.1.b, MP.1.d, MP.1.e, MP.2.c, MP.3.a, MP.4.a

Multiplying 0.160 kg by 1,000 converts it to mg.

$0.160 \times 1{,}000 = 160$ mg

$T = 0$, *Weight* = 40 mg

$T = 20$ s, *Weight* = 80 mg

$T = 40$ s, *Weight* = 160 mg

Therefore, it takes 40 s for the substance to weigh 0.160 kg.

17. **C**; **DOK Level:** 2; **Content Topics:** Q.2.a, Q.2.e; **Practices:** MP.1.a, MP.1.e

Total liters required = (3 × 448 L) + (2 × 236 L) = 1,816 L. Set up an equation to help with conversion, or simply divide by 1,000:

Method 1

$1{,}816 \div 1{,}000 = 1.816$ L

Method 2 (equation)

$\dfrac{1\ kL}{1{,}000\ L} = \dfrac{x}{1{,}816\ L}$; $1{,}000x = 1{,}816$;

$x = \dfrac{1{,}816}{1{,}000}$; $x = 1.816$ kL

All other answer choices result from incorrect conversion of units.

18. **D**; **DOK Level:** 2; **Content Topics:** Q.2.a, Q.2.e, Q.3.c; **Practices:** MP.1.a, MP.1.e

Total volume of pond water:

(5 × 10 ml) + (5 × 1 ml) + (5 × 0.1 ml) = 55.5 ml

Convert to cL by dividing 55.5 by 10 to get 5.55 cL.

19. **A**; **DOK Level:** 2; **Content Topics:** Q.2.a, Q.2.e, Q.3.c; **Practices:** MP.1.a, MP.1.e

$1\ kL = \dfrac{1}{1{,}000}$ L; $17\ L \div 1{,}000 = 0.017$ kL

When converting from a smaller unit to a larger unit, use division. Answer choices C and D use multiplication instead of division.

20. **A**; **DOK Level:** 2; **Content Topics:** Q.2.a, Q.2.e, Q.3.c; **Practices:** MP.1.a, MP.1.e

Paint required for 4 walls = 450 L × 4 = 1,800 L. Next, convert 1,800 L to kL by dividing $\dfrac{1{,}800\ L}{1{,}000} = 1.8$ kL.

Paint left over = 2 kL − 1.8 kL = 0.2 kL

Answer choice B represents the amount of paint required to cover one wall. Answer choice C represents the amount of paint required to cover all four walls. Answer choice D is the amount of paint that was purchased.

ANSWER KEY

Answer Key

UNIT 2 (continued)

21. C; DOK Level: 2; **Content Topics:** Q.2.a, Q.2.e, Q.3.c; **Practices:** MP.1.a, MP.1.b, MP.1.d, MP.1.e, MP.2.c, MP.3.a, MP.4.a

Total yards walked = (875 × 3) + (2,625 × 2)
$$= 2,625 + 5,250$$
$$= 7,875 \text{ yards}$$

Set up an equation to aid in the conversion:
$$\frac{1}{1,760} = \frac{x}{7,875}$$
$$1,760x = 7,875$$
$$1x \approx 4.47 \text{ miles, which rounds to 4.5 miles}$$

Incorrect answer choices A, B, and D result from improper conversion of units.

22. B; DOK Level: 2; **Content Topics:** Q.2.a, Q.2.e, Q.3.c; **Practices:** MP.1.a, MP.1.b, MP.1.d, MP.1.e, MP.2.c, MP.3.a

Total ribbon needed = 18 × 24 = 432 inches.

Set up an equation to aid in the conversion:
$$\frac{1 \; ft}{12 \; inches} = \frac{x}{432 \; inches}$$
$$12x = 432$$
$$1x = 36 \text{ ft}$$

Other answer choices result from improper conversion of units.

23. D; DOK Level: 3; **Content Topics:** Q.2.a, Q.2.e, Q.3.a, Q.3.c; **Practices:** MP.1.a, MP.1.b, MP.1.d, MP.1.e, MP.2.c, MP.3.a, MP.4.a

Set up an equation to aid in the conversion:
$$\frac{39 \; inches}{24 \; hours} = \frac{x}{1 \; hour}$$
$$24x = 39$$
$$1x = 1.625 \text{ inches}$$

In 1 h (60 min), the plant grows 1.625 inches.

Set up a second equation to see how far the plant grows in 60 seconds (1 minute):
$$\frac{1.625 \; inches}{60 \; min} = \frac{x}{1 \; min}$$
$$60x = 1.625 \text{ inches}$$
$$1x = 0.027 \text{ inch}$$

Other answer choices result from improper conversion of units.

24. D; DOK Level: 2; **Content Topics:** Q.2.a, Q.2.e, Q.3.a, Q.3.c; **Practices:** MP.1.a, MP.1.b, MP.1.d, MP.1.e, MP.2.c, MP.3.a, MP.4.a

In 24 hours, the plant grows 39 inches. In 24 × 2 = 48 hours, the plant grows 39 × 2 = 78 inches.

The numerical value in answer choice A represents the height of the plant after 1 minute. Answer choice B represents the height of the plant after 1 hour. Answer choice C is the number of hours that have elapsed.

LESSON 2, pp. 34–37

1. D; DOK Level: 2; **Content Topics:** Q.2.a, Q.2.e, Q.4.a, Q.4.c, Q.4.d; **Practices:** MP.1.a, MP.1.b, MP.1.d, MP.1.e

P = 40 yd × 4 sides = 160 yd

2. D; DOK Level: 2; **Content Topics:** Q.2.a, Q.2.e, Q.4.a, Q.4.c, Q.4.d; **Practices:** MP.1.a, MP.1.b, MP.1.d, MP.1.e

P = (2 × 120 yd) + (2 × 80 yd) = 400 yd

3. A; DOK Level: 2; **Content Topics:** Q.2.a, Q.2.e, Q.4.c, Q.5.a; **Practices:** MP.1.a, MP.1.b, MP.1.d, MP.1.e, MP.2.c, MP.3.a, MP.4.a

Rectangle:
$$P = 2l + 2w$$
$$P = 2l + 2(16 \text{ ft})$$
$$72 \text{ ft} = 2l + 32 \text{ ft}$$

Rearranging the equation above gives:
$$2l = 72 \text{ ft} - 32 \text{ ft}$$
$$2l = 40 \text{ ft}, \; 1l = 20 \text{ ft}$$

Incorrect answer choice C represents 2 lengths. Answer choice B represents 2 widths. Answer choice D represents the difference in the perimeter and one length of the yard.

4. C; DOK Level: 1; **Content Topics:** Q.2.a, Q.2.e, Q.4.c, Q.5.a; **Practices:** MP.1.a, MP.1.b, MP.1.d, MP.1.e

Perimeter of the garden = 2l + 2w
$$= 2(4 \text{ ft}) + 2(4 \text{ ft})$$
$$= 16 \text{ ft}$$

Answer choices A, B, and D result from incorrect use of the perimeter formula.

5. D; DOK Level: 1; **Content Topics:** Q.2.a, Q.2.e, Q.4.a, Q.4.d; **Practices:** MP.1.a, MP.1.b, MP.1.d, MP.1.e

Total amount of fencing required = perimeter of the garden + perimeter of yard

Perimeter of fencing = 16 ft + 72 ft = 88 ft

Answer choices A, B, and C result from incorrect use of the perimeter formula.

6. A; DOK Level: 2; **Content Topics:** Q.2.a, Q.2.e, Q.4.a, Q.4.c; **Practices:** MP.1.a, MP.1.b, MP.1.d, MP.1.e, MP.2.c, MP.3.a, MP.4.a

Perimeter of rectangle = 2l + 2w
$$54 \text{ cm} = 2(16 \text{ cm}) + 2(w)$$
$$2w = 54 \text{ cm} - 32 \text{ cm}$$
$$2w = 22 \text{ cm}$$
$$1w = 11 \text{ cm}$$

7. C; DOK Level: 3; **Content Topics:** Q.2.a, Q.2.e, Q.5.a, Q.5.c; **Practices:** MP.1.a, MP.1.b, MP.1.d, MP.1.e, MP.2.c, MP.3.a, MP.4.a

Volume of a cube = l × l × l
$$27 = l \times l \times l$$
$$1l = 3 \text{ ft}$$

Surface area of 1 face = 3 ft × 3 ft = 9 ft

Since a cube has six equal faces, area = 9 ft × 6 = 54 ft²

Answer choice A represents the surface area of one face of the cube. Answer choices B and D were derived from inaccurate mathematical operations.

8. A; DOK Level: 1; **Content Topics:** Q.2.a, Q.2.e, Q.4.c, Q.5.a; **Practices:** MP.1.a, MP.1.b, MP.1.d, MP.1.e, MP.2.c, MP.3.a, MP.4.a

To find the width of a figure with an area of 64 square ft and a length of 16 ft, use the formula for area of a rectangle:
$$\text{Area} = l \times w$$
$$64 = 16 \times w$$
$$64 = 16w$$
$$4 = w$$

9. B; DOK Level: 1; **Content Topics:** Q.2.a, Q.2.e, Q.4.a, Q.4.c; **Practices:** MP.1.a, MP.1.b, MP.1.d, MP.1.e

Dividing the perimeter of a square by 4 gives you the length of each side, so that 20 ft ÷ 4 = 5 ft. Answer choices A, C, and D result from incorrect calculation.

10. **D**; **DOK Level:** 2; **Content Topics:** Q.2.a, Q.2.e, Q.5.a, Q.5.c; **Practices:** MP.1.a, MP.1.b, MP.1.d, MP.1.e, MP.2.c
Volume = $l \times w \times h$
Volume = 12 cm × 12 cm × 12 cm = 1,728 cm³

11. **C**; **DOK Level:** 2; **Content Topics:** Q.2.a, Q.2.e, Q.5.a, Q.5.c; **Practices:** MP.1.a, MP.1.b, MP.1.d, MP.1.e, MP.2.c
Container A: 15 cm × 15 cm × 24 cm = 5,400 cm³
Container B: 12 cm × 12 cm × 20 cm = 2,880 cm³
Difference: 5,400 cm³ − 2,880 cm³ = 2,520 cm³

12. **D**; **DOK Level:** 3; **Content Topics:** Q.2.a, Q.2.e, Q.5.a, Q.5.c; **Practices:** MP.1.a, MP.1.b, MP.1.d, MP.1.e, MP.2.c, MP.3.a, MP.4.a
Volume to be transported: 8,000 cm³
Volume of Container A: 5,400 cm³
Volume of Container B: 2,880 cm³
Volume of Container C: 1,728 cm³

Methods of Transporting Sand	Cost
A. 7 Units of Container C: 12,096 cm³	$700
B. 3 Units Container B: 8,640 cm³	$300
C. 1 Unit Container A: 5,400 cm³	$100
D. 2 Units Container A: 10,800 cm³	$200

8,000 cm³ sand fits into 3 units of Container B, 2 units of Container A, or 7 units of Container C. The cheapest option is to use 2 units of Container A, since this only costs $200.

13. **B**; **DOK Level:** 3; **Content Topics:** Q.2.a, Q.2.e, Q.5.a, Q.5.c; **Practices:** MP.1.a, MP.1.b, MP.1.d, MP.1.e, MP.2.c, MP.3.a, MP.4.a
The goal here is to figure out the surface area of both boxes.
Box A:
Surface Area = 6 × ($l \times w$)
$\quad\quad\quad\quad$ = 6 × 12.5 × 12.5
$\quad\quad\quad\quad$ = 937.5 cm²
Box B:
Note that Length $\quad$ = 3 × 12.5 = 37.5
Surface Area $\quad\quad$ = 6 × (37.5 × 37.5)
$\quad\quad\quad\quad\quad\quad$ = 8,437.5 cm²
Total Surface Area = 937.5 + 8,437.5 = 9,375 cm²
Since one gallon paints 1,000 cm³, we will need at least 10 gallons to cover this surface area.

14. **C**; **DOK Level:** 2; **Content Topics:** Q.2.a, Q.2.e, Q.5.a, Q.5.c; **Practices:** MP.1.a, MP.1.b, MP.1.d, MP.1.e, MP.2.c, MP.3.a, MP.4.a
Surface area of a cube = 6 ($l \times l$)
$\quad\quad\quad\quad\quad$ 600 ft² = 6 ($l \times l$)
$\quad\quad\quad\quad$ 600 ÷ 6 = $l \times l$
$\quad\quad\quad\quad\quad\quad$ 100 = $l \times l$
$\quad\quad\quad\quad$ $\sqrt{100} = \sqrt{(l \times l)}$
$\quad\quad\quad\quad\quad\quad$ 10 = l
Volume of a cube = $l \times l \times l$
$\quad\quad\quad\quad\quad\quad$ = 10 ft × 10 ft × 10 ft
$\quad\quad\quad\quad\quad\quad$ = 1,000 cubic feet
All answer choices are in the correct units, but choices A, B, and D have incorrect number values. The number 10 represents the length of each side, while 100 represents the area of each face. Answer choice D is derived from incorrect computation.

15. **D**; **DOK Level:** 2; **Content Topics:** Q.2.a, Q.2.e, Q.5.a, Q.5.c; **Practices:** MP.1.a, MP.1.b, MP.1.d, MP.1.e, MP.2.c, MP.3.a
The amount of water that can fit in Pool A is equal to the volume of Pool A.
Volume of Pool A = $l \times w \times h$ = 15 ft × 20 ft × 4 ft = 1,200 ft³.

16. **B**; **DOK Level:** 2; **Content Topics:** Q.2.a, Q.2.e, Q.5.a, Q.5.c; **Practices:** MP.1.a, MP.1.b, MP.1.d, MP.1.e, MP.2.c, MP.3.a, MP.4.a
Volume of Pool B = $l \times w \times h$
$\quad\quad\quad$ 1,200 ft³ = 15 ft × 16 ft × (x)
$\quad\quad\quad$ 1,200 ft³ = 240x
$\quad$ 1,200 ÷ 240 = x
$\quad\quad\quad\quad\quad\quad$ x = 5 ft

17. **C**; **DOK Level:** 2; **Content Topics:** Q.2.a, Q.2.e, Q.5.a, Q.5.c; **Practices:** MP.1.a, MP.1.b, MP.1.d, MP.1.e, MP.2.c, MP.3.a, MP.4.a
Pool A is a rectangular prism. Find the area of each face, then add them together.
Top face:$\quad\quad$ 15 ft × 20 ft = 300 ft²
Bottom face: 15 ft × 20 ft = 300 ft²
Left face:$\quad\quad$ 4 ft × 15 ft = 60 ft²
Right face:$\quad\quad$ 4 ft × 15 ft = 60 ft²
Front face:$\quad\quad$ 4 ft × 20 ft = 80 ft²
Back face:$\quad\quad$ 4 ft × 20 ft = 80 ft²
Total surface area = 300 ft² + 300 ft² + 60 ft² + 60 ft² + 80 ft² + 80 ft² = 880 ft²

18. **B**; **DOK Level:** 3; **Content Topics:** Q.2.a, Q.2.e, Q.5.a, Q.5.c; **Practices:** MP.1.a, MP.1.b, MP.1.d, MP.1.e, MP.2.c, MP.3.a, MP.4.a
Pool B is a rectangular prism. Find the area of each face, then add them together.
Top face:$\quad\quad$ 15 ft × 16 ft = 240 ft²
Bottom face: 15 ft × 16 ft = 240 ft²
Left face:$\quad\quad$ 5 ft × 15 ft = 75 ft²
Right face:$\quad\quad$ 5 ft × 15 ft = 75 ft²
Front face:$\quad\quad$ 5 ft × 16 ft = 80 ft²
Back face:$\quad\quad$ 5 ft × 16 ft = 80 ft²
Total surface area = 240 ft² + 240 ft² + 75 ft² + 75 ft² + 80 ft² + 80 ft² = 790 ft², so the surface area of Pool B (790 ft²) is less than the surface area of Pool A (880 ft²).

19. **D**; **DOK Level:** 2; **Content Topics:** Q.2.a, Q.2.e, Q.5.a, Q.5.c; **Practices:** MP.1.a, MP.1.b, MP.1.d, MP.1.e, MP.2.c, MP.3.a
Volume = $l \times w \times h$
Volume = 12 ft × 14 ft × 10 ft
Volume = 1,680 ft³

20. **B**; **DOK Level:** 2; **Content Topics:** Q.2.a, Q.2.e, Q.5.a, Q.5.c; **Practices:** MP.1.a, MP.1.b, MP.1.d, MP.1.e, MP.2.c, MP.3.a
If volume of addition is a cube, then:
Volume = $l \times l \times l$
$\quad$ 512 ft³ = 8 ft × 8 ft × 8 ft
$\quad\quad\quad\quad$ l = 8 ft
The value of x is 8 ft.
Answer choices A, C, and D are derived from incorrect use of the formula for volume.

21. **C**; **DOK Level:** 2; **Content Topics:** Q.2.a, Q.2.e, Q.5.a, Q.5.c; **Practices:** MP.1.a, MP.1.b, MP.1.d, MP.1.e, MP.2.c, MP.3.a, MP.4.a
First figure the volume of Owen's garage.
Volume = $l \times w \times h$
Volume = 12 ft × 14 ft × 10 ft
Volume = 1,680 ft³
Add the volume of Owen's garage to the volume of the addition supplied in question 20, so that 1,680 ft³ + 512 ft³ = 2,192 ft³.

Answer Key

UNIT 2 *(continued)*

22. A; DOK Level: 2; **Content Topics:** Q.2.a, Q.2.e, Q.5.a, Q.5.c, Q.5.f; **Practices:** MP.1.a, MP.1.b, MP.1.d, MP.1.e, MP.2.c, MP.3.a, MP.4.a
New height of drop ceiling = 10 − 2 = 8 ft.
New volume without the addition = 8 ft × 12 ft × 14 ft.
Volume = 1,344 ft³.

LESSON 3, pp. 38–41

1. D; DOK Level: 2; **Content Topics:** Q.2.a, Q.2.e, Q.6.c, Q.7.a; **Practices:** MP.1.a, MP.1.b, MP.1.c, MP.1.d, MP.1.e, MP.2.c, MP.3.a
The range of the data set is 9 − 1 = 8.

2. C; DOK Level: 2; **Content Topics:** Q.2.a, Q.2.e, Q.6.c, Q.7.a; **Practices:** MP.1.a, MP.1.b, MP.1.c, MP.1.d, MP.1.e, MP.2.c, MP.3.a
To find the mean, sum all numbers and divide by 10 to get 4.6. Answer option A is the mode, while option B is the median. Option D results from dividing 46 by 9, rather than by 10.

3. A; DOK Level: 2; **Content Topics:** Q.2.a, Q.2.e, Q.6.c, Q.7.a; **Practices:** MP.1.a, MP.1.b, MP.1.c, MP.1.d, MP.1.e, MP.2.c, MP.3.a
To find the range of a data set, one needs to identify the least and greatest data points, then subtract the smallest number from the largest number. In this case, it would be 97 − 68 = 29.

4. C; DOK Level: 2; **Content Topics:** Q.2.a, Q.2.e, Q.6.c; **Practices:** MP.1.a, MP.1.b, MP.1.c, MP.1.d, MP.1.e, MP.2.c, MP.3.a
The mode is the most frequently occurring number in a data set. In this case, 85 occurs twice.

5. C; DOK Level: 2; **Content Topics:** Q.2.a, Q.2.e, Q.6.c, Q.7.a; **Practices:** MP.1.a, MP.1.b, MP.1.c, MP.1.d, MP.1.e, MP.2.c, MP.3.a
To find the median in a data set, order data points from least to greatest. In this arrangement, the middle number will be the median. The middle number here is 85. Elena's grade is 75, so the difference between the two numbers is: 85 − 75 = 10. The other answer choices result from choosing different middle values, or from not arranging the data set in increasing order.

6. A; DOK Level: 2; **Content Topics:** Q.2.a, Q.2.e, Q.6.c, Q.7.a; **Practices:** MP.1.a, MP.1.b, MP.1.c, MP.1.d, MP.1.e, MP.2.c, MP.3.a
The mode is the most common number in a data set. In this case, the number 85 is listed twice—more than any other number—so it is the mode. The mean is the average of a data set. In this case, the data set sums to 912. By dividing 912 by the number of scores, 11, you receive a mean of 82.9. Subtract 82.9 from 85 to find a difference of 2.1 between the mode and mean. Other response options occur through an incorrect finding of mode.

7. A; DOK Level: 2; **Content Topics:** Q.2.a, Q.2.e, Q.6.c, Q.7.a; **Practices:** MP.1.a, MP.1.b, MP.1.c, MP.1.d, MP.1.e, MP.2.c, MP.3.a
To find the median in a data set, order data points from least to greatest. In this arrangement, the middle number or numbers will be the median. In this case, the two middle numbers are $11,820 and $18,560. Adding these numbers and dividing them by two gives a median of $15,190. The other answer choices result from choosing different middle values, not arranging the data set in increasing order, or not recognizing that the median covers only the first 6 months of sales.

8. C; DOK Level: 2; **Content Topics:** Q.2.a, Q.2.e, Q.6.c, Q.7.a; **Practices:** MP.1.a, MP.1.b, MP.1.c, MP.1.d, MP.1.e, MP.2.c, MP.3.a
The formula for calculating mean is as follows:
$$Mean = \frac{Sum\ of\ all\ data\ values}{Number\ of\ data\ entries}$$
So, $Mean = \frac{121,630}{6}$, or $20,271.66, which rounds to $20,272.
Other answer choices take the sum of the entire year as opposed to the specified period of July through December.

9. D; DOK Level: 2; **Content Topics:** Q.2.a, Q.2.e, Q.6.c, Q.7.a; **Practices:** MP.1.a, MP.1.b, MP.1.c, MP.1.d, MP.1.e, MP.2.c, MP.3.a
To find the range of a data set, arrange all data points from least to greatest and then subtract the smallest number from the largest number. In this case, it would be $26,890 − $7,200 = $19,690. Other response options occur through incorrect determination of highest and lowest scores in the set.

10. B; DOK Level: 2; **Content Topics:** Q.2.a, Q.2.e, Q.6.c, Q.7.a; **Practices:** MP.1.a, MP.1.b, MP.1.c, MP.1.d, MP.1.e, MP.2.c, MP.3.a
To find the mean in a data set, sum all data values and divide by the quantity of data entries. In this case, add sales from each month and divide by 12 (the number of months) to arrive at a mean sales total of $18,170.83. To find the median, order data points from least to greatest. In this arrangement, the middle number will be the median. In this instance, you have two middle numbers, $18,560 and $19,300, which you must sum and then divide by two to find the average between them of $18,930. Subtract $18,170.83 from $18,930 to get a difference of $759.17 between the mean and median.

11. D; DOK Level: 2; **Content Topics:** Q.2.a, Q.2.e, Q.6.c, Q.7.a; **Practices:** MP.1.a, MP.1.b, MP.1.c, MP.1.d, MP.1.e, MP.2.c, MP.3.a
To find the range of a data set, identify the least and greatest data points and then subtract the smallest number from the largest number. In this case, the smallest number in the data set is 0.25. The largest number in the data set is 7.5. To find the range, subtract 0.25 from 7.5, so that 7.5 − 0.25 = 7.25.

12. C; DOK Level: 2; **Content Topics:** Q.2.a, Q.2.e, Q.6.c; **Practices:** MP.1.a, MP.1.b, MP.1.c, MP.1.d, MP.1.e, MP.2.c, MP.3.a
To find the range of a data set, arrange all data points from least to greatest and then subtract the smallest number from the largest number. In this case, the smallest number in the data set is 2.25. The largest number in the data set is 7. To find the range, subtract 2.25 from 7, so that 7 − 2.25 = 4.75.

13. **B**; **DOK Level:** 2; **Content Topics:** Q.2.a, Q.2.e, Q.6.c; **Practices:** MP.1.a, MP.1.b, MP.1.c, MP.1.d, MP.1.e, MP.2.c, MP.3.a

To find the median in a data set, order data points from least to greatest. Arranging numbers from smallest to largest gives 0.25, 0.5, 0.75, 1.5, 2, 3, 3. The median is the middle number, in this case 1.5.

14. **D**; **DOK Level:** 2; **Content Topics:** Q.2.a, Q.2.e, Q.6.c; **Practices:** MP.1.a, MP.1.b, MP.1.c, MP.1.d, MP.1.e, MP.2.c, MP.3.a

To find the mean in a data set, sum all data and divide by the quantity of data values. In this case, sum the values from Wednesday and divide by 5:

Mean (Wednesday) = $\frac{17}{5}$ = 3.4

Next, sum the values from Sunday and also divide by 5:

Mean (Sunday) = $\frac{29}{5}$ = 5.8

Subtract the mean for Wednesday (3.4) from the mean for Sunday (5.8), so that 5.8 − 3.4 = 2.4.

15. **C**; **DOK Level:** 2; **Content Topics:** Q.2.a, Q.2.e, Q.6.c; **Practices:** MP.1.a, MP.1.b, MP.1.c, MP.1.d, MP.1.e, MP.2.c, MP.3.a

To determine the mode in a data set, find the most common number. In this case, 5.5 is listed more than any other number, so it is the mode.

16. **C**; **DOK Level: 2**; **Content Topics:** Q.2.a, Q.2.e, Q.6.c, Q.7.a; **Practices:** MP.1.a, MP.1.b, MP.1.c, MP.1.d, MP.1.e, MP.2.c, MP.3.a

To find the mean in a data set, sum all data and divide by the quantity of data values. In this case, add the Pirates' scores to get 92 and then divide by their number of games—6—to find that the mean scoring, or average number of points they scored per game, is 15.3. Answer options A and D feature incomplete data sets, while answer option B provides the mean for the opponents' scoring.

17. **B**; **DOK Level:** 2; **Content Topics:** Q.2.a, Q.2.e, Q.6.c, Q.7.a; **Practices:** MP.1.a, MP.1.b, MP.1.c, MP.1.d, MP.1.e, MP.2.c, MP.3.a

To find the median in a data set, order data points from least to greatest. Arranging numbers from smallest to largest gives 0, 6, 12, 14, 21, and 30. Because this is an even-numbered data set, take and average the middle two numbers of the data set to find the median. In this case, the average of 12 and 14 is 13.

18. **D**; **DOK Level:** 2; **Content Topics:** Q.2.a, Q.2.e, Q.6.c, Q.7.a; **Practices:** MP.1.a, MP.1.b, MP.1.c, MP.1.d, MP.1.e, MP.2.c, MP.3.a

To find the mean in a data set, sum all data and divide by the quantity of data values. In this case, add the 3 supplied scores (75 + 100 + 70) to get 245. Next, multiply 85% by 4 scores to get 340 total points. Subtract 245 from 340 so that 340 − 245 = 95% remaining score.

19. **C**; **DOK Level:** 2; **Content Topics:** Q.2.a, Q.2.e, Q.6.c, Q.7.a; **Practices:** MP.1.a, MP.1.b, MP.1.c, MP.1.d, MP.1.e, MP.2.c, MP.3.a

To find the mean in a data set, sum all data and divide by the quantity of data values. In this case, multiply 10 people by their average score of 80 = 800 points. Next, multiply the 15 remaining students by their average score of 65 = 975 points. Add 800 points and 975 to get 1,775 points. Divide 1,755 by 25 students to get an average score of 71.

20. **$150**; **DOK Level:** 2; **Content Topics:** Q.2.a, Q.2.e, Q.6.c; **Practices:** MP.1.a, MP.1.b, MP.1.c, MP.1.d, MP.1.e, MP.2.c, MP.3.a, MP.4.a

$Mean = \dfrac{Sum\ of\ all\ data}{Number\ of\ data\ entries}$

First find the partial sum by adding $100 + $50 + $200 = $350. Next, multiply $125 × 4 = $500. From there, subtract $350 from $500 so that $500 − $350 = $150.

21. **$150**; **DOK Level:** 2; **Content Topics:** Q.2.a, Q.2.e, Q.6.c; **Practices:** MP.1.a, MP.1.b, MP.1.c, MP.1.d, MP.1.e, MP.2.c, MP.3.a, MP.4.a

The range of a data set is the largest data entry minus the smallest entry. In this case, range = $200 − $50 = $150.

22. **B**; **DOK Level:** 2; **Content Topics:** Q.2.a, Q.2.e, Q.6.c; **Practices:** MP.1.a, MP.1.b, MP.1.c, MP.1.d, MP.1.e, MP.2.c, MP.3.a

The mode in a data set is the most frequently occurring number. Since 7 people have 3 pets, it has the highest frequency and therefore is the mode.

23. **C**; **DOK Level:** 2; **Content Topics:** Q.2.a, Q.2.e, Q.6.c; **Practices:** MP.1.a, MP.1.b, MP.1.c, MP.1.d, MP.1.e, MP.2.c, MP.3.a

To find the median, arrange each data point in increasing order so that: 1, 1, 2, 2, 2, 2, 2, 3, 3, 3, 3, 3, 3, 4, 4, 5 Because it is an odd data set, the median is the middle number. In this case, the median is 3.

24. **A**; **DOK Level:** 3; **Content Topics:** Q.2.a, Q.2.e, Q.6.c; **Practices:** MP.1.a, MP.1.b, MP.1.c, MP.1.d, MP.1.e, MP.2.c, MP.3.a

To find the mean, multiply and add the frequencies across each category for a total of 46. Next, divide 46 by the total number of entries, 17, to find that the mean = 2.7.

25. **A**; **DOK Level:** 2; **Content Topics:** Q.2.a, Q.2.e, Q.6.c; **Practices:** MP.1.a, MP.1.b, MP.1.c, MP.1.d, MP.1.e, MP.2.c, MP.3.a

Answer option A is the only option in which subtracting the smallest number from the largest gives 6.5.

26. **D**; **DOK Level:** 2; **Content Topics:** Q.2.a, Q.2.e, Q.6.c, Q.7.a; **Practices:** MP.1.a, MP.1.b, MP.1.c, MP.1.d, MP.1.e, MP.2.c, MP.3.a

To find the range of a data set, identify the least and greatest data points, and then subtract the smallest number from the largest number. In this case, the smallest number in the data set is 20:58. The largest number in the data set is 26:10. To find the range, subtract 20:58 from 26:10, so that 26:10 − 20:58 = 5:12, or 5 minutes and 12 seconds. (Note: rename 1 minute in 26:10 to get 25:70.)

LESSON 4, pp. 42–45

1. **C**; **DOK Level:** 2; **Content Topics:** Q.3.c, Q.3.d, Q.8.b; **Practice:** MP.2.c

The probability of spinning a 1, 4, or 5 is $\frac{3}{5}$ or 60%. Since this percentage is greater than 50% but less than 100%, it makes the chances of spinning a 1, 4 or 5 likely.

2. **C**; **DOK Level:** 1; **Content Topics:** Q.3.c, Q.3.d, Q.8.b; **Practices:** MP.1.e, MP.2.c

The spinner has 5 equally sized sections, one of which is labeled with the number 3. The probability of spinning and landing on the number 3 is 1:5.

Answer Key

UNIT 2 (continued)

3. **B; DOK Level:** 2; **Content Topics:** Q.2.a, Q.2.e, Q.3.c, Q.8.b; **Practices:** MP.1.e, MP.2.c
There are three striped wedges and three white wedges, for a total of 6 wedges that are either white or striped from the 8 total wedges. Then, 6:8 can be reduced to 3:4.

4. **D; DOK Level:** 2; **Content Topics:** Q.2.a, Q.2.e, Q.3.c, Q.8.b; **Practices:** MP.1.e, MP.2.c
There are two yellow wedges and three striped wedges, for a total of 5 wedges that are either yellow or striped from the 8 total wedges.

5. **C; DOK Level:** 2; **Content Topics:** Q.2.a, Q.2.e, Q.3.c, Q.8.b; **Practices:** MP.1.e, MP.2.c
The probability of the spinner landing on a white or a yellow wedge is the combination of the white and yellow wedges on the spinner divided by the total number of wedges on the spinner. The number of white and yellow wedges is 5, and the total number of wedges on the spinner is 8, so that probability is $\frac{5}{8}$.

6. **A; DOK Level:** 3; **Content Topics:** Q.2.a, Q.2.e, Q.3.c; **Practices:** MP.1.a, MP.1.b, MP.1.d, MP.1.e, MP.2.c, MP.4.a
This question involves the concept of compound probability, or the likelihood that two events will occur. To determine compound probability, you first must determine the probability of each single event. Here, the likelihood that the spinner will land on a yellow wedge is 2:8, which simplifies to 1:4. The likelihood that the spinner will land on a white wedge is 3:8. Next, multiply $\frac{1}{4} \times \frac{3}{8} = \frac{3}{32}$, which can be expressed as .09.

7. **B; DOK Level:** 2; **Content Topics:** Q.2.a, Q.2.e, Q.3.c, Q.8.b; **Practices:** MP.1.e, MP.2.c
The probability that Jenna will pick a black marble is the number of black marbles out of the total marbles. There are 5 black marbles and 12 total marbles, so the probability is $\frac{5}{12}$ that Jenna will pick a black marble.

8. **D; DOK Level:** 2; **Content Topics:** Q.2.a, Q.2.e, Q.3.c, Q.3.d, Q.8.b; **Practices:** MP.1.b, MP.1.e, MP.2.c
Once Jenna removes the striped and black marbles from the bag, she has 10 total marbles. She removed one of the original 7 striped marbles, leaving only 6. Therefore, the probability of Jenna picking a striped marble on the third event is 6 out of 10, or 60%.

9. **B; DOK Level:** 2; **Content Topics:** Q.2.a, Q.3.c, Q.8.b; **Practices:** MP.1.a, MP.1.b
The experimental probability of picking a striped marble is 2 out 3, or $\frac{2}{3}$.

10. **D; DOK Level:** 2; **Content Topics:** Q.2.a, Q.2.e, Q.3.c, Q.3.d, Q.8.b; **Practices:** MP.1.e, MP.2.c
All of the wedges in this spinner are either yellow or odd. Therefore, there is a 100% chance of spinning and landing on either a yellow wedge or an odd number.

11. **C; DOK Level:** 1; **Content Topic:** Q.3.c, Q.8.b; **Practices:** MP.1.e, MP.2.c
Spinning a second time is an independent event. That means whatever is spun the first time has no affect on what is spun the next time. Since there is only one wedge of the spinner with the number 4, the probability that Marta will spin a 4 on her second spin (or any spin) is 1:6.

12. **C; DOK Level:** 2; **Content Topics:** Q.2.a, Q.2.e, Q.3.c, Q.8.b; **Practices:** MP.1.e, MP.2.c
There are three white wedges on the spinner, and two other wedges with the numbers 2 and 6, for a total of 5 wedges. Therefore, Marta has a 5:6 probability of landing on 6, 2, or a white wedge.

13. **A; DOK Level:** 1; **Content Topic:** Q.3.c, Q.8.b; **Practices:** MP.1.e, MP.2.c
Rolling a die for a second time is an independent event. That means whatever is rolled the first time has no affect on what is rolled the next time. Since there is only one side of the die with a number 2, the probability that Chuck will roll a 2 on his second turn (or any turn) is 1:6.

14. **A; DOK Level:** 2; **Content Topics:** Q.2.a, Q.2.e, Q.3.c, Q.8.b; **Practices:** MP.1.e, MP.2.c
Since this question is asking about the experimental probability, we need to look at the results of Chuck's experiment. So far, he has only rolled the dice two times and each time has ended up with an odd number. Therefore, the number of outcomes so far has only been one (odd) and the number of favorable outcomes has only been odd. The experimental probability of Chuck landing on an odd number is 1:1.

15. **B; DOK Level:** 2; **Content Topic:** Q.3.c, Q.3.d, Q.8.b; **Practices:** MP.1.e, MP.2.c
Three of the six sides of the die are even numbers. The probability that Chuck will roll an even number is 3:6, or 50%.

16. **B; DOK Level:** 2; **Content Topic:** Q.3.c, Q.8.b; **Practices:** MP.1.e, MP.2.c
For Chuck to win the game, he must roll a 4. The probability of Chuck rolling a 4 is 1:6.

17. **A; DOK Level:** 2; **Content Topics:** Q.2.a, Q.2.e, Q.3.c, Q.8.b; **Practices:** MP.1.e, MP.2.c
Ryan saw 15 blue cars and 25 red cars, for a total of 40 cars that were either blue or red. He surveyed 100 cars in all, so there is a 0.40 chance that the next car he spots will be either blue or red.

18. **B; DOK Level:** 2; **Content Topics:** Q.2.a, Q.2.e, Q.3.c, Q.3.d, Q.8.b; **Practices:** MP.1.e, MP.2.c
Ten of the cars Ryan surveyed were neither black, blue, red, nor white. The probability that the next car will also not be one of those four colors is 10%.

19. **C; DOK Level:** 2; **Content Topics:** Q.2.a, Q.2.e, Q.3.c, Q.8.b; **Practices:** MP.1.e, MP.2.c
Of the 100 cars surveyed, Ryan saw black cars more often than any other color. Therefore, black cars have the greatest probability of being seen next.

20. **C; DOK Level:** 2; **Content Topics:** Q.2.a, Q.2.e, Q.3.d, Q.8.b; **Practices:** MP.1.e, MP.2.c
50 of the cars Ryan surveyed are a color other than black or white. The probability that the next car will be one of those colors is 50%.

21. D; DOK Level: 2; **Content Topics:** Q.2.a, Q.2.e, Q.3.c, Q.8.b; **Practices:** MP.1.e, MP.2.c

Julian has only picked three marbles, two of which have been red. Since this question is about experimental probability, Julian has a $\frac{2}{3}$ chance of picking a red marble on his next turn.

22. B; DOK Level: 2; **Content Topic:** Q.8.a; **Practices:** MP.1.e, MP.2.c

There are four digits in your PIN. For the first digit, you have 10 numbers from which to choose (0 through 9). For the second digit, you will only have 9 numbers to choose from since you used one of them for the first digit. For the third digit, you have 8 numbers left from which to choose, and there are going to be 7 numbers left for your final digit. To find the total number of combinations you must multiply the possibilities for each choice. 10 × 9 × 8 × 7 = 5,040 possible combinations for your PIN number.

23. C; DOK Level: 3; **Content Topic:** Q.8.a; **Practices:** MP.1.e, MP.2.c, MP.3.c, MP.5.a

You need to multiply to find the total number of possible outcomes, eliminating answer options B and D. Since she cannot use the same number twice, option A is also incorrect.

LESSON 5, *pp. 46–49*

1. B; DOK Level: 2; **Content Topics:** Q.6.a, Q.6.c; **Practices:** MP.1.a, MP.3.a

By comparing the two bars that show sales of soft drinks and water from innings 1 through 5 and innings 6 through 9, you see that early sales were about $650 versus later-game sales of $450, for a decrease of $200 during the game. Options A and C both show increases, which are inaccurate. Option D shows a decrease, but a larger one of $300.

2. C; DOK Level: 2; **Content Topics:** Q.6.a, Q.6.c; **Practices:** MP.1.a, MP.3.a, MP.4.c

By analyzing all three categories and trends within and across them, you see that hot dogs showed a decrease of $500 in sales from innings 1 through 5 to innings 6 through 9. Option A is incorrect because soft drinks and water sold better at the start of the game than toward the end; Option B is likewise incorrect because soft drinks and water sold better in innings 6 through 9 than did hot dogs; Option D is incorrect because all products decreased, rather than increased, in sales in the latter part of the game.

3. Students should circle 1960 and 2000 on the graph.
DOK Level: 2; **Content Topic:** Q.6.c; **Practices:** MP.1.a, MP.2.c

The bars for both 1960 and 2000 hover around the 4,500 mark.

4. The bar on the graph should be drawn to reflect a 2010 population of 3,500.
DOK Level: 3; **Content Topics:** Q.2.a, Q.2.e, Q.6.a, Q.6.c; **Practices:** MP.1.a, MP.3.a, MP.4.a, MP.4.c

The population in 1970 was about 7,000 people. Half of 7,000 is 3,500. The bar for the year 2010 should extend to 3,500.

5. Students should circle 55 on the *x*-axis.
DOK Level: 2; **Content Topic:** Q.6.a, Q.6.c; **Practices:** MP.1.a, MP.3.a, MP.4.c

The highest overall annual salaries are concentrated above the 55-year-old age range.

6. Students should circle 60 on the *y*-axis.
DOK Level: 2; **Content Topic:** Q.6.c; **Practices:** MP.1.a, MP.2.c

A 45-year-old employee can expect to earn about $60,000 at the company.

7. The dot should appear at (30; 80).
DOK Level: 3; **Content Topics:** Q.2.a, Q.2.e, Q.6.a, Q.6.c; **Practices:** MP.1.a, MP.3.a, MP.4.a, MP.4.c

First look along the horizontal axis and find age 30. This age isn't numbered but can be found directly between the 25 and 35 ages. From that point, go straight up until you hit the line for an $80,000 annual salary.

8. Circle: Raleigh, NC; Dallas, TX; Boston, MA; Houston, TX; San Francisco, CA; Seattle, WA; San Jose, CA; Denver, CO; and Salt Lake City, UT;
DOK Level: 3; **Content Topics:** Q.6.a, Q.6.c; **Practices:** MP.1.a, MP.3.a, MP.4.c

The cities of Raleigh, NC; Dallas, TX; Boston, MA; Houston, TX; San Francisco, CA; Seattle, WA; San Jose, CA; Denver, CO; and Salt Lake City, UT, all fall in the half of the scatter plot devoted to healthy markets. The placement on the scatter plot of Houston, Boston, Raleigh, and Dallas suggests they are more closely related to "humming" markets, while Seattle, San Francisco, San Jose, Denver, and Salt Lake City are closer to "booming" real estate markets.

9. Students should plot a point on the graph at (25, 50).
DOK Level: 1; **Content Topic:** Q.6.c; **Practices:** MP.1.a, MP.2.c

The asking price change is plotted on the *x*-axis. An increase of 25% is halfway between 20 and 30 on the horizontal scale. Heathy market rank is plotted on the *y*-axis. A rank of 50 is halfway up the vertical scale.

10. Students should place a check mark next to the name of Don Meredith.
DOK Level: 3; **Content Topics:** Q.2.a, Q.2.e, Q.6.a, Q.6.c; **Practices:** MP.1.a, MP.3.a, MP.4.a, MP.4.c

Meredith is the only color commentator with two separate stints on *Monday Night Football*—from 1970 to 1974 and again from 1977 to 1985. Those separate stints are noted by two unconnected bars next to his name, suggesting a separation of three years between appearances.

11. Students should circle the names of Mike Tirico, Jon Gruden, and Lisa Salters.
DOK Level: 2; **Content Topics:** Q.2.a, Q.2.e, Q.6.a, Q.6.c; **Practices:** MP.1.a, MP.3.a, MP.4.a, MP.4.c

Tirico, Gruden, and Salters are the only announcers with bars that extended through the year 2012.

12. Students should place an X next to the names of Keith Jackson, Fred Williamson, Joe Namath, Lisa Guerrero, Sam Ryan, and Joe Theismann.
DOK Level: 2; **Content Topics:** Q.2.a, Q.2.e, Q.6.a, Q.6.c; **Practices:** MP.1.a, MP.3.a, MP.4.a, MP.4.c

Keith Jackson (1970), Fred Williamson (1974), Joe Namath (1985), Lisa Guerrero (2003), Sam Ryan (2005), and Joe Theismann (2005) all had the shortest length of bars on the graph, indicating they were with *Monday Night Football* for only a single season.

Answer Key

UNIT 2 (continued)

13. Students should draw a box around the name of Frank Gifford.
DOK Level: 2; **Content Topics:** Q.2.a, Q.2.e, Q.6.a, Q.6.c; **Practices:** MP.1.a, MP.3.a, MP.4.a, MP.4.c
Gifford is the only announcer with a two-colored bar, indicating he served as play-by-play announcer from 1971 to 1986 and as color commentator from 1986 to 1997.

14. Students should place a star next to the name of Lynn Swann.
DOK Level: 2; **Content Topics:** Q.2.a, Q.2.e, Q.6.a, Q.6.c; **Practices:** MP.1.a, MP.3.a, MP.4.a, MP.4.c
The green bars indicate announcers who served as sideline reporters. To determine the answer, you must read along the y-axis to find the sideline reporter with the earliest tenure. That's Swann, who started as a sideline reporter on *Monday Night Football* in 1994.

15. Students should underline the name of Al Michaels.
DOK Level: 2; **Content Topics:** Q.2.a, Q.2.e, Q.6.a, Q.6.c; **Practices:** MP.1.a, MP.3.a, MP.4.a, MP.4.c
The blue bars indicate broadcasters who served as play-by-play announcers. Of those, Michaels had the longest tenure, on *Monday Night Football* from 1986 to 2006, a span of 20 years.

16. Student should circle Gray Squirrels.
DOK Level: 2; **Content Topic:** Q.6.c; **Practices:** MP.1.a, MP.2.c
Gray Squirrels were the only animals that increased in population over the 5 years between 2005 and 2010.

17. Students should circle the opossum.
DOK Level: 1; **Content Topic:** Q.6.c; **Practices:** MP.1.a, MP.2.c
There is not a bar for the year 2010 for the opossum, indicating that none was seen in the park that year.

18. Students should circle Computer Specialist.
DOK Level: 2; **Content Topics:** Q.2.a, Q.2.e, Q.6.c; **Practices:** MP.1.a, MP.2.c
The bars indicate that about 3,200 women work in retail. There are about 6,500 women who work as computer specialists in Centre City, or twice the number of women who work in retail.

19. Students should circle September.
DOK Level: 1; **Content Topic:** Q.6.c; **Practices:** MP.1.a, MP.2.c
In September, the lines for both Anchorage and the United States meet, indicating that the average rainfall was about the same for both during that month.

20. Students should underline February.
DOK Level: 2; **Content Topics:** Q.2.a, Q.2.e, Q.6.c; **Practices:** MP.1.a, MP.2.c
The top (green) line represents the rainfall for the U.S. The lowest point is in February.

21. Students should circle June, July, and August.
DOK Level: 2; **Content Topics:** Q.2.a, Q.2.e, Q.6.c; **Practices:** MP.1.a, MP.2.c
Three dots on the graph—representing the sunlight totals for June, July, and August—are above or slightly below the 18 figure on the y-axis, indicating sunlight of more than 17 hours.

LESSON 6, pp. 50–53

1. B; DOK Level: 2; **Content Topic:** Q.6.a; **Practices:** MP.2.c
Determine the part of the circle that represents customers who wanted to buy ice cream. Together, the parts of the graph for ice cream and chicken sandwich are about one-fourth, or 25%, of the circle. Each of those two menu items has about the same size part of the customers. So, about half of 25%, or about 12%, of people wanted to buy ice cream.

2. C; DOK Level: 2; **Content Topic:** Q.6.a; **Practices:** MP.1.a, MP.1.d, MP.1.e, MP.2.c
Determine the part of the circle that represents customers who wanted to buy cheeseburgers. The part of the graph for cheeseburgers is more than one-fourth and less than one-half. Only one answer option, $\frac{1}{3}$, is reasonable given that understanding.

3. D; DOK Level: 2; **Content Topic:** Q.6.a; **Practices:** MP.2.c
Read the circle graph to determine the percentage of the population that uses each type of fuel. Gas is used by 25% of the population and wood stove is used by 15% of the population, so a total of 25% + 15% = 40% of the population uses those two sources. This is not more than 50%. Oil is used by 35% of the population and electricity is used by 15% of the population, so a total of 35% + 15% = 50% of the population uses those two sources. This is not more than 50%. Wood stove is used by 15% of the population and oil is used by 35% of the population, so a total of 15% + 35% = 50% of the population uses those two sources. This is not more than 50%. Oil is used by 35% of the population and gas is used by 25% of the population, so a total of 35% + 25% = 60% of the population uses those two sources. This is more than 50%.

4. D; DOK Level: 2; **Content Topic:** Q.6.a; **Practices:** MP.1.a, MP.1.b, MP.2.c, MP.3.a
Read the circle graph to determine the percentage of the population that uses each type of fuel. Wood stove is used by 15% of the population and gas is used by 25% of the population. These percentages are not equal. Electricity is used by 15% of the population and other sources are used by 10% of the population. These percentages are not equal. Oil is used by 35% of the population and gas is used by 25% of the population. These percentages are not equal. Electricity is used by 15% of the population and wood stove is used by 15% of the population. These percentages are equal.

5. A; DOK Level: 2; **Content Topics:** Q.2.a, Q.2.e, Q.6.a; **Practices:** MP.1.a, MP.1.d, MP.1.e, MP.2.c
To find the percentage of the population that uses a source other than gas, subtract the percentage that *does* use gas from 100%. Since 25% of the population uses gas, 100% − 25% = 75% of the population uses a source other than gas. Alternately, find the sum of the percentages for sources other than gas: 35% + 15% + 15% + 10% = 75%.

6. C; DOK Level: 2; **Content Topics:** Q.2.a, Q.2.e, Q.6.a; **Practices:** MP.1.a, MP.1.e, MP.2.c
To find the percentage of the population that uses a source other than a wood stove, subtract the percentage that *does* use a wood stove from 100%. Since 15% of the population uses gas, 100% − 15% = 85% of the population uses a source other than gas. Alternately, find the sum of the percentages for sources other than gas: 35% + 25% + 15% + 10% = 85%.

7. C; **DOK Level:** 1; **Content Topic:** Q.6.a; **Practices:** MP.1.a, MP.1.d, MP.1.e, MP.2.c

The circle graph shows the population, so half of the population is represented by half of the circle. The section for Democrat is half of the circle, so half of the population voted for the Democratic Party.

8. C; **DOK Level:** 2; **Content Topics:** Q.2.a, Q.2.e, Q.6.a; **Practices:** MP.1.a, MP.1.d, MP.1.e, MP.2.c

Together, the part of the population that voted for either Independent or Republican candidates is slightly less than half of the circle. So, the percentage that voted for either Independent or Republican candidates is slightly less than 50%. Therefore, 45% is the only reasonable answer.

9. B; **DOK Level:** 2; **Content Topics:** Q.2.a, Q.2.e, Q.6.a; **Practices:** MP.1.a, MP.1.d, MP.1.e, MP.2.c

From question 8 we know that about 45% of the population voted Independent or Republican. This means that the Other section is about 50% − 45% = 5%. The Republican section is about twice the size of the Independent section, so it is reasonable to say that the Independent percentage is $45 \div (x + 2x) = 45 \div 3x = 15\%$. Taken together, about 5% voted Other and about 15% voted Independent for a total of 20%.

10. B; **DOK Level:** 3; **Content Topics:** Q.2.a, Q.2.e, Q.6.a; **Practices:** MP.1.a, MP.1.d, MP.1.e, MP.2.c

From question 9, we know that about 15% of the voters voted Independent. Calculate 15% of 200 to find the number of people in Middlesburg who voted Independent: 15% = 0.15; 0.15 × 200 = 30. Alternately, think: 15% of 100 = 15, so 15% of 200 must be 2(15) = 30.

11. C; **DOK Level:** 2; **Content Topics:** Q.2.a, Q.2.e, Q.6.a; **Practices:** MP.1.a, MP.1.d, MP.1.e, MP.2.c

Consider each statement and compare it to the information in the circle graph. There were 25 people who said they prefer walking. Since 25 out of 100 people is 25%, more than 20% of people prefer walking. The first statement is not accurate. Next, since 8 people prefer walking and 20 prefer swimming, the second statement is not accurate. In addition, there were 20 people who said they prefer swimming, so there were 100 − 20 = 80 people who prefer an exercise other than swimming. The fourth statement is not accurate. There were 25 people who said they prefer walking and 25 people who said they prefer running, so a total of 25 + 25 = 50 people said they prefer either running or walking. Fifty out of 100 is equal to 50%, or half, so the third statement is accurate.

12. C; **DOK Level:** 2; **Content Topics:** Q.2.a, Q.2.e, Q.6.a; **Practices:** MP.1.a, MP.1.d, MP.1.e, MP.2.c

Twenty-five out of 100 people prefer running, which is equal to $\frac{25}{100}$ or $\frac{1}{4}$. So, to find the fraction of people who prefer an exercise other than running, subtract $\frac{1}{4}$ from 1: $1 - \frac{1}{4} = \frac{4}{4} - \frac{1}{4} = \frac{3}{4}$. Alternately, find the sum of the people who chose an exercise other than running and write that number as the numerator of a fraction with a denominator of 100: $\frac{25 + 20 + 10 + 8 + 7 + 5}{100} = \frac{75}{100} = \frac{3}{4}$.

13. D; **DOK Level:** 2; **Content Topic:** Q.6.a; **Practices:** MP.1.a, MP.1.d, MP.1.e, MP.2.c, MP.4.c

The part of the circle that represents red maple is between one-fourth and one-half. It is closer to one-half of the circle than it is to one-fourth of the circle, so 40% is the most reasonable answer.

14. B; **DOK Level:** 3; **Content Topics:** Q.2.a, Q.2.e, Q.6.a; **Practices:** MP.1.a, MP.1.d, MP.1.e, MP.2.c, MP.4.c

The part of the circle that represents ash is slightly less than one-fourth. So, 20% is a reasonable estimate of the percentage of trees that are ash. Use the equation **base × rate = part**, where the base is 400 trees, the rate is 20% or 0.2, and the part is the unknown number of ash trees. Multiply: 400 × 0.2 = 80.

15. A; **DOK Level:** 2; **Content Topics:** Q.2.a, Q.2.e, Q.6.a; **Practices:** MP.1.a, MP.1.d, MP.1.e, MP.2.c, MP.4.c

Ash is close to one-fourth of the circle, so is too large. Similarly, chestnut and dogwood each appear to be about half the size of the ash part of the circle, so each of those trees is about $\frac{1}{8}$. Pin oak is about $\frac{1}{6}$ of the circle.

16. C; **DOK Level:** 1; **Content Topics:** Q.2.a, Q.2.e, Q.6.a; **Practices:** MP.1.a, MP.1.d, MP.1.e

The red maple tree is the only option that represents more than one-quarter of the graph.

17. D; **DOK Level:** 2; **Content Topics:** Q.2.a, Q.2.e, Q.6.a; **Practices:** MP.1.a, MP.1.b, MP.1.d, MP.1.e, MP.2.c

There are 40% of students who speak three languages (English, Spanish, and Chinese), and 25% of students who speak four languages (English, Spanish, Chinese, and French). Find the sum of these two percentages: 40% + 25% = 65%.

18. C; **DOK Level:** 2; **Content Topics:** Q.2.a, Q.2.e, Q.6.a; **Practices:** MP.1.a, MP.1.b, MP.1.d, MP.1.e, MP.2.c

The percentage of students who do not speak Chinese is the sum of the percentage of students who speak only English (20%) and the percentage of students who speak only English and Spanish (15%). Add: 20% + 15% = 35%. Alternately, subtract the percentage of students who speak English, Spanish, Chinese, and French (25%) or English, Spanish, and Chinese (40%) from the total, 100%: 100% − 25% − 40% = 35%.

19. D; **DOK Level:** 2; **Content Topics:** Q.2.a, Q.2.e, Q.6.a; **Practices:** MP.1.a, MP.1.b, MP.1.d, MP.1.e, MP.2.c

Consider each statement and compare it to the information in the circle graph. Only one part of the circle graph shows students who speak French. That part of the circle is 25%. Since 25% is much less than half, the first statement is not accurate. Three parts of the circle graph show students who speak Spanish: English, Spanish, Chinese, and French (25%); English, Spanish, and Chinese (40%); and English and Spanish (15%). So, 15% + 40% + 25% = 80% of students speak Spanish. Since 80% is much greater than one-fourth, the second statement is not accurate. Three parts of the circle graph show students who speak two or more languages: English, Spanish, Chinese, and French (25%); English, Spanish, and Chinese (40%); and English and Spanish (15%). So, 15% + 40% + 25% = 80% of students speak two or more languages. Since 80% is much greater than half, the fourth statement is not accurate. Finally, each part of the circle includes students who speak English. So, 100% of students speak English; the fourth statement is accurate.

Answer Key

UNIT 2 (continued)

20. A; DOK Level: 2; Content Topics: Q.2.a, Q.2.e, Q.6.a;
Practices: MP.1.a, MP.1.d, MP.1.e, MP.2.c
Examining the graph carefully shows that only choice A is correct. Answer B is incorrect because 65% of students speak Chinese. Answer choice C is incorrect as only 25% of students speak French. Answer choice D is incorrect as English and Spanish are represented on the graph.

21. C; DOK Level: 2; Content Topics: Q.2.a, Q.2.e, Q.6.a;
Practices: MP.1.a, MP.1.d, MP.1.e, MP.2.c
Diego spends 25% of his money on food. Use the equation **base × rate = part**, where the base is $100, the rate is 25% or 0.25, and the part is the unknown amount spent on food. Multiply: $100 × 0.25 = $25.

22. C; DOK Level: 2; Content Topics: Q.2.a, Q.2.e, Q.6.a;
Practices: MP.1.a, MP.1.d, MP.1.e, MP.2.c
Diego saves 5% of his money. Use the equation **base × rate = part**, where the base is $2,200, the rate is 5% or 0.05, and the part is the unknown amount put into savings. Multiply: $2,200 × 0.05 = $110.

23. D; DOK Level: 2; Content Topics: Q.2.a, Q.2.e, Q.6.a;
Practices: MP.1.a, MP.1.b, MP.1.d, MP.1.e, MP.2.c
Consider each statement and compare it to the information in the circle graph. Diego spends 25% of his monthly income on food. Since 25% is less than half, the first statement is not accurate. Next, Diego spends 15% on transportation and 5% on miscellaneous expenses, so he spends a total of 15% + 5% = 20% on those two expenses. Since 20% is less than the percentage that Diego spends on food (25%), the second statement is not accurate. In addition, Diego spends 15% on transportation and 15% on clothing costs. Since the two percentages are equal, the third statement is not accurate. Finally, Diego spends 25% on food and 35% on rent, for a total of 25% + 35% = 60% on those two expenses. Since 60% is the largest part of Diego's expenses, the fourth statement is accurate.

LESSON 7, pp. 54–57

1. B; DOK Level: 1; Content Topic: Q.6.b, Q.7.a;
Practices: MP.1.a, MP.2.c, MP.4.c
The mode is the data value with the greatest number of occurrences, or in this case the number of siblings most commonly reported by students in the class. On a dot plot, this is represented by the data value that the greatest number of corresponding dots (3 siblings, or answer option B). Answer option A corresponds to the median number of siblings. Answer option C is the number of students (5) at the modal data value (3). Answer option D is the range.

2. A; DOK Level: 2; Content Topics: Q.2.a, Q.2.e, Q.6.b, Q.7.a; **Practices:** MP.1.a, MP.1.b, MP.4.a, MP.4.c
There are 16 siblings, and so the median value will be halfway between the values of the 8th and 9th data points, which are 2 and 3, respectively. The median value, then, is the average of those two values, or 2.5. The rationale for the other choices are as described for the previous question.

3. B; DOK Level: 2; Content Topics: Q.6.b, Q.7.a;
Practices: MP.1.a, MP.1.b, MP.2.c, MP.4.c
Each bar in the histogram represents the number of visitors for the associated month. The highest bar occurs in the range 9–12 weeks. The second highest bar occurs in the range 13–16 weeks. Answer choice B is the only choice containing weeks 9–12 and 13–16.

4. B; DOK Level: 2; Content Topics: Q.6.b, Q.7.a;
Practices: MP.1.a, MP.1.b, MP.2.c, MP.4.c
The median scores are denoted by the bars in the middle of the boxes. Comparison of the four boxes shows that Chef 2 (answer option B) has the highest median score.

5. D; DOK Level: 2; Content Topics: Q.6.b, Q.7.a;
Practices: MP.2.c, MP.4.c
The upper quartile corresponds to the top of each box. The chef with the box whose top is the highest is chef 4 (answer option D).

6. B; DOK Level: 2; Content Topics: Q.6.b, Q.7.a;
Practices: MP.1.a, MP.4.c
There are 30 tosses, the median will be located between the 15th and 16th instances in an ordered list; both values are 5, so the median is 5. Other answer options are derived from an incorrect median.

7. A; DOK Level: 2; Content Topics: Q.6.b, Q.7.a;
Practices: MP.1.a, MP.1.b, MP.2.c, MP.4.a, MP.4.c
The mode is the value with the largest number of instances. The total with the largest number of dots associated with it is 6 (answer option D). The other choices represent the remaining integer points between the lower and upper quartiles.

8. A; DOK Level: 2; Content Topics: Q.2.a, Q.2.e, Q.6.b, Q.7.a; **Practices:** MP.1.a, MP.1.b, MP.1.e, MP.4.a, MP.4.c
In the plot, the minimum value is 2 (answer option A). The maximum value is 8 (option D), the mode and range are 6 (option C), and 3 has a high frequency (option B).

9. C; DOK Level: 3; Content Topics: Q.6.b, Q.7.a;
Practices: MP.1.a, MP.1.b, MP.1.e, MP.2.c, MP.3.a, MP.4.c
There is only one possible combination of dice rolls that gives a total of 2 (1 + 1). Likewise, there is only one possible combination of dice rolls that gives a total of 8 (4 + 4). There are two possible combinations that give a total of 3 (1 + 2, or 2 + 1); likewise there are only two possible combinations that give 7 (4 + 3 and 3 + 4). There are three possible combinations that total 4 (1 + 3, 2 + 2, and 3 + 1) and 6 (2 + 4, 3 + 3, and 4 + 2). There are four combinations that give 5 (1 + 4, 2 + 3, 3 + 2, and 4 + 1). Since the number that can be rolled with the greatest number of possible combinations is 5, one would expect the mode of a large number of tosses to be 5.

10.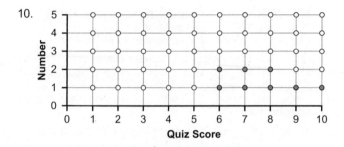

DOK Level: 2; **Content Topics:** Q.6.b;
Practices: MP.1.a, MP.4.c
One must count the number of instances of each score; this can be simplified by placing the list in increasing order. There are, for example, two instances of a score of 6 and two instances of a score of 7, and so on. Once the frequencies of each score have been tabulated, place the appropriate number of dots above each score value.

11.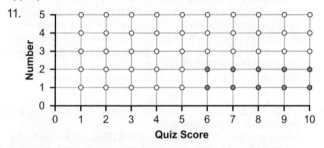

DOK Level: 3; **Content Topics:** Q.2.a, Q.2.e, Q.6.b, Q.7.a;
Practices: MP.1.a, MP.1.b, MP.1.e, MP.3.a, MP.4.a, MP.4.c
This can be done numerically. In order to have a mean of 8 after taking ten quizzes, the sum of the quiz scores must total 80. The scores on the first eight total 61, so the sum of the scores of the final two must be at least 19. This can be done by getting a 9 on one, and a 10 on the other. (A mean of at least 8 also could be attained by scoring 10 on each, but the question asks for the minimum scores.) Adding the two dots gives the resulting dot plot.

12. **C; DOK Level:** 3; **Content Topics:** Q.2.a, Q.2.e, Q.6.b, Q.7.a; **Practices:** MP.1.a, MP.1.b, MP.1.e, MP.2.c, MP.3.a, MP.4.a, MP.4.c
The range specified *excludes* the first two intervals and the final two intervals. The number of rods corresponding to these four intervals adds to 15 out of the total of 53, for a percentage of 28.3%. Choice A corresponds to the rejection of the first and last intervals only. Choice B corresponds to the rejection of the last two intervals only. Choice D corresponds to the rejection of the last and first *three* intervals.

13. **A; DOK Level:** 1; **Content Topic:** Q.6.b, Q.7.a;
Practices: MP.1.a, MP.4.c
To determine the mode, find the bar on the histogram that extends higher than any other bar. That tells you the mode, or the most frequent age group of viewers.

14. **C; DOK Level:** 2; **Content Topics:** Q.6.b, Q.7.a;
Practices: MP.1.a, MP.1.b, MP.4.c
To find the median, first order the numbers from lowest to highest (18, 20, 22, 22, 23, 25, 25, 26, 29, 29, 29, 30, 31, 33, 34, 34, 35, 37, 39). Since there are 19 data points, the median value will be at the 10th data point (29).

15. **D; DOK Level:** 2; **Content Topics:** Q.6.b, Q.7.a;
Practices: MP.1.a, MP.1.b, MP.4.c
To determine the range, identify the fewest words per minute and the most words per minute. The fewest words per minute is 18, and the most is 39. Subtract 18 from 39: 39 − 18 = 21.

16. **C; DOK Level:** 2; **Content Topics:** Q.6.b, Q.7.a;
Practices: MP.1.a, MP.1.b, MP.4.c
To determine the mode, find the bar on the histogram that extends higher than any other bar. That tells you the mode, or the most common amount of words typed per minute by students in the keyboarding class.

17. **A; DOK Level:** 2; **Content Topics:** Q.6.b, Q.7.a;
Practices: MP.1.a, MP.1.b, MP.2.c, MP.4.c
Regardless of whether one is using the range or the difference between the lower and upper quartile to judge how well a thermostat maintains a relatively constant temperature, thermostat 1 (option A) is best.

18. **C; DOK Level:** 2; **Content Topics:** Q.6.b, Q.7.a;
Practices: MP.1.a, MP.1.b, MP.2.c, MP.4.c
The median is represented by the bar in the middle of the box. The thermostat with the median closest to the set value of 68° is thermostat 3.

19. **D; DOK Level:** 2; **Content Topics:** Q.6.b, Q.7.a;
Practices: MP.1.a, MP.1.b, MP.2.c, MP.4.c
The end points of the lines extending from the box in the plot represent the minimum and maximum values; the range is the difference. The thermostat with the largest range is, then, number 4 (option D).

20. **A; DOK Level:** 2; **Content Topics:** Q.6.b, Q.7.a;
Practices: MP.1.a, MP.1.b, MP.2.c, MP.4.c
The end points of the lines extending from the box in the plot represent the minimum and maximum values; the range is the difference. The thermostat with the smallest range is then number 1 (option A).

UNIT 3 ALGEBRA, FUNCTIONS, AND PATTERNS

LESSON 1, *pp. 58–61*
1. **D; DOK Level:** 1; **Content Topics:** Q.2.a; Q.2.e;
Practices: MP.1.a, MP.1.b, MP.4.a
If her brother's apartment is 39 miles from her house, then 3 times that number is 117 miles (choice D). Choice A *divides* the 39 miles by 3 rather than multiplying it. Choice B *subtracts* 3 from 39 rather than multiplying, while choice C *adds* 3 to the 39.

2. **B; DOK Level:** 2; **Content Topics:** Q.2.a, Q.2.e, A.1.b;
Practices: MP.1.a, MP.4.a
Substituting the specified values for x and y into the numerator gives $9(12) − 3 = 105$. Dividing that by the 5 in the denominator gives 21 miles (choice B). Choice A results when the numerator is incorrectly calculated using $9(x − y)$. Choice C results from treating the numerator as $(9x + y)$. Choice D results from neglecting to divide the correct numerator by 5 in the denominator.

Answer Key

3. D; DOK Level: 2; **Content Topic:** A.1.c; **Practices:** MP.1.a, MP.1.b, MP.2.a

If *b* is the number of boys, then twice the number of boys is 2*b*, and 15 fewer than that number is 2*b* − 15 (choice D). Choice A is twice the number of boys divided by 15, rather than *reduced* by 15. Choice B begins by taking *half* the number of boys, rather than *twice* the number. Choice C is 15 *more* than twice the number of boys, rather than 15 less.

4. B; DOK Level: 2; **Content Topic:** A.1.c; **Practices:** MP.1.a, MP.1.b, MP.2.a

If there are originally 3 cases, each with 12 boxes, then there are a total of (3)(12) boxes in all. If there are 50 packs in each box, then the total number of packs is 50 times the number of boxes, or (3)(12)(50). That result times the number of pencils in a pack (*p*) gives the original total number of pencils. Since Julia removed one pencil, the number left is (3)(12)(50)*p* − 1 (choice B). Choice A adds the various factors that go into the original number of pencils, rather than *multiplying* them. Choice C *divides* by the number of pencils per pack to get the original number, rather than *multiplying*. Choice D assumes Julia *adds* a pencil to the original number, rather than *removing* a pencil.

5. D; DOK Level: 2; **Content Topic:** A.1.c; **Practices:** MP.1.a, MP.1.b, MP.2.a

If *x* and *y* are the number of miles Edward drove on Wednesday and Thursday, respectively, then (*x* + *y*) is the combined number of miles he drove those days. If he drove 4 times that many miles on Tuesday, then he drove 4(*x* + *y*) (choice D). Choice A assumes he drove 4 times the number of miles he drove on Thursday plus the number of miles he drove on Wednesday, neglecting to multiply the miles on Wednesday by 4. Choice B *divides* 4 by the combined number of miles, rather than *multiplying* by 4 that combined number. Choice C assumes Edward drove $\frac{1}{4}$ the combined miles, rather than 4 times the combined number.

6. C; DOK Level: 2; **Content Topics:** Q.2.a, Q.2.e; **Practices:** MP.1.a, MP.1.b, MP.4.a

Let *a* = the admission fee for an adult. Then, $\frac{a}{2}$ + 4 represents the admission fee for a child. The total amount paid is $12\left(\frac{a}{2} + 4\right) + 4a = 6a + 48 + 4a = 10a + 48$. (choice C).

7. C; DOK Level: 2; **Content Topics:** Q.2.a, Q.4.a, A.1.a, A.1.c; **Practices:** MP.1.a, MP.4.b

The perimeter of the triangle is the sum of the lengths of the three sides: (2*b* + 1) + (*b*) + (−4 + 3*b*). Combining like terms gives (2*b* + *b* + 3*b*) + (1 − 4) = 6*b* − 3 (choice C).

8. A; DOK Level: 2; **Content Topic:** A.1.c; **Practices:** MP.1.a, MP.1.b, MP.2.a

Since *x* and *y* are the ages of the two grandchildren, their combined ages is (*x* + *y*), and twice their combined ages is 2(*x* + *y*). The grandfather's age is 5 years greater than that, so is 2(*x* + *y*) +5 (choice A). Choice B begins by taking *half* of the combined ages, rather than *twice* the combined ages. Choice C divides by the 5 years, rather than adding 5 years to the combined ages. Choice D assumes the grandfather's age is 5 years *less* than twice the combined ages, rather than 5 years *greater*.

9. B; DOK Level: 2; **Content Topics:** Q.2.a, Q.2.e; **Practices:** MP.1.a, MP.1.b, MP.4.a

Let *a* = the number of adult tickets; then $\frac{1}{3}a + 56 = \frac{a}{3} + 56$ represents the number of children's tickets sold. Option D inverts the fraction, while option C divides the product of 56 and the number of adult tickets by 3. Option A uses the proper expression, albeit with a minus sign instead of an addition sign.

10. B; DOK Level: 2; **Content Topics:** Q.2.a, Q.2.e; **Practices:** MP.1.a, MP.1.b, MP.4.a

Let *y* = the number of students in the sophomore class; then the number of students in the freshman class can be described as $\frac{3y}{4}$. Options A and D multiply and either add or subtract 4, rather than divide, by 4. Option C inverts the expression.

11. B; DOK Level: 1; **Content Topics:** Q.2.a, Q.2.e, A.1.b; **Practices:** MP.1.a, MP.4.a

If *x* = 4, then *x* + 2*x* = 4 + 8 = 12. Multiplying that result by 3 gives 36 (choice B). Choice A can come either from multiplying the (*x* + 2*x*) term by 4 instead of 3, or by incorrectly summing the (*x* + 2*x*) term to give 4*x*, rather than 3*x*. Choice C is the result of treating the factor in parentheses as (1 + 2*x*). Choice D corresponds to a multiplication error of a factor of 2.

12. C; DOK Level: 1; **Content Topics:** Q.2.a, Q.2.e, A.1.b; **Practices:** MP.1.a, MP.4.a

There are 207 tickets sold for the $15 seats, for sales of (207)($15) = $3,105. There are 134 tickets sold for the $25 seat, for sales of (134)($25) = $3,350. Adding the two gives ($3,105 + $3,350) = $6,455 (choice C).

13. C; DOK Level: 2; **Content Topic:** A.1.g; **Practices:** MP.1.a, MP.1.b

If *w* is the width of the rectangle, then 3 times the width is 3*w*, and 3 less than that quantity—the length—is 3*w* − 3. The area of the rectangle is the product of the width (*w*) and the length (3*w* − 3), giving choice C as the result: *w*(3*w* − 3). Choice A is the expression for the length of the rectangle. Choice B is one-half the area of the rectangle. Choice D is one-half the length of the rectangle.

14. A; DOK Level: 3; **Content Topic:** A.1.c; **Practices:** MP.1.a, MP.1.b, MP.1.e, MP.2.a, MP.2.c, MP.3.a

This question requires working backward from the information given. Time *t* is 45 minutes less than one-half the time spent on Project B. That means that (*t* + 45) is one-half the time spent on Project B. That, in turn, means that 2(*t* + 45) is the time spent on Project B. Multiplying the terms in parenthesis by the factor of 2 gives choice A: 2*t* + 90. Choice B is 45 less than twice the time spent on Project A. Choice C is twice the time spent on Project A *divided* by 45. Choice D is 45 less than one-half the time spent on project A—the result one would get if one switched the times for the two projects.

15. C; DOK Level: 2; **Content Topic:** A.1.c; **Practices:** MP.1.a, MP.1.b

The sum of the second and third numbers is (*x* + *y*). One-half of that value is $\frac{(x + y)}{2}$ or choice C. Choice A is twice the sum of the two numbers. Choice B is 2 divided by the difference of the two numbers. Choice D is twice the sum of the two numbers, the same as choice A, but expressed differently.

ANSWER KEY

16. D; **DOK Level:** 2; **Content Topics:** Q.2.a, Q.2.e;
Practices: MP.1.a, MP.1.b, MP.4.a
If the cyclist rode 30 miles on Sunday, 3 times the number of miles he rode on Sunday will be 90 miles. Twenty (20) miles fewer than that result will be 70 miles.

17. C; **DOK Level:** 2; **Content Topics:** Q.2.a, Q.2.e;
Practices: MP.1.a, MP.1.b, MP.4.a
If Leo's sister is 23, 2 times the age of his sister is 46. Reducing that by 21 gives 25.

18. B; **DOK Level:** 2; **Content Topics:** Q.2.a, Q.2.e;
Practices: MP.1.a, MP.1.b, MP.4.a
If there are 374 male students, then one-half that number is 187. Increasing that number by 56 gives 243.

19. B; **DOK Level:** 2; **Content Topics:** Q.2.a, Q.2.e;
Practices: MP.1.a, MP.1.b, MP.4.a
If 9 pairs of men's shoes were sold, 4 times that number is 36. Twelve (12) more than that result gives 48.

20. A; **DOK Level:** 2; **Content Topics:** Q.2.a, Q.2.e;
Practices: MP.1.a, MP.1.b, MP.4.a
If Antonio swam 15 laps, twice that number of laps is 30. Eight (8) fewer than that result gives 22.

21. B; **DOK Level:** 3; **Content Topics:** Q.2.a, Q.2.e;
Practices: MP.1.a, MP.1.b, MP.1.e, MP.2.c, MP.3.a, MP.4.a
If 45 students scored at or below average, then twice that number is 90. Thirty-four (34) fewer than that result is 56. That is the number of students who scored above average.

22. A; **DOK Level:** 3; **Content Topics:** Q.2.a, Q.2.e;
Practices: MP.1.a, MP.1.b, MP.1.e, MP.2.c, MP.3.a, MP.4.a
If the distance from Christina's home to work (33 miles) is 15 miles less than 4 times the distance from her home to her parents' home, then 48 miles (33 + 15) is 4 times the distance from her home to her parents' home. That means that the distance from her home to her parents' is 12 miles (48 ÷ 4).

23. B; **DOK Level:** 2; **Content Topics:** Q.2.a, A.1.b;
Practice: MP.1.a
Substituting in −3 for x, the term in parentheses becomes [3 − 2(−3)] = 3 − (−6) = 3 + 6 = 9. The entire expression is, as a result, $4y − 8(9) = 4y − 72$ (choice B).

24. A; **DOK Level:** 2; **Content Topics:** Q.2.a, Q.2.e;
Practices: MP.1.a, MP.1.b, MP.4.a
If she deposited $84, one-half that amount is $42. Then $5 less than that result is $37 (choice A). Choice B is one-half the amount Jada deposited, neglecting to subtract the specified $5. Choice C is the amount Jada deposited reduced by $5 and doubled. Choice D is $5 less than *all* of the amount Jada deposited that day.

25. D; **DOK Level:** 2; **Content Topic:** A.1.j; **Practices:** MP.1.a, MP.1.b
The quotient of the second and third numbers is $\left(\frac{x}{y}\right)$. Three (3) times that quotient is choice D: $3\left(\frac{x}{y}\right)$. Choice A is one-third of the product of the second and third numbers. Choice B is 3 divided by the sum of the two numbers. Choice C is the third number (y) added to the quotient of 3 and x.

26. A; **DOK Level:** 3; **Content Topics:** Q.2.a, A.1.a, A.1.c;
Practices: MP.1.a, MP.1.b, MP.4.b
Two-thirds of the width of the rectangle is $\left(\frac{2}{3}\right)w$; 6 more than that result is the length of the rectangle: $\left(\frac{2}{3}\right)w + 6$. The perimeter is twice the width added to twice the length: $2w + \left(\frac{4}{3}\right)w + 12$. Rewriting $2w$ as $\left(\frac{6}{3}w\right)$, the final result becomes choice A: $\left(\frac{10}{3}\right)w + 12$.

27. C; **DOK Level:** 3; **Content Topics:** Q.1.b, Q.2.a, A.1.a;
Practices: MP.1.a, MP.4.b
Substituting $y = 2x$ into the numerator gives $2x(x + 4)$. Substituting $y = 2x$ into the denominator gives $x(2x + 4)$, which can be rewritten as $2x(x + 2)$. Noting that both numerator and denominator have factors of $2x$ that cancel each other, the result is choice C: $\frac{(x + 4)}{(x + 2)}$.

28. B; **DOK Level:** 2; **Content Topics:** Q.2.a, A.1.e, A.1.i;
Practices: MP.1.a, MP.4.a
If $x = 2$, then $x^2 = 4$. If $y = −1$, then $y^2 = 1$. Substituting those values into the expression gives choice B: $\frac{(4 − 1)}{(4 + 1)} = \frac{3}{5}$.

LESSON 2, *pp. 62–65*

1. B; **DOK Level:** 2; **Content Topics:** Q.3.a, A.1.j, A.2.b, A.2.c; **Practices:** MP.1.a, MP.1.e, MP.2.a, MP.2.c
Let t represent the price of lobster. The price of the crab lettuce wraps is $10. The price of the lobster, t, is $4 more than one-third the price of the crab lettuce wraps, or $4 more than $\frac{1}{3}(10)$, which is $\frac{1}{3}(10) + 4$. So, $t = \frac{1}{3}(10) + 4$.

2. D; **DOK Level:** 2; **Content Topics:** Q.2.a, Q.2.e, Q.3.a, A.1.c, A.2.b, A.2.c; **Practices:** MP.1.a, MP.1.b, MP.1.e, MP.2.a, MP.2.c, MP.4.a
Let t represent the total cost of the lobster tails. The lobster bisque costs $8 per cup, so the total cost of the two cups of lobster bisque was 2($8) = $16. Since Leon's family spent a total of $70, $t + 16 = 70$. Subtract 16 from both sides of the equation to solve for t; $t = 54$. Answer B provides the price of each of the three lobster tails, rather than the overall price. Answers A and C use incorrect equations.

3. D; **DOK Level:** 2; **Content Topics:** A.1.j, A.2.a, A.2.c; **Practices:** MP.1.a, MP.1.e, MP.2.a, MP.2.c
Since the goal is to find the second number, let x represent the second number. The other number is 5 times the value of the second number, or $5x$. The sum of the numbers x and $5x$ is 72, so $x + 5x = 72$. Group the like terms: $6x = 72$.

4. B; **DOK Level:** 2; **Content Topics:** A.2.b, A.2.c; **Practices:** MP.1.a, MP.1.e, MP.2.a, MP.2.c
Let r represent the amount John spent in restaurants. He spent $55 more than twice the amount he spent on groceries, y. $55 more than twice y is $55 more than $2y$, or $55 + 2y$. So, $r = 55 + 2y$.

5. D; **DOK Level:** 2; **Content Topics:** Q.3.d, A.1.j, A.2.b, A.2.c; **Practices:** MP.1.a, MP.1.e, MP.2.a, MP.2.c
The total cost of the printer was the price of the printer and 6% sales tax. The price of the printer was p. Patricia paid 6% sales tax on the price p, which is equal to $0.06p$. So, $p + 0.06p = 105.97$.

Answer Key

UNIT 3 (continued)

6. B; DOK Level: 2; **Content Topics:** A.2.b, A.2.c;
Practices: MP.1.a, MP.1.e, MP.2.a, MP.2.c
Let a represent the price of an adult ticket. The price of a child's ticket, $26, is $3 less than half the price of an adult ticket, a. Half the price of an adult ticket is $\frac{1}{2}a$, so $3 less than half the price of an adult ticket is $\frac{1}{2}a - 3$. Therefore, $\frac{1}{2}a - 3 = 26$.

7. A; DOK Level: 2; **Content Topics:** A.2.a, A.2.b, A.2.c;
Practices: MP.1.a, MP.1.e, MP.2.a, MP.2.c
Let h represent Rachel's husband's weekly earnings. Rachel earns twice as much as her husband, or $2h$. The sum of their earnings is $h + 2h$, so $h + 2h = 1,050$. Group like terms: $3h = 1,050$.

8. B; DOK Level: 2; **Content Topics:** Q.2.a, Q.2.e, A.2.a, A.2.b, A.2.c; **Practices:** MP.1.a, MP.1.b, MP.1.e, MP.2.a, MP.2.c, MP.4.a
Let x represent the number of hours Steven worked this week. Last week, Steven worked 33 hours. One-third of 33 hours is $\frac{1}{3}(33)$, and 2 more than that 33 is $\frac{1}{3}(33) + 2$. So, $x = \frac{1}{3}(33) + 2 = 11 + 2 = 13$. Steven worked 13 hours this week.

9. C; DOK Level: 2; **Content Topics:** A.2.b, A.2.c;
Practices: MP.1.a, MP.1.e, MP.2.a, MP.2.c
There are 36 inches in a yard, so the number of inches, i, is 36 times the number of yards, y, and $36y = i$.

10. C; DOK Level: 2; **Content Topics:** A.2.b, A.2.c;
Practices: MP.1.a, MP.1.e, MP.2.a, MP.2.c
Let x = the number of people who listed baseball as their favorite sport, so that $3x - 13 = 419$. Add 13 to both sides so that $3x = 432$. Divide 432 by 3 to determine that $x = 144$. Check your answer by substituting 144 in the equation: $3(144) - 13 = 419$, which comes to $432 - 13 = 419$.

11. A; DOK Level: 2; **Content Topics:** A.2.b, A.2.c;
Practices: MP.1.a, MP.1.e, MP.2.a, MP.2.c
To solve for this equation, work backward. First, subtract 92 from 515 so that he has $515 - 92 = 423$ comics after he sold half of them. Next, double 423 for the original amount to get $423 \times 2 = 846$.

12. D; DOK Level: 2; **Content Topics:** Q.2.a, Q.2.e, A.1.j, A.2.a, A.2.c; **Practices:** MP.1.a, MP.1.e, MP.2.a, MP.2.c
Let x represent the greater number. The lesser number is two-thirds of the greater number, or $\frac{2}{3}x$. The sum of the numbers is 55, so $x + \frac{2}{3}x = 55$. Multiply both sides of the equation by 3 to eliminate the fraction: $3x + 2x = 165$. Group like terms: $5x = 165$. Divide both sides by 5: $x = 33$.

13. B; DOK Level: 2; **Content Topics:** Q.2.a, Q.2.e, A.1.j, A.2.a, A.2.b, A.2.c; **Practices:** MP.1.a, MP.1.d, MP.1.e, MP.2.a, MP.2.c
Let x represent the amount that Karleen's mother spent. One-fourth of what Karleen's mother spent is $\frac{1}{4}x$, so $65.25 more than that is $\frac{1}{4}x + 65.25$. Karleen and her mother spent a total of $659, so $x + \frac{1}{4}x + 65.25 = 659$. Multiply both sides of the equation by 4 to eliminate the fraction: $4x + x + 261 = 2,636$. Group like terms and subtract 261 from both sides: $5x = 2,375$. Divide both sides by 5: $x = 475$. So, Karleen's mother spent $475, and Karleen spent $659 - $475 = $184.00.

14. B; DOK Level: 2; **Content Topics:** Q.2.a, Q.2.e, A.1.j, A.2.a, A.2.b, A.2.c; **Practices:** MP.1.a, MP.1.e, MP.2.a, MP.2.c
Let x be the number of boxes of crackers. So, Emma spent $3.35x$ on crackers. Emma bought 3 bottles of ginger ale for $2.29, so she spent $3 \times $2.29 = 6.87 on ginger ale. Since Emma spent a total of $23.62, the sum of the cost of crackers and the cost of ginger ale is $23.62, and $3.35x + 6.87 = 23.62$. Subtract 6.87 from both sides of the equation: $3.35x = 16.75$. Divide both sides of the equation by 3.35: $x = 5$.

15. C; DOK Level: 2; **Content Topics:** Q.2.a, Q.2.e, A.1.j, A.2.a, A.2.b, A.2.c; **Practices:** MP.1.a, MP.1.e, MP.2.a, MP.2.c
Let x be the number of boxes of cereal. The total cost of the boxes of cereal is $2.69x$, and the store pays $53.80 for a carton of boxes. So, $2.69x = 53.80$. Divide both sides of the equation by 2.69: $x = 20$.

16. D; DOK Level: 2; **Content Topics:** Q.3.a, A.2.b, A.2.c;
Practices: MP.1.a, MP.1.e, MP.2.a, MP.2.c
Let t represent the number of hours the barge traveled. The distance, 60 miles, is equal to the rate, 15 miles per hour, multiplied by the time, t. So, $60 = 15t$.

17. B; DOK Level: 2; **Content Topics:** Q.2.a, Q.2.e, A.2.a, A.2.b, A.2.c; **Practices:** MP.1.a, MP.1.b, MP.1.e, MP.2.a, MP.2.c, MP.4.a
Let x represent the number of miles that Brian biked. Ben biked 11 miles more than Brian, so Ben biked $x + 11$ miles. They rode a total of 107 miles, so $x + x + 11 = 107$, or $2x + 11 = 107$. Subtract 11 from both sides: $2x = 96$. Divide both sides by 2: $x = 48$.

18. B; DOK Level: 2; **Content Topics:** Q.2.a, Q.2.e, A.2.a, A.2.b, A.2.c; **Practices:** MP.1.a, MP.1.b, MP.1.e, MP.2.a, MP.2.c, MP.4.a
Let x represent the cost of each desk. Mrs. Logan ordered 12 desks, so the total cost of the desks was $12x$. She ordered 20 chairs at $30 each, so the total cost of the chairs was $20 \times $30 = $600. In all, the desks and chairs cost $1,260, so $12x + 600 = 1,260$. Subtract 600 from both sides of the equation: $12x = 660$. Divide both sides of the equation by 12: $x = 55$.

19. **C**; **DOK Level:** 2; **Content Topics:** Q.2.a, A.1.a, A.2.a, A.2.b; **Practices:** MP.1.a, MP.1.b, MP.1.e, MP.2.a, MP.2.c, MP.4.a

Substitute $\frac{1}{2}$ for y in the equation and then solve for x.

$4 - 2(3x - y) = 5x - 2\frac{1}{3}$

$4 - 2\left(3x - \frac{1}{2}\right) = 5x - 2\frac{1}{3}$

$4 - 6x + 1 = 5x - 2\frac{1}{3}$

$5 - 6x = 5x - 2\frac{1}{3}$

$7\frac{1}{3} = 11x$

$\frac{22}{3} = 11x$

$\frac{2}{3} = x$

Answers A and D result from incorrect equations. Answer B results from incorrect use of the negative sign.

20. **B**; **DOK Level:** 3; **Content Topics:** Q.2.a, Q.2.e, A.1.j, A.2.a, A.2.b, A.2.c; **Practices:** MP.1.a, MP.1.b, MP.1.e, MP.2.a, MP.2.c

Let d be the number of dimes. Let n be the number of nickels. Since the total number of coins is 12, $d + n = 12$. Each dime has a value of $0.10, so the total value of the dimes is $0.10d$. Each nickel has a value of $0.05, so the total value of the nickels is $0.05n$. In all, the coins have a value of $0.95, so $0.10d + 0.05n = 0.95$. Solve the first equation for n: $d + n = 12$, so $n = 12 - d$. Substitute $(12 - d)$ for n in the second equation: $0.10d + 0.05n = 0.95$, so $0.10d + 0.05(12 - d) = 0.95$. Apply the distributive property: $0.10d + 0.6 - 0.05d = 0.95$. Group like terms and subtract 0.6 from both sides: $0.05d = 0.35$. Divide both sides by 0.05: $d = 7$, so there are 7 dimes.

21. **A**; **DOK Level:** 2; **Content Topics:** A.1.c, A.2.b; **Practices:** MP.1.a, MP.1.e, MP.2.a, MP.2.c

One of the numbers is x. Twice that number is $2x$, and 8 less than that is $2x - 8$. The sum of the numbers is 40, so $x + 2x - 8 = 40$. Group like terms: $3x - 8 = 40$, or $3x + (-8) = 40$. To solve the equation, add 8 to both sides, so that $3x = 48$. Next, divide by 3 on both sides to find that $x = 16$.

22. **B**; **DOK Level:** 2; **Content Topics:** Q.2.a, Q.2.e, A.1.j, A.2.a, A.2.b, A.2.c; **Practices:** MP.1.a, MP.1.e, MP.2.a, MP.2.c

Let x be the cost of one cone. So, the cost of 5 cones is $5x$. The total bill, $15.37, is the cost of the cones and the amount of the sales tax, so $5x + 0.87 = 15.37$. Subtract 0.87 from both sides of the equation: $5x = 14.50$. Divide both sides by 5: $x = 2.90$.

23. **A**; **DOK Level:** 2; **Content Topics:** Q.2.a, Q.2.e, A.1.j, A.2.a, A.2.b, A.2.c; **Practices:** MP.1.a, MP.1.e, MP.2.a, MP.2.c

The cell phone costs $49.99 at Store B. Twice that is $2(\$49.99) = \$99.98$, and \$10 less than that is \$89.98.

24. **D**; **DOK Level:** 2; **Content Topics:** Q.2.a, Q.2.e, A.1.j, A.2.a, A.2.b, A.2.c; **Practices:** MP.1.a, MP.1.b, MP.1.d, MP.1.e, MP.2.a, MP.2c, MP.4.a

Let x be the number of children's tickets. Find the cost of a child's ticket. An adult's ticket is $9. Half that price is $\frac{1}{2}(9)$, and \$2 more than that is $\frac{1}{2}(9) + 2$. Simplify: $\frac{1}{2}(9) + 2 = 4.5 + 2 = 6.5$. So, a child's ticket costs \$6.50. Melanie bought 4 adults tickets, which cost $4(\$9) = \$36$, and some children's tickets, which cost $6.50x. The total cost of the tickets was $75, so $6.50x + 36 = 75$. Subtract 36 from both sides of the equation: $6.5x = 39$. Divide both sides by 6.5: $x = 6$.

25. **B**; **DOK Level:** 2; **Content Topics:** Q.2.a, Q.2.e, Q.3.d, A.1.j, A.2.a, A.2.b, A.2.c; **Practices:** MP.1.a, MP.1.b, MP.1.d, MP.1.e,MP.2.a, MP.2c, MP.4.a

Let x be Juan's sales. In the first earning option, Juan earns $200 plus 15% of sales, or $200 + 0.15x$. In the second earning option, Juan earns $300 plus 10% of sales, or $300 + 0.10x$. When both options pay the same amount, the two earning options are equal, and $200 + 0.15x = 300 + 0.10x$. Subtract 200 from both sides: $0.15x = 100 + 0.10x$. Subtract $0.10x$ from both sides: $0.05x = 100$. Divide both sides by 0.05: $x = 2,000$.

26. **B**; **DOK Level:** 2; **Content Topics:** Q.2.a, Q.2.e, A.2.a, A.2.b, A.2.c; **Practices:** MP.1.a, MP.1.b, MP.1.d, MP.1.e, MP.2.a, MP.2c, MP.4.a

Let x be the amount Michael contributed. Twice that is $2x$, and \$25 less than that is $2x - 25$. The sum of Andrew's and Michael's contributions was $200, so $x + 2x - 25 = 200$. Group like terms and subtract 25 from both sides of the equation: $3x = 225$. Divide both sides by 3: $x = 75$. So, Michael contributed $75, while Andrew contributed $20(75) - \$25 = \$125$.

27. **B**; **DOK Level:** 2; **Content Topics:** Q.2.a, Q.2.e, A.2.a, A.2.b, A.2.c; **Practices:** MP.1.a, MP.1.b, MP.1.d, MP.1.e, MP.2.a, MP.2c, MP.4.a

Let x be Madeleine's age. Half of Madeleine's age is $\frac{1}{2}x$, and 4 more than that is $\frac{1}{2}x + 4$. The sum of Xavier's and Madeleine's ages is 28, so $x + \frac{1}{2}x + 4 = 28$. Multiply both sides of the equation by 2 to eliminate the fraction: $2x + x + 8 = 56$. Group like terms and subtract 12 from both sides: $3x = 48$. Divide both sides of the equation by 3: $x = 16$. So, Madeleine is 16 and Xavier is $28 - 16 = 12$ years old. In 2 years, Xavier will be $12 + 2 = 14$ years old.

28. **A**; **DOK Level:** 2; **Content Topics:** Q.2.a, Q.2.e, A.2.a, A.2.b, A.2.c; **Practices:** MP.1.a, MP.1.b, MP.1.e, MP.2.a, MP.2c, MP.4.a

Let x be Beth's student loan payment. Four times that amount is $4x$, and \$74 less than that is $4x - 74$. The total of Beth's bill is $486, so $x + 4x - 74 = 486$. Group like terms and add 74 to both sides of the equation: $5x = 560$. Divide both sides by 5: $x = 112$.

29. **C**; **DOK Level:** 2; **Content Topics:** Q.2.a, Q.2.e, A.2.a, A.2.b, A.2.c; **Practices:** MP.1.a, MP.1.b, MP.1.e, MP.2.a, MP.2c, MP.4.a

Let x be Ann's weekly salary. Joe earns $874 per week. Twice that is $2(874)$, and \$543 less than that amount is $2(874) - 543$. So, $x = 2(874) - 543$. Simplify: $x = 1,748 - 543 = 1,205$.

Answer Key

UNIT 3 (continued)

LESSON 3, pp. 66–69

1. B; DOK Level: 1; **Content Topics:** Q.2.b, Q.4.a, Q.4.c; **Practices:** MP.1.a, MP.4.a
The side length is the square root of the area given (121 square feet). The square root of 121 is that number which, when multiplied by itself, equals 121. Using a calculator, or reasoning by inspection, shows the number to be 11.

2. C; DOK Level: 2; **Content Topics:** Q.2.a, Q.2.b, Q.2.e, Q.4.a, Q.4.c; **Practices:** MP.1.a, MP.1.b, MP.4.a
If the original side length is a, then the initial area is a^2. If the side length is doubled to $2a$, the area increases to $(2a)^2 = 2^2a^2 = 4a^2$. As a result, the area increases from its original value of 121 square feet to 484 square feet (choice C). Alternately, one could use the answer from question 1 (11 ft), double it (to get 22 ft), and square that result. Choice A is twice the original area, choice B is three times the original area, and choice D is five times the original area.

3. C; DOK Level: 1; **Content Topic:** Q.2.b; **Practices:** MP.1.a, MP.4.a
The square root of 144 is the number that, when multiplied by itself, produces 144. Using a calculator, or reasoning by inspection, that number is 12 (choice C). Choices A, B, and D are evenly spaced integers distributed around the correct answer.

4. B; DOK Level: 2; **Content Topic:** Q.2.a, Q.2.c, Q.2.e, A.1.e; **Practices:** MP.1.a, MP.4.a
Using a calculator, find that the square root of 7,788 is 88.2496…, which, rounded to the nearest hundredth, is 88.25 (choice B). Choice A is the result of rounding down to the nearest hundredth. Choices C and D are the same as choices A and B, aside from a misreading of the ones digit as a 9.

5. C; DOK Level: 1; **Content Topics:** Q.2.a, Q.2.c; **Practices:** MP.1.a, MP.4.a
The volume of a cube is the cube of the side length, in this case, 29 cm. The volume of the cube is $29 \times 29 \times 29 = 24{,}389$ (choice C). Choice A is three times the side length. Choice B is the square of the side length. Choice D is 841 (the square of the side lengths) squared.

6. B; DOK Level: 1; **Content Topics:** Q.2.b, Q.4.a; **Practices:** MP.1.a, MP.4.a
The side length is the square root of the area of 6.7 sq ft. Using a calculator, the square root is 2.5884…, which, rounded to the nearest tenth of a foot, is 2.6 (choice B).

7. B; DOK Level: 2; **Content Topic:** Q.2.b; **Practices:** MP.1.a, MP.4.a
$5^2 = 25$ so $\sqrt{25} = 5$, and $6^2 = 36$, so $\sqrt{36} = 6$. If we order the square roots: $\sqrt{25}, \sqrt{33}, \sqrt{36}$, we see that $\sqrt{33}$ falls between 5 and 6.

8. C; DOK Level: 1; **Content Topics:** Q.2.a, Q.2.b, Q.4.a, Q.4.c; **Practices:** MP.1.a, MP.4.a
The area of a square is the side length squared. The value of 7.8 squared is $7.8 \times 7.8 = 60.84$.

9. A; DOK Level: 3; **Content Topics:** Q.2.a, Q.2.b, Q.2.e; **Practices:** MP.1.a, MP.1.b, MP.1.e, MP.2.c, MP.3.a, MP.4.a, MP.4.b, MP.5.a, MP.5.b, MP.5.c
If the width of the living room is taken to be x, then the length of the living room is $1.5x$. The area of the room is the product of the length and width, or $1.5x^2 = 216$. Dividing both sides by 1.5 sets the equation as $x^2 = 144$. Taking the square root of both sides gives a value for x, the width of the room, of 12 feet. The length is 50% more than that, or 18 feet.

10. B; DOK Level: 2; **Content Topic:** Q.2.a, Q.2.c, Q.2.e; **Practices:** MP.1.a, MP.4.a
The set of integers that solves the equation is 4, −4, since both square to equal 16. In choice A, the 4 squares to equal 16, but −2 squares only to 4, not 16. Choices C and D, when multiplied by each other, equal 16. However, neither squares to equal 16.

11. C; DOK Level: 3; **Content Topics:** Q.2.a, Q.2.c, Q.2.e, Q.5.a; **Practices:** MP.1.a, MP.1.b, MP.1.e, MP.3.a, MP.4.a
If the width of the container is taken to be x, then the height is also x, and the length is $5x$. The volume is the product of the width, height, and length, or $5x^3$. Setting that equal to the volume given, 2,560 cubic feet, and dividing each side by 5 gives the equation $x^3 = 512$. Taking the cube root of both sides gives a value for x, the width of the container, of 8 feet. The height is also 8 feet, while the length is 5 times the width, or 40 feet.

12. B; DOK Level: 3; **Content Topics:** Q.2.a, Q.2.b, Q.2.e, Q.4.a; **Practices:** MP.1.a, MP.1.b, MP.1.e, MP.3.a, MP.4.a
The square of 19 is 361. The square root of 169 is 13. Subtract 13 from 361 so that $361 - 13 = 348$ for the correct answer.

13. D; DOK Level: 3; **Content Topics:** Q.2.a, Q.2.b, Q.2.e, Q.4.a; **Practices:** MP.1.a, MP.1.b, MP.1.e, MP.3.a, MP.4.a
If the width of the field is taken to be x, then the length of the field is $1.6x$. The area is the product of the width and length, or $1.6x^2$. Equating that to the given area, 4,000 square yards, and dividing both sides by 1.6, gives the equation $x^2 = 2{,}500$. Taking the square root of both sides gives a value for x, the width of the field, of 50 yards. The length is 60% longer than that, or 80 yards. $1.6 \times 50 = 1$

14. A; DOK Level: 2; **Content Topics:** Q.2.a, Q.2.c, Q.5.e, Q.5.a; **Practices:** MP.1.a, MP.1.b, MP.1.d, MP.1.e, MP.2.c, MP.4.a
The volume of the table is the cube of its side length: $4^3 = 64$. The volume of the hollow cube is the cube of its side length: $1.5^3 = 3.375$. The total volume of glass used is the difference between the volume of the table and the volume of the hollow center: $64 - 3.375 = 60.625$ cubic feet (Choice A).

15. D; DOK Level: 2; **Content Topics:** Q.2.a, Q.2.b, Q.5.a; **Practices:** MP.1.a, MP.1.b, MP.1.e, MP.3.a, MP.4.a
If the lengths of the three sides are a, b, and c, respectively, the initial volume is abc. If each side is increased by a factor of three, the new volume is $(3a)(3b)(3c) = 3^3abc = 27abc$. That is larger than the original volume by a factor of 27 (choice D).

16. B; DOK Level: 2; **Content Topics:** Q.2.a, Q.2.b, Q.4.a; **Practices:** MP.1.a, MP.1.b, MP.3.a, MP.4.a
If the lengths of the two sides are a and b, then the initial area is the product of the two, ab. Doubling the length of the two sides gives a new area of $(2a)(2b) = 2^2ab = 4ab$. That is 4 times the original area (choice B).

17. **C**; **DOK Level:** 3; **Content Topics:** Q.2.a, Q.2.b, Q.2.e;
Practices: MP.1.a, MP.1.b, MP.1.e, MP.2.c, MP.3.a, MP.4.b
Taking the square root of both sides of the equation, and noting that the square root of 4 can be either 2 or −2, gives the result $2 - \sqrt{x + 2} = 2$ or $2 - \sqrt{x + 2} = -2$.
Subtract 2 from each side of both equations: $-\sqrt{x + 2} = 0$ or $-\sqrt{x + 2} = -4$. Divide each side of both equations by −1: $\sqrt{x + 2} = 0$ or $\sqrt{x + 2} = 4$. Square both sides of each equation: $x + 2 = 0$ or $x + 2 = 16$. Subtract 2 from each side of both equations: $x = -2$ or $x = 14$.
Since 14 is the only answer that can correspond to a person's age, that is the correct choice (C).

18. **A**; **DOK Level:** 2; **Content Topic:** Q.2.b; **Practices:** MP.1.a, MP.4.a
The two possible solutions to the equation are $x = 5$ and −5. (Both, when squared, give 25 as the result.) The product of 5 and −5 is −25 (choice A).

19. **D**; **DOK Level:** 3; **Content Topics:** Q.2.a, Q.2.b, Q.5.a;
Practices: MP.1.a, MP.1.b, MP.1.e, MP.3.a, MP.4.b
Taking the square root of both sides of the equation, and noting that the square root of 64 can be either 8 or −8, one finds that $x - 1$ can equal 8 or −8. If one solves using the positive value, $x = 9$. If one solves using the negative value, $x = -7$. The product of the two solutions is −63 (choice D).

20. **D**; **DOK Level:** 2; **Content Topics:** Q.2.a, Q.2.b, Q.2.c, Q.2.e; **Practices:** MP.1.a, MP.1.b, MP.1.d, MP.3.e, MP.2.c, MP.4.a
The cube root of 64 is 4. The square of the cube root of 64 is $4^2 = 16$. The square root of 64 is 8. The cube of the square root of 64 is $8^3 = 512$. $\frac{512}{16} = 32$, so the cube of the square root is 32 times greater than the square of the cube root. (Choice D)

21. **C**; **DOK Level:** 3; **Content Topic:** Q.2.ba; **Practices:** MP.1.a, MP.1.b, MP.1.e, MP.3.a, MP.4.b
Taking the square root of both sides, one finds that x in $x - 6$ equals either 2 or −2. For the positive value one finds the solution $x = 8$. For the negative value one finds the solution $x = 4$. The product of the two solutions is 32 (choice C).

22. **B**; **DOK Level:** 3; **Content Topics:** Q.2.a, Q.2.b, Q.2.c, Q.5.a; **Practices:** MP.1.a, MP.3.a, MP.4.a
Taking the square root of the given area of 30.25 square inches gives the length of 5.5 inches. Cubing that result (5.5 × 5.5 × 5.5) gives the volume of 166.38 cubic inches. Rounding that to the nearest cubic inch gives the result 166 cubic inches (choice B).

23. **C**; **DOK Level:** 1; **Content Topics:** Q.2.b, Q.4.a;
Practices: MP.1.a, MP.4.a
Taking the square root of the area of 2,000 square inches gives the side length, 44.721 inches. Rounding that to the nearest inch gives 45 inches (choice C).

24. **C**; **DOK Level:** 2; **Content Topics:** Q.2.a, Q.2.c, Q.2.e, Q.5.a; **Practices:** MP.1.a, MP.4.a
If the width of a side is 18 inches, the width, expressed in feet, is 1.5 feet. The volume is the cube of the width (1.5 × 1.5 × 1.5), or 3.375 cubic feet. Rounded to the nearest tenth of a cubic foot, that gives 3.4 cubic feet (choice C).

25. **D**; **DOK Level:** 2; **Content Topics:** Q.2.a, Q.2.c, Q.2.e;
Practices: MP.1.a, MP.1.b, MP.1.e, MP.3.a, MP.4.a
Since each block is 2 inches wide, it will take 6 × 6 = 36 blocks to make a square that is a foot long and a foot wide. It will take 6 of these squares to make a cube, so the total number of blocks in the stack will be 6^3, or 216 blocks (choice D).

26. **A**; **DOK Level:** 2; **Content Topics:** Q.2.a, Q.2.b, Q.2.e;
Practices: MP.1.a, MP.1.b, MP.1.e, MP.2.c, MP.3.a, MP.4.b
Substituting in the value $F = 41$, noting that (41 − 32) is 9, and 9^2 is 81, one gets the result that $(25)(81) = (81)C^2$. Cancelling the 81 on both sides of the equation leaves $C^2 = 25$. That means that, mathematically, C can be 5 or −5. Since 41 °F is above freezing, the equivalent temperature in degrees Celsius must be positive.

27. **B**; **DOK Level:** 2; **Content Topics:** Q.2.a, Q.2.c, Q.2.e;
Practices: MP.1.a, MP.3.a, MP.4.a, MP.4.b
Substituting in the height $D = 1,350$, and dividing both sides of the equation by 400, one gets the result that $t^3 = 3.375$. Taking the cube root of both sides gives the answer $t = 1.5$ seconds.

28. **D**; **DOK Level:** 1; **Content Topic:** Q.2.c; **Practices:** MP.1.a, MP.4.a
There is no real solution. Answers A and B, when squared, provide positive 16, while answer C equals positive 64, leaving answer D as the only possible response. There is no real solution because any real number, when squared, cannot equal a negative number.

29. **B**; **DOK Level:** 1; **Content Topic:** Q.2.c; **Practices:** MP.1.a, MP.4.a
The cube of negative numbers are themselves negative, and so the cube root of a negative number exists and is negative. In this case, the cube root of −64 is the negative of the cube root of +64, or −4. Note that +4 is not a solution since the cube of +4 is positive.

30. **B**; **DOK Level:** 3; **Content Topics:** Q.2.a, Q.2.b, Q.2.e, Q.4.a; **Practices:** MP.1.a, MP.1.b, MP.1.e, MP.3.a, MP.4.a
If the length of the room is taken to be x, then the width is $\frac{3}{4}x$. The area is the product of the length and width, or $\frac{3}{4}x^2$. Setting that equal to the area given, 192 square feet, and dividing both sides by $\frac{4}{3}$, one gets the equation $x^2 = 256$. Taking the square root of both sides gives $x = 16$ feet, which is the length. The width of the room is $\frac{3}{4}$ of that, or 12 feet.

31. **A**; **DOK Level:** 3; **Content Topics:** Q.2.a, Q.2.c, Q.2.e, Q.5.a; **Practices:** MP.1.a, MP.1.b, MP.1.e, MP.3.a, MP.4.a
If the depth of the box is taken to be x, then the width is also x, and the length is $3x$. The volume is the product of the depth, width, and length, or $3x^3$. Setting this equal to the volume given, 192 cubic inches, and dividing both sides by the factor of 3, gives the result $x^3 = 64$. Solving for x gives the result $x = 4$ inches for the depth. The width is also 4 inches, and the length is three times the depth, or 12 inches.

32. **B**; **DOK Level:** 3; **Content Topics:** Q.2.a, Q.2.b, Q.2.e;
Practices: MP.1.a, MP.1.b, MP.1.e, MP.2.c, MP.3.a, MP.4.a, MP.4.b
When the ball hits the ground, $h = 0$. Setting $h = 0$ in the equation provided, and rearranging, gives the result $4.9t^2 = 9.8$. Dividing both sides by 4.9 gives the result $t^2 = 2$, for a value of t of 1.414 seconds. Rounding to the nearest tenth of a second gives the final answer of 1.4 seconds.

Answer Key

UNIT 3 (continued)

33. D; DOK Level: 3; Content Topics: Q.2.b, Q.2.d;
Practices: MP.1.a, MP.1.e. MP.3.a, MP.4.b
The expression is not a real number if the quantity in the square root is not less than zero. That will happen for any number, x, where x^2 is less than 1.5. The values $x = -1$, $x = 0$, and $x = 1$ are all clearly meet the requirement; the square of less than 1.5. The other integers given, including -2 and -3, all produce values, when squared, greater than 1.5.

34. C; DOK Level: 3; Content Topics: Q.2.a, Q.2.b, Q.2.e, Q.4.a; **Practices:** MP.1.a, MP.1.b, MP.1.e, MP.3.a, MP.4.a
The square of 14 = 196 and the square of 21 = 441. Add 196 + 441 to get 637. Next, determine the square root of 49 (7). Subtract 7 from 637 to get $630.

35. C; DOK Level: 1; Content Topics: Q.2.a, Q.2.b, Q.2.c, Q.4.d; **Practices:** MP.1.a, MP.4.a,
The square root of a negative number is not a real number, so the value of x for $x^2 = -49$ is not a real number. (Choice C). Choice A is the cube root of a positive number, and $x = 2$. Choice B is the cube root of a negative number, and $x = -3$. Choice D is the square root of a positive number, and $x = 11$ or $x = -11$.

LESSON 4, pp. 70–73

1. C; DOK Level: 1; Content Topics: Q.1.c, Q.2.e;
Practice: MP.1.a
Converting to scientific notation requires moving the decimal point from its initial position to directly right of the ones digit (5). The number of places the decimal point moves, in this case, is 4. Since the decimal place moves to the *left*, the exponent of 10 is *positive* 4. The answer is then 5.76×10^4 (choice C). The remaining choices result from miscounting the number of places the decimal point moves.

2. B; DOK Level: 2; Content Topics: Q.1.c, Q.2.a, Q.2.e;
Practices: MP.1.a, MP.4.a
Dividing the amount of grass seed (150 pounds) by the total area (57,600 sq. ft.) gives an answer of about 0.0026 pounds per sq. ft. Converting this to scientific notation requires moving the decimal point 3 places to the *right*, making the exponent a -3 (*negative*). The result, then, is 2.6×10^{-3} (choice B). Remaining choices result from miscounting the number of places the decimal point moves.

3. A; DOK Level: 1; Content Topics: Q.1.c, Q.2.a, Q.4.a;
Practice: MP.1.a, MP.4.a
The decimal point is moved to a point just to the right of the first nonzero digit (5). That requires moving the decimal point four places to the right. As a result, the number, expressed using scientific notation, is 5×10^{-4} (choice A). The 10 is raised to a *negative* power because the decimal point was moved to the *right*. Choices B and C result from a miscounting of the number of places the decimal point was moved. Choice D changes the sign of the exponent.

4. C; DOK Level: 1; Content Topics: Q.2.a, Q.2.b, Q.2.e;
Practices: MP.1.a, MP.4.a
The quantity 3^4 is the same as $3 \times 3 \times 3 \times 3$, which equals 81. The option closest to 81 is choice C. Choice A is the option closest to 3^3. Choices B and D are multiples of 10 that bracket the correct answer.

5. C; DOK Level: 1; Content Topic: Q.1.c; **Practice:** MP.1.a
The total number of students is the sum of the two quantities: $3^4 + 2^6$ (choice C). Choice A is the sum of the bases $(2 + 3)$, raised to the sum of the exponents $(4 + 6)$. Choice B is the product of the two bases, raised to the sum of the exponents. Choice D is the product of the two quantities.

6. A; DOK Level: 2; Content Topic: Q.1.c; **Practices:** MP.1.a, MP.1.b, MP.4.a
Any nonzero positive numbers raised to the power of zero is always equal to 1. So 4^0 is equal to 1. Choice A is one such case; 5^0 is also equal to 1. Choice B is 5 raised to the 1st power, which is equal to 5. Choice C is 5 raised to the power of -1, which is the reciprocal of 5, or $\frac{1}{5}$. Choice D is 4 raised to the first power, or 4.

7. D; DOK Level: 2; Content Topic: A.1.a, A.1.f; **Practices:** MP.1.a, MP.4.b
Multiplying the two terms inside the parentheses by the preceding quantity, $4x$, gives: $4x^3 + 8xy$ (choice D). Choice A neglects to multiply the second term by the preceding factor. Choice B drops a factor of x in the product with the first term. Choice C neglects to include the x from the preceding factor in the product with the second term.

8. C; DOK Level: 2; Content Topic: Q.6.c; **Practice:** MP.1.a
Scanning through the table, note that Jupiter has the mass value with the largest exponent (27). If there were additional mass values with the same exponent, the leading numbers would need to be compared to determine that which is largest. Since Jupiter has the only mass with the largest exponent, it has the largest mass among the planets listed.

9. A; DOK Level: 2; Content Topic: Q.6.c; **Practice:** MP.1.a
Again, scanning through the table, note that the mass values with the smallest exponents are for Mercury and Mars (23). The leading numbers or the two planets are 3.3 and 6.42, respectively. Since 3.3 is smaller than 6.42, the mass of Mercury (3.3×10^{23} kg) is less than the mass of Mars (6.42×10^{23} kg). That means Mercury has the least mass among the planets listed.

10. B; DOK Level: 2; Content Topics: Q.1.c, Q.2.a, Q.2.b, Q.2.e, Q.6.c; **Practices:** MP.1.a, MP.2.c, MP.4.a
The mass of Jupiter divided by the mass of Mars is (1.899×10^{27} kg) $\div$ (6.42×10^{23} kg). This can be rearranged to read $\left(\frac{1.899}{6.42}\right) \cdot \left(\frac{10^{27}}{10^{23}}\right)$. The first factor in parentheses rounds to 0.3. The second factor can be rewritten as $10^{(27-23)}$, or 10^4. The result, then, is 0.3×10^4 or, rewritten in proper scientific notation, 3×10^3. (Moving the decimal point to the *right* by one place requires reducing the exponent by one.)

11. A; DOK Level: 2; Content Topics: Q.1.c, Q.2.a, Q.2.b, Q.2.e, Q.6.c; **Practices:** MP.1.a, MP.2.c, MP.4.a
To find the sum of numbers in scientific notation, the first step is to write each number using the same power of 10. Write each mass in terms 10^{27} kg by moving the decimal point the appropriate number of places to the *left*. Mercury: 0.00033×10^{27}; Venus: 0.00487×10^{27}; Earth: 0.00597×10^{27}; Mars: 0.000642×10^{27}; Jupiter: 1.899×10^{27}; Saturn 0.568×10^{27}; Uranus: 0.0868×10^{27}; Neptune: 0.102×10^{27}. The sum of the masses is 2.667612×10^{27}, which is about 2.7×10^{27}.

12. **B**; **DOK Level:** 3; **Content Topics:** Q.2.a, A.1.a, A.1.e, A.1.f; **Practices:** MP.1.a, MP.1.b, MP.1.e, MP.4.b
The numerical coefficients of all three terms (5, −15, 10) have, as a largest common factor, 5. The variable portions of each term all have x^3 as a common factor. As a result, $5x^3$ can be factored out of the expression; placing the $5x^3$ in front, and dividing the three terms inside the parentheses by $5x^3$ gives the correct choice.

13. **D**; **DOK Level:** 3; **Content Topics:** Q.2.a, A.1.a, A.1.d; **Practices:** MP.1.a, MP.1.b, MP.1.e, MP.3.a, MP.4.b
Expanding the second term in the numerator by multiplying the x^2 coefficient by the expression in parentheses gives $x^4 − 2x^3$. Adding this to the first term in the numerator $(x^4 + 5x^3)$ gives $2x^4 + 3x^3$. Dividing each term by the x^3 in the denominator gives $2x + 3$, the correct choice.

14. **C**; **DOK Level** 3; **Content Topics:** Q.2.a, A.1.a, A.1.d, A.1.f; **Practices:** MP.1.a, MP.1.b, MP.1.e, MP.3.a, MP.4.b
Expanding the first term by multiplying through by the factor of 3 gives $(6x^2 − 3)$. Subtracting the second term, $(5x^2 + x − 3)$, from that result gives $(6x^2 − 5x^2 − x − 3 + 3) = (x^2 − x)$. Noting that a factor of x can be factored out of the parentheses, one gets $x(x − 1)$.

15. **C**; **DOK Level:** 2; **Content Topics:** Q.2.c, A.1.i; **Practices:** MP.1.a, MP.1.b, MP.3.a, MP.4.b
Substituting the −1 for x in the numerator, gives $(−1)^3 = (−1) × (−1) × (−1) = −1$. Substituting the −1 for x in the denominator gives $[(−1)^3 − 1] = [−1 − 1] = −2$. Since the numerator and denominator are both negative, the quotient is positive and therefore greater than zero.

16. **D**; **DOK Level:** 2; **Content Topics:** Q.2.c, Q.2.d, A.1.i; **Practices:** MP.1.a, MP.1.b, MP.3.a, MP.4.b
Substituting in the −1 for x in the numerator gives $(−1)^3 = −1$. Doing the same for the denominator gives $[(−1)^3 + 1] = [−1 + 1] = 0$. Since the denominator is zero, the result is undefined.

17. **D**; **DOK Level:** 2; **Content Topics:** Q.2.b, Q.2.d, A.1.i; **Practices:** MP.1.a, MP.1.b, MP.3.a, MP.4.b
Substituting −1 for x in the numerator gives $(−1 − 1)^4 = (−2)^4 = 16$. Doing likewise for the denominator gives $[(−1)^2 − 1] = [1 − 1] = 0$. Since the denominator is zero, the expression is undefined.

18. **C**; **DOK Level:** 1; **Content Topics:** Q.1.c, Q.2.e, Q.6.c; **Practices:** MP.1.a, MP.2.c
The distance between Saturn and the sun is given in the table as 1.4335×10^9 km. To write this in expanded form, note that the exponent of 10 is +9 (positive), which means that the decimal point must be moved 9 places to the right. Doing so, and filling in the trailing zeros, leads to choice C. The remaining choices represent results obtained by miscounting the number of places that the decimal point moved.

19. **B**; **DOK Level:** 2; **Content Topics:** Q.1.c, Q.2.a, Q.2.e, Q.6.c; **Practices:** MP.1.a, MP.2.c, MP.4.a
The difference in distances can be found by subtracting the sun-to-Venus distance from the sun-to-Jupiter distances: $(7.786 \times 10^8$ km$) − (1.082 \times 10^8$ km$)$. In general, the smaller number would have to be rewritten so that it was expressed using the same power of 10 as the larger number, but since both numbers use the same exponent, that is not needed here. One can rearrange the numerical expression to read $(7.786 − 1.082) \times 10^8$ km $= 6.704 \times 10^8$ km (choice B). Choices A and C represent incorrect adjustments to the power of 10. Choice D incorrectly sums the powers of 8 for the two numbers, which would be correct for multiplication, but not for the subtraction required here.

20. **C**; **DOK Level:** 1; **Content Topics:** Q.1.c, Q.2.e; **Practice:** MP.1.a
Since $10^5 = 1 \times 10^5$, and the exponent (5) is *positive*, one must move the decimal point 5 places to the *right* and fill in the trailing zeros. The result is 100,000 (choice C). The remaining choices result from miscounting the number of places that the decimal point must move.

21. **B**; **DOK Level:** 1; **Content Topic:** Q.1.c; **Practices:** MP.1.a, MP.4.b
Raising a number or quantity by a negative power is the same as dividing by the same number to the *positive* power. In this case, the exponent is −4, so the procedure is to invert the expression and switch the exponent to +4: $\frac{1}{b^4}$ (choice B). Choice A neglects to invert the expression. Choice C incorrectly brings the negative sign from the exponent. Choice D incorrectly interprets the expression as raising $(−b)$ to the +4 power.

22. **D**; **DOK Level:** 1; **Content Topics:** Q.1.c, Q.2.e; **Practice:** MP.1.a
Focusing first on the exponent of 10, the power of −10 *(negative)* implies that the decimal point must be moved 10 places to the *left*, filling in with zeros as needed. In this case, that results in nine zeros between the decimal point and the first nonzero digit (choice D). The remaining choices result from miscounting the number of places that the decimal point must move.

23. **C**; **DOK Level:** 1; **Content Topics:** Q.1.c, Q.2.e; **Practice:** MP.1.a
Converting to scientific notation requires moving the decimal point from its initial point (immediately to the right of the ones digit) to a location immediately following the leading digit of the number (the first 4). The exponent of the 10 corresponds to the number of places the decimal must move (9), and since the decimal point moves *left*, the exponent is *positive* (+9). The result is choice C. Other choices result from miscounting the number of places the decimal point must move.

24. **C**; **DOK Level:** 2; **Content Topic:** Q.1.c; **Practices:** MP.1.a, MP.1.b
To maintain the value of a number expressed in this way, for every place a decimal point moves to the left, the exponent must increase by 1. In this case, moving it one place to the left requires increasing the exponent by one: 0.4404×10^{10}. Moving it one place to the right requires *decreasing* the exponent by 1: 44.04×10^8. Both numbers have the same value as the original.

Answer Key

UNIT 3 *(continued)*

25. D; DOK Level: 1; **Content Topics:** Q.2.a, Q.2.b;
Practices: MP.1.a, MP.1.b, MP.4.a
The easiest way to find x is to note that $81 = 9 \times 9$, and that $9 = 3 \times 3$. This means that $81 = (3 \times 3) \times (3 \times 3) = 3^4$. Hence $x = 4$. One can also find the answer by inspection, multiplying 3 by 3, and that result by 3 again, and so forth, until one finds the number of times 3 has to appear as a factor in the product (4 times) to get to the result of 81.

26. C; DOK Level: 2; **Content Topics:** Q.2.a, Q.2.e;
Practices: MP.1.a, MP.4.a
The number of students at Shadyside is written as 2^9. Either by using a calculator or by finding the product of nine factors of 2, $2^9 = 512$ students. Sunnyside has 3 times that number of students, or $3 \times 512 = 1,536$ students (choice C).

27. B; DOK Level: 3; **Content Topic:** Q.2.b; **Practices:**
MP.1.a, MP.1.b, MP.1.e, MP.3.a, MP.4.b, MP.5.a, MP.5.c
Multiplying (-5) by an even exponent, such as 2, always will result in a positive number, meaning choice A is incorrect and choice B is correct. Through a similar argument, one can see that if multiplying (-5) by an odd power, the result always will be negative, eliminating choice C as a possibility. Choice D is also incorrect since any nonzero number raised to the power of 0 is 1.

28. C; DOK Level: 3; **Content Topics:** Q.2.a, Q.2.b;
Practices: MP.1.a, MP.1.b, MP.1.e, MP.3.a, Mp.4.b, MP.5.a, MP.5.c
Since the base numbers are the same, one can combine the factors by keeping the same base and adding the exponents: $(3^x)(3^x) = (3)^{2x}$. Since that quantity is equal to 3, and 3 is equal to 3^1, equating the exponents means that $2x = 1$, or $x = \frac{1}{2}$ (choice C). The other choices can be eliminated by direct substitution. For choice A, $(3^{-1})(3^{-1}) = \left(\frac{1}{3}\right)\left(\frac{1}{3}\right) = \frac{1}{9}$. For choice B, $(3^0)(3^0) = (1)(1) = 1$. For choice D, $(3^1)(3^1) = (3)(3) = 9$.

29. D; DOK Level: 3; **Content Topics:** Q.2.a, Q.2.d, A.1.d;
Practices: MP.1.a, MP.1.b, MP.1.e, MP.2.c, MP.3.a, Mp.4.b, MP.5.c
The expression will be undefined anywhere one of the terms represents a zero in the denominator. For the first term, $(x^3 + 27)$, the one and only value where it is zero is $x = -3$. For the second term, since x^4 is always positive, the term can *never* be zero. Finally, for the third term, the one and only value of x where the term is zero is for $x = -1$. There are, therefore, two values where the expression is undefined, -3 and -1, and their product is $+3$ (choice D).

30. B; DOK Level: 2; **Content Topics:** Q.1.c, Q.2.a, Q.2.e, Q.6.c; **Practices:** MP.1.a, MP.2.c, MP.4.a
There are 60 seconds in 1 minute and 60 minutes in 1 hour, so there are $60 \times 60 = 3,600$ seconds in 1 hour. $3,600 \times 5 \times 10^{13} = 18,000 \times 10^{13} = 1.8 \times 10^{17}$ (choice B).

LESSON 5, *pp. 74–77*

1. D; DOK Level: 2; **Content Topics:** Q.2.a, Q.2.e, Q.6.c, A.7.b; **Practices:** MP.1.a, MP.1.b
The train travels 60 miles for every hour it travels. Since it had gone 260 miles after 4 hours, after 5 hours it will have gone $(260 + 60)$ miles $= 320$ miles. The remaining choices are regularly spaced values between the distances at 4 and 5 hours, respectively.

2. A; DOK Level: 2; **Content Topics:** Q.2.a, Q.2.e, Q.6.c, A.7.b; **Practice:** MP.1.a
Since the train travels 60 miles every hour, and it is 80 miles from Station A after one hour, it must have been 20 miles (80 miles – 60 miles) from the station when it began the trip. The remaining choices are regularly spaced values between the correct answer and the distance after one hour.

3. A; DOK Level: 2; **Content Topics:** Q.2.a, Q.6.c, A.1.b, A.2.c, A.7.b; **Practice:** MP.1.a
There are a number of ways to identify the correct relationship. A quick way is to note that at $x = 0$, only one equation—choice A— gives the correct result for y (-2). That eliminates choices B, C, and D. Substitution of other values in the table confirm that choice A is the correct one.

4. C; DOK Level: 1; **Content Topics:** Q.2.a, Q.6.c, A.1.b, A.7.b; **Practice:** MP.1.a
Substituting $x = 6$ into the equation $y = 3x - 2$ gives $y = (3)(6) - 2 = 18 - 2 = 16$ (choice C). The remaining choices are numbers distributed uniformly around the correct answer.

5. B; DOK Level: 3; **Content Topics:** Q.2.a, Q.2.b;
Practices: MP.1.a, MP.1.b, MP.1.e, MP.2.c, MP.3.a
The latter three numbers in the pattern are all multiples of 3, suggesting that the rule is to multiply the previous number by 3. Multiplying the fourth term (27) by two more factors of 3 ($3 \times 3 = 9$) gives 243. Choices A and C are the terms just after and just before the correct term, respectively. Choice D is a repeat of the third term.

6. D; DOK Level: 2; **Content Topics:** Q.2.a, A.1.b;
Practice: MP.1.a
Setting $f(x)$ equal to 1 gives the equation $1 = \frac{1}{2}x$. Multiplying both sides by 2 gives the result $x = 2$. Choice C is the result one gets by substituting 1 in for x. Choices A and B are the same as C and D, aside from a sign error.

7. B; DOK Level: 2; **Content Topic:** Q.2.a, Q.2.b, Q.6.c, A.1.b, A.1.e, A.1.i, A.7.a, A.7.b; **Practices:** MP.1.a, MP.1.b, MP.4.a
The number of blocks on a side progress from 1 to 2 to 3 to 4. It is apparent that the next stack in the sequence will be a 5×5 stack, which will have 25 blocks (choice B). The remaining choices represent stacks with incorrect numbers of blocks on a side (3×6, 4×8, 6×7, respectively).

8. A; DOK Level: 2; **Content Topic:** Q.2.a, Q.2.e, Q.6.c, A.7.a, A.7.b; **Practices:** MP.1.a, MP.1.b, MP.1.e, MP.2.a, MP.2.c, MP.3.a, MP.4.a, MP.5.c
The second term is five less than the first term and twice the first term. The third term is <u>not</u> five less than the second term, but it <u>is</u> twice the second term. The remaining numbers confirm that the rule is to multiply the previous term by 2. Remaining choices represent numbers that are multiples of 20 between -80 and the correct choice.

9. **C**; **DOK Level:** 2; **Content Topics:** Q.2.a, Q.2.b, Q.6.c, A.1.e, A.7.b, A.7.c; **Practices:** MP.1.a, MP.1.b, MP.2.c, MP.4.a
At $x = 0$, $f(x)$ equals 50. As one moves away from $x = 0$ by 1 in either direction, $f(x)$ will drop by 1, to $f(x) = 50 - 1 = 49$.

10. **C**; **DOK Level:** 2; **Content Topic:** Q.2.a; **Practices:** MP.1.a, MP.1.b, MP.2.c
Multiplying terms by 2 results in correct totals for subsequent terms. Adding 4 only works when going from 4 to 8 (second number to third number in the sequence), while subtracting and dividing don't work for any of the numbers in the sequence.

11. **B**; **DOK Level:** 3; **Content Topic:** Q.2.a; **Practices:** MP.1.a, MP.1.b, MP.1.e, MP.2.c, MP.3.a
The numbers of circles in the three patterns shown are 9, 7, and 5, respectively. The number is decreasing by 2 for each term. The fourth term will have $5 - 2 = 3$ circles, and the fifth term (choice B) will have $3 - 2 = 1$ circle. The remaining choices are evenly spaced numbers distributed around the correct answer.

12. **B**; **DOK Level:** 3; **Content Topic:** Q.2.a; **Practices:** MP.1 .a, MP.1.b, MP.1.e, MP.2.c, MP.3.a
Each successive term is 3 less than the previous. The sixth term will be, therefore, −18, and the seventh term will be −21 (choice B). The remaining choices are terms in the pattern evenly distributed around the correct term.

13. **D**; **DOK Level:** 2; **Content Topics:** Q.2.a, A.7.c; **Practice:** MP.1.a
Any value of x less than or equal to 8 will produce a value for $f(x)$ that is greater or equal to 1. Any value of x greater than 8 will produce a result less than 1. Among the terms in the sequence, only 9 (as the fraction $\frac{8}{9}$) will produce values of $f(x)$ less than 1.

14. **C**; **DOK Level:** 3; **Content Topic:** Q.2.a; **Practices:** MP.1.a, MP.1.b, MP.1.e, MP.2.c, MP.3.a
The 1st, 2nd, and 3rd terms shown have 1, 4, and 9 triangles, respectively. From that pattern, the rule can be established as: the nth term will have n^2 triangles. The next term is the 4th, and so will have be composed of $4^2 = 16$ triangles.

15. **A**; **DOK Level:** 2; **Content Topics:** Q.2.a, Q.2.c; **Practices:** MP.1.a, MP.1.b
Setting $y = x$ gives the equation $x = x^3$, which reduces to $x^2 = 1$. There are two possible values for x: −1 and +1. Of these, only +1 appears as an option (choice A).

16. **A**; **DOK Level:** 1; **Content Topics:** Q.2.a, Q.2.e, A.1.b; **Practices:** MP.1.a, MP.2.a, MP.4.a
The time it takes to travel a given distance is the distance divided by 55. Dividing 220 by 55 gives 4 (choice A). The remaining choices are regularly spaced values smaller in magnitude than the correct answer.

17. **D**; **DOK Level:** 1; **Content Topics:** Q.2.a, Q.2.e, Q.3.d, A.1.b; **Practices:** MP.1.a, MP.2.a
Substituting in $N = 5{,}000$, one gets a value of $I = (0.01)(5{,}000) = 50$ (choice D).

18. **A**; **DOK Level:** 2; **Content Topics:** Q.2.a, Q.2.e, A.1.b; **Practices:** MP.1.a, MP.2.a, MP.4.b
Setting $F = 80°C$ in the equation, one gets $80 = \frac{9}{5}C + 32$; subtracting 32 from each side and multiplying by $\frac{5}{9}$ gives $C = \frac{5}{9}(48) = 26.7$ (choice A).

19. **D**; **DOK Level:** 2; **Content Topics:** Q.2.a, Q.2.e, Q.3.d, A.1.b; **Practices:** MP.1.a, MP.2.a, MP.4.a
The rate required to get $250 in interest can be found by substituting $I = 250$ into the equation and solving for r. The result is $r = \frac{250}{(1000)\,(5)} = 0.05$. Converting this into percent gives 5%. Interest rates less than 5% will give less than $250 interest, and rates greater than 5% will give more.

20. **D**; **DOK Level:** 2; **Content Topics:** Q.2.a, Q.2.b, A.1.e, A.7.c; **Practices:** MP.1.a, MP.1.b, MP.2.c, MP.4.b
For the function to be less than $\frac{1}{2}$, $(x^2 + 1)$ must be greater than 2, or x^2 must be greater than 1. That means that x must be either greater than 1, or less than −1. Option D provides a fraction of $\frac{1}{5}$, which is less than $\frac{1}{2}$. The other answer options provide fractions equal to $\frac{1}{2}$ or the whole-number value of 1.

21. **C**; **DOK Level:** 2; **Content Topics:** Q.2.a, Q.2.b, Q.2.e, Q.6.c, A.1.e, A.7.a, A.7.b; **Practices:** MP.1.a, MP.1.b, MP.2.a, MP.2.c, MP.4.a
Substituting $d = 1$ eliminates choice A as a possibility; 1.2 ≠ 0.8. Substituting $d = 2$ eliminates choice B (1.8 ≠ 1.2), as well as choice D (3.2 ≠ 1.2). Choice C, however, works for all values shown. Note: Since the data is quadratic, the answer cannot be A or B because they are linear equations.

22. **A**; **DOK Level:** 1; **Content Topics:** Q.2.a, Q.2.b, Q.2.e, Q.6.c, A.1.e, A.7.b; **Practices:** MP.1.a, MP.2.a
Substituting $d = 5$ into the equation gives $5 - (0.2)(5^2) = 5 - (0.2)(25) = 5 - 5 = 0$ (choice A). The remaining choices are equally spaced numbers between the correct answer and 0.8.

23. **C**; **DOK Level:** 2; **Content Topics:** Q.2.a, Q.2.b, A.1.e, A.7.c; **Practices:** MP.1.a, MP.2.c
Substituting $x = 1$ into the function gives a result of 4. One could substitute the various choices into the equation to find another that gives the same output, and one would find that the correct choice is −1 (choice C). Alternately, one could note that $f(x) = 4 = 3x^2 + 1$ implies that $3x^2 = 3$, or $x^2 = 1$, which has both +1 and −1 as solutions. One also could note upfront that since x only appears in the equation as x^2, any number substituted for x will yield the same value as that when substituting $-x$.

24. **A**; **DOK Level:** 3; **Content Topic:** Q.2.a; **Practices:** MP.1.a, MP.1.b, MP.1.e, MP.2.c, MP.3.a
One has to note two things—first that the magnitudes of the numbers double for each term, and second, that the signs alternate. This is precisely what happens if each term is multiplied by −2. The next three terms will be, as a result, −64, 128, and −256. The value of −256 represents the eighth term. Choice B is the seventh term, and choices C and D represent the seventh and eighth terms with sign errors.

25. **D**; **DOK Level:** 2; **Content Topics:** Q.2.a, Q.2.b, Q.6.c, A.7.b; **Practice:** MP.1.a
Since $y = x^2$, the missing value of x is the square root of 4. That means x could take on the value of either −2 or +2. Since +2 is the only value represented in the options, choice D is the correct one. (The x-values as listed also appear in increasing order, suggesting the positive root is the one desired.)

Answer Key

UNIT 3 *(continued)*

26. B; DOK Level: 2; **Content Topics:** Q.2.a, Q.2.e, Q.6.c, A.1.b, A.2.c, A.7.a, A.7.b; **Practices:** MP.1.a, MP.1.b, MP.2.a, MP.2.c, MP.4.a
Substituting the value $d = 0$ eliminates choice D as a possibility. Substituting $d = 10$ eliminates choices A and C as possibilities (neither 15.7 nor 14.7 equals the value in the table, 29.4). However, substitution of all values into choice B gives results consistent with the table.

27. B; DOK Level: 2; **Content Topics:** Q.2.a, Q.2.b, Q.2.e, Q.6.c, A.1.b, A.7.b; **Practices:** MP.1.a, MP.1.b, MP.1.e, MP.2.a, MP.2.c, MP.4.a, MP.4.b
Solving the equation for a gives $a = 2h \div t^2$. Using the data in the table, one can calculate a value of a for each point. For example, the first point gives $a = 2(4) \div (0.5)^2 = 8 \div (.25) = 32$. Doing the same calculation for the other points gives the identical result of 32. So $a = 32$. Alternatively, one can substitute any pair of values of t and h into the formula and solve for a.

LESSON 6, pp. 78–81

1. A; DOK Level: 2; **Content Topics:** Q.2.a, A.2.a; **Practices:** MP.1.a, MP.1.b, MP.1.e, MP.4.b
To find the value of x that makes the equation true, solve the equation for x. First, expand the parentheses on the right side of the equation by applying the distributive property. Multiply each term inside the parentheses by -2: $8x = -2(3) - 2(-2x)$. Simplify: $8x = -6 + 4x$. Subtract $4x$ from both sides of the equation: $8x - 4x = -6 + 4x - 4x$. Simplify: $4x = -6$. Divide both sides by 4: $\frac{4x}{4} = \frac{-6}{4}$. Simplify: $x = -1.5$.
Other responses result from use of incomplete or incorrect operations (for example, failing to multiply $-2x$ by -2).

2. B; DOK Level: 2; **Content Topics:** Q.2.a, A.2.a; **Practices:** MP.1.a, MP.1.b, MP.1.e, MP.4.b
To solve the equation for m, begin by expanding the parentheses on both sides of the equation: $2(m) + 2(3) = 5(6) - 5(2m)$. Simplify: $2m + 6 = 30 - 10m$. Add $10m$ to both sides of the equation: $2m + 10m + 6 = 30 - 10m + 10m$. Simplify: $12m + 6 = 30$. Subtract 6 from both sides of the equation: $12m + 6 - 6 = 30 - 6$. Simplify: $12m = 24$. Divide both sides by 12: $\frac{12m}{12} = \frac{24}{12}$. So, $m = 2$. Other responses result from use of incomplete or incorrect operations (for example, subtracting—rather than adding—$10m$ from both sides of the equation).

3. C; DOK Level: 2; **Content Topics:** Q.2.a, A.2.a; **Practices:** MP.1.a, MP.1.b, MP.1.e, MP.4.b, MP.5.c
To find the value of x that makes the equation true, solve the equation for x. First, expand the parentheses on the left side of the equation by applying the distributive property. Multiply each term inside the parentheses by 0.5: $0.5(4x) - 0.5(8) = 6$. Simplify: $2x - 4 = 6$. Next, add 4 to each side of the equation: $2x - 4 + 4 = 6 + 4$. Simplify: $2x = 10$. Finally, divide both sides of the equation by 2: $\frac{2x}{2} = \frac{10}{2}$. So, $x = 5$.

4. A; DOK Level: 2; **Content Topics:** Q.2.a, A.2.a; **Practices:** MP.1.a, MP.1.b, MP.1.e, MP.4.b
To solve the equation for x, begin by multiplying each term within the parentheses by 3: $3\left(\frac{2}{3}x\right) + 3(4) = -5$. Simplify: $2x + 12 = -5$. Subtract 12 from both sides of the equation: $2x + 12 - 12 = -5 - 12$. Simplify: $2x = -17$. Divide both sides by 2: $\frac{2x}{2} = \frac{-17}{2}$. So, $x = -8.5$.

5. C; DOK Level: 1; **Content Topics:** Q.2.a, Q.2.e, A.2.a, A.2.b; **Practices:** MP.1.a, MP.1.b, MP.1.e, MP.2.a, MP.4.a
Since Drew is 17, $17 = \frac{1}{2}t + 3$. Subtract 3 from both sides of the equation: $17 - 3 = \frac{1}{2}t + 3 - 3$. Simplify: $14 = \frac{1}{2}t$.
Multiply both sides of the equation by 2: $2(14) = (2)\frac{1}{2}t$. Simplify: $28 = t$.

6. B; DOK Level: 2; **Content Topics:** Q.2.a, Q.2.e, A.2.a, A.2.b, A.2.c; **Practices:** MP.1.a, MP.1.b, MP.1.e, MP.2.a, MP.5.c
To solve the equation for x, begin by expanding the parentheses on both sides of the equation: $0.25(3x) - 0.25(8) = 2(0.5x) + 2(4)$. Simplify: $0.75x - 2 = x + 8$. Subtract x from both sides of the equation: $0.75x - x - 2 = x - x + 8$. Simplify: $-0.25x - 2 = 8$. Add 2 to both sides of the equation: $-0.25x - 2 + 2 = 8 + 2$. Simplify: $-0.25x = 10$. Divide both sides of the equation by $-0.25x$: $\frac{-0.25x}{-0.25} = \frac{10}{-0.25}$. So, $x = -40$.

7. A; DOK Level: 2; **Content Topics:** Q.2.a, A.2.a; **Practices:** MP.3.a
To find the value of w that makes the equation true, solve the equation for w. Begin by multiplying each quantity inside the parentheses by -2: $10w + 8 - 2(3w) - 2(-4) = -12$. Simplify: $10w + 8 - 6w + 8 = -12$. Group like terms together: $4w + 16 = -12$. Subtract 16 from each side of the equation: $4w + 16 - 16 = -12 - 16$. Simplify: $4w = -28$. Divide both sides of the equation by 4: $\frac{4w}{4} = \frac{-28}{4}$. So, $w = -7$.

8. A; DOK Level: 2; **Content Topics:** Q.2.a, A.2.a; **Practices:** MP.5.a, MP.5.c
To solve the equation for b, begin by expanding the parentheses: $12b - 2(b) - 2(-1) = 6 - 4b$. Simplify: $12b - 2b + 2 = 6 - 4b$. Next, group like terms: $10b + 2 = 6 - 4b$. Add $4b$ to both sides of the equation: $10b + 4b + 2 = 6 - 4b + 4b$. Simplify: $14b + 2 = 6$. Subtract 2 from both sides of the equation: $14b + 2 - 2 = 6 - 2$. Simplify: $14b = 4$. Divide both sides by 14 and simplify: $\frac{14b}{14} = \frac{4}{14} = \frac{2}{7}$.

9. B; DOK Level: 2; **Content Topics:** Q.2.a, A.2.a; **Practices:** MP.1.a, MP.1.b, MP.1.e, MP.4.b
If $(x - 4)$ is 5 more than $3(2x + 1)$, then $(x - 4) = 3(2x + 1) + 5$. To solve for x, begin by expanding the parentheses: $x - 4 = 3(2x) + 3(1) + 5$. Simplify: $x - 4 = 6x + 3 + 5$. Group like terms: $x - 4 = 6x + 8$. Subtract $6x$ from both sides of the equation: $x - 6x - 4 = 6x - 6x + 8$. Simplify: $-5x - 4 = 8$. Add 4 to both sides of the equation: $-5x - 4 + 4 = 8 + 4$. Simplify: $-5x = 12$. Divide both sides of the equation by -5: $\frac{-5x}{-5} = \frac{12}{-5}$. So, $x = -2.4$.

10. **A**; **DOK Level:** 3; **Content Topics:** Q.2.a, A.2.a; **Practices:** MP.1.a, MP.1.b, MP.1.e, MP.4.b
To determine whose answer is correct, solve the equation. Begin by multiplying each term within the parentheses by the quantity outside the parentheses: $-2(4x) - 2(-5) = 3x - 6 + x$. Simplify: $-8x + 10 = 4x - 6$. Subtract $4x$ from both sides of the equation: $-8x - 4x + 10 = 4x - 4x - 6$. Simplify: $-12x + 10 = -6$. Subtract 10 from both sides of the equation: $-12x + 10 - 10 = -6 - 10$. Simplify: $-12x = -16$. Divide both sides of the equation by -12: $\frac{-12x}{-12} = \frac{-16}{-12} = \frac{4}{3}$. So, Ameila is correct.

11. **D**; **DOK Level:** 2; **Content Topics:** Q.2.a, A.2.a; **Practices:** MP.1.a, MP.1.b, MP.1.e, MP.4.b
To solve for q, begin by multiplying each term within the parentheses by the quantity outside of the parentheses: $0.1q - 0.2(3q) - 0.2(4) = -0.3(5q) - 0.3(3)$. Simplify: $0.1q - 0.6q - 0.8 = -1.5q - 0.9$. Group like terms: $-0.5q - 0.8 = -1.5q - 0.9$. Add $1.5q$ to both sides of the equation: $-0.5q + 1.5q - 0.8 = -1.5q + 1.5q - 0.9$. Simplify: $q - 0.8 = -0.9$. Add 0.8 to both sides of the equation: $q - 0.8 + 0.8 = -0.9 + 0.1$. Simplify: $q = -0.1$.

12. **1**; **DOK Level:** 2; **Content Topics:** Q.2.a, A.2.a; **Practices:** MP.1.a, MP.1.b, MP.1.e, MP.4.a
To begin, multiply each term within the parentheses by the quantity outside of the parentheses: $\frac{1}{2}(7y) - \frac{1}{2}(4) + y = 3y - \frac{1}{2}(6) - \frac{1}{2}(-5y)$. Simplify: $\frac{7}{2}y - 2 + y = 3y - 3 + \frac{5}{2}y$. Write $3y$ and y as fractions with denominators of 2: $\frac{7}{2}y - 2 + \frac{2}{2}y = \frac{6}{2}y - 3 + \frac{5}{2}y$. Combine like terms: $\frac{9}{2}y - 2 = \frac{11}{2}y - 3$. Subtract $\frac{11}{2}y$ from both sides of the equation: $\frac{9}{2}y - \frac{11}{2}y - 2 = \frac{11}{2}y - \frac{11}{2}y - 3$. Simplify: $-\frac{2}{2}y - 2 = -3$. Write the fraction in lowest terms and add 2 to each side of the equation: $-y - 2 + 2 = -3 + 2$. Simplify: $-y = -1$. Multiply both sides of the equation by -1: $y = 1$.

13. **−24**; **DOK Level:** 2; **Content Topics:** Q.2.a, A.2.a; **Practices:** MP.1.a, MP.1.b, MP.1.e, MP.4.a
To begin, multiply each term within the parentheses by the quantity outside the parentheses: $8k(4) - 8k(6) - 2k = 16(3) - 16(k)$. Simplify: $32k - 48k - 2k = 48 - 16k$. Group like terms: $-18k = 48 - 16k$. Add $16k$ to each side of the equation: $-18k + 16k = 48 - 16k + 16k$. Simplify: $-2k = 48$. Divide both sides of the equation by -2: $\frac{-2k}{-2} = \frac{48}{-2}$. So, $k = -24$.

14. **2.5**; **DOK Level:** 2; **Content Topics:** Q.2.a, Q.2.e, Q.4.a, A.2.a, A.2.b; **Practices:** MP.1.a, MP.1.b, MP.1.e, MP.2.a, MP.4.a
Since the perimeter of the triangle is 9.5 feet, $9.5 = x + 2(3x - 4)$. To solve for x, begin by multiplying the terms within the parentheses by 2: $9.5 = x + 2(3x) - 2(4)$. Multiply: $9.5 = x + 6x - 8$. Combine like terms: $9.5 = 7x - 8$. Add 8 to both sides of the equation: $9.5 + 8 = 7x - 8 + 8$. Simplify: $17.5 = 7x$. Divide both sides of the equation by 7: $\frac{17.5}{7} = \frac{7x}{7}$. So, $x = 2.5$.

15. **−2.2**; **DOK Level:** 2; **Content Topics:** Q.2.a, A.2.a; **Practices:** MP.1.a, MP.1.b, MP.1.e, MP.4.a
To begin, multiply each term within the parentheses by the quantity outside of the parentheses: $4(2.25a) + 4(0.75) = 12(2a) + 12(3)$. Multiply: $9a + 3 = 24a + 36$. Subtract $24a$ from both sides of the equation: $9a - 24a + 3 = 24a - 24a + 36$. Simplify: $-15a + 3 = 36$. Subtract 3 from each side of the equation: $-15a + 3 - 3 = 36 - 3$. Simplify: $-15a = 33$. Divide both sides of the equation by -15: $\frac{15a}{-15} = \frac{33}{-15}$. So, $a = -2.2$.

16. **6**; **DOK Level:** 2; **Content Topics:** Q.2.a, A.2.a; **Practices:** MP.1.a, MP.1.b, MP.1.e, MP.4.a
To begin, multiply each term within the parentheses by the quantity outside of the parentheses: $-\frac{1}{5}z - \frac{1}{5}(12) = \frac{2}{5}(9) - \frac{2}{5}(3z)$. Multiply: $-\frac{1}{5}z - \frac{12}{5} = \frac{18}{5} - \frac{6}{5}z$. Add $\frac{6}{5}z$ to each side of the equation: $-\frac{1}{5}z + \frac{6}{5}z - \frac{12}{5} = \frac{18}{5} - \frac{6}{5}z + \frac{6}{5}z$. Simplify: $\frac{5}{5}z - \frac{12}{5} = \frac{18}{5}$. Write the fraction in lowest terms and add $\frac{12}{5}$ to each side of the equation: $z - \frac{12}{5} + \frac{12}{5} = \frac{18}{5} + \frac{12}{5}$. Simplify: $z = \frac{30}{5} = 6$.

17. **1.25**; **DOK Level:** 2; **Content Topics:** Q.2.a, Q.2.e, A.2.a, Q.3.a, A.2.b; **Practices:** MP.1.a, MP.1.b, MP.1.e, MP.2.a, MP.4.a
Since 5,500 gallons of water remain in the pool, $5,500 = 9,250 - 60(50t)$. To solve for t, begin by multiplying to remove the parentheses: $5,500 = 9,250 - 3,000t$. Subtract 9,250 from both sides of the equation: $5,500 - 9,250 = 9,250 - 9,250 - 3,000t$. Simplify: $-3,750 = -3,000t$. Divide both sides of the equation by -3000: $\frac{-3750}{-3000} = \frac{-3000t}{-3000}$, so $t = 1.25$. The pool has been emptying for 1.25 hours.

18. **B**; **DOK Level:** 1; **Content Topics:** Q.2.a, Q.4.a, A.2.a; **Practices:** MP.1.a, MP.1.b, MP.1.e, MP.2.a, MP.4.a
Since the perimeter of the rectangle is 35 inches, $2x + 2(4x - 2) = 35$. To solve for x, begin by multiplying each term inside the parentheses by 2: $2x + 2(4x) - 2(2) = 35$. Simplify: $2x + 8x - 4 = 35$. Group like terms: $10x - 4 = 35$. Add 4 to both sides of the equation: $10x - 4 + 4 = 35 + 4$. Simplify: $10x = 39$. Divide both sides of the equation by 10: $x = 3.9$.

19. **B**; **DOK Level:** 3; **Content Topics:** Q.2.a, A.2.a; **Practices:** MP.4.a, MP.3.a
Begin by multiplying each term inside the parentheses by 5: $10y - 12 = 5(2y) + 5(3) - y$. Simplify: $10y - 12 = 10y + 15 - y$. Group like terms: $10y - 12 = 9y + 15$. Add 12 to each side of the equation: $10y - 12 + 12 = 9y + 15 + 12$. Simplify: $10y = 9y + 27$. Subtract $9y$ from each side of the equation: $10y - 9y = 9y - 9y + 27$. Simplify: $y = 27$.

UNIT 3 *(continued)*

20. D; DOK Level: 2; **Content Topics:** Q.2.a, A.2.a;
Practices: MP.1.a, MP.1.b, MP.1.e, MP.2.a, MP.4.a
To solve the equation, begin by expanding the parentheses:
$4\left(\frac{1}{8}t\right) + 4(2) = 2(t) - 2(8) - \frac{1}{2}t$. Simplify: $\frac{4}{8}t + 8 =$
$2t - 16 - \frac{1}{2}t$. To write the fractions with like denominators,
write the fraction $\frac{4}{8}$ in lowest terms, and write $2t$ as a
fraction with a denominator of 2: $\frac{1}{2}t + 8 = \frac{4}{2}t - 16 - \frac{1}{2}t$.
Group like terms: $\frac{1}{2}t + 8 = \frac{3}{2}t - 16$. Subtract $\frac{3}{2}t$ from
both sides of the equation: $\frac{1}{2}t - \frac{3}{2}t + 8 = \frac{3}{2}t - \frac{3}{2}t - 16$.
Simplify: $-\frac{2}{2}t + 8 = -16$. Simplify the fraction and subtract
8 from both sides of the equation: $-t + 8 - 8 = -16 - 8$.
Simplify: $-t = -24$. Multiply both sides of the equation by -1:
$t = 24$.

21. A; DOK Level: 1; **Content Topics:** Q.2.a, Q.2.e, Q.4.a,
A.2.b; **Practices:** MP.1.a, MP.1.b, MP.1.e, MP.2.a, MP.4.a
Since the length of the fencing is 65 feet, $2x + 2(x + 7.5) =$
65. Multiply the terms inside of the parentheses by 2: $2x +$
$2x + 2(7.5) = 65$. Simplify: $4x + 15 = 65$. Subtract 15 from
both sides of the equation: $4x + 15 - 15 = 65 - 15$. Simplify:
$4x = 50$. Divide both sides of the equation by 4: $\frac{4x}{4} = \frac{50}{4}$, so
$x = 12.5$.

22. C; DOK Level: 2; **Content Topics:** Q.2.a, A.2.a;
Practices: MP.1.a, MP.1.b, MP.1.e, MP.3.a, MP.3.b, MP.4.a
To find the value of a, complete Keira's next step in the
solution. Keira previously found that $12x - 20 = -2x - 14$.
To group together the variable terms, she must have added
$2x$ to both sides of the equation: $12x + 2x - 20 = -2x +$
$2x - 14$. Simplify: $14x - 20 = -14$. Since a represents the
x-coefficient, a is equal to 14.

23. C; DOK Level: 2; **Content Topics:** Q.2.a, A.2.a;
Practices: MP.1.a, MP.1.b, MP.1.e, MP.4.a, MP.5.a
To find the error in Quentin's solution, solve the equation for
y and compare each step to Quentin's solution. Begin by
expanding the parentheses: $0.5(7y) - 0.5(6) = 2(2y) + 2(1)$.
Simplify: $3.5y - 3 = 4y + 2$. This is Quentin's first step, so the
error is not in Step 1. Next, subtract $4y$ from both sides of the
equation: $3.5y - 4y - 3 = 4y - 4y + 2$. Simplify: $-0.5y - 3 = 2$.
This is Quentin's second step, so the error is not in Step 2.
Add 3 to both sides of the equation: $-0.5y - 3 + 3 = 2 + 3$.
Simplify: $-0.5y = 5$. Quentin subtracted 3 from the right side
of the equation in Step 3. So, the error is in Step 3. Step 4,
although correct, produces and incorrect answer because of
the error in step 3.

24. C; DOK Level: 2; **Content Topics:** Q.2.a, A.2.a;
Practices: MP.1.a, MP.1.b, MP.1.e, MP.4.a
To solve the equation for b, begin by expanding the
parentheses: $10 - 3(2b) - 3(4) = -4b - 2(5) - 2(-b)$.
Simplify:
$10 - 6b - 12 = -4b - 10 + 2b$. Group like terms: $-2 - 6b =$
$-2b - 10$. Add $2b$ to both sides of the equation:
$-6b + 2b - 2 = -2b + 2b - 10$. Simplify: $-4b - 2 = -10$. Add
2 to both sides of the equation: $-4b - 2 + 2 = -10 + 2$.
Simplify: $-4b = -8$. Divide both sides of the equation by -4:
$\frac{-4b}{-4} = \frac{-8}{-4}$. So, $b = 2$.

25. A; DOK Level: 2; **Content Topics:** Q.2.a, A.2.a;
Practices: MP.1.a, MP.1.b, MP.1.e, MP.4.a, MP.5.a
To find the error in Lisa's solution, solve the equation for x and
compare each step to Lisa's solution. Begin by expanding the
parentheses: $\frac{1}{4}(2x) + \frac{1}{4}(12) = 3\left(\frac{1}{4}x\right) - 3(2)$. Simplify: $\frac{2}{4} + 3 =$
$\frac{3}{4}x - 6$. Lisa did not multiply -2 by 3, so the error is in Step 1.
All of the other steps (2 through 4), although correct, produce
an incorrect answer because of the error in Step 1.

26. A; DOK Level: 2; **Content Topics:** Q.2.a, A.2.a;
Practices: MP.1.a, MP.1.b, MP.1.e, MP.4.a
To find the value of n that makes the equation true, solve
the equation for n. First, multiply each term inside the
parentheses by quantities outside of the parentheses:
$0.2(6n) + 0.2(5) = 0.5(2n) - 0.5(8) + 3$. Simplify: $1.2n + 1 =$
$n - 4 + 3$. Group like terms: $1.2n + 1 = n - 1$. Subtract n from
both sides of the equation: $1.2n - n + 1 = n - n - 1$. Simplify:
$0.2n + 1 = -1$. Subtract 1 from both sides of the equation:
$0.2n + 1 - 1 = -1 - 1$. Simplify: $0.2n = -2$. Divide both sides
of the equation by 0.2: $\frac{0.2n}{0.2} = \frac{-2}{0.2}$. So, $n = -10$.

27. C; DOK Level: 2; **Content Topics:** Q.2.a, A.2.a;
Practices: MP.1.a, MP.1.b, MP.1.e, MP.4.a
To find the value of w that makes the equation true, solve
the equation for w. First, multiply each term inside the
parentheses by quantities outside of the parentheses:
$3w - 2(.05w) - 2(1) = -4(2) - 4(w)$. Simplify:
$3w - w - 2 = -8 - 4w$. Group like terms: $2w - 2 = -8 - 4w$.
Add $4w$ to both sides, so that $2w - 2 + 4w = -8 - 4w + 4w$.
Simplify: $6w - 2 = -8$. Add 2 to both sides so that
$6w = -6$. Divide both sides of the equation by 6 to find that
$w = -1$.

28. B; DOK Level: 2; **Content Topics:** Q.2.a, A.2.a; **Practices:**
MP.1.a, MP.1.b, MP.1.e, MP.4.a
Begin by expanding the parentheses: $2x + 3(5) - 3(x) - 12 = 4x$
$+ 4(2)$. Simplify: $2x + 15 - 3x - 12 = 4x + 8$. Group like terms:
$-x + 3 = 4x + 8$. Subtract $4x$ from both sides of the equation:
$-x - 4x + 3 = 4x - 4x + 8$. Simplify: $-5x + 3 = 8$. Subtract 3 from
both sides of the equation: $-5x + 3 - 3 = 8 - 3$. Simplify: $-5x = 5$.
Divide both sides of the equation by -5. $x = -1$.

LESSON 7, pp. 82–85
1. A; DOK Level: 2; **Content Topics:** Q.2.a, A.2.a, A.2.d;
Practices: MP.1.a, MP.1.b, MP.1.e, MP.2.c, MP.4.a
In this system of equations, neither equation is easily solved
for a variable and neither variable has coefficients that are
multiples of each other. To solve this system, find the least
common multiple of the coefficients of one of the variables.
The least common multiple of 2 and 3 (y-variable) is 6. In
order to eliminate the y-terms, multiply the first equation by
3, and multiply the second equation by 2. Then add these
two new equations together:

$$3(3x + 2y = -5) \longrightarrow 9x + 6y = -15$$
$$2(4x - 3y = -18) \longrightarrow \underline{8x - 6y = -36}$$
$$17x = -51$$
$$x = -3$$

Substitute −3 for x in either of the original equations: $3(−3) + 2y = −5$. Multiply: $−9 + 2y = −5$. Add 9 to both sides of the equation: $2y = 4$. Divide both sides of the equation by 2: $y = 2$. Alternately, multiply the first equation by 4 and the second equation by −3 and then add the new equations to eliminate the x-terms. Then solve for y and substitute this value into one of the original equations to solve for x.

2. **C**; **DOK Level:** 2; **Content Topics:** Q.2.a, A.2.a, A.2.d; **Practices:** MP.1.a, MP.1.b, MP.1.e, MP.2.c, MP.4.a
Begin by writing the second equation in the form $Ax + By + C$: $7x + 3y = 1$. The y-coefficients have opposite signs, so find the lowest common multiple of the y-coefficients. The LCM of 2 and 3 is 6. Multiply the first equation by 3 and multiply the second equation by 2. Then add the resulting equations together:

$$3(3x − 2y = 7) \longrightarrow 9x − 6y = 21$$
$$2(7x + 3y = 1) \longrightarrow \underline{14x + 6y = 2}$$
$$23x = 23$$
$$x = 1$$

Substitute 1 for x in either of the original equations: $3(1) − 2y = 7$. Multiply: $3 − 2y = 7$. Subtract 3 from both sides of the equation: $−2y = 4$. Divide both sides of the equation by −2: $y = −2$. Alternately, multiply the first equation by 7 and the second equation by −3 and then add the new equations to eliminate the x-terms. Then solve for y and substitute this value into one of the original equations to solve for x.

3. **D**; **DOK Level:** 2; **Content Topics:** Q.2.a, A.2.a, A.2.d; **Practices:** MP.1.a, MP.1.b, MP.1.e, MP.2.c, MP.4.a
To solve this system by linear combination, add the two equations together: $6x + 0y = 30$. Divide both sides of the equation by 6: $x = 5$. Substitute 5 for x in either of the original equations: $2(5) + y = 13$. Multiply: $10 + y = 13$. Subtract 10 from both sides of the equation: $y = 3$. To solve this system by substitution, solve the first equation for y: $y = 13 − 2x$. Substitute $13 − 2x$ for y in the second equation: $4x − (13 − 2x) = 17$. Simplify: $6x − 13 = 17$. Add 13 to both sides of the equation: $6x = 30$. Divide both sides of the equation by 6: $x = 5$. Substitute 5 for x in either of the original equations to solve for y.

4. **C**; **DOK Level:** 2; **Content Topics:** Q.2.a, A.2.a, A.2.d; **Practices:** MP.1.a, MP.1.b, MP.1.e, MP.2.c, MP.4.a
To solve this system by linear combination, multiply the first equation by 2: $6x − 4y = 28$. Add the new equation to the second equation: $7x + 0y = 14$. Divide both sides of the equation by 7: $x = 2$. Substitute 2 for x in either of the original equations: $2 + 4y = −14$. Subtract 2 from both sides of the equation: $4y = −16$. Divide both sides of the equation by 4: $y = −4$. To solve this system by substitution, solve the second equation for x: $x = −4y − 14$. Substitute $−4y − 14$ for x in the first equation: $3(−4y − 14) − 2y = 14$. Simplify: $−12y − 42 − 2y = 14$. Group like terms together: $−14y − 42 = 14$. Add 42 to both sides of the equation: $−14y = 56$. Divide both sides of the equation by −14: $y = −4$. Substitute $y = −4$ into either original equation to find that $x = 2$.

5. **A**; **DOK Level:** 2; **Content Topics:** Q.2.a, Q.2.e, A.2.a, A.2.b, A.2.d; **Practices:** MP.1.a, MP.1.b, MP.1.e, MP.2.a, MP.2.c, MP.4.a
To solve this system by linear combination, begin by writing the second equation in the form $Ax + By = C$: $4x + y = −2$. Multiply the second equation by 2: $8x + 2y = −4$. Add the new equation to the first equation: $14x + 0y = −14$. Divide both sides of the equation by 14: $x = −1$. Substitute −1 for x in either of the original equations: $4(−1) + y = −2$. Solve: $y = 2$. To solve this system by substitution, solve the second equation for y: $y = −4x − 2$. Substitute $−4x − 2$ for y in the first equation: $6x − 2(−4x − 2) = −10$. Multiply: $6x + 8x + 4 = −10$, so $14x + 4 = −10$. Subtract 4 from both sides of the equation: $14x = −14$. Divide both sides of the equation by 14: $x = −1$. Substitute $x = −1$ into either original equation to find that $y = 2$.

6. **D**; **DOK Level:** 1; **Content Topics:** Q.2.a, A.2.a, A.2.d; **Practices:** MP.1.b, MP.1.e, MP.2.c, MP.4.a
To solve a system by linear combination, the coefficients of one of the variables should be opposites. For this system, the lowest common multiple of the x-coefficients is 10 and the lowest common multiple of the y-coefficients is 12. To eliminate the x-terms, the first equation could be multiplied by 5 or −5, and the second equation could be multiplied by −2 or 2. None of those corresponds to available answer options. To eliminate the y-terms, the first equation could be multiplied by 4 and the second equation could be multiplied by 3. So, answer choice D is correct.

7. **B**; **DOK Level:** 2; **Content Topics:** Q.2.a, A.2.a, A.2.d; **Practices:** MP.1.a, MP.1.b, MP.1.e, MP.2.c, MP.4.a
To solve this system by linear combination, multiply the first equation by 4 and the second equation by 3. Then add these two new equations together:

$$4(2x − 3y = 8) \longrightarrow 8x − 12y = 32$$
$$3(5x + 4y = −3) \longrightarrow \underline{15x + 12y = −9}$$
$$23x = 23$$
$$x = 1$$

Substitute 1 for x in either of the original equations: $2(1) − 3y = 8$. Multiply: $2 − 3y = 8$. Subtract 2 from both sides of the equation: $−3y = 6$. Divide both sides of the equation by −3: $y = −2$. This system could also be solved by multiplying the first equation by 5 and the second equation by −2, and then adding the new equations to eliminate the x-terms. Then solve for y and substitute this value into one of the original equations to solve for x.

8. **A**; **DOK Level:** 2; **Content Topics:** Q.2.a, A.2.a, A.2.d; **Practices:** MP.1.a, MP.1.b, MP.1.e, MP.2.c, MP.3.a, MP.4.a
Since the sum of Darnell's new equations does not have a y-term, Darnell multiplied the original equations by factors that would eliminate the y-terms. The lowest common multiple of the y-terms is 15, so Darnell multiplied the first equation by 3 or −3, and the second equation by 5 or −5. The y-terms in the original equations have the same signs, so the factors by which the equations are multiplied must have opposite signs. Therefore, Darnell multiplied the first equation by 3 and the second equation by −5. Check: $3(4x − 5y = −7) \longrightarrow 12x − 15y = −21$. $−5(7x − 3y = 5) \longrightarrow −35x + 15y = −25$. The sum of these new equations is $−23x + 0y = −46$.

Answer Key

9. C; DOK Level: 2; **Content Topics:** Q.2.a, A.2.a, A.2.d;
Practices: MP.1.a, MP.1.b, MP.1.e, MP.2.c, MP.4.a
In this system of equations, neither equation is easily solved for a variable and neither variable has coefficients that are multiples of each other. To solve this system, find the least common multiple of the coefficients of one of the variables. The least common multiple of 5 and 2 is 10. In order to eliminate the y-terms, multiply the first equation by 2, and multiply the second equation by 5. Then add these two new equations together:

$$2(4x - 5y = -6) \longrightarrow \quad 8x - 10y = -12$$
$$5(3x + 2y = -16) \longrightarrow \quad \underline{15x + 10y = -80}$$
$$23x = -92$$
$$x = -4$$

Substitute -4 for x in either of the original equations: $4(-4) - 5y = -6$. Multiply: $-16 - 5y = -6$. Add 16 to both sides of the equation: $-5y = 10$. Divide both sides of the equation by -5: $y = -2$. Alternately, multiply the first equation by 3 and the second equation by -4 and then add the new equations to eliminate the x terms. Then solve for y and substitute this value into one of the original equations to solve for x.

10. A; DOK Level: 2; **Content Topics:** Q.2.a, Q.2.e, Q.6.c, A.2.a, A.2.b, A.2.d; **Practices:** MP.1.a, MP.1.b, MP.1.e, MP.2.a, MP.2.c, MP.4.a
This system is best solved using linear combination. Multiply the first equation by -2 so that the y-coefficients will be opposites: $-30a - 16c = -616$. Add this new equation to the second equation: $-8a + 0c = -96$. Divide both sides of the equation by -8: $a = 12$. Since the question asks for the number of adults, it is not necessary to solve for c.

11. D; DOK Level: 2; **Content Topics:** Q.2.a, A.2.a, A.2.d;
Practices: MP.1.a, MP.1.b, MP.1.e, MP.2.c, MP.4.a
This system can be solved using either substitution or linear combination. To solve using substitution, solve the first equation for y by subtracting $2x$ from each side: $-y = 3 - 2x$. Multiply both sides by -1: $y = 2x - 3$. Substitute $2x - 3$ for y in the second equation: $3x - 2(2x - 3) = 2$. Multiply: $3x - 4x + 6 = 2$. Group like terms and subtract 6 from both sides of the equation: $-x = -4$. So, $x = 4$. Substitute 4 for x in either of the original equations and solve for y: $2(4) - y = 3$. Multiply: $8 - y = 3$. Subtract 8 from both sides of the equation: $-y = -5$. So, $y = 5$. To solve this system by linear combination, multiply the first equation by -2: $-4x + 2y = -6$. Add this new equation to the second equation to eliminate the y-terms: $-x + 0y = -4$, so $x = 4$. Substitute 4 for x in either of the original equations to solve for y.

12. C; DOK Level: 2; **Content Topics:** Q.2.a, A.2.a, A.2.d;
Practices: MP.1.a, MP.1.b, MP.1.e, MP.2.c, MP.4.a
This system can be solved using substitution or linear combination, but since the y-coefficients of the two equations are opposites, it is easier to solve using linear combination. Add the two equations: $6x + 0y = 12$. Divide both sides of the equation by 6: $x = 2$. Substitute 2 for x in either of the original equations: $4(2) + 2y = 2$. Multiply: $8 + 2y = 2$. Subtract 8 from both sides of the equation: $2y = -6$. Divide both sides of the equation by 2: $y = -3$.

13. B; DOK Level: 2; **Content Topics:** Q.2.a, A.2.a, A.2.d;
Practices: MP.1.a, MP.1.b, MP.1.e, MP.2.c, MP.4.a
This system is more easily solved using linear combination. To begin, write the second equation in the form $Ax + By = C$: $5x - 2y = -22$. Since the y-coefficients are multiples of each other, multiply the second equation by 2 and leave the first equation as it is: $10x - 4y = -44$. Add this new equation to the first equation: $13x + 0y = -26$. Divide both sides of the equation by 13: $x = -2$. Substitute -2 for x in either of the original equations: $3(-2) + 4y = 18$. Multiply: $-6 + 4y = 18$. Add 6 to both sides of the equation: $4y = 24$. Divide both sides of the equation by 4: $y = 6$. Alternately, multiply the first equation by 5 and the second equation by -3 and add the new equations to eliminate the x-terms. Then solve for y and substitute that value into an original equation to solve for x.

14. A; DOK Level: 2; **Content Topics:** Q.2.a, A.2.a, A.2.d;
Practices: MP.1.a, MP.1.b, MP.1.e, MP.2.c, MP.4.a
This system is more easily solved using linear combination. Multiply the first equation by 4 and the second equation by 5 to make the y-coefficients opposites. Then add the new equations together:

$$4(7x + 5y = -2) \longrightarrow \quad 28x + 20y = -8$$
$$5(3x - 4y = -7) \longrightarrow \quad \underline{15x - 20y = -35}$$
$$43x = -43$$
$$x = -1$$

Substitute -1 for x in either of the original equations: $7(-1) + 5y = -2$. Multiply: $-7 + 5y = -2$. Add 7 to both sides of the equation: $5y = 5$. So, $y = 1$. Alternately, multiply the first equation by 3 and the second equation by -7 and then add the new equations to eliminate the x terms. Then solve for y and substitute this value into one of the original equations to solve for x.

15. D; DOK Level: 2; **Content Topics:** Q.2.a, A.2.a, A.2.d;
Practices: MP.1.a, MP.1.b, MP.1.e, MP.2.c, MP.4.a
This system is more easily solved using linear combination. Multiply either equation by -1 to make the y-coefficients opposites. Then add the new equations together.

$$4x + 5y = 2 \longrightarrow \quad 4x + 5y = 2$$
$$2x + 5y = -4 \longrightarrow \quad \underline{-2x - 5y = 4}$$
$$2x = 6$$
$$x = 3$$

Substitute 3 for x in either of the original equations: $4(3) + 5y = 2$. Multiply: $12 + 5y = 2$. Subtract 12 from each side of the equation: $5y = -10$. So, $y = -2$. Alternately, multiply the second equation by -2 and then add the new equations to eliminate the x-terms. Then solve for y and substitute this value into one of the original equations to solve for x.

16. D; DOK Level: 2; **Content Topics:** Q.2.a, A.2.a, A.2.d;
Practices: MP.1.a, MP.1.b, MP.1.e, MP.2.c, MP.3.a, MP.4.a
Since the sum of Liam's new equations does not have an x-term, Liam multiplied the original equations by factors that would eliminate the x-terms. The lowest common multiple of the x-terms is 45, so Liam multiplied the first equation by 5 or -5, and the second equation by 9 or -9. The x-terms in the original equations have the same signs, so the factors by which the equations are multiplied must have opposite signs. Check -5 and 9:

$$-5(9x - 4y = 2) \longrightarrow \quad -45x + 20y = -10$$
$$9(5x - 3y = -2) \longrightarrow \quad \underline{-45x - 27y = -18}$$
$$-7y = -28$$

Although the *x*-terms have been eliminated, the new equation does not match Liam's equation, so the signs of the factors must be incorrect. Check 5 and −9:

$$5(9x − 4y = 2) \longrightarrow −45x − 20y = 10$$
$$−9(5x − 3y = −2) \longrightarrow \underline{−45x + 27y = 18}$$
$$7y = 28$$

17. **C; DOK Level:** 2; **Content Topics:** Q.2.a, A.2.a, A.2.d; **Practices:** MP.1.a, MP.1.b, MP.1.e, MP.2.a, MP.2.c, MP.4.a
This system can be solved using either substitution or linear combination. Since the *y*-coefficients have opposite signs, multiply the first equation by 2 and the second equation by 3 to solve by linear combination. Then add the new equations to eliminate the *y*-terms:

$$2(10x + 3y = 8) \longrightarrow 20x + 6y = 16$$
$$3(4x − 2y = 16) \longrightarrow \underline{12x − 6y = 48}$$
$$32x = 64$$
$$x = 2$$

Substitute 2 for *x* in either of the original equations: $10(2) + 3y = 8$. Multiply: $20 + 3y = 8$. Subtract 20 from both sides of the equation: $3y = −12$. So, $y = −4$. Alternately, multiply the first equation by 4 and the second equation by −10 and then add the new equations to eliminate the *x*-terms. Then solve for *y* and substitute this value into one of the original equations to solve for *x*. To solve by substitution, solve the second equation for *y*: $y = 2x − 8$. Substitute $2x − 8$ for *y* in the first equation to find that $x = 2$. Then substitute that value for *x* in either of the original equations to find that $y = −4$.

18. **C; DOK Level:** 3; **Content Topics:** Q.2.a, A.2.a, A.2.d; **Practices:** MP.1.a, MP.1.b, MP.1.e, MP.2.c, MP.3.a, MP.4.a, MP.5.a, MP. 5.c
To solve a system by linear combination, multiply one or both equations by factor(s) that will result in opposite coefficients for the same variable. Multiplying the first equation by 5 and the second equation by −3 will result in an *x*-coefficient of 15 in the first equation and −15 in the second equation. Since these coefficients are opposites, adding the new equations will eliminate the *x*-terms. So, Scott is correct. Multiplying the first equation by 3 and the second equation by −4 will result in a *y*-coefficient of −24 in the first equation and 24 in the second equation. Since these coefficients are opposites, adding the new equations will eliminate the *y*-terms. So, Craig is also correct.

19. **A; DOK Level:** 2; **Content Topics:** Q.2.a, A.2.a, A.2.d; **Practices:** MP.1.a, MP.1.b, MP.1.e, MP.2.a, MP.2.c, MP.4.a
This system is more easily solved using linear combination. Since the *y*-coefficients are multiples and opposites of each other, multiply the first equation by 2 and leave the second equation as it is. Then add the equations to eliminate the *y*-terms:

$$2(2x − 3y = 7) \longrightarrow 4x − 6y = 14$$
$$\underline{4x + 6y = 26}$$
$$8x = 40$$
$$x = 5$$

Substitute 5 for *x* in either of the original equations: $2(5) − 3y = 7$. Multiply: $10 − 3y = 7$. Subtract 10 from both sides of the equation: $−3y = −3$. So, $y = 1$. Alternately, multiply the first equation by −2 and leave the second equation as it is, then add the equations to eliminate the *x*-terms. Then solve for *y* and substitute this value into one of the original equations to solve for *x*.

20. **B; DOK Level:** 3; **Content Topics:** Q.2.a, A.2.a, A.2.d; **Practices:** MP.1.a, MP.1.b, MP.1.e, MP.2.c, MP.3.a, MP.4.a, MP.5.a, MP. 5.c
To identify the step in which Hannah made an error, examine the work in each step. In Step 1, Hannah multiplied the first equation by 3 and the second equation by −4 in order to eliminate the *y*-variables. This approach was correct. Her computations also were correct, so there is no error in Step 1. In Step 2, Hannah added together the new equations from Step 1. This approach was correct. However, Hannah made a computation error when adding the constant terms. The sum of −6 + 20 is 14, not −14. Therefore, the error was in Step 2. Although she correctly performed Steps 3 and 4, the ordered pair of (−2, 2) does not solve the system.

21. **D; .DOK Level:** 2; **Content Topics:** Q.2.a, Q.2.e, Q.6.c, A.2.a, A.2.b, A.2.d; **Practices:** MP.1.a, MP.1.b, MP.1.e, MP.2.a, MP.2.c, MP.4.a
This system is more easily solved using linear combination. Since the question asks for the number of reams of paper, *r*, multiply each equation by a factor that will cancel out the *b*-terms. Multiply the first equation by 5 and the second equation by −3, then add the new equations together:

$$5(4r + 3b = 205) \longrightarrow 20r + 15b = 1,025$$
$$−3(7r + 5b = 355) \longrightarrow \underline{−21r − 15b = −1,065}$$
$$−r = −40$$
$$r = 40$$

So, the office manager will order 40 reams of paper. Alternately, solve the system by multiplying the first equation by 7 and the second equation by −4. Add the new equations together to eliminate the *r*-terms and solve for *b*. Then substitute $b = 15$ into either original equation to find that $r = 40$.

22. **B; DOK Level:** 2; **Content Topics:** Q.2.a, A.2.a, A.2.d; **Practices:** MP.1.a, MP.1.b, MP.1.e, MP.2.a, MP.2.c, MP.4.a
This system can be solved using either substitution or linear combination. To solve by substitution, begin by solving the first equation for *x* or *y*. Solve for *y*: $2y = 6 − 2x$, so $y = 3 − x$. Substitute $3 − x$ for *y* in the second equation: $5(3 − x) = 19 − 4x$. Multiply: $15 − 5x = 19 − 4x$. Add $4x$ to both sides of the equation: $15 − x = 19$. Subtract 15 from both sides of the equation: $−x = 4$. So, $x = −4$. Substitute −4 for *x* in either of the original equations: $2(−4) + 2y = 6$. Multiply: $−8 + 2y = 6$. Add 8 to both sides of the equation: $2y = 14$. So, $y = 7$. To solve this system using linear combination, begin by writing the second equation in the form $Ax + By = C$: $4x + 5y = 19$. Multiply the first equation by −2 to produce *x*-coefficients that are opposites: $−4x − 4y = −12$. Add this new equation to the second equation: $y = 7$. Substitute 7 for *y* in either original equation to find that $x = −4$.

Answer Key

UNIT 3 *(continued)*

23. A; **DOK Level:** 2; **Content Topics:** Q.2.a, A.2.a, A.2.d; **Practices:** MP.1.a, MP.1.b, MP.1.e, MP.2.a, MP.2.c, MP.4.a
This system is more easily solved using linear combination. Since neither variable has coefficients that are multiples of each other, either variable can be eliminated. Find the lowest common multiple of the y-coefficients to eliminate the y-terms. The lowest common multiple of 2 and 5 is 10. Multiply the first equation by 5 and the second equation by -2, then add the new equations together:
$$5(7x + 2y = -11) \longrightarrow 35x + 10y = -55$$
$$-2(3x + 5y = 16) \longrightarrow \underline{-6x - 10y = -32}$$
$$29x = -87$$
$$x = -3$$
Substitute -3 for x in either of the original equations: $7(-3) + 2y = -11$. Multiply: $-21 + 2y = -11$. Add 21 to both sides of the equation: $2y = 10$. So, $y = 5$. Alternately, multiply the first equation by 3 and the second equation by -7, then add the new equations to eliminate the x-terms. Then solve for y and substitute this value into one of the original equations to solve for x.

24. D; **DOK Level:** 2; **Content Topics:** Q.2.a, Q.2.e, A.2.a, A.2.b, A.2.d; **Practices:** MP.1.a, MP.1.b, MP.1.e, MP.2.a, MP.2.c, MP.4.a
This system can be solved using substitution or linear combination. To solve using substitution, solve the first equation for either variable. Then substitute that value into the second equation to solve for the other variable. Solve for h: $h = 1,200 - c$. Substitute $1,200 - c$ for h in the second equation: $3c + 8(1,200 - c) = 5,600$. Multiply: $3c + 9,600 - 8c = 5,600$. Group like terms and subtract 9,600 from both sides of the equation: $-5c = -4,000$. Divide both sides of the equation by -5: $c = 800$. Substitute 800 for c in either of the original equations: $800 + h = 1,200$, so $h = 400$. To solve using linear combination, multiply the first equation by -3: $-3c - 3h = -3,600$. Add this new equation to the second equation to eliminate the c terms: $0c + 5h = 2,000$. Divide both sides of the equation by 5: $h = 400$. Substitute this value into either of the original equations to find that $c = 800$.

25. D; **DOK Level:** 3; **Content Topics:** Q.2.a, A.2.a, A.2.d; **Practices:** MP.1.a, MP.1.b, MP.1.e, MP.2.a, MP.2.c, MP.4.a
Substitute 2 for x in the second equation and solve for y: $5(2) + 4y = 14$. Multiply: $10 + 4y = 14$. Subtract 10 from both sides of the equation: $4y = 4$. Divide both sides of the equation by 4: $y = 1$. Substitute 1 for y and 2 for x in the first equation: $9(2) + a(1) = 25$. Multiply: $18 + a = 25$. Subtract 18 from both sides of the equation: $a = 7$.

LESSON 8, pp. 86–89

1. C; **DOK Level:** 2; **Content Topics:** Q.2.a, Q.2.e, Q.4.a, A.1.a, A.1.g; **Practices:** MP.1.a, MP.1.b, MP.1.e, MP.2.a, MP.2.c, MP.4.a,
$$\text{Area} = l \times w$$
$$\text{Area} = w \,(w - 2)$$
$$48 = w^2 - 2w$$
$$w^2 - 2w - 48 = 0$$
Answer choice A represents the width squared, which is appropriate for a square but not a rectangle. Choice B results from inaccurate use of a sign. Choice D results from not using the correct formula for area.

2. D; **DOK Level:** 2; **Content Topics:** Q.2.a, Q.2.e, Q.4.a, A.1.a, A.1.g; **Practices:** MP.1.a, MP.1.b, MP.1.e, MP.2.a, MP.2.c, MP.4.a, MP.4.b
$$w^2 - 2w - 48 = 0$$
$$w^2 - 8w + 6w - 48 = 0$$
$$w(w - 8) + 6(w + 8) = 0$$
$$(w - 8)(w + 6) = 0$$
$w - 8 = 0$, so $w = 8$; likewise, $w + 6 = 0$, so $w = -6$. Answer choices A and C result from not properly solving for the variables. Because the width cannot be negative (answer choice B), the correct answer is 8.

3. B; **DOK Level:** 2; **Content Topics:** Q.2.a, Q.2.e, A.1.a; **Practices:** MP.1.a, MP.1.b, MP.1.e, MP.2.c, MP.4.a
Take the square root of both sides to get:
$$z - 3 = \sqrt{10}$$
$$z = \sqrt{10} + 3$$
Answer choices A, C, and D result from inaccurately rearranging the equation.

4. C; **DOK Level:** 2; **Content Topics:** Q.2.a, Q.2.e, Q.5.a; **Practices:** MP.1.a, MP.1.b, MP.1.e, MP.2.c, MP.4.a
Expand the brackets using FOIL, so that:
$\underline{F}$irst: $x(x) = x^2$
$\underline{O}$uter: $x(-4) = -4x$
$\underline{I}$nner: $5(x) = 5x$
$\underline{L}$ast: $5(-4) = -20$
This can be represented by the following equation:
$x^2 - 4x + 5x - 20 = x^2 + 1x - 20$. Answer choice A results from an incorrect sign for the c variable, choice B results from inaccurate b values, and choice D results from an incorrect sign for the b variable.

5. D; **DOK Level:** 2; **Content Topics:** Q.2.a, Q.2.e, A.1.a, A.1.g, A.4.b; **Practices:** MP.1.a, MP.1.b, MP.1.e, MP.2.a, MP.2.c, MP.4.a
$$\text{Area of a square} = \text{side} \times \text{side}$$
$$= (x - 4)\,(x - 4)$$
$$= x^2 - 4x - 4x + 16$$
$$= x^2 - 8x + 16$$
Answer choices A, B, and C result from inaccurate expansion of $x - 4$.

6. A; **DOK Level:** 2; **Content Topics:** Q.2.a, Q.2.e, A.1.a, A.1.g, A.4.b; **Practices:** MP.1.a, MP.1.b, MP.1.e, MP.2.a, MP.2.c, MP.4.a, MP.4.b
$$\text{Area} = (x + 2)\,(x - 5)$$
Use the FOIL method to determine the area of the rectangle:
$\underline{F}$irst: $x(x) = x^2$
$\underline{O}$uter: $x(-5) = -5x$
$\underline{I}$nner: $2(x) = 2x$
$\underline{L}$ast: $2(-5) = -10$
Expression: $x^2 - 3x - 10$

7. C; **DOK Level:** 2; **Content Topics:** Q.2.a, Q.2.e, A.1.a, A.1.g, A.4.b; **Practices:** MP.1.a, MP.1.b, MP.1.e, MP.2.c, MP.4.a, MP.4.b
Plug each solutions pair into the equation to determine the pair that makes the equation true. Only answer choice C makes it true.

8. B; DOK Level: 2; **Content Topics:** Q.2.a, Q.2.e, A.1.a, A.4.b, A.1.g; **Practices:** MP.1.a, MP.1.b, MP.1.e, MP.2.c, MP.4.a

Total students = x

Pencils each student has = $x + 5$

Total number of pencils in the room = $x(x + 5) = x^2 + 5x$

Answer choices A and D result from incomplete expansion of brackets. Answer choice C results from inaccurate use of signs.

9. A; DOK Level: 2; **Content Topics:** Q.2.a, Q.2.e, Q.5.a; **Practices:** MP.1.a, MP.1.b, MP.1.e, MP.2.c, MP.4.a

First, find two factors of the third term (-21) that have a sum equal to the coefficient of the middle term (-7, 3). Use the variable x as the first term in each factor and the integers as the second terms.

$x^2 - 4x - 21$

$x^2 + 3x - 7x - 21$

$x(x + 3) - 7(x + 3)$

$(x + 3)(x - 7) = 0$

$(x + 3) = 0$, or $(x - 7) = 0$

10. A; DOK Level: 2; **Content Topics:** Q.2.a, Q.2.e, A.1.a, A.1.g, A.4.b; **Practices:** MP.1.a, MP.1.b, MP.1.e, MP.2.c, MP.4.a, MP.4.b

First, find two factors of the third term (-20) that have a sum equal to the coefficient of the middle term (10, -2). Use the variable x as the first term in each factor and the integers as the second terms so that:

$x^2 + 8x - 20 = 0$

$x^2 + 10x - 2x - 20 = 0$

$x(x + 10) - 2(x + 10) = 0$

$(x + 10)(x - 2) = 0$

Since $x + 10 = 0$, $x = -10$; likewise, since $x - 2 = 0$, $x = 2$. Since -10 is the only value listed in the responses, it is the correct answer.

Answer choices B and C result from inaccurately factoring values, while answer choice D uses an correct sign.

11. B; DOK Level: 2; **Content Topics:** Q.2.a, Q.2.e, A.1.a, A.1.g, A.4.b; **Practices:** MP.1.a, MP.1.b, MP.1.e, MP.2.a, MP.2.c, MP.4.a, MP.4.b

Factor the equation to determine the sides of the square. Begin by finding two factors of the third term (9) that have a sum equal to the coefficient of the middle term (6). in this case, those numbers are 3, 3. Next, use the variable x as the first term in each factor and the integers as the second terms so that:

$x^2 + 6x + 9 = 0$

$x^2 + 3x + 3x + 9 = 0$

$x(x + 3) + 3(x + 3) = 0$

$(x + 3)(x + 3) = 0$

Each side of the square is $x + 3$.

Answer choices A, C, and D result from improperly factoring the equation. To check whether your answer is correct, try to square your result. If the original equation is obtained, then you have factored correctly.

12. B; DOK Level: 2; **Content Topics:** Q.2.a, Q.2.e, A.1.a, A.4.a, A.4.b, A.1.g; **Practices:** MP.1.a, MP.1.b, MP.1.e, MP.2.a, MP.2.c, MP.4.a

Let the first integer be x and let the second integer be $x + 1$.

$(x)(x + 1) = 42$

$x^2 + 1x = 42$

$x^2 + 1x - 42 = 0$

Answer choices A, C, and D result from improperly factoring the equation. Answer choice D has an incorrect sign for the c value in the equation. Answer choices A and C have incorrect b values.

13. D; DOK Level: 2; **Content Topics:** Q.2.a, Q.2.e, Q.4a, A.1.a, A.1.g, A.4.a, A.4.b; **Practices:** MP.1.a, MP.1.b, MP.1.e, MP.2.a, MP.2.c, MP.4.a, MP.4.b

First, find the area of the square.

Area of square = $l \times w$

$49 = (x + 4)(x + 4)$

$49 = x^2 + 8x + 16$

$0 = x^2 + 8x + 16 - 49$

$0 = x^2 + 8x + - 33$

Next, factor the equation to determine the sides of the square. Begin by finding two factors of the third term (-33) that have a sum equal to the coefficient of the middle term (8). In this case, those numbers are 11 and -3. Next, use the variable x as the first term in each factor and the integers as the second terms so that:

$x^2 + 8x - 33 = 0$

$x^2 + 11x - 3x - 33 = 0$

$x(x + 11) - 3(x + 11) = 0$

$(x + 11)(x - 3) = 0$

Since $x + 11 = 0$, $x = -11$; likewise, since $x - 3 = 0$, $x = 3$. A measurement cannot be negative, so use $x = 3$ for the next step. If $x = 3$, $x + 4 = 7$, which would make the area 49 square feet as stated in the problem. Other answer choices then can be eliminated.

14. D; DOK Level: 2; **Content Topics:** Q.2.a, Q.2.e, A.1.a, A.1.d, A.4.a, A.4.b, A.1.f, A.1.g; **Practices:** MP.1.a, MP.1.b, MP.1.e, MP.2.a, MP.2.c, MP.4.a, MP.4.b

Let the first integer be x and the second integer be $x + 1$.

$x^2 + (x + 1)^2 = 113$

$x^2 + x^2 + 2x + 1 = 113$

$2x^2 + 2x - 112 = 0$

Next, factor out 2 from each of the terms, so that:

$2[x^2 + x - 56] = 0$

From there, find two factors of the third term (-56) that have a sum equal to the coefficient of the middle term (1). in this case, those numbers are 8 and -7. Next, use the variable x as the first term in each factor and the integers as the second term so that: $2[(x - 7)(x + 8)] = 0$.

The integers are 7 and 8. Other answer choices do not produce 113 when summed and squared, so they may be eliminated.

15. A; DOK Level: 2; **Content Topics:** Q.2.a, Q.2.e, A.1.a, A.1.d, A.4.a, A.4.b, A.1.f, A.1.g; **Practices:** MP.1.a, MP.1.b, MP.1.e, MP.2.a, MP.2.c, MP.4.a, MP.4.b

Let the first odd integer be x and the second integer be $x + 2$. Find the product of the integers, then solve for x.

$x(x + 2) = 35$

$x^2 + 2x = 35$

$x^2 + 2x - 35 = 0$

Next, find two factors of the third term (-35) that have a sum equal to the coefficient of the middle term (2). In this case, those numbers are 7 and -5. Next, use the variable x as the first term in each factor and the integers as the second terms so that:

$x^2 + 7x - 5x - 35 = 0$

$x(x + 7) - 5(x + 7) = 0$

$(x + 7)(x - 5) = 0$

Since $x + 7 = 0$, $x = -7$. To make it consecutive, it must be positive 7. Lastly, since $x - 5 = 0$, $x = 5$. Other answer choices do not multiply with a consecutive integer to produce 35, so they may be eliminated.

Answer Key

UNIT 3 *(continued)*

16. D; DOK Level: 2; Content Topics: Q.2.a, Q.2.e, A.1.a, A.1.d, A.1.g, A.4.a, A.4.b; **Practices:** MP.1.a, MP.1.b, MP.1.e, MP.2.a, MP.2.c, MP.4.a, MP.4.b
Let the first integer be x and the second be $x + 2$. Find the product of the integers and set up an equation:
$x(x + 2) = 48$
$x^2 + 2x = 48$
$x^2 + 2x - 48 = 0$
Answer choices A, B, and C have incorrect b values.

17. C; DOK Level: 2; Content Topics: Q.2.a, Q.2.e, A.1.a, A.1.d, A.1.f, A.1.g, A.4.a, A.4.b; **Practices:** MP.1.a, MP.1.b, MP.1.e, MP.2.a, MP.2.c, MP.4.a, MP.4.b
Let x be the length of the rectangle. Therefore, $x - 4$ is the width of the rectangle. The area of a rectangle is the product of its length and width, so $x(x - 4) = 165$. Expand the parentheses and subtract 165 from each side of the equation: $x^2 - 4x - 165 = 0$. Find the two numbers whose product is −165 and whose sum is −4. The numbers are −15 and 11. So, $(x - 15)(x + 11) = 0$. Therefore, $x - 15 = 0$ or $x + 11 = 0$, and $x = 15$ or $x = -11$. Since a length must have a positive value, $x = 15$ and the length of the rectangle is 15 feet.

18. B; DOK Level: 2; Content Topics: Q.2.a, Q.2.e, Q.3.a, A.1.a, A.1.d, A.1.f, A.1.g, A.4.a, A.4.b; **Practices:** MP.1.a, MP.1.b, MP.1.e, MP.2.a, MP.2.c, MP.4.a, MP.4.b
When the object hits the ground, its height will be zero, therefore, $h = 0$ may be represented by:
$-4.9t^2 + 19.6t + 58.8 = 0$. Solve for t to find the time that $h = 0$. Factor, dividing the entire equation by −4.9 to make factoring easier:
$-4.9[t^2 - 4t - 12] = 0$
Next, find two factors of the third term (−12) that have a sum equal to the coefficient of the middle term (−4). In this case, those numbers are 2 and −6. Next, use the variable x as the first term in each factor and the integers as the second terms so that:
$-4.9[t^2 - 6t + 2t - 12] = 0$
$-4.9[t(t - 6) + 2(t - 6)] = 0$
$(t - 6)(t + 2) = 0$
Since $t - 6 = 0$, $t = 6$; likewise, since $t + 2 = 0$, $t = -2$
Since time cannot equal −2s in reality, the object hits the ground at $t = 6$s after being propelled in the air.
Answer choice A is incorrect as time cannot be negative. Answer choice C results from incorrect factoring, and answer choice D represents the b value in the standard quadratic equation.

19. C; DOK Level: 2; Content Topics: Q.2.a, Q.2.e, Q.3.a, A.1.a, A.4.a, A.1.f, A.1.g, A.4.b; **Practices:** MP.1.a, MP.1.b, MP.1.e, MP.2.a, MP.2.c, MP.4.a, MP.4.b
Set the equation equal to zero: $t^2 - 2t - 8 = 0$.
Next, find two factors of the third term (−8) that have a sum equal to the coefficient of the middle term (−2). In this case, those numbers are 2 and −4. Next, use the variable x as the first term in each factor and the integers as the second terms so that: $(t + 2)(t - 4) = 0$.
Since $t + 2 = 0$, $t = -2$; likewise, since $t - 4 = 0$, $t = 4$.
Because, in this context, a negative time does not exist, the ball hits the ground at $t = 4$s.

20. D; DOK Level: 2; Content Topics: Q.2.a, Q.2.e, A.1.a; **Practices:** MP.1.a, MP.1.b, MP.1.e, MP.2.c, MP.4.a
Reset the expression as: $(x + 6)(x + 6)$. Next, solve by using the FOIL method:
*F*irst: $x(x) = x^2$
*O*uter: $x(6) = 6x$
*I*nner: $6(x) = 6x$
*L*ast: $6(6) = 36$
Expression: $x^2 + 6x + 6x + 36 = x^2 + 12x + 36$
Choices A, B, and C partially result from incorrect expansion of last terms. Answer choice B also results from incorrect expansion of outer and inner terms.

21. 890 kg; DOK Level: 2; Content Topics: Q.2.a, Q.2.e, Q.5.a; **Practices:** MP.1.a, MP.1.b, MP.1.e, MP.2.a, MP.2.c, MP.4.a, MP.4.b
$809,600 = x^2 + 20x - 300$
$x^2 + 20x - 300 - 809,600 = 0$
$x^2 + 20x - 809,900 = 0$
Begin with the formula: $\dfrac{-b \pm \sqrt{b^2 - 4ac}}{2a}$
Next, substitute values so that:
$a = 1$
$b = 20$
$c = -809,900$
$x = \dfrac{[-20 \pm \sqrt{[20^2 - 4(1)(-809,900)]}}{2(1)}$
$x = \dfrac{[-20 \pm \sqrt{3,240,000]}}{2}$
$x = \dfrac{[-20 \pm 1,800]}{2}$
$x = \dfrac{-20 + 1,800}{2} = \dfrac{1780}{2} = 890$ or $x = \dfrac{-20 - 1,800}{2}$
$x = \dfrac{-1,820}{2}$
$x = -910$.
Since, in this context, it is impossible to sell negative units of products, $x = 890$ kg.

22. $300; DOK Level: 2; Content Topics: Q.2.a, Q.2.e, Q.5.a; **Practices:** MP.1.a, MP.1.b, MP.1.e, MP.2.c, MP.4.a
If no products are sold, $x = 0$. Plugging this value into the equation gives:
$R = x^2 + 20x - 300$
$R = (0)^2 + 20(0) - 300$
$R = -300$
The company loses $300 when no products are sold.

23. $11,700; DOK Level: 2; Content Topics: Q.2.a, Q.2.e, Q.4.a, A.1.a, A.1.g, A.4.a, A.4.b; **Practices:** MP.1.a, MP.1.b, MP.1.e, MP.2.a, MP.2.c, MP.4.a, MP.4.b
When 100 kg of product are sold, $x = 100$. Plugging this value into the equation gives:
$R = x^2 + 20x - 300$
$R = 100^2 + 20(100) - 300$
$R = 10,000 + 2,000 - 300$
$R = 12,000 - 300$
$R = $11,700$

24. B; DOK Level: 3; **DOK Level:** 2; **Content Topics:** Q.2.a, Q.2.e, Q.3.a, A.1.a, A.1.d, A.1.f, A.1.g, A.4.a, A.4.b; **Practices:** MP.1.a, MP.1.b, MP.1.e, MP.2.a, MP.2.c, MP.4.a, MP.4.b

When the object hits the ground, its height will be zero, therefore, $h = 0$ may be represented by:

Brian
$-16t^2 + 160 = 0$
$-16t^2 = -160$
Divide each side by -16, so that $t^2 = 10$
$t = \sqrt{10}$

Ball
$-16t^2 - 48t + 160 = 0$
$-16 [t^2 + 3t - 10] = 0$
Next, find two factors of the third term (-10) that have a sum equal to the coefficient of the middle term (3). in this case, those numbers are 5 and -2. Next, use the variable x as the first term in each factor and the integers as the second terms so that:
$-16 [t^2 + 5t - 2t - 10] = 0$
$-16 [t(t + 5) - 2(t + 5)] = 0$
$(t + 5)(t - 2) = 0$
Since $t - 2 = 0$, $t = 2$. Also, since $t + 5 = 0$, $t = -5$. Since a negative time does not exist in reality, $t = 2$. Therefore, the difference in time is $\sqrt{10} - 2$.

25. D; DOK Level: 3: **Content Topics:** Q.2.a, Q.2.e, Q.4.a, A.1.a, A.1.d, A.1.f, A.1.g, A.4.a, A.4.b; **Practices:** MP.1.a, MP.1.b, MP.1.e, MP.2.a, MP.2.c, MP.4.a, MP.4.b

Set up an equation to represent the triangle.
Let the shorter side, $x - 6 = a$
Let the longer side, $x = b$
Let the hypotenuse, $2(x - 6) - 6 = c$
The Pythagorean theorem ($a^2 + b^2 = c^2$) can be used to find the missing side of a triangle:
$(x - 6)^2 + x^2 = (2x - 18)^2$
$x^2 - 12x + 36 + x^2 = 4x^2 - 72x + 324$
Rearrange the equation and group like terms so that: $2x^2 - 12x + 36 = 4x^2 - 72x + 324$. Next, add $12x$ to each side so that: $2x^2 + 36 = 4x^2 - 60x + 324$. Then, subtract 324 from each side so that: $2x^2 - 288 = 4x^2 - 60x$. Then, subtract $2x^2$ from each side so that: $-288 = 2x^2 - 60x$. Set the equation to 0, so that: $2x^2 - 60x + 288 = 0$. Next, factor 2 from the equation so that: $2[x^2 - 30x + 144] = 0$. Next, find two factors of the third term (144) that have a sum equal to the coefficient of the middle term (-30). In this case, those numbers are -24, -6. Next, use the variable x as the first term in each factor and the integers as the second terms so that:
$2[(x - 6) (x - 24)] = 0$
$x = 6$, or $x = 24$
Recall that $x =$ longer side of triangle
If the longer side $= 6$, shorter leg would have to be ($x - 6 = 0$). Since the side of the triangle cannot be zero units, $x = 24$ units.
Longer Leg (x) = 24 units
Shorter leg ($x - 6$) = 24 − 6 = 18 units
Hypotenuse $2(x - 6) - 6 = 2(24 - 6) - 6 = 30$ units.
Length of the yarn ball = Perimeter of the triangle = 24 units + 18 units + 30 units = 72 units.

26. B; DOK Level: 2; **Content Topics:** Q.2.a, Q.2.e, Q.4.a, A.1.a, A.1.f, A.1.g, A.4.a, A.4.b; **Practices:** MP.1.a, MP.1.b, MP.1.e, MP.2.c, MP.4.a

Solve using the FOIL method:
*F*irst: $x(x) = x^2$
*O*uter: $x(-8) = -8x$
*I*nner: $-8(x) = -8x$
*L*ast: $-8(-8) = 64$
Expression: $x^2 - 16x + 64$

27. B; DOK Level: 2; **Content Topics:** Q.2.a, Q.2.e, Q.5.a; **Practices:** MP.1.a, MP.1.b, MP.1.e, MP.2.a, MP.2.c, MP.4.a, MP.4.b

$A = (w) (w + 8)$
$84 = w^2 + 8w$
$w^2 + 8w - 84 = 0$
Next, find two factors of the third term (-84) that have a sum equal to the coefficient of the middle term (8). In this case, those numbers are 14 and -6. Next, use the variable x as the first term in each factor and the integers as the second terms so that:
$w^2 + 14w - 6w - 84 = 0$
$(w + 14) (w - 6) = 0$
$w = -14$, or $w = 6$
Since the side of a rectangle cannot be negative, $w = 6$. The longer side of the rectangle is $w + 8 = 6 + 8 = 14$ feet.

LESSON 9, *pp. 90–93*

1. C; DOK Level: 2; **Content Topics:** Q.2.a, A.1.a, A.1.f, A.1.h; **Practices:** MP.1.a, MP.1.b, MP.1.e, MP.4.b

To add rational expressions with unlike denominators, rewrite the expressions so that they have like denominators. Begin by completely factoring the expressions to make sure each expression is simplified: $\frac{3}{x + 1} + \frac{x - 2}{x^2 - 4} = \frac{3}{x + 1} + \frac{x - 2}{(x + 2)(x - 2)}$. Since the second addend can be simplified to $\frac{1}{x + 2}$, the lowest common denominator is the product of the two denominators, $(x + 1)(x + 2)$. Multiply the numerator and denominator of the first expression by $(x + 2)$ and the numerator and denominator of the second expression by $(x + 1)$ to rewrite each expression with like denominators: $\frac{3(x + 2)}{(x + 1)(x + 2)} + \frac{1(x + 1)}{(x + 1)(x + 2)}$. Add: $\frac{3(x + 2)}{(x + 1)(x + 2)} + \frac{1(x + 1)}{(x + 1)(x + 2)} = \frac{3(x + 2) + (x + 1)}{(x + 1)(x + 2)}$. Use the distributive property, then group like terms: $\frac{3(x + 2) + (x + 1)}{(x + 1)(x + 2)} = \frac{3x + 6 + x + 1}{(x + 1)(x + 2)} = \frac{4x + 7}{(x + 1)(x + 2)}$.

2. A; DOK Level: 2; **Content Topics:** Q.2.a, A.1.a, A.1.f, A.1; **Practices:** MP.1.a, MP.1.b, MP.1.e, MP.4.b

Begin by factoring each expression to make sure it is simplified. The expression on the left-hand side of the equation is factored. The expression on the right-hand side of the equation has a denominator that is not factored: $y^2 + 5y - 6 = (y - 1)(y + 6)$. Since the denominator on the left-hand side is a factor of the denominator on the right-hand side, the LCD is $(y - 1)(y + 6)$. Multiply each side of the equation by the LCD: $(y - 1)(y + 6) \cdot \frac{5}{y - 1} = (y - 1)(y + 6) \cdot \frac{-10}{(y - 1)(y + 6)}$. Divide out common factors: $(y - 1)(y + 6) \cdot \frac{5}{y - 1} = (y - 1)(y + 6) \cdot \frac{-10}{(y - 1)(y + 6)}$. Simplify: $5(y + 6) = -10$. Multiply: $5y + 30 = -10$. Subtract 30 from each side: $5y = -40$. Divide each side by 5: $y = -8$.

UNIT 3 *(continued)*

3. C; DOK Level: 2; Content Topics: Q.2.a, A.1.a, A.1.f, A.1.h; **Practices:** MP.1.a, MP.1.b, MP.1.e, MP.4.b
To find the lowest common denominator of rational expressions, begin by factoring the denominators. The denominator of the second expression is completely factored, but $x^2 - 6x = 9 = (x - 3)(x - 3)$. Since the denominator of one expression is a factor of the denominator of the other expression, the lowest common denominator is $(x - 3)(x - 3)$. Answer choice A is the denominator of the second expression and the factor that is common to both denominators. Answer choice B is the result of an error in factoring $x^2 - 6x + 9$. Answer choice D is the product of the two denominators, but it is not the lowest common denominator.

4. A; DOK Level: 2; Content Topics: Q.2.a, A.1.a, A.1.f, A.1.h; **Practices:** MP.1.a, MP.1.b, MP.1.e, MP.4.b
To subtract rational expressions with unlike denominators, rewrite the expressions so that they have like denominators. as shown in Problem 3: $\dfrac{4x}{(x - 3)(x - 3)} - \dfrac{3(x - 3)}{(x - 3)(x - 3)}$. Subtract the numerators: $\dfrac{4x - 3(x - 3)}{(x - 3)(x - 3)}$. Use the distributive property and combine like terms:
$\dfrac{4x - 3(x - 3)}{(x - 3)(x - 3)} = \dfrac{4x - 3x + 9}{(x - 3)(x - 3)} = \dfrac{x + 9}{(x - 3)(x - 3)}$.

5. A; DOK Level: 2; Content Topics: Q.2.a, A.1.a, A.1.f, A.1.h; **Practices:** MP.1.a, MP.1.b, MP.1.e, MP.4.b
To add rational expressions, rewrite the expressions with like denominators. Begin by completely factoring each expression to ensure that the expressions are in their simplified forms. The second expression is completely factored, but the denominator of the first expression is not in its factored form: $\dfrac{x - 2}{x^2 + x - 6} = \dfrac{x - 2}{(x + 3)(x - 2)}$. The common factor $(x - 2)$ can be divided out of the numerator and the denominator, and the simplified expression is $\dfrac{1}{x + 3}$. The simplified expressions have like denominators, so add the numerators and keep the denominator: $\dfrac{1}{x + 3} + \dfrac{4x}{x + 3} = \dfrac{4x + 1}{x + 3}$.

6. B; DOK Level: 2; Content Topics: Q.2.a, A.1.a, A.1.f, A.1.h; **Practices:** MP.1.a, MP.1.b, MP.1.e, MP.4.b
To divide rational expressions, multiply by the reciprocal of the divisor: $\dfrac{x^2 - 16}{x} \div \dfrac{x^2 - x - 12}{x + 3} = \dfrac{x^2 - 16}{x} \cdot \dfrac{x + 3}{x^2 - x - 12}$.
Multiply numerators and denominators:
$\dfrac{x^2 - 16}{x} \cdot \dfrac{x + 3}{x^2 - x - 12} = \dfrac{(x^2 - 16)(x + 3)}{x(x^2 - x - 12)}$. Factor numerator and denominator and divide out common factors:
$\dfrac{(x^2 - 16)(x + 3)}{x(x^2 - x - 12)} = \dfrac{(x - 4)(x + 4)(x + 3)}{x(x + 3)(x - 4)} = \dfrac{x + 4}{x}$.

7. A; DOK Level: 2; Content Topics: Q.2.a, A.1.a, A.1.f, A.1.h; **Practices:** MP.1.a, MP.1.b, MP.1.e, MP.4.a, MP.4.b
To solve the equation for x, the rational expressions must have like denominators. Before finding the lowest common denominator, factor the expressions: $\dfrac{x + 1}{3x + 3} = \dfrac{x + 1}{3(x + 1)} = \dfrac{1}{3}$. Rewrite the equation with the simplified expression: $\dfrac{5}{x} + \dfrac{1}{3} = \dfrac{2}{x}$. The lowest common denominator of x and 3 is $3x$, so multiply each expression by $3x$: $3x \cdot \dfrac{5}{x} + 3x \cdot \dfrac{1}{3} = 3x \cdot \dfrac{2}{x}$. Simplify: $15 + x = 6$. Subtract 15 from each side of the equation: $x = -9$.

8. B; DOK Level: 3; Content Topics: Q.2.a, A.1.a, A.1.f, A.1.h; **Practices:** MP.1.a, MP.1.b, MP.1.e, MP.3.c, MP.4.a, MP.4.b, MP.5.a
Examine each step in Evan's solution. In Step 1, Evan factors the numerator: $12 - 3x = 3(4 - x)$. He also factors the denominator: $(x + 1)(x + 4)$. This step is correct. In Step 2, Evan factors -1 from the numerator: $3(4 - x) = -3(x - 4)$. So, Evan did not factor the numerator correctly and the error was in Step 2. The remaining steps of Evan's solution correctly work with the incorrect expression from Step 2.

9. C; DOK Level: 2; Content Topics: Q.2.a, A.1.a, A.1.f, A.1.h; **Practices:** MP.1.a, MP.1.b, MP.1.e, MP.4.a, MP.4.b
To solve this equation, multiply each expression by the lowest common denominator. Since $x^2 - 9 = (x + 3)(x - 3)$, the lowest common denominator is $(x + 3)(x - 3)$. Multiply each expression by the lowest common denominator:
$(x + 3)(x - 3) \cdot \dfrac{2}{x + 3} + (x + 3)(x - 3) \cdot \dfrac{2}{x - 3} = (x + 3)(x - 3) \cdot \dfrac{20}{x^2 - 9}$ Simplify: $2(x - 3) + 2(x + 3) = 20$. Multiply: $2x - 6 + 2x + 6 = 20$. Group like terms: $4x = 20$. Divide both sides of the equation by 4: $x = 5$.

10. B; DOK Level: 2; Content Topics: Q.2.a, A.1.a, A.1.f, A.1.h; **Practices:** MP.1.a, MP.1.b, MP.1.e, MP.4.a, MP.4.b
To multiply a rational expression by a polynomial, write the polynomial as a rational expression with a denominator of 1: $\dfrac{8x}{x^2 + 10x + 16} \cdot (x + 2) = \dfrac{8x}{x^2 + 10x + 16} \cdot \dfrac{(x + 2)}{1}$.
Multiply numerators and denominators:
$\dfrac{8x}{x^2 + 10x + 16} \cdot \dfrac{(x + 2)}{1} = \dfrac{8x(x + 2)}{x^2 + 10x + 16}$.
Factor, and divide out common factors:
$\dfrac{8x(x + 2)}{x^2 + 10x + 16} = \dfrac{8x(x + 2)}{(x + 2)(x + 8)} = \dfrac{8x}{(x + 8)}$.

11. A; DOK Level: 2; Content Topics: Q.2.a, Q.2.e, A.1.a, A.1.f, A.1.h; **Practices:** MP.1.a, MP.1.b, MP.1.e, MP.2.a, MP.4.a, MP.4.b
To find the number of consecutive tests on which Alicia must score 100%, solve the equation for x. First, multiply the rational numbers in the equation ($0.85 \times 4 = 3.4$. 3.4 is the aggregate of Alicia's first four test scores): $0.90 = \dfrac{3.4 + x}{4 + x}$. Next, multiply both sides of the equation by the lowest common denominator, $4 + x$: $(4 + x) \cdot 0.90 = (4 + x) \cdot \dfrac{3.4 + x}{4 + x}$. Simplify: $3.6 + 0.9x = 3.4 + x$. Subtract 3.4 and 0.9x from each side: $0.2 = 0.1x$. Divide each side by 0.1: $x = 2$. Alicia must score 100% on the next two tests to raise her average to 90%.

12. C; DOK Level: 2; Content Topics: Q.2.a, A.1.a, A.1.f, A.1.h; **Practices:** MP.1.a, MP.1.b, MP.1.e, MP.4.b
To find the lowest common denominator, begin by simplifying both sides of the equation. The terms in the left-hand side of the equation are completely factored. The numerator and denominator of the expression on the right-hand side of the equation have a common factor of 2: $\frac{12}{2x+8} = \frac{2(6)}{2(x+4)} = \frac{6}{x+4}$. None of the denominators have common factors, so the lowest common denominator is $(5)(1)(x+4)$, or $5(x+4)$.

13. B; DOK Level: 2; Content Topics: Q.2.a, A.1.a, A.1.f, A.1.h; **Practices:** MP.1.a, MP.1.b, MP.1.e, MP.4.b
To solve the equation, multiply both sides of the equation by the lowest common denominator, $5(x+4)$: $\cancel{5}(x+4) \cdot \frac{x}{\cancel{5}} + 5(x+4) \cdot 1 = 5\cancel{(x+4)} \cdot \frac{2(6)}{2\cancel{(x+4)}}$. Simplify: $x(x+4) + 5(x+4) = 30$. Multiply: $x^2 + 4x + 5x + 20 = 30$. Combine like terms: $x^2 + 9x - 10 = 0$. Since $(-1)(10) = -10$ and $(-1) + 10 = 9$, $x^2 + 9x - 10 = (x-1)(x+10) = 0$, so $x = 1$ or $x = -10$.

14. A; DOK Level: 3; Content Topics: Q.2.a, A.1.a, A.1.f, A.1.h; **Practices:** MP.1.a, MP.1.b, MP.1.e, MP.4.b, MP.5.a, MP.5.c
To determine who is correct, find the lowest common denominator of the expressions. Begin by completely factoring each expression: $\frac{x^2-25}{x^2+7x+10} + \frac{4x+8}{x^2+4x-5}$ $= \frac{(x+5)(x-5)}{(x+5)(x+2)} + \frac{4(x+2)}{(x+5)(x-1)}$. Next, in each expression, identify any common factors in the numerator and denominator, and cancel out those common factors: $\frac{\cancel{(x+5)}(x-5)}{\cancel{(x+5)}(x+2)} + \frac{4(x+2)}{(x+5)(x-1)}$. Finally, examine the factors in the denominators of the two expressions. There are no common factors, so the lowest common denominator is the product of the two simplified denominators, or $(x+2)(x+5)(x-1)$. Therefore, Emma is correct. Consider the two reasons given for Emma's correct lowest common denominator. In answer choice A, the reason for the lowest common denominator is that the common factor of $(x+5)$ can be divided out from the first addend. This is the correct approach to dividing out factors. In answer choice C, the reason for the lowest common denominator is that the common factor of $(x+5)$ can be divided out of the numerator of the first expression and the denominator of the second expression. However, common factors must be divided out of a single expression when adding or subtracting. Answer choices B and D are incorrect because Marco is incorrect.

15. C; DOK Level: 2; Content Topics: Q.2.a, A.1.a, A.1.f, A.1.h; **Practices:** MP.1.a, MP.1.b, MP.1.e, MP.4.b
To solve the equation, begin by finding the lowest common denominator. The first step is to completely factor each side of the equation. The terms on the left-hand side of the equation are completely factored. However, the numerator and denominator of the expression on the right-hand side have a common factor of $(x+6)$: $\frac{x+6}{x^2-36} = \frac{x+6}{(x+6)(x-6)} = \frac{1}{x-6}$. So, the lowest common denominator is $(x-6)$. Multiply each side of the equation by the lowest common denominator: $(x-6) \cdot 3 + \cancel{(x-6)} \cdot \frac{4}{\cancel{x-6}} = \cancel{(x-6)} \frac{x+6}{\cancel{(x+6)}\,\cancel{(x-6)}}$. Simplify: $3x - 18 + 4 = 1$. Add 18 and subtract 4 from each side: $3x = 15$. Divide each side by 3: $x = 5$.

16. A; DOK Level: 2; Content Topics: Q.2.a, A.1.a, A.1.f, A.1.h; **Practices:** MP.1.a, MP.1.b, MP.1.e, MP.4.b
To divide rational expressions, multiply by the reciprocal of the divisor: $\frac{x^2+2x-15}{7x^2} \div (x-3) = \frac{x^2+2x-15}{7x^2} \cdot \frac{1}{(x-3)}$. Multiply numerators and denominators: $\frac{x^2+2x-15}{7x^2} \cdot \frac{1}{(x-3)} = \frac{x^2+2x-15}{7x^2(x-3)}$. Factor, and divide out common factors: $\frac{x^2+2x-15}{7x^2(x-3)} = \frac{(x+5)(x-3)}{7x^2\cancel{(x-3)}} = \frac{x+5}{7x^2}$.

17. A; DOK Level: 2; Content Topics: Q.2.a, A.1.a, A.1.f, A.1.h; **Practices:** MP.1.a, MP.1.b, MP.1.e, MP.4.b
To subtract rational expressions, rewrite the expressions with like denominators. To determine the lowest common denominator, begin by completely factoring each expression. The expression $\frac{2}{x+4}$ is completely factored. The numerator and denominator of the expression $\frac{x^2-25}{x^2+9x+20}$ have a common factor of $(x+5)$: $\frac{x^2-25}{x^2+9x+20} = \frac{(x+5)(x-5)}{(x+5)(x+4)} = \frac{(x-5)}{(x+4)}$. The simplified expressions have like denominators of $(x+4)$, so add the numerators and keep the denominator: $\frac{x^2-25}{x^2+9x+20} - \frac{2}{x+4} = \frac{x-5}{x+4} - \frac{2}{x+4} = \frac{x-7}{x+4}$.

18. C; DOK Level: 2; Content Topics: Q.2.a, A.1.a, A.1.f, A.1.h; **Practices:** MP.1.a, MP.1.b, MP.1.e, MP.4.b
To solve the equation, begin by finding the lowest common denominator. The denominator of $\frac{2}{6x+12}$ can be rewritten as $6(x+2)$, so the lowest common denominator for the equation is $6(x+2)$. Multiply each side of the equation by the lowest common denominator: $6\cancel{(x+2)} \cdot \frac{3}{\cancel{x+2}} + 6\cancel{(x+2)} \cdot \frac{2}{6\cancel{(x+2)}} = \cancel{6}(x+2) \cdot \frac{5}{\cancel{6}}$. Simplify: $6(3) + 2 = 5(x+2)$. Multiply: $18 + 2 = 5x + 10$. Combine like terms and subtract 10 from each side: $10 = 5x$. Divide each side by 5: $x = 2$.

19. A; DOK Level: 2; Content Topics: Q.2.a, A.1.a, A.1.f, A.1.h; **Practices:** MP.1.a, MP.1.b, MP.1.e, MP.4.b
To solve the equation, begin by finding the lowest common denominator. The denominator of $\frac{4}{x^2-9}$ can be rewritten as $(x+3)(x-3)$, so the lowest common denominator for the equation is $(x+3)(x-3)$. Multiply each side of the equation by the lowest common denominator: $(x+3)\cancel{(x-3)} \cdot \frac{3}{\cancel{x-3}} + (x+3)(x-3) \cdot 1 = \cancel{(x+3)}\cancel{(x-3)} \cdot \frac{4}{\cancel{(x+3)}\cancel{(x-3)}}$. Simplify: $3(x+3) + x^2 - 9 = 4$. Multiply: $3x + 9 + x^2 - 9 = 4$. Combine like terms and subtract 4 from each side: $x^2 + 3x - 4 = 0$. Since $(4)(-1) = -4$ and $4 + (-1) = 3$, $x^2 + 3x - 4 = (x-1)(x+4) = 0$, so $x = 1$ or $x = -4$.

Answer Key

UNIT 3 *(continued)*

20. D; **DOK Level:** 2; **Content Topics:** Q.2.a, A.1.a, A.1.f, A.1.h; **Practices:** MP.1.a, MP.1.b, MP.1.e, MP.4.b
To solve the equation, begin by finding the lowest common denominator. The denominator of $\frac{3x - 29}{x^2 - 13 + 42}$ can be rewritten as $(x - 6)(x - 7)$, so the lowest common denominator for the equation is $(x - 6)(x - 7)$. Multiply each side of the equation by the lowest common denominator: $(x - 6)(x - 7)\frac{x + 2}{x - 6} = (x - 6)(x - 7)\frac{3x - 29}{(x - 6)(x - 7)}$. Simplify: $(x - 7)(x + 2) = 3x - 29$. Multiply: $x^2 - 5x - 14 = 3x - 29$. Subtract $3x$ and add 29 to each side: $x^2 - 8x + 15 = 0$. Since $(-3)(-5) = 15$ and $-3 + (-5) = -8$, $x^2 - 8x + 15 = (x - 3)(x - 5) = 0$, and $x = 3$ or $x = 5$.

21. A; **DOK Level:** 2; **Content Topics:** Q.2.a, A.1.a, A.1.f, A.1.h; **Practices:** MP.1.a, MP.1.b, MP.1.e, MP.4.b
To simplify, first factor out the largest common factors from the various terms: $\frac{2(4x^2 - 9)}{(x^2 - 1)} \cdot \frac{3(x - 1)}{2(2x + 3)}$. Next, note any terms involving the difference between perfect squares, e.g., $(4x^2 - 9)$ and $(x^2 - 1)$, because they are easily factored: $\frac{2(2x - 3)(2x + 3)}{(x - 1)(x + 1)} \cdot \frac{3(x - 1)}{2(2x + 3)}$. Canceling identical terms in the numerator and denominator gives the result: $\frac{3(2x - 3)}{(x + 1)}$ (choice A).

22. D; **DOK Level:** 1; **Content Topics:** Q.2.a, A.1.f; **Practices:** MP.1.a, MP.1.b, MP.1.e, MP.4.b
To find the lowest common denominator of each equation, completely factor both sides. In answer choice A, $\frac{7}{2x + 8} = \frac{7}{2(x + 4)}$ and $\frac{3}{3x - 9} = \frac{\cancel{3}}{\cancel{3}(x - 3)}$, so the lowest common denominator is $2(x + 4)(x - 3)$. In answer choice B, $\frac{2x - 4}{x^2 + 2x - 8} = \frac{2(x - 2)}{(x + 4)(x - 2)}$, so the lowest common denominator is $(x + 4)(x - 2)$. In answer choice C, $\frac{x + 3}{x^2 - 9} = \frac{x + 3}{(x + 3)(x - 3)}$ and $\frac{x + 5}{x^2 + 2x - 15} = \frac{x + 5}{(x + 5)(x - 3)}$, so the lowest common denominator is $(x - 3)$. In answer choice D, $\frac{6}{3x + 12} = \frac{3(2)}{\cancel{3}(x + 4)}$ and $\frac{x^2 - 16}{x^2 + x - 12} = \frac{(x + 4)(x - 4)}{(x - 3)(x + 4)}$, so the lowest common denominator is $(x + 4)(x - 3)$.

23. A; **DOK Level:** 3; **Content Topics:** A.1.a, A.1.f, A.1.h; **Practices:** MP.1.a, MP.1.b, MP.1.d, MP.1.e, MP.2.c, MP.3.a, MP.4.a
In order for an expression *not* to change the lowest common denominator of $\frac{n}{(x + a)} + \frac{m}{(x + b)}$, its simplified denominator must be either $(x + a)$, $(x + b)$, or $(x + a)(x + b)$. In answer choice A, the denominator of $(x - b)$ does not cancel with any factor in the numerator. So, adding the expression $\frac{2(x + b)}{x - b}$ would change the lowest common denominator. In answer choice B, the numerator factors to $(x - a)(x - a)$ and the denominator factors to $(x - a)(x + a)$. One $(x - a)$ factor in the numerator cancels with the $(x - a)$ factor in the denominator. This leaves $\frac{(x - a)}{(x + a)}$, which will not change the lowest common denominator. For answer choice C, the denominator factors to $(x + b)(x + b)$. The $(x + b)$ in the numerator cancels with one of the $(x + b)$ factors in the denominator to leave $\frac{1}{(x + b)}$, which will not change the lowest common denominator. In answer choice D, the denominator factors to $2(x + a)$. The 2 in the numerator cancels with the 2 in the denominator to leave $\frac{(x - a)}{(x + a)}$, which will not change the lowest common denominator.

24. B; **DOK Level:** 2; **Content Topics:** Q.2.a, Q.2.e, A.1.a, A.1.f, A.1.h; **Practices:** MP.1.a, MP.1.b, MP.1.e, MP.2.a, MP.4.a, MP.4.b
To find the number of milliliters of 25% alcohol solution the chemist needs to add, solve the equation for m. First, multiply to eliminate the parentheses: $0.15 = \frac{0.1(100) + 0.25m}{100 + m} = \frac{10 + 0.25m}{100 + m}$. Next, multiply each side by the lowest common denominator, $100 + m$: $(100 + m) \cdot 0.15 = (100 + m) \cdot \frac{10 + 0.25m}{100 + m}$. Multiply: $15 + 0.15m = 10 + 0.25m$. Subtract 10 and $0.15m$ from each side: $5 = 0.1m$. Divide each side by 0.1: $m = 50$. The chemist must add 50 mL of the 25% alcohol solution.

25. C; **DOK Level:** 2; **Content Topics:** Q.2.a, A.1.a, A.1.f, A.1.h; **Practices:** MP.1.a, MP.1.b, MP.1.e, MP.4.b
To subtract rational expressions, rewrite them with like denominators. To find the lowest common denominator, begin by simplifying each expression: $\frac{x^2 + 4x}{3x + 12}$ can be simplified to $\frac{x(x + 4)}{3(x + 4)}$. From there, factor out the $x + 4$ terms in the numerator and denominator so that it reads: $\frac{x}{3} - \frac{4x}{x + 7}$. Multiply the two terms in the denominator to find the common denominator of $3(x + 7)$. Next, rewrite each expression using the lowest common denominator, applying $x + 7$ to both the numerator and denominator on the left side of the expression and 3 to the numerator and denominator on the right side so that: $\frac{x^2 + 7x - 12x}{3x + 21}$. Combine like terms: $\frac{x^2 - 5x}{3x + 21}$.

26. C; **DOK Level:** 2; **Content Topics:** Q.2.a, A.1.a, A.1.d, A.1.f; A.1.h, A.4.a; **Practices:** MP.1.a, MP.1.b, MP.1.e, MP.4.b
To simplify, begin by multiplying numerators and denominators: $\frac{x^2 + 6x - 16}{3x + 15} \cdot \frac{x^2 - 25}{x^2 - 4x + 4} = \frac{(x^2 + 6x - 16)(x^2 - 25)}{(3x + 15)(x^2 - 4x + 4)}$. Completely factor the numerator and denominator: $\frac{(x^2 + 6x - 16)(x^2 - 25)}{(3x + 15)(x^2 - 4x + 4)} = \frac{(x + 8)(x - 2)(x + 5)(x - 5)}{(3x + 5)(x - 2)(x - 2)}$. Divide out common factors: $\frac{(x + 8)(x - 2)(x + 5)(x - 5)}{3(x + 5)(x - 2)(x - 2)} = \frac{(x + 8)(x - 5)}{3(x - 2)}$.

27. C; DOK Level: 2; Content Topics: Q.2.a, A.1.a, A.1.f, A.1.h; **Practices:** MP.1.a, MP.1.b, MP.1.e, MP.4.b

To simplify the expression, begin by factoring each denominator: $\frac{2}{5(x-2)} + \frac{x+1}{(x-5)(x-2)} + \frac{1}{-(x-2)}$. The lowest common denominator is $5(x-2)(x-5)$. Rewrite addition of a negative quantity as subtraction, and rewrite the expression with the LCD:

$\frac{2(x-5)}{5(x-2)(x-5)} + \frac{5(x+1)}{5(x-5)(x-2)} - \frac{1(5)(x-5)}{5(x-5)(x-2)}$.

Add: $\frac{2(x-5) + 5(x+1) - 1(5)(x-5)}{5(x-2)(x-5)}$.

Find the products in the numerator: $\frac{2x - 10 + 5x + 5 - 5x + 25}{5(x-2)(x-5)}$. Combine like terms:

$\frac{2x + 20}{5(x-2)(x-5)}$.

28. B; DOK Level: 3; Content Topics: Q.2.a, A.1.a, A.1.f, A.1.h; **Practices:** MP.1.a, MP.1.b, MP.1.e, MP.3.c, MP.4.a, MP.4.b, MP.5.a

Examine each step of Rebecca's solution. In Step 1, Rebecca multiplied each side of the equation by the lowest common denominator, $5(x-3)$: $5(x-3) \cdot \frac{x}{x-3} + 5(x-3) \cdot \frac{1}{5} = 5(x-3) \cdot \frac{3}{x-3}$. This step is correct. In Step 2, Rebecca finds the products from Step 1: $5x + (x - 15) = 5(3)$. Rebecca made an error multiplying $5(x-3) \cdot \frac{1}{5}$, and wrote the product as $x - 15$ rather than $x - 3$. The error is in Step 2.

LESSON 10, pp. 94–97

1. D; DOK Level: 2; Content Topics: Q.4.a, A.3.d; **Practices:** MP.1.a, MP.2.a

Let w represent the width of the plywood. The area of a rectangle is the product of its length and width, so the area of the plywood is $25w$. Since the area must be greater than 100 square feet, $25w \geq 100$. Answer choice A subtracts the width from the length and uses an incorrect inequality symbol. Answer choice B adds the width to the length. Answer choice C uses an incorrect inequality symbol.

2. C; DOK Level: 1; Content Topics: Q.2.a, Q.2.e, Q.4.a, A.3.d; **Practices:** MP.1.a, MP.1.e, MP.2.a, MP.4.b

The area of a rectangle is equal to length × width. The length is 25 feet and the width is represented by w, so the area of the rectangle is $25w$. Since the area is greater than 100 square feet, $25w \geq 100$. Divide each side of the inequality by 25 to solve for w: $w \geq 4$. Answer choices A, B, and D use an incorrect inequality symbol.

3. B; DOK Level: 1; Content Topic: A.3.b; **Practice:** MP.4.c

The closed circle on −3 indicates that −3 is part of the solution set. The arrow points to the right, so the graph shows the inequality $x \geq -3$. The graph of answer choice A would show a closed circle on 3 with an arrow also pointing to the right. The graph of answer choice C would show a closed circle on −3 with an arrow pointing to the left. The graph of answer choice D would show an open circle on −3 with an arrow pointing to the right.

4. D; DOK Level: 1; Content Topics: Q.2.a, Q.2.e, Q.4.a, A.3.d; **Practices:** MP.1.a, MP.1.e, MP.2.a, MP.4.b

Solve the inequality as you would solve an equation. Subtract 5 from each side of the inequality: $x + 5 - 5 < 14 - 5$. Simplify: $x < 9$. Answer choice A has an incorrect sign for the constant. Answer choices B and C are the result of adding 5 to each side of the inequality and using an incorrect inequality sign.

5. C; DOK Level: 1; Content Topic: A.3.b; **Practice:** MP.4.c

A closed circle on the graph of an inequality means that the number is included in the solution set. So, an inequality that is graphed on a number line using a closed circle must be either "less than or equal to" (≤) or "greater than or equal to" (≥). Therefore, only answer choice C would be graphed on a number line using a closed circle.

6. D; DOK Level: 2; Content Topics: Q.2.a, A.3.a, A.3.b; **Practices:** MP.1.a, MP.1.e, MP.4.a, MP.4.c

To graph the inequality, begin by solving it for x. First, multiply to eliminate the parentheses: $4x - 4 \geq 8$. Add 4 to each side of the inequality: $4x \geq 12$. Divide each side by 3: $x \geq 3$. The inequality sign means "greater than or equal to," so it is graphed using a closed circle on 3 with an arrow pointing to the right. Answer choice A represents the inequality $x \leq -1$. Answer choice B represents the inequality $x < 3$. Answer choice C represents the inequality $x > -1$.

7. B; DOK Level: 2; Content Topics: Q.2.a, A.3.a; **Practices:** MP.1.a, MP.1.e, MP.4.a

To solve the inequality, isolate the variable on one side of the inequality sign. First, subtract $5x$ from each side so that $-3x + 3 \leq 4$. Next, subtract 3 from each side so that $-3x \geq 1$. Divide each side by −3 and change the direction of the inequality symbol because you are dividing by a negative: $x \leq -\frac{1}{3}$. Answer choice A uses an incorrect inequality symbol. Answer choice C is the result of multiplying by −3 instead of dividing and failing to change the direction of the inequality symbol. Answer choice D is the result of multiplying by 3 instead of dividing by −3 and using an incorrect inequality symbol.

8. D; DOK Level: 1; Content Topic: A.3.b; **Practice:** MP.4.c

The closed circle on −1 shows that −1 is included in the solution set. The arrow points to the left, so the graph shows the inequality $x \leq -1$. The graph of answer choice A would show an open circle on 1 with an arrow pointing to the right. The graph of answer choice B would show a closed circle on −1 with an arrow pointing to the right. The graph of answer choice C would show an open circle on −1 with an arrow pointing to the left.

9. A; DOK Level: 2; Content Topics: Q.2.a, A.3.a; **Practices:** MP.1.a, MP.1.e, MP.4.a

To solve the inequality, isolate the variable on one side of the inequality symbol. Add 7 to each side of the inequality so that $2x \geq 22$. Next, divide each side by 2 so that $x \geq 11$. Answer choice B is the result of failing to divide by 2. Answer choice C is the result of changing the direction of the inequality symbol. Answer choice D is the result of both failing to divide by 2 and changing the direction of the inequality symbol.

Answer Key

10. A; DOK Level: 2; **Content Topics:** Q.2.a, A.3.a, A.3.d; **Practices:** MP.1.a, MP.1.e, MP.2.a, MP.4.b
Let x be the number. Four times the number, $4x$, added to 3 is greater than 2 less than five times the number, or $5x - 2$. So, the inequality is $4x + 3 > 5x - 2$.

11. C; DOK Level: 2; **Content Topics:** Q.2.a, Q.2.e, A.3.a, A.3.c, A.3.d; **Practices:** MP.1.a, MP.1.e, MP.2.a, MP.4.b
Let x be the number of minutes Stacy talks. Stacy pays \$12 per month plus \$0.10 per minute, or $12 + 0.1x$. She budgets \$25 per month for her cell phone bill, so the amount she pays must be less than or equal to \$25, which is represented by the inequality $12 + 0.1x \leq 25$. Subtract 12 from each side: $0.1x \leq 13$. Multiply each side by 10: $x \leq 130$.

12. C; DOK Level: 2; **Content Topics:** Q.2.a, Q.2.e, A.3.a, A.3.c, A.3.d; **Practices:** MP.1.a, MP.1.e, MP.2.a, MP.4.b
Let x be the price of 1 gallon of milk. Lydia purchased 3 gallons of milk, or $3x$. Her total was more than \$9, so $3x > 9$. Divide each side by 3: $x > 3$. The lowest possible price that is greater than \$3 is \$3.01. Answer choices A and B are less than \$3, so Lydia's total would be less than \$9. Answer choice D would result in a total greater than \$9, but \$3.50 is not the lowest possible price.

13. A; DOK Level: 2; **Content Topics:** Q.2.a, Q.2.e, Q.7.a, A.3.c, A.3.d; **Practices:** MP.1.a, MP.1.e, MP.2.a, MP.4.b
To find an average, divide the total by the number of values. Dylan's average score would be the total score from the three games divided by the number of games. If x is Dylan's score on the third game, his average is $\frac{122 + 118 + x}{3}$. Since Dylan wants his average to be at least 124, $\frac{122 + 118 + x}{3} \geq 124$. Multiply each side by 3: $122 + 118 + x \geq 372$. Combine like terms: $240 + x \geq 372$. Subtract 240 from each side $x \geq 132$.

14. $x > -1$; DOK Level: 1; **Content Topic:** A.3.b; **Practice:** MP.4.c
The open circle on -1 indicates that -1 is not part of the solution set. The arrow points to the right. So, $x > -1$.

15. $x \leq 2$; DOK Level: 1; **Content Topic:** A.3.b; **Practice:** MP.4.c
The closed circle on 2 indicates that 2 is part of the solution set. The arrow points to the left. So, $x \leq 2$.

16. $x > -3$; DOK Level: 2; **Content Topics:** Q.2.a, A.3.a; **Practices:** MP.1.a, MP.1.e, MP.4.a
Subtract 2 from each side so that $6x > 3x - 9$. Subtract $3x$ from each side: $3x > -9$. Divide: $x > -3$.

17. $y \geq -4$; DOK Level: 2; **Content Topics:** Q.2.a, A.3.a; **Practices:** MP.1.a, MP.1.e, MP.4.a
Add 2 to each side so that $4y \leq 7y + 12$. Subtract $7y$ from each side so that $-3y \leq 12$. Divide and change the direction of the inequality symbol because you are dividing by a negative number: $y \geq -4$.

18. $30c \leq 1{,}000$; DOK Level: 2; **Content Topics:** Q.2.a, Q.2.e, Q.7.a, A.3.c, A.3.d; **Practices:** MP.1.a, MP.1.e, MP.2.a, MP.4.b
Each cinder block weighs 30 pounds, so the total weight of the cinder blocks is $3c$. Since the maximum load is 1,000 pounds, $30c \leq 1{,}000$.

19. $3m > 18$; DOK Level: 2; **Content Topics:** Q.2.a, Q.2.e, A.3.c, A.3.d; **Practices:** MP.1.a, MP.1.e, MP.2.a, MP.4.b
Matthew will jog m miles. He will run twice as many miles as he jogs, so he will run $2m$ miles. The combined distance, $m + 2m$, must be more than 18, so $m + 2m > 18$, or $3m > 18$.

20. 16; DOK Level: 2; **Content Topics:** Q.2.a, Q.2.e, Q.4.a, A.3.c, A.3.d; **Practices:** MP.1.a, MP.1.e, MP.2.a, MP.4.b
The area of a rectangle is the product of its length (or height) and width, or lw. Since the mural will be 15 feet high, the area of the mural is $15w$. The mural can have an area of no more than 240 square feet, so $15w \leq 240$. Divide: $w \leq 16$. So the maximum width of the mural is 16 feet.

21. D; DOK Level: 2; **Content Topics:** Q.2.a, Q.2.e, Q.7.a, A.3.a, A.3.c, A.3.d; **Practices:** MP.1.a, MP.1.e, MP.2.a, MP.4.b
To find an average, divide the total by the number of values. Brit's average score would be the total score from her four quizzes divided by the number of quizzes. If x is Brit's score on the fourth test, her average is $\frac{45 + 38 + 47 + x}{4}$. Since Brit wants her average to be at least 44, $\frac{45 + 38 + 47 + x}{4} \geq 44$. Multiply each side by 4: $45 + 38 + 47 + x \geq 176$. Combine like terms: $130 + x \geq 176$. Subtract 130 from each side $x \geq 46$.

22. D; DOK Level: 2; **Content Topics:** Q.2.a, Q.2.e, A.3.c, A.3.d; **Practices:** MP.1.a, MP.1.e, MP.2.a, MP.4.b
Let x be the original number of T-shirts. The number of T-shirts remaining is equal to the number sold subtracted from the original number, or $x - 156$. Since the number of T-shirts remaining is less than 34, $x - 156 < 34$. Add 156 to each side: $x < 190$.

23. D; DOK Level: 2; **Content Topics:** Q.2.a, Q.2.e, A.3.a, A.3.c, A.3.d; **Practices:** MP.1.a, MP.1.e, MP.2.a, MP.4.b
Let x be Gabe's monthly sales. Gabe's total earnings are the sum of his base salary, \$1,500, and his commission, 3% of sales or $0.03x$. For Gabe to earn at least \$3,000, $1{,}500 + 0.03x \geq 3{,}000$. Subtract 1,500 from each side: $0.03x \geq 1{,}500$. Divide each side by 0.03: $x \geq 50{,}000$. Answer choices A, B, and C are the result of computational errors involving either the conversion of percent to decimal or division by a decimal.

24. A; DOK Level: 2; **Content Topics:** Q.2.a, Q.2.e, A.3.c, A.3.d; **Practices:** MP.1.a, MP.1.e, MP.2.a, MP.4.b
Let y be the number of points that Allen scored in the second round. He scored 10 points in the first round. In the second round, he scored less than 2 times the number of points that he scored in the first round, or less than $2(10)$. So, $y < 20$. Answer choices B and D represent the result of failing to multiply by 2 and/or using an incorrect inequality sign. Answer choice C represents "less than or equal to 2 times the number of points he scored in the first round."

25. **D**; **DOK Level:** 2; **Content Topics:** Q.2.a, Q.2.e, A.3.a, A.3.c, A.3.d; **Practices:** MP.1.a, MP.1.e, MP.2.a, MP.4.b
Let x be the number of boxes of noodles. The first box costs $1.60. Each additional box costs $0.95, so the cost of the additional boxes is $0.95(x − 1)$. The total cost of the boxes of noodles is $1.60 + 0.95(x − 1)$. Therefore, the maximum number of boxes of noodles Jax can buy with $4.50 is given by $1.60 + 0.95(x − 1) ≤ 4.50$. Multiply to eliminate the parentheses: $1.60 + 0.95x − 0.95 ≤ 4.50$. Combine like terms: $0.95x + 0.65 ≤ 4.50$. Subtract 0.65 from each side so that $0.95x ≤ 3.85$. Divide: $x ≤ 4.05$. Since the number of boxes must be a whole number, the maximum number of boxes that Jax can buy is 4.

26. **B**; **DOK Level:** 2; **Content Topics:** Q.2.a, Q.2.e, A.3.a, A.3.c, A.3.d; **Practices:** MP.1.a, MP.1.e, MP.2.a, MP.4.b
Let x be the price of the boots. Therefore, the price of the jacket is $2\frac{1}{2}x$ or $2.5x$. The sum of the price of the boots and the price of the jacket cannot be more than $157.50, so $x + 2.5x ≤ 157.50$. Combine like terms: $3.5x ≤ 157.50$. Divide each side by 3.5: $x ≤ 45$.

27. **A**; **DOK Level:** 2; **Content Topics:** Q.2.a, Q.2.e, A.3.a, A.3.c, A.3.d; **Practices:** MP.1.a, MP.1.e, MP.2.a, MP.4.b
Let x be the number of yards Michael swam on Monday. On Tuesday, Michael swam 400 less than $3x$, or $3x − 400$. Over the two days, Michael swam $x + (3x − 400)$ yards. The number of yards Michael swam over the two days was less than 2,000, so $x + (3x − 400) < 2,000$. Combine like terms: $4x − 400 < 2,000$. Add 400 to each side: $4x < 2,400$. Divide: $x < 600$. Since Michael swam less than 600 yards on Monday, he could have swam 500 yards.

28. **B**; **DOK Level:** 2; **Content Topics:** Q.2.a, Q.2.e, Q.7.a, A.3.a, A.3.c, A.3.d; **Practices:** MP.1.a, MP.1.e, MP.2.a, MP.4.b
To find an average, divide the total by the number of values. Since Jose has the same number of at-bats in each year, his combined batting average can be found by computing the average of his batting averages from the two years. If x is Jose's batting average this year, his combined batting average for the two years is $\frac{0.266 + x}{2}$. Since Jose wants a combined batting average greater than 0.300, $\frac{0.266 + x}{2} ≥ 0.300$. Multiply each side by 2: $0.266 + x ≥ 0.600$. Subtract 0.266 from each side $x ≥ 0.334$. Answer choice A is the average of 0.266 and 0.300. Answer choices C and D both would result in a combined batting average greater than 0.300 but are not the minimum batting average that Jose could have.

29. **D**; **DOK Level:** 2; **Content Topics:** Q.2.a, Q.2.e, A.3.c, A.3.d; **Practices:** MP.1.a, MP.1.e, MP.2.a, MP.4.b
Let x be the price of the magazine. There is a 6% tax on her purchase, so the total amount she spends is $(8.99 + x) + 0.06 \cdot (8.99 + x)$, or $1.06(8.99 + x)$. The total amount that Elena spends on the book and the magazine must be less than or equal to $15, so the inequality $1.06(8.99 + x) ≤ 15$ represents the maximum price of the magazine.

30. **B**; **DOK Level:** 2; **Content Topics:** Q.2.a, Q.2.e, A.3.a, A.3.c, A.3.d; **Practices:** MP.1.a, MP.1.e, MP.2.a, MP.4.b
Let x be the number of students enrolled in the class last year. Therefore, 30 fewer than twice as many as last year can be represented by the expression $2x − 30$. Since the enrollment cannot exceed 100, $2x − 30 ≤ 100$. Add 30 to each side: $2x ≤ 130$. Divide by 2: $x ≤ 65$. Answer choice A is the result of subtracting 30 from each side instead of adding. Answer choice C is the result of subtracting 30 from 100. Answer choice D is the maximum enrollment this year.

31. **D**; **DOK Level:** 2; **Content Topics:** Q.2.a, Q.2.e, A.3.a, A.3.c, A.3.d; **Practices:** MP.1.a, MP.1.e, MP.2.a, MP.4.b
Let x be the amount each friend paid. Since the three friends split the bill evenly, $3x$ is the total amount that the three friends paid. The bill was less than $45, so $3x < 45$. Divide: $x < 15$. The greatest amount less than $15 is $14.99, so the greatest amount each friend could have paid is $14.99.

32. **C**; **DOK Level:** 2; **Content Topics:** Q.2.a, Q.2.e, Q.7.a, A.3.a, A.3.c, A.3.d; **Practices:** MP.1.a, MP.1.e, MP.2.a, MP.4.b
To find an average, divide the total by the number of values. Leah's average score is the total of her scores divided by the number of scores. If x is Leah's score on her fifth test, her average is $\frac{78 + 85 + 82 + 74 + x}{5}$. Since Leah wants an average score of at least 80%, $\frac{78 + 85 + 82 + 74 + x}{5} ≥ 80$. Multiply each side by 5: $78 + 85 + 82 + 74 + x ≥ 400$. Combine like terms: $319 + x ≥ 400$. Subtract 319 from each side: $x ≥ 81$. Leah needs a score of at least 81 on the fifth test. Answer choice D would give Leah an average score greater than 80, but is not the minimum score she needs. Answer choices A and B would give Leah an average score of less than 80.

LESSON 11, *pp. 98–101*

1. **D**; **DOK Level:** 1; **Content Topic:** A.5.a; **Practice:** MP.1.a
Point G is located 3 units to the right of the origin, which is represented by a positive number, and 3 units below the origin, which is represented by a negative number. So point G is located at $(3, −3)$. The ordered pair $(3, −4)$ describes the location 3 units to the right of the origin and 4 units below the origin. The ordered pair $(4, −3)$ describes the location 4 units to the right of the origin and 3 units below the origin. The ordered pair $(−3, 3)$ describes the location 3 units to the left of the origin and 3 units above the origin.

2. **A**; **DOK Level:** 2; **Content Topics:** Q.2.a, A.5.a; **Practices:** MP.1.a, MP.1.e
Point G is located at 3 units to the right of the origin and 3 units below the origin, at $(3, −3)$. To translate the point up 1 unit, add 1 to the y-coordinate, which is $−3$: $−3 + 1 = −2$. To translate the point left 2 units, subtract 2 from the x-coordinate, which is 3: $3 − 2 = 1$. So, the new location of point G is $(1, −2)$. The point $(−2, 1)$ confuses the x- and y-coordinates of the translated point. The point $(4, −5)$ is 1 unit right and 2 units down from point G. The point $(1, −4)$ incorrectly moves 1 unit down and 2 units left from point G.

Answer Key

UNIT 3 (continued)

3. A; DOK Level: 1; Content Topic: A.5.a; Practice: MP.1.a
Point D is located 2 units to the right of the origin and 5 units above the origin. Both of these directions are represented by positive numbers, so point D is located at (2, 5). The ordered pair (5, 2) describes the location 5 units to the right of the origin and 2 units above the origin. The ordered pair (−5, 2) describes the location 5 units to the left of the origin and 2 units above the origin. The ordered pair (−2, −5) describes the location 2 units to the left of the origin and 5 units below the origin.

4. D; DOK Level: 2; Content Topic: A.5.a; Practices: MP.1.a, MP.1.d, MP.3.a
The missing point will be on the same vertical line as point C, so the point will be the same distance from the y-axis and will have the same x-coordinate as point C. Point C is located 1 unit to the right of the origin, so its x-coordinate is 1. The missing point will be on the same horizontal line as point B, so the point will be the same distance from the x-axis and will have the same y-coordinate as point C. Point B is located 5 units below the origin, so its y-coordinate is −5. Therefore, the missing point is located at (1, −5). The point (1, 5) is located above point C. The point (−5, −1) is located on the left side of the rectangle, between points A and B. The point (−5, 1) is the location of point A.

5. D; DOK Level: 2; Content Topic: A.5.a; Practices: MP.1.a, MP.1.d, MP.3.a
A rectangle has two sets of parallel sides. In order for the missing point and point C to form a side parallel with the side formed by points E and F, the relationship between the missing point and point C must be the same as the relationship between points E and F. Point E is 3 units below and 2 units to the left of point F. So, the missing point is 3 units below and 2 units to the left of point C. Point C is located at (1, 1), so the missing point is located at (−1, −2). The remaining points do not form sides with point C that are parallel to the side formed by points E and F.

6. A; DOK Level: 2; Content Topics: Q.2.a, A.5.a; Practices: MP.1.a, MP.1.e
Point D is located 2 units to the right of the origin and 5 units above the origin, at (2, 5). To translate the point 5 units down, subtract 5 from the y-coordinate, which is 5 − 5 = 0. To translate the point right 2 units, add 2 to the x-coordinate, which is 2 + 2 = 4. So, the new location of point D is (4, 0). The point (0, 4) confuses the x- and y-coordinates of the translated point. The point (−3, 3) is 5 units left and 2 units down from point D. The point (0, 0) is 2 units left and 5 units down from point D.

7. D; DOK Level: 2; Content Topics: Q.2.a, A.5.a; Practices: MP.1.a, MP.1.e
Point C is located 1 unit to the right of the origin and 1 unit above the origin, at (1, 1). To translate the point 2 units down, subtract 2 from the y-coordinate, which is 1 − 2 = −1. The x-coordinate does not change. So, the new location of point C is (1, −1). The point (−1, 1) confuses the x- and y-coordinates of the translated point, or is the result of translating point C 2 units left. The point (1, 3) is 2 units up from point C. The point (3, 1) confuses the x- and y-coordinates of the point 2 units up from point C, or is the result of translating point C two units right.

8. C; DOK Level: 1; Content Topic: A.5.a; Practices: MP.1.a, MP.1.e
Quadrant 2 is the top left quadrant of the coordinate grid. Quadrant 2 is to the left of the y-axis and above the x-axis, so points in quadrant 2 have a negative x-coordinate and a positive y-coordinate. So, the point (−2, 5) is in quadrant 2. The point (2, 3) is in quadrant 1, the top right quadrant. The point (−4, −3) is in quadrant 3, the bottom left quadrant. The point (1, −6) is in quadrant 4, the bottom right quadrant.

9. B; DOK Level: 2; Content Topics: Q.2.a, A.5.a; Practices: MP.1.a, MP.1.e
Frank started at the point 4 units to the right of the origin and 3 units below the origin, at (4, −3). To move 1 unit down, subtract 1 from the y-coordinate, which is −3 − 1 = −4. To move right 2 units, add 2 to the x-coordinate, which is 4 + 2 = 6. So, Frank's new location is (6, −4). The point (−4, 6) confuses the x- and y-coordinates of the translated point. The point (3, −1) is 1 unit left and 2 units up from Frank's starting point. The point (−1, 3) confuses the x- and y-coordinates of the point.

10. C; DOK Level: 2; Content Topics: Q.2.a, A.5.a; Practices: MP.1.a, MP.1.e
To show a translation of 3 units down, subtract 3 from the y-coordinate. The y-coordinate is −6, so the y-coordinate of the translated point is −6 − 3 = −9. There is no change right or left, so the x-coordinate is still x and the translated point is located at (x, −9).

11. B; DOK Level: 2; Content Topics: Q.2.a, A.5.a; Practices: MP.1.a, MP.1.e
Point M is located 3 units to the left of the origin and 2 units below the origin, at (−3, −2). To translate the point 2 units up, add 2 to the y-coordinate, which is −2 + 2 = 0. To translate the point right 3 units, add 3 to the x-coordinate, which is −3 + 3 = 0. So, the new location of point M is (0, 0). The point (−1, −1) is 1 unit up and 2 units to the right of point M. The point (0, −1) is 1 unit up and 3 units to the right of point M. The point (0, −5) is 3 units down and 3 units to the right of point M.

12. C; DOK Level: 2; Content Topics: Q.2.a, A.5.a; Practices: MP.1.a, MP.1.e
Point K is located 1 unit to the right of the origin and 2 units above the origin, at (1, 2). Point M is located 3 units to the left of the origin and 2 units below the origin, at (−3, −2). Moving from point M to point K, the x-coordinate increases by 1 − (−3) = 4 and the y-coordinate increases by 2 − (−2) = 4. Both of these changes are represented by positive numbers, so the translation moved the point 4 units up and 4 units to the right. A translation of 2 units up and 3 units to the right would put the point at (0, 0). A translation of 3 units up and 3 units to the right would put the point at (0, 1). A translation of 5 units up and 4 units to the right would put the point at (1, 3).

13. A; DOK Level: 3; Content Topics: Q.2.a, A.5.a; **Practices:** MP.1.a, MP.1.e

Each side of the square is 4 units long. So, the center of the square is 2 vertical units and 2 horizontal units from each corner of the square. Starting from point M, move 2 units up and 2 units to the right to find the center. The center of the square, point N, is located 1 unit to the left of the origin and 0 units above or below the origin, at $(-1, 0)$. To translate the point 1 unit up, add 1 to the y-coordinate, which is $0 + 1 = 1$. To translate the point 2 units to the left, subtract 2 units from the x-coordinate, which is $-1 - 2 = -3$. So, the new location of point N is $(-3, 1)$. The point $(0, -2)$ is located 1 unit to the right and 2 units below the original point. The point $(1, 1)$ is located 2 units to the right and 1 unit above the original point.

14. C; DOK Level: 1; Content Topic: A.5.a; **Practices:** MP.1.a, MP.1.e

Quadrant 3 is the bottom left quadrant of the coordinate grid. Quadrant 3 is to the left of the y-axis and below the x-axis, so points in quadrant 3 have a negative x-coordinate and a negative y-coordinate. So, the point $(-3, -2)$ is in quadrant 3. The point $(2, 3)$ is in quadrant 1, the top right quadrant. The point $(-2, 3)$ is in quadrant 2, the top left quadrant. The point $(3, -2)$ is in quadrant 4, the bottom right quadrant.

15. C; DOK Level: 2; Content Topic: A.5.a; **Practices:** MP.1.a, MP.1.d, MP.3.a

The missing point will be on the same vertical line as the top left point, so the point will be the same distance from the y-axis and will have the same x-coordinate as that point. The top left point is located 3 units to the left of the origin, so its x-coordinate is -3. The missing point will be on the same horizontal line as the bottom right point, so the point will be the same distance from the x-axis and will have the same y-coordinate as that point. The bottom right point is located 5 units below the origin, so its y-coordinate is -5. Therefore, the missing point is located at $(-3, -5)$. The point $(4, -3)$ is located on the right side of the rectangle, between the two points shown. The point $(-3, -4)$ has the correct x-coordinate but the y-coordinate is incorrect and fails to complete the rectangle. The point $(-5, -3)$ confuses the x- and y-coordinates of the correct point.

16. D; DOK Level: 2; Content Topic: A.5.a; **Practice:** MP.1.a

If line segments were drawn to connect the existing points on the coordinate grid, there would be a horizontal line segment 2 units below the origin, a vertical line segment 4 units to the right of the origin, and a diagonal line segment moving downward from left to right. The vertical line and horizontal line segments form a right angle, making the triangle a right triangle. The triangle is not equilateral because the horizontal line segment is 7 units long and the vertical line segment is 3 units long. The triangle is not obtuse because none of the angles is larger than a right angle. The triangle is not isosceles because the diagonal line segment is not the same length as either of the other two line segments.

17. B; DOK Level: 2; Content Topic: A.5.a; **Practices:** MP.1.a, MP.1.d, MP.3.a

Moving a point up or down changes its y-coordinate. To translate a point down 2 units, subtract 2 units from the original y-coordinate. So, to find the original location of a point that has been translated 2 units down, add 2 units to the final y-coordinate.

18. C; DOK Level: 2; Content Topic: A.5.a; **Practices:** MP.1.a, MP.1.d

Point R is located 2 units to the right of the origin, which is represented by a positive number. So, its x-coordinate is 2. Point T is located 5 units below the origin, which is represented by a negative number. So, its y-coordinate is -5. Therefore, point V is located at $(2, -5)$.

19. A; DOK Level: 3; Content Topics: Q.2.a, A.5.a; **Practices:** MP.1.a, MP.1.e

Point U is located 4 units to the right of the origin, which is represented by a positive number, and 5 units below the origin, which is represented by a negative number. So, point U is located at $(4, -5)$. To find the new x-coordinate, substitute 4 for x in $x - 5$: $4 - 5 = -1$. To find the new y-coordinate, substitute -5 for y in $y + 3$: $-5 + 3 = -2$. So, the ending location of point U is $(-1, -2)$.

20. A; DOK Level: 1; Content Topic: A.5.a; **Practice:** MP.1.a

Point X, $(-2, -1)$, has a negative x-coordinate and a negative y-coordinate. So, moving 6 units to the right of -2 gives an x-coordinate of $-2 + 6 = 4$ and moving 3 units down from -1 gives a y-coordinate of $-1 + (-3) = -4$.

21. D; DOK Level: 2; Content Topic: A.5.a; **Practices:** MP.1.a, MP.1.e

Point W is located at $(-2, 2)$, so expanding it 1 unit left and 1 unit up gives coordinates of $(-3, 3)$. The coordinate $(2, 3)$ is where point Z is located after it moves 1 unit right and 1 unit up. The coordinate $(-1, 1)$ is where point W is located after it moves 1 unit right and 1 unit down. The coordinate $(2, -2)$ is where point Y is located after it moves 1 unit right and 1 unit down.

22. B; DOK Level: 2; Content Topics: Q.2.a, A.5.a; **Practices:** MP.1.a, MP.1.e

Point Z lies in Quadrant 1 (the upper right) since it has both positive x- and y-coordinates. Moving in a counterclockwise manner, Point W lies in Quadrant 2, the top left quadrant. Quadrant 2 is to the left of the y-axis and above the x-axis, so points in quadrant 2 have a negative x-coordinate and a positive y-coordinate. Point X lies in Quadrant 3, located in the bottom left quadrant of the coordinate grid. Quadrant 3 is to the left of the y-axis and below the x-axis, so points in quadrant 3 have a negative x-coordinate and a negative y-coordinate. Point Y lies in Quadrant 4, the bottom right quadrant of the coordinate grid. Quadrant 4 is to the right of the y-axis and below the x-axis, so points in quadrant 4 have a positive x-coordinate and a negative y-coordinate.

23. A; DOK Level: 2; Content Topics: Q.2.a, A.5.a; **Practices:** MP.1.a, MP.1.e

Point Z moves 3 units to the right, which means its x-coordinate changes while the y-coordinate remains the same. So, its new location is $(4, 2)$. The other coordinates occur with moves 3 units to the right of the other points, W, X, and Y.

Answer Key

UNIT 3 (continued)

LESSON 12, *pp. 102–105*

1. B; **DOK Level:** 1; **Content Topics:** Q.2.a, Q.2.e, A.1.b; **Practices:** MP.1.a, MP.1.e, MP.4.a
If points on a graph satisfy an equation, then they make the equation true. Substitute the values for x and y for each ordered pair into each equation. Start with the ordered pair $(−3, 3)$. For Choice A, $x − y = 0$, $−3 − (3) = −6$. Since $−6 ≠ 0$, the points do not satisfy the equation $x − y = 0$. Similarly, for Choice C, $x − y = −1$, $−3 − (3) = −6$. Since $−6 ≠ 1$, the points do not satisfy the equation $x − y = −1$. For Choice D, $x + y = 1$, $−3 + (3) = 0$. Since $0 ≠ 1$, the points do not satisfy the equation $x + y = 1$. However, for Choice B, $x + y = 0$, since $−3 + (3) = 0$, the points satisfy the equation $x + y = 0$.

2. C; **DOK Level:** 2; **Content Topics:** Q.2.a, Q.2.e, A.1.b; **Practices:** MP.1.a, MP.1.e, MP.4.a
Use the equation $d = \sqrt{(x_2 − x_1)^2 + (y_2 − y_1)^2}$, where $x_2 = 2$, $x_1 = −3$, $y_2 = −2$, and $y_1 = 3$. Substitute the values and solve.
$d = \sqrt{(2 − (−3))^2 + (−2 − 3)^2}$
$d = \sqrt{(5)^2 + (−5)^2}$
$d = \sqrt{25 + 25}$
$d = \sqrt{50}$
$d ≈ 7.1$

3. C; **DOK Level:** 1; **Content Topics:** Q.2.a, Q.2.e, A.1.b; **Practices:** MP.1.a, MP.1.e, MP.4.a
If an ordered pair is a solution to an equation, then it makes the equation true. Substitute the values for x and y for each ordered pair into the equation. For Choice A $(4, 8)$, $\frac{1}{2}x = \frac{1}{2}(4) = 2$. Since $2 ≠ 8$, $(4, 8)$ is not a solution of the equation. For Choice B $(1, 3)$, $\frac{1}{2}x = \frac{1}{2}(1) = \frac{1}{2}$. Since $3 ≠ \frac{1}{2}$, $(1, 3)$ is not a solution of the equation. For Choice D $(1, 2)$, $\frac{1}{2}x = \frac{1}{2}(1) = \frac{1}{2}$. Since $2 ≠ \frac{1}{2}$, $(1, 2)$ is not a solution of the equation. For Choice C $(4, 2)$, $\frac{1}{2}x = \frac{1}{2}(4) = 2$. Since $2 = 2$, $(4, 2)$ is a solution of the equation.

4. A; **DOK Level:** 2; **Content Topics:** Q.2.a, Q.2.e, A.1.b; **Practices:** MP.1.a, MP.1.d, MP.1.e, MP.2.c, MP.4.a
Since $(2, y)$ is a solution to $−x = y + 1$, substitute 2 for x and then solve for y: $−2 = y + 1$. To solve for y, subtract 1 from both sides of the equation: $−2 − 1 = y$, so $−3 = y$.

5. C; **DOK Level:** 2; **Content Topics:** Q.2.a, Q.2.e, A.1.b; **Practices:** MP.1.a, MP.1.d, MP.1.e, MP.2.c, MP.4.a
Since $(x, −3)$ is a solution of $2x + 2y = −8$, substitute $−3$ for y and then solve for x: $2x + 2(−3) = −8$. Simplify: $2x − 6 = −8$. To solve for x, begin by adding 6 to both sides of the equation: $2x = −8 + 6$, so $2x = −2$. Divide both sides of the equation by 2. $x = −1$.

6. D; **DOK Level:** 1; **Content Topics:** Q.2.a, Q.2.e, A.1.b; **Practices:** MP.1.a, MP.1.e, MP.4.a
If a graph of an equation passes through a point on the coordinate grid, then the ordered pair makes the equation true. Substitute the values for x and y for each ordered pair into the equation. For Choice A, $(1, −1)$, $4 − 3x = 4 − 3(1) = 4 − 3 = 1$. Since $1 ≠ −1$, the point does not satisfy the equation $y = 4 − 3x$. For Choice B, $(4, 8)$, $4 − 3x = 4 − 3(4) = 4 − 12 = −8$. Since $−8 ≠ 8$, the point does not satisfy the equation $y = 4 − 3x$. For Choice C, $(3, 1)$, $4 − 3x = 4 − 3(3) = 4 − 9 = −5$. Since $−5 ≠ 1$, the point does not satisfy the equation $y = 4 − 3x$. For Choice D, $(2, −2)$, $4 − 3x = 4 − 3(2) = 4 − 6 = −2$. Since $−2 = −2$, the point satisfies the equation $y = 4 − 3x$.

7. C; **DOK Level:** 2; **Content Topics:** Q.2.a, Q.2.e, A.1.b; **Practices:** MP.1.a, MP.1.d, MP.1.e, MP.2.c, MP.4.a
Since $(x, 1)$ is a solution of $2x − y = 5$, substitute 1 for y and then solve for x: $2x − 1 = 5$. To solve for x, begin by adding 1 to both sides of the equation: $2x = 5 + 1$, so $2x = 6$. Divide both sides of the equation by 2. $x = 3$.

8. C; **DOK Level:** 2; **Content Topics:** Q.2.a, Q.2.e, A.1.b, A.5.a; **Practices:** MP.1.a, MP.1.d, MP.1.e, MP.4.a
For each graph, find a point through which the line passes. Then check if that point satisfies the equation $x + 2y = 2$. Graph A passes through the point $(3, −3)$. Substitute: $3 + 2(−3) = 3 − 6 = −3$. So, the first graph does not show the equation $x + 2y = 2$. Graph B passes through $(0, 0)$. Substitute: $0 + 2(0) = 0$. So, the second graph does not show the equation $x + 2y = 2$. Graph D passes through $(0, 2)$. Substitute: $0 + 2(2) = 0 + 4 = 4$. So, the fourth graph does not show the equation. Graph C passes through $(0, 1)$. Substitute: $0 + 2(1) = 0 + 2 = 2$. The graph may show the equation $x + 2y = 2$. Check another point. The graph also passes through $(2, 0)$. Substitute: $2 + 2(0) = 2$. Since two points on the line satisfy the equation, the graph shows the equation $x + 2y = 2$.

9. $y = −\frac{1}{2}x − 2$, $y = \frac{3}{2}x − 2$, $y = \frac{1}{2}x + 2$; **DOK Level:** 2; **Content Topics:** Q.2.a, Q.2.e, A.1.b, A.5.a; **Practices:** MP.1.a, MP.1.d, MP.1.e, MP.4.a
Find a point through which each lines passes. Then check the equation that each line satisfies. Side PR passes through the point $(−2, −1)$. This point satisfies the equation $y = −\frac{1}{2}x − 2$ because $−\frac{1}{2}(−2) − 2 = 1 − 2 = −1$. Side QR passes through the point $(2, 1)$. This point satisfies the equation $y = \frac{3}{2}x − 2$ because $\frac{3}{2}(2) − 2 = 3 − 2 = 1$. Side PQ passes through the point $(−2, 1)$. This point satisfies the equation $y = \frac{1}{2}x + 2$ because $\frac{1}{2}(−2) + 2 = 1$.

10. (4,4), (0, −2), (−4,0); **DOK Level:** 2; **Content Topics:** A.5.a, A.5.d; **Practices:** MP.1.a, MP.1.e, MP.4.a
The solution of a system of linear equations is the point at which the graphs of the equations intersect. Sides PQ and QR intersect at $(4, 4)$. These sides lie on the lines $y = \frac{1}{2}x + 2$ and $y = \frac{3}{2}x − 2$, so $(4, 4)$ is the solution of that pair of equations. Sides PR and QR intersect at $(0, −2)$. These sides lie on the lines $y = −\frac{1}{2}x − 2$ and $y = \frac{3}{2}x − 2$, so $(0, −2)$ is the solution of that pair of equations. Sides PQ and PR intersect at $(−4, 0)$. These sides lie on the lines $y = \frac{1}{2}x + 2$ and $y = −\frac{1}{2}x − 2$, so $(−4, 0)$ is the solution of that pair of equations.

11. **(0,2) and (-6, -1); (2,1) and (6,7); (2,-3) and (8, -6);** **DOK Level:** 1; **Content Topics:** Q.2.a, Q.2.e, A.1.b; **Practices:** MP.1.a, MP.1.e, MP.4.a

If a graph of an equation passes through a point on the coordinate grid, then the ordered pair makes the equation true. Substitute the values for x and y for each ordered pair into each equation. The points $(0, 2)$ and $(-6, -1)$ make the equation $y = \frac{1}{2}x + 2$ true, because $\frac{1}{2}(0) + 2 = 0 + 2 = 2$ and $\frac{1}{2}(-6) + 2 = -3 + 2 = -1$. The points $(2, 1)$ and $(6, 7)$ make the equation $y = \frac{3}{2}x - 2$ true, because $\frac{3}{2}(2) - 2 = 3 - 2 = 1$ and $\frac{3}{2}(6) - 2 = 9 - 2 = 7$. The points $(2, -3)$ and $(8, -6)$ make the equation $y = -\frac{1}{2}x - 2$ true because $-\frac{1}{2}(2) - 2 = -1 - 2 = -3$ and $-\frac{1}{2}(8) - 2 = -4 - 2 = -6$.

12. **D**; **DOK Level:** 2; **Content Topics:** Q.2.a, Q.2.e, A.1.b; **Practices:** MP.1.a, MP.1.e, MP.4.a

Use the equation $d = \sqrt{(x_2 - x_1)^2 + (y_2 - y_1)^2}$, where $x_2 = 4$, $x_1 = 0$, $y_2 = 7$, and $y_1 = 0$. Substitute the values and solve.
$d = \sqrt{(4 - 0)^2 + (7 - 0)^2}$
$d = \sqrt{(4)^2 + (7)^2}$
$d = \sqrt{16 + 49}$
$d = \sqrt{65}$
$d \approx 8.1$

13. **A**; **DOK Level:** 2; **Content Topics:** Q.2.a, Q.2.e, A.1.b; **Practices:** MP.1.a, MP.1.e, MP.4.a

Use the equation $d = \sqrt{(x_2 - x_1)^2 + (y_2 - y_1)^2}$, where $x_2 = -3$, $x_1 = -2$, $y_2 = -8$, and $y_1 = -5$. Substitute the values and solve.
$d = \sqrt{(-3 - (-2))^2 + (-8 - (-5))^2}$
$d = \sqrt{(-1)^2 + (-3)^2}$
$d = \sqrt{1 + 9}$
$d = \sqrt{10}$
$d \approx 3.2$

14. **A**; **DOK Level:** 1; **Content Topics:** Q.2.a, Q.2.e, A.1.b; **Practices:** MP.1.a, MP.1.e, MP.4.a

If a graph of an equation passes through a point on the coordinate grid, then the ordered pair makes the equation true. Substitute the values for x and y for each ordered pair into the equation. For choice A, $(1, -3)$, $-2(1) - 1 = -2 - 1 = -3$. So, the graph passes through $(1, -3)$. Test the other points. For choice B, $(1, -2)$, since $-2(1) - 1 = -3$, and $-3 \neq -2$, the line does not pass through $(1, -2)$. For choice C, $(0, 1)$, since $-2(0) - 1 = 0$, $0 - 1 = -1$, and $-1 \neq 1$, the line does not pass through $(0, 1)$. For choice D, $(-1, 2)$, since $-2(-1) - 1 = 1$, $2 - 1 = 1$, and $1 \neq 2$, the line does not pass through $(-1, 2)$.

15. **B**; **DOK Level:** 2; **Content Topics:** Q.2.a, Q.2.e, A.1.b; **Practices:** MP.1.a, MP.1.e, MP.4.a

Use the equation $d = \sqrt{(x_2 - x_1)^2 + (y_2 - y_1)^2}$, where $x_2 = -4$, $x_1 = -3$, $y_2 = 5$, and $y_1 = -2$.
$d = \sqrt{(-4 - (-3))^2 + (5 - (-2))^2}$
$d = \sqrt{(-1)^2 + 7^2}$
$d = \sqrt{1 + 49}$
$d = \sqrt{50}$
$d \approx 7.1$

16. **A**; **DOK Level:** 2; **Content Topics:** Q.2.a, Q.2.e, A.1.b, A.2.d, A.5.d; **Practices:** MP.1.a, MP.1.e, MP.4.a

The solution of a set of linear equations is the point at which the graphs of the equations intersect. Begin by finding the point of intersection of each pair of graphs and testing that point in each equation. In answer choice A, the graphs intersect at the point $(1, 0)$. For $2x - y = 2$, $2(1) - 0 = 2$. For $y = -x + 1$, $-1 + 1 = 0$. So, the point $(1, 0)$ lies on both lines. In answer choice B, the graphs intersect at the point $(0, 1)$. For $2x - y = 2$, $2(0) - 1 = -1$. Since $-1 \neq 2$, the point $(0, 1)$ does not lie on the line $2x - y = 2$, so $(0, 1)$ cannot be the point of intersection of the graphs. In answer choice C, the lines intersect at the point $(0, -1)$. For $2x - y = 2$, $2(0) - (-1) = 0 + 1 = 1$. Since $1 \neq 2$, the point $(0, -1)$ does not lie on the line $2x - y = 2$, so $(0, -1)$ cannot be the point of intersection of the graphs. In answer choice D, the lines intersect at $(-1, -1)$. For $2x - y = 2$, $2(-1) - (-1) = -2 + 1 = -1$. Since $-1 \neq 2$, the point $(-1, -1)$ does not lie on the line $2x - y = 2$, so $(-1, -1)$ cannot be the point of intersection of the graphs.

17. **C**; **DOK Level:** 2; **Content Topics:** Q.2.a, Q.2.e, A.1.b, A.5.d; **Practices:** MP.1.a, MP.1.e, MP.4.a

To identify which equation is shown in the graph, determine whether the point $(4, 48)$ makes the equation true. Substitute the values for x and y for the ordered pair into each equation. For choice A $12x + y = 0$, $12(4) + 48 = 48 + 48 = 96$. Since $96 \neq 0$, the line $12x + y = 0$ does not pass through the point $(4, 48)$. For choice B $4x - 5y = 0$, $4(4) - 5(48) = 16 - 240 = -224$. Since $-224 \neq 0$, the line $4x - 5y = 0$ does not pass through the point $(4, 48)$. For choice C $12x - y = 0$, $12(4) - 48 = 48 - 48 = 0$. So, the line $12x - y = 0$ passes through the point $(4, 48)$. Finally, for choice D $4x + 5y = 0$, $4(12) + 5(48) = 48 + 240 = 288$. Since $288 \neq 0$, the line $4x + 5y = 0$ does not pass through the point $(4, 48)$. Therefore, since only the line $12x - y = 0$ passes through the given point, that is the equation of the *Revenue* line.

18. **C**; **DOK Level:** 2; **Content Topics:** Q.2.a, Q.2.e, A.1.b, A.5.a, A.5.d; **Practices:** MP.1.a, MP.1.e, MP.4.a

To identify which equation is shown in the graph, identify a point on the graph and determine which equation is true for that point. Since Rachel's start-up expenses total $150, the line passes through the point $(0, 150)$. Substitute the values for x and y for the ordered pair into each equation. For choice A, $x - 2y = 150$, $0 - 2(150) = 0 - 300 = -300$. Since $-300 \neq 150$, the line $x - 2y = 150$ does not pass through the point $(0, 150)$. For choice B, $x + 2y = 150$, $0 + 2(150) = 0 + 300 = 300$. Since $300 \neq 150$, the line $x + 2y = 150$ does not pass through the point $(0, 150)$. For choice C, $2x - y = -150$, $2(0) - 150 = 0 - 150 = -150$. So, the line $2x - y = -150$ passes through the point $(0, 150)$. Finally, for choice D, $2x - y = 150$, $2(0) - 150 = 0 - 150 = -150$. Since $-150 \neq 150$, the line $2x - y = 150$ does not pass through the point $(0, 150)$. Therefore, since only the line $2x - y = -150$ passes through the given point, that is the equation of the *Expenses* line.

Answer Key

UNIT 3 (continued)

19. B; DOK Level: 2; **Content Topics:** Q.2.a, Q.2.e, A.1.b, A.2.d, A.5.a, A.5.d; **Practices:** MP.1.a, MP.1.e, MP.3.a, MP.4.a

The number of pounds of fudge is the x-value of the ordered pair that represents the solution of the set of equations. The solution of a set of equations is the intersection of the graphs of the equations. The revenue and expense lines intersect near the point (15, 180). The x-coordinate of the point of intersection is 15, so Rachel must sell 15 pounds of fudge to reach the breakeven point. Answer choice A (18) is the result of misreading the y-coordinate of the point of intersection. Answer choices C (10) and D (8) are the result of misreading the graph or not understanding how to find the solution of a set of equations.

LESSON 13, pp. 106–109

1. D; DOK Level: 2; **Content Topics:** Q.2.a, Q.2.e, Q.6.c, A.1.i, A.5.a, A.5.b; **Practices:** MP.1.a, MP.1.b, MP.1.e, MP.3.a, MP.4.a

To find the slope of line G, use the formula for slope:
$$m = \frac{y_2 - y_1}{x_2 - x_1}$$
Next, identify points on the line from the grid: (−2, 1) and (4, 4) and insert them into the slope formula:
$$m = \frac{4 - 1}{4 - (-2)} = \frac{3}{6} = \frac{1}{2}$$

2. C; DOK Level: 2; **Content Topics:** Q.2.a, Q.2.e, Q.6.c, A.1.i, A.5.b, A.5.c, A.6.a, A.6.b; **Practices:** MP.1.a, MP.1.b, MP.1.e, MP.3.a, MP.4.a

The formula for slope is $y = mx + b$. The y-intercept is 2, so, using the slope of $\frac{1}{2}$, the equation of the line is $y = \frac{1}{2}x + 2$.

3. A; DOK Level: 2; **Content Topics:** Q.2.a, Q.2.e, Q.6.c, A.1.i; **Practices:** MP.1.a, MP.1.b. MP.1.e, MP.3.a, MP.4.a

Find the slope by plugging the points into the formula for slope, and solving:
$$m = \frac{y_2 - y_1}{x_2 - x_1} \text{ so that } m = \frac{3 - 4}{2 - (-4)} = \frac{-1}{6}$$

4. D; DOK Level: 2; **Content Topics:** Q.2.a, Q.2.e, Q.6.c, A.1.i, A.6.a, A.6.b; **Practices:** MP.1.a, MP.1.b. MP.1.e, MP.3.a, MP.4.a

Slope of a line $= \dfrac{y_2 - y_1}{x_2 - x_1}$
$$= \frac{-4 - (-2)}{-3 - (-1)} = \frac{-2}{-2} = 1$$

5. B; DOK Level: 2; **Content Topics:** Q.2.a, Q.2.e, Q.6.c, A.1.i, A.6.a, A.6.b; **Practices:** MP.1.a, MP.1.b. MP.1.e, MP.3.a, MP.4.a

The only choice shown with a slope of $\frac{1}{2}$ is $y = \frac{1}{2}$ −3, so it is parallel to $y = \frac{1}{2}x + 3$. Since slope is m in $y = mx + b$, in $y = \frac{1}{2}x + 3$, $\frac{1}{2}$ = the slope.

6. C; DOK Level: 2; **Content Topics:** Q.2.a, Q.2.e, Q.6.c, A.1.i, A.5.b, A.5.c, A.6.a, A.6.b; **Practices:** MP.1.a, MP.1.b. MP.1.e, MP.3.a, MP.4.a

Use the slope formula $y = mx + b$ to solve, solve for b: $-2 = -1(4) + b$, so $b = 2$. Use the equation $y = -x + 2$. If $x = 2$, then $y = 0$, so point L is at (0, 2).

7. A; DOK Level: 3; **Content Topics:** Q.2.a, Q.2.e, Q.6.c, A.1.i, A.5.b, A.5.c, A.6.a, A.6.b; **Practices:** MP.1.a, MP.1.b. MP.1.e, MP.3.a, MP.4.a

Equation of a line $y = mx + b$
$$m = \frac{y_2 - y_1}{x_2 - x_1}$$
$$m = \frac{1 - 5}{5 - (-5)} = \frac{-4}{10} = \frac{-2}{5}$$
Next, find b, by substituting the value for m in the equation $y = mx + b$, where $y = 5$ and $x = -5$
$$5 = \frac{-2}{5}(-5) + b$$
$$5 = \frac{10}{5} + b$$
$$5 = 2 + b$$
$$b = 5 - 2 = 3$$
By substituting these values, one then can find the equation of the line.
$$y = mx + b$$
$$y = \frac{-2}{5}x + 3$$

8. D; DOK Level: 2; **Content Topics:** Q.2.a, Q.2.e, Q.6.c, A.1.i, A.5.b, A.5.c, A.6.a, A.6.b; **Practices:** MP.1.a, MP.1.b. MP.1.e, MP.3.a, MP.4.a, MP.4.c

Recall that the slope of a line refers to the steepness of a line. The intercept (b) is the point at which the line crosses the y-axis, which in this case has a value of 20. Here, then, the initial fee $= b = \$20$, and the slope is $\frac{\text{rise}}{\text{run}} = \frac{30}{1} = 30$. So, the equation of the line is $y = 30x + 20$.

9. C; DOK Level: 2; **Content Topics:** Q.2.a, Q.2.e, Q.6.c, A.1.i; **Practices:** MP.1.a, MP.1.b. MP.1.e, MP.3.a, MP.4.a

Pick any two points on the line and record the x- and y-values. For example, $(x_1, y_1) = (-3, -3)$; $(x_2, y_2) = (3, -2)$
By plugging the values above into the formula, the equation below is obtained:
$$m = \frac{-2 - (-3)}{3 - (-3)} = \frac{1}{6}$$

10. D; DOK Level: 2; **Content Topics:** Q.2.a, Q.2.e, Q.6.c, A.1.i; **Practices:** MP.1.a, MP.1.b. MP.1.e, MP.3.a, MP.4.a

Recall that the slope of the roof $= \frac{\text{rise}}{\text{run}}$
$$\frac{1}{3} = \frac{4}{\text{run}}.$$
Next, solve $\frac{1}{3} = \frac{4}{x}$ for x to find that $x = 12$ (the run). The span is $12 \times 2 = 24$.

11. D; DOK Level: 2; **Content Topics:** Q.2.a, Q.2.e, Q.6.c, A.1.i; **Practices:** MP.1.a, MP.1.b. MP.1.e, MP.3.a, MP.4.a

Note that when a line has a positive slope, it moves upward left to right as the y-values increase. Only line D meets this requirement. When a line decreases in y-values as it moves left to right, it has a negative slope (as in lines A and B).

12. C; DOK Level: 2; **Content Topics:** Q.2.a, Q.2.e, Q.6.c, A.1.i; **Practices:** MP.1.a, MP.1.b, MP.1.e, MP.3.a, MP.4.a

Vertical lines have an undefined slope because the denominator is 0, and division by 0 is undefined. Line C fulfills this requirement.

13. A; DOK Level: 2; **Content Topics:** Q.2.a, Q.2.e, Q.6.c, A.1.i, A.5.b, A.5.c, A.6.a, A.6.b; **Practices:** MP.1.a, MP.1.b, MP.1.e, MP.3.a, MP.4.a

$15 per month is charged regardless of the number of minutes Kaylia uses, so this is the constant value: $b = 15$. $0.10 is charged for every minute used, so the total charge depends on the number of minutes used: $0.1x$.
$y = mx + b$
$y = 0.1x + 15$
In the above equation, the slope is 0.1.

14. B; DOK Level: 3; **Content Topics:** Q.2.a, Q.2.e, Q.6.c, A.1.i, A.5.b, A.5.c, A.6.a, A.6.b; **Practices:** MP.1.a, MP.1.b, MP.1.e, MP.3.a, MP.4.a

Use the equation from problem 13. Since Kaylia uses 200 minutes, substitute 200 for x and solve for y.
$y = 0.1x + 15$
$y = 0.1(200) + 15$
$y = 20 + 15$
$y = 35$
If Kaylia uses 200 minutes in a month, her bill will be $35.

15. 4.5 feet; DOK Level: 2; **Content Topics:** Q.2.a, Q.2.e, Q.6.c, A.1.i **Practices:** MP.1.a, MP.1.b. MP.1.e, MP.3.a, MP.4.a

Slope of the ladder $= \dfrac{\text{rise}}{\text{run}} = \dfrac{18}{4} = 4.5$

16. 2; DOK Level: 2; **Content Topics:** Q.2.a, Q.2.e, Q.6.c, A.1.i, A.5.a, A.5.b; **Practices:** MP.1.a, MP.1.b. MP.1.e, MP.3.a, MP.4.a

Find the slope by plugging the provided values into the formula for slope: $\dfrac{y_2 - y_1}{x_2 - x_1} = \dfrac{3 - (-3)}{4 - 1} = \dfrac{6}{3} = 2$.

17. $\dfrac{4}{5}$; DOK Level: 2; **Content Topics:** Q.2.a, Q.2.e, Q.6.c, A.1.i; **Practices:** MP.1.a, MP.1.b. MP.1.e, MP.3.a, MP.4.a

Find the slope by plugging the provided values into the formula for slope: $\dfrac{y_2 - y_1}{x_2 - x_1} = \dfrac{4 - 0}{3 - (-2)} = \dfrac{4}{5}$

18. B; DOK Level: 2; **Content Topics:** Q.2.a, Q.2.e, Q.6.c, A.1.i; **Practices:** MP.1.a, MP.1.b. MP.1.e, MP.3.a, MP.4.a

Note that the rate of change is the same as the slope.
$m = \dfrac{400 \text{ km} - 300 \text{ km}}{8 \text{ h} - 6 \text{ h}} = \dfrac{100 \text{ km}}{2 \text{ h}} = 50 \text{ km/h}$

19. C; DOK Level: 2; **Content Topics:** Q.2.a, Q.2.e, Q.6.c, A.1.i; **Practices:** MP.1.a, MP.1.b, MP.1.e, MP.3.a, MP.4.a

The rate at which the helicopter rises is the slope, so m = 90t. The helicopter takes off from 200ft, so $b = 200$. The equation of the line is $x = 90(t) + 200$.

20. D; DOK Level: 2; **Content Topics:** Q.2.a, Q.2.e, Q.6.c, A.1.i **Practices:** MP.1.a, MP.1.b. MP.1.e, MP.3.a, MP.4.a

Option A: Set up a table of x (time elapsed) and y-values (temperature)
Option B: Find the equation of the line and plug in the value, $time = 6\ h$
Option C: At midnight, 6 hours has elapsed. Since the temperature drops 4°F per hour, determine the temperature change by multiplying these values together.
Temperature change = 6 × 4 = 24°F
Temperature at midnight is 90°F − 24°F = 66°F

21. A; DOK Level: 2; **Content Topics:** Q.2.a, Q.2.e, Q.6.c, A.1.i; **Practices:** MP.1.a, MP.1.b. MP.1.e, MP.3.a, MP.4.a

Option A: Use the **point-slope formula** to find the equation of the line:
$y - y_1 = m(x - x_1)$
$y - 90 = -4(x - 0)$
$y = -4x + 90$ or $y = 90 - 4x$
Option B: Recall that the slope is the rate of change. Temperature is decreasing by 4, so our slope is −4. The b value represents the temperature when $t = 0$, which is 90.
$y = mx + b$
$y = -4x + 90$

22. C; DOK Level: 3; **Content Topics:** Q.2.a, Q.2.e, Q.6.c, A.1.i; **Practices:** MP.1.a, MP.1.b. MP.1.e, MP.3.a, MP.4.a

At 4:30 A.M., 10.5 hours has elapsed since sunset. To determine if the plant is still alive, find out if the temperature has been below 60°F for more than 2 hours. After 7.5 hours, the temperature drops to 60°F. The plant dies 2 hours after that ($t = 9.5$ hours). Since the temperature does not rise again for 1 hour, Maria's plant has died.

LESSON 14, *pp. 110–113*

1. A; DOK Level: 1; **Content Topics:** Q.6.c, A.5.b, A.5.b, A.6.a, A.6.c; **Practices:** MP.1.a, MP.2.c

The equation for the given line is in slope-intercept form, with the slope specified as −3. Lines parallel to the given line also will have a slope of −3. Using the point-slope formula, with the slope of −3 and the point (−2, 2), the equation for the parallel line is $y - 2 = -3(x + 2)$ (choice A). Choices B and D have the reciprocal of the correct slope, and choices C and D have the x- and y-values of the specified point switched.

2. A; DOK Level: 1; **Content Topics:** A.5.b, A.6.b; **Practices:** MP.1.a, MP.2.c

Again, the slope of the given line is −3. Lines perpendicular to the given line will have slopes that are the negative reciprocal of −3, or $+\dfrac{1}{3}$. Again, using the point-slope form of the equation with the specified point (−2, 2), one gets $(y - 2) = \dfrac{1}{3}(x + 2)$ (choice A). Choices B and D have the reciprocal of the correct slope, and choice C has the incorrect y-value.

3. B; DOK Level: 1; **Content Topics:** A.5.b, A.6.c; **Practices:** MP.1.a, MP.2.c

The given equation is already in slope-intercept form, $y = mx + b$, and so the slope of the given line is $m = \dfrac{1}{2}$. Any line parallel to the given line will have that same slope. Choice B is the only equation that meets that condition. Choice A swaps the 2 and the 3 in the given equation. Choice C represents a line perpendicular to the given line. Choice D has the same y-intercept, but twice the slope.

4. C; DOK Level: 1; **Content Topics:** A.5.b, A.6.c; **Practices:** MP.1.a, MP.2.c

The slope in the given equation is −2. Lines perpendicular to the given line will have a slope that is the negative reciprocal of −2, or $+\dfrac{1}{2}$. Choice C is the only equation to meet that condition.

UNIT 3 *(continued)*

5. A; DOK Level: 2; **Content Topics:** Q.2.a, Q.2.d, Q.6.c, A.5.a, A.5.b, A.6.c; **Practices:** MP.1.a, MP.1.b, MP.2.c, MP.4.a, MP.5.c

The two lines that are parallel must have identical slopes. Of all the lines shown, only lines *A* and *B* have negative slopes. Line *C* has a slope that is undefined, line *D* has a positive slope, and line *E* has a slope of zero. So lines *A* and *B* must be the two lines that have the same slope, and so are parallel.

6. D; DOK Level: 2; **Content Topics:** Q.2.a, Q.6.c, A.5.a, A.5.b, A.6.c; **Practices:** MP.1.a, MP.1.b, MP.2.c, MP.3.a

The slope of the line through points *N* and *P* can be found by dividing the change in *y* going from *N* to *P* (+4) by the corresponding change in *x* (+5), giving a slope of $\frac{4}{5}$. Lines parallel to that given line must have the same slope and so, for equations written in slope-intercept form, the coefficient of *x* must be $\frac{4}{5}$. Choice D is the only equation that meets that requirement.

7. B; DOK Level: 2; **Content Topics:** Q.2.a, Q.6.c, A.5.a, A.5.b, A.6.c; **Practices:** MP.1.a, MP.1.b, MP.2.c, MP.3.a

The slope of the line through points *M* and *P* can be found by dividing the change in *y* going from *M* to *P* (−2) by the corresponding change in *x* (+7), giving a slope of $-\frac{2}{7}$. Lines parallel to that given line must have the same slope of $-\frac{2}{7}$ (choice B). Choice A is the reciprocal of the correct answer, while choice C is the negative of the correct answer. Choice D is the negative reciprocal of the correct slope, making it equal to the slope of a line *perpendicular* to the given line.

8. D; DOK Level: 2; **Content Topics:** Q.2.a, Q.6.c, A.5.a, A.5.b, A.6.c; **Practices:** MP.1.a, MP.1.b, MP.2.c, MP.3.a

The slope of the line through points *M* and *P* is, again, $-\frac{2}{7}$. Lines perpendicular to that given line must have a slope that is the negative reciprocal of $-\frac{2}{7}$, or $\frac{7}{2}$ (choice D). Choice A is the negative of the correct answer, while choice C is the reciprocal of the correct answer. Choice B is equal to the slope of the given line, making it equal to the slope of a line *parallel* to the given line.

9. *y = 2x*; DOK Level: 3; **Content Topics:** Q.2.a, Q.6.c, A.5.a, A.5.b, A.6.a, A.6.c; **Practices:** MP.1.a, MP.1.b, MP.1.c, MP.1.d, MP.1.e, MP.2.c, MP.3.a, MP.4.a

Since the line between points *A* and *B* and the line between points *C* and *D* form the opposite sides of a rectangle, they must be parallel, and have equal slopes. The slope of the line between *A* and *B* can be found from their coordinates by using the formula for slope and solving: $\frac{y_2 - y_1}{x_2 - x_1} = \frac{4 - 0}{0 - (-2)} = \frac{4 - 0}{0 + 2} = \frac{4}{2} = 2$. This is also the slope of the line between *C* and *D*. Since the given information states explicitly that the line between *C* and *D* passes through the origin, it must have a *y*-intercept of 0. That means the equation of that line is *y = 2x*.

10. −0.5; DOK Level: 2; **Content Topics:** Q.2.a, Q.6.c, A.5.a, A.5.b, Q.6.c; **Practices:** MP.1.a, MP.1.b, MP.2.c, MP.3.a, MP.4.a

Since the line through points *B* and *C* form one end of a rectangle, it must be perpendicular to the adjacent sides of the rectangle (the line through *A* and *B*). The slope of the line through *A* and *B* already has been determined to be +2, and so the slope of the line through *B* and *C* must be the negative reciprocal of 2, or $-\frac{1}{2}$. Expressing that in decimal form gives −0.5.

11. (1.6, 3.2); DOK Level: 3; **Content Topics:** Q.2.a, Q.6.c, A.5.a, A.5.b, A.6.c; **Practices:** MP.1.a, MP.1.b, MP.1.c, MP.1.d, MP.1.e, MP.2.c, MP.3.a, MP.4.a, MP.5.c

The equation of the line that goes through points *C* and *D* is *y = 2x*. The equation of the line passing through *B* and *C* is $y = -\frac{1}{2}x + 4$. These two lines cross at point *C*, where $2x = -\frac{1}{2}x + 4$. Rearranging the equation gives $\frac{5}{2}x = 4$, so $x = \frac{8}{5} = 1.6$. Substituting that value of *x* into *y = 2x* gives a corresponding value of *y* = 2(1.6) = 3.2. As a result, the coordinates of point *C* are (1.6, 3.2).

12. (−0.4, −0.8); DOK Level: 3; **Content Topics:** Q.2.a, Q.6.c, A.5.a, A.5.b, A.6.c; **Practices:** MP.1.a, MP.1.b, MP.1.c, MP.1.d, MP.1.e, MP.2.c, MP.3.a, MP.4.a, MP.5.c

The equation of the line that goes through points *C* and *D* is *y = 2x*. Because it is perpendicular to the slope of line through *B* and *C*, the equation of the line passing through *A* and *D* has a slope of $-\frac{1}{2}$ and passes through the point (−2, 0). The equation of that latter line is, therefore, $(y - 0) = -\frac{1}{2}[x - (-2)]$, or $y = -\frac{1}{2}x - 1$. These two lines cross at point *D*, where $2x = -\frac{1}{2}x - 1$. Rearranging the equation gives $\frac{5}{2}x = -1$, $x = -\frac{2}{5} = -0.4$. Substituting that value of *x* into *y = 2x* gives a corresponding value of *y* = 2(−0.4) = −0.8. As a result, the coordinates of point *D* are (−0.4, −0.8).

13. A; DOK Level: 2; **Content Topics:** Q.2.a, Q.6.c, A.5.a, A.5.b, A.6.c; **Practices:** MP.1.a, MP.1.b, MP.1.e, MP.2.c

The slope of the line between points *A* and *B* is the change in *y* (1) divided by the change in *x* (3), or $\frac{1}{3}$. Since the line between *B* and *C* is perpendicular to the line between *A* and *B*, the slope of the line passing through points *B* and *C* must be the negative reciprocal of $\frac{1}{3}$, or −3 (choice A). Choice B is the reciprocal of the correct answer, choice C is the slope of line AB, and choice D is the negative of the correct answer.

14. D; DOK Level: 3; **Content Topics:** Q.2.a, Q.6.c, A.5.a; **Practices:** MP.1.a, MP.1.b, MP.1.e, MP.2.c, MP.3.a, MP.4.a

The line passing through points *B* and *C* has a slope of −3 and goes through the point (3, 1). Substituting those values into the slope-intercept form of a line (*y = mx + b*) gives 1 = (−3)(3) + *b* = −9 + *b*. Solving for *b* gives a value of *b* = 10, or choice D. Answer choice A results from use of an incorrect sign, while answer choices B and C result from errors in operation or computation.

15. D; **DOK Level:** 3; **Content Topics:** Q.2.a, Q.6.c, A.5.a, A.5.b, A.6.c; **Practices:** MP.1.a, MP.1.b, MP.1.c, MP.1.d, MP.1.e, MP.2.c, MP.3.a, MP.4.a, MP.5.c

The slope of the line between (0, −4) and (3, 2) is $\frac{[(2) - (-4)]}{(3 - 0)} = \frac{(6)}{(3)} = 2$. The slope of the line between (−3, −2) and (0, 4) is $\frac{[(4) - (-2)]}{[(0) - (-3)]} = \frac{(6)}{(3)} = 2$. Since they have the same slope, those two lines are parallel, as would be the case if the figure were a rectangle. In the same way, the slopes of the line between (0, 4) and (3, 2), and the line between (−3,−2) and (0, −4), are both $-\frac{2}{3}$. So those lines are also parallel. However, if the figure were a rectangle, each side would also be perpendicular to its adjacent sides and the slope of adjacent sides would be negative reciprocal. Since the negative reciprocal of $-\frac{2}{3}$ is $\frac{3}{2}$ not 2, the adjacent sides are not perpendicular, and choice D is correct.

16. C; **DOK Level:** 3; **Content Topics:** Q.2.a, A.5.b, A.6.b, A.6.c; **Practices:** MP.1.a, MP.1.b, MP.1.c, MP.1.d, MP.1.e, MP.2.c, MP.3.a, MP.4.a, MP.5.c

The slope of the line through points A and B is $\frac{7 - 3}{2 - 1} = 4$. The equation of the line is $(y - 3) = 4(x - 1) = 4x - 4$. Solving for y gives $y = 4x - 1$. Since the new line is parallel to the given line, it will have the same slope (4), and if the y-intercept of −1 is increased by 2 as required by the question, the new y-intercept will be +1. As a result, the equation of the new line will be $y = 4x + 1$. (choice C). Choices A and B have the slope inverted; choice B also has an incorrect y-intercept. Choice D has the correct slope, but an incorrect y-intercept.

17. B; **DOK Level:** 2; **Content Topics:** Q.2.a, Q.2.e, Q.6.c, A.5.a, A.5.b, A.6.a; **Practices:** MP.1.a, MP.1.b, MP.2.a, MP.2.c

The slope of the line that passes through points A and B is the change in y (6 ft) divided by the change in x (−12 ft), based on the coordinate system specified in the question and figure. That slope, $-\frac{1}{2}$, combined with the fact that the line crosses the y-axis at $y = 6$, leads to the equation $y = -\frac{1}{2}x + 6$ (choice B). Choice A has the correct slope, but the negative of the correct y-intercept. Choices C and D have the slope inverted, and choice C has the incorrect y-intercept as well.

18. A; **DOK Level:** 2; **Content Topics:** Q.2.e, Q.6.c, A.5.a, A.5.b, A.6.c; **Practices:** MP.1.a, MP.1.b, MP.2.c

Since the rug is rectangular in shape, the line through points B and C is perpendicular to the line through points A and B. This means that the slope of the line through B and C will be the negative reciprocal of the slope through A and B. In this case, the negative reciprocal of $-\frac{1}{2}$ is 2, or answer option A. Answer option B is the negative of the slope, while answer option C is the slope of a line that passes through points A and B. Answer option D doesn't apply the negative reciprocal.

19. B; **DOK Level:** 3; **Content Topics:** Q.2.a, Q.2.e, Q.6.c, A.5.a; **Practices:** MP.1.a, MP.1.b, MP.1.c, MP.1.d, MP.1.e, MP.2.c, MP.3.a, MP.4.a, MP.5.c

The slope of the line connecting points B and C is 2. That means that the change in x is half the change in y. The change in y can be found by subtracting the distance between the lower left-hand corner to point B (6 ft) from the total length of that wall (14 ft), a difference of 8 ft. And the corresponding change in x is the distance d. So d, the change in x, half the change in y is $\frac{8 ft}{2} = 4$ ft. The other answer options are possibilities that may ensue from incorrect operations or computation.

LESSON 15, *pp. 114–117*

1. B; **DOK Level:** 1; **Content Topics:** A.5.a, A.5.e; **Practices:** MP.1.a, MP.1.b, MP.2.c

The curve crosses the y-axis at $y = c$, where c is the constant term in the equation. In the case of the right-hand curve, that is $y = -24$ (choice B).

2. A; **DOK Level:** 2; **Content Topics:** Q.2.a, Q.6.c, A.4.a, A.5.a, A.5.e; **Practices:** MP.1.a, MP.1.b, MP.4.a, MP.5.c

Setting the left-hand expression equal to zero and multiplying through by 2 gives: $x^2 + 8x + 8 = 0$. The equation does not factor, so one must use the quadratic formula $\left(x = \frac{-b \pm \sqrt{b^2 - 4ac}}{2a}\right)$. The resulting x-values are: $x = \frac{-8 \pm \sqrt{64 - 32}}{2} = \frac{-8 \pm \sqrt{32}}{2} = \frac{-8 \pm 5.656}{2} = \frac{-4 \pm 2.828}{1}$, which leads to rounded values of −6.8 and −1.2 (choice A). Remaining answer choices are uniformly distributed, nearby points.

3. C; **DOK Level:** 1; **Content Topics:** A.5.a, A.5.e; **Practices:** MP.1.a, MP.1.b, MP.2.c

The curve crosses the y-axis when $x = 0$. For this equation, substituting $x = 0$ into the equation of $y = 2x^2 - 5x + 3$ gives $y = +3$ (choice C).

4. D; **DOK Level:** 2; **Content Topics:** Q.2.a, A.5.a, A.5.e; **Practices:** MP.1.a, MP.1.b, MP.1.d, MP.4.a

The coefficient of the x^2 term (a) determines whether a quadratic function goes through a maximum or minimum. In this case, $a < 0$, which means the function goes through a maximum. The x-value of the maximum is given by $\frac{-b}{2a}$. In this case, that is equal to $\frac{-12}{2(-3)} = +2$. Therefore, choice D is the correct answer.

5. B; **DOK Level:** 3; **Content Topics:** Q.2.a, Q.2.e, Q.6.c, A.1.g, A.4.b, A.5.a, A.5.e; **Practices:** MP.1.a, MP.1.b, MP.1.c, MP.1.d, MP.1.e, MP.2.a, MP.2.c, MP.3.a, MP.4.a, MP.5.a

The equation has the form $y = ax^2 + bx + c$. Since the ball is thrown horizontally, its maximum value occurs at $x = 0$, which means that $b = 0$. That eliminates choices C and D. At $x = 6$, the value of y equals 0. Only choice B satisfies that condition, so choice B is the correct one.

6. D; **DOK Level:** 2; **Content Topics:** Q.6.c, A.5.e; **Practices:** MP.1.a, MP.1.b, MP.2.c, MP.5.a

Quadratic functions with $a < 0$ are characterized by curves that go through maxima rather than minima; negative values of a turn a curve upside down. Of the curves shown, B, D, and E feature maxima (choice D). Curves A and C feature minima, and therefore must have values of $a > 0$.

Answer Key

7. B; DOK Level: 2; **Content Topics:** Q.6.c, A.5.e; **Practices:** MP.1.a, MP.1.b, MP.1.d, MP.2.c, MP.5.a
If $b = 0$, the location of the maximum or minimum of the curve $\left(x = \frac{-b}{2a}\right)$ also must be zero, regardless of the values of a or c. Of the curves shown, those featuring maxima or minima at $x = 0$ include curves B and D (choice B).

8. A; DOK Level: 2; **Content Topics:** Q.6.c, A.5.e; **Practices:** MP.1.a, MP.1.b, MP.2.c, MP.5.a
The location of the maximum or minimum of a quadratic function occurs at $x = \frac{-b}{2a}$. If $\left(\frac{b}{2a}\right)$ is positive, then the maximum or minimum occurs at a *negative* value of x on the graph. Only Curve A has a vertex with a negative x-value.

9. A; DOK Level: 3; **Content Topics:** Q.6.c, A.5.e; **Practices:** MP.1.a, MP.1.b, MP.2.c, MP.5.a
Negative values of a imply curves that go through maxima (and turn upside down), in this case, curves B, D, and E. The higher the *magnitude* of a, the steeper the curve. Of the three curves with $a < 0$, curve B is the steepest, and so its equation features the most negative value of a.

10. (−2, 0), (2, 0), and (0, −2); DOK Level: 2; **Content Topics:** Q.2.a, Q.6.c, A.5.a, A.5.e; **Practices:** MP.1.a, MP.1.b, MP.1.d, MP.2.c, MP.3.a, MP.4.b, MP.4.c, MP.5.a
The function crosses the y-axis when $x = 0$; substituting $x = 0$ into $y = \frac{1}{2}x^2 - 2$ gives $y = \frac{1}{2}(0)^2 - 2$ or $y = 0 - 2$, so that $y = -2$. The function crosses the x-axis when $y = 0$; substituting, that gives $0 = \frac{1}{2}x^2 - 2$. Add −2 to both sides so that $2 = \frac{1}{2}x^2$, or $x^2 = 4$. That gives two more points: (−2, 0) and (2, 0). The minimum occurs at $x = \frac{-b}{2a}$, where, in this case, the coefficient of the x-term (b), is 0. The point at $x = 0$ has already been determined: (0, −2). So there are only three points to plot.

11. (0, 3), (−1, 0), (−3, 0), (−2, −1); DOK Level: 2; **Content Topics:** Q.2.a, Q.6.c, A.5.a, A.5.e; **Practices:** MP.1.a, MP.1.b, MP.1.d, MP.2.c, MP.3.a, MP.4.b, MP.4.c, MP.5.c
Substitute $x = 0$ into $y = x^2 + 4x + 3$, so that it gives $y = 0^2 + 4(0) + 3$ and $y = 3$, giving the first point: (0, 3). Next, when $y = 0$, substitute $y = 0$ into $x^2 + 4x + 3 = 0$; factoring the equation gives $(x + 1)(x + 3) = 0$. That leads to two solutions for x (−1 and −3), giving two more points: (−1, 0) and (−3, 0). The minimum occurs at $x = \frac{-b}{2a} = \frac{-4}{(2 \cdot 1)} = -2$. Find the corresponding y-value by substitution: $y = (-2)^2 + 4(-2) + 3$ so that $y = -1$, giving a fourth point: (−2, −1).

12. (0, 3), (3, 0), (−1, 0), (1, 4); DOK Level: 2; **Content Topics:** Q.2.a, Q.6.c, A.5.a, A.5.e; **Practices:** MP.1.a, MP.1.b, MP.1.d, MP.2.c, MP.3.a, MP.4.b, MP.4.c, MP.5.c
Substitute $x = 0$ into $y = -x^2 + 2x + 3$, so that $y = -0^2 + 2(0) + 3$ and $y = 3$, giving the first point: (0, 3). Next, when $y = 0$, $-x^2 + 2x + 3 = 0$; factoring gives $(-x + 3)(x + 1) = 0$. That leads to two more solutions for x (3 and −1), giving two more points: (3, 0) and (−1, 0). The minimum occurs at $x = \frac{-b}{2a} = \frac{(-2)}{(-2)} = 1$. The corresponding y-value is, by substitution, 4, giving a fourth point (1, 4).

13. (−1, −3), (0, −2), (1, 0), (2, 3); DOK level: 3; **Content Topics:** Q.2.a, Q.6.c, A.5.a, A.5.e; **Practices:** MP.1.a, MP.1.b, MP.1.d, MP.2.c, MP.3.a, MP.4.c, MP.5.c
For each given point, there will be a corresponding point that also lies on the curve, with the same y-value, located the same horizontal distance from the minimum as the given point, but in the opposite direction. The given point (−2, −3) is horizontally located half a unit to the left of the minimum ($x = -2$ compared to $x = -1.5$). So the reflected point will be located half a unit to the right of the minimum (−1.5 + 0.5 = −1), at the same y-value (−3), making the point (−1, −3). Similarly, since the given point (−3, −2) is 1.5 units to the left of the minimum, the reflected point will be 1.5 units to the right (−1.5 + 1.5 = 0), giving a point (0, −2). Likewise, the point (−4, 0), will have a corresponding point 2.5 units to the right of the minimum at $y = 0$: (1, 0). The last point (−5, 3) has a corresponding point 3.5 units right of the minimum at (2, 3).

14. (1, 4), (4, 1), (−1, −4); DOK Level: 3; **Content Topics:** Q.2.a, Q.6.c, A.5.a, A.5.e; **Practices:** MP.1.a, MP.1.b, MP.1.d, MP.2.c, MP.3.a, MP.4.c, MP.5.c
For the point (3, 4), which is one unit to the right of the maximum, there will be a corresponding point one unit to the left of the maximum ($x = 1$), also with $y = 4$: (1, 4). For the point (0, 1), which is two units to the left of the maximum, there will be a corresponding point two units to the right of the maximum ($x = 4$), also at $y = 1$: (4, 1). For the point (5, −4), which is three units to the right of the maximum, there will be a corresponding point three units to the left of the maximum ($x = -1$), also at $y = -4$: (−1, −4).

15. (0, −4), (−3, −1), (2, 4); DOK Level: 3; **Content Topics:** Q.2.a, Q.6.c, A.5.a, A.5.e; **Practices:** MP.1.a, MP.1.b, MP.1.d, MP.2.c, MP.3.a, MP.4.c, MP.5.c
For the point (−2, −4), which is one unit to the left of the minimum, there will be a corresponding point one unit to the right of the minimum ($x = 0$), also with $y = -4$: (0, −4). For the point (1, −1), which is two units to the right of the minimum, there will be a corresponding point two units to the left of the minimum ($x = -3$), also at $y = -1$: (−3, −1). For the point (−4, 4), which is three units to the left of the minimum, there will be a corresponding point three units to the right of the minimum ($x = 2$), also at $y = 4$: (2, 4).

16. D; DOK Level: 2; **Content Topics:** Q.2.a, A.1.f, A.4.a A.5.a, A.5.e; **Practices:** MP.1.a, MP.1.b, MP.1.d, MP.4.b
The curve crosses the x-axis when $y = 0$. Setting the expression in x to zero and dividing both sides by −2 gives: $x^2 + 2x - 3 = 0$. This factors into $(x + 3)(x - 1) = 0$. The solutions to this are $x = -3$, and $x = +1$ (choice D). Remaining choices represent the answers of the correct magnitudes but with varying mixes of sign errors.

17. D; DOK Level: 1; **Content Topics:** A.1.e, A.5.a, A.5.e; **Practices:** MP.1.a, MP.1.d, MP.2.c
The curve crosses the y-axis when $x = 0$, so that $y = -2(0)^2 - 4(0) + 6$. When simplified, only the final term (c) remains, so $y = +6$ (choice D). Choice A has the correct magnitude but the incorrect sign. Choices B and C represent the coefficient of the x^2 term (a) with and without the negative sign, respectively.

18. C; DOK Level: 2; Content Topics: Q.2.a, A.5.a, A.5.e; **Practices:** MP.1.a, MP.1.b, MP.4.a
The x-value of the minimum is given by $\frac{-b}{2a}$ or, in this case, $\frac{-(-4)}{2(-2)} = -1$ (choice C). Choice B has the correct magnitude but the incorrect sign. Choices A and D represent $\frac{-b}{a}$, without and with the negative sign, respectively.

19. B; DOK Level: 3; Content Topics: Q.2.a, Q.6.c, A.5.a, A.5.e; **Practices:** MP.1.a, MP.1.b, MP.1.d, MP.2.c, MP.3.a, MP.5.a
The portion of the curve that is given includes the point $(-2, 3)$. That point is four units to the left of the x-value where the minimum occurs. The other point where $y = 3$ will occur, by symmetry, the same distance to the right of the minimum, or four units to the right of $x = 2$. The result is $x = 6$ (choice B). The other choices represent a uniform distribution of x-values around the correct answer.

20. D; DOK Level: 3; Content Topics: Q.2.a, Q.2.e, Q.6.c, A.1.g, A.4.a, A.5.a, A.5.e; **Practices:** MP.1.a, MP.1.b, MP.1.c, MP.1.d, MP.2.c, MP.3.a, MP.4.b, MP.5.c
When the second player catches the ball, $y = 6$. Substitute 6 into the equation so that $6 = -\frac{1}{144}x^2 + x + 6$. Next, subtract 6 from both sides and multiply through by -144 so that: $x^2 - 144x = 0$. The two solutions correspond to the point the ball is thrown ($x = 0$) and the point the ball is caught ($x = 144$). The distance between the two players is, then, 144 ft (choice D).

21. B; DOK Level: 2; Content Topics: Q.2.a, Q.2.e, Q.6.c, A.1.g, A.5.a, A.5.e; **Practices:** MP.1.a, MP.1.b, MP.1.c, MP.1.d, MP.4.a
The maximum of the curve is located at $x = \frac{-b}{2a}$, where $b = 1$ and $a = \frac{-1}{144}$. Substituting, the x-value of the maximum is 72 feet (choice B). One also could use symmetry; since $y = 6$ at both $x = 0$ and $x = 144$, the maximum has to be at the average of the two x-values: $\frac{(0 + 144)}{2}$.

22. C; DOK Level: 1; Content Topics: Q.2.a, Q.2.e, Q.6.c, A.1.e, A.1.g, A.5.a, A.5.e; **Practices:** MP.1.a, MP.4.a
Substituting $x = 72$ into the equation $y = -\frac{1}{144}(72)^2 + 72 + 6$ gives a y-value of 42 feet.

23. C; DOK Level: 3; Content Topics: Q.2.a, Q.2.e, A.5.a, A.5.e; **Practices:** MP.1.a, MP.1.b, MP.1.d, MP.1.e, MP.3.a, MP.4.a, MP.5.c
The equation representing the path is still a quadratic function, so the symmetry with respect to the maximum still exists regardless of how far the ball is thrown. If the ball returns to the same height it was thrown, the horizontal distance between where it is thrown and where it is caught will always be twice the distance from where it is thrown and where it attains its peak height. As a result, any change that causes a 20-foot increase in the distances in which it achieves its peak height will result in a total distance increasing by 40 feet (choice C). Choice A assumes no impact on the total distance. Choice B assumes the total distance increases by the same amount as the horizontal distance to where the peak height is attained. Choice D continues the sequence of numbers established by the previous three choices.

LESSON 16, *pp. 118–121*
1. D; DOK Level: 1; Content Topics: Q.2.a, Q.6.c, A.5.e; **Practices:** MP.1.a, MP.2.c, MP.4.a
The value at which the curve crosses the x-axis can be determined from the graph or by noting that the numerator in $y = \frac{x-2}{x+1}$, $x - 2$, goes to 0 when $x = 2$ (choice D). Choice A is the opposite of the correct answer, and also the y-value of the y intercept. Choice B is the x-value at which the function is undefined. Choice C is the next integer in the sequence following choices A and B.

2. B; DOK Level: 2; Content Topics: Q.2.a, Q.6.c, A.5.e; **Practices:** MP.1.a, MP.1.b, MP.4.a
Inspection of the function shows that the denominator in $y = \frac{x-2}{x+1}$, $x + 1$, goes to 0 when $x = -1$ (choice B). This is consistent with the graphical representation of the function, where the curves show radical behavior as they approach $x = -1$, both from below and above. The remaining choices parallel those of question 1.

3. D; DOK Level: 3; Content Topics: Q.6.c, A.1.i, A.5.e; **Practices:** MP.1.a, MP.1.b, MP.1.e, MP.2.c, MP.3.a, MP.4.a, MP.4.c, MP.5.b, MP.5.c
The graph shows that, for large values of x (such as 3, 4, and so on), the function is positive. That eliminates choices A and B since, for large values of x, the numerators of those choices are both negative, and the denominators of both are positive. The graph also shows that the function is undefined (denominator goes to zero) at $x = 1$ and $x = -1$, indicating that the denominators go to 0 for those values of x. That eliminates choice C, leaving choice D as the only possible option.

4. B; DOK Level: 3; Content Topics: Q.6.c, A.1.i, A.5.e; **Practices:** MP.1.a, MP.1.b, MP.1.e, MP.2.c, MP.3.a, MP.4.a, MP.4.c, MP.5.b, MP.5.c
The graph shows that the numerator takes on zero values at $x = 0$, $x = -1$, and 2; that eliminates choices A and C. Choices B and D are both consistent with the fact that the function is undefined at $x = 1$. The graph shows that, for large values of x, the function is positive. That eliminates choice D, which is negative. However, it is consistent with choice B, the correct answer.

5. A; DOK Level: 1; Content Topics: Q.6.c, A.5.e; **Practices:** MP.1.a, MP.2.c
By inspection of the graph, the only x-value with a positive corresponding y-value is x_1. The function is increasing slightly at x_3 (choice C), but retains a negative value. The function value for choices B and D are negative.

6. C; DOK Level: 2; Content Topics: Q.6.c, A.5.e; **Practices:** MP.1.a, MP.2.c
The graph shows that the function is decreasing (the curve is moving downward, from left to right) at x_1, x_2, and x_4. Only at x_3 (choice C) is the function increasing.

7. D; DOK Level: 2; Content Topics: Q.6.c, A.5.e; **Practices:** MP.1.a, MP.2.c
The curve goes through a *minimum* between x_2 and x_3 (choice C), and does not change direction to the left of x_1 (choice A), or between x_1 and x_2. The only maximum occurs between x_3 and x_4 (choice D).

UNIT 3 *(continued)*

8. C; DOK Level: 2; **Content Topics:** Q.2.a, Q.6.c, A.5.e; **Practices:** MP.1.a, MP.2.c, MP.4.a

The curve crosses the *y*-axis when *x* is zero. Substituting $x = 0$ into the equation $y = -x^3 - 2x^2$ gives $y = 0$ (choice C). Choice A is a point at which the curve crosses the *x*-axis; choice D is the opposite of that *x*-value. Choice B is the integer intermediate between choices A and C

9. D; DOK Level: 2; **Content Topics:** Q.2.a, Q.6.c, A.1.f, A.5.e; **Practices:** MP.1.a, MP.1.b, MP.1.e, MP.2.c, MP.4.a, MP.4.b

To find where the curve intercepts the *x*-axis, one has to solve the equation: $-x^3 - 2x^2 = 0$. Solving this is simplified by factoring out $-x^2$ from the expression: $-x^2(x + 2) = 0$. This makes it clear that the two solutions are $x = 0$ and $x = -2$ (choice D). Choices A and C each contain one of the solutions, but not both. Choice B contains one of the solutions (-2) but also the opposite (2) of that solution.

10. B; $y = \dfrac{x(x - 1)}{(x + 1)}$; **DOK Level:** 3; **Content Topics:** Q.2.a, A.1.i, A.5.e; **Practices:** MP.1.a, MP.1.b, MP.1.e, MP.2.c, MP.3.a, MP.4.a, MP.4.c, MP.5.c

The graphed function crosses the *x*-axis at $x = 0$ and $x = 1$, indicating that the numerator goes to 0 at those points. By plugging $x = 0$ and $x = 1$ into each equation, you find that it results in a numerator of 0 using both values with only equations B and F. Further, both of those functions are undefined at $x = -1$, consistent with the graph. At large values of *x*, such as 4, the function in the graph is positive, as is the case in equation B. However, equation F is *negative* at large values of *x*. So the correct choice is equation B.

11. A; $y = \dfrac{(x + 1)(x - 1)}{x}$; **DOK Level:** 3; **Content Topics:** Q.2.a, A.1.i, A.5.e; **Practices:** MP.1.a, MP.1.b, MP.1.e, MP.2.c, MP.3.a, MP.4.a, MP.4.c, MP.5.c

The graphed function crosses the *x*-axis at $x = -1$ and $x = 1$, indicating that the numerator becomes 0 at those points. That eliminates all of the equations except for A and D. Both functions are undefined at $x = 0$, which is consistent with the graph. At large values of *x*, such as 4, the function in the graph is positive, indicating that equation A, which is also positive for large values of *x*, is the correct one.

12. C; $y = -\dfrac{1}{x}$; **DOK Level:** 3; **Content Topics:** Q.2.a, A.1.i, A.5.e; **Practices:** MP.1.a, MP.1.b, MP.1.e, MP.2.c, MP.3.a, MP.4.a, MP.4.c, MP.5.c

The graphed function never crosses the *x*-axis, so any terms in the numerator never equal 0. That eliminates all choices except for equation C. The function is undefined at $x = 0$, indicating that the denominator becomes 0 at that point, consistent with equation C. At large positive values of *x*, such as 2, the graph shows the function to be negative, also consistent with equation C.

13. F; $y = \dfrac{-x(x - 1)}{(x + 1)}$; **DOK Level:** 3; **Content Topics:** Q.2.a, A.1.i, A.5.e; **Practices:** MP.1.a, MP.1.b, MP.1.e, MP.2.c, MP.3.a, MP.4.a, MP.4.c, MP.5.c

The graphed function crosses the *x*-axis at $x = 0$ and $x = 1$, indicating that the numerator goes to 0 at those points. By plugging $x = 0$ and $x = 1$ into each equation, you find that it results in a numerator of 0 using both values with only equation B and equation F. Both functions are undefined at $x = -1$, consistent with the graph. At large values of *x*, such as 3, the function in the graph is negative, as is the case with equation F. Equation B is *positive* at large values of *x*. So the correct choice is equation F.

14. E; $y = \dfrac{x(x + 1)}{(x - 1)}$; **DOK Level:** 3; **Content Topics:** Q.2.a, A.1.i, A.5.e; **Practices:** MP.1.a, MP.1.b, MP.1.e, MP.2.c, MP.3.a, MP.4.a, MP.4.c, MP.5.c

The function in the graph crosses the *x*-axis at $x = -1$ and $x = 0$, indicating that the numerator goes to 0 at those points. By plugging $x = -1$ and $x = 0$ into each equation, you find that it results in a numerator of 0 using both values with only equation E. That function is undefined at $x = 1$ since the denominator is 0 at that point, also consistent with the graph. At large values of *x*, such as 2, both the function in the graph and equation E are positive.

15. D; $y = \dfrac{-(x + 1)(x - 1)}{x}$; **DOK Level:** 3; **Content Topics:** Q.2.a, A.1.i, A.5.e; **Practices:** MP.1.a, MP.1.b, MP.1.e, MP.2.c, MP.3.a, MP.4.a, MP.4.c, MP.5.c

The function in the graph crosses the *x*-axis at $x = 1$ and $x = -1$, indicating that the numerator goes to 0 at those points. By plugging $x = 1$ and $x = -1$ into each equation, you find that it results in a numerator of 0 using both values with only equations A and D. Both those choices are functions that are undefined at $x = 0$, consistent with the graph. The graph shows that, as *x* increases to large positive values, such as 3, the function grows negative. This leaves equation D as the correct answer.

16. C; DOK Level: 3; **Content Topics:** Q.6.c, A.1.i, A.5.e; **Practices:** MP.1.a, MP.1.b, MP.1.e, MP.2.c, MP.3.a, MP.4.a, MP.4.c, MP.5.b, MP.5.c

The function in the graph crosses the *x*-axis only at $x = 1$, indicating that the numerator goes to 0 at that point. That eliminates choices B and D. The functions in choices A and C both are undefined at $x = 0$ and $x = -1$, since the denominators go to 0 at those points. For values that are to the left of $x = -1$, the function in the graph has a negative value, consistent with the equation in choice C. Choice A is positive at those points (two negatives make a positive), eliminating that choice as a possibility.

17. C; DOK Level: 3; **Content Topic:** A.7.b; **Practices:** MP.1.a, MP.1.b, MP.1.e, MP.2.c, MP.3.a, MP.5.c

The curve in graph *B* features two *y*-values for every value of *x* greater than zero. The curve in graph *D* has three *y*-values for $x = 0$; in other words, the *y*-axis crosses the curve at three different points. That eliminates both *B* and *D* (choices A and D). The curves in both graphs *A* and *C* never have more than one *y*-value for any given *x*-value, making choice C the correct one.

18. B; DOK Level: 3; **Content Topics:** Q.6.c, A.1.i, A.5.e; **Practices:** MP.1.a, MP.1.b, MP.1.e, MP.2.c, MP.3.a, MP.4.a, MP.4.c, MP.5.b, MP.5.c

The curve crosses the x-axis at $x = -1$, consistent with choices B and D. Both those choices represent functions that are undefined at $x = 0$ and 1. For large values of x, such as 2 or 3, only choice B represents a function that is negative, consistent with the graph.

19. D; DOK Level: 3; **Content Topics:** Q.6.c, A.1.i, A.5.e; **Practices:** MP.1.a, MP.1.b, MP.1.e, MP.2.c, MP.3.a, MP.4.a, MP.4.c, MP.5.b, MP.5.c

The function in the graph crosses the x-axis at $x = -1$ and $x = 0$, indicating that the numerators go to 0 at those points. By plugging $x = -1$ and $x = 0$ into each equation, you find that it results in a numerator of 0 using both values with only answer choices B and D. The functions of answer choices B and D are undefined at $x = 1$, consistent with the graph. For large values of x, such as 3 and 4, the function is negative, showing that D is the correct choice.

20. C; DOK Level: 3; **Content Topics:** Q.2.a, A.1.e, A.5.e; **Practices:** MP.1.a, MP.1.b, MP.1.e, MP.2.c, MP.3.a, MP.4.a, MP.5.c

The function crosses the y-axis when x equals 0. Substituting $x = 0$ into the equation gives $y = 10$, which, because it's positive, eliminates choices A and B. By substituting very small numbers, such as +0.1 and −0.1, for x in the equation, one finds that the function is decreasing at that point, making choice C the correct one.

LESSON 17, *pp. 122–125*

1. B; DOK Level: 2; **Content Topics:** Q.6.a, Q.6.c, A.5.e, A.7.a, A.7.c, A.7.d; **Practices:** MP.1.a, MP.1.b, MP.1.d, MP.1.e, MP.4.c

At $x = 0$, the quadratic function has a value of −1. At $x = 3$, the quadratic function has a value of 3.5. So, the average rate of change of the function is $\frac{4.5}{3} \approx 1.5$. The rate of change of a linear function represented algebraically, in function notation, is given by the x-coefficient. So, compare the x-coefficient of the function in each answer choice to 1.5. Only answer choice B has an x-coefficient (0.5) that is less than 1.5.

2. A; DOK Level: 2; **Content Topics:** Q.6.a, Q.6.c, A.5.e, A.7.a, A.7.c, A.7.d; **Practices:** MP.1.a, MP.1.b, MP.1.d, MP.1.e, MP.4.c

The rate of change of a linear function represented in function notation is the x-coefficient. So, the rate of change of $f(x) = -2x - 3$ is −2. Find the average rate of change of the quadratic equation over each interval and compare to −2. In answer choice A, $f(-4) = 7$ and $f(0) = -1$. So, the average rate of change is $\frac{7 - (-1)}{-4 - 0} = \frac{8}{-4} = -2$. So, the average rate of change (−2) of the quadratic function over the interval $x = -4$ to $x = 0$ is the same as the rate of change of the function $f(x) = -2x - 3$. In answer choice B, $f(-4) = 7$ and $f(-2) = 1$, so the average rate of change is $\frac{7 - 1}{-4 - (-2)} = \frac{6}{-2} = -3$. In answer choice C, $f(-3) = 3.5$ and $f(2) = 1$, so the average rate of change is $\frac{3.5 - 1}{-3 - 2} = \frac{2.5}{-5} = -0.5$. In answer choice D, $f(0) = -1$ and $f(4) = 7$, so the average rate of change is $\frac{7 - (-1)}{4 - 0} = \frac{8}{4} = 2$.

3. B; DOK Level: 1; **Content Topics:** Q.6.a, Q.6.c, A.5.e, A.7.a, A.7.c, A.7.d; **Practices:** MP.1.a, MP.1.b, MP.1.d, MP.1.e

The y-intercept of a function is the value of the function when $x = 0$. For the function represented in the table, the y-intercept (where $x = 0$) is also 0. For the function represented algebraically, $f(0) = 6(0) + 4$ is 4. So, the y-intercept of the function represented algebraically is greater than the y-intercept of the function represented in the table.

4. B; DOK Level: 2; **Content Topics:** Q.6.a, Q.6.c, A.5.e, A.7.a, A.7.c, A.7.d; **Practices:** MP.1.a, MP.1.b, MP.1.d, MP.1.e

The rate of change of a linear function represented algebraically is the x-coefficient. In the function $f(x) = 6x + 4$, the x-coefficient is 6, so the rate of change of the function is 6. For the function represented in the table, $f(0) = 0$ and $f(1) = 3$. So, the average rate of change is $\frac{3 - 0}{1 - 0} = 3$, and the rate of change of the function represented algebraically is greater than the average rate of change of the function represented in the table.

5. C; DOK Level: 2; **Content Topics:** Q.6.a, Q.6.c, A.5.e, A.7.a, A.7.c, A.7.d; **Practices:** MP.1.a, MP.1.b, MP.1.d, MP.1.e

The rate of change of a linear function represented algebraically is the x-coefficient. In the function $f(x) = 6x + 4$, the x-coefficient is 6, so the rate of change of the function is 6. For the function represented in the table, $f(0) = 0$ and $f(2) = 12$. So, the average rate of change is $\frac{12 - 0}{2 - 0} = 6$, and the rate of change of the function represented algebraically is equal to the average rate of change of the function represented in the table.

6. A; DOK Level: 2; **Content Topics:** Q.6.a, Q.6.c, A.5.e, A.7.a, A.7.c, A.7.d; **Practices:** MP.1.a, MP.1.b, MP.1.d, MP.1.e

The rate of change of a linear function represented algebraically is the x-coefficient. In the function $f(x) = 6x + 4$, the x-coefficient is 6, so the rate of change of the function is 6. For the function represented in the table, $f(1) = 3$ and $f(3) = 27$. So, the average rate of change is $\frac{27 - 3}{3 - 1} = 12$, and the rate of change of the function represented algebraically is less than the average rate of change of the function represented in the table.

7. A; DOK Level: 2; **Content Topics:** Q.6.a, Q.6.c, A.5.e, A.7.a, A.7.c, A.7.d; **Practices:** MP.1.a, MP.1.b, MP.1.d, MP.1.e, MP.4.c

The y-intercept of a function is the value of the function when $x = 0$. For the function represented in the table (where $x = 0$), the y-intercept is 0. For the function represented algebraically, $f(0) = -9(0) - 1 = -1$. So, the y-intercept of the function represented algebraically is less than the y-intercept of the function represented in the table.

8. C; DOK Level: 2; **Content Topics:** Q.6.a, Q.6.c, A.5.e, A.7.a, A.7.c, A.7.d; **Practices:** MP.1.a, MP.1.b, MP.1.d, MP.1.e, MP.4.c

The rate of change of a linear function represented algebraically is the x-coefficient. In the function $f(x) = -9x - 1$, the x-coefficient is −9, so the rate of change of the function is −9. For the function represented in the table $f(-2) = 12$ and $f(-1) = 3$. So, the average rate of change is $\frac{12 - 3}{-2 - (-1)} = -9$, and the rate of change of the function represented algebraically is equal to the average rate of change of the function represented in the table.

Answer Key

UNIT 3 *(continued)*

9. D; **DOK Level:** 1; **Content Topics:** Q.6.a, Q.6.c, A.5.e, A.7.a, A.7.c, A.7.d; **Practices:** MP.1.a, MP.1.b, MP.1.d, MP.1.e, MP.4.c

The y-intercept of a function that is represented in a graph is the y-value of the point where the graph crosses the y-axis. So, the y-intercept of the function represented in the graph is 1. The y-intercept of a function that is represented algebraically is the constant term, or b. In answer choice A, the y-intercept is −2. In answer choice B, the y intercept is 2. In answer choice C, the y-intercept is −1. In answer choice D, the y-intercept is 1.

10. C; **DOK Level:** 2; **Content Topics:** Q.6.a, Q.6.c, A.5.e, A.7.a, A.7.c, A.7.d; **Practices:** MP.1.a, MP.1.b, MP.1.d, MP.1.e, MP.4.c

The x-intercept of a function that is represented in a graph is the x-value of the point where the graph crosses the x-axis. So, the x-intercept of the function represented in the graph is 2. The x-intercept of a function that is represented algebraically is the value of x for which the value of the function is 0. Set $f(x) = 0$ for each answer choice and solve for x. For answer choice A, $0 = x + 1$, so $x = -1$. For answer choice B, $0 = \frac{3}{2}x - 1$, so $\frac{3}{2}x = 1$ and $x = \frac{2}{3}$. For answer choice C, $0 = -x + 2$, so $x = 2$. For answer choice D, $0 = -\frac{3}{2}x - 2$, so $x = -\frac{4}{3}$.

11. D; **DOK Level:** 2; **Content Topics:** Q.6.c, A.5.e, A.7.c, A.7.d; **Practices:** MP.1.a, MP.1.b, MP.1.d, MP.1.e, MP.4.c

The maximum value of the function represented in the graph is 5. Compare this value to the maximum values of the functions represented algebraically in the answer choices. In answer choices A and B, the coefficients of the x^2 terms are positive, so the graphs open upward and the graphs do not have maximum values. In answer choices C and D, the coefficients of the x^2 terms are negative, so the graphs open downward and the graphs have maximum values. In answer choice C, the y-intercept is 3, so the maximum is 3. In answer choice D, the y-intercept is 5, so the maximum is 5.

12. B; **DOK Level:** 3; **Content Topics:** Q.2.a, Q.2.e, Q.6.c, A.5.e, A.7.a, A.7.d; **Practices:** MP.1.a, MP.1.b, MP.1.d, MP.1.e, MP.2.a, MP.2.b, MP.4.c

The speed of Car 1 is represented by the slope of the graph. Choose two points on the graph and find the ratio of the vertical change to the horizontal change. The graph passes through (3, 150) and (0,0), so slope $m = \frac{150 - 0}{3 - 0} = 50$. Car 1 is traveling at a speed of 50 miles per hour. The speed of Car 2 is represented by the x-coefficient of the equation, which is 45. So, Car 1 is traveling at a greater speed, because the slope of the line of the graph is greater than 45.

13. D; **DOK Level:** 3; **Content Topics:** Q.6.c, A.5.e, A.7.a, A.7.d; **Practices:** MP.1.a, MP.1.b, MP.1.d, MP.1.e, MP.4.c

The rate of change of the function represented in the graph is the slope of the graph, or the ratio of the vertical change to the horizontal change. The line passes through the points (0, −2) and (5, 0). Find the slope: $\frac{0 - (-2)}{5 - 0} = \frac{2}{5} = 0.4$. The rate of change of a function represented algebraically is the x-coefficient, so the rate of change of the function $f(x) = 0.75x - 1$ is 0.75. Therefore, the rate of change of the function represented in the graph is less than the rate of change of the function $f(x) = 0.75x - 1$. The y-intercept of a function represented in a graph is the y-value of the point at which the graph crosses the y-axis, so the y-intercept of the function represented in the graph is −2. The y-intercept of a function represented algebraically is the constant term, b, so the function $f(x) = 0.75x - 1$ has a y-intercept of −1. Therefore, the y-intercept of the function represented in the graph is less than the y-intercept of the function $f(x) = 0.75x - 1$.

14. B; **DOK Level:** 3; **Content Topics:** Q.2.a, Q.6.c, A.5.e, A.7.a, A.7.c, **Practices:** MP.1.a, MP.1.b, MP.1.d, MP.1.e, MP.2.c, MP.4.c

The rate of change of the function represented in the graph is the slope of the graph, or the ratio of the vertical change to the horizontal change. The line passes through the points (0, −2) and (5, 0). Find the slope: $\frac{0 - (-2)}{5 - 0} = \frac{2}{5} = 0.4$.

Since the slope of the graph of the function $g(x)$ is twice the slope of the graph of the function represented in the graph, its slope is $2(0.4) = 0.8$. The y-intercept of a function represented in a graph is the y-value of the point at which the graph crosses the y-axis, so the y-intercept of the function represented in the graph is −2. So, the y-intercept of the graph of $g(x)$ is also −2. Therefore, $g(x) = 0.8x - 2$. Test each ordered pair to see if it makes the equation true. For answer choice A, $g(-10) = 0.8(-10) - 2 = -8 - 2 = -10$. Therefore, (−10, 6) is not on the graph of $g(x)$. For answer choice B, $g(-5) = 0.8(-5) - 2 = -4 - 2 = -6$. Therefore, (−5, −6) is on the graph of $g(x)$. For answer choice C, $g(5) = 0.8(5) - 2 = 4 - 2 = 2$. Therefore, (5, −2) is not on the graph of $g(x)$. For answer choice D, $g(10) = 0.8(10) - 2 = 6$. Therefore, (10, −10) is not on the graph of $g(x)$.

15. D; **DOK Level:** 2; **Content Topics:** Q.2.a, Q.6.c, A.5.e, A.7.c, A.7.d; **Practices:** MP.1.a, MP.1.b, MP.1.d, MP.1.e, MP.2.c, MP.4.c, MP.5.a

The function represented in the graph has a minimum value of −3, when $x = -2$. The function represented by the equation $f(x) = x^2 - 2$ has a minimum value of −2. Therefore, Alaina is incorrect because the function represented in the graph has a minimum value of −3 and the function $f(x) = x^2 - 2$ has a minimum value of −2.

16. C; DOK Level: 2; **Content Topics:** Q.2.a, Q.6.c, A.5.e, A.7.a, A.7.c, A.7.d; **Practices:** MP.1.a, MP.1.b, MP.1.d, MP.1.e, MP.2.c, MP.4.c

The average rate of change of the function represented in the graph is the ratio of the vertical change to the horizontal change over the interval from $x = -3$ to $x = 0$. When $x = -3$, $y = -1$. When $x = 0$, $y = 5$. Find the rate of change: $\frac{5 - (-1)}{0 - (-3)} = \frac{6}{3} = 2$. The rate of change of a linear function represented algebraically is the x-coefficient. So, the linear function that has the same rate of change as the average rate of change of the function represented in the graph over the interval from $x = -3$ to $x = 0$ has an x-coefficient of 2. Therefore, $f(x) = 2x - 6$ has the same rate of change as the average rate of change of the quadratic function over the given interval.

17. D; DOK Level: 2; **Content Topics:** Q.2.a, Q.6.c, A.5.e, A.7.a, A.7.c, A.7.d; **Practices:** MP.1.a, MP.1.b, MP.1.d, MP.1.e, MP.2.c, MP.4.c

The rate of change of a linear function is the ratio of the vertical change to the horizontal change. The function represented in the table has a rate of change of $\frac{5 - 6}{-2 - (-4)} = \frac{-1}{2} = -0.5$. Therefore, the given function has the same rate of change as the function represented in the table. The y-intercept of a function is the y-value when the x-value is 0, so the y-intercept of the function represented in the table is 4. Therefore, the given function has a greater y-intercept (5) than the function represented in the table.

18. B; DOK Level: 2; **Content Topics:** Q.2.a, Q.6.c, A.5.e, A.7.a, A.7.c, A.7.d; **Practices:** MP.1.a, MP.1.b, MP.1.d, MP.1.e, MP.2.c, MP.4.c

The x-intercept of a function is the x-coordinate of the point where the function crosses the x-axis, or the value of x when the function has a value of 0. For the function represented in the table, the rate of change of the function is $\frac{5 - 6}{-2 - (-4)} = \frac{-1}{2} = -0.5$ and the y-intercept is 4, so the function can be represented algebraically as $f(x) = -0.5x + 4$. When the function has a value of 0, $0 = -0.5x + 4$, so $0.5x = 4$ and $x = 8$. Therefore, the x-intercept of the function represented in the table is 8. For the function $f(x) = x + 8$, when the function has a value of 0, $0 = x + 8$ and $x = -8$. For the function $f(x) = 0.25x - 2$, when the function has a value of 0, $0 = 0.25x - 2$ and $x = 8$. So, the function $f(x) = 0.25x - 2$ has the same x-intercept as the function represented in the table and Sam is correct.

19. B; DOK Level: 2; **Content Topics:** Q.2.a, Q.6.c, A.5.e, A.7.a, A.7.c, A.7.d; **Content Practices:** MP.1.a, MP.1.b, MP.1.d, MP.1.e, MP.2.c, MP.4.c

The function represented in the table has a rate of change of $\frac{5 - 6}{-2 - (-4)} = \frac{-1}{2} = -0.5$. Since the rate of change is negative, the function is decreasing. The rate of change of the function represented by the ordered pairs is $\frac{1 - (-1)}{-2 - (-6)} = \frac{2}{4} = 0.5$. So, the function represented by the ordered pairs is increasing at the same rate that the function represented in the table is decreasing.

UNIT 4 GEOMETRY

LESSON 1, *pp. 126–129*

1. A; DOK Level: 2; **Content Topics:** Q.2.a, Q.2.e, Q.4.a, A.2.a, A.2.b, A.2.c; **Practices:** MP.1.a, MP.1.b, MP.1.d, MP.1.e, MP.2.a, MP.4.a, MP.4.b

The perimeter of a square is given by the formula $P = 4s$. The perimeter of the square is 34 feet, so $34 = 4s$. Divide each side by 4: $s = 8.5$. Answer choice B is the result of dividing the area of the rectangle by 4. Answer choice C is the result of dividing the perimeter of the rectangle by 2. Answer choice D is the perimeter of the square.

2. B; DOK Level: 2; **Content Topics:** Q.2.a, Q.2.e, Q.4.a, A.2.a, A.2.b, A.2.c; **Practices:** MP.1.a, MP.1.b, MP.1.d, MP.1.e, MP.2.a, MP.4.a, MP.4.b

The perimeter of a triangle is the sum of its side lengths. Since an isosceles triangle has two congruent sides, $P = b + 2s$. Substitute 28 for P and 8 for b: $28 = 8 + 2s$. Subtract 8 from each side: $20 = 2s$. Divide each side by 2: $s = 10$. Answer choice A is the result of dividing 28 by 2 and then subtracting 8. Answer choice C is the result of adding $28 + 8$ and dividing the sum by 2. Answer choice D is the sum of the lengths of the two sides.

3. 24; DOK Level: 2; **Content Topics:** Q.2.a, Q.4.a, A.2.a, A.2.b, A.2.c; **Practices:** MP.1.a, MP.1.b, MP.1.d, MP.1.e, MP.2.a, MP.4.a, MP.4.b

The perimeter of a triangle is the sum of the lengths of its sides. Since the perimeter is 64 inches, $20 + 20 + b = 64$. Combine like terms and subtract 40 from each side: $b = 24$.

4. 16; DOK Level: 2; **Content Topics:** Q.2.a, Q.4.a, A.2.a, A.2.b, A.2.c; **Practices:** MP.1.a, MP.1.b, MP.1.d, MP.1.e, MP.2.a, MP.4.a, MP.4.b

The area of a triangle is $\frac{1}{2}bh$. The base of the triangle is $64 - 20 - 20 = 24$ inches, so $192 = \frac{1}{2}(24)h$. Multiply: $192 = 12h$. Divide each side by 12: $h = 16$.

5. 4; DOK Level: 2; **Content Topics:** Q.2.a, Q.4.a, A.2.a, A.2.b, A.2.c; **Practices:** MP.1.a, MP.1.b, MP.1.d, MP.1.e, MP.2.a, MP.4.a, MP.4.b

The area of a triangle is $\frac{1}{2}bh$. In a right triangle, the sides that form the right angle are the base and the height. Since the area is 30 cm², $\frac{1}{2}(15)(h) = 30$. Multiply: $7.5h = 30$.

Divide each side by 7.5: $h = 4$.

6. 8; DOK Level: 3; **Content Topics:** Q.2.a, Q.4.a, A.2.a, A.2.b, A.2.c; **Practices:** MP.1.a, MP.1.b, MP.1.d, MP.1.e, MP.2.a, MP.4.a, MP.4.b.

The area of a rectangle is lw. Since the length is 2 times its width, substitute $2w$ for l in the formula. So, $A = (2w)(w)$. Since the area is 32 in²., $32 = 2w^2$. Divide each side by 2: $16 = w^2$. Take the positive square root of each side: $w = 4$, so $l = 2(4)$, or 8.

Answer Key

UNIT 4 *(continued)*

7. 22; DOK Level: 3; **Content Topics:** Q.2.a, Q.2.e, Q.4.a, Q.4.d, A.2.a, A.2.c; **Practices:** MP.1.a, MP.1.b, MP.1.d, MP.1.e, MP.2.a, MP.4.a, MP.4.b.

The area of a square is the square of its side length. Since the area of each quilt square is $\frac{1}{4}$ ft^2, $\frac{1}{4} = s^2$. Take the positive square root of each side: $s = \frac{1}{2}$. There are 10 squares in each row, so the width of the quilt is $10 \times \frac{1}{2} = 5$ feet. There are 12 rows, so the length of the quilt is $12 \times \frac{1}{2} = 6$ feet. The perimeter of the quilt is $2(l + w)$, so $P = 2(5 + 6) = 2 (11) = 22$.

8. C; DOK Level: 1; **Content Topics:** Q.2.a, Q.4.a, Q.4.c; **Practices:** MP.1.a, MP.1.e

The perimeter of the parallelogram cannot be determined because the width is unknown. Use the square to find the perimeter of the two figures. The perimeter of a square is equal to $4s$. Since $s = 16$, the perimeter is $4(16) = 64$ cm. Answer choice A is the result of multiplying the side length of the square by 2 instead of by 4. Answer choice B is the result of adding $16 + 8$ and multiplying the sum by 2. Answer choice D is the result of multiplying 16×8.

9. A; DOK Level: 2; **Content Topics:** Q.2.a, Q.2.e, Q.4.a, Q.4.c, A.2.a, A.2.b, A.2.c; **Practices:** MP.1.a, MP.1.b, MP.1.d, MP.1.e, MP.2.a, MP.4.a, MP.4.b

The area of the rectangle is equal to the area of the triangle, $\frac{1}{2}(12)(9)$ or 54 in^2. So, 54 in.^{2} is the area of each figure

10. B; DOK Level: 2; **Content Topics:** Q.2.a, Q.4.a, A.2.a, A.2.b, A.2.c; **Practices:** MP.1.a, MP.1.b, MP.1.d, MP.1.e, MP.4.a, MP.4.b.

The area of a triangle is given by the formula $A = \frac{1}{2}bh$. Substitute the area and height into the formula and solve for the base: $86.6 = \frac{1}{2}b(17.32)$. Multiply both sides by 2: $173.2 = 17.32b$. Divide both sides by 17.32: $b = 10$.

11. C; DOK Level: 2; **Content Topics:** Q.2.a, Q.4.a, A.2.a, A.2.b, A.2.c; **Practices:** MP.1.a, MP.1.b, MP.1.d, MP.1.e, MP.4.a, MP.4.b.

An equilateral triangle has three congruent sides. To find one side, the base, substitute 86.6 for A and 17.32 for h in the formula $A = \frac{1}{2}bh$. Solve for b to find that the triangle has a base of 10. The perimeter of a triangle is the sum of the side lengths, so the perimeter of the equilateral triangle is $3b = 3(10) = 30$.

12. B; DOK Level: 2; **Content Topics:** Q.2.a, Q.4.a, Q.4.c, A.2.a, A.2.b, A.2.c; **Practices:** MP.1.a, MP.1.b, MP.1.d, MP.1.e, MP.4.a, MP.4.b.

The area of a parallelogram is given by the formula $A = bh$. Substitute 58 for A and 5 for b: $58 = 5h$. Divide each side of the equation by 5: $h = 11.6$.

13. A; DOK Level: 2; **Content Topics:** Q.2.a, Q.4.a, A.2.a, A.2.b, A.2.c; **Practices:** MP.1.a, MP.1.b, MP.1.d, MP.1.e, MP.4.a, MP.4.b.

The perimeter of a square is equal to four times its side length, or $4s$. Substitute 0.5 for P in the formula $P = 4s$ and divide both sides of the equation by 4 to solve for s: $0.5 = 4s$, so $s = 0.125$. Answer choice B is the result of dividing the perimeter by 2. Answer choice C is the result of multiplying the side length by 2. Answer choice D is the result of using the given perimeter as the side length of a square and multiplying it, rather than dividing it, by 4.

14. A; DOK Level: 2; **Content Topics:** Q.2.a, Q.2.e, Q.4.a, A.2.a, A.2.b, A.2.c; **Practices:** MP.1.a, MP.1.b, MP.1.d, MP.1.e, MP.2.a, MP.4.a, MP.4.b.

To find the width of the swimming pool, first find its area by dividing the total cost of the cover by the cost per square foot: $76.80 ÷ $0.15 = 512$. Next, substitute 512 for A and 32 for l in the formula $A = lw$: $512 = 32w$. Divide both sides by w: $w = 16$.

15. B; DOK Level: 2; **Content Topics:** Q.2.a, Q.2.e, Q.4.a, A.2.a, A.2.b, A.2.c; **Practices:** MP.1.a, MP.1.b, MP.1.d, MP.1.e, MP.2.a, MP.4.a, MP.4.b.

Substitute the minimum and maximum areas and the length into the formula $A = lw$ to find the minimum and maximum widths. If $A = 30$, then $30 = 7w$ and w is about 4.28 feet. If $A = 40$, then $40 = 7w$ and w is about 5.71. Only answer choice B, 4.4 feet, falls within the range of 4.28 to 5.71.

16. A; DOK Level: 2; **Content Topics:** Q.2.a, Q.4.a, A.2.a, A.2.b, A.2.c; **Practices:** MP.1.a, MP.1.b, MP.1.d, MP.1.e, MP.2.a, MP.4.a, MP.4.b.

For each answer choice use the perimeter formula to determine the width, and then calculate the area. If the length is 2 feet, then the width is 10 feet and the area is $(2)(10) = 20$. If the length is 3 feet, then the width is 9 feet and the area is $(3)(9) = 27$. If the length is 4 feet, then the width is 8 feet and the area is $(4)(8) = 32$. If the length is 5 feet, then the width is 7 feet and the area is $(5)(7) = 35$. Only 20 is less than 24, so the length could be 2 feet.

17. A; DOK Level: 2; **Content Topics:** Q.2.a, Q.4.a, Q.4.c, A.2.a, A.2.b, A.2.c; **Practices:** MP.1.a, MP.1.b, MP.1.d, MP.1.e, MP.2.a, MP.4.a, MP.4.b.

Only the area of the square can be determined from the information provided: $A = s^2 = 6^2 = 36$. Use the area of the square to determine the missing dimensions of the other figures. For the parallelogram, $A = bh$. Since the area is 36 cm^2 and the height is 9 cm, $36 = 9b$ and $b = 4$ cm. For the triangle, $A = \frac{1}{2}bh$. Since the area is 36 cm^2 and the height is 6 cm, $36 = \frac{1}{2}(6)b$, so $36 = 3b$ and $b = 12$ cm. For the rectangle, $A = lw$. Since the area is 36 cm^2 and the width is 4.5 cm, $36 = 4.5l$ and $l = 8$. So, of the given choices, on choice A, base of triangle, is a dimension of 12.

18. **B**; **DOK Level:** 2; **Content Topics:** Q.2.a, Q.4.a, Q.4.c, A.2.a, A.2.b, A.2.c; **Practices:** MP.1.a, MP.1.b, MP.1.d, MP.1.e, MP.2.a, MP.4.a, MP.4.b.

Using the square, the area of each figure is $6^2 = 36$ cm². Use the area of the square to determine the missing dimensions needed to find the perimeter. For the parallelogram, $A = bh$, so $36 = 9b$ and $b = 4$. Therefore, $P = 2(10 + 4) = 2(14) = 28$ cm. For the triangle, $A = \frac{1}{2}bh$, so $36 = \frac{1}{2}b(6)$ and $b = 12$. Therefore, $P = 8 + 10 + 12 = 30$ cm. For the rectangle, $A = lw$, so $36 = 4.5l$ and $l = 8$. Therefore, $P = 2(4.5 + 8) = 2(12.5) = 25$ cm.

19. **C**; **DOK Level:** 2; **Content Topics:** Q.2.a, Q.4.a, Q.4.c, A.2.a, A.2.b, A.2.c; **Practices:** MP.1.a, MP.1.b, MP.1.d, MP.1.e, MP.2.a, MP.4.a, MP.4.b.

The perimeter of the square is $4(6) = 24$ cm. All four of the figures have the same area. Using the square, the area of each figure is $6^2 = 36$ cm². The difference between the area and perimeter of the square is $36 - 24 = 12$. Use the area of the square to determine the missing dimensions needed to find the perimeter. For the parallelogram, $A = bh$, so $36 = 9b$ and $b = 4$. Therefore, $P = 2(10 + 4)$ $2(14) = 28$ cm. The difference between the area and perimeter of the parallelogram is $36 - 28 = 8$. For the triangle, $A = \frac{1}{2}bh$, so $36 = \frac{1}{2}b(6)$ and $b = 12$. Therefore, $P = 8 + 10 + 12 = 30$ cm. The difference between the area and perimeter of the triangle is $36 - 30 = 6$. For the rectangle, $A = lw$, so $36 = 4.5l$ and $l = 8$. Therefore, $P = 2(4.5 + 8) = 2(12.5) = 25$ cm. The difference between the area and perimeter of the rectangle is $36 - 25 = 11$. Therefore, the square has the greatest difference between area and perimeter (12).

20. **D**; **DOK Level:** 2; **Content Topics:** Q.2.a, Q.4.a, A.2.a, A.2.b, A.2.c; **Practices:** MP.1.a, MP.1.b, MP.1.d, MP.1.e, MP.2.a, MP.4.a, MP.4.b, MP.5.a.

A parallelogram has two pair of congruent sides, so the perimeter of a parallelogram can be determined if the side length of each pair of sides is known. The area of a parallelogram is equal to the product of its base and height, so the area of a parallelogram cannot be determined from the side lengths alone. Therefore, the perimeter of the parallelogram can be determined, but the area cannot. The perimeter of the parallelogram is equal to $2(11) + 2(14) = 50$, so answer D is correct.

21. **A**; **DOK Level:** 3; **Content Topics:** Q.2.a, Q.4.a, A.2.a, A.2.c; **Practices:** MP.1.a, MP.1.b, MP.1.d, MP.1.e, MP.4.a, MP.4.b.

Use $A = \frac{1}{2}bh$ to find the measure of the base of the isosceles triangle, where $A = 75$ and $h = 7.5$. So $75 = \frac{1}{2}b(7.5)$. Multiply each side by 2: $150 = 7.5b$. Divide each side by 7.5: $b = 20$. Therefore, the base of each right triangle is $\frac{1}{2}(20) = 10$ inches.

22. **D**; **DOK Level:** 2; **Content Topics:** Q.2.a, Q.4.a, A.2.a, A.2.b, A.2.c; **Practices:** MP.1.a, MP.1.b, MP.1.d, MP.1.e, MP.2.a, MP.4.a, MP.4.b.

Each triangle has an area of 30 cm². Use the formula for area, $A = \frac{1}{2}bh$, and the height of each triangle to determine its base. For Triangle 1, $30 = \frac{1}{2}b(5)$. Multiply each side by 2: $60 = 5b$, so $b = 12$. For Triangle 2, $30 = \frac{1}{2}b(15)$. Multiply each side by 2: $60 = 15b$, so $b = 4$. For Triangle 3, $30 = \frac{1}{2}b(6)$. Multiply each side by 2: $60 = 6b$, so $b = 10$. For Triangle 4, $30 = \frac{1}{2}b(4)$. Multiply each side by 2: $60 = 4b$, so $b = 15$. Therefore, Triangle 4 has the longest base.

23. **B**; **DOK Level:** 2; **Content Topics:** Q.2.a, Q.4.a, A.2.a, A.2.b, A.2.c; **Practices:** MP.1.a, MP.1.b, MP.1.d, MP.1.e, MP.2.a, MP.4.a, MP.4.b.

Each triangle has an area of 30 cm². Use the formula for area, $A = \frac{1}{2}bh$, and the height of each triangle to determine its base. Then add the base to the other two side lengths to find the perimeter. For Triangle 1, $30 = \frac{1}{2}b(5)$. Multiply each side by 2: $60 = 5b$, so $b = 12$. The perimeter of Triangle 1 is $5 + 13 + 12 = 30$ cm. For Triangle 2, $30 = \frac{1}{2}b(15)$. Multiply each side by 2: $60 = 15b$, so $b = 4$. The perimeter of Triangle 2 is $18 + 16 + 4 = 38$ cm. For Triangle 3, $30 = \frac{1}{2}b(6)$. Multiply each side by 2: $60 = 6b$, so $b = 10$. The perimeter of Triangle 3 is $11 + 8 + 10 = 29$ cm. For Triangle 4, $30 = \frac{1}{2}b(4)$. Multiply each side by 2: $60 = 4b$, so $b = 15$. The perimeter of Triangle 4 is $5 + 17 + 15 = 37$ cm. Therefore, Triangle 2 has the greatest perimeter.

24. **B**; **DOK Level:** 2; **Content Topics:** Q.2.a, Q.4.a, A.2.a, A.2.b, A.2.c; **Practices:** MP.1.a, MP.1.b, MP.1.d, MP.1.e, MP.2.a, MP.4.a, MP.4.b.

For each rectangle, substitute its area and width into the formula $A = lw$ and solve for the width. For answer choice A, $32 = 6w$, so w is about 5.66. For answer choice B, $40 = 7w$, so w is about 5.74. For answer choice C, $45 = 8w$, so w is 5.625. For answer choice D, $50 = 9w$, so w is about 5.56. Therefore, the rectangle described in answer choice B has the greatest length.

25. **D**; **DOK Level:** 3; **Content Topics:** Q.2.a, Q.4.a, A.2.a, A.2.b, A.2.c; **Practices:** MP.1.a, MP.1.b, MP.1.d, MP.1.e, MP.2.a, MP.4.a, MP.4.b.

An isosceles triangle has two congruent sides. The given side, with length 12, could be one of the congruent sides, or it could be the third side. If the given side is one of the congruent sides, then another side must measure 12, and the third side must measure $48 - 12 - 12 = 24$. If the given side is the third side, then the sum of the two congruent sides is $48 - 12 = 36$, and each of the congruent sides measures $36 \div 2 = 18$. Therefore, the sides could measure 12, 12, 24, or 12, 18, 18. They cannot, however, measure 30.

Answer Key

LESSON 2, pp. 130–133

1. D; DOK Level: 2; **Content Topics:** Q.4.e, A.4.a;
Practices: MP.1.a, MP.2.b, MP.4.b
Solve $10^2 + 2^2 = c^2$ to find that $c^2 = 104$ and $c \approx 10.2$ ft.

2. B; DOK Level: 2; **Content Topics:** Q.4.e, A.4.a;
Practices: MP.1.a, MP.2.b, MP.4.b.
Solve $12^2 + 2^2 = c^2$ to find that $c^2 = 148$ and $c \approx 12.17$ ft, which rounds to 12.2 ft.

3. 8.25; DOK Level: 2; **Content Topics:** Q.4.e, A.4.a;
Practices: MP.1.a, MP.2.b, MP.4.b.
Imagine that $\overline{AB}$ is the hypotenuse of a right triangle with vertices A, B, and $(3, -3)$. Solve $8^2 + 2^2 = c^2$ to find that $c \approx 8.25$.

4. 10.05; DOK Level: 2; **Content Topics:** Q.4.e, A.4.a;
Practices: MP.1.a, MP.2.b, MP.4.b
Imagine that $\overline{AC}$ is the hypotenuse of a right triangle with vertices A, C, and $(5, -4)$. Solve $1^2 + 10^2 = c^2$ to find that $c \approx 10.05$.

5. 7.21; DOK Level: 2; **Content Topics:** Q.4.e, A.4.a;
Practices: MP.1.a, MP.2.b, MP.4.b
First find the difference between the x-coordinates: $2 - (-4) = 6$. Then find the difference between the y-coordinates: $0 - 4 = -4$. Use the Pythagorean Theorem: $6^2 + (-4)^2 = c^2$. Simplify: $36 + 16 = c^2$, so $c^2 = 52$. Therefore, $c \approx 7.21$, which is the difference between points J and L.

6. 6; DOK Level: 2; **Content Topics:** Q.4.e, A.4.a;
Practices: MP.1.a, MP.2.b, MP.4.b
First find the difference between the x-coordinates: $2 - (-4) = 6$. Then find the difference between the y-coordinates: $0 - 0 = 0$. Use the Pythagorean Theorem: $6^2 + 0^2 = c^2$. Simplify: $36 + 0 = c^2$, so $c^2 = 36$. Therefore, $c = 6$, which is the distance between points K and L.

7. 17.21; DOK Level: 2; **Content Topics:** Q.4.e, A.4.a;
Practices: MP.1.a, MP.1.e, MP.2.b, MP.4.b.
First find the difference between the x-coordinates: $-4 - (-4) = 0$. Then find the difference between the y-coordinates: $0 - 4 = -4$. Use the Pythagorean Theorem: $0^2 + (-4)^2 = c^2$. Simplify: $0 + 16 = c^2$, so $c^2 = 16$. Therefore, $c = 4$. Next, add the sides together to find the perimeter of a triangle. $6 + 4 + 7.21 = 17.21$.

8. D; DOK Level: 3; **Content Topics:** Q.4.e, A.4.a;
Practices: MP.1.a, MP.2.b, MP.3.c, MP.4.b, MP.5.a
Ella added the square of 4(16) to the square of 10(100), rather than subtracting 16 from 100. By doing so, Ella got a total of 116 instead of the correct total of 84. The square root of 84 is ≈ 9.165, which rounds to 9.17.

9. A; DOK Level: 2; **Content Topics:** Q.4.e, A.4.a;
Practices: MP.1.a, MP.2.b, MP.4.b
Solve $4^2 + 4^2 = c^2$ to find that $c^2 = 32$ and $c \approx 5.656$ inches, which rounds to 5.66 inches.

10. C; DOK Level: 2; **Content Topics:** Q.4.e, A.4.a;
Practices: MP.1.a, MP.2.b, MP.4.b
Solve $16^2 + b^2 = 21^2$ to find that $256 + b^2 = 441$. Subtract 256 from 441 so that $b^2 = 185$ and $b \approx 13.6$.

11. D; DOK Level: 2; **Content Topics:** Q.4.e, A.4.a;
Practices: MP.1.a, MP.2.b, MP.4.b.
Solve $75^2 + 63^2 = c^2$ to find the hypotenuse. Add $5,625 + 3,969 = c^2$ so that $c^2 = 9,594$. Therefore, $c \approx 97.9$.

12. C; DOK Level: 2; **Content Topics:** Q.4.e, A.4.a;
Practices: MP.1.a, MP.2.b, MP.4.b.
Solve $11^2 + 3^2 = c^2$ to find the hypotenuse. Therefore, $121 + 9 = c^2$, so $c^2 = 11.4$.

13. B; DOK Level: 2; **Content Topics:** Q.4.e, A.4.a;
Practices: MP.1.a, MP.2.b, MP.4.b
Solve $6.5^2 + b^2 = 7.9^2$ to find the other leg so that $42.25 + b^2 = 62.41$. Subtract 42.25 from 62.41 so that $b^2 = 20.16$ and $b \approx 4.49$, which rounds to 4.5.

14. D; DOK Level: 2; **Content Topics:** Q.4.e, A.4.a;
Practices: MP.1.a, MP.2.b, MP.4.b
Solve $5^2 + 8^2 = c^2$ to find the hypotenuse. Add $25 + 64 = c^2$ so that $c^2 = 89$. Therefore, $c \approx 9.4$.

15. B; DOK Level: 2; **Content Topics:** Q.4.e, A.4.a;
Practices: MP.1.a, MP.2.b, MP.4.b
Solve $55^2 + 40^2 = c^2$ to find the hypotenuse. Add $3,025 + 1,600 = c^2$ so that $c^2 = 4,625$ and $c \approx 68$. Next, convert 68 from inches to feet by dividing it by 12, so that you arrive at 5.67 feet, which rounds to 6 feet.

16. C; DOK Level: 3; **Content Topics:** Q.4.e, A.4.a;
Practices: MP.1.a, MP.1.e, MP.2.b, MP.4.b.
Check to see which measurements fit into $a^2 + b^2 = c^2$.
$6^2 + 8.5^2 = 108.25$
$c^2 = 108.25$
$c \approx 10.4$
None of the other options fits the formula.

17. A; DOK Level: 2; **Content Topics:** Q.4.e, A.4.a;
Practices: MP.1.a, MP.2.b, MP.4.b
Solve $30^2 + 17^2 = c^2$ to find the walkway in the garden. Add $900 + 289 = c^2$ so that $c^2 = 1,189$. Therefore, $c \approx 34.48$, which rounds to 34.5.

18. B; DOK Level: 2; **Content Topics:** Q.4.e, A.4.a;
Practices: MP.1.a, MP.2.b, MP.4.b
Solve $12^2 + b^2 = 40^2$ so that $144 + b^2 = 1,600$. Subtract 144 from 1,600 so that $b^2 = 1,456$ and $b \approx 38.16$, which rounds to 38.2.

19. B; DOK Level: 2; **Content Topics:** Q.4.e, A.4.a;
Practices: MP.1.a, MP.2.b, MP.4.b
Solve $12^2 + b^2 = 15^2$ so that $144 + b^2 = 225$. Subtract 144 from 225 so that $b^2 = 81$ and $b = 9$.

20. A; DOK Level: 2; **Content Topics:** Q.4.e, A.4.a;
Practices: MP.1.a, MP.2.b, MP.4.b
Solve $16^2 + b^2 = 18^2$ so that $256 + b^2 = 324$. Subtract 256 from 324 so that $b^2 = 68$ and $b \approx 8.2$.

21. C; DOK Level: 2; **Content Topics:** Q.4.e, A.4.a;
Practices: MP.1.a, MP.2.b, MP.4.b
Solve $6^2 + b^2 = 18^2$ so that $36 + b^2 = 324$. Subtract 36 from 324 so that $b^2 = 288$ and $b \approx 16.97$.

22. D; DOK Level: 2; **Content Topics:** Q.4.e, A.4.a;
Practices: MP.1.a, MP.2.b, MP.4.b
Solve $15^2 + 15^2 = c^2$ to find the width of the dollhouse. Add $225 + 225 = c^2$ so that $c^2 = 450$. Therefore, $c \approx 21.2$.

23. A; DOK Level: 2; **Content Topics:** Q.4.e, A.4.a;
Practices: MP.1.a, MP.2.b, MP.4.b
Solve $15^2 + 15^2 = c^2$ to find the width of the dollhouse. Add $225 + 225 = c^2$ so that $c^2 = 450$. Therefore, $c \approx 21.2$. To find the perimeter of the triangular section, add the length of all three sides: $15 + 15 + 21.2 = 51.2$.

24. **B**; **DOK Level:** 3; **Content Topics:** Q.4.e, A.4.a; **Practices:** MP.1.a, MP.1.d, MP.1.e, MP.2.b, MP.2.c, MP.4.b
To find the perimeter, add all of the outer measurements of the dollhouse, including that of the base (which is not labeled in the picture, but found in question 21 above). 15 + 15 + 18 + 18 + 21.2 = 87.2 inches.

LESSON 3, pp. 134–137

1. **B**; **DOK Level:** 2; **Content Topics:** Q.2.a, Q.4.c; **Practices:** MP.1.a, MP.1.e, MP.2.c, MP.4.a
The perimeter of a regular polygon is the product of its side length and number of sides. The figure has 6 sides, so $s = 27 \div 6 = 4.5$ feet. Answer choice A is the result of finding the side length of a figure with 8 sides. Answer choice C is the result of finding the side length of a figure with 5 sides. Answer choice D is the result of subtracting 6 from 27.

2. **B**; **DOK Level:** 2; **Content Topics:** Q.2.a, Q.4.c; **Practices:** MP.1.a, MP.1.d, MP.1.e, MP.2.c, MP.4.a
The perimeter of an irregular polygon is the sum of its side lengths. To find an unknown side length, subtract the known side lengths from the perimeter: $s = 27 - (7.5 + 3 + 2 + 5.5 + 5) = 27 - 23 = 4$. The length of the side of the regular polygon is the perimeter divided by the number of sides: $27 \div 6 = 4.5$ feet. Subtract: $4.5 - 4 = 0.5$ foot. There are 12 inches in a foot, so 0.5 foot = $(0.5)(12) = 6$ inches. Answer choice A is the result of converting 0.5 foot to 5 inches. Answer choice C is the result of incorrectly calculating the length of the unknown side in either figure. Answer choice D is the length of the unknown side in the irregular figure.

3. **A**; **DOK Level:** 1; **Content Topics:** Q.2.a, Q.4.c; **Practices:** MP.1.a, MP.1.e, MP.2.c, MP.4.a
The perimeter of an irregular polygon is the sum of its side lengths. To find an unknown side length, subtract the known side lengths from the perimeter: $s = 32 - 5 - 12 - 2 - 10 = 3$. Answer choice B is the result of a computation error. Answer choice C is the result of dividing the sum of the given side lengths by 5. Answer choice D is the result of dividing 32 by 5.

4. **C**; **DOK Level:** 2; **Content Topics:** Q.2.a, Q.4.c; **Practices:** MP.1.a, MP.1.e, MP.2.c, MP.4.a
The perimeter of a regular polygon is the product of its side length and number of sides. A pentagon has 5 sides, so $s = 32 \div 5 = 6.4$ meters. Other answers result from computation errors or incorrect assumptions about number of sides.

5. **A**; **DOK Level:** 2; **Content Topics:** Q.2.a, Q.2.e, Q.4.c; **Practices:** MP.1.a, MP.1.e, MP.2.c, MP.4.a
To find the length of the path between the fountain and the snack bar, subtract the lengths of the other sections of the path from the total length of the path: $135 - (40 + 45 + 20) = 135 - 105 = 30$. So, the path between the fountain and the snack bar is 30 yards long.

6. **A**; **DOK Level:** 2; **Content Topics:** Q.2.a, Q.4.c; **Practices:** MP.1.a, MP.1.e, MP.2.c, MP.4.a
The perimeter of a regular polygon is equal to the product of its side length and number of sides. Find the side length of each regular polygon by dividing its perimeter by its number of sides. For answer choice A, side length = $36 \div 4 = 9$ feet. For answer choice B, side length = $32 \div 8 = 4$ feet. For answer choice C, side length = $30 \div 6 = 5$ feet. For answer choice D, side length = $35 \div 5 = 7$ feet. So, the figure described in answer choice A has the greatest side length.

7. **B**; **DOK Level:** 2; **Content Topics:** Q.2.a, Q.4.c; **Practices:** MP.1.a, MP.1.e, MP.2.c, MP.4.a
The perimeter of an irregular polygon is the sum of its side lengths. To find the missing side length, subtract the known side lengths from the perimeter: $70 - (8 + 11 + 10 + 8 + 10 + 5) = 70 - 52 = 18$.

8. **C**; **DOK Level:** 2; **Content Topics:** Q.2.a, Q.4.c; **Practices:** MP.1.a, MP.1.e, MP.2.c, MP.4.a
The perimeter of a regular polygon is the product of its side length and number of sides. To find the number of sides, divide the perimeter by the side length: $21 \div 3.5 = 6$.

9. **B**; **DOK Level:** 2; **Content Topics:** Q.2.a, Q.4.c; **Practices:** MP.1.a, MP.1.b, MP.1.d, MP.1.e, MP.2.c, MP.4.a
The perimeter of a regular polygon is the product of its side length and number of sides. So, the perimeter of the regular octagon is $(2.5)(8) = 20$ inches. Since Eli uses the same piece of wire, the perimeter of the regular pentagon also must be 20 inches. Divide the perimeter by the number of sides: $20 \div 5 = 4$ inches.

10. **C**; **DOK Level:** 1; **Content Topics:** Q.2.a, Q.4.c; **Practices:** MP.1.a, MP.1.b, MP.1.e, MP.4.a
The perimeter of a regular polygon is the product of its side length and number of sides. The perimeter of the regular pentagon is $(7.5)(5) = 37.5$. Answer choice A is the result of computing the perimeter of a four-sided regular polygon with side length 7.5. Answer choice B is the sum of the given sides of the irregular polygon. Answer choice D is the result of computing the perimeter of a six-sided regular polygon with side length 7.5.

11. **A**; **DOK Level:** 1; **Content Topics:** Q.2.a, Q.4.c; **Practices:** MP.1.a, MP.1.b, MP.1.d, MP.1.e, MP.4.a
To find the missing side length in the irregular polygon, first find its perimeter by finding the perimeter of the regular polygon: $(5)(7.5) = 37.5$. Subtract the known side lengths of the irregular polygon from its perimeter: $37.5 - (10 + 9 + 6 + 6.5) = 6$.

12. **A**; **DOK Level:** 2; **Content Topics:** Q.2.a, Q.4.c; **Practices:** MP.1.a, MP.1.b, MP.1.d, MP.1.e, MP.4.a
The perimeter of the irregular polygon is the sum of its side lengths. To find the combined length of the two unknown sides, subtract the known side lengths from the perimeter: $33.5 - (7 + 10 + 2 + 6.5) = 33.5 - 25.5 = 8$ inches. Next, since the two unknown side lengths are equal, divide their combined length by 2: $8 \div 2 = 4$ cm. Answer choice B is the result of a computation error. Answer choice C is the result of failing to divide the combined length of the sides by 2. Answer choice D is the result of multiplying the combined length by 2 rather than dividing by 2.

Answer Key

13. C; DOK Level: 3; Content Topics: Q.2.a, Q.4.c;
Practices: MP.1.a, MP.1.b, MP.1.d, MP.1.e, MP.2.c, MP.3.a,
MP.4.a
To find the missing side length of the irregular hexagon
(right), you need to know its perimeter. Answer choice A
tells you that both figures have the same perimeter, but
since one side length of each polygon is unknown, you do
not know the perimeter of either. Answer choice B tells you
the perimeter of the quadrilateral, but does not specify the
relationship between the two perimeters. Answer choice C
tells you the perimeter of both polygons. Answer choice D
provides enough information to determine the perimeter
of the quadrilateral, but does not specify the relationship
between the two perimeters.

14. B; DOK Level: 3; Content Topics: Q.2.a,Q.2.e, Q.4.c;
Practices: MP.1.a, MP.1.b, MP.1.d, MP.1.e, MP.2.c, MP.4.a
The perimeter of the regular octagon is the product of its
side length and number of sides, so the perimeter is (8)
(3.5) = 28 cm. The ribbon is 40 cm long, so 40 − 28 = 12 cm
remain. This length is equal to the perimeter of the hexagon.
Divide the perimeter by the number of sides to find the side
length of the hexagon: 12 ÷ 6 = 2 cm. Answer choice A is
the result of dividing the length of the remaining ribbon,
12, by 8. Answer choice C is the result of dividing the extra
ribbon by 5 sides (to fit around a pentagon). Answer choice
D is the result of dividing the length of the ribbon by 8.

15. D; DOK Level: 3; Content Topics: Q.2.a, Q.4.c;
Practices: MP.1.a, MP.1.b, MP.1.d, MP.1.e, MP.2.c, MP.3.b,
MP.4.a, MP.5.b
The perimeter of a regular polygon is the product of its side
length and number of sides. The number of sides must be
a whole number, but the side length can be any positive
rational number. Therefore, Ethan is incorrect because,
since (2.25)(8) = 18, the polygon could have 8 sides with a
side length of 2.25 feet.

16. 40; 5; DOK Level: 2; Content Topics: Q.2.a, Q.4.c;
Practices: MP.1.a, MP.1.b, MP.1.d, MP.1.e, MP.2.c, MP.4.a
An octagon has 8 sides and (5)(8) = 40. So, the octagon
has a perimeter of 40 inches and a side length of 5 inches.

17. hexagon; 54; DOK Level: 2; Content Topics: Q.2.a,
Q.4.c; **Practices:** MP.1.a, MP.1.b, MP.1.d, MP.1.e, MP.2.c,
MP.4.a
A hexagon has 6 sides and (6)(9) = 54. So, a hexagon with
a perimeter of 54 cm has a side length of 9 cm.

18. octagon; 1.5; DOK Level: 2; Content Topics: Q.2.a,
Q.4.c; **Practices:** MP.1.a, MP.1.b, MP.1.d, MP.1.e, MP.2.c,
MP.4.a
An octagon has 8 sides and (8)(1.5) = 12, so an octagon
with a perimeter of 12 inches has a side length of
1.5 inches.

19. 7; 4.5; DOK Level: 2; Content Topics: Q.2.a, Q.4.c;
Practices: MP.1.a, MP.1.b, MP.1.d, MP.1.e, MP.2.c, MP.4.a
Since (7)(3.5) = 31.5, a regular 7-sided figure with a
perimeter of 31.5 cm has a side length of 4.5 cm.

20. A; DOK Level: 2; Content Topics: Q.2.a, Q.2.e, Q.4.c;
Practices: MP.1.a, MP.1.b, MP.1.d, MP.1.e, MP.2.c, MP.4.a
The perimeter of a regular polygon is the product of its side
length and number of sides. The fence has a perimeter
of 108 feet and it has 6 sides, so the length of each side
is 108 ÷ 6 = 18 feet. The length of the side of the fence is
6 feet greater than the length of the side of the pool, so
the side of the pool is 18 − 6 = 12 feet. Answer choice B is
the side length of the fence. Answer choice C is the result
of adding 6 to the side length of the fence. Answer choice
D is the result of subtracting 6 from 108 and dividing the
difference by 6.

21. B; DOK Level: 3; Content Topics: Q.2.a, Q.4.c;
Practices: MP.1.a, MP.1.b, MP.1.d, MP.1.e, MP.2.c, MP.4.a
The perimeter of an irregular polygon is the sum of its side
lengths. A pentagon has 5 sides. At least one side measures 3
inches, and at least one side measures 9 inches. All other side
lengths are between 3 inches and 9 inches. If the figure has
4 sides that measure 3 inches each and 1 side that measures
9 inches, its perimeter is: 3 + 3 + 3 + 3 + 9 = 21 inches. If the
figure has 4 sides that measure 9 inches each and 1 side that
measures 3 inches its perimeter: 3 + 9 + 9 + 9 + 9 = 39 inches.
The perimeter of the figure must be between 21 inches and
39 inches. Only answer choice B, 24 inches, falls within this
range.

22. B; DOK Level: 3; Content Topics: Q.2.a, Q.4.c;
Practices: MP.1.a, MP.1.b, MP.1.d, MP.1.e, MP.2.c, MP.4.a
The perimeter of an irregular polygon is the sum of its side
lengths. Add: 3 + 1 + 2.5 + 3.5 + 3.5 + 2.5 = 16 m. Multiply
the perimeter of the irregular polygon by 1.5 to find the
perimeter of the regular polygon: (1.5)(16) = 24 m. Since the
regular polygon has 8 sides, divide the perimeter by 8 to
find the side length: 24 ÷ 8 = 3 m.

LESSON 4, pp. 138–141

1. D; DOK Level: 2; Content Topics: Q.2.a, Q.2.e, Q.4.b,
A.2.a, A.2.b, A.2.c; **Practices:** MP.1.a, MP.1.b, MP.2.e,
MP.2.c, MP.4.a, MP.4.b
The circumference of a circle is the product of its diameter
and π. Substitute 25.9 for C in the formula $C = \pi d$ and solve
for d: 25.9 = 3.14d. Divide each side by 3.14: $d \approx 8.25$ inches.

2. A; DOK Level: 3; Content Topics: Q.2.a, Q.2.e, Q.4.b,
A.2.a, A.2.b; **Practices:** MP.1.a, MP.1.b, MP.1.d, MP.1.e,
MP.2.c, MP.4.a, MP.4.b
The circumference of a circle is the product of its diameter
and π. Substitute 25.9 for C in the formula $C = \pi d$ and solve
for d: 25.9 = 3.14d. Divide each side by 3.14: d = 8.25 inches.
If Elizabeth uses 35 stones, the total length of the stones will
be 35 × 8.25 = 289 inches. There are 12 inches in 1 foot, so
divide the number of inches by 12: 289 ÷ 12 = 24.1 ft. So, the
garden path will be about 24 feet.

3. 18.84; DOK Level: 1; Content Topics: Q.2.a, Q.4.b;
Practices: MP.1.a, MP.1.b, MP.1.d, MP.1.e, MP.2.c, MP.4.a
The circumference of a circle is given by $C = \pi d$. Since the
diameter of a circle is twice its radius, $d = 2 \times 3 = 6$.
So, $C = 3.14 \times 6 \approx 18.84$ inches.

4. **43.96**; **DOK Level:** 2; **Content Topics:** Q.2.a, Q.4.b; **Practices:** MP.1.a, MP.1.b, MP.1.d, MP.1.e, MP.2.c, MP.4.a
The radius of the larger circle is 3 + 4 = 7 inches. Since the diameter of a circle is twice its radius, the diameter is 2 × 7 = 14 inches. The circumference of a circle is given by $C = \pi d$. So, $C = 3.14 \times 14 \approx 43.96$ inches.

5. **94.2**; **DOK Level:** 1; **Content Topics:** Q.2.a, Q.2.e, Q.4.b; **Practices:** MP.1.a, MP.1.b, MP.1.e, MP.2.c, MP.4.a
The circumference of a circle is given by $C = \pi d$. Since the diameter is 30 inches, $C = 3.14 \times 30 \approx 94.2$ inches.

6. **4**; **DOK Level:** 2; **Content Topics:** Q.2.a, Q.2.e, Q.4.b, A.2.a, A.2.b, A.2.c; **Practices:** MP.1.a, MP.1.b, MP.1.e, MP.2.c, MP.4.a, MP.4.b
The circumference of a circle is given by $C = \pi d$. Substitute 25.12 for C and solve for d: 25.12 = 3.14d. Divide each side by 3.14: $d = 8$. The diameter of a circle is twice the radius, so $r = 8 \div 2 = 4$ inches.

7. **6**; **DOK Level:** 2; **Content Topics:** Q.2.a, Q.2.e, Q.4.b, A.2.a, A.2.b, A.2.c; **Practices:** MP.1.a, MP.1.b, MP.1.e, MP.2.c, MP.4.a, MP.4.b
The circumference of a circle is given by $C = \pi d$. Substitute 19 for C and solve for d: 19 = 3.14d. Divide each side by 3.14: $d = 6.0509...$, so $d \approx 6$.

8. **C**; **DOK Level:** 1; **Content Topics:** Q.2.a, Q.2.e, Q.4.b; **Practices:** MP.1.a, MP.1.b, MP.1.d, MP.1.e, MP.2.c, MP.4.a
The area of a circle is given by $A = \pi r^2$. Since the diameter of the circle is 132 cm, the radius of the circle is 132 ÷ 2 = 66 cm. Substitute 66 for r to find the area: $3.14 \times 66^2 \approx 13{,}678$ cm².

9. **D**; **DOK Level:** 2; **Content Topics:** Q.2.a, Q.2.e, Q.4.b; **Practices:** MP.1.a, MP.1.b, MP.1.d, MP.1.e, MP.2.c, MP.4.a
The area of a circle is given by $A = \pi r^2$. Since the diameter of the circle is 12 ft, the radius of the circle is 12 ÷ 2 = 6 ft. Substitute 6 for r to find the area: $3.14 \times 6^2 \approx 113.04$ ft².

10. **A**; **DOK Level:** 2; **Content Topics:** Q.2.a, Q.4.b, A.2.a, A.2.c; **Practices:** MP.1.a, MP.1.b, MP.1.d, MP.1.e, MP.2.c, MP.4.a, MP.4.b
The circumference of a circle is given by $C = \pi d$. Substitute 50.24 for C and solve for d: 50.24 = 3.14d. Divide each side by 3.14: $d = 16$ inches. Since the radius of a circle is one-half its diameter, $r = 16 \div 2 = 8$ inches.

11. **A**; **DOK Level:** 1; **Content Topics:** Q.2.a, Q.2.e, Q.4.b; **Practices:** MP.1.a, MP.1.b, MP.1.d, MP.1.e, MP.2.c, MP.4.a
The frame is 2 inches wide, so it extends 2 inches in either direction from the mirror. Determine the diameter of the mirror alone by subtracting 4 inches from the diameter of the mirror and frame. The diameter of the mirror is 11 − 4 = 7. Since the radius of a circle is one-half its diameter, $r = d \div 2 = 3.5$ inches.

12. **B**; **DOK Level:** 1; **Content Topics:** Q.2.a, Q.2.e, Q.4.b; **Practices:** MP.1.a, MP.1.b, MP.1.d, MP.1.e, MP.2.c, MP.4.a
The diameter of the mirror is 11 − 4 = 7. Since the radius of a circle is one-half its diameter, $r = d \div 2 = 3.5$ inches. Since $A = \pi r^2$, the area of the mirror is $3.14 \times 3.5^2 = 38.5$ inches.

13. **C**; **DOK Level:** 2; **Content Topics:** Q.2.a, Q.2.e, Q.4.b; **Practices:** MP.1.a, MP.1.b, MP.1.d, MP.1.e, MP.2.c, MP.4.a
The area of the frame only is the difference between the area of the mirror and frame and the area of the mirror alone. The diameter of the mirror is 11 − 4 = 7. Since the radius of a circle is one-half its diameter, $r = d \div 2 = 3.5$ inches. Since $A = \pi r^2$, the area of the mirror is $3.14 \times 3.5^2 = 38.465$ inches. Since the diameter of the mirror and frame is 11 inches, the radius of the mirror and frame is 11 ÷ 2 = 5.5 inches. Substitute 5.5 for r and calculate the area: $\pi r^2 = 3.14 \times 5.5^2 = 94.985$. Subtract the area of the mirror from the area of the mirror and frame: 94.985 − 38.465 = 56.52, which rounds to 56.5 square inches.

14. **A**; **DOK Level:** 1; **Content Topics:** Q.2.a, Q.2.e, Q.4.b; **Practices:** MP.1.a, MP.1b, MP.1.e, MP.2.c, MP.4.a
The circumference of a circle is given by $C = \pi d$. The diameter of the mirror and frame is 11 inches, so the circumference is $3.14 \times 11 \approx 34.54$ inches.

15. **B**; **DOK Level:** 3; **Content Topics:** MP.1.a, MP.1.b, MP.1.d, MP.1.e, MP.2.c, MP.4.a, MP.4.b; **Practices:** Q.2.a, Q.2.e, Q.4.b, A.2.a, A.2.b, A.2.c
The diameter of the mirror is 11 − 4 = 7. Since the radius of a circle is one-half its diameter, $r = d \div 2 = 3.5$ inches. Since $A = \pi r^2$, the area of the original mirror is $3.14 \times 3.5^2 = 38.5$ inches. Therefore, the area of the second mirror is 1.5 × 38.5 = 57.75 inches. Substitute 57.75 for A and solve for r: 57.75 = 3.14r^2. Divide each side by 3.14: $r^2 = 18.39$. Take the square root of each side: $r = 4.3$ inches. The diameter of a circle is twice its radius, so $d = 2 \times 4.3 \approx 8.6$ inches.

16. **C**; **DOK Level:** 1; **Content Topics:** Q.2.a, Q.2.e, Q.4.b; **Practices:** MP.1.a, MP.1b, MP.1.e, MP.2.c, MP.4.a
The area of a circle is given by $A = \pi r^2$. Substitute 4 for r and calculate the area: $A = 3.14 \times 4^2 \approx 50.24$ square feet.

17. **B**; **DOK Level:** 3; **Content Topics:** Q.2.a, Q.2.e, Q.4.b; **Practices:** MP.1.a, MP.1b, MP.1.e, MP.2.c, MP.4.a
The area of a circle is given by $A = \pi r^2$. So, the area of the tablecloth is $3.14 \times 4^2 = 50.24$ square feet. The diameter of the table is 6 feet, so the radius of the table is 6 ÷ 2 = 3 feet. Substitute 3 for r to find the area of the table: $\pi r^2 = 3.14 \times 3^2 = 28.26$ square feet. To find the number of square feet of tablecloth that will hang over the edge of the table, subtract the area of the table from the area of the tablecloth: 50.24 − 28.26 ≈ 21.98 square feet.

18. **B**; **DOK Level:** 2; **Content Topics:** Q.2.a, Q.2.e, Q.4.b; **Practices:** MP.1.a, MP.1b, MP.1.d, MP.1.e, MP.2.c, MP.4.a
Since the piece of fabric must be 2 inches wider than the pillow all the way around, the diameter of the fabric that Jonna will need is 15 + 2 + 2 = 19 inches. Therefore, the radius of the fabric is 19 ÷ 2 = 9.5 inches. The area of a circle is given by $A = \pi r^2$, so substitute 9.5 for r and calculate the area: $3.14 \times 9.5^2 = 283.4$ square inches.

19. **D**; **DOK Level:** 2; **Content Topics:** Q.2.a, Q.2.e, Q.4.b, A.2.a, A.2.b, A.2.c; **Practices:** MP.1.a, MP.1b, MP.1.d, MP.1.e, MP.2.c, MP.4.a, MP.4.b
The circumference of a circle is given by $C = \pi d$. Since the circumference of one circle is 37.68 inches, 37.68 = 3.14d. Divide each side by 3.14: $d = 12$ inches. To find the number of circles, divide the length of the banner by the diameter of one circle: 60 ÷ 12 = 5 circles to tie together.

Answer Key

UNIT 4 (continued)

20. B; **DOK Level:** 2; **Content Topics:** Q.2.a, Q.2.e, Q.4.b;
Practices: MP.1.a, MP.1b, MP.1.d, MP.1.e, MP.2.c, MP.4.a
The area of a circle is given by $A = \pi r^2$. The radius of a circle is one-half its diameter, so divide the diameter of each pool by 2 to find its radius. For the smaller section of the pool, $r = 10 \div 2 = 5$, and $A = 3.14 \times 5^2 = 78.5$ square meters. For the larger section of the pool, $r = 15 \div 2 = 7.5$, and $A = 3.14 \times 7.5^2 = 176.625$. Add the two areas together to find the total area of the pool: $176.625 + 78.5 = 255.125$, which rounds downward to 255.

21. C; **DOK Level:** 2; **Content Topics:** Q.2.a, Q.2.e, Q.4.b;
Practices: MP.1.a, MP.1b, MP.1.d, MP.1.e, MP.2.c, MP.4.a
Since 100 cm = 1 m, if the diameter of the second section is increased by 45 cm, it brings its diameter to 10.45. So, its new radius is $10.45 \div 2 = 5.225$ meters. The area of a circle is given by $A = \pi r^2$, so the new area of the smaller section is $3.14 \times 5.225^2 = 85.724$. For the larger section of the pool, $r = 15 \div 2 = 7.5$, and $A = 3.14 \times 7.5^2 = 176.625$. Add the two areas together: $176.625 + 85.724 \approx 262.35$ square meters.

22. B; **DOK Level:** 2; **Content Topics:** Q.2.a, Q.2.e, Q.4.b;
Practices: MP.1.a, MP.1b, MP.1.e, MP.2.c, MP.4.a
The circumference of a circle is given by $C = \pi d$. The diameter of the larger circle is $2 \times 6 = 12$, so its circumference is $3.14 \times 12 = 37.68$ inches. The diameter of the smaller circle is $2 \times 2 = 4$, so its circumference is $3.14 \times 4 = 12.56$ inches. Divide: $37.68 \div 12.56 = 3$. So, the circumference of the larger circle is 3 times the circumference of the smaller circle. The area of a circle is given by $A = \pi r^2$. The radius of the larger circle is 6 inches, so its area is $3.14 \times 6^2 = 113.04$ square inches. The radius of the smaller circle is 2 inches, so its area is $3.14 \times 2^2 = 12.56$ square inches. Divide: $113.04 \div 12.56 = 9$. So, the area of the larger circle is 9 times the area of the smaller circle.

23. D; **DOK Level:** 2; **Content Topics:** Q.2.a, Q.2.e, Q.4.b;
Practices: MP.1.a, MP.1b, MP.1.d, MP.1.e, MP.2.c, MP.4.a
The area of a circle is given by $A = \pi r^2$. For the smaller circle, substitute 5 for r and calculate the area: $3.14 \times 5^2 = 78.5$ square inches. For the larger circle, substitute 6 for r and calculate the area: $3.14 \times 6^2 = 113.04$ square inches. Subtract to find the difference between the two areas: $113.04 - 78.5 = 34.54$ square inches.

24. D; **DOK Level:** 2; **Content Topics:** Q.2.a, Q.2.e, Q.4.b;
Practices: MP.1.a, MP.1b, MP.1.d, MP.1.e, MP.2.c, MP.4.a
The circumference of a circle is given by $C = \pi d$. The diameter of each front tire is 3.5 inches, so the circumference of each front tire is $3.14 \times 3.5 = 10.99$ inches. Since there are two tires, multiply the circumference by 2: $10.99 \times 2 = 21.98$ inches, which rounds upward to 22 inches.

25. D; **DOK Level:** 2; **Content Topics:** Q.2.a, Q.2.e, Q.4.b;
Practices: MP.1.a, MP.1b, MP.1.d, MP.1.e, MP.2.c, MP.4.a
The area of a circle is given by $A = \pi r^2$. The radius of the circle is one-half its diameter, so substitute $1 \div 2 = 0.5$ for r and calculate the area: $3.14 \times 0.5^2 \approx 0.79$ square feet.

26. A; **DOK Level:** 3; **Content Topics:** Q.2.a, Q.2.e, Q.4.b;
Practices: MP.1.a, MP.1b, MP.1.d, MP.1.e, MP.2.c, MP.4.a
The radius of the circle is one-half its diameter, so substitute $1 \div 2 = 0.5$ for r and calculate the area: $3.14 \times 0.5^2 = 0.79$ square feet. The window is a rectangle, so the area of the window is $lw = 3 \times 2 = 6$ square feet. To determine the percent of the area of the window that is covered by the sunshield, divide the area of the sunshield by the area of the window and multiply by 100: $0.79 \div 6 \times 100 \approx 13\%$.

LESSON 5, pp. 142–145

1. D; **DOK Level:** 3; **Content Topics:** Q.4.a, Q.4.b, Q.4.d;
Practices: MP.1.a, MP.1.b, MP.1.c, MP.1.d
Note that since the actual tablecloth is twice as large as this sample, we need to multiply each value by 2 to get 10 ft and 16 ft. To find the area of the rectangular portion, use $l \times w$ so that A = 10 ft × 16 ft = 160 ft². Next, find the area of each semicircle by using the formula $\frac{1}{2}\pi r^2$. Multiply so that $= \frac{1}{2}(3.14)(5^2) = 39.25$. Since there are two semicircles, multiply this value by 2: $39.25 \times 2 = 78.5$ ft². Finally, add the areas of the figures = 160 ft² + 78.5 ft² = 238.5 ft².

2. A; **DOK Level:** 2; **Content Topics:** Q.4.a, Q.4.b, Q.4.d;
Practices: MP.1.a, MP.1.b, MP.1.c, MP.1.d
Use the formula for area (πr^2). The diameter of 5 ft ÷ 2 = a radius of 2.5 ft. So, (3.14)(2.5)(2.5) = an area of 19.625 ft², which rounds upward to 19.63 ft².

3. C; **DOK Level:** 3; **Content Topics:** Q.4.a, Q.4.d;
Practices: MP.1.a, MP.1.b, MP.1.c, MP.1.d, MP.3.a
To determine the area, this figure may be divided into 3 smaller rectangles running horizontally.
<u>**Area of rectangle #1**</u> = $l \times w$
$\qquad$ = 20 ft × 5 ft = 100 ft²
<u>**Area of rectangle #2**</u> = $l \times w$
$\qquad$ = 14 ft × 6 ft
$\qquad$ = 84 ft²
<u>**Area of rectangle #3**</u> = $l \times w$
$\qquad$ = 7 ft × 5 ft
$\qquad$ = 35 ft²
Total area of figure = 100 ft² + 84 ft² + 35 ft² = 219 ft².

4. B; **DOK Level:** 3; **Content Topics:** Q.4.a, Q.4.b, Q.4.d;
Practices: MP.1.a, MP.1.b, MP.1.c, MP.1.d, MP.3.a
To determine the perimeter, add each side of the figure so that P = 5 ft + 6 ft + 6 ft + 9 ft + 7 ft + 5 ft + 18 ft + 20 ft = 76 ft.

5. D; **DOK Level:** 3; **Content Topics:** Q.4.a, Q.4.b, Q.4.d;
Practices: MP.1.a, MP.1.b, MP.1.c, MP.1.d, MP.3.a
Area each of circle = πr^2 = (3.14)(3 cm)(3 cm) = 28.26 cm²
and 2 circles × 28.26 cm² = 56.52 cm²
56.52 cm² + 226.1 cm² = 282.62 cm²

6. C; **DOK Level:** 3; **Content Topics:** Q.4.a, Q.4.b, Q.4.d;
Practices: MP.1.a, MP.1.b, MP.1.c, MP.1.d, MP.3.a
Area of the entire pizza = πr^2, so (3.14)(8)(8) = 200.96 square inches. The area of 1 slice of pizza = (200.96 ÷ 8) = 25.12 square inches. Next, figure the pizza eaten = 25.12 × 3 = 75.36 square inches. Finally, subtract the pizza eaten from the total pizza so that 200.96 − 75.36 = 125.6 square inches.

7. B; DOK Level: 3; **Content Topics:** Q.4.a, Q.4.d;
Practices: MP.1.a, MP.1.b, MP.1.c, MP.1.d, MP.3.a
Find the area of the bathroom floor, then divide by the area of each tile. The area of the floor equals the area of the rectangle and the area of the square. The area of the rectangle = 80 inches × 64 inches = 5,120 square inches and the area of the square = 40 inches × 40 inches = 1,600 square inches. The total area of floor = 5,120 + 1,600 = 6,720 square inches. The area of each tile = $l \times w$ = 8 inches × 8 inches = 64 square inches. Total tiles required = 6,720 ÷ 64 = 105 tiles.

8. C; DOK Level: 3; **Content Topics:** Q.4.a, Q.4.b, Q.4.d;
Practices: MP.1.a, MP.1.b, MP.1.c, MP.1.d, MP.3.a
To find the figure's total area, first determine the area of the rectangular base: 30 m × 5 m = 150 m². Next, find the area of the triangle using the formula of $\frac{1}{2}bh$ so that 0.5 × 30m × 3m = 45 m². Add the areas to find the total area of the figure = 150 m² + 45 m² = 195 m².

9. B; DOK Level: 3; **Content Topics:** Q.4.a, Q.4.b, Q.4.d;
Practices: MP.1.a, MP.1.b, MP.1.c, MP.1.d, MP.3.a
The formula for the area of a circle the is $A = \pi r^2$. To find the area of one of the larger circles, first determine the diameter of one of the circles. The overall diameter is 22 m, so 22 ÷ 2 = 11. From there, you can find the radius by taking one-half of 11. Next, use the formula for area so that (3.14)(5.5)(5.5) = 94.98 m², which rounds upward to 95 m².

10. C; DOK Level: 3; **Content Topics:** Q.4.a, Q.4.b, Q.4.d;
Practices: MP.1.a, MP.1.b, MP.1.c, MP.1.d, MP.3.a
The area of the garden bed equals the area of all three circles. To find the area of one of the larger circles, first determine the diameter of one of the circles. The overall diameter is 22 m, so 22 ÷ 2 = 11. From there, you can find the radius by taking one-half of 11. Next, use the formula for area so that (3.14)(5.5)(5.5) = 94.98 m². Finally, multiply the area of the one circle by 2 to get an overall area of the two larger circles of 189.96. From there, determine the area of the smaller circle. Use the formula πr^2 so that (3.14)(4)(4) = 50.24 m². Lastly, add the two areas: 189.96 m² + 50.24 m² = 240.2 m², which rounds to 240 m².

11. C; DOK Level: 3; **Content Topics:** Q.4.a, Q.4.b, Q.4.d;
Practices: MP.1.a, MP.1.b, MP.1.c, MP.1.d, MP.3.a
The formula for the area of a circle is $A = \pi r^2$. To find the diameter of a large circle with about the same area, divide the overall area from question 10 above (240 m²) by 3.14 to get the radius squared, 76.43 m². Then, take the square root of 76.43 to find the radius, 8.7 m. Finally, double the radius to find that the diameter of the new, larger bed is 17.4 m.

12. C; DOK Level: 3; **Content Topics:** Q.4.a, Q.4.b, Q.4.d;
Practices: MP.1.a, MP.1.b, MP.1.c, MP.1.d, MP.3.a
The formula for the area of a circle is $A = \pi r^2$. To find the area of one of the larger circles, first determine the diameter of one of the circles. The overall diameter is 22 m, so 22÷ 2 = 11. From there, you can find the radius by taking one-half of 11. Next, use the formula for area so that (3.14)(5.5)(5.5) = 94.98 m², which rounds upward to 95 m². Since there are two larger circles, double the area of the one—95 m²—to arrive at 190 m². Next, to find the area of one of the smaller circles, determine the diameter of one of them. The overall diameter is 8 m, so you can find the radius by taking one-half of 8 (4). Next, use the formula for area so that (3.14)(4)(4) = 50.24 m², which rounds to 50 m². Since there are two smaller circles, double the area to arrive at 100 m². Add the combined areas of the smaller circles and larger circles: (100 m² + 190 m² = 290 m²).

13. B; DOK Level: 3; **Content Topics:** Q.4.a, Q.4.b, Q.4.d;
Practices: MP.1.a, MP.1.b, MP.1.c, MP.1.d, MP.3.a
The area of the extension will be the area of the rectangle minus the semicircle included in the rectangle that is already part of the garden area. First, find the area of the rectangle by multiplying the two sides (8 x 10 = 80 m²). Next, use the formula for area of a semicircle and the radius (one-half of the diameter, or 4 m). $\frac{1}{2}$(3.14)(4)(4) = 25.12 m². Subtract the area of the semicircle from the area of the rectangle. 80 − 25.12 = 54.88

14. B; DOK Level: 3; **Content Topics:** MP.1.a, MP.1.b, MP.1.c, MP.1.d, MP.3.a; **Practices:** Q.4.a, Q.4.b, Q.4.d
The formula for area of semicircle = $\frac{1}{2}(\pi r^2)$. Next, use what you know about the diameter (6 cm) to find the radius (one-half of the diameter, or 3 cm), so that $\frac{1}{2}$(3.14)(3 cm)(3 cm) = 14.13 cm²

15. B; DOK Level: 3; **Content Topics:** Q.4.a, Q.4.b, Q.4.d;
Practices: MP.1.a, MP.1.b, MP.1.c, MP.1.d, MP.3.a
To find the area of the entire figure, you must determine the area of the semicircle and then add it to the area of the rectangle. In this case, you can find area of the rectangle by multiplying the two sides (6 × 13 = 78 cm²). Next, find the area of the semicircle, using the diameter (6 cm) to find the radius (one-half of the diameter, or 3 cm), so that $\frac{1}{2}$(3.14)(3 cm)(3 cm) = 14.13 cm². Finally, add the area of the rectangle and the area of the semicircle so that 14.13 cm² + 78 cm² = 92.13 cm².

16. C; DOK Level: 3; **Content Topics:** Q.4.a, Q.4.b, Q.4.d;
Practices: MP.1.a, MP.1.b, MP.1.c, MP.1.d, MP.3.a
The perimeter of a semicircle is πr, or (3.14)(3 cm) = 9.42 cm. The perimeter of the rectangle is 13 cm + 13 cm + 6 cm = 32 cm. Next, add 9.42 cm + 32 cm = 41.42 cm.

17. D; DOK Level: 3; **Content Topics:** Q.4.a, Q.4.b, Q.4.d;
Practices: MP.1.a, MP.1.b, MP.1.c, MP.1.d, MP.3.a
The length of the rectangle and the diameter of the semicircle become 12 cm, so to find the area of the rectangle, use 12 cm × 13 cm = 156 cm². Next, use the following formula to find the area of the semicircle = $\frac{1}{2}(\pi r^2)$, so that (3.14)(6 cm)(6 cm) = 56.52 cm². Finally, add to find the area of the total figure: 156 cm² + 56.52 cm² = 212.52 cm².

Answer Key

UNIT 4 (continued)

18. A; DOK Level: 2; **Content Topics:** Q.4.a, Q.4.d;
Practices: MP.1.a, MP.1.b, MP.1.c, MP.1.d, MP.3.a
Height of triangle = 27 ft − 15.25 ft = 11.75 ft.

19. C; DOK Level: 3; **Content Topics:** Q.4.a, Q.4.d;
Practices: MP.1.a, MP.1.b, MP.1.c, MP.1.d, MP.3.a
To find the area of the figure, you first must find the area of the triangle, then find the area of the rectangle, and then add the areas of the two figures together.
Area of rectangle = 15.25 ft × 14 ft = 213.5 ft².
Area of triangle = (14 ft × 11.75 ft) ÷ 2 = 82.25 ft².
Finally, add the areas: 213.5 ft² + 82.25 ft² = 295.75 ft².

20. C; DOK Level: 3; **Content Topics:** Q.4.a, Q.4.d;
Practices: MP.1.a, MP.1.b, MP.1.c, MP.1.d, MP.3.a
Use the Pythagorean theorem ($a^2 + b^2 = c^2$) to calculate the hypotenuse of the triangle, so that $c^2 = 11.75^2 + 7^2$ (to get 7, take one-half of the base of 14 in order to form a right triangle) = 187.0625. Take the square root of 187 to find that c = 13.68 ft. Next, add to find the perimeter of the figure: 13.68 + 13.68 + 15.25 + 14 + 15.25 = 71.86 ft, which rounds to 71.9 ft.

21. A; DOK Level: 3; **Content Topics:** Q.4.a, Q.4.d;
Practices: MP.1.a, MP.1.b, MP.1.c, MP.1.d, MP.3.a
Add the lengths of the sides to find the perimeter of the rectangle: 14 + 14 + 15.25 + 15.25 = 58.5 ft. Next, add the side lengths to find the perimeter of the triangle: 14 + 14 + 14 = 42 ft. Finally, add the perimeters of both figures to find that 58.5 ft + 42 ft = 100.5 ft.

22. C; DOK Level: 3; **Content Topics:** Q.4.a, Q.4.b, Q.4.d;
Practices: MP.1.a, MP.1.b, MP.1.c, MP.1.d, MP.3.a
To find the area of the entire shape, first find the area of rectangular portion: 18 inches × 24 inches = 432 square inches. Next, find the area of the circles: $2(\pi r^2) = 2(3.14)(9)(9)$ = 508.68 square inches. Finally, sum the areas: 432 + 508.68 = 940.68. To the nearest square inch, the area is 941 square inches.

23. B; DOK Level: 3; **Content Topics:** Q.4.a, Q.4.b, Q.4.d;
Practices: MP.1.a, MP.1.b, MP.1.c, MP.1.d, MP.3.a
The area the children wish to paint will be the rectangular portion plus one circular portion. The area of the rectangular portion = 18 inches × 24 inches = 432 square inches. The area of 1 circular portion = $(\pi r^2) = (3.14)(9)(9)$ = 254.34 square inches. Add the two areas: 432 square inches + 254.34 square inches to find 686.34 square inches.

24. C; DOK Level: 3; **Content Topics:** Q.4.a, Q.4.b, Q.4.d;
Practices: MP.1.a, MP.1.b, MP.1.c, MP.1.d, MP.3.a
We know that the area of the entire figure is 940.68 square inches. So, divide the total area by the area that each paint container covers: $\frac{940.68 \text{ square inches}}{100 \text{ square inches}}$ = 9.4068 containers of paint. In order to fully coat the figure, you need to have at least 10 containers of paint.

25. C; DOK Level: 3; **Content Topics:** Q.4.a, Q.4.b, Q.4.d;
Practices: MP.1.a, MP.1.b, MP.1.c, MP.1.d, MP.3.a
To find the new area of the rectangular portion: 48 in × 18 inches = 864 square inches. Next, find the area of the two circles, using the formula $2(\pi r^2)$, so that $A = 2(3.14)(9)(9)$ = 508.68. Finally, add the two areas: 864 square inches + 508.68 square inches to get 1,372.68 square inches, which rounds upward to 1,372.7 square inches.

LESSON 6, pp. 146–149

1. C; DOK Level: 2; **Content Topics:** Q.3.b, Q.3.c;
Practices: MP.1.a, MP.1.b, MP.1.d
Set up a proportional relationship, and ensure you use the same units.
$\frac{\text{Actual rug}}{\text{Floor plan}} = \frac{5 \text{ feet}}{1 \text{ inch}} = \frac{8}{x}$
$8 \div 5x = x = 1.6$ inches

2. B; DOK Level: 2; **Content Topics:** Q.3.b, Q.3.c;
Practices: MP.1.a, MP.1.b, MP.1.d
$\frac{\text{Actual length}}{\text{Floor plan}} = \frac{5 \text{ feet}}{1 \text{ inch}} = \frac{x}{3}$
$x = 15$ feet

3. D; DOK Level: 3; **Content Topics:** Q.3.b, Q.3.c;
Practices: MP.1.a, MP.1.b, MP.1.d
Set up a proportional relationship for the photograph to the enlargement (x) as detailed below:
$\frac{6}{4} = \frac{x}{12}$; $x = \frac{72}{4} \rightarrow x = 18$

4. D; DOK Level: 2; **Content Topics:** Q.3.b, Q.3.c;
Practices: MP.1.a, MP.1.b, MP.1.d
Set up a proportional relationship according to the scale from the question:
$\frac{5.5 \text{ miles}}{1 \text{ inch}} = \frac{x}{3.5 \text{ inches}}$
$x = 19.25$ miles
Therefore, the actual distance in miles between the two towns is 19.25 miles.

5. A; DOK Level: 2; **Content Topics:** Q.3.b, Q.3.c;
Practices: MP.1.a, MP.1.b, MP.1.d
Set up a proportional relationship to represent the situation:
$\frac{1 \text{ inch}}{25 \text{ miles}} = \frac{x}{350 \text{ miles}}$
$x = 14$ inches

6. C; DOK Level: 2; **Content Topics:** Q.3.b, Q.3.c;
Practices: MP.1.a, MP.1.b, MP.1.d
Set up a proportional relationship to represent the problem:
$\frac{\text{Map}}{\text{Actual}} = \frac{2 \text{ inches}}{3.2 \text{ miles}} = \frac{x}{19.2 \text{ miles}}$
So, 38.4 inches = 3.2x and x = 12 inches.

7. D; DOK Level: 2; **Content Topics:** Q.3.b, Q.3.c;
Practices: MP.1.a, MP.1.b, MP.1.d
$\frac{\text{Map}}{\text{Actual}} = \frac{2}{6.5} = \frac{3.25}{x}$
Cross-multiply to find that 21.125 = 2x. Then, x = 10.56 km, which rounds upward to 10.6 km.

8. D; DOK Level: 2; **Content Topics:** Q.3.b, Q.3.c;
Practices: MP.1.a, MP.1.b, MP.1.d
To calculate the difference in kilometers of driving from Blue Harbor to Dodgeville through Westfield (BWD) versus driving from Blue Harbor to Dodgeville through Crawford (BCD), we first must calculate each distance individually.
BWD = 3.25 cm + 3 cm = 6.25 cm
BCD = 2.75 cm + 3.25 cm = 6 cm
Next, find the difference between the two routes so that BWD − BCD = 6.25 cm − 6 cm = 0.25 cm. Use the calculated difference above to convert the scaled distance from centimeters to kilometers.
$\frac{6.5 \text{ km}}{2 \text{ cm}} = \frac{x \text{ km}}{0.25 \text{ cm}}$
Cross-multiply to find that 1.625 = 2x and x = 0.8 km.

9. B; DOK Level: 2; Content Topics: Q.3.b, Q.3.c;
Practices: MP.1.a, MP.1.b, MP.1.d
To calculate the scale of the map, set up the following conversion equation:

$$\frac{\text{Map}}{\text{Actual}} = \frac{4 \text{ cm}}{48 \text{ km}} = \frac{1 \text{ cm}}{12 \text{ km}}$$

Therefore, the scale is 1 cm = 12 km.

10. D; DOK Level: 2; Content Topics: Q.3.b, Q.3.c;
Practices: MP.1.a, MP.1.b, MP.1.d
Set up an equation to represent the relationship:
Dimension 1:

$$\frac{\text{Map}}{\text{Actual}} = \frac{0.5 \text{ inch}}{5 \text{ ft}} = \frac{1 \text{ inch}}{x}$$

So, 5 ft ÷ 0.5 = x = 10 ft
Dimension 2:

$$\frac{\text{Map}}{\text{Actual}} = \frac{0.5 \text{ inch}}{5 \text{ ft}} = \frac{1.5 \text{ inches}}{x}$$

So, 7.5 ft ÷ 0.5 = x = 15 ft
The dimensions of the deck are 10 ft by 15 ft.

11. A; DOK Level: 2; Content Topics: Q.3.b, Q.3.c;
Practices: MP.1.a, MP.1.b, MP.1.d
Use the scale factor to set up a proportion and solve for x.

$$\frac{\frac{7}{8}}{x} = \frac{0.5}{5}, \text{ so } 0.5x = 4.375$$

$x = 8.75$
The length of the longer side of the bathroom is $8\frac{3}{4}$ ft.

12. A; DOK Level: 2; Content Topics: Q.3.b, Q.3.c;
Practices: MP.1.a, MP.1.b, MP.1.d
To find the dimensions of the actual bathroom, find the width by setting up the following equation:

$$\frac{5 \text{ ft}}{0.5 \text{ inch}} = \frac{W \text{ ft}}{0.75 \text{ inch}}$$

So, 5 ft x .75 inch = 3.75 feet and 3.75 ÷ 0.5 = W = 7.5 ft. The width of the bathroom is $7\frac{1}{2}$ ft. Using the length calculated in question 11, the dimensions are $7\frac{1}{2}$ feet by $8\frac{3}{4}$ feet.

13. B; DOK Level: 3; Content Topics: Q.3.b, Q.3.c;
Practices: MP.1.a, MP.1.b, MP.1.d
Set up an equation to determine the distance that Stacey travels:

$$\frac{\text{Map}}{\text{Actual}} = \frac{3 \text{ cm}}{18 \text{ km}} \times \frac{10 \text{ cm}}{x}$$

Cross-multiply to find that 180 ÷ 3 = x = 60 km.
Set up a second equation to solve for time:

$$\frac{90 \text{ km}}{1 \text{ h}} \times \frac{60 \text{ km}}{x}$$

After cross-multiplying, you find that x = .667 hour or 40 minutes.

14. D; DOK Level: 2 Content Topics: Q.3.b, Q.3.c;
Practices: MP.1.a, MP.1.b, MP.1.d
To calculate the length of the 55-foot building's shadow, set up the following proportion:

$$\frac{\text{Shadow}}{\text{Pole}} = \frac{31.9 \text{ ft}}{22 \text{ ft}} \times \frac{x}{55 \text{ ft}}$$

Cross-multiply to find that 1,754.5 ft = 22x and divide to find that x = 79.75, which rounds to 79.8 ft.

15. A; DOK Level: 2; Content Topics: Q.3.b, Q.3.c;
Practices : MP.1.a, MP.1.b, MP.1.d
The height of the second animal is calculated by using the following equation:

$$\frac{4.2 \text{ ft}}{3.8 \text{ ft}} \times \frac{h}{6.8 \text{ ft}}$$

Cross-multiply to find that 28.56 ft = 3.8h and divide to find that h = 7.5 ft. The second animal is 7.5 ft tall.

16. C; DOK Level: 2; Content Topics: Q.3.b, Q.3.c;
Practices: MP.1.a, MP.1.b, MP.1.d
Set up an equation to help solve for the unknown:

$$\frac{\text{Scale}}{\text{Actual}} = \frac{1 \text{ inch}}{32 \text{ inches}} = \frac{x}{106.8 \text{ inches}}$$

Cross-multiply to find that 108.8 inches = 32x and divide to find that x = 3.4 inches.

17. C; DOK Level: 2; Content Topics: Q.3.b, Q.3.c;
Practices: MP.1.a, MP.1.b, MP.1.d
Set up an equation to help solve for the unknown:

$$\frac{2 \text{ cm}}{5 \text{ yd}} = \frac{22 \text{ cm}}{x}$$

Cross-multiply to find that 110 ÷ 2 = x = 55 yards. If the perimeter of the square measures 55 yards, then one side measures 55 ÷ 4 = 13.75 yards.

18. B; DOK Level 2; Content Topics: Q.3.b, Q.3.c;
Practices: MP.1.a, MP.1.b, MP.1.d
Recall that scale is simply a proportion. In this case, the scale can be represented by:

Scale = $\dfrac{\text{Drawing Measure}}{\text{Actual Measure}}$ so that $\dfrac{3 \text{ inches}}{30 \text{ ft}} = \dfrac{1 \text{ inch}}{10 \text{ ft}}$. The scale of the map is 1 inch:10 ft.

19. D; DOK Level: 2; Content Topics: Q.3.b, Q.3.c;
Practices: MP.1.a, MP.1.b, MP.1.d
Set up an equation to help solve for the unknown:

$$\frac{0.5 \text{ inch}}{6.5 \text{ ft}} = \frac{1 \text{ inch}}{x}$$

Cross-multiply to find that 6.5 = .5x, and then divide to find that x = 13 ft. The dimensions of the new deck would be 13 feet by 13 feet.

20. C; DOK Level: 2; Content Topics: Q.3.b, Q.3.c;
Practices: MP.1.a, MP.1.b, MP.1.d
Recall that the dimensions in a similar figure are always proportional. The scale factor is simply the proportion that relates the two triangles to each other.
Set up an equation to determine the scale factor:

$$\frac{\overline{CB}}{\overline{GF}} = \frac{1.25}{0.625} = 2$$

Because the scale factor is 2, the lines on Triangle 1 are twice as long as the lines on Triangle 2.

21. B; DOK Level: 3; Content Topics: Q.3.b, Q.3.c;
Practices: MP.1.a, MP.1.b, MP.1.d
Recall that the dimensions in a similar figure are always proportional. The scale factor is simply the proportion that relates the carpets to one another.
Set up an equation to determine the scale factor:

$$\frac{\text{Larger Carpet}}{\text{Smaller Carpet}} = \frac{18 \text{ ft}}{10 \text{ ft}} = 1.8$$

Each side of the smaller carpet is 1.8 times shorter than the longer carpet. The missing width of the shorter carpet: 9 ft ÷ 1.8 = 5 ft. Alternately, because the length of the larger carpet (18 ft) is twice its width (9 ft), you can assume that the width of the smaller carpet would be one-half of the smaller length (10 ft), or 5 ft.

UNIT 4 *(continued)*

LESSON 7, pp. 150–153

1. C; DOK Level: 1; **Content Topics:** Q.2.a, Q.2.e, Q.5.b; **Practices:** MP.1.a, MP.1.b, MP.1.d, MP.1.e, MP.4.a
The volume of a cylinder is the product of the area of its base and its height, or $V = \pi r^2 h$. Since the diameter and height of Pool A are provided, find the volume of Pool A. The radius of Pool A is equal to 0.5 × 20 = 10 feet. Substitute 3.14 for π, 10 for r and 4 for h: $3.14 \times 10^2 \times 4 = 3.14 \times 100 \times 4 = 1,256$ ft³. Answer choice A is the product of the square of the radius and the height. Answer choice B is result of using 4 as the radius, squaring it, multiplying by the diameter of the pool and then multiplying again by 3.14. Answer choice D is the result of using a radius of 20 feet.

2. B; DOK Level: 2; **Content Topics:** Q.2.a, Q.2.e, Q.5.b; **Practices:** MP.1.a, MP.1.b, MP.1.d, MP.1.e, MP.4.b
The volume of a cylinder is the product of the area of its base and its height, or $V = \pi r^2 h$. To find the height of a cylinder with known volume and radius, divide the volume by πr^2. Since the volume of Pool B is equal to the volume of Pool A, $V = 1,256$ ft³. The radius of Pool B is half its diameter, or 8 feet. So, the height of the cylinder is $1,256 \div (3.14 \times 8^2) = 1,256 \div 200.96 = 6.25$ feet. The remaining answer choices are the result of errors in computing the volume or the height.

3. A; DOK Level: 1; **Content Topics:** Q.2.a, Q.2.e, Q.5.b; **Practices:** MP.1.a, MP.1.b, MP.1.d, MP.1.e, MP.4.a
The volume of a cylinder is the product of the area of its base and height, or $V = \pi r^2 h$. Substitute 1.5 for r and 10 for h: $V = 3.14 \times 1.5^2 \times 10 = 70.65$ in³.

4. B; DOK Level: 2; **Content Topics:** Q.2.a, Q.2.e, Q.5.b; **Practices:** MP.1.a, MP.1.b, MP.1.d, MP.1.e, MP.2.a, MP.4.a
The volume of a cylinder is the product of the area of its base and its height, or $V = \pi r^2 h$. The cylinder has a diameter of 10 meters, so its radius is 0.5 × 10 meters = 5 meters. Substitute 5 for r and 7 for h: $V = 3.14 \times 5^2 \times 7 = 549.5$ m³.

5. A; DOK Level: 1; **Content Topics:** Q.2.a, Q.2.e, Q.5.a; **Practices:** MP.1.a, MP.1.b, MP.1.d, MP.1.e, MP.4.a
The volume of a prism is the product of the area of its base and its height. For a cube, since the length, width, and height are equal, the volume is the cube of the side length. Since the question asks for the volume in cubic feet, rename 18 inches as 1.5 ft. The volume is 1.5 × 1.5 × 1.5 = 3.375 ft³, which rounds to 3 ft.

6. A; DOK Level: 2; **Content Topics:** Q.2.a, Q.5.a; **Practices:** MP.1.a, MP.1.b, MP.1.d, MP.1.e, MP.4.a
The surface area of a prism is the sum of the areas of its surfaces. Since a cube has 6 congruent faces, the surface area is equal to 6 times the area of the base. The base is a square, so its area is equal to the side length (18 inches = 1.5 ft) multiplied by itself: 6(1.5)(1.5) = 13.5 ft² ≈ 14 ft².

7. B; DOK Level: 2; **Content Topics:** Q.2.a, Q.2.e, Q.5.a, A.2.a, A.2.b, A.2.c; **Practices:** MP.1.a, MP.1.b, MP.1.d, MP.1.e, MP.4.a, MP.4.b
The volume of a rectangular prism is the product of its length, width, and height, or $V = lwh$. To find the length, substitute 97.5 for V, 2.5 for w, and 13 for h, then solve for l: 97.5 = (2.5)(13)l. Multiply: 97.5 = 32.5l. Divide: l = 3.

8. C; DOK Level: 2; **Content Topics:** Q.2.a,Q.2.e, Q.5.c; **Practices:** MP.1.a, MP.1.b, MP.1.d, MP.1.e, MP.4.a
The amount of cardboard needed is equal to the surface area of the triangular prism. The prism has 2 triangular surfaces with base 10 cm and height 10 cm, 2 rectangular surfaces with length 50 cm and width 10 cm, and 1 rectangular surface with length 50 cm and width 14 cm. So, the surface area is $2\left(\frac{1}{2}\right)(10)(10) + 2(10)(50) + 14(50)$. Multiply: 100 + 1,000 + 700. Add: 1,800 cm².

9. D; DOK Level: 2; **Content Topics:** Q.2.a, Q.5.a; **Practices:** MP.1.a, MP.1.b, MP.1.d, MP.1.e, MP.4.a, MP.5.b
The volume of a cube is equal to the product of its length, width, and height. Since the length, width, and height of a cube are equal, volume is equal to the cube of the side length, or s^3. The surface area of a cube is 6 times the area of its base. The area of a square base is s^2, so the surface area of a cube is $6s^2$. Find the side length for which the surface area is less than the volume. For answer choice A, volume = 0.5^3 = 0.125 and surface area = $6(0.5)^2$ = 1.5. For answer choice B, volume = 2^3 = 8 and surface area = $6(2)^2$ = 24. For answer choice C, volume = 5^3 = 125 and surface area = $6(5)^2$ = 150. For answer choice D, volume = 8^3 = 512 and surface area = $6(8)^2$ = 384.

10. C; DOK Level: 2; **Content Topics:** Q.2.a, Q.5.b, A.2.a, A.2.c; **Practices:** MP.1.a, MP.1.b, MP.1.d, MP.1.e, MP.2.a, MP.4.a, MP.4.b
The volume of a cylinder is given by $V = \pi r^2 h$. So, substitute 235.5 for V and 3 for h to solve for r: 235.5 = 3.14 × r^2 × 3. Multiply: 235.5 = 9.42r^2. Divide each side by 9.42: r^2 = 25. Take the square root of each side: r = 5. Now, use the radius to find the diameter. The diameter is twice the radius, so d = 2(5) = 10 inches.

11. D; DOK Level: 2; **Content Topics:** Q.2.a, Q.2.e, Q.5.b., A.2.a, A.2.b, A.2.c; **Practices:** MP.1.a, MP.1.b, MP.1.d, MP.1.e, MP.2.a, MP.4.a, MP.4.b
The area of cardboard needed is equal to the sum of the area of one base and the lateral area. The lateral area is equal to the area of a rectangle whose length is equal to the circumference of the circle and whose width is equal to the height of the cylinder, so the lateral area is (31.4)(20) = 628 square centimeters. Since the circumference is equal to $2\pi r$, the $r = \frac{31.4}{2 \times 3.14} = 5$. So, the area of the base is 3.14 × 5^2 = 78.5. Therefore, the area of cardboard needed is 628 + 78.5 = 706.75 cm², which rounds to 707 cm².

12. B; DOK Level: 2; **Content Topics:** Q.2.a, Q.2.e, Q.5.b., A.2.a, A.2.b, A.2.c; **Practices:** MP.1.a, MP.1.b, MP.1.d, MP.1.e, MP.2.a, MP.4.a, MP.4.b
To find the circumference of the second cylinder, first find the volume of the first cylinder. The volume of a cylinder is given by $V = \pi r^2 h$. Since the circumference is equal to $2\pi r$, the $r = \frac{31.4}{2 \times 3.14} = 5$. Substitute 5 for r and 20 for h: $V = 3.14 \times 5^2 \times 20 = 1,570$ cm³. Next, substitute 1,570 for V and 15 for h in the formula for volume and solve for r: 1,570 = 3.14 × r^2 × 15, so $r^2 = \frac{1,570}{3.14 \times 15} = 33.33$ and r is about 5.77 centimeters. The circumference of the cylinder is equal to $2\pi r$, or 2(3.14)(5.77), which is about 36.2 cm.

13. **D**; **DOK Level:** 2; **Content Topics:** Q.2.a, Q.5.a, Q.5.c., A.2.a, A.2.b, A.2.c; **Practices:** MP.1.a, MP.1.b, MP.1.d, MP.1.e, MP.2.a, MP.4.a, MP.4.b
The volume of a triangular prism is the product of the area of its base and its height. Since the height is given, dividing the volume by the height will give the area of the base. The volume of the triangular prism is equal to the volume of the rectangular prism, which is equal to lwh, or $16 \times 5 \times 3$, which is equal to 240 in^3. Divide 240 by 12 to find the area of the base of the triangular prism: $240 \div 12 = 20$.

14. **C**; **DOK Level:** 2; **Content Topics:** Q.2.a, Q.2.e, Q.5.a; **Practices:** MP.1.a, MP.1.b, MP.1.d, MP.1.e, MP.2.c, MP.4.a
The volume of a rectangular prism is the product of its length, width, and height. Since the fish tank is filled only halfway, use $0.5(15) = 7.5$ inches as the height. Multiply: $24 \times 10 \times 7.5 = 1,800$ cubic inches. Answer choice A is the result of doubling the height instead of taking one-half. Answer choice B is the volume of the entire fish tank. Answer choice D is the result of multiplying each dimension by 0.5.

15. **C**; **DOK Level:** 2; **Content Topics:** Q.2.a, Q.2.e, Q.5.b, A.2.a, A.2.b, A.2.c; **Practices:** MP.1.a, MP.1.b, MP.1.d, MP.1.e, MP.2.a, MP.4.a, MP.4.b
A can has the shape of a cylinder. The volume of a cylinder is given by $V = \pi r^2 h$. The diameter of the can is 3 inches, so substitute $3 \div 2 = 1.5$ for r and 28.26 for V and solve for h: $28.26 = 3.14 \times 1.5^2 \times h$. Multiply: $28.26 = 7.065h$. Divide: $h = 4$. Answer choice A is the result of using 3 inches as the radius of the can. Answer choice B is the result of using 3 inches as the radius and failing to square the radius. Answer choice D is the result of failing to square the radius.

16. **A**; **DOK Level:** 2; **Content Topics:** Q.2.a, Q.2.e, Q.5.b; **Practices:** MP.1.a, MP.1.b, MP.1.d, MP.1.e, MP.2.a, MP.4.a
The volume of a cylinder is given by $V = \pi r^2 h$. Substitute 3.5 for r and 10 for h: $V = 3.14 \times 3.5^2 \times 10 = 384.65$ cm^3, which rounds upward to 384.7 cm. Answer choice B is the result of multiplying the radius by 2 rather than squaring it. Answer choice C is the result of dividing $\pi r^2 h$ by 2. Answer choice D is the result of failing to square the radius.

17. **D**; **DOK Level:** 2; **Content Topics:** Q.2.a, Q.2.e, Q.5.b; **Practices:** MP.1.a, MP.1.b, MP.1.d, MP.1.e, MP.2.a, MP.4.a
The lateral area of a cylinder is the area of the rectangle whose length is equal to the circumference of the circular base and whose width is equal to the height of the cylinder. The cup has a radius of 3.5, so its circumference is $2(3.5)(3.14) = 21.98$ cm. So, the lateral area is $(21.98)(10) = 219.8$, or about 220 cm^2.

18. **B**; **DOK Level:** 3; **Content Topics:** Q.2.a, Q.2.e, Q.5.a, Q.5.b; **Practices:** MP.1.a, MP.1.b, MP.1.d, MP.1.e, MP.2.c, MP.4.a
To find the amount of empty space in the box, find the difference between the volume of the box and the total volume of the cans. The volume of each can is given by $V = \pi r^2 h$. Substitute 2 for r and 5 for h: $V = 3.14 \times 2^2 \times 5 = 62.8$ cubic inches. There are 40 cans, so the total volume of the cans is $40(62.8) = 2,512$ cubic inches. The volume of the box is lwh or $18 \times 10 \times 28$, which is equal to 5,040 cubic inches. Subtract to find the amount of empty space: $5,040 - 2,512 = 2,528$ cubic inches.

19. **B**; **DOK Level:** 2; **Content Topics:** Q.2.a, Q.2.e, Q.5.b; **Practices:** MP.1.a, MP.1.b, MP.1.d, MP.1.e, MP.2.c, MP.4.a
The number of cubic inches of potting soil that Kaya uses is equal to the amount of potting soil that would be needed to fill a cylindrical-shaped flowerpot with a height of $24 - 3 = 21$ inches. The radius of the cylinder is equal to one-half the diameter, or $0.5(18)$, which is 9 inches. The volume of a cylinder is given by $V = \pi r^2 h$. Substitute 9 for r and 21 for h: $V = 3.14 \times 9^2 \times 21 = 5,341.14$ cubic inches, or about 5,340 cubic inches.

20. **C**; **DOK Level:** 3; **Content Topics:** Q.2.a, Q.2.e, Q.5.a, A.2.a, A.2.b, A.2.c; **Practices:** MP.1.a, MP.1.b, MP.1.d, MP.1.e, MP.2.a, MP.2.c, MP.4.a, MP.4.b
The volume of a prism is the product of its length, width, and height. Since the volume is equal to 4,050 in^3., $x(2x)(25) = 4,050$. Multiply: $50x^2 = 4,050$. Divide each side by 50: $x^2 = 81$. Take the square root of each side: $x = 9$. Since x is the width, the length (base) is $2(9) = 18$ inches. Answer choice A is the result of dividing x by 2 instead of multiplying. Answer choice B is the value of x, which represents the width. Answer choice D is the result of multiplying the width by 3 instead of by 2.

21. **A**; **DOK Level:** 3; **Content Topics:** Q.2.a, Q.2.e, Q.5.a; **Practices:** MP.1.a, MP.1.b, MP.1.d, MP.1.e, MP.2.c, MP.4.a
Since the volume of the prism is 4,050 in^3., $x(2x)(25) = 4,050$ and $x = 9$ inches. Therefore, the prism is 9 inches wide and $2(9) = 18$ inches long. The surface area of the prism is the total area of its rectangular faces. There are two faces that measure 9 inches by 18 inches. There are two faces that measure 9 inches by 25 inches. There are two faces that measure 18 inches by 25 inches. So, the surface area is equal to $2(9 \times 18) + 2(9 \times 25) + 2(18 \times 25)$. Multiply: $2(162) + 2(225) + 2(450) = 324 + 450 + 900 = 1,674$ in^3.

LESSON 8, pp. 154–157

1. **A**; **DOK Level:** 1; **Content Topics:** Q.2.a, Q.2.e, Q.5.d; **Practices:** MP.1.a, MP.1.b, MP.1.d, MP.1.e, MP.2.c, MP.4.a
The volume of a cone is given by $V = \frac{1}{3}\pi r^2 h$. The diameter and height of Shed A are given, so use the diameter to find the radius and calculate the volume of Shed A: $r = 100 \div 2 = 50$ ft radius, so $V = \frac{1}{3} \times 3.14 \times 50^2 \times 16 = 41,866.66$ ft^3, which rounds to 41,867 ft^3.

2. **C**; **DOK Level:** 2; **Content Topics:** Q.2.a, Q.2.e, Q.5.d, A.2.a, A.2.b, A.2.c; **Practices:** MP.1.a, MP.1.b, MP.1.d, MP.1.e, MP.2.a, MP.2.c, MP.4.a, MP.4.b
To find the diameter of Shed B, use the volume to calculate the radius and then double the radius. The volume of Shed B is equal to the volume of Shed A: $V = \frac{1}{3} \times 3.14 \times 50^2 \times 16 = 41,867$ ft^3. Substitute 41,867 for V and 25 for h in the formula $V = \frac{1}{3}\pi r^2 h$ and then solve for r: $41,867 = \frac{1}{3} \times 3.14 \times r^2 \times 25$. Multiply: $41,867 = 26.167r^2$. Divide: $r^2 = 1,600$. Take the square root of each side: $r = 40$ feet. So, the diameter is $40 \times 2 = 80$ feet.

Answer Key

3. **B**; **DOK Level:** 2; **Content Topics:** Q.2.a, Q.2.e, Q.5.e; **Practices:** MP.1.a, MP.1.b, MP.1.d, MP.1.e, MP.2.c, MP.4.a
The volume of a sphere is equal to $\frac{4}{3}\pi r^3$. Since the diameter of a sphere is twice its radius, the radius of the sphere is 15 ÷ 2 = 7.5 inches. Substitute 7.5 for r to find the volume: $\frac{4}{3} \times 3.14 \times (7.5)^3 = 1{,}766.25$. So the volume of the beach ball is about 1,770 cubic inches.

4. **A**; **DOK Level:** 1; **Content Topics:** Q.2.a, Q.5.d; **Practices:** MP.1.a, MP.1.b, MP.1.d, MP.1.e, MP.2.c, MP.4.a
The volume of a square pyramid is one-third the product of the area of its base and its height ($V = \frac{1}{3}Bh$). The area of the base is 36 cm² and the height is 9 cm, so the volume is $\frac{1}{3}(36)(9) = 108$ cm³.

5. **A**; **DOK Level:** 2; **Content Topics:** Q.2.a, Q.5.e, A.2.a, A.2.c; **Practices:** MP.1.a, MP.1.b, MP.1.d, MP.1.e, MP.2.a, MP.2.c, MP.4.a, MP.4.b
The surface area of a sphere is equal to $4\pi r^2$. Since the sphere has a surface area of about 28.26 cubic inches, $4 \times 3.14 \times r^2 = 28.26$. Multiply: $12.56r^2 = 28.26$. Divide: $r^2 = 2.25$. Take the square root of each side: $r = 1.5$.

6. **B**; **DOK Level:** 2; **Content Topics:** Q.2.a, Q.5.d, A.2.a, A.2.c; **Practices:** MP.1.a, MP.1.b, MP.1.d, MP.1.e, MP.2.a, MP.2.c, MP.4.a, MP.4.b
The volume of a pyramid is given by $\frac{1}{3}Bh$. The area of the base is 8 × 8 = 64 square feet, and the volume is 64 cubic feet, so $\frac{1}{3}(64)h = 64$. Multiply each side by 3: $64h = 192$. Divide each side by 64: $h = 3$.

7. **C**; **DOK Level:** 2; **Content Topics:** Q.2.a, Q.5.d, A.2.a, A.2.c; **Practices:** MP.1.a, MP.1.b, MP.1.d, MP.1.e, MP.2.a, MP.2.c, MP.4.a, MP.4.b
The surface area of a prism is given by $B + \frac{1}{2}Ps$. The area of the base is 64 feet, the perimeter is 4(8) = 32 feet, and the surface area is 144 square feet, so $\frac{1}{2}(32)s + 64 = 144$. Multiply: $16s + 64 = 144$. Subtract 64 from each side: $16s = 80$. Divide: $s = 5$.

8. **A**; **DOK Level:** 2; **Content Topics:** Q.2.a, Q.2.e, Q.5.d; **Practices:** MP.1.a, MP.1.b, MP.1.d, MP.1.e, MP.2.c, MP.4.a
The volume of a cone is given by $V = \frac{1}{3}\pi r^2 h$. The radius of the cone is equal to one-half the diameter, so $r = 6 ÷ 2 = 3$. Substitute 3 for r and 10 for h and solve for the volume: $V = \frac{1}{3} \times 3.14 \times 3^2 \times 10$. Multiply: $V = 94.2$ cubic centimeters, which rounds to 94 cubic centimeters.

9. **B**; **DOK Level:** 2; **Content Topics:** Q.2.a, Q.2.e, Q.5.d; **Practices:** MP.1.a, MP.1.b, MP.1.d, MP.1.e, MP.2.c, MP.4.a
The cone does not have a circular base, so the amount of paper used is equal to the area of the curved surface of the cone, $\pi r s$. The radius is equal to one-half the diameter, so $r = 6 ÷ 2 = 3$. Substitute 3 for r and 10.4 for s: $3.14 \times 3 \times 10.4 = 97.97$ cm², which rounds to 98 cm².

10. **C**; **DOK Level:** 2; **Content Topics:** Q.2.a, Q.2.e, Q.5.d; **Practices:** MP.1.a, MP.1.b, MP.1.d, MP.1.e, MP.2.c, MP.4.a
The volume of a cone is given by $V = \frac{1}{3}\pi r^2 h$. The radius of a cone is half its diameter, so the radius of the medium cone is 8 ÷ 2 = 4 cm and the radius of the large cone is 10 ÷ 2 = 5 cm. For the medium cone, substitute 4 for r and 12 for h: $V = \frac{1}{3} \times 3.14 \times 4^2 \times 12 = 200.96$ cm³. For the large cone, substitute 5 for r and 14 for h: $V = \frac{1}{3} \times 3.14 \times 5^2 \times 14 = 366.33$ cm³. Subtract to find the difference: 366.33 − 200.96 = 165.37 which rounds to 165 cm³.

11. **A**; **DOK Level:** 2; **Content Topics:** Q.2.a, Q.2.e, Q.5.d; **Practices:** MP.1.a, MP.1.b, MP.1.d, MP.1.e, MP.2.c, MP.4.a
The volume of a cone is given by $V = \frac{1}{3}\pi r^2 h$. The radius of a cone is half its diameter, so the radius of the original cone is 6 ÷ 2 = 3 cm and the radius of the new cone is 5 ÷ 2 = 2.5 cm. For the original cone, substitute 3 for r and 10 for h: $V = \frac{1}{3} \times 3.14 \times 3^2 \times 10 = 94.2$ cm³. For the new cone, substitute 2.5 for r and 9 for h: $V = \frac{1}{3} \times 3.14 \times 2.5^2 \times 9 = 58.9$ cm³. Subtract to find the difference: 94.2 − 58.9 = 35.3 cm³, which rounds to 35 cm³.

12. $V = \frac{1}{3} \times \pi \times 5^2 \times 8 \approx 209$ in³.; **DOK Level:** 3; **Content Topics:** Q.2.a, Q.5.d, A.2.c; **Practices:** MP.1.a, MP.1.b, MP.1.d, MP.1.e, MP.2.a, MP.2.c, MP.4.a
The volume of a cone is given by $V = \frac{1}{3}\pi r^2 h$. The diameter of the cone is 10 inches, so the radius is 10 ÷ 2 = 5 inches. The height of the cone is 8 inches. Substitute 5 for r and 8 for h, and then multiply to find the volume:
$V = \frac{1}{3} \times \pi^2 \times 5^2 \times 8 = 209$ in³.

13. $V = \frac{1}{3} \times 144 \times 15 = 720$ ft³; **DOK Level:** 1; **Content Topics:** Q.2.a, Q.5.d, A.2.c; **Practices:** MP.1.a, MP.1.b, MP.1.d, MP.1.e, MP.2.a, MP.2.c, MP.4.a
The volume of a prism is given by $V = \frac{1}{3}Bh$. The base edge is 12 feet, so the area of the base is $12^2 = 144$. The height is 15 feet. Substitute 144 for B and 15 for h and multiply to find the volume: $V = \frac{1}{3} \times 144 \times 15 = 720$ ft³.

14. **C**; **DOK Level:** 1; **Content Topics:** Q.2.a, Q.2.e, Q.5.d; **Practices:** MP.1.a, MP.1.b, MP.1.d, MP.1.e, MP.2.c, MP.4.a
The volume of a pyramid is one-third the product of the area of its base and its height, or $V = \frac{1}{3}Bh$. For Pyramid A, the base has an area of $6^2 = 36$ square feet, and the height is 7 feet. So, the volume is $\frac{1}{3}(36)(7) = 84$ cubic feet.

15. **D**; **DOK Level:** 1; **Content Topics:** Q.2.a, Q.2.e, Q.5.d; **Practices:** MP.1.a, MP.1.b, MP.1.d, MP.1.e, MP.2.c, MP.4.a
The volume of a pyramid is one-third the product of the area of its base and its height, or $V = \frac{1}{3}Bh$. For Pyramid B, the base has an area of $10^2 = 100$ square feet, and the height is 6 feet. So, the volume is $\frac{1}{3}(100)(6) = 200$ cubic feet.

16. **A**; **DOK Level:** 2; **Content Topics:** Q.2.a, Q.2.e, Q.5.d, A.2.a, A.2.b, A.2.c; **Practices:** MP.1.a, MP.1.b, MP.1.d, MP.1.e, MP.2.a, MP.2.c, MP.4.a, MP.4.b
Pyramid C has the same volume as Pyramid A, so its volume is 84 cubic feet (from question 14). Pyramid C has the same base edge length as Pyramid B, so its base edge length is 10 feet. Substitute 84 for V and $10^2 = 100$ for B in the formula for volume of a pyramid: $\frac{1}{3}(100)h = 84$. Multiply each side by 3: $100h = 252$. Divide by 100: $h = 2.52$ feet, which rounds to 2.5 ft.

17. **A**; **DOK Level:** 3; **Content Topics:** Q.2.a, Q.2.e, Q.5.e; **Practices:** MP.1.a, MP.1.b, MP.1.d, MP.1.e, MP.2.c, MP.4.a
The surface area of a sphere is $4\pi r^2$. The radius of the lantern is 12 inches, so the surface area is $4 \times 3.14 \times 12^2 = 1{,}808.64$ in^2. The area of a circle is πr^2, so the area of the circular hole is $3.14 \times 3^2 = 28.26$ in^2. Subtract the area of the hole from the surface area of the lantern: $1{,}808.64 - 28.26 = 1{,}780.38$ in^2., which rounds to 1,780 in^2.

18. **D**; **DOK Level:** 2; **Content Topics:** Q.2.a, Q.2.e, Q.5.d, A.2.a, A.2.b, A.2.c; **Practices:** MP.1.a, MP.1.b, MP.1.d, MP.1.e, MP.2.a, MP.2.c, MP.4.a, MP.4.b
The volume of a cone is given by $V = \frac{1}{3}\pi r^2 h$. The radius is $10 \div 2 = 5$, so substitute 550 for V and 5 for r and solve for h: $550 = \frac{1}{3} \times 3.14 \times 5^2 \times h$. Multiply: $550 \approx 26h$. Divide: $h \approx 21$ inches.

19. **B**; **DOK Level:** 2; **Content Topics:** Q.2.a, Q.5.d; **Practices:** MP.1.a, MP.1.b, MP.1.d, MP.1.e, MP.2.c, MP.4.a
The volume of a square pyramid is given by $V = \frac{1}{3}Bh$. Since there are 12 inches in 1 foot, 2 feet 6 inches is equal to 2.5 feet and 3 feet 3 inches is equal to 3.25 feet. The area of the base is the square of the side length, so $B = 2.5^2 = 6.25$ ft^2. Substitute 6.25 for B and 3.25 for h to calculate the volume: $V = \frac{1}{3}(6.25)(3.25) = 6.77$ ft^3. To the nearest cubic inch, the volume of the pyramid is 7 cubic feet.

20. **C**; **DOK Level:** 2; **Content Topics:** Q.2.a, Q.2.e, Q.5.d, A.2.a, A.2.b, A.2.c; **Practices:** MP.1.a, MP.1.b, MP.1.d, MP.1.e, MP.2.a, MP.2.c, MP.4.a, MP.4.b
The volume of a cone is given by $V = \frac{1}{3}\pi r^2 h$. The radius is $16 \div 2 = 8$, so substitute 803.84 for V and 8 for r and solve for h: $803.84 = \frac{1}{3} \times 3.14 \times 8^2 \times h$. Multiply: $803.84 = 67h$. Divide: $h = 12$ ft.

21. **B**; **DOK Level:** 2; **Content Topics:** Q.2.a, Q.2.e, Q.5.d, A.2.a, A.2.b, A.2.c; **Practices:** MP.1.a, MP.1.b, MP.1.d, MP.1.e, MP.2.a, MP.2.c, MP.4.a, MP.4.b
The surface area of a cone is the sum of the area of its circular base and the area of its curved surface, or $\pi r^2 + \pi rs$. So, $563 = \pi r^2 + \pi rs$. Substitute $16 \div 2 = 8$ for the radius and solve for s, the slant height. $563 = 3.14 \times 8^2 + 3.14 \times 8s$. Multiply: $563 = 200.96 + 25.12s$. Subtract: $362.04 = 25.12s$. Divide: $s = 14.41$ feet. Since there are 12 inches in 1 foot: 0.41 ft $= 12 \times 0.41 \approx 5$ inches. The slant height is about 14 feet 5 inches.

22. **C**; **DOK Level:** 1; **Content Topics:** Q.2.a, Q,2,e, Q.5.d; **Practices:** MP.1.a, MP.1.b, MP.1.d, MP.1.e, MP.2.c, MP.4.a
The volume of a square pyramid is given by $V = \frac{1}{3}Bh$. Since the height and base edge length are known for Greenhouse A, calculate the volume of Greenhouse A. Substitute $8^2 = 64$ for B and 9 for h: $V = \frac{1}{3}(64)(9) = 192$ cubic feet.

23. **D**; **DOK Level:** 2; **Content Topics:** Q.2.a, Q,2,e, Q.5.d, A.2.a, A.2.b. A.2.c; **Practices:** MP.1.a, MP.1.b, MP.1.d, MP.1.e, MP.2.a, MP.2.c, MP.4.a, MP.4.b
The area of wood needed for Greenhouse B is its base area. The volume of a pyramid is one-third the product of its base area and area, so use the formula for the volume of a pyramid to solve for the base area. The volume of Greenhouse B is equal to the volume of Greenhouse A: $V = \frac{1}{3}(64)(9) = 192$ cubic feet. Substitute 192 for V and 16 for h into the formula for volume and solve for B: $192 = \frac{1}{3}B(16)$. Multiply each side by 3: $576 = 16B$. Divide each side by 16: $B = 36$ square feet.

24. **D**; **DOK Level:** 2; **Content Topics:** Q.2.a, Q,2,e, Q.5.d; **Practices:** MP.1.a, MP.1.b, MP.1.d, MP.1.e, MP.2.c, MP.3.a, MP.4.a
The amount of glass needed for each greenhouse is the total area of the triangular faces, because the base of each greenhouse will be made of wood. The total area of the triangular faces of a square pyramid is $\frac{1}{2}ps$. For Greenhouse A, the total area of the triangular faces is $\frac{1}{2}(4 \times 8)(9.5) = 152$ square feet. For Greenhouse B, we know from question 23 that the base area is 36 square feet, so 1 side is 6 feet. Therefore, the total area of the triangular faces is $\frac{1}{2}(4 \times 6)(7.2) = 86.4$ square feet. Therefore, the total area of the triangular faces of Greenhouse A is greater than the total area of the triangular faces of Greenhouse B, and the architect should choose the design for Greenhouse B.

LESSON 9, pp. 158–161
1. **C**; **DOK Level:** 1; **Content Topics:** Q.2.a, Q.2.e, Q.5.a; **Practices:** MP.1.a, MP.2.c, MP.4.a
The lower part of the shed is a rectangular prism, 20 feet by 20 feet, and 12 feet high. The volume is the product of those three dimensions: $(20)(20)(12) = 4{,}800$ cubic feet (choice C).

2. **B**; **DOK Level:** 2; **Content Topics:** Q.2.a, Q.2.e, Q.5.a, Q.5.d, Q.5.f; **Practices:** MP.1.a, MP.2.c, MP.4.a
The volume of the pyramid is $\left(\frac{1}{3}\right)Bh$, where $B = 900$ feet (the base is the product of s^2, or 30×30) and $h = 12$ feet. Substituting gives a volume of 3,600 cubic feet. Adding that to the volume of the lower part (4,800 cubic feet from question 1) gives a total of 8,400 cubic feet (choice B).

Answer Key

UNIT 4 (continued)

3. C; DOK Level: 2; Content Topics: Q.2.a, Q.2.e, Q.5.b, Q.5.d, Q.5.f; **Practices:** MP.1.a, MP.1.b, MP.4.a
Add the volume of the cone and the volume of the cylinder to find the volume of the container. Cone: $V = \frac{1}{3}\pi r^2 h$, so that $\frac{1}{3}(3.14)(3^2)(4) = 37.68$ cubic centimeters. Cylinder: $V = \pi r^2 h$, so that $= (3.14)(3^2)(12) = 339.12$ cubic centimeters. Combining the two volumes and rounding to the nearest centimeter gives 377 cubic centimeters (choice C).

4. D; DOK Level: 2; Content Topics: Q.2.a, Q.2.e, Q.5.c, Q.5.f; **Practices:** MP.1.a, MP.2.c, MP.4.a
The front face of the stage can be broken into two rectangles, the base, which is 30 cm by 5 cm, and the step, which is 12 cm by 16 cm. The areas of the two sections are 150 cm² and 192 cm², respectively, for a combined area of 342 cm². The volume is that area multiplied by the depth of 16 cm, or 5,472 cm³ (choice D).

5. B; DOK Level: 2; Content Topics: Q.2.a, Q.2.e, Q.5.d; **Practices:** MP.1.a, MP.4.a
The volume of the cone is $V = \frac{1}{3}\pi r^2 h = \frac{1}{3}(3.14)(25)^2(8) = 5{,}233.3$ cubic feet (choice B).

6. D; DOK Level: 2; Content Topics: Q.2.a, Q.2.e, Q.5.b, Q.5.f; **Practices:** MP.1.a, MP.4.a
The volume of the cylindrical part of the restaurant is $V = \pi r^2 h$, where $r = 25$ and $h = 12$. Substituting gives a volume of 23,550 cubic feet. Adding the volume of the cone (5,233 cubic feet from question 5) to the volume of the cylindrical part of the restaurant gives 28,783 cubic feet (choice D).

7. B; DOK Level: 3; Content Topics: Q.2.a, Q.2.e, Q.5.b, Q.5.f; **Practices:** MP.1.a, MP.4.a
The new radius of the building is 24 feet. The new height of the cone-shaped section is 7 feet. The height of the cylinder-shaped section does not change. The volume of the cone is $V = \frac{1}{3}\pi r^2 h = \frac{1}{3}(3.14)(24)^2(7) = 4{,}220.16$ cubic feet. The volume of the cylindrical part of the restaurant is $V = \pi r^2 h$, where $r = 24$ and $h = 12$. Substituting gives a volume of 21,703.68 cubic feet. So, the total volume of the restaurant is $4{,}220.16 + 21{,}703.68 = 25{,}923.84$ cubic feet. Subtract from the original volume of 28,783 to find the decrease in volume: $28{,}783 - 25{,}924 = 2{,}859$ cubic feet.

8. A; DOK Level: 3; Content Topics: Q.5.b, Q.5.d, Q.5.f, A.1.a, A.1.c, A.1.g, A.2.c, A.4.b; **Practices:** MP.1.a, MP.1.b, MP.1.d, MP.2.a, MP.2.c, MP.3.a, MP.4.b, MP.5.c
The surface area of the cylindrical wall is $2\pi rh$; the area of the floor is not included as the question does not ask for it. The area of the conical ceiling is πrs; again, the area of the circular base is not relevant to the problem. Combining the two areas gives $(2\pi rh + \pi rs)$. Factoring out πr gives $\pi r(2h + s)$ (choice A).

9. C; DOK Level: 2; Content Topics: Q.2.a, Q.2.e, Q.5.a, Q.5.b, Q.5.f; **Practices:** MP.1.a, MP.2.c, MP.4.a
The volume of the table top is the product of its length, width, and thickness: $(4)(8)(0.5) = 16$ cubic feet. The volume of one leg is $\pi r^2 h$, where $r = 0.25$ feet and $h = 4$ feet: $V = (3.14)(.25)^2(4) = 0.785$ cubic feet. There are four legs so the total volume of the table and legs is $(16) + 4(0.785) = 19.1$ cubic feet (choice C).

10. D; DOK Level: 2; Content Topics: Q.2.a, Q.2.e, Q.5.a, Q.5.b, Q.5.f; **Practices:** MP.1.a, MP.2.c, MP.4.a
The weight of the table top is 50 pounds per cubic foot times the volume (16 cubic feet), or 800 pounds. The weight of the legs is 120 pounds per cubic foot times the total volume of the legs (3.14 cubic feet), or 376.8 pounds, which rounds to 377 pounds. The total weight is the sum of the two, or 1,177 pounds (choice D).

11. A; DOK Level: 2; Content Topics: Q.2.a, Q.2.e, Q.5.a, Q.5.b, Q.5.f; **Practices:** MP.1.a, MP.2.c, MP.4.a
The area of the top surface of the table is $4 \times 8 = 32$ square feet. The area of the front edge is $4 \times 0.5 = 2$ square feet, and the area of the side edge is $8 \times 0.5 = 4$ square feet. Combining those gives 38 square feet. For each of those surfaces, there are opposing surfaces not visible in the figure, so the total surface area of the table top is twice that, or 76 square feet. The surface area of each table leg is $2\pi rh$, where $r = 0.25$ and $h = 4$. Substitute so that $2(3.14)(.25)(4) =$ a surface area of 6.28 square feet per leg, or 25.12 square feet, which rounds to 25 square feet. Add the surface area of the table (76 square feet) to the surface area of the legs (25 square feet) to get a total surface area of 101 square feet.

12. C; DOK Level: 2; Content Topics: Q.2.a, Q.2.e, Q.5.a, Q.5.b, Q.5.f; **Practices:** MP.1.a, MP.2.c, MP.4.a
The total area that is varnished is the top of the table, measuring $4 \times 8 = 32$ square feet; two sides of the table, each measuring $8 \times 0.5 = 4$ square feet for a total of 8 square feet; two sides of the table, each measuring $4 \times 0.5 = 2$ square feet for a total of 4 square feet; and 4 lateral surfaces, each measuring $2 \times 3.14 \times .25 \times 4 = 6.28$ square feet for a total of 25.12 square feet. Add to find the total area of the table that is varnished: $32 + 8 + 4 + 25.12 = 69.12$ square feet, which rounds downward to 69 square feet.

13. B; DOK Level: 3; Content Topics: Q.5.b, Q.5.e, Q.5.f, A.1.a, A.1.c, A.1.g, A.2.c, A.4.b; **Practices:** MP.1.a, MP.1.b, MP.1.c, MP.1.d, MP.1.e, MP.2.a, MP.3.a, MP.4.b, MP.5.c
The volume of the cylindrical portion is $\pi r^2 h$, where $r = R$ and the height h of the cylindrical part is $h = (H - R)$, so that $V = \pi R^2 (H - R)$. The volume of the hemispherical portion is $\left(\frac{4}{3}\right)\pi r^3 \div 2$ (or one-half of the sphere) $= \left(\frac{2}{3}\right)\pi r^3$, where again $r = R$. Adding the two and expanding the term for the cylindrical portion gives $V = \pi R^2 H - \pi R^3 + \left(\frac{2}{3}\right)\pi R^3 = \pi R^2 H - \left(\frac{1}{3}\right)\pi R^3$. Factoring out πR^2 gives $V = \pi R^2\left(H - \frac{1}{3}R\right)$ (choice B).

14. **C**; **DOK Level:** 3; **Content Topics:** Q.5.a, Q.5.c, Q.5.f, A.1.a, A.1.c, A.1.g, A.2.c, A.4.b; **Practices:** MP.1.a, MP.1 b, MP.1.d, MP.2.a, MP.3.a, MP.4.b, MP.5.c

The volume of the rectangular prism is given by LWh. The volume of the triangular prism is given by $\frac{1}{2}W(H-h)L$. Combining the two gives the total volume of $\frac{1}{2}LW(H+h)$ (choice C).

15. **D**; **DOK Level:** 2; **Content Topics:** Q.2.a, Q.2.e, Q.5.a; **Practices:** MP.1.a, MP.1.d, MP.2.c, MP.4.a, MP.5.c

The bottom of the monument is a square prism, which means that the base is a 50 ft × 50 ft square. Given that the height is 400 ft, the volume then will be (50)(50)(400) = 1,000,000 cubic feet (choice D).

16. **C**; **DOK Level:** 2; **Content Topics:** Q.2.a, Q.2.e, Q.5.d, Q.5.f; **Practices:** MP.1.a, MP.1.d, MP.2.c, MP.4.a

The volume of the small pyramid at the top is $\left(\frac{1}{3}\right)(50)^2(60)$ = 50,000 cubic feet. Adding that to the volume of the lower portion of the monument gives 1,050,000 cubic feet (choice C).

17. **D**; **DOK Level:** 3; **Content Topics:** Q.2.a, Q.2.e, Q.5.a, Q.5.d, Q.5.f; **Practices:** MP.1.a, MP.1.b, MP.1.c, MP.1.d, MP.2.c, MP.4.a

The side faces of the monument are rectangles, 50 feet wide and 400 feet high. The area of each is, then, (50)(400) = 20,000 square feet. There are four such rectangles making up the sides of the monument, for a total area of 80,000 square feet. The area of the triangles making up the top requires calculation of the slant height using the vertical height (60 ft) and the half of the width of the base $\left(\frac{1}{2}\times\right.$ 50 = 25 ft$\left.\right)$. By the Pythagorean Theorem, the slant height is $60^2 + 25^2 = s^2$, or the square root of $(60^2 + 25^2)$, or 65 ft. The area of one of the triangles making up the top is, then $\left(\frac{1}{2}\right)(50)(65)$ = 1,625 square feet. There are four such triangles, for a total area of 6,500 square feet. Adding the area of the sides and the top then gives (80,000 + 6,500) = 86,500 square feet (choice D).

18. **C**; **DOK Level:** 2; **Content Topics:** Q.2.a, Q.2.e, Q.5.b, Q.5.e, Q.5.f; **Practices:** MP.1.a, MP.2.c, MP.4.a

The volume of the hemisphere forming the top of the water tower is $\left(\frac{1}{2}\right)\left(\frac{4}{3}\right)\pi r^3$, where $r = 24$ ft. Substitute so that $\left(\frac{1}{2}\right)\left(\frac{4}{3}\right)\pi r^3 = \left(\frac{1}{2}\right)\left(\frac{4}{3}\right)(3.14)(24^3)$ = 28,938 cubic feet, which rounds to 28,940 cubic feet. The volume of the cylindrical part is $\pi r^2 h$, where $r = 4$ ft (one-half of the diameter of 8 ft) and $h = 40$ ft. Substitute so that $\pi r^2 h = (3.14)(4^2)(40)$ = 2,009.6 cubic feet, which rounds to 2,010 cubic feet. Adding the two volumes (28,940 + 2,010) gives 30,950 cubic feet (choice C).

19. **A**; **DOK Level:** 3; **Content Topics:** Q.2.a, Q.2.e, Q.5.d, Q.5.f; **Practices:** MP.1.a, MP.1.b, MP.2.c, MP.3.a, MP.4.a, MP.5.c

The total volume of the figure is 45,350 cubic feet. The tower holds 36,280 cubic feet of water.
$\frac{45,350}{36,280} = 0.8 = 80\%$.

20. **C**; **DOK Level:** 2; **Content Topics:** Q.2.a, Q.2.e, Q.5.b, Q.5.e, Q.5.f; **Practices:** MP.1.a, MP.2.c, MP.4.a

The surface area of a hemisphere is half that of the entire sphere, so is equal to $2\pi r^2$, where $r = 24$. This gives a surface area of 3,617 square feet. The lateral surface area of the cylinder is $2\pi rh$, where $r = 4$ and $h = 40$, giving a volume of 1,004.8 square feet, which rounds to 1,005 square feet. Summing the two areas (3,617 + 1,005) and rounding to the nearest 10 square feet gives 4,620 square feet (choice C).

21. **B**; **DOK Level:** 3; **Content Topics:** Q.2.a, Q.2.e, Q.5.d, Q.5.f; **Practices:** MP.1.a, MP.1.b, MP.1.d, MP.2.c, MP.3.a, MP.4.a, MP.5.c

The surface area is $\frac{1}{2} \times 4 \times 3.14 \times 24^2$ = 3,617.28 square feet. Each gallon of paint covers 400 square feet, so divide the surface area by 400: 3,617.28 ÷ 400 = 9.0432. Since only whole gallons of paint can be purchased, it will take 10 gallons of paint.

Index

A

Absolute value, 10–13
Acute triangle, 126
Addition
  on calculator, xii
  of decimals, 22–26
  of exponential numbers, 70–73
  of fractions, 14, 17
  of integers, 10–13
  of rational expressions, 90–93
  of whole numbers, 6–9, 28
Algebra
  algebraic expressions and variables,
    58–61
  comparison of functions, 122–125
  coordinate grid, 98–101
  equations, 62–65
  evaluation of functions, 118–121
  exponents and scientific notation,
    70–73
  factoring, 86–89
  graphing linear equations, 102–105
  graphing quadratic equations,
    114–117
  patterns and functions, 74–77
  Pythagorean Theorem, xiv, 130–133,
    158
  quadratic formula, xiv, 86, 114
  rational expressions and equations,
    90–93
  simple interest, xiv
  slope, xiv, 106–109
  slope-intercept form of equation of a
    line, xiv, 106
  solving and graphing inequalities,
    94–97
  solving one-variable equations, 78–81
  solving two-variable equations, 82–85,
    102–105
  squaring, cubing, and taking roots,
    66–69
  standard form of quadratic equation, xiv
  using slope to solve geometric
    problems, 110–113
Algebraic expressions
  functions written as, 118, 122–125
  inequalities, 94–97
  solving, 58–61, 70
Angles
  of congruent and similar figures, 146
  of polygons, 126
Area
  of circle, 138–145
  of composite plane figures, 142–145
  lateral area, 150
  of parallelogram, xiv
  of quadrilaterals, 126–129
  of rectangle, 34–37, 60, 67–70, 86, 89,
    94, 126
  of square, 66–68, 87–88
  of trapezoid, xiv
  of triangles, 126–129, 133
  See also **Surface area**
Average rate of change, 109, 122–125

B

Bar graphs, 46–49
Base of percent, 26
Bases
  of solid figures, 150, 152, 154
  of triangles, 126, 128–129
Box plots, 54–57

C

Calculator, xii–xiii, 58, 66
Cancel, 70, 82, 90
Capacity, 30–31, 33
Certain event, 42
Circle graphs, 50–53
Circles, 138–141, 144–145
Circumference, 138–141, 152
Clear key, xii–xiii
Coefficients, 82, 114
Common denominator, 14, 90–93
Common terms, 90–93
Composite plane figures, 142–145
Composite solids, 158–161
Computer, GED® Test on, xiv–xv
Cones, xiv, 154–157
Congruent figures, 144, 146–149
Congruent sides, 34, 80, 126
Constant rate of change, 122
**Content Practices, solving algebraic
  expressions**, 70
Content Topics
  absolute value of integers, 10
  area and circumference of circles, 138
  composite solids, 158
  computing volume and surface area, 154
  displaying/interpreting data, 54
  ordered pairs, 98
  solving systems of linear equations, 82
Converting metric units, 30–33
Converting U.S. customary units, 31, 33
Coordinate grid
  finding slope and equations of lines,
    106–108
  graphing linear equations, 102–105
  graphing quadratic equations, 114–117
  parts of, 98–101
  solving geometric problems, 110–113
Cube roots, xiii, 66–69
Cubic units, 34, 150
Cup, 16, 31
Cylinder, xiv, 150–153, 159–160

D

Measurement/Data analysis
  bar and line graphs, 46–49
  circle graphs, 50–53
  dot plots, histograms, and box plots,
    54–57
  length, area, and volume, 34–37

mean, median, mode, and range, 38–41
measurement and units of measure,
    30–33
probability, 42–45
Data sets, 38–41
Decimal point, 22, 30, 70
Decimals
  operations with, 22–25
  values in circle graphs as, 50
  writing as percent, 26
Denominator, 14, 18, 26, 90, 92, 118
Diameter, 138–141, 143–145, 150–152, 154
Distance between two points, 17, 58,
    60–61, 64, 72–74, 76–77, 102, 104,
    113, 115, 117, 131–132, 135, 147
Distance formula, 30, 102
Distribution, 54
Distributive property, 78, 81, 90
Dividend, 6, 14–17, 22
Division
  on calculator, xii
  of decimals, 22–25
  of exponential numbers, 70–73
  of fractions, 15–17
  of integers, 10, 13
  involving scientific notation, 70
  of rational expressions, 90–93
  of whole numbers, 6–9
Divisor, 6, 14–17, 22
Dot plots, 54–57
Double-bar graph, 46, 49

E

Elimination method, 82–85
Enter key, xii–xiii
Equations
  finding equation of a line, 106–107,
    112–113
  graphing linear equations, 102–105
  one-variable linear equations, 62–65,
    78–81
  proportions, 18–21
  for Pythagorean Theorem, 130–133
  quadratic formula, xiv, 86, 114
  rational equations, 90–93
  slope-intercept form of equation of a
    line, xiv, 106
  slope-point form of equation of a line,
    106, 110
  standard form of quadratic equation,
    xiv, 86
  two-variable linear equations, 82–85
Events, 42
Experimental probability, 42, 44–45
Exponents, xii–xiii, 70–73

F

Faces, 154, 157
Factoring, 86–93
Factors, 86–93

Favorable outcomes, 42
FOIL method, 86
Formulas
    area of a square, 66
    area of circle, 138
    area of parallelogram, xiv
    area of polygons, 34
    area of quadrilaterals, 94, 126
    area of trapezoid, xiv
    area of triangle, 126
    circumference, 138
    distance, 30
    distance between two points, 102
    percent formula, 26
    perimeter of polygons, 126, 134
    Pythagorean Theorem, xiv, 130–131
    quadratic formula, xiv, 114
    simple interest, xiv
    slope-intercept form of equation of a
        line, xiv, 106
    slope of a line, xiv, 106
    slope-point form of equation of a line,
        106, 110
    surface area of cone, xiv, 154
    surface area of cylinder, xiv
    surface area of prism, xiv, 34
    surface area of pyramid, xiv, 154
    surface area of sphere, xiv, 154
    volume of cone, 154
    volume of cylinder, xiv
    volume of prism, xiv
    volume of pyramid, 154
    volume of solids, 34
    volume of sphere, 154
Fraction bar, 14
Fractions
    entering into calculator, xii–xiii
    operations with, 14–17
    probability written as, 42–43, 45
    rational numbers as, 90–93
    ratios written as, 18–20
    values in circle graphs as, 50, 52
    writing as percent, 26–29
Functions
    comparing, 122–125
    evaluating and graphing, 118–121
    patterns, 74–77

G

GED® Mathematical Reasoning Test, x
GED® Test
    on computer, vi–vii
    subjects and question types, iv–v.
        See also question types on
        GED® Test
Geometry
    area of quadrilaterals, xiv
    circles, 138–141
    composite figures, 142–145
    composite solids, 158–161
    prisms and cylinders, 150–153
    pyramids, cones, and spheres,
        154–157

Pythagorean Theorem, xiv, 130–133
    scale drawings, 146–149
    solving problems with slope, 110–113
    triangles and quadrilaterals, 126–129
Graphing
    inequalities, 94–97
    linear equations, 102–105
    quadratic equations, 114–117
Graphs
    bar and line graphs, 46–49
    circle graphs, 50–53
    dot plots, histograms, and box plots,
        54–57
    of functions, 118–122, 124–125
    of linear equations, 102–105, 122
    of quadratic equations, 114–117, 122
Greater than (>), 94
Greater than or equal to (≥), 94

H

Height
    of cylinders, 150, 152
    of parallelogram, 126
    slant height of cones and pyramids,
        154–155, 157
    of triangles, 126–127, 129, 145
Histograms, 54–57
Hypotenuse, 130

I

Impossible event, 42
Improper fractions, 14
Inequalities, 94–97
Input, 118
Inside the Items
    checking solutions to equations, 78
    comparison of functions, 122
    interpreting functions, 118
    slope of a line, 110
Integers, 118, 122, 10–13
Intercepts, 118
Interest, xiv
Inverse operations, 62–65, 78–81,
    126–129
Irregular polygons, 134–137
Isosceles triangle, 80, 100, 126, 129

K

Keys of graphs, 46, 48–49
Key words, 2, 6, 10, 14, 58

L

Lateral area, 150, 153
Length, 30–37, 54, 56, 60–61, 66–71,
    80–81, 86–88, 94, 102, 104, 126–142,
    145–151, 153–154, 156–157

Less than (<), 94
Less than or equal to (≤), 94
Likely event, 42
Linear combination method, 82–85
Linear equations
    graphing, 102–105
    with one variable, 62–65, 78–81
    with two variables, 82–85
Linear functions, 122–125
Line graphs, 46, 49
Lines
    parallel and perpendicular, 110
    slope-intercept form of equation of a
        line, xiv, 106
    slope of, xiv, 106–113
    slope-point form of equation of a line,
        106, 110
Line segment, 98
Lower quartile, 54
Lowest common denominator (LCD),
    90–93
Lowest common multiple (LCM), 82

M

Making Assumptions, 90
Mathematical patterns, 74–77
Maximum of functions, 118–119, 122,
    124
Maximum of quadratic equation,
    114–117
Maximum value of data set, 54
Mean, 38–41
Measurement
    length, area, and volume, 34–37
    U.S. customary and metric systems,
        30–33
Median, 38–41, 54
Metric system, 30–33
Minimum of functions, 118, 125
Minimum value of data set, 54
Minimum value of quadratic equation,
    114–117
Mixed numbers, xiii, 14, 16–17
Mode, 38–41, 54
Multiplication
    on calculator, xii
    of decimals, 22–25
    of exponential numbers, 70, 73
    of expressions with FOIL method, 86
    of fractions, 14, 16
    of integers, 10, 12–13
    of rational expressions, 90–93
    of whole numbers, 6–9

N

Negative numbers
    entering on calculator, xii–xiii
    operations with, 10–13, 78–81
    square and cube roots of, 66–69
Number line, 10, 12, 16–17, 54, 94–96

Index

INDEX

Surface area
of composite plane figures, 142–145
of composite solids, 158–161
of cylinder, xiv
of prism, xiv, 34–37, 150–151, 153
of pyramid, cone, sphere, xiv, 154
Symmetry, 114, 116

T

Tables
of function values, 118, 122, 123, 125
reading, 2, 6
Terms
of factors, 86
in ratios, 18
Test-Taking Tech
hot spot items, 114
negative and subtraction signs, 58
on-screen calculator, 66
use of mouse, 26
Test-Taking Tips, xv
checking answers, 46
converting units of measure, 30
ensuring understanding of questions, 134
estimating values in circle graphs, 50
information for solving geometry problems, 126
labeling ratios, 18
mean, median, and mode, 38
Pythagorean Theorem, 130
reducing fractions, 14
required information in questions, 34
solid figures and volume, 150
underlining key words, 2
using answer choices, 74, 102
writing probability answers, 42
Theoretical probability, 42–45
Three-dimensional figures
composite solids, 158–161
pyramids, cones, and spheres, 154–157

rectangular prism, xiv, 34, 37, 66, 68, 151, 158
surface area of, 150–153
volume, 34–37, 150–153
TI-30XS calculator, xii–xiii, 58, 66
Toggle key, xii
Translations, 98, 100–101
Trapezoid, xiv
Triangles, 59, 76, 80, 104, 126–129, 130, 143, 145. *See also* **Pythagorean Theorem; Right triangle**
Two-dimensional figures
area of trapezoid, xiv
circles, 138–141, 144–145
composite plane figures, 142–145
pentagon, 134, 136–137
polygons, 34–37, 134–137
quadrilaterals, 126–129, 136
rectangles, 34–37, 60, 67–70, 86, 89, 94, 126
triangles, 34, 59, 76, 80, 104, 126–129, 143, 145
Two-variable linear equations, 82–85, 102–105

U

Undefined points, 118
Unit rate, 18–20
Unlike fractions, 14–17
Upper quartile, 54
U.S. customary measurement, 30–33
Using Logic
analysis of composite figures, 142
checking decimal answers, 22
checking solutions to inequalities, 94
finding equation of a line, 106
FOIL method, 86
opposite operations, 6
using common knowledge, 146
value of variables, 62

V

Variables
in algebraic expressions, 58–61
isolating on one side of an equation, 62–65, 78, 126
in linear equations, 78–85
in quadratic equations, 114
Volume
of composite solids, 158–161
of cylinders and prisms, 150–153
of pyramids, cones, and spheres, 154–157
of rectangular prism, 34–37, 66–69

W

Whole numbers, 2–5, 7–10, 22, 50, 136

X

X-axis, 46–47, 98, 101, 114, 117–119
X-intercept, 118, 123, 125

Y

Y-axis, 46–47, 98, 112, 119
Y-intercept, 106, 112–114, 123–125

Z

Zero
as characteristic of quadratic equations, 86, 114
as integer, 10–13
as place holders, 22